Critical Acclaim for Nafeez Ahmed's *The War on Truth*

"Nafeez Ahmed's understanding of the post 9/11 power game, its lies, illusions and dangers, is no less than brilliant. Everyone should read this wise and powerfully illuminating book."
—John Pilger, Frank H.T. Rhodes Professor, Cornell University;
author, *The New Rulers of the World*

"Nafeez Ahmed's book demonstrates brilliantly that the war on freedom is inseparable from the war on truth. That is why the struggle for freedom and democracy must simultaneously be a struggle for truth. It is no accident that Gandhi's tool for freedom was *satyagraha*—the force of truth—exercised through non-cooperation with the violence and injustice of the empire."
—Vandana Shiva, director, Research Foundation for Science,
Technology and Natural Resource Policy in New Delhi, and International
Forum on Globalization in San Francisco; 1993 Winner of Alternative Nobel Prize

"*The War on Truth* is a monumental work of breathtaking scope and detail. Copiously documented, this book puts 9/11 in its historical context and shows that the American people have been subjected to a massive disinformation campaign. Every American interested in politics, history, and truth should read it. Of all the possible conspiracy theories about 9/11, the most unbelievable of all is the official conspiracy theory about Osama bin Laden and 19 fanatic Muslim hijackers taking the government of the United States completely by surprise and getting 'lucky.' *The War on Truth* completely explodes this official myth and reveals the incredible hypocrisy and brazen lies of the government's hand-picked self-investigators of the so-called '9/11 Commission.' If you are a real patriot concerned for your country's future, you must read this book and keep it handy as a reference."
—Robert M. Bowman, Lt. Col., US Air Force (ret.); former director of
Advanced Space Programs Development ("Star Wars"),
Air Force Space Division, under Presidents Ford and Carter

"*The War on Truth* is an outstanding book on arguably the most important issue of our times. I hope it receives the widespread attention it so richly deserves."
—Robert W. McChesney, professor of communication, University of Illinois;
author, *The Problem of the Media*

"The new book by Nafeez Ahmed, based on very extensive and deep research, is by far the best on the 9/11 syndrome. Articulating and documenting what many feel, and empowering them into action, the book will have an impact on entrenched US empire elites unwilling and unable to take it on."
—Johan Galtung, professor of peace studies; director TRANSCEND

"In *The War on Truth*, Nafeez Ahmed, with as usual excellent documentation, maps out the logistical interlocks of Western power and international terrorism. The conclusions he draws, following clearly from the wealth of evidence he presents, is that al-Qaeda terrorism is an integral lead-function of the global corporate market system in its expansion without limit of border or life, a system that works precisely by not being understood."
—John McMurtry, professor of philosophy, University of Guelph;
fellow, Royal Society of Canada

NAFEEZ MOSADDEQ AHMED

THE WAR
ON TRUTH

9/11, DISINFORMATION, AND THE
ANATOMY OF TERRORISM

OLIVE
BRANCH
PRESS

An imprint of Interlink Publishing, Inc.
Northampton, Massachusetts

*For those who died on 9/11, for their grieving families and friends,
and for all victims of terrorism.*

First published in 2005 by

OLIVE BRANCH PRESS
An imprint of Interlink Publishing Group, Inc.
46 Crosby Street, Northampton, Massachusetts 01060
www.interlinkbooks.com

Library of Congress Cataloging-in-Publication Data
Ahmed, Nafeez Mosaddeq.
The war on truth : 9/11, disinformation, and the anatomy of terrorism /
by Nafeez Mosaddeq Ahmed.   p. cm.
Includes bibliographical references and index.
ISBN 1-56656-596-0 (pbk.)
1. Terrorism—Government policy—United States 2. Intelligence service—United States.
3. September 11 Terrorist Attacks, 2001. 4. War on Terrorism, 2001– 5. United States—Foreign relations—1993–2001. 6. United States—Foreign relations—2001–
7. Terrorism—History—20th Century. I. Titles.
HV6432.A432 2005
973.931—dc22   2005000358

Cover image © AP/Wide World Photos

Printed and bound in Canada by Webcom

1 2 3 4 5 6 7 8 9 10

To request our complete 40-page full-color catalog,
please call us toll free at **1-800-238-LINK,** visit our
website at **www.interlinkbooks.com**, or write to
Interlink Publishing
46 Crosby Street, Northampton, MA 01060
e-mail: info@interlinkbooks.com

TABLE OF CONTENTS

Acknowledgements ix
Preface xi

"Terrorism is a part of the dark side of globalization. It is a part of doing business in the world, business we as Americans are not going to stop doing."

—Secretary of State Colin Powell
"New Terror Task Force," CBS News, May 8, 2001

"It has been said that the intelligence agencies have to be right 100 percent of the time and the terrorists only have to get lucky once. This explanation for the devastating attacks of September 11th, simple on its face, is wrong in its value. Because the 9/11 terrorists were not just lucky once: they were lucky over and over again."

—American citizen Mindy Kleinberg,
whose husband died in the World Trade Center on September 11, 2001

"I also became angry at my government.... There were people, people in responsible positions, who failed us.... Some of those people are still in responsible positions in government. Perhaps they shouldn't be."

—American citizen Stephen Push,
whose wife died in the plane that crashed into the Pentagon on September 11, 2001

"Political language... is designed to make lies sound truthful and murder respectable, and to give an appearance of solidity to pure wind."

—George Orwell, Politics and the English Language

Acknowledgments

This work follows on from my first book, *The War on Freedom: How & Why America Was Attacked, September 11, 2001*. Originally intended to be an updated edition of that text, the amount of new material and revisions made to the text warranted releasing the final product as a completely new book. This book follows a similar format to that of *The War on Freedom*. While retaining the analysis and information in that volume, this greatly revised text contains extensive new material and about double the data of my text in the previous book. As with *The War on Freedom*, this book combines original research with the pioneering work of other numerous researchers on 9/11, drawing amply on academic studies, expert opinion, and open sources.

I must thank all those who broke new ground in researching the September 11, 2001 terrorist attacks, often at great personal cost. Their work has provided invaluable inspiration and information for this study. Specific researchers who should be mentioned are Michael C. Ruppert, Jared Israel, and Michel Chossudovsky, who for me provided the first and most fundamental pieces of an increasingly complex puzzle regarding the 9/11 attacks. While I disagree with much of Israel's other work, the subsequent work of Ruppert and Chossudovsky has continued to provide a powerful pool of expert data and analysis. Paul Thompson, Derek Mitchell, and the online Center for Cooperative Research must be thanked for providing the most comprehensive databank of reference material on 9/11, allowing researchers such as myself to easily locate and verify crucial documentation. Chossudovsky's Centre for Research on Globalisation in Canada must be credited for providing an up-to-date and comprehensive source of current affairs news and resources. Kyle Hence of the national citizen's oversight group, 911 Citizens Watch, and Carol Brouillet of The People's Investigation of 9/11 in San Francisco, deserve my utmost gratitude for their unending attempts to promote the cause and my work. Bill Douglas and William Clark also deserve thanks for their activism at the forefront of the 9/11 truth movement. All the other activists and researchers on 9/11, similarly, have my sincere gratitude. I would also like to thank journalist Roger Trilling for most fruitful information sharing and discussions.

I must thank my Italian agent and editor Vincenzo Ostuni and my UK agent Jonny Pegg, for their highly-valued sincerity, professionalism, and unceasing support.

I must thank my father-in-law, Shabbir Gheewalla, not only for research assistance that involved burning the midnight oil until the oil ran out and he couldn't see farther than his glasses, but for working hard on the practical side to literally save me and this book from the ashes. If I forget to mention my mother-in-law, Nasira, I'd be in even bigger trouble because I'd lose out on some of the greatest meals I've ever had—since I have no intention of dieting for the next year, she does indeed have my most heartfelt, genuine gratitude. Both Shabbir and Nasira were there for us at rock bottom—to them I owe more than I can imagine. I have to thank both my sisters-in-law too, Sukaina and Fatema; Sukaina for being so supportive during times when it felt like we were sliding into oblivion, despite her own worries and headaches; and Fatema for being such a caring and thoughtful grown-up (sometimes, anyway!).

I would like to express utmost gratitude and love to my wife Akeela for enduring the worst times while I was buried in both myself and *The War on Freedom*, for enduring even worse times in the aftermath, and for standing beside me despite everything. She has been my most valuable source of support, advice, and solace when I had already given up hope, and she continues to be the one who keeps me going. There are two other very special people who I must thank—the first is my beautiful daughter Amina, whose cuteness keeps me sane; the last, but not least, is Akeela's bump, whose cuteness is currently keeping us both waiting impatiently. To them this book is dedicated, because without them, without their constant sacrifices and love, this book would never have existed.

Preface

On September 11, 2001, a catastrophe occurred that signaled unprecedented transformations in world order. As yet, the precise nature of these transformations and their implications for the future of international relations—as well as of Western democracy—cannot be easily predicted. The events of that horrific day have scarred the public mind. But to this day, little is known about how or why. There has as yet been no meaningful, full-scale, and powerful independent inquiry into the events of that day. As this study will reveal, both the official Congressional inquiry and the 9/11 National Commission have failed dismally to provide a comprehensive and accurate accounting of the events of 9/11 and those responsible for them. Consequently, the US government's failure to anticipate and prevent these terrorist attacks continues to be somewhat of an enigma.

The world has, indeed, changed forever—but not necessarily in the way described by the majority of academic and media commentators. Scholarship on the September 11, 2001, terrorist attacks against the United States from an appropriately critical perspective is unfortunately lacking. As yet, there have been very few studies of the failure of both the domestic US national security apparatus and the international network of military intelligence agencies to effectively anticipate and prevent the 9/11 attacks.[1] Correspondingly, the wider context of this failure in terms of the structure, capabilities, and policies of the US national security apparatus as determined by political actors in successive US administrations is little understood.

This gap in scholarship extends to other issues such as the complex relations between US security policy (including of course multiple spheres of operation, namely domestic and foreign), worldwide terrorist networks, and other states/nations who to varying degrees may be categorized as friendly and/or unfriendly to US interests. In this respect, a proper understanding of the failure of the US national security apparatus with regards to 9/11 must proceed from an understanding of the wider political and institutional framework vis-à-vis domestic and foreign policies motivated by the issue of national security. This to some extent would lead us to examine problems related to US foreign policies toward friendly/unfriendly states in terms of national security, and how this impacts—both historically and currently—on the activities and motivations of terrorist networks, particularly of course al-Qaeda and the terrorist attack on 9/11.

This study adopts a thematic and chronological analysis of the events of 9/11, the responses of US government, military, and intelligence agencies, as well as the historical, strategic, and economic context of current US policy. However, my analysis extends to not only the US, but also to the wider matrix of Western policies toward al-Qaeda. I examine the development of US and Western policy prior to the 9/11 terrorist attacks in relation not only to Afghanistan, but also to the surrounding region, and to states harboring al-Qaeda terror networks. In particular, I analyze the hidden extended web of interests and actors connecting Western state policy with international terrorism, including intricate ties between oil interests, the Bush family, powerful Saudis, the bin Laden family, and Pakistani military intelligence—as well as systematic financial, military, and intelligence linkages between Western power and al-Qaeda's network throughout the post-Cold War era. I review in detail the information received by the US intelligence community concerning the impending 9/11 attacks and critically assess the community's—and the government's—response. I also review the terrorist attacks themselves, including how they occurred, in order to uncover the causes of the failure of US air defense to prevent them. The geostrategic context of the "War on Terror" as such is revealed with a discussion of the grand military-economic strategy behind longterm US national security policy. I also provide a much wider perspective of the complex relations between the West and terrorism in the post-Cold War period. While the focus is on 9/11, detailed information on previous terrorist attacks against US targets is included, scrutinized in relation to longstanding Western foreign and national security policies, and placed in their geopolitical context. In my final analysis and summary of findings, I take the liberty of outlining some conclusions—as I do in relevant sections throughout the work—but as always attempt to keep as close as possible to merely conducting an exegesis of the data itself.

Throughout this work, I have been deeply conscious of the sanitizing effect of the official inquiries, namely the Joint Inquiry of the House and Senate, and the investigation conducted by the government-appointed National Commission on Terrorist Attacks Upon the United States (later referred to simply as the 9/11 Commission or the Commission). Both are deemed to be fruitful and genuine attempts to arrive at an independent understanding of the events of 9/11. There is no doubt that some important information has been revealed through these official processes. However, the vast majority of the data discussed in this book, well documented though it is, has been either ignored or actively obfuscated by both inquiries. Indeed, in creating this work, my intention was to provide the public with a fairly comprehensive and reliable reference source on the events of 9/11, their causes, consequences, and their wider geopolitical background. The implications of this data are largely at odds with the narrative endorsed by the official inquiries, a narrative constructed to absolve state power of any real responsibility for the rise of international terrorism, including the events of 9/11.

My basic thesis is fairly simple: that 9/11—not to mention many previous terrorist attacks—was a direct product of US and Western policy, or rather a myriad of Western policies implemented not only during the Cold War, but seamlessly throughout the post-Cold War period. A detailed investigation discloses that US and Western policy can be found behind every single element of the 9/11 attacks, from the failures of the US security apparatus that facilitated them to the outcomes of US and Western regional alliances with states harboring al-Qaeda. Indeed, it is my opinion that this thesis is not a contentious inference from questionable data, but a simple corollary of a wide variety of documented facts. Unsurprisingly, such a politically incorrect conclusion—despite the wealth of documentation upon which it is based—has been studiously ignored by the official inquiries.

The study attempts to compile and analyze the work of other researchers in light of my own original research. Due to the inherently controversial nature of the subject matter, I have chosen quite deliberately to attempt to grant as much space as possible to my sources to allow them, effectively, to speak for themselves. Simultaneously, I have avoided overemphasis on my own personal conclusions, preferring instead to assess rigorously the factual record and its most immediate implications. This method minimizes the possibility that I have misrepresented crucial data that is often stunningly at odds with the conventional wisdom. Thus, although I attempt to outline what seem to me the most obvious deductions from the available facts, the actual value of my work is in the facts themselves. The readers, ultimately, are free to draw their own overarching conclusions.

The reader will have gathered by now that throughout this study there is a recognition that the official narrative of events surrounding 9/11 espoused by the US and other governments—and generally supported by the mass media—suffers from a large variety of inconsistencies. The existence of these "holes" in the official narrative has fueled the burgeoning growth of all kinds of theories about 9/11, most of them vacuous, a few of potential value, and almost all lacking in factual substantiation. The rapid proliferation of such often conflicting (and sometimes absurd) narratives continues, due to the ongoing lack of proper academic research into 9/11 combined with the lack of a meaningful, full-scale independent inquiry. Indeed, the US government's active opposition to a successful independent inquiry—continuing despite the Joint Congressional Inquiry and 9/11 Commission—only aggravates public concerns, fueling speculation as to possible reasons for such a policy. In this respect, I have written the study in a manner that I hope provides the reader with immediate access to the most important documentation available on 9/11 from a geopolitical perspective, serving as a corrective companion to the findings of the official inquiries—an alternative, but comprehensive and authoritative 9/11 report. Consequently, I deliberately avoid indulging in too much theoretical speculation of any kind, preferring instead to focus on the collation and documentation of relevant facts and credible reports, while highlighting their obvious implications. I leave it to my readers, and to other researchers, to think further on the lines of inquiry pursued in this study.

In this ambiguous political climate, it is fair to suggest that properly conducted independent research has the potential to contribute to constructing a new and more accurate narrative of 9/11, one that is able to account for anomalies in the official narrative and supersede more spurious theories. Another central goal of this study, therefore, based on the essential lines of inquiry discussed above, is to contribute to ultimately constructing a more accurate narrative of 9/11 than currently exists. Whatever one's perspective on the analysis and findings of this study, it is hoped that it helps to pave the way for a new and much needed investigation of 9/11. The overarching goal of this work, in this vein, is a moral one: to contribute toward uncovering the truth about 9/11, thereby establishing a factual basis by which justice and accountability can be rigorously pursued, so that an atrocity of that scale can never again occur.

PART ONE
THE GEOPOLITICS OF TERRORISM

In this introductory chapter, our focus is on the political and historical background to the 9/11 attacks. Our purpose here is to develop an understanding of the variety of foreign policies implemented by the US both currently and historically, motivated fundamentally by national security concerns, toward friendly/unfriendly states vis-à-vis international terrorism. Key states of this kind are the subject of ambiguous US security policies. The implications of these policies with respect to the operations of international terrorist networks (specifically al-Qaeda) and states harboring and/or repressing these networks, as well as the actual and/or potential relationship of these implications to 9/11, will also be explored.

1.

AFGHANISTAN AND "INTERNATIONAL TERRORISM"

It is widely known that the roots of contemporary international terrorism originate in Afghanistan—a major theater of conflict during the Cold War—when the United States sponsored the Afghan mujahideen in their bid to repel the Soviet occupation of the country. Indeed, some of the same Afghan rebel factions sponsored by the United States eventually became instrumental in the forging of an international network of CIA-trained terrorists united under the banner of Osama bin Laden's "al-Qaeda." While this historical link between US/Western foreign policy and the prevalence of international terrorism today is often acknowledged, being the subject of a wide variety of popular political exposés, not only is its actual course rarely understood, but its contemporary continuities are virtually unknown. Western involvement in Afghanistan during the Cold War was, in fact, merely the beginning of a relationship that has continued to blossom long after the demise of the Soviet Union, notwithstanding the tide of bloodshed that has arisen in its wake. But to understand the extent to which international terrorism is so intimately interconnected with US and Western foreign policy, it is essential to examine precisely how this complex relationship evolved since its war-ravaged birth.

"International Terrorism" as Ideological Construct

In the summer of 1979, a group of powerful elites from various countries gathered at an international conference in Jerusalem to promote and exploit the idea of "international terrorism." The forum, officially known as the Jerusalem Conference on International Terrorism (JCIT), was organized by Benjamin Netanyahu, currently Israeli Minister of Finance, on behalf of the Jonathan Institute. The Institute was established in honor of the memory of Netanyahu's brother, Lt. Col. Jonathan Netanyahu, an Israeli officer killed by a stray bullet during an IDF raid in the Occupied Territories.[1]

Over two decades ago, the JCIT established the ideological foundations for the "War on Terror." The JCIT's defining theme was that international terrorism constituted an organized political movement whose ultimate origin was in the Soviet Union. All terrorist groups were ultimately products of, and could be traced back to, this single source, which—according to the JCIT—provided financial, military, and logistical assistance to disparate terrorist movements around the globe. The mortal danger to Western security and democracy posed by the worldwide scope of this international terrorist movement required an appropriate worldwide anti-terrorism offensive, consisting of the mutual coordination of Western military intelligence services.[2]

But as Philip Paull documents extensively in his Masters thesis at San Francisco State University, the JCIT's own literature and use of source documentation was profoundly flawed. It heavily cited, for instance, statistics purporting to demonstrate a drastic ten-fold increase in incidents of international terrorism between 1968–78—but as Paull shows, these figures were deliberately concocted and inflated, and contradicted original CIA data illustrating a decline in terrorist incidents.[3] It also routinely relied on techniques of blatant disinformation, misquoting and misrepresenting Western intelligence reports, as well as recycling government-sponsored disinformation published in the mainstream media.[4] Paull thus concludes that the 1979 JCIT was:

> ... a successful propaganda operation... the entire notion of "international terrorism" as promoted by the Jerusalem Conference rests on a faulty, dishonest, and ultimately corrupt information base.... The issue of international terrorism has little to do with fact, or with any objective legal definition of international terrorism. The issue, as promoted by the Jerusalem Conference and used by the Reagan administration, is an ideological and instrumental issue. It is the ideology, rather than the reality, that dominates US foreign policy today.[5]

The new ideology of "international terrorism" justified the Reagan administration's shift to "a renewed interventionist foreign policy," and legitimized a "new alliance between right-wing dictatorships everywhere" and the government. "These military dictatorships and repressive governments have long used the word 'terrorist' to characterize the opposition to their rule." Thus, the administration had moved to "legitimate *their* politics of state terrorism and repression," while also alleviating pressure for the reform of the intelligence community and opening the door for "aggressive and sometimes illegal intelligence action," in the course of fighting the international terrorist threat.[6]

But if the target of the administration's anti-terrorist program was not real, what in fact was the administration targeting? According to former State Department official Richard Barnet, the inflation of Soviet-sponsored "international terrorism" was useful precisely for demonizing threats to the prevailing US-dominated capitalist economic system:

> Even the word "communist" has been applied so liberally and so loosely to revolutionary or radical regimes that any government risks being so characterised if it adopts one or more of the following policies which the State Department finds distasteful: nationalisation of private industry, particularly foreign-owned corporations, radical land reform, autarchic

trade policies, acceptance of Soviet or Chinese aid, insistence upon following an anti-American or non-aligned foreign policy, among others.[7]

Who exactly were the primary architects of the JCIT's "international terrorism" project? According to Paull, "present and former members of the Israeli and United States governments, new right politicians, high-ranking former United States and Israeli intelligence officers, the anti-détente, pro-cold war group associated with the policies of Senator Henry M. Jackson, a group of neoconservative journalists and intellectuals…, and reactionary British and French politicians and publicists."[8] Particular prominent individuals who participated in the JCIT included:

Menachem Begin, then Prime Minister of Israel and former Irgun "terrorist"
Benzion Netanyahu, then Cornell University professor emeritus
Shimon Peres, then leader of the Israeli Labor Party
Gen. Chaim Herzog, former Israeli military intelligence chief
Maj. Gen. Meir Amit, former Israeli military intelligence chief
Lt. Gen. Aharon Yariv, former Israeli military intelligence chief
Maj. Gen. Schlomo Gazit, former Israeli military intelligence chief
Paul Johnson, former editor of *New Statesman*
Honorable Sir Hugh Fraser, Conservative MP and former British
    Undersecretary of State for Colonies
Henry M. Jackson, influential right-wing Senator from the State of
    Washington
Richard Pipes, a professor and Russian expert in President Reagan's
    National Security Council
Ray S. Cline, former Deputy Director for Intelligence at the CIA
Maj. Gen. George J. Keegan, former US Air Force Intelligence chief
George Bush Sr., former CIA Director and then Presidential candidate
    who later became President[9]

Coincidentally, it is Bush Sr.'s son, George W. Bush, who, taking the presidency after Bill Clinton, has most effectively overseen the enforcement of an entire domestic and international American political program based principally on the ideology of "international terrorism." The only significant difference here is that the contemporary doctrine underlying the new "War on Terror" is based not on inflating the threat posed by the now defunct Soviet Union, but on projecting a new transnational Islamist threat, Osama bin Laden's al-Qaeda. However, the underlying logic of the late Bush administration's centralization of "international terrorism" is the same as that promoted by George Bush Sr. and the JCIT. In the words of civil liberties attorney Frank J. Donner: "The primary contemporary candidate for expanded intelligence operations is terrorism, a phenomenon that has profoundly shocked popular consciousness in all countries in the West, even those that are not so far theaters of terrorism. Its intent as a tactic is to generate fear, and it has unquestionably succeeded."[10]

Yet another coincidence is that the JCIT, the first major political conference to articulate the concept of "international terrorism" and legitimize the US government's use of the concept as a tool of statecraft, was held almost simultaneously with the inception of a series of fateful US covert operations in Afghanistan—operations that constituted the beginning of a dangerous new alliance between the West and a collection of organizations which we now know as the West's greatest terrorist enemy. It is an unfortunate irony that at the same time US, Israeli, and British elites were actively constructing "international terrorism" as an ideology, the US government, by exploiting tensions resulting from Soviet policy, was already involved in forging ties with the very individuals who went on to form today's most powerful international terrorist network.

Midwives to the Devil's Birth—the Cold War

In 1978, the Soviet Union was deeply involved in Afghanistan's politics. In April of that year, Nur Muhammad Taraki and his party—the People's Democratic Party of Afghanistan (PDPA)—spearheaded a coup d'etat, toppling the government of Muhammad Daud. In a single day, Daud was assassinated and his government overthrown. The coup was precipitated by Daud's draconian attempts to minimize his domestic opposition by arresting most of the PDPA's leadership. Undoubtedly, the PDPA was a Soviet-sponsored entity. Many of its leaders had studied or received military training in the USSR. The party itself, which had split into two factions in 1967, only reunited in 1977 under Soviet pressure.

Under the PDPA, Afghanistan became exclusively dependent on Soviet aid and was subjected to a fairly comprehensive program of socio-economic reform. Some of the most significant elements of this reform program included the elimination of usury and inequalities in land-ownership; the cancelation of mortgage debts of agricultural laborers, tenants, and small landowners; widespread educational projects such as literacy courses, especially for women; the printing of textbooks in many languages; the training of large numbers of teachers; and the establishment of hundreds of new schools, hospitals, and nurseries for orphans.

While it is important to acknowledge the beneficial import of such reforms, it is certainly crucial to note what the PDPA lacked. Because Taraki's regime was essentially the result of a military coup undertaken by a small faction, it lacked democratic institutions sufficient to provide meaningful rapport with the majority of the Afghan people. Despite the relative success of many reforms, the regime ultimately failed to engender participation in the political process. Much of the problem was directly related to the fact that the

PDPA was, ultimately, a secular institution sponsored by a secular power, the Soviet Union, with little sympathy for the Islamic sentiments of Afghanistan's majority Muslim people. In this context, Islam became a tool of powerful social classes in Afghanistan threatened by PDPA reforms, who wished to consolidate their privilege.

This basic gap between the government and the people was compounded by the revolutionary nature of the regime's modernizing programs, which included a large-scale land-redistribution policy designed to grant land to 200,000 rural families. The policy promised to contribute fundamentally to greater equality, but simultaneously exacerbated social conflicts. The policy was in flat contradiction to the interests of rich landowners and others benefiting from positions of power within the traditional feudal system, many of whom happened to be Muslim clergy.[11] As the New York Times noted, the need to protect Islamic practice was "being used by some Afghans who actually object more to President Taraki's plans for land reforms and other changes in this feudal society."[12] Although—as The Economist observed—"no restrictions had been imposed on religious practice" by Taraki's regime,[13] the perception among many Afghans that the Soviet-oriented PDPA regime was a form of foreign occupation designed to challenge the country's Muslim traditions was fueled by the activities of these local clergy. The PDPA's lack of rapport with the population exacerbated this problem.

As early as June 1979, and perhaps earlier, the United States had already commenced a series of covert operations in Afghanistan designed to exploit the potential for social conflict. According to Zbigniew Brzezinski, former National Security Adviser under the Carter Administration, US involvement had begun long before the Soviet Union invaded Afghanistan on December 27, 1979. Citing Brzezinski, Agence France Press reported that "the United States launched a covert operation to bolster anti-Communist guerrillas in Afghanistan at least six months before the 1979 Soviet invasion of the country.... 'We actually did provide some support to the mujahideen before the invasion' [said Brzezinski]."[14] Indeed, he also confirmed that US strategy was designed to provoke a Soviet invasion: "We did not push the Russians into invading, but we knowingly increased the probability that they would. That secret operation was an excellent idea. The effect was to draw the Russians into the Afghan trap."[15] Brzezinski's revelations have been corroborated by former CIA Director Robert Gates in his memoirs From the Shadows, where he writes that US intelligence began sponsoring an Afghan rebellion in Afghanistan six months before Soviet intervention.[16]

This seems to have been a carefully crafted attempt to foster unrest among Afghan factions led by elements of the feudal-based clergy—who were largely divorced from national political groups—with the aim of destabilizing the Soviet-supported PDPA. Exploiting the sentiments of powerful and wealthy religious leaders, the US actively recruited local warlords to form mercenary rebel groups. The US strategy directly aggravated conflict between the government and rebels. The PDPA's response was also unhelpful, involving the arrest and execution of both real and suspected enemies, setting off the first major refugee flows to neighboring Pakistan. The inclusion of innocent civilians in the government's response fueled the claims of local religious leaders and seemed to lend credence to the legitimacy of their opposition to the PDPA. Subsequently, local revolts broke out in different parts of the country in response to perceived government repression. But the role of local power-holders in this US-sponsored rebellion, whose interests depended fundamentally on the traditional Afghan feudal system, was critical. As the BBC concluded after its reporter spent four months with members of the rebel movement, these power-holders were "fighting to retain their feudal system and stop the Kabul government's left-wing reforms which [are] considered anti-Islamic."[17] The result was a deepening bifurcation of Afghan society under the combination of Soviet-backed PDPA rule and US-sponsored rebellion.[18]

In December 1979 the USSR conducted a full-scale invasion to counter the US destabilization program. In turn, the US escalated its covert support of the rebels, with the CIA allying with Pakistani military intelligence to provide them military aid and training. Afghan analyst Dr. Nour Ali observes that "hundreds of high ranking Afghan politicians and technocrats as well as army officers including generals entered into Pakistan with the hope of organizing the needed resistance to oppose the invader in order to liberate Afghanistan." The US government "in collusion with Pakistan's leaders took abusive advantage of the opportunity." Ali outlines three fundamental objectives behind the US strategy:

(i) to rule out the creation of any responsible and independent Afghan organization among Afghans, interacting directly with Washington, to support Afghan resistance, (ii) to repulse the Red Army by using exclusively the blood of Afghans, and (iii) to make of Afghanistan a satellite if not an integrated part of Pakistan in return for Pakistani leaders' services, but in complete disregard to Afghan people's sovereignty and sacrifices.[19]

Central to the US-sponsored operation was the attempt to manufacture an extremist religious ideology by amalgamating local Afghan feudal traditions with Islamic rhetoric: "Predominant themes were that Islam was a complete socio-political ideology, that holy Islam was being violated by the atheistic Soviet troops, and that the Islamic people of Afghanistan should reassert their independence by overthrowing the leftist Afghan regime propped up by Moscow."[20]

Among the myriad of policies designed to generate the desired level of extremism, the US funded—to the tune of millions of dollars—the production and distribution in Afghanistan of school textbooks promoting the war-values of murder and fanaticism. "The primers," reports the *Washington Post*, "which were filled with talk of jihad and featured drawings of guns, bullets, soldiers and mines, have served since then as the Afghan school system's core curriculum. Even the Taliban used the American-produced books." The *Post* cited anonymous US officials admitting that the textbooks "steeped a generation in violence."[21]

The US role in cultivating extremism was therefore particularly crucial. As noted by Central Asia expert Selig Harrison of the Woodrow Wilson International Center for Scholars: "I warned them that we were creating a monster. They told me these people were fanatical, and the more fierce they were the more fiercely they would fight the Soviets."[22] The US government was thus fully cognizant of the nature of the monster it had created. As noted by Washington journalist Ken Silverstein, contributing editor of *Harper's Magazine*:

> Though Reagan called the rebels "freedom fighters," few within the government had any illusions about the forces that the United States was backing. The mujahidin fighters espoused a radical brand of Islam—some commanders were known to have thrown acid in the faces of women who refused to wear the veil—and committed horrific human rights violations in their war against the Red Army.[23]

The extremist religious "jihadi" ideology cultivated in CIA-sponsored training programs was interspersed with tribal norms, giving rise to a distinctly distorted system of war-values garbed with "Islamic" jargon.

Osama bin Laden played a crucial role in this process. His father, Sheikh Muhammad bin Laden, was founder of the formidable bin Laden construction dynasty, which soon became "legendary in Arab construction, in the Saudi kingdom, the Gulf emirate of Ras al-Khaimah and in Jordan, for major road, airport and other infrastructure projects," according to ABC News correspondent and Middle East specialist John K. Cooley. "The firm attracted engineering talent from all over the world and rapidly amassed a huge fortune." By 1966, the bin Laden conglomerate of companies "was the biggest private contractor of its kind in the world." And by the late 1970s, "one of Sheikh Muhammad's young sons, Usama, was running much of the business. Under his guidance, the group maintained its reputation for professional excellence and 'can do' spirit in large projects. Usama bin Laden's inherited share of the family fortune was soon augmented by huge earnings."[24]

Ahmed Rashid—the Pakistan, Afghanistan, and Central Asia correspondent for the *Far Eastern Economic Review* and the *Daily Telegraph* (London)—noted in the *Pittsburgh Post-Gazette* that Osama bin Laden and his family were deeply involved in the US-backed Afghan rebellion against Soviet occupation: "[His family] backed the Afghan struggle and helped fund it; when Osama bin Laden decided to join the non-Afghan fighters with the Mujaheddin, his family responded enthusiastically."[25]

Cooley reports that Osama bin Laden's activities in Afghanistan occurred "with the full approval of the Saudi regime and the CIA."[26] Under contract with the CIA, he and the family company built the multi-billion dollar caves known as the Tora Bora complex:

> He brought in engineers from his father's company and heavy construction equipment to build roads and warehouses for the Mujaheddin. In 1986, he helped build a CIA-financed tunnel complex, to serve as a major arms storage depot, training facility and medical center for the Mujaheddin, deep under the mountains close to the Pakistan border.[27]

Cooley points out further that

> Through his own personal reputation as a pious Muslim who favored the cause of Wahabi Islamism, and through involvement of the bin Laden companies in construction and renovation at the holy shrines of Mecca and Medina, he seemed to both Saudi intelligence and the CIA an ideal choice for the leading role he began to play. Bin Laden began to pay, with his own company and funds, for recruitment, transportation and training of the Arab volunteers who flocked, first to Peshawar, and to Afghanistan.... By 1985 bin Laden had collected enough millions from his family and company wealth... to organize al-Qaida.[28]

"Delighted by his impeccable Saudi credentials," records Cooley, "the CIA gave Usama free rein in Afghanistan, as did Pakistan's intelligence generals."[29] According to Michael Springmann, former head of the US Visa Bureau in Jeddah, the CIA and Saudi Arabia had a joint policy to facilitate the influx of bin Laden recruits for terrorist training in the United States:

> In Saudi Arabia I was repeatedly ordered by high-level State Department officials to issue visas to unqualified applicants.... These were, essentially, people who had no ties either to Saudi Arabia or to their own country. I complained bitterly at the time there. I returned to the US, I complained to the State Department here, to the General Accounting Office, to the Bureau of Diplomatic Security and to the Inspector General's office. I was met with silence. What I was protesting was, in reality, an effort to bring recruits, rounded up by Osama Bin Laden, to the US for terrorist training by the CIA. They would then be returned to Afghanistan to fight against the then-Soviets.[30]

During the same period, Gulbuddin Hekmatyar was a key Afghan operative receiving huge amounts of CIA-supplied funds through Pakistan's Inter-Services Intelligence (ISI), amounting to approximately a half-billion dollars per year throughout the 1980s. Saudi Arabia contributed by supplying roughly equal sums.[31] The Pakistani ISI served as the intermediary through which the CIA funneled arms, planning, and training to the Afghan rebels. Under President Reagan's March 1985 National Security Decision Directive 166, the *Washington Post* notes that the Afghan war aimed to "defeat Soviet troops in Afghanistan through covert action and encourage a Soviet withdrawal." The covert operation included "a dramatic increase in arms supplies—a steady rise to 65,000 tons annually by 1987," along with "a 'ceaseless stream' of CIA and Pentagon specialists who traveled to the secret headquarters of Pakistan's ISI on the main road near Rawalpindi, Pakistan. There the CIA specialists met with Pakistani intelligence officers to help plan operations for the Afghan rebels."[32] The Pakistani ISI thus became an integral instrument of US foreign policy in the region, becoming a "parallel structure wielding enormous power over all aspects of government."[33]

The result was not merely a working partnership between the American and Pakistani intelligence agencies, but a subservient relationship in which the CIA maintained overall directive dominance over an ISI that pursued policies within the strategic framework established by its principal donor, the United States. According to *Jane's Defense Weekly*, the ISI operatives in contact with al-Qaeda had received assistance from "American Green Beret commandos and Navy SEALS in various US training establishments." Over 10,000 mujahideen were "trained in guerrilla warfare and armed with sophisticated weapons." By 1988, *Jane's* reports that "with US knowledge, Bin Laden created Al-Qaeda (The Base): a conglomerate of quasi-independent Islamic terrorist cells spread across at least 26 countries." But in the meantime, "Washington turned a blind eye to Al-Qaeda."[34]

Simultaneously, those policies pursued by Saudi Arabia and Pakistan, overseen by the United States, were instrumental in the construction of an international Islamist financial empire of incredible sophistication. Osama bin Laden played a key role in the establishment of this mafia-style network. In an extensive four-year investigation of this subject including the use of official intelligence sources, prize-winning Swiss television journalist Richard Labeviere—a specialist in Middle East and African affairs—found that although covertly committed to the Saudi brand of Wahabism, this network was eager to expand its power and wealth. The network provided the CIA with the ability to recruit, finance, and train terrorist groups throughout the Muslim world. The goal of these policies was to destabilize nationalist and Communist movements that threatened US interests, and one of their major successes was aiding the Muslim Brotherhood of Egypt to undermine Nasser. His pan-Arab nationalism was religious heresy to the Wahabis and politically unacceptable to the CIA, which feared—apart from the rise of regional independence—the prospects of a pro-Soviet Egypt. Extremists in Pakistan were thus mobilized by the CIA in tandem with the Saudis to proliferate extremist sects in Afghanistan, Pakistan, Algeria, Yemen, Indonesia, the Philippines, and elsewhere. Simultaneously, organized-criminal financial centers intertwined with the latter were established in Malaysia, Madagascar, South Africa, Nigeria, Latin America, Switzerland, the United Kingdom, Turkestan, and elsewhere. The ultimate aim of all this was to counter nationalist movements and Soviet influence.[35]

Nurturing Terror's Mastermind—After the Cold War

After the departure of Soviet troops from Afghanistan and the collapse of the Soviet Union in 1989, the anti-Soviet Afghan factions began competing for power. Although in 1991 the US and the USSR formally agreed to jointly cease aiding any faction in Afghanistan, the US Department of State had remained anxious about who might emerge as the winner of this competition. According to Labeviere, European intelligence sources reveal that the CIA and the Saudis—intent on securing a regime commensurate with their joint regional interests—agreed that they did not want to give up "the assets of such a profitable collaboration," referring to the Cold War Afghan–US alliance controlled significantly by Osama bin Laden. Accordingly, in 1991, the CIA, Saudi intelligence, and bin Laden held a series of meetings. Although exactly what was agreed upon remains secret, Labeviere reports that the CIA remained determined to maintain its influence in Afghanistan, "the vital route to Central Asia where the great oil companies were preparing the energy eldorado for the coming millenium." The Saudis were also intent on preserving the bin Laden–Pakistan alliance "at all costs," which was agreeable for the US in order to ensure a regional stalwart against influence from Shi'ite Iran.[36]

Labeviere's findings are corroborated by other credible sources. After the Soviet withdrawal from Afghanistan in 1989, Osama bin Laden "returned for a short period to Saudi Arabia to tend to the family construction business at its Jeddah head office."[37] Even after 1991 when Saudi security held on to bin Laden's passport purportedly "to prevent or at least discourage his contact with extremists he had worked with... during the Afghan jihad," he had considerable influence in Saudi royal circles: "After Iraq's invasion of Kuwait he lobbied the Saudi royal family to organize civil defense in the kingdom and to raise a force from among the Afghan war veterans to fight Iraq."[38]

The Saudi regime turned down his offer, instead accepting the influx of 300,000 US soldiers. According to Gerald Posner—a leading investigative journalist who contributes regularly to NBC's *Today Show*—this was the key point at which bin Laden decided to become an enemy of the Saudi regime. But in April 1991, according to a classified US intelligence report, then head of Saudi intelligence services Prince Turki al-Faisal struck a secret deal with bin Laden—despite his being under house arrest for his opposition to the presence of US soldiers. Under the deal, although the regime would publicly disown him, bin Laden was permitted to leave Saudi Arabia with his funding and supporters. Moreover, the regime would continue to fund his activities on condition that he did not target the Saudi kingdom itself.[39] Posner's account of a secret agreement between bin Laden and Saudi intelligence, known to US intelligence, confirms the general tenor of Labeviere's findings. Citing European intelligence sources, however, Labeviere, goes further in suggesting that the CIA was integrally involved in the 1991 Saudi–bin Laden agreement. Even by Posner's account though, it is difficult to avoid the conclusion of at least tacit US connivance in the agreement, since US intelligence was clearly aware of the deal but did nothing about it.

Although the Cold War had ended, the conflict in Afghanistan had not. According to Barnette Rubin of the Council on Foreign Relations, "the massive arms supplies still held by both the Soviet-aided army and the Islamic resistance fighters (backed by the US, with help from Pakistan, Saudi Arabia and others)" continued to fuel the fighting between the numerous rebel factions.[40] As per their secret 1991 agreement, the United States, Saudi Arabia, and Pakistan continued to be active in attempting to manipulate the conflict to their own ends. Thus, in August 1992, ongoing rocketing by the forces of Gulbuddin Hekmatyar—who was then sponsored by Pakistan and the US—had driven half a million civilians from the capital city, Kabul, and killed over 2,000 people. According to Human Rights Watch, by the end of the year, "international interest in the conflict had all but vanished and Afghanistan appeared to be on the brink of a humanitarian catastrophe," while Hekmatyar masterminded the escalation of terror, "carried out with US and Saudi financed weaponry."[41]

Hekmatyar, however, was not solely responsible for the violence. Every single rebel faction—for instance, under Ahmed Shah Masoud, Burhanuddin Rabbani, Abdul Rashid Dostum, Abdul Ali Mazari, and Abdul Karim Khalili— was equally responsible for the violence that raged between 1992 and 1996.

Atrocities by a loose confederation of factions known as the Northern Alliance, which after 1996 also became known as the "United Front," were of exactly the same nature as those committed by the later Taliban regime. British Middle East specialist Robert Fisk refers in the *Independent* to "the whole bloody, rapacious track record of the killers in the 'Alliance,'" a "gang of terrorists.... The Northern Alliance, the confederacy of warlords, patriots, rapists and torturers who control a northern sliver of Afghanistan,... have done their [fair share of] massacres on home turf, in Afghanistan. Just like the Taliban...."[42] He points out that "it remains a fact that from 1992 to 1996, the Northern Alliance was a symbol of massacre, systematic rape, and pillage.... The Northern Alliance left [Kabul] in 1996 with 50,000 dead behind it."[43]

Sidney Jones, executive director of the Asia division of Human Rights Watch, notes that Northern Alliance commanders, "whose record of brutality raises questions about their legitimacy inside Afghanistan," were responsible for gross violations of human rights throughout their reign over much of Afghanistan from 1992 to 1996, including "summary executions, burning of houses, and looting, principally targeting ethnic Pashtuns and others suspected of supporting the Taliban." The Alliance "amassed a deplorable record of attacks on civilians between the fall of the Najibullah regime in 1992 and the Taliban's capture of Kabul in 1996."[44]

But control of Afghanistan by Northern Alliance warlords was being increasingly challenged by the Taliban forces, supported by Pakistan and Saudi Arabia. In the early 1990s, the Taliban did not exist as a coherent politico-military faction or movement. Rather, a number of factions such as Harakat-e Islami and Mohammad Nabi Mohammadi operated independently without a centralized command center. By mid-1994, the members of these factions joined together to form the Taliban movement, which finally conquered the capital city of Kabul in 1996. Oliver Roy, a scholar of modern Islamic politics and a consultant to the French Ministry of Foreign Affairs, observed that the Taliban victory "was largely orchestrated by the Pakistani secret service [ISI] and the oil company Unocal, with its Saudi ally Delta." At this time, he reported, Pakistan's support for the Taliban was also approved by public and private Saudi authorities and the CIA.[45]

But around the same time, in May 1996, Osama bin Laden was offered protection by Pakistan on condition that he firmly align himself and his forces with the Taliban—he promptly moved to Afghanistan. The next month, bin Laden and senior al-Qaeda colleague Abu Zubaida met with senior Pakistani military officials, including Mushaf Ali Mir, who later became Pakistani Air Force chief one year before 9/11. According to bin Laden, the al-Qaeda–Taliban alliance brokered by Pakistan was "blessed by the Saudis," who had already been funding both the Taliban and al-Qaeda.[46]

The Rise of the Taliban under US Auspices
The Taliban was recognized as Afghanistan's legitimate government by only three key governments, Pakistan, Saudi Arabia, and the United Arab Emirates—all key US/Western clients.[47] While sometimes condemning atrocious Taliban policies in rhetoric, the West in practice consistently turned a blind eye to the support of the Taliban by its own allies.

Barnett Rubin, for instance, reports that the professed US policy of promoting peace in Afghanistan has "suffered from a variety of internal contradictions. US policy toward Iran conflicts with US stated policy toward Afghanistan, and is one of the reasons that many in the region believe the US supports the Taliban." Rubin notes: "If the US is in fact supporting the joint Pakistani–Saudi backing of the Taliban in some way, even if not materially, then it has in effect decided to make Afghanistan the victim of yet another proxy war—this time aimed at Iran rather than the USSR." The professed commitment to support the UN as a vehicle of peace in Afghanistan was similarly flawed due to the "congressional refusal to allocate funds for UN dues or the US share of peacekeeping expenses." Worse still, Rubin notes: "The US has not described and criticized in a straightforward manner the specific types of external interference occurring in Afghanistan," from Pakistan and Saudi Arabia, for instance. "Public statements by the State Department condemn such interference but never specify who is undertaking it."[48]

Considerable evidence suggests that these seemingly contradictory policies can in fact be explained by a single factor: sponsorship. From 1994 to 1998, the United States supported the Taliban as a vehicle of sustained and directed American involvement in the region. Between 1999 and 2000, US government support continued despite growing cautions and finally began to wane and even reversed by 2001.

Indeed, US interests in Afghanistan have always been extremely pertinent, as noted by Elie Krakowski, former special assistant to the US Assistant Secretary of Defense for International Security Policy (1982–88), a man who "knows more about Afghanistan than just about any man on American soil," according to Tony Snow of Fox News. Afghanistan, writes Krakowski,

> is the crossroads between what Halford MacKinder called the world's Heartland and the Indian subcontinent... It owes its importance to its location at the confluence of major routes. A boundary between land power and sea power, it is the meeting point between opposing forces larger than itself. Alexander the Great used it as a path to conquest. So did the Moghuls. An object of competition between the British and Russian empires in the 19th century, Afghanistan became a source of controversy between the American and Soviet superpowers in the 20th. With the collapse of the Soviet Union, it has become an important potential opening to the sea for the landlocked new states of Central Asia. The presence of large oil and gas deposits in that area has attracted countries and multinational corporations.... Because Afghanistan is a major strategic pivot what happens there affects the rest of the world.[49]

According to Amnesty International, "many Afghanistan analysts believe that the United States has had close political links with the Taleban militia. They refer to visits by Taleban representatives to the United States in recent months and several visits by senior US State Department officials to Kandahur, including one immediately before the Taleban took over Jalalabad." Amnesty refers, for instance, to a comment by the *Guardian*: "Senior Taleban leaders attended a conference in Washington in mid-1996 and US diplomats regularly traveled to Taleban headquarters." The *Guardian* reported that although such "visits can be explained... the timing raises doubts as does the generally approving line which US officials take toward the Taleban."[50] Further revelations were disclosed by Agence France Presse as follows:

> In the months before the Taliban took power [in 1996], former US
> Assistant Secretary of State for South Asia Robin Raphel waged an intense
> round of shuttle diplomacy between the powers with possible stakes in the
> [UNOCAL] project. "Robin Raphel was the face of the Unocal pipeline,"
> said an official of the former Afghan government who was present at some
> of the meetings with her.... In addition to tapping new sources of energy,
> the [project] also suited a major US strategic aim in the region: isolating its
> nemesis Iran and stifling a frequently mooted rival pipeline backed by
> Tehran, experts said.[51]

Amnesty goes on to confirm that recent

> accounts of the madrasas (religious schools) which the Taleban attended
> in Pakistan indicate that these [Western] links [with the Taleban] may
> have been established at the very inception of the Taleban movement...
> In an interview broadcast by the BBC World Service on 4 October 1996,
> Pakistan's then Prime Minister Benazir Bhutto affirmed that the madrasas
> had been set up by Britain, the United States, Saudi Arabia and Pakistan
> during the Jihad, the Islamic resistance against Soviet occupation of
> Afghanistan.[52]

According to Selig Harrison, an expert on US relations with Asia, the creation of
the Taliban was "actively encouraged by the [Pakistani] ISI and the CIA."[53] Thus,
when the Taliban consolidated its rule in 1996, US State Department
spokesperson Glyn Davies explained that the US found "nothing objectionable"
in the event. US approval was further revealed by Chairman of the Senate Foreign
Relations Subcommittee on the Near East and South East Senator Hank Brown,
who announced: "The good part of what has happened is that one of the factions
at last seems capable of developing a new government in Afghanistan."[54] After a
visit by the head of Saudi intelligence, Prince Turki, to Islamabad and Kandahar,
US ally Saudi Arabia funded and equipped the Taliban march on Kabul.[55]

Many US experts on Afghanistan concede that the rise of the Taliban
occurred with the covert support of the US state. Agence France Presse, for
instance, cites Radha Kumar of the Council on Foreign Relations reporting that
the Taliban

> was brought to power with Washington's silent blessing as it dallied in an
> abortive new 'Great Game' in central Asia...Keen to see Afghanistan
> under strong central rule to allow a US-led group to build a multi-billion-
> dollar oil and gas pipeline, Washington urged key allies Pakistan and Saudi
> Arabia to back the militia's bid for power in 1996, analysts said.... The

United States encouraged Saudi Arabia and Pakistan to support the Taliban, certainly right up to their advance on Kabul…. One key reason for US interest in the Taliban was a 4.5-billion-dollar oil and gas pipeline that a US-led oil consortium planned to build across war-ravaged Afghanistan…. [The oil] consortium feared there could be no pipeline as long as Afghanistan, battered by war since the Soviet withdrawal in 1989, was split among rival warlords.[56]

Professor William O. Beeman, an anthropologist who is director of Middle East studies at Brown University specializing in Islamic Central Asia, similarly observes that

It is no secret, especially in the region, that the United States, Pakistan and Saudi Arabia have been supporting the fundamentalist Taliban in their war for control of Afghanistan for some time. The US has never openly acknowledged this connection, but it has been confirmed by both intelligence sources and charitable institutions in Pakistan.[57]

Professor Beeman, a long-time observer of Afghan affairs, observes that the US-backed Taliban "are a brutal fundamentalist group that has conducted a cultural scorched-earth policy" in Afghanistan. Extensive documentation shows that the Taliban have "committed atrocities against their enemies and their own citizens…. So why would the US support them?" Beeman concludes that the answer to this question "has nothing to do with religion or ethnicity—but only with the economics of oil. To the north of Afghanistan is one of the world's wealthiest oil fields, on the Eastern Shore of the Caspian Sea in republics formed since the breakup of the Soviet Union." Caspian oil needs to be trans-shipped out of the landlocked region through a warm water port. The "simplest and cheapest" pipeline route is through Iran—but Iran is an "enemy" of the US, for a variety of strategic reasons, largely due to the regime's aversion toward regional US designs. As Beeman notes: "The US government has such antipathy to Iran that it is willing to do anything to prevent this." The alternative route is one that passes through Afghanistan and Pakistan, which "would require securing the agreement of the powers-that-be in Afghanistan"—the Taliban. Such an arrangement would also benefit Pakistani elites, "which is why they are willing to defy the Iranians." Therefore, as far as the US was concerned, the solution was "for the anti-Iranian Taliban to win in Afghanistan and agree to the pipeline through their territory."[58]

"The Taliban will probably develop like the Saudis," commented one US diplomat in 1997, highlighting the US vision for a "free Afghanistan." "There will be Aramco [a consortium of oil companies controlling Saudi oil], pipelines, an emir, no parliament and lots of Sharia law. We can live with that."[59] Thus, in December 1997, Taliban representatives were invited as guests to the Texas headquarters of UNOCAL to negotiate their support of the pipeline. Meanwhile, UNOCAL had already begun training Afghans in the skills required for pipeline construction, with US government approval

> A senior delegation from the Taleban movement in Afghanistan is in the United States for talks with an international energy company that wants to construct a gas pipeline from Turkmenistan across Afghanistan to Pakistan…A spokesman for the company, Unocal, said the Taleban were expected to spend several days at the company's headquarters in Sugarland, Texas…. A BBC regional correspondent says the proposal to build a pipeline across Afghanistan is part of an international scramble to profit from developing the rich energy resources of the Caspian Sea…. Unocal… has commissioned the University of Nebraska to teach Afghan men the technical skills needed for pipeline construction. Nearly 140 people were enrolled last month in Kandahar and Unocal also plans to hold training courses for women in administrative skills. Although the Taleban authorities only allow women to work in the health sector, organisers of the training say they haven't so far raised any objections.[60]

The Taliban: Gateway to Riches?

Strategic and economic interests, therefore, motivated what the *Guardian* referred to as "the generally approving line that US officials take toward the Taleban." Elaborating, CNN reported that the "United States wants good ties [with the Taliban] but can't openly seek them while women are being repressed"—hence they could be sought covertly.[61]

The Inter Press Service (IPS) reported that underscoring "the geopolitical stakes, Afghanistan has appeared prominently in US government and corporate planning about routes for pipelines and roads opening the ex-Soviet republics on Russia's southern border to world markets." Hence, amid the fighting, "some Western businesses are warming up to the Taliban" despite the movement's responsibility for terror, massacres, abductions, and impoverishment. "Leili Helms, a spokeswoman for the Taliban in New York, told IPS that one US company, Union Oil of California (Unocal), helped to arrange the visit last week of the movement's acting information, industry and mines ministers. The three officials met lower-level State Department officials before departing for France, Helms said." "Several US and French firms are interested in developing gas lines through central and southern Afghanistan, where the 23 Taliban-controlled states" just happen to be located, as Helms added, to the "chance" convenience of Western companies.[62] Helms was hired by the Taliban to be their PR representative in Washington. She happens to be well versed in the clandestine workings of US intelligence agencies—her uncle, Richard Helms, is a former director of the CIA.[63]

An October 1996 article appearing in the German daily *Frankfurter*

Rundschau reported that UNOCAL "has been given the go-ahead from the new holders of power in Kabul to build a pipeline from Turkmenistan via Afghanistan to Pakistan. It would lead from Krasnovodsk on the Caspian Sea to Karachi on the Indian Ocean coast." UN diplomats in Geneva believed that the war in Afghanistan was the result of a struggle between Turkey, Iran, Pakistan, Russia, and the United States "to secure access to the rich oil and natural gas of the Caspian Sea."[64] Other companies jubilantly interested in exploiting Caspian oil included AMOCO, BP, Chevron, EXXON, and Mobile.[65]

It is in this context that Franz Schurmann, professor emeritus of history and sociology at the University of California, referred to "Washington's discreet backing of the Taliban," noting the announcement in May 1996 "by UNOCAL that it was preparing to build a pipeline to transport natural gas from Turkmenistan to Pakistan through Western Afghanistan... UNOCAL's announcement was premised on an imminent Taliban victory."[66]

It therefore comes as no surprise to see the *Wall Street Journal* reporting that the main regional interest of US/Western elites was to convert Afghanistan into "a prime transshipment route for the export of Central Asia's vast oil, gas and other natural resources.... Like them or not, the Taliban are the players most capable of achieving peace in Afghanistan at this moment in history."[67] Meanwhile, the *New York Times* reported that "The Clinton Administration has taken the view that a Taliban victory... would act as a counterweight to Iran... and would offer the possibility of new trade routes that could weaken Russian and Iranian influence in the region."[68]

In a similar vein, the *International Herald Tribune* reported that in the summer of 1998, "the Clinton administration was talking with the Taleban about potential pipeline routes to carry oil and natural gas out of Turkmenistan to the Indian Ocean by crossing Afghanistan and Pakistan."[69]

P. Stobdan, research fellow at the Institute for Defense Studies and Analysis (IDSA) in New Delhi, reported in the Institute's journal *Strategic Analysis* that

> The US government fully backed the route as a useful option to free the Central Asian states from Russian clutches and prevent them getting close to Iran. The project was also perceived as the quickest and cheapest way to bring out Turkmen gas to the fast growing energy market in South Asia. To help it canvass for the project, Unocal hired the prominent former diplomat and secretary of state, Henry Kissinger, and a former US ambassador to Pakistan, Robert Oakley, as well as an expert on the Caucasus, John Maresca.... The president of Unocal even speculated that the cost of the construction would be reduced by half with the success of the Taliban movement and formation of a single government.

Worse still, this corporate endeavor, backed wholeheartedly by the US government, involved direct, material support of the Taliban: "It was reported by the media that the US oil company had even provided covert material support to help push the militia northward against Rabbani's forces." However, UNOCAL indefinitely suspended work on the pipeline in August 1998.[70] It took three more months for the oil company to pull out of the CentGas consortium, which had been organized to build the proposed pipeline.[71]

UNOCAL has repeatedly denied further interest in the trans-Afghan pipeline project—however, those denials are misleading. The *Business Recorder* reported in March 2000, for instance, that UNOCAL had continued to display keen interest behind-the-scenes:

> UNOCAL is trying to again jump into the Turkmenistan gas pipeline project it had quit about a year ago on account of alleged gross abuse of human rights in Afghanistan. The US company is in dialogue with the Afghan authorities seeking guaranteed protection for its personnel while working on the Afghani terrain, reliable sources told *Business Recorder*. This is an interesting manoeuvre on the part of the company since Afghanistan has been under severe US sanctions for being a patron of terrorists.[72]

UNOCAL was not alone in its dealings with the Taliban. The notorious US energy corporation Enron, which had close ties to the government, was also deeply involved. Enron performed the preliminary feasibility study on the gas pipeline, which was paid for with a $750,000 grant from the US Agency for Trade and Development.[73]

US intelligence sources and former Enron officials have confirmed that Enron "gave the Taliban millions of dollars," apparently with the US government's blessings, "in a no-holds-barred bid to strike a deal for an energy pipeline in Afghanistan—while the Taliban were already sheltering Osama bin Laden."

Atul Davda, who worked as a senior director for Enron's International Division until the company's collapse, stated that "Enron had intimate contact with Taliban officials. Building the pipeline was one of the corporation's prime objectives." One CIA insider commented that "Enron was wooing the Taliban and was willing to make the Taliban a partner in the operation of a pipeline through Afghanistan. Enron proposed to pay the Taliban large sums of money in a 'tax' on every cubic foot of gas and oil shipped through the pipeline." More than $400 million was paid by Enron for the feasibility study on the pipeline, "a large portion" of which "was payoffs to the Taliban," according to the CIA source. An FBI official similarly confirmed that "When Clinton was bombing Bin Laden camps in Afghanistan in 1998, Enron was making payoffs to Taliban and Bin Laden operatives to keep the pipeline project alive. And there's no way that anyone could NOT have known of the Taliban and Bin Laden connection at that time, especially Enron."[74]

Other sources indicate that key governmental and intelligence officials of successive US administrations were fully aware of Enron's flirtations with the Taliban—and thereby al-Qaeda—and actively supported the corporation's regional operations. "A captured Al Qaida document reveals that US energy companies were secretly negotiating with the Taliban to build a pipeline," reports US attorney and former Justice Department prosecutor John Loftus.

> The document was obtained by the FBI but was not allowed to be shared with other agencies in order to protect Enron... Multiple sources confirm that American law enforcement agencies were deliberately kept in the dark and systematically prevented from connecting the dots before 9/11 in order to aid Enron's secret and immoral Taliban negotiations.
>
> The suppressed Al Qaida document tends to support recent claims of a cover-up made by several mid-level intelligence and law enforcement figures. Their ongoing terrorist investigations appear to have been hindered during the same sensitive time period while the Enron Corporation was still negotiating with the Taliban. An inadvertent result of the Taliban pipeline cover-up was that the Taliban's friends in Al Qaida were able to complete their last eight months of preparations for 9/11 while the Enron secrecy block was still in force.
>
> Although the latest order to block investigations allegedly resulted from Enron's January 2002 appeal to Vice President Dick Cheney, it appears that there were at least three previous block orders, each building upon the other, stretching back for decades and involving both Republican and Democratic administrations.[75]

It should be noted of course that the US government was well aware that the Taliban had been harboring Osama bin Laden since June 1996, as revealed by official documents. Bin Laden was expelled by Sudan to Afghanistan in early 1996 at US insistence. He had publicly declared war against the US in August 1996. He had lauded that year's bombings in Saudi Arabia, which killed 19 US servicemen, as "praiseworthy terrorism," promising future attacks against US targets in November 1996 and confessing complicity in attacks on US military personnel in Somalia in 1993 and Yemen in 1992. There was already a mass of evidence linking him to the 1995 bombing of a US military barracks in Riyadh; the 1993 World Trade Center attacks; and a 1994 assassination plot against President Clinton in the Philippines.[76] Nevertheless, with US government blessings, UNOCAL and Enron showered the Taliban with millions of dollars to further the pipeline negotiations, with apparently no concern for the potential consequences in terms of the financial support of a regime hosting the al-Qaeda terrorist network.

Even members of the US government have criticized covert US support of the terror-hosting Taliban. One should note, for instance, the authoritative testimony of US Congressman Dana Rohrabacher, who has been involved with

Afghanistan since the early 1980s when he worked in the White House as special assistant to then US President Ronald Reagan. He is now a senior member of the US House International Relations Committee and has been involved in US policy toward Afghanistan for some 20 years. In 1988, he traveled to Afghanistan to mingle with mujahideen fighters and participated in the battle of Jalalabad against the Soviets. In Congressional hearings in April 1999, he testified before a Senate Foreign Relations Subcommittee as follows:

> Having been closely involved in US policy toward Afghanistan for some twenty years, I have called into question whether or not this administration has a covert policy that has empowered the Taliban and enabled this brutal movement to hold on to power. Even though the President and the Secretary of State have voiced their disgust at the brutal policies of the Taliban, especially their repression of women, the actual implementation of US policy has repeatedly had the opposite effect.

After documenting a large number of factors indicating a concrete degree of US support of the Taliban, Rohrabacher concluded his statement:

> I am making the claim that there is and has been a covert policy by this administration to support the Taliban movement's control of Afghanistan.... [T]his amoral or immoral policy is based on the assumption that the Taliban would bring stability to Afghanistan and permit the building of oil pipelines from Central Asia through Afghanistan to Pakistan.... I believe the administration has maintained this covert goal and kept the Congress in the dark about its policy of supporting the Taliban, the most anti-Western, anti-female, anti-human rights regime in the world. It doesn't take a genius to understand that this policy would outrage the American people, especially America's women. Perhaps the most glaring evidence of our government's covert policy to favor the Taliban is that the administration is currently engaged in a major effort to obstruct the Congress from determining the details behind this policy. Last year in August, after several unofficial requests were made of the State Department, I made an official request for all diplomatic documents concerning US policy toward the Taliban, especially those cables and documents from our embassies in Pakistan and Saudi Arabia. As a senior Member of the House International Relations Committee I have oversight responsibility in this area. In November, after months of stonewalling, the Secretary of State herself promised before the International Relations Committee that the documents would be forthcoming. She reconfirmed that promise in February when she testified before our Committee on the State Department budget. The Chairman of the Committee, Ben Gilman, added his voice to the record in support of my document request. To this time, we have received nothing. There can only be two explanations.

Either the State Department is totally incompetent, or there is an ongoing cover-up of the State Department's true fundamental policy toward Afghanistan. You probably didn't expect me to praise the State Department at the end of this scathing testimony. But I will. I don't think the State Department is incompetent. They should be held responsible for their policies and the American people should know, through documented proof, what they are doing.[77]

The extent of this support is shocking. "Impressed by the ruthlessness and willingness of the then-emerging Taliban to cut a pipeline deal," reported Ahmed Rashid in his Yale University study *Taliban*, "the State Department and Pakistan's Inter-Services Intelligence agency agreed to funnel arms and funding to the Taliban in their war against the ethnically Tajik Northern Alliance. As recently as 1999, US taxpayers paid the entire annual salary of every single Taliban government official."[78]

As late as 2000, hearings in the House of Representatives' International Relations Committee confirmed that US support of the Taliban was secured through the Pakistani ISI:

[T]he United States has been part and parcel to supporting the Taliban all along, and still is.... You have a military government in Pakistan now that is arming the Taliban to the teeth.... Let me note; that [US] aid has always gone to Taliban areas.... We have been supporting the Taliban, because all our aid goes to the Taliban areas. And when people from the outside try to put aid into areas not controlled by the Taliban, they are thwarted by our own State Department....

At a time when the Taliban were vulnerable, the top person of this administration, Mr. Inderfurth, and Bill Richardson, personally went to Afghanistan and convinced the anti-Taliban forces not to go on the offensive and, furthermore, convinced all of the anti-Taliban forces, their supporters, to disarm them and to cease their flow of support for the anti-Taliban forces.... At that same moment, Pakistan initiated a major resupply effort, which eventually saw the defeat, and caused the defeat, of almost all of the anti-Taliban forces in Afghanistan.[79]

As Afghan scholar Dr. Nour Ali notes, in supporting the Taliban, the US had intended "to cross Afghanistan from Pakistan" in order

(i) to sway Iran;
(ii) to expand its power beyond the Amou Daria to control the resources of Central Asia;
(iii) to influence the Federation of Russia from South, and the mainland China from North West, as and when required.

The logic of the underlying strategy premised US regional leverage on the installation of "a servile government," which would allow the US "to influence the overall politics and economics of the region in accordance with its imperialistic objectives."[80]

The End of an Affair

The US, therefore, had never disengaged from Afghanistan. US regional interference continued to occur by proxy through Saudi Arabia and Pakistan. This triangular relationship was clearly fundamental to the development of the infrastructure essential to the survival and growth of the al-Qaeda terrorist network. While this triangular relationship responsible for the ongoing existence of al-Qaeda continues to exist, the US relationship with the Taliban regime in Afghanistan faced significant turbulence at the dawn of the new millennium. US policymakers had, it seems, realized that the Taliban was unlikely to play the role of a friendly "servile government." As Ahmed Rashid points out:

> The UNOCAL project was based on the premise that the Taliban were going to conquer Afghanistan. This premise was fed to them by various countries like Saudi Arabia, Pakistan and elements within the US administration. Essentially it was a premise that was very wrong, because it was based on conquest, and would therefore make it absolutely certain that not only would they not be able to build the pipeline, but they would never be able to have that kind of security in order to build the pipeline.[81]

Rashid further notes that after 1998 an increasingly anti-American worldview "appeared to dominate the thinking of senior Taliban leaders." They became "increasingly vociferous against the Americans, the UN, the Saudis and Muslim regimes around the world," and their language "increasingly reflected the language of defiance Bin Laden had adopted and which was not an original Taliban trait."[82]

The US was in other words beginning to recognize that the Taliban's penchant for extreme tribalistic brutality served to escalate the inter-factional conflict, destabilizing the country unremittingly, and contributing to an escalating cycle of violence. The regime no longer seemed capable of providing the security essential for the trans-Afghan pipeline. As the Taliban grew increasingly uncooperative, US policy grew increasingly hostile. Matters were made worse, according to the *Oil & Gas International*, when "the Taliban demanded more than the $100 million a year in rent for the pipeline route in the form of the construction of roads, water supplies, telephone lines, and electricity power lines, as well as a tap in the pipeline to provide oil and gas for Afghanistan." In response, "Unocal balked, and finally dropped its plans...."[83]

Thus, by the end of 1998, the US had begun to see the Taliban's intransigence as a potential obstacle to US interests. This growing perception among US policymakers was reflected in burgeoning plans for a military operation against the Taliban—long before 9/11. Frederick Starr, chairman of the Central Asia-Caucasus Institute at Johns Hopkins's Nitze School of Advanced International Studies, reported in December 2000 in the *Washington Post* that

> ... the United States has quietly begun to align itself with those in the Russian government calling for military action against Afghanistan and has toyed with the idea of a new raid to wipe out Osama bin Laden. Until it backed off under local pressure, it went so far as to explore whether a Central Asian country would permit the use of its territory for such a purpose.[84]

Starr's insight should not be in question. A specialist in Central Asia, his director at Johns Hopkins was Assistant Secretary of Defense Paul Wolfowitz. In his *Post* report, Starr further noted that meetings between US, Russian, and Indian government officials occurred at the end of 2000 "to discuss what kind of government should replace the Taliban.... [T]he United States is now talking about the overthrow of a regime that controls nearly the entire country, in the hope it can be replaced with a hypothetical government that does not exist even on paper."[85]

The extensive military planning for a war on Afghanistan was also noted by Canadian journalist Eric Margolis, a specialist in Middle East and Central Asian affairs with firsthand experience of Afghanistan. In a December 2000 edition of the *Toronto Sun*, he reported that

> Such an attack would probably include US Delta Force and Navy Seals, who would join up with Russia's elite Spetsnaz and Alpha commandos in Tajikistan, the Central Asian state where Russia has military bases and 25,000 troops. The combined forces would be lifted by helicopters, and backed by air support, deep into neighboring Afghanistan to attack Bin Laden's fortified base in the Hindu Kush mountains.[86]

By March 2001, *Jane's Intelligence Review* confirmed that India had joined "Russia, the USA and Iran in a concerted front against Afghanistan's Taliban regime... Several recent meetings between the newly instituted Indo-US and Indo-Russian joint working groups on terrorism led to this effort to tactically and logistically counter the Taliban." The United States, Russia, India, and Iran were already providing military, intelligence, and logistical support to anti-Taliban forces in Afghanistan. "Military sources indicated that Tajikistan and Uzbekistan are being used as bases to launch anti-Taliban operations by India and Russia."[87]

In May 2001, US State Department, Iranian, German, and Italian officials met in Geneva to discuss "a strategy to topple the Taliban and replace the theocracy with a 'broad-based government.'"[88]

By June 2001, the public affairs magazine *India Reacts* reported the escalation of joint US–Russian plans to conduct a military assault on Afghanistan. According to Indian officials:

India and Iran will only play the role of "facilitator" while the US and Russia will combat the Taliban from the front with the help of two Central Asian countries, Tajikistan and Uzbekistan.... Tajikistan and Uzbekistan will lead the ground attack with a strong military backup of the US and Russia. Vital Taliban installations and military assets will be targeted. India and Iran will provide logistic support.

In a Moscow meeting in early June, "Russian President Vladimir Putin [had] already hinted of military action against the Taliban to CIS nations." According to diplomats, the formation of this anti-Taliban front "followed a meeting between US Secretary of State Colin Powell and Russian Foreign Minister Igor Ivanov and later between Powell and Indian foreign minister Jaswant Singh in Washington. Russia, Iran and India have also held a series of discussions and more diplomatic activity is expected."[89]

Flirting with the Enemy

At the same time that intensive preparations for war against the Taliban were being pursued, the Bush administration attempted to save its relationship with the regime. The *Pakistan Observer* reported, for instance, that in July 2001, "Christina Rocca, the US Assistant Secretary of State for South Asia" had a meeting with Taliban officials in Islamabad and "announced $43 million in food and shelter aid, bringing to $124 million the US contribution to the IDPs this year alone." This "humanitarian assistance" was granted "without any accountability." The meeting followed several other secretive meetings between US government and Taliban officials, "including a visit by seven US officials to Kabul in late April preceded by another visit by three US officials earlier in that month, before the terror struck America on September 11." The visits led many observers to speculate about the Bush administration's "cautious engagement with Taliban even as they were under stringent sanctions by Washington and the UN Security Council."[90]

"Cautious engagement" appears to have also been the Clinton administration's official policy. In April 1998, United Press International (UPI) reported that "American UN Representative Bill Richardson will visit the war-torn nation on a trip to south Asia that begins Friday.... Richardson will be joined on his mission, which US officials say is an attempt to draw the Taliban militia and the coalition of forces in the north into preliminary peace talks, by

Assistant Secretary of State Carl Inderfurth and White House aide Bruce Riedel."[91] UPI reported a year later in August 1999 that

> The United States and Afghanistan's ruling Taliban militia have been talking to each other despite tensions that have marked their relations ever since the Taliban appeared on the Afghan scene about five years ago.... "The talks with Taliban are usually held in Islamabad, Washington or New York where the Taliban U.N. representative lives," said the US Embassy spokesman. "The two sides have also held talks on the fringes of international conferences and seminars," he said.[92]

By March 2000, UPI reported that a series of US-backed negotiations with the Taliban and other factions had begun to explore the possibility of a political compromise that would herald an end to the devastating factional war, paving the way for regional security—a factor critically necessary to fulfill regional US designs:

> Senior officials of Afghanistan's ruling Taliban militia are also expected to participate in the talks. Officials at Pakistan's ministry for foreign affairs say the talks are part of the so-called two-plus-six process, initiated by the United Nations with US support. The United States and Russia participate in these talks as two guarantors while six countries that neighbor Afghanistan discuss various options to "end the fighting."[93]

Shortly after taking power in January 2001, the Bush administration escalated this negotiation process. US and Taliban diplomatic representatives met several times in February 2001 in Washington, Berlin, and Islamabad. The last meeting between US and Taliban representatives took place in August 2001—five weeks before the attacks on New York and Washington, DC. Christina Rocca, then head of Central Asian affairs at the US Department of State, met the Taliban ambassador to Pakistan in Islamabad.[94]

Until now, former French intelligence officer Jean-Charles Brisard and intelligence analyst Guillaume Dasquié report, "the oil and gas reserves of Central Asia have been controlled by Russia. The Bush government wanted to change all that." However, confronted with the Taliban's refusal to accept US conditions, "this rationale of energy security changed into a military one." In an interview in Paris, Brisard noted that "At one moment during the negotiations, the US representatives told the Taliban, either you accept our offer of a carpet of gold, or we bury you under a carpet of bombs."

Describing the key theme of some of the several meetings that occurred in 2001, the intelligence analysts record that

> Several meetings took place this year under the arbitration of Francesc Vendrell, personal representative of UN Secretary-General Kofi Annan, to

discuss the situation in Afghanistan. Representatives of the US government and Russia, and the six countries that border with Afghanistan, were present at these meetings. Sometimes, representatives of the Taliban also sat around the table.[95]

The three Americans at one of these meetings in Berlin in July were Tim Simons, a former US Ambassador to Pakistan, Karl "Rick" Inderfurth, a former Assistant Secretary of State for South Asian affairs, and Lee Coldren, who headed the office of Pakistan, Afghan, and Bangladesh affairs in the State Department until 1997. These meetings, called "6+2" due to the number of states involved (six Central Asian neighbors, plus the new partners, Russia and the US), have also been confirmed by the former Pakistani Minister for Foreign Affairs, Niaz Naik, who was present at the meetings.

In an interview for French television in early November 2001, Naik testified that during a meeting in Berlin in July 2001, the discussions focused on "... the formation of a government of national unity. If the Taliban had accepted this coalition, they would have immediately received international economic aid. And the pipelines from Kazakhstan and Uzbekistan would have come." Naik clarified that one of the US representatives at the meetings, Tom Simons, openly threatened the Taliban: "Simons said, 'either the Taliban behave as they ought to, or Pakistan convinces them to do so, or we will use another option.' The words Simons used were 'a military operation.'"[96]

There were several signs throughout the same period, according to the *Guardian*, that US war plans were reaching their fruition. US defense official Dr. Jeffrey Starr visited Tajikistan in January 2001. US Rangers were training special troops inside Kyrgyzstan, and there were reports that Tajik and Uzbek special troops were training in Alaska and Montana. On May 16, Gen. Tommy Franks visited Dushanbe to describe Tajikistan as "a strategically significant country," offering military aid and receiving Tajikistan's application to join NATO's Partnership for Peace. Reliable western military sources said that a US war plan "existed on paper by the end of the summer to attack Afghanistan from the north." By July 8, the Afghan opposition, Pakistani diplomats, and senior staff from the British Foreign Office, "were gathering at Weston Park under UN auspices for private teach-ins on the Afghan situation."[97]

Former State Department official Lee Coldren confirmed to the *Guardian* that "there was some discussion of the fact that the United States was so disgusted with the Taliban that they might be considering some military action." Naik, described by Tim Simons himself as "a friend for years" and "an honourable diplomat," also told the newspaper:

The Americans indicated to us that in case the Taliban does not behave and in case Pakistan also doesn't help us to influence the Taliban, then the

United States would be left with no option but to take an overt action against Afghanistan. I told the Pakistani government, who informed the Taliban via our foreign office and the Taliban ambassador here.

When asked whether he could be sure that the American officials were passing ideas from the Bush administration rather than their own views, Naik clarified that: "What the Americans indicated to us was perhaps based on official instructions. They were very senior people. Even in 'track two' people are very careful about what they say and don't say." Naik also cited Tim Simons declaring that action against bin Laden was imminent: "This time they were very sure. They had all the intelligence and would not miss him this time. It would be aerial action, maybe helicopter gunships, and not only overt, but from very close proximity to Afghanistan."[98] In an interview with BBC News, Naik elaborated on this information:

> Niaz Naik, a former Pakistani Foreign Secretary, was told by senior American officials in mid-July that military action against Afghanistan would go ahead by the middle of October.... US officials told him of the plan at a UN-sponsored international contact group on Afghanistan which took place in Berlin.... The wider objective, according to Mr. Naik, would be to topple the Taleban regime and install a transitional government of moderate Afghans in its place—possibly under the leadership of the former Afghan King Zahir Shah.

Citing the information he received in July 2001, the former Pakistani Minister of Foreign Affairs further stated that "Washington would launch its operation from bases in Tajikistan, where American advisers were already in place," and "Uzbekistan would also participate in the operation... 17,000 Russian troops were on standby." He was also told that "if the military action went ahead it would take place before the snows started falling in Afghanistan, by the middle of October at the latest." The 9/11 attacks provided ample pretext to implement these plans—"after the World Trade Center bombings, this pre-existing US plan had been built upon and would be implemented within two or three weeks."[99]

On September 9, 2001, only two days prior to the impending al-Qaeda attacks, President George W. Bush was presented with detailed military plans to invade Afghanistan and topple the Taliban. The plans, outlined in a National Security Presidential Directive, discussed a global campaign of military, diplomatic, and intelligence action, including an ultimatum to the Taliban:

> President Bush was expected to sign detailed plans for a worldwide war against al-Qaida two days before Sept. 11 but did not have the chance before the terrorist attacks in New York and Washington, US and foreign sources told NBC News.

The document, a formal National Security Presidential Directive, amounted to a "game plan to remove al-Qaida from the face of the Earth," one of the sources told NBC News' Jim Miklaszewski.

The plan dealt with all aspects of a war against al-Qaida, ranging from diplomatic initiatives to military operations in Afghanistan, the sources said on condition of anonymity. In many respects, the directive, as described to NBC News, outlined essentially the same war plan that the White House, the CIA and the Pentagon put into action after the Sept. 11 attacks. The administration most likely was able to respond so quickly to the attacks because it simply had to pull the plans "off the shelf," Miklaszewski said.[100]

In context with the previous documentation, this war plan had clearly been prepared through a meticulous process of consultation occurring over at least several months (probably at least a year), involving the Pentagon, CIA, and the State Department—along with other security and intelligence agencies. Indeed, according to Francis Boyle, professor of international law at the University of Illinois, the war on Afghanistan constituted the execution of "an operational War Plan... that had been in the works for at least the past four years" prior to 9/11. He reports that a US war on Afghanistan

had been war-gamed by the Pentagon going back to 1997... Right around September 11, two US Aircraft carrier task forces conveniently arrived in the Persian Gulf right at the same time on "rotation." Obviously, preplanned. Just before September 11, the UK had put together what was billed as the "largest armada since the Falklands War" and had it steaming toward Oman, where now 23,000 UK troops are on maneuvers. This had been planned for at least 3 years. Also, the US "Bright Star" operation is currently going on in Egypt. 23,000 US troops plus an additional 17,000 from NATO and its associates. This had been planned at least two years ago. Finally, NATO just landed 12,000 troops into Turkey. This had been planned for at least two years.

"September 11," he concluded, "is either a pretext or a trigger or both."[101]

2.

TERRORISM AND STATECRAFT PART I

Terror Networks and US Intelligence

According to a former CIA analyst cited by Labeviere in his *Dollars for Terror*: "The policy of guiding the evolution of Islam and of helping them against our adversaries worked marvelously well in Afghanistan against the Red Army. The same doctrines can still be used to destabilize what remains of Russian power, and especially to counter the Chinese influence in Central Asia."[1]

In other words, the CIA had always seen vast potential to use the terrorist network established by bin Laden during the Cold War in an international framework in the post-Cold War era against Russian and Chinese power, i.e. in Eastern Europe, the Balkans, and Central Asia. From the beginning of US policy in Afghanistan, the CIA had hoped that the network of terrorists being spawned by Osama bin Laden with assistance from Saudi Arabia and Pakistan would continue to be used after the Afghan war against Soviet occupation. Indeed, US intelligence maintained its co-optation of al-Qaeda by proxy as a means of expanding US power in the Balkans wars.

The degree to which al-Qaeda provides an often convenient—if highly dangerous—instrument of Western statecraft for the orchestration of illegal and corrupt covert operations can be understood in this context. In the cases discussed below, al-Qaeda is shown to be not an "enemy" to be fought and eliminated, but rather an unpredictable intelligence asset to be controlled, manipulated, and co-opted as much as possible to secure covert strategic ends.

Labeviere's book, with meticulous documentation, places all this in the context of an ongoing US policy that aims to selectively foster "Islamic" militancy to secure various strategic and economic interests around the world. Labeviere documents a "short-sighted" policy that at first did not anticipate the degree to which al-Qaeda would turn against the US, but even after reaping the bloody fruits of its own policy continued to signal a green light to its allies funneling finances and arms to al-Qaeda. The maintenance of such a green light seems based on the calculation that the policy would ultimately suit US interests far better than the alternative option: pursuing meaningful measures to crack down on bin Laden's network, including intense pressure on its own regional allies. Al-Qaeda, he reports, "was protected because the network was designed to serve US foreign policy and military interests." He adds that

US diplomacy is in the habit of using religious movements against Communism and any other obstacle to its hegemonic objectives...

After the collapse of the Soviet empire, this policy persisted without any major setback until the Gulf War. Mainly intended to safeguard the American oil supply, that police action caused a great trauma in the Arab-Muslim world. Armed Islamism then started to question the guidance of its protective father....

Shortly after the Gulf War, armed Islamism turned against its principal creator who, in spite of all, did not give up his paternalistic reflex. Indeed, although in the uncomfortable position of the attacker attacked, the United States still continues unabated its policy of supporting the multifarious explosion of an ascendant Islamism, its terrorist excesses and its business networks that are extremely ramified (if not entirely melded into the circuits of the legal economy).[2]

US policy in the Balkans provides a surprising confirmation of Labeviere's thesis and provides a profoundly powerful explanation of how Western foreign policies directly undermine Western national security by forming alliances with the very forces of terror that are so threatening. Although this material is well documented, its crucial implications are largely ignored by the majority of academic and media commentators.

Our Military Intelligence Asset in Bosnia and the 1993 World Trade Center Bombing

Successive US administrations have used al-Qaeda to pursue strategic interests in the Balkans. A further examination of this issue, however, reveals that the US–al-Qaeda alliance in the Balkans has been instrumental in facilitating successive terrorist attacks against US targets. Nevertheless, the alliance continues to exist to this day. As the London *Spectator* noted:

America's role in backing the Mujahideen a second time in the early and mid-1990s is seldom mentioned.... From 1992 to 1995, the Pentagon assisted with the movement of thousands of Mujahideen and other Islamic elements from Central Asia into Europe, to fight alongside Bosnian Muslims against the Serbs.... If Western intervention in Afghanistan created the Mujahideen, Western intervention in Bosnia appears to have globalised it.[3]

Much of the details of the alliance have been authoritatively documented in the official Dutch inquiry into the 1995 Srebrenica, which contains an in-depth report on Western intelligence in the Bosnian conflict by Professor Cees Wiebes of Amsterdam University. In a review of the Wiebes report for the London *Guardian*, British political scientist Professor Richard Aldrich of the University of

Nottingham described the Dutch inquiry's most salient findings, based on five years of unrestricted access to Dutch intelligence files and interviews with key officials:

Now we have the full story of the secret alliance between the Pentagon and radical Islamist groups from the Middle East designed to assist the Bosnian Muslims—some of the same groups that the Pentagon is now fighting in "the war against terrorism." Pentagon operations in Bosnia have delivered their own "blowback."

The policy created a "vast secret conduit of weapons smuggling though Croatia" and was "in flagrant violation of the UN security council arms embargo against all combatants in the former Yugoslavia." The conduit was arranged by the intelligence agencies of "the US, Turkey and Iran, together with a range of radical Islamist groups, including Afghan mojahedin." British intelligence services obtained documents on the secret alliance early on in the Bosnian war, but turned a blind eye. Aldrich continues:

Arms purchased by Iran and Turkey with the financial backing of Saudi Arabia made their way by night from the Middle East. Initially aircraft from Iran Air were used, but as the volume increased they were joined by a mysterious fleet of black C-130 Hercules aircraft. The report stresses that the US was "very closely involved" in the airlift. Mojahedin fighters were also flown in, but they were reserved as shock troops for especially hazardous operations.... Rather than the CIA, the Pentagon's own secret service was the hidden force behind these operations... American Awacs aircraft covered crucial areas and were able to turn a blind eye to the frequent nightime comings and goings at Tuzla.[4]

The secret arms shipments from Iran began in 1992, and were first discovered by the CIA on September 4, 1992. An Iran Air Boeing 747 was found at Zagreb airport in Croatia containing arms, ammunition, anti-tank rockets, communication equipment, uniforms, and helmets for the Bosnian Muslim Army. Around 30,000 soldiers were armed and equipped by Iran and Turkey in one three to five-month period in late 1993 in this manner.[5] US military intelligence at first tacitly consented to the conduit, but then later actively supported it. On April 27, 1994, President Clinton "decided to give a green light to the arms supplies."[6]

This secret US-backed conduit between Iran, Turkey, Saudi Arabia, and the Bosnian Muslims was also used to fly in al-Qaeda mujihadeen forces connected to Osama bin Laden from Afghanistan, Algeria, Chechnya, Yemen, Sudan, and elsewhere. The US played a very direct role in facilitating this influx. According to one authoritative report from London's International Media Corporation affiliated to Washington, DC's International Strategic Studies Association: "The Mujahedin landing at Ploce are reported to have been mujahideen accompanied by US Special Forces equipped with high-tech communications equipment." Intelligence sources indicated that "the mission of the US troops was to establish a command, control, communications and intelligence network to coordinate and support Bosnian Muslim offensives—in concert with Mujahideen and Bosnian Croat forces." The US military, in other words, was actively coordinating on the ground with several thousand members of bin Laden's al-Qaeda network in Bosnia.[7] Consequently, as estimated by US Lt. Col. John Sray who worked as an intelligence officer in Sarajevo in 1994: "Approximately 4,000 Mujihadeen, supported by Iranian special operations forces, have been continually intensifying their activities in central Bosnian for more than two years."[8] According to Yossef Bodansky, Director of the Congressional Task Force on Terrorism and Unconventional Warfare, most reliable intelligence estimates indicate that the number of al-Qaeda affiliated mujahideen operating in Bosnia at this time was more than 10,000.[9]

In a succinct overview of this policy, Director of the Centre for Research on Globalisation (CRG) Professor Michel Chossudovsky of the University of Ottawa finds that "The evidence amply confirms that the CIA never severed its ties to the 'Islamic Militant Network.' Since the end of the Cold War, these covert intelligence links have not only been maintained, they have in fact become increasingly sophisticated."[10] According to the London-based International Media Corporation, for example, "the US Central Intelligence Agency (CIA) had full knowledge of the operation" to fly in and equip hundreds of mujahideen into Bosnia-Herzegovina. Indeed, "the CIA believed that some of the 400 had been detached for future terrorist operations in Western Europe."[11]

Chossudovsky also refers to a lengthy Congressional report by the Republican Party Committee (RPC) in 1997 confirming that the Clinton administration "helped turn Bosnia into a militant Islamic base." Among the radical groups involved in the scheme was "one Sudan-based 'humanitarian organization,' called the Third World Relief Agency [TWRA]" which was "a major link in the arms pipeline to Bosnia." TWRA, however, was reportedly "connected with such fixtures of the Islamic terror network as Sheik Omar Abdel Rahman (the convicted mastermind behind the 1993 World Trade Center bombing) and Osama bin Laden, a wealthy Saudi émigré believed to bankroll numerous militant groups."[12]

In other words, the US–al-Qaeda alliance in Bosnia seems to have played a key role in preventing US action to apprehend the mastermind of the first World Trade Center bombing in 1993, Sheik Omar Abdel-Rahman (otherwise known as the "blind sheik") before the attack occurred. The blind sheik was utilized by the CIA in the Afghan war against the Soviets due to his influence over the mujahideen. Having arrived in the US on a CIA-sponsored visa, he was described by US intelligence officials as "a valuable asset."[13]

He had been a close companion of Osama bin Laden during the war against the Soviet occupation of Afghanistan.[14] As *Newsweek* reported: "the sheik had slipped into the United States with the protection of the CIA, which saw the revered cleric as a valuable recruiting agent for the Mooj [Afghan Mujahideen]. Investigators trying to track down the blind sheik 'had zero cooperation from the intelligence community, zero,' recalled a federal investigator in New York."[15]

US intelligence analyst Mary Anne Weaver observes that the CIA and State Department "overlooked his anti-Western message and incitement to holy war because they wanted him to help unify the mujahideen groups."[16] Yet the blind sheik was one of the most outspoken advocates of "jihad" against the West, in particular against America, preaching his message freely throughout the 1980s in Pakistan, Egypt, Saudi Arabia, Turkey, Germany, England, and even the United States.[17]

Citing an investigative report by *New York* magazine, the Associated Press described how this relationship proceeded in some detail:

> The CIA sponsored Sheik Omar Abdel-Rahman's visits to 'jihad offices' around the United States starting in 1986...
>
> The "jihad," or holy war, offices were American outposts for the CIA-funded Mujahedeen fighting the occupying Soviets. The war ended in 1989.... Although Abdel-Rahman's name should have been added to the State Department's list of terrorist suspects after he was acquitted in connection with the 1981 assassination of Egyptian President Anwar Sadat, that did not happen until 1987. Between 1986 and 1990, he received at least three visas to enter the United States. Eventually he received permanent resident status.[18]

But Sheik Omar's involvement in the Afghan war against the Soviets does not explain why he continued to gain entry into the US after that war had ended in 1989. The Associated Press noted that: "In 1990, a CIA officer serving at the US Embassy in Sudan... approved Abdel-Rahman's tourist visa, the State Department determined in 1993."[19] The blind sheik's green card was approved shortly after December despite the fact that the State Department by November 1990 had actually revoked his visa, advising the INS to attempt to locate him—but evidently not to expel him, for once the INS found him, it granted him a green card for permanent US residency.[20]

After the Afghan war was over, however, the blind sheik remained a significant intelligence asset, playing an instrumental role in recruiting mujahideen for Bosnia at least as early as 1993—the year of the first WTC terror attack. According to London's *Compass* magazine:

> The Al-Kifah, or Struggle, Refugee Center in New York, which used to recruit and raise funds for Mujahedeen headed for Afghanistan, last year

announced it was switching its operations to Bosnia. It was established in the mid-1980s by Egyptian Mustafa Rahman as a joint venture with Sheikh Omar Abdel-Rahman, spiritual leader of Gamaat al-Islamiya.[21]

But financial flows going through the same center were being used to contribute funds for domestic terrorist attacks. As the *New York Times* reported, "the World Trade Center bombing [1993] was financed through money coming from the Alkifah Refugee Center in Brooklyn."[22] Indeed, as late as the summer of 1993 Egyptian President Hosni Mubarak confirmed that Sheik Rahman was connected to the CIA.[23]

The blind sheik's central role in recruiting mujahideen for the covert US-backed pipeline in Bosnia demonstrates his continuing importance to US intelligence agencies despite the demise of the Cold War—even though he was on the State Department's terrorism watch list. Meanwhile, he was masterminding the 1993 bombing of the World Trade Center. For instance, when El Sayyid Nosair—a leading member of the blind sheik's al-Salaam Mosque—shot and killed radical rightwing Rabbi Meir Kahane in November 1990, the FBI refused to investigate the blind sheik's role in the murder due to his immunity as a CIA asset. The matter was revealed in a conversation between a 20-year veteran FBI agent and his top undercover operative:

> "Why aren't we going after the Sheik [Adbel Rahman]?" demanded the undercover man.
> "It's hands off," answered the agent.
> "Why?" asked the operative.
> "It was no accident that the Sheik got a visa and that he's still in the country," replied the agent, visibly upset. "He's here under the banner of national security, the State Department, the NSA, and the CIA."
> The agent pointed out that the Sheik had been granted a tourist visa, and later a green card, despite the fact that he was on a State Department terrorist watch-list that should have barred him from the country. "He's an untouchable," concluded the agent.[24]

The refusal to investigate the blind sheik was maintained in spite of the fact that Nosair was being monitored by the FBI as a suspected terrorist, and that following the shooting of Rabbi Kahane an FBI raid on El Sayyid Nosair's accommodation discovered detailed documentation of the blind sheik's World Trade Center bombing plot. William Norman Grigg reported in the *New American* that

> ... the FBI seized and impounded 49 boxes of documents from Nosair's New Jersey apartment; the cache included bomb-making instructions, a hit list of public figures (including Kahane), paramilitary training

materials, detailed pictures of famous buildings (including the World Trade Center), and sermons by Sheik Omar urging his followers to "destroy the edifices of capitalism."[25]

The Los Angeles Times similarly noted that the FBI had "discovered manuals for building bombs. They found photos of the World Trade Center, the Empire State Building and the Washington Monument and a text advocating terrorists strikes on American soil." According to one senior investigator the collection of documents amounted to "a road map" to the World Trade Center bombing plot. But they "sat" in an FBI locker "untranslated in about 50 storage boxes." Only after the detonation of the bomb in the World Trade Center did "the FBI finally open the boxes."[26]

Indeed, the key organizer of the 1993 WTC bombing plot was an Egyptian intelligence officer, Emad Ali Salem, who was at that time a longstanding FBI informant paid over $2 million for his infiltration of the blind sheik's al-Qaeda cell. Salem was called in by the prosecution as a government witness in the trial of the conspirators.[27] Throughout his surveillance of the blind sheik's cell long before the blast on February 26, Salem had secretly tape-recorded more than 1,000 conversations at various meetings with the cell's members. Salem had worked with fellow FBI informant Mahmoud Zaki Zakhary, who had infiltrated the Sheik's cell since January 10, 1990. Through their informants, the FBI "knew every residence, office and meeting which occurred between the Sheik and his followers for a period of three and a half years."[28]

Reporting on the release and discovery of the tapes, Newsday observed that

The Federal informant who allegedly foiled the plot to bomb the Holland Tunnel and the United Nations Building secretly tape recorded his conversations with Federal prosecutors and agents....

Emad Salem, the shadowy Government informant—who videotaped Muslim Fundamentalists as they allegedly conspired to bomb a variety of city landmarks—made at least forty audiotapes of his discussions with FBI and Federal authorities, sources say. Law enforcement officials discovered the tapes last month while they were gathering items from Salem's apartment, sources say. Joyce London, lawyer for suspect Tariq El-Hassan, called the tapes "'a gold mine' because they will show jurors how the case was spawned, and will possibly bolster an entrapment defense. It's going to lay out exactly how the deal was set up—what instructions he (Salem) was given, and how far he was told to go to ensnare these people," she said. Prosecutors concede that the conversations may become a potent weapon for defense attorneys, damaging the informant's credibility and strengthening the defense's theory that the FBI instigated the plot... Defense lawyers have blasted away at the credibility of Salem, accusing him of entrapping suspects in the plot that the FBI engineered. Salem worked as an FBI informant before the World Trade

Center bombing, and then was recruited to infiltrate the Muslim militant community after the February 26th explosion.[29]

According to defense lawyers for the eight Arabs accused of masterminding the plot, the tapes proved that FBI informant Salem was the pivotal orchestrator of the scheme: "Salem was wired before, after and during every meeting. It is known that Salem was involved in the initial discussions, provided the safe houses in which bombs were allegedly manufactured, helped purchase the firearms and other materials that were to be used in the attacks."[30] By mid-February, Salem had even arranged "the massive chemical bomb that would kill six and injure more than 1000 at the Trade Center, brewed in barrels hidden in the Jersey City storage unit." As usual, the wired Salem reported the bombing arrangement to his FBI handlers.[31] Renowned defense attorney William Kunstler described the implications of the transcripts of Salem's recorded conversations:

> I've read a lot of the tapes by now—transcriptions of the tapes which were just furnished to me today. Before I came here, I read some of them, and they are things like... having him [Salem] say: "Well, I think we ought to bomb the George Washington Bridge. That's a very good target. It would make the commuters raise hell with this Government of ours."
> And so then says [conspirator] Siddig Ali: "Yeah?"
> [Salem]: "And I think" so and so...
> [Ali]: "Yeah?"
> ... and so on. That's the way it goes, virtually throughout these hundreds of pages of transcriptions. There are a hundred and fifty hours of tapes.[32]

Indeed, in one of the post-attack recordings a conversation between FBI informant Salem and his handler FBI Special Agent John Anticev reveals both Salem's and the Bureau's involvement in constructing the bomb that blew up the World Trade Center:

> FBI: But ah basically nothing has changed. I'm just telling you for my own sake that nothing, that this isn't a salary but you got paid regularly for good information. I mean the expenses were a little bit out of the ordinary and it was really questioned. Don't tell Nancy I told you this. [Nancy Floyd is another FBI agent who worked with Salem]
> SALEM: Well, I have to tell her of course.
> FBI: Well then, if you have to, you have to.
> SALEM: Yeah, I mean because the lady was being honest and I was being honest and everything was submitted with receipts and now it's questionable.
> FBI: It's not questionable, it's like a little out of the ordinary.
> SALEM: Okay. I don't think it was. If that what you think guys, fine, but

I don't think that because we was start already building the bomb which is went off in the World Trade Center. It was built by supervising supervision [sic] from the Bureau and the DA and we was all informed about it and we know what the bomb start to be built. By who? By your confidential informant. What a wonderful great case![sic]...[33]

In a further extraordinary report, the New York Times revealed that the FBI had precise advanced warning of the attack. Nevertheless, no action was taken against the blind sheik's cell. Instead, FBI agents originally proposed a bizarre plan to thwart the bombing plot by replacing the explosives with a harmless powder. "The informer was to have helped the plotters build the bomb and supply the fake powder, but the plan was called off by an FBI supervisor," and the FBI refused to act to prevent the bombing. On the tapes, Salem recalls that the FBI planned on "building the bomb with a phony powder and grabbing the people who was [sic] involved in it." But, he said, the powder scheme was canceled and "we didn't do that." Salem is also heard criticizing FBI agents for ignoring his warnings of the World Trade Center bombing: "You saw this bomb went off and you... know that we could avoid that.... You get paid, guys, to prevent problems like this from happening."[34] Why had the FBI failed to act on its firsthand evidence of the bombing plot by apprehending the blind sheik and his circle of plotters? The answer seems to be, as one FBI agent observed, that he was under the protection of "the State Department, the NSA, and the CIA"— in other words, "an untouchable."

It was the blind sheik's status as a CIA asset vis-à-vis the Bosnian conflict that appears to be the primary reason he was granted effective immunity by US intelligence agencies despite being implicated in criminal acts and terrorist plots. His involvement in a covert US operation to transfer al-Qaeda militants to the Balkans in order to escalate the destabilization of Yugoslavia granted him free reign to pursue criminal and terrorist activities within the US, to the point that even after the bombing, high-level elements of the US government were extremely reluctant to prosecute him—perhaps for fear of revealing the extent of post-Cold War US co-optation of al-Qaeda. Jack Blum, investigator for the Senate Foreign Relations Subcommittee, complained that: "One of the big problems here is that many suspects in the World Trade Center bombing were associated with the Mujahadeen. And there are components of our government that are absolutely disinterested in following that path because it leads back to people we supported in the Afghan war"—and, crucially, to people whom the government continued to support in the Bosnian war.[35]

Our Military Intelligence Asset in Kosovo, Macedonia, and the 1998 Embassy Bombings in Kenya and Tanzania

US officials were well aware of the implications of their post-Cold War alliance with al-Qaeda in the Balkans. They knew that one of bin Laden's top lieutenants was commanding a league of operatives in Bosnia, which during the 1990s had thus become a "staging area and safe haven" for al-Qaeda. Nevertheless, a conscious decision was made to continue allowing the growth and activities of al-Qaeda mujahideen in Europe throughout the 1990s.[36]

Extensive military intelligence training and assistance was provided to the KLA during the Kosovo conflict in the late 1990s by both American and British forces. This training continued despite the fact that it was documented in a 1999 Congressional report by the US Senate Republican Party Committee that the KLA is closely involved with

> The extensive Albanian crime network that extends throughout Europe and into North America, including allegations that a major portion of the KLA finances are derived from that network, mainly proceeds from drug trafficking; and Terrorist organizations motivated by the ideology of radical Islam, including assets of Iran and of the notorious Osama bin-Ladin—who has vowed a global terrorist war against Americans and American interests.[37]

Indeed, as early as 1998, the US State Department listed the KLA as a terrorist organization connected to al-Qaeda.[38] Other US intelligence reports prove that not only is the KLA funded from afar by al-Qaeda, numerous KLA fighters have trained in al-Qaeda camps in Afghanistan and Albania, and numerous al-Qaeda mujahideen have joined the ranks of the KLA. The reports substantiate a "link" between bin Laden and the KLA, "including a common staging area in Tropoje, Albania, a center for Islamic terrorists." KLA-sponsored border crossings into Kosovo from Albania of hundreds of foreign fighters include "veterans of the militant group Islamic Jihad from Bosnia, Chechnya and Afghanistan," carrying forged Macedonian Albanian passports.[39]

As Ralf Mutschke, assistant director of Interpol's Criminal Intelligence Directorate, testified before Congress in December 2000: "In 1998, the US State Department listed the KLA as a terrorist organization, indicating that it was financing its operations with money from the international heroin trade and loans from Islamic countries and individuals, among them allegedly Osama bin Laden." Mutschke also confirmed that Osama bin Laden sent one of his top military commanders to Kosovo to lead "an elite KLA unit during the Kosovo conflict."[40]

While much of the KLA's funds came from Osama bin Laden as reported by Mutschke, and while KLA fighters were trained in al-Qaeda camps, US and British military intelligence personnel actively mingled with the al-Qaeda backed KLA, providing them further extensive training and assistance. The *Sunday Times* reported that since March 1999: "American intelligence agents have admitted they helped to train the Kosovo Liberation Army before NATO's bombing of Yugoslavia." CIA officers were "developing ties with the KLA and giving American military training manuals and field advice on fighting the Yugoslav army and Serbian police" under the cover of ceasefire monitors. The US military gave KLA commanders—including no doubt Osama's own military commander in Kosovo—"satellite telephones and global positioning systems." KLA commanders also "had the mobile phone number of General Wesley Clark, the NATO commander."[41] The *Herald* also disclosed that

> Both the UK and the US set up clandestine camps inside Albania to teach the KLA effective guerilla tactics.... Despite government denials on both sides of the Atlantic, SAS [British Special Forces] and US Delta Force instructors were used to train Kosovar Volunteers in weapons handling, demolition and ambush techniques, and basic organization.[42]

Former Drugs Enforcement Administration (DEA) undercover agent Michael Levine comments that US support for the KLA, which is effectively al-Qaeda's arm in the Balkans, has had direct repercussions for the United States in terms of drugs and terrorism. Levine—a 26-year veteran of undercover work for four federal agencies and the recipient of many Justice and Treasury Department awards including the International Narcotics Enforcement Officer Association's Octavio Gonzales Award—observes that US policy in Kosovo was

> simply insane... My contacts within the DEA are quite frankly terrified, but there's not much they can say without risking their jobs. These guys have a network that's active on the streets of this country.... They're the worst elements of society that you can imagine, and now, according to my sources in drug enforcement, they're politically protected.

As Levine points out, the US armed and funded "the worst elements of the Mujahideen in Afghanistan—drug traffickers, arms smugglers, anti-American terrorists. We later paid the price when the World Trade Center was bombed, and we learned that some of those responsible had been trained by us. Now we're doing the same thing with the KLA."

The same has been noted by Yousef Bodansky, director of the Congressional anti-terrorism task force, who also notes that the KLA and its Albanian mafia allies constitute a vital arm of Osama bin Laden's terrorist network within the US, providing broad financial and logistical support for operations.

> The role of the Albanian Mafia, which is tightly connected to the KLA, is laundering money, providing technology, safe houses, and other support to terrorists within this country...
>
> This isn't to say that the Albanians themselves would carry out the actual terrorist operations. But there are undoubtedly "sleeper" agents within the Albanian networks, and they can rely upon those networks to provide

them with support. In any case, a serious investigation of the Albanian mob isn't going to happen, because they're "our boys"—they're protected.

The KLA–Albanian mafia network camouflages the "blonde-haired, blue-eyed Bosnians and Albanians who are bin Laden operatives. After the last attack we're all looking for Arab suspects, but it's not going to be that easy."[43]

Former KLA forces continue to be active in Macedonia under the banner of the NLA—largely at the instigation of US military intelligence. Long after the end of the Kosovo conflict and the demise of the Milosovic regime in Yugoslavia, the BBC reported near the end of January 2001 that Western Special Forces were still training KLA guerrillas. According to foreign diplomatic sources, the former KLA had "several hundred fighters in the 5km-deep military exclusion zone on the boundary between Kosovo and the rest of Serbia..." In addition:

• Certain Nato-led K-For forces were not preventing the guerrillas taking mortars and other weapons into the exclusion zone
• The guerrilla units had been able to hold exercises there, including live-firing of weapons, despite the fact that K-For patrols the zone
• Western special forces were still training the guerrillas, as a result of decisions taken before the change of government in Yugoslavia.[44]

In May 2001, US diplomat Robert Fenwick—head of the Organization for Security and Cooperation in Europe—held a secret meeting in Prizren, Kosovo, with Albanian and former KLA (NLA) leaders, to which Macedonian officials were not invited. According to James Bisset—former Canadian Ambassador to Yugoslavia, Bulgaria, and Albania (1990–1992)—the meeting made clear that "the United States was backing the Albanian terrorist cause." One month later, 400 former NLA fighters were surrounded by Macedonian security forces in the town of Aracinovo near the capital, Skopje. Just as they began moving in, suddenly NATO ordered them to pull back. Subsequently, US Army buses from Camp Bondsteel, Kosovo, swept in to escort the NLA fighters to safety.[45]

By August 2001, Scott Taylor—Canada's top war reporter, former soldier and editor of *Esprit de Corps Military Magazine*—reported in detail on how he witnessed firsthand in Tetovo the clandestine American and British support for the ethnic Albanian guerrillas at the height of their anti-Macedonia insurgency. Noting that such support is vehemently denied by officials, Taylor pointed out that

there is no denying the massive amount of materiel and expertise supplied by NATO to the guerrillas...
   The UCK [NLA] commanders welcomed me with a shout of, "God bless America and Canada too for all that they have provided to us!" In the well constructed UCK bunkers overlooking the besieged city of Tetovo,

there is ample evidence of US military hardware. Everything from sidearms and sniper rifles to menacing-looking grenade launchers are emblazoned with a "Made in the USA" logo.

An abundant stock of sophisticated night vision goggles provides the UCK with a tremendous tactical advantage over the Macedonian security forces. By nightfall, the Macedonians are compelled to hole-up in their bunkers while the UCK roam with impunity throughout the Tetovo streets. "Snake" Arifaj, a 22-year-old platoon commander with the UCK, proudly displayed his unit's impressive arsenal and said, "Thanks to Uncle Sam, the Macedonians are no match for us."

The extent of US support to the guerrillas was highlighted in early August 2001 when the Macedonian government loudly protested the delivery of supplies by two US helicopters to an Albanian village in the mountains above Tetovo. US spokesmen said the helicopters were only providing much needed humanitarian assistance. The reality of the matter, however, was revealed by a local NLA commander known only as "Commandant Mouse," who confirmed that the supplies had consisted of "heavy mortars and ammunition" to the NLA. As if to vindicate his claim, on August 16 the NLA began firing 120mm and 82mm mortars at Tetovo. Taylor, who witnessed the mortar attacks, argues that their duration and intensity proves that the NLA is receiving a continuous and abundant supply of ammunition. US military assistance to the ethnic Albanian guerrillas was also more direct. According to Taylor: "The US also frequently used their tactical helicopters to gather intelligence inside Macedonia, without authorization from the Macedonian government. The sight of the US choppers prompted the ethnic Albanian villagers to cheer wildly, waving their arms to encourage 'their' airforce."[46]

In what appeared to be a welcome turnaround to this policy, in summer 2001 President George W. Bush signed two decrees purportedly depriving "Albanian extremists who were threatening the stability of Macedonia" of all financial or material support, and barring them from entry into the United States. But as George Szamuely reported:

The US decrees were more rhetoric than reality. As an Irish Times report put it sarcastically: "Commander Rrustem... earned fame during the Kosovo war as one of the most successful guerrilla commanders. He has since become a favourite with NATO commanders, whose glowing commendations line the walls of his office. Certainly if the Americans have reservations about him they have yet to show it: on Tuesday two separate US army teams came to his base to train his men."[47]

On June 22, 2002, a secret European intelligence report, leaked through the respected Dutch military analysis firm the Clingendael Institute to Dutch

National Radio, documented ongoing US arms and training to the NLA. The report confirmed the German *Hamburger Abendblatt's* story that 17 military advisers from the Virginian-based private US defense contractor Military Professionals Resources Inc. (MPRI) accompanied the NLA fighters evacuated from Aracinovo. The Dutch report also reveals that high-level US officials maintained constant telephone connection with the NLA rebels. The conversations were recorded by European intelligence. Although the conversations ceased when US intelligence uncovered the tapping, the communications were restored after special computers with phone technology were supplied by the US to the NLA.[48]

Simultaneously, however, the US-backed NLA remains the most prominent wing of Osama bin Laden's al-Qaeda in the Balkans. According to Yossef Bodansky, Director of Congress' Task Force on Terrorism, the Albanian network is headed by Muhammad al-Zawahiri, the engineer brother of Ayman al-Zawahiri who is bin Laden's right-hand man and mentor. According to Fatos Klosi—head of Shik, the Albanian intelligence services—a major al-Qaeda network was established in Albania in 1998 under the cover of various Muslim charities serving as a springboard for European operations. The network, Klosi noted, had "already infiltrated other parts of Europe from bases in Albania through traffic in illegal immigrants, who have been smuggled by speedboat across the Mediterranean to Italy in large numbers."[49]

The Macedonian Ministry of the Interior has provided the US National Security Council with a detailed report on al-Qaeda activity in the Kumanovo-Lipkovo region of Macedonia, including lists of operatives' names and in particular the role of two units, one consisting of 120 al-Qaeda connected fighters, the other of 250. Members of the NLA units are not only Macedonian and Kosovar Albanians, but also mujahideen from Turkey, Saudi Arabia, Pakistan, Jordan, and Chechnya, some trained in al-Qaeda camps in Afghanistan. The US has done little in response. "Officials at the NSC and CIA were polite and received the information with thanks, but little else has happened," noted one Macedonian official.[50]

Yugoslav intelligence, working on behalf of Interpol, has corroborated these findings, noting that: "The American CIA has also been made aware that last year the mujahedeen had a training camp in the village of Tropoja in northern Albania." On October 23, 2001, Interpol released a report personally linking Osama bin Laden to the Albanian mafia. Interpol also documented that one of bin Laden's senior lieutenants was commander of an elite Albanian unit operating in Kosovo in 1999. Macedonian intelligence, however, complains that NATO political pressure and direct US interference constitutes the biggest obstacle to investigating the al-Qaeda presence in the region.[51]

So powerful is the al-Qaeda presence in the Balkans that Osama bin Laden himself was issued a Bosnia-Herzegovina passport in 1993—the same time that the Pentagon was actively organizing the influx of al-Qaeda mujahideen to fight with the Bosnian Muslim Army—by the Bosnian embassy in Vienna, according to the Bosnian Muslim weekly *Dani* reporting on September 24, 1999. In the summer of 1998, a joint CIA-Albanian intelligence operation discovered that mujahideen units from at least half a dozen Middle East countries were streaming across the border into Kosovo from bases in Albania. According to Albanian intelligence chief Fatos Klosi, bin Laden had actually visited Albania himself to oversee al-Qaeda's consolidation. The Yugoslav news agency *Tanjug* confirmed the same in April 2000, noting that he had landed in Kosovo from Albania: "Until recently, Bin Laden was training a group of almost 500 mujahadeen from Arab countries around the Albanian towns of Podgrade and Korce for terrorist actions in Kosovo." *Tanjug* added that a contingent of 2000 "extremists" planned "to set off a new wave of violence."[52]

These reports are considered credible by Interpol. As reported by the Swiss financial daily *Neue Zürcher Zeitung*, Gwen McClure of Interpol's Criminal Subdivision officially informed a group of parliamentarians from NATO countries on October 23, 2001, of bin Laden's entrenched infiltration of the region, including his meeting in Albania during which he established "many structures and networks... for propaganda and fundraising activities and for providing the Algerian armed groups with logistical support."[53]

Citing Albanian intelligence sources, the Toronto-based Centre for Peace in the Balkans (CPB) confirms that: "One of the leaders of an elite KLA unit was Muhammed al-Zawahiri, the brother of Dr. Ayman al-Zawahiri, a leader in an Egyptian Jihad organization and a military commander of Osama bin Laden." Kosovo, the CPB observes, is "a paradox where several mortal enemies... Osama bin Laden and the CIA—are standing shoulder to shoulder training the KLA."[54] Elaborating on the al-Zawahiri connection, the Macedonian daily *Dnevnik* cited intelligence sources reporting that a group of "50 mujahideen" had entered Macedonia via Kosovo and "taken up positions in the mountains of Skopaska Crna Gora nearby Skopje.... An Egyptian national, the younger brother of Ayman al-Zawahiri—the commander of al-Qaeda responsible for the Balkan operations—is in charge of the terrorist groups that recently entered Macedonia." Intelligence sources noted that the plan to expand al-Qaeda operations in the Balkans is being supervised by Ayman, while his younger brother Muhammed is charged with recruiting mujahideen. *Dnevnik* noted that the NLA's 113 Brigade named Ismet Jashar along with the rapid intervention unit Baruti were "stationed at a Kosovo training camp near the village of Ropotovo in the US-run sector. Zawahiri was in charge of the terrorist training camp."[55]

On October 16, Macedonia's *Novosti* cited sources in the Russian peacekeeping force in Kosovo who corroborated the above:

A training camp of Albanian militants functions near the village of Ropotovo, close to Kosovska Kamenica, in the Yugoslav province of Kosovo, which is controlled by the American force, sources from the Russian peacekeeping force in Kosovo reported.... According to [the sources], the camp is now training 50 Afghan and Algerian mujahideen, led by Zaiman Zawahiri. He is reportedly the brother of one of the closest associates of international terrorist Osama bin Laden. This camp prepares militants for terrorist formations in Kosovo and Macedonia.[56]

According to the Arabic daily al-Sharq al-Awsat (April 16, 1999), sources linked to bin Laden in London revealed that Ayman al-Zawahiri himself, leader of the Egyptian Islamic Jihad, "is currently" in Albania. "Al-Zawahiri and Abu-al-Faraj travelled to Albania some weeks ago, heading a company of Arab mujahideen," even though Albania "is now in the grip of US intelligence."[57]

So, precisely who is Ayman al-Zawahri? He is on the FBI's "Most Wanted Terrorist" list, which refers to him as having "been indicted for his alleged role in the August 7, 1998, bombings of the US Embassies in Dar es Salaam, Tanzania, and Nairobi, Kenya.... The Rewards For Justice Program, United States Department of State, is offering a reward of up to $25 million for information leading directly to the apprehension or conviction of Ayman Al-Zawahiri."[58] Al-Zawahiri is described as bin Laden's top deputy, but even that, according to the Guardian, perhaps understates his significance in al-Qaeda. 9/11 hijackers Atta and Khalid al-Midhar were reportedly members of al-Zawahiri's Islamic Jihad. He was also implicated in the 1981 assassination of Anwar Sadat. Intelligence analysts believe that he now controls much of bin Laden's terrorist finances, operations, plans, and resources. In Afghanistan, al-Zawahiri has reportedly acted as bin Laden's spokesman. His main terrorist vehicle, Egyptian Islamic Jihad, has been linked with the Islamic Group of Egypt, who perpetrated the 1993 World Trade Center bombing. Indeed, he appeared in a video alongside bin Laden in which they threatened retaliation against the US for imprisoning the blind sheik. According to the State Department's 1997 Patterns of Global Terrorism, al-Zawahiri is leader of the Vanguards of Conquest, believed to have perpetrated the 1997 Luxor massacre and a 1995 assassination attempt against Egyptian President Mubarak.[59]

Despite this well-documented and notorious record of terror, al-Zawahiri was granted asylum in the 1990s by a variety of European countries, including Denmark and Switzerland. But most shockingly, he was even granted residence in the United States, according to an expert testifying before the House of Representatives Judiciary Subcommittee on Immigration in January 2000, who said "that he was one of a number of Islamist activists who had been granted green card status by the US immigration service."[60]

Indeed, as the New York Times reported, he traveled to and in the US in 1995 to raise funds for al-Qaeda, gathering thereby approximately half a million dollars. Although he reportedly used a false name, there is no doubt that his receipt of a right of residency from the US State Department directly facilitated his entry and tour of the US. His travels to the US were facilitated by al-Qaeda operative Ali Mohamed—a naturalized American born in Egypt—then US Army Special Forces officer and FBI informant.[61]

In 1984, Mohamed was expelled from Egyptian Special Forces as a religious extremist. He contacted the CIA, "offering to be a spy," according to one US official. The CIA judged him unreliable and dropped him as a source, the official said. He was later placed on a US government watch list, according to US officials.[62] He should therefore have been banned from entry into the US—like Sheik Omar.

A report in the *Wall Street Journal* further indicates that the FBI and the CIA were aware of Mohamed's mingling with terrorists. He nevertheless obtained a US visa, married an American woman, became a US citizen, settled in California and eventually became a US Army Sergeant by 1986. Until 1989, he was lecturing on the Middle East at the US Army's John F. Kennedy Special Warfare Center and School at Fort Bragg, North Carolina. The US Army and the CIA declined to comment when asked by *Journal* reporters about whether Mohamed was working for the CIA in the US proxy war against the Soviets in Afghanistan. San Jose obstetrician Ali Zaki, a close friend of Mohamed, was more forthcoming: "Everyone in the community knew he was working as a liaison between the CIA and the Afghan cause."[63]

Mohamed's relations to the US military and intelligence community thereafter are unclear. According to a report in the *Raleigh News & Observer*:

> Mohamed's relationship with the FBI and intelligence services remains wrapped in secrecy. His plea agreement is sealed, as are many of the court documents and much of the testimony. Mohamed was expected to testify—but did not—at the trial at which the four others were convicted. Mohamed and his lawyer have declined all interview requests.

The same report notes evidence suggesting that the CIA used Mohamed as an agent. In 1988, while still on active duty, he visited Afghanistan on leave where he fought the Soviets and made contact with Osama bin Laden, apparently with CIA sponsorship. Honorably discharged in 1989, Mohamed joined the US Army Reserves for another five years—i.e. until 1994. Documents from US court cases prove that while either on active duty or as a member of the US Army Reserves, Mohamed continued to travel abroad to meet with Osama bin Laden and his colleagues, as well as train al-Qaeda members within America. Retired Lt. Col. Robert Anderson, who was also at Fort Bragg, testifies that despite informing his superiors of Mohamed's activities in relation to terrorists, nothing was done. In 1988, Mohamed had even openly admitted to Anderson and others that he was to participate in the war against Soviet occupation in Afghanistan. As the *News & Observer* notes, "it was highly irregular, if not illegal, for an active-duty US soldier to fight in a foreign war." Anderson submitted an intelligence report to his superiors two weeks before Mohamed's departure that was completely ignored. The silence of his superiors led him to conclude that Mohamed was indeed "sponsored" by US intelligence.[64]

To this day, there remains a cloud of secrecy maintained by the US government about Mohamed's role, his simultaneous ties with US military intelligence and al-Qaeda, and how long this continued. Astonishingly, Mohamed was apparently permitted by the US military intelligence community to continue his terrorist activities unhindered through the 1990s. As the Associated Press observed:

> It remains unclear how Mohamed managed to enter the United States and join the Army in the 1980s, despite the CIA's misgivings. Equally unclear is how he was able to maintain his terror ties in the 1990s without being banished by either side, even after the Special Forces documents he stole turned up in the 1995 New York trial. The State Department, CIA, and FBI declined to answer questions about Mohamed. Officials have refused to discuss how much he has helped in their investigations as he awaits sentencing, which has been postponed indefinitely.[65]

Why the resounding official silence? "Mohamed was quiet but with a ferocious temper and very religious.... This echoes court testimony by admitted al-Qaeda members earlier this year about the man they called 'Abu Mohamed al Amriki'—Mohamed the American," reported the *News & Observer*.[66] Crucially, Mohamed—who was indicted for his role in organizing the 1998 embassy bombings—was under strict surveillance by the FBI. The US terrorism analysis journal *IntelWire* reports that: "The FBI was already well aware of Ali Mohamed, whom they had interrogated [in the early 1990s], according to trial testimony and published accounts.... Ali Mohamed trained some of the World Trade Center and 'Day of Terror' plotters in firearms use during 1989, an act which was photographed by the FBI at the time."[67] Curiously, even after the 1993 WTC bombing and the 1994 conviction of some of Ali Mohamed's trainees—all monitored by the FBI at the shooting range including Mahmud Abouhalima and Mohammed Salameh for the previous year's terrorist attack—Mohamed was permitted to continue his activities unhindered.[68]

Indeed, as early as 1990, the FBI found top-secret US Army documents that Mohamed had given to an al-Qaeda operative convicted in 1993 WTC trials. An FBI inventory showed that the documents, which resurfaced along with Mohammed's theft of them in the 1993 WTC trial, included highly sensitive material from the Joint Chiefs of Staff and the Commander in Chief of the

Army's Central Command. A former Special Forces officer confirmed that the action had certainly compromised US policy in Afghanistan. As US counterterrorism expert Steve Emerson points out:

> Federal law enforcement officials say that Mohammed's role and association with the Islamic militants surfaced in connection with the World Trade Center bombing trials in 1994 and 1995. He was named on a list of some 118 potential unindicted co-conspirators in the World Trade Center bombing conspiracy released by federal prosecutors.[69]

But although Mohamed's clandestine support to al-Qaeda was thus apparent, nothing was done to sanction him. According to the News & Observer, the reason was simple: "From 1981 until his arrest in September 1998, Mohamed was in contact with the US government.... 'He was an active source for the FBI, a double agent,' said Larry Johnson, a former CIA agent and director of counterterrorism at the State Department during the first Bush administration."[70] As Nabil Sharef, a former Egyptian intelligence officer, told the Wall Street Journal, the CIA must have been well aware of Mohamed's activities with al-Qaeda: "For five years he was moving back and forth between the US and Afghanistan. It's impossible the CIA thought he was going there as a tourist."[71]

Indeed, a US court ruling released in January 2001 revealed that FBI surveillance of the al-Qaeda cell behind the 1998 embassy bombings—including its contact with Mohamed—was extensive. Federal Judge Leonard Sand's decision in New York "reveals that US intelligence agents knew as early as April of 1996, more than two years prior to the bombing, that Osama bin Laden's terrorist organisation had established a presence in Kenya." In August 1997, Kenyan and US agents jointly searched the Nairobi home of Wadih el-Hage, a close associate of Osama bin Laden now indicted for the 1998 terror attacks. According to Judge Sand's ruling, "Important intelligence information" on the impending plot "was obtained in the course of that search." El Hage, who lived in Nairobi from 1994 until 1997, was clearly under intensive FBI surveillance— he was "questioned extensively by the FBI upon his return to the United States in September 1997, almost a year before the bombings." The evidence of FBI monitoring of el-Hage before the 1998 attack came to light in the court disclosure of "the 1996–97 Nairobi telephone monitoring of suspected bin Laden operatives" which emerged from el-Hage's "motion to suppress evidence obtained through eavesdropping." In other words, telephone communications among el-Hage and others were tapped by US intelligence:

> According to US prosecutors, the wiretapping revealed that Kenya-based members of bin Laden's organisation were providing false passports and other documents to fellow conspirators. Coded telephone numbers were also being passed to and from the headquarters of al Qaeda, the Arabic

name for bin Laden's network. The al Qaeda cell in Nairobi, likewise, warned other members of the organisation when investigators were closing in on them.

The wiretapping, it seems, had disclosed extensive information on the key conspirators behind the plot and its multiple organizers. It is certainly hard to imagine how the substance of the unfolding plan could have been missed and why US intelligence failed to apprehend the plotters. Indeed, the US State Department

> has already acknowledged that it was warned of a planned bomb attack on the Nairobi embassy nine months before the actual explosion...Mustafa Mahmoud Said Ahmed, an Egyptian national, had gone to the Nairobi embassy in November 1997 and told intelligence agents there that he knew of a group planning to detonate a truck bomb inside the diplomats parking garage. Ahmed's warning, which largely foretold the circumstances of the attack nine months later, was relayed to the State Department by the CIA.[72]

In his own guilty plea, Mohamed confirmed that he had maintained telephone contact with el-Hage from 1996 to 1998—the same period of FBI surveillance of el-Hage and his telephone communications.[73] Moreover, el-Hage's own address book—which was seized by the FBI in the 1997 search of his Nairobi home— included a contact number for Mohamed.[74] There can be no doubt then that during the two years before the 1998 bombings, the FBI was aware of Mohamed's connections to the Kenyan bomb plot, the details of which he was trying to conceal from the FBI—even though he was at that time an FBI informant. But again, he faced no appropriate sanctions. Mohamed, it seemed, had a green light from his US intelligence backers to do as he pleased. That green light, in turn, allowed him to act as escort for bin Laden's deputy, al-Zawahiri, during the 1990s, permitting him to establish a network of al-Qaeda sleeper cells in the country.

More than 10,000 pages of Egyptian state security documents obtained by the *Sunday Times* demonstrate that "Islamic fundamentalists under the command of Ayman Al-Zawahiri... established sleeper cells across the western world and were plotting sophisticated attacks." Among al-Zawahiri's operatives in the US "in the early 1990s were a communications specialist, a special forces officer, two wealthy doctors and a chain of fundraisers.... A base in Santa Clara, California, was used from 1990 to coordinate communications with terrorists' cells around the world, including Bin Laden's Sudanese base. Other operatives were based in New York."[75]

Mohamed's connections to al-Zawahiri appear to have not ended there. In fact, they seem to have continued in connection with the US–al-Qaeda alliance in the Balkans. This was revealed in an extraordinary report by veteran US intelligence and counterterrorist official Yossef Bodansky, currently the US Congress' terrorism expert, director of research of the International Strategic Studies Association, and former senior consultant to the Defense and State Departments. According to Bodansky writing in February 1998, intelligence sources revealed

> ... discussions between the Egyptian terrorist leader Dr. Ayman al-Zawahiri and an Arab-American known to have been both an emissary of the CIA and the US Government in the 1980s. Egypt's President Husni Mubarak is convinced this information is accurate and has already undertaken major steps to address the challenge. Moreover, to-date, the independent sources that provided this information have proven highly reliable and forthcoming....
>
> In the first half of November 1997, Ayman al-Zawahiri, the leader of the Jihad Organization and the Vanguard of Conquest terrorist organizations, met a man called Abu-Umar al-Amriki [al-Amriki means the American] at a camp near Peshawar on the Pakistan-Afghanistan border. High-level Islamist leaders insist that in this meeting Abu-Umar al-Amriki made al-Zawahiri an offer: The US will not interfere with nor intervene to prevent the Islamists' rise to power in Egypt if the Islamist Mujahedin currently in Bosnia-Herzegovina [B-H] refrain from attacking the US forces. Moreover, Abu-Umar al-Amriki promised a donation of $50 million (from undefined sources) to Islamist charities in Egypt and elsewhere.
>
> This was not the first meeting between Abu-Umar al-Amriki and al-Zawahiri. Back in the 1980s, Abu-Umar al-Amriki was openly acting as an emissary for the CIA with various Arab Islamist militant/terrorist movements then operating under the wings of the Afghan Jihad. In the late 1980s, in one of his meetings with al-Zawahiri, Abu-Umar al-Amriki suggested that al-Zawahiri would "need $50 million to rule Egypt." At the time, al-Zawahiri interpreted this assertion as a hint that Washington would tolerate his rise to power if he could raise this money.
>
> Thus, the mention of the magic figure—$50 million—by Abu-Umar al-Amriki in the November 1997 meeting has been interpreted by al-Zawahiri and the entire Islamist leadership, including Shaykh Usamah bin Ladin, as a reaffirmation of the discussions with the CIA in the late 1980s. The Islamist leaders are convinced that in November 1997, Abu-Umar al-Amriki was speaking for the CIA—that is the uppermost echelons of the Clinton Administration.... [T]here is no doubt that the November 1997 meeting between Abu-Umar al-Amriki and al-Zawahiri took place.[76]

Who was "al-Amriki"? There is only one other person on the historical record matching this description—Ali Mohamed, otherwise known by his al-Qaeda contemporaries as "Abu Mohamed al Amriki," was an Arab-American who acted as a CIA emissary to al-Qaeda during the Cold War and who had previously handled al-Zawahiri in the 1980s and '90s. Given that there is no other person of this description on the record, it is almost certain that "Abu Umar al-Amriki" refers to "Abu Mohamed al Amriki." Notably, Egyptian press reports on the CIA-al-Zawahiri meeting described by Bodansky—drawing on Egyptian intelligence and other sources—state only that the CIA emissary was known as "al-Amriki," suggesting that Bodansky's addition of "Umar" is perhaps mistaken.[77]

If true, Bodansky's report suggests that throughout the 1990s until the 1998 embassy bombing, Mohamed was working for the CIA. Shockingly, through "al-Amriki" the CIA had offered firstly to fund al-Qaeda to the tune of $50 million through the vehicle of bin Laden's right-hand man al-Zawahiri and secondly to allow al-Qaeda to target the secular regime of Hosni Mubarak. The condition for this deal was simply that al-Qaeda mujahideen "refrain from attacking the US forces" in the Balkans.

It is legitimate to question whether or not the deal was struck—the previous documentation on the Balkans suggests it was. In December 1997, al-Zawahiri's Jihad Group issued a special bulletin threatening an apocalyptic war on American and Israeli targets on a global scale. As Bodansky noted, at first sight the Jihad bulletin "seems to suggest that the US request for al-Zawahiri not to strike out is not being heeded to." But on further reflection, "al-Amriki was talking only about al-Zawahiri's not striking out against the US forces in B-H [Bosnia-Herzegovina]. *Nothing was said about transferring the Islamist Jihad to other 'fronts': Egypt, Israel, or the heart of America, for that matter.*"[78]

Although the CIA displayed a clear red light to al-Zawahiri for anti-US operations in the Balkans, it did not display a red light for anti-US operations anywhere else. In other words, the CIA's offer to al-Qaeda was explicitly an arrangement for al-Qaeda to cease targeting US interests in the Balkans. But by not signaling a clear red light for anti-US operations outside the Balkans, the CIA–al-Zawahiri agreement suggests the existence of an implicit decision to tolerate al-Qaeda's targeting of US interests everywhere else—including, for that matter, in Africa, New York, and Washington, DC. It is plausible to conclude that effectively, the CIA–al-Zawahiri agreement amounted to a green light to al-Qaeda to launch attacks in Egypt and, indeed, anywhere except the Balkans, as well as a promise to not interfere in such attacks.

In hindsight, the activities of the mujahideen in the Balkans supports the conclusion that al-Qaeda accepted the offer, and the US government assented to it. Thus, on November 17, 1997, Ayman al-Zawahiri's forces conducted the terrorist attack in Luxor killing nearly 70 innocent Western tourists, which undermined the very economic foundations of the Mubarak regime by damaging Egypt's tourist industry.[79] According to Bodansky, "The virtually deafening silence of the Clinton administration" in response to the Luxor massacre "had to reassure Zawahiri and bin Laden that Abu-Umar al-Amriki had spoken with its backing, and a rejuvenated call to arms followed."[80]

Ayman al-Zawahiri along with his brother, Muhammad al-Fawahiri, is currently deeply active in the Balkans, recruiting and training mujahideen to join the ranks of the US-backed KLA/NLA. Not only is al-Qaeda refraining from targeting US interests in the Balkans, they are actively working with US military intelligence and utilizing US military assistance to secure covert US interests. Simultaneously, however, al-Qaeda attacks on US targets elsewhere continued unabated—and reached a new height of bloodshed on 9/11. Nevertheless, apparently, the US–al-Qaeda alliance in the Balkans—and with it the CIA–al-Zawahiri agreement—continues seamlessly in the post-9/11 era.

At face value, this revelation represents perhaps one of the most fatal holes in the official "War on Terror" narrative so far. "Al-Amriki" was apparently connected to the CIA throughout his terrorist career, including during his involvement in the 1998 embassy bombings. Moreover, his primary role appears to have been that of a CIA–al-Qaeda go-between facilitating at least one strategic policy agreement between the two blocs. His meeting with al-Zawahri is also significant in another respect and illustrates once again the extent to which al-Qaeda's utility to the US as an asset for covert operations outweighs any Western interest in genuinely eliminating the terrorist network. US intelligence clearly was fully aware of al-Zawahiri's whereabouts and movements. Rather than making any attempt to arrest him or to at least alert Egyptian security to his location so that they could do so, no effort at all was made to apprehend him. Instead, the CIA sent its emissary to forge a mutually convenient post-Cold War pact with the devil. It is thus beyond doubt that despite the demise of the Cold War, the Western strategic alliance with al-Qaeda never ceased. Rather, it merely shifted to a new theater of military operations— from Afghanistan to Eastern Europe, Central Asia, and the Balkans. The strategic objective of the policy is the destabilization of the last remaining vestiges of Russian power in this region and the consolidation of Anglo-American hegemony in Eurasia.

Al-Qaeda terrorism throughout the post-Cold War period is therefore not merely a form of "blowback" from past Western military intelligence operations supporting the mujahideen during the Cold War. It is entirely contemporaneous "blowback" from ongoing Anglo-American ties with Osama bin Laden's international al-Qaeda terrorist network throughout the post-Cold War era. It is these covert ties that have fundamentally compromised the attempts by Western intelligence operatives to fully investigate, apprehend, and shut down the al-Qaeda terrorist network.

Indeed, the 1998 embassy bombings provide an unambiguous historical example of how the sheer existence of these ties to al-Qaeda seems to lead the US government to systematically obstruct legitimate inquiries into the network and turn a blind eye to credible warnings of the network's anti-Western terrorist attacks. On the one hand, it is probable that the bombings were a direct product of the secret CIA–al-Zawahiri agreement, which firstly granted an effective green light to the escalation of al-Qaeda anti-US terrorist operations by not showing a red light, and secondly which promised $50 million of unchecked financial assistance for al-Qaeda to use as it pleased. On the other hand, it is probable that the bombings were able to occur because investigations into al-Qaeda would inevitably be hindered, once more as a consequence of the US–al-Qaeda strategic alliance in the Balkans sealed in the CIA–al-Zawahiri agreement to turn a blind eye to non-Balkan al-Qaeda operations.

Although the State Department originally maintained it had received no specific warnings before the simultaneous August 7 explosions, a spokesman acknowledged that "the CIA had relayed two reports about Mustafa Mahmoud Said Ahmed to the department nearly a year" prior to the attacks. Ahmed had "walked into the Nairobi embassy last November and told American intelligence officials that he knew of a group planning to detonate a bomb-laden truck inside the diplomats' parking garage." Kenyan interrogators were told by Ahmed that he had "taken surveillance photos of the embassy for the attack, which was to involve stun grenades and several vehicles." This information—which detailed the entire 1998 bombing plot—was also passed to US officials, who failed to apprehend him and allowed Kenya to deport him to Tanzania where he actually participated in the operation.[81]

The CIA warnings followed hot on the heels of the FBI's strict surveillance of the Kenyan al-Qaeda cell at least since 1996, through which the US government was fully alert to the fact that al-Qaeda was planning an attack in Kenya. In the spring of 1998, a month after the latter warnings were received by the State Department from the CIA, the Clinton administration's own Ambassador to the Republic of Kenya, Prudence Bushnell, personally warned then Secretary of State Madeleine Albright of an imminent terrorist attack being planned against the US embassy in Nairobi. For several months, Ambassador Bushnell had been demanding tighter security at the embassy from the State Department in response to mounting terrorist threats and a warning that she was the target of the assassination plot. Her demands were based on a mass of ominous FBI and CIA information on the al-Qaeda Kenya threat. Intelligence sources confirm that "the CIA and FBI kept US Ambassador to Kenya Prudence Bushnell and her staff fully informed about the warnings and the possible threat."[82]

These warnings were obviously credible—and their implication, Ambassador Bushnell illustrates, was clear. But the State Department responded to her requests in the negative, citing "lack of money." Ambassador Bushnell replied that the State Department policy was "endangering the lives of embassy personnel." Indeed, an in-depth New York Times investigation of events in the year before the attacks "based on interviews with officials throughout the US government," proved that Ambassador Bushnell's warnings "were more intense, more well-founded, more specific, and more forcefully expressed than has previously been known." The review found that

- The CIA repeatedly told State Department officials in Washington and in the Kenya Embassy that there was an active terrorist cell in Kenya connected to Osama bin Laden, the Saudi exile who is accused of masterminding the attack.
- The CIA and FBI investigated at least three terrorist threats in Nairobi in the year before the bombing and took one seriously enough to send a counter-terrorism team from CIA headquarters. The agency ultimately concluded that threat was unfounded, but some officials believe the inquiry was botched, and the agency's inspector general is investigating how it was handled.
- State Department officials brushed aside Gen. Anthony Zinni, commander of the US Central Command, who had visited Nairobi on his own and warned that the Nairobi embassy was an easy and tempting target for terrorists. Zinni's offer to send his own specialists to review security in Nairobi was turned down by the State Department.
- The State Department had... adopted a strategy of improving the handful of embassies it believed were at greatest risk. Nairobi was not one of them.

This was in spite of similar warnings from other senior government officials. Gen. Zinni, for instance, "sent a cable to the State Department warning that the embassy was vulnerable to a terrorist attack after having seen security conditions at the embassy for himself." He offered to send in "a security team from CentCom to review security at the embassy, but his offer was turned down." Instead, the State Department belatedly sent its own team to conduct a security review as late as March 1998. Despite concluding that a host of new security measures were required worth a mere $500,000—measures which would have foiled the bombing plot including "the installation of a new fence around the front parking lot, upgrading perimeter surveillance, and construction of a fence in front of the embassy's front entrance"—the government failed to implement them for half a year, until the bombings occurred. This failure was unconscionable. The State Department clearly had sufficient funds for tightening security for embassies at risk of attack. Furthermore, Zinni's authoritative assessment plus classified cable traffic and intelligence reports demonstrated that the US embassy in Nairobi was at grave risk. Based on credible warnings, "the United States had growing evidence that the embassy was a target of terrorist plots, and that terrorists hostile to American interests were active in Kenya." According to the *Times*, when el-Hage's Nairobi home was raided in August 1997 by Kenyan police, CIA, and FBI officials, they discovered a letter "describing the existence of an 'East African cell' of bin Laden's group." The letter, which "set off alarm bells," combined with the previously discussed telephone monitoring of the Kenyan cell, led US officials to expect "an upcoming attack by bin Laden's Kenyan operatives... the CIA and FBI believed at the time that they had uncovered a potentially dangerous terrorist group linked to bin Laden."[83]

Also among the warnings reaching the State Department passed through Ambassador Bushnell was one in the summer of 1997, picked up by the CIA's Nairobi-based officers from an informant who stated that the Nairobi branch of an Islamic charity, the al-Haramain Foundation, was plotting terrorist attacks against Americans. The informant also warned that an al-Qaeda cell was plotting to blow up the US embassy in Nairobi. The threat was relayed to the embassy by the CIA's station chief in Nairobi. Senior US diplomats at the embassy "wanted the CIA to ask the Kenyan authorities to arrest the group's members immediately." On October 31, 1997, Kenyan police "arrested nine Arabs connected to Al-Haramain, and seized the group's files." The threat was taken so seriously that "the CIA took the unusual step of sending a team of counter-terrorism specialists from its Langley, Va., headquarters to Nairobi to investigate." Finding no evidence of a terrorist plot from al-Haramain's files, the CIA counterterrorism experts "wanted to question the Al-Haramain members in jail." But, bizarrely, the CIA station chief blocked any further inquiry, refusing "to ask the Kenyans for access to the Al-Haramain suspects" on the pretext of protecting US "relations with the Kenyans." Even more strangely, senior officials at CIA headquarters acquiesced—"they said the decision was ultimately his, and he held his ground." The nine were subsequently deported by Kenyan authorities. Members of the CIA counterterrorism team were "furious" and have harshly criticized the block, complaining that "their investigation had been dangerously short-circuited… they were unable to conduct a thorough investigation without talking to the suspects themselves." The decision was, indeed, completely unjustified—intelligence officials already "believed at the time that members of the charity were tied to bin Laden." As one State Department official remarked, the decision was not normal CIA protocol: "Why would you *not* want to interview them?" he asked.[84]

The State Department, however, anxious not to incriminate itself, denies having received any such information detailing the extent of this advanced warning. But that denial is refuted by senior intelligence and law enforcement officials:

> The State Department, said one intelligence official, was briefed about the presence of bin Laden's operatives in Kenya "before, during and after" the August 1997 raid on el Hage's house. Over the next year, intelligence officials said the CIA sent the State Department numerous reports detailing the activities of el Hage and others linked to bin Laden in Kenya. "Some of those reports referred to Osama bin Laden in the first paragraph," recalled one US intelligence official.[85]

Unsurprisingly then, US defense lawyers in the New York trial of four al-Qaeda operatives charged with the 1998 embassy bombings argued that the US government had failed to act on the credible warnings of the plot, not because they were insufficient in themselves, but because "the US government had reckless disregard for human life."[86]

The root mechanism of the government's failure was, therefore, not a lack of significant intelligence or a deficiency in interagency cooperation. On the contrary, advanced warning of the 1998 plot was sufficient to prevent it. But for unexplained reasons, the government failed to act. Now, however, we have the beginnings of a plausible—if highly unsavory—explanation. The US pact with the devil in the Balkans, driven by strategic interests, inevitably entails that the devil must be permitted to continue its activities on behalf of the US without significant interference. Thus, the imperative to secure those strategic interests inexorably leads the US to tolerate and turn a blind eye to the "blowback" of its unruly asset, if not indeed to actively protect it.

But the 1998 embassy bombings were not the only terrorist attack that appears to be directly connected to the 1997 CIA–al-Zawahiri agreement to pursue a US–al-Qaeda alliance in the Balkans. Intelligence sources reveal that Mohammed Atta had met with the US military intelligence asset al-Zawahiri in Afghanistan prior to the 9/11 terrorist attacks. According to *Time* magazine, "Atta and several others in the group" responsible for the attacks "met with senior Al Qaida leaders, most notably Ayman al-Zawahiri. The Egyptian Islamic Jihad leader is belived to be Bin Laden's deputy, and the top operational commander of Al Qaida's networks.[87] But even after 9/11, the US–al-Qaeda alliance in the Balkans, commandeered by al-Qaeda's terrorist mastermind al-Zawahiri, persists.

3.

TERRORISM AND STATECRAFT PART II

I n the current climate of the "War on Terror," it is distinctly unfashionable, if not indeed repulsive, to suggest that Osama bin Laden and his international terrorist network are actually creatures of the intelligence services. Contrary to the conventional wisdom, however, al-Qaeda's utility as a military intelligence asset for implementing illicit covert operations in pursuit of elite interests is a widespread phenomenon. We have already seen examples of covert Anglo-American support for al-Qaeda in Bosnia and Kosovo. But al-Qaeda has been manipulated and co-opted by intelligence services closely allied to the West in many other areas. To illustrate this state of affairs, we will examine cases of conflict in the Caucasus, Algeria, and the Philippines.

The Russian–Chechen Conflict and the 1999 Moscow Apartment Bombings

From 1994–96, Russia waged a brutal war to crush Chechnya's plea for self-determination. Although the Chechen resistance succeeded in repelling the invasion, Russian forces had slaughtered 100,000 Chechens, wounded 240,000, and scattered 17 million anti-personnel land mines across the country.[1] This mass destruction had been achieved through the use of "mass artillery, rocket barrages, and airstrikes to smash Chechen villages and towns," along with the use of "wide scale torture," culminating in "most of Chechnya" being "razed to [the] ground."[2]

Ironically, Russia's war had been supported by its former Cold War foe, the United States. President Clinton had "lent Yeltsin $11 billion to finance the operation," and "even went to Moscow, lauded Yeltsin, likened Russia's savage repression of tiny Chechnya to America's civil war, and had the effrontery to call Yeltsin 'Russia's Abraham Lincoln.'" The extent of US support for Russia's campaign again came to light when in 1996, "Clinton reportedly ordered the CIA to supply Moscow top-secret electronic targeting devices that allowed the Russians to assassinate Chechen President, Dzhokar Dudayev, while he was conducting peace negotiations with Moscow on his cell phone." After the war, Russia and Chechnya signed a treaty granting the latter de facto independence and recognizing an August 31, 1996, agreement stipulating that a popular referendum be held in Chechnya on December 31, 2001, to determine the country's future. But in 1999, Russia launched another attack on Chechnya, violating both the 1996 treaty and the 1990 CFE treaty.[3]

The new war was justified as a response to a devastating terrorist attack blamed on Chechnen guerrillas—in September 1999, bombs exploded in apartment blocks in Moscow and other cities, killing over 200 people. But although the Russian government immediately pinpointed the role of "terrorists" connected to the Chechen resistance, charging six Chechen men, according to the London *Economist* "No clear evidence has yet been found for who was responsible for those bombs, and no one has claimed responsibility."[4]

But it was not long before a variety of Russian insiders and observers emerged to reveal that the 1999 Chechen terrorist plot was in fact of Russia's own making. At the beginning of 2000, the London *Independent* obtained a videotape in which Russian officer Lt. Galtan stated: "I know who is responsible for the bombings in Moscow [and Dagestan]. It is the FSB [Russian security service], in cooperation with the GRU [Russian military intelligence service], that is responsible for the explosions in Volgodonsk and Moscow."[5] An investigation by Channel 4's *Dispatches* confirmed that on September 22, 1999, a third bomb was discovered in the basement of a block of flats 100 miles south of Moscow. Local residents had noticed two men and a woman acting suspiciously and called the local police, who then arrested them. The police discovered explosive devices hidden in what appeared to be bags of sugar. It was soon discovered that the suspects planting the devices were Russian FSB agents.[6]

According to Russian bomb squad officer Yuri Tkachenko, who defused the third bomb, "It was a live bomb," made of hexagen, the same explosive as the Moscow apartment bombs. Its detonator had been set for 5:30 AM, and would probably have killed most of the 250 tenants of the block of flats it was planted in. Boris Kagarlitsy, a member of the Russian Institute for Comparative Politics, stated that "FSB officers were caught red-handed while planting the bomb. They were arrested by the police and they tried to save themselves by showing FSB identity cards." According to the first man to enter the basement, Police Inspector Andrei Chernyshev:

> It was about 10 in the evening. There were some strangers who were seen leaving the basement. We were told about the men who came out from the basement and left the car with a licence number which was covered with paper. I went down to the basement. This block of flats had a very deep basement which was completely covered with water. We could see sacks of sugar and in them some electronic device, a few wires and a clock. We were shocked. We ran out of the basement and I stayed on watch by the entrance and my officers went to evacuate the people.

Despite the arrest of the FSB officers by the police, they were quietly released when the secret service's Moscow headquarters intervened. The *Observer* reports that the next day, in an attempt to cover-up the discovery, "the FSB in Moscow announced that there had never been a bomb, only a training exercise."[7] But there had been a bomb. According to Pavel Voloshin, an investigative reporter for the *Novaya Gazeta* newspaper, additional evidence of the bomb's existence emerged in his interviews with paratroopers assigned to guard the "sugar" sacks at a nearby military base. One soldier, Voloshin relates, "took a sample to a military commander schooled in explosives who said it was definitely hexagen."[8]

Russian involvement in the terror bombings was suggested again when Sergei Stepashin, Russian Interior and Prime Minister for most of the previous year, told British correspondent Patrick Cockburn that

> Russia made its plans to invade Chechnya six months before the bombing of civilian targets in Russia and the Chechen attack on Dagestan which were the official pretext for launching the war. His account wholly contradicts the official Russian version... which claims that it was only as a result of "terrorist" attacks last August and September [1999] that Russia invaded Chechnya.

According to Stepashin, the plan to send the Russian army into Chechnya "had been worked out in March [1999]," and he had played a central role in organizing the military build up before the invasion. The latter, he said, "had to happen even if there were no explosions in Moscow." Cockburn points out: "The revelation by Mr. Stepashin, that Russia planned to go to war long before it has previously admitted, lends support to allegations in the Russian press that the invasion of Dagestan in August and the bombings in September were arranged by Moscow to justify its invasion of Chechnya."[9]

But Boris Kagarlitsky of the Institute of Comparative Politics at the Russian Academy of Sciences further stated in the *Novaya Gazeta* that the bombings in Moscow and elsewhere were arranged by Russian intelligence agencies: "He says they used members of a group controlled by Shirvani Basayev, brother of the Chechen warlord Shamil Basayev, to plant the bombs" which "killed 300 people in Buikask, Moscow and Volgodonsk in September." According to Cockburn, Kagarlitsky was "drawing on a source with close knowledge of the GRU." Kagarlitsky also revealed that the "invasion of Dagestan by Shamil Basayev himself in August was pre-arranged with a senior Kremlin leader at a meeting in France in July." The underlying motive for these covert operations "was the need for the political leadership in the Kremlin to control the succession of Boris Yeltsin," who by "last summer" "was deeply unpopular," and whose "family and associates feared for their freedom and their fortunes if a president hostile to their interests was elected this June." Cockburn also draws attention to a crucial June 6, 1999, report in the Swedish daily *Svenska Dagbladet* by the paper's Moscow correspondent Jan Blomgren, disclosing that

> ... one option being considered by the Kremlin and its associates was "terror bombings in Moscow which could be blamed on the Chechens."

This was four months before the first bomb. Mr. Blomgren told the *Independent* that his sources, whom he cannot name, were familiar with discussions within the political elite.[10]

After Russian elites made the decision to orchestrate a terror bombing, according to Kagarlisky, in July 1999

> ... a meeting took place in the south of France attended by Alexander Voloshin, head of the presidential administration, Shamil Basayev, the Chechen warlord, and Anton Surikov, a former official belonging to the army special services. Both sides had interests in common. Mr. Basayev's political fortunes had ebbed in Chechnya and might be restored by a small war. The Kremlin was also in need of an outside enemy. According to Mr. Kagarlitsky they agreed that Mr. Basayev would launch a military foray into Dagestan and that Russia would respond by invading northern Chechnya up to the Terek river.

Basayev's forces thus invaded Dagestan at Russian instigation on August 8, 1999. "The next day Vladimir Putin replaced Stepashin as prime minister." However, the invasion of Dagestan "did not go as planned." Basayev's forces "were beaten off but, according to the Russian magazine *Profile*, were virtually escorted back to the Chechen border by two Russian helicopters." The invasion was also

> insufficient to mobilise Russian public opinion...
> It was the wave of anger and hatred among Russians against Chechens, universally blamed for the attacks, that gave Mr. Putin the backing he needed to invade Chechnya. An unknown figure when appointed, with just 2 per cent support in the polls, he was soon the leading candidate to win the presidency. In December Mr. Yeltsin was able to retire more gracefully than seemed possible six months before and Mr. Putin became acting president.[11]

Russian co-optation of Baseyev and the Chechen resistance is longstanding. Cockburn notes for instance that: "In 1992–93 he is widely believed to have received assistance from the GRU when he and his brother Shirvani fought in Abkhazia, a breakaway part of Georgia. Russia did not want to act overtly against Georgia but covertly supported a battalion of volunteers led by Mr. Basayev."[12]

Forbes senior editor and historian Paul Klebnikov in his book, *Godfather of the Kremlin*, notes the widely acknowledged fact that "Kremlin oligarch Boris Berezovsky gave the al Qaeda-connected Chechen terrorist leader Shamil Basayev $1 million prior to the 1999 Dagestan incursion that triggered the latest Chechen conflict." Klebnikov reports that

Berezovsky, together with other members of the Yeltsin inner circle, had long maintained a secret relationship with Chechen extremists...

To the extent Berezovsky represented the interests of the Yeltsin regime in Chechnya, the Kremlin had been undermining the [Chechen] moderates, supporting the extremists financially and politically, and consequently sowing the seeds of conflict... the Berezovsky strategy with the Chechen warlords was a deliberate attempt to fan the flames of war.

According to Kagarlitsky writing in *Novaya Gazeta* (January 24, 2000), Shamil Basayev and his brother have long been special agents of the Main Intelligence Directorate of the Russian General Staff. In an article titled "Who Blew Up Russia" in the February 2000 edition of *Versiya*, another researcher Pyotr Praynishnikov reported that "Chechnya's terrorists had been trained by the GRU—by Russia's SPETSNAZ (special diversionary troops)." The Basayev brothers, Shamil and Shirvani, were "both recruited as agents by the Main Intelligence Directorate of the Russian General Staff (GRU) in 1991–2." Indeed, Basayev was initially recruited by the GRU to "organize kidnappings, bombings and airline hijackings in Russia and Abkhazia." In 1992, Basayev and his men were allowed by Russian guards to travel freely across the borders into Chechnya.[13]

According to R. P. Eddy, former director of counterterrorism at the White House National Security Council, at the end of the Afghan war in 1989, "a multinational force of mujahadin slithered into Chechnya" led by "Omar Ibn al Khattab, who had trained in bin Laden's camps. Bin Laden and Khattab enjoyed an unusually close theological affinity, and exchanged personnel and resources." Khattab was appointed operations chief "under the overall commander, Shamil Basayev. Like Khattab, Basayev had trained in al Qaeda camps and was personally close to bin Laden."[14] Basayev himself has admitted to reporters that he "visited training camps in Afghanistan three times in the early 1990s to study the tactics of guerrilla warfare. In Chechnya, he and Khattab built their own training camp in the village of Serzhen-Yurt, complete with advanced communications equipment."[15]

Since the mid-1990s, bin Laden has funded Chechen guerrilla leaders Basayev and Khattab, sidelining the moderate Chechen majority, "to the tune of several millions of dollars per month" according to the *Asia Times*:

Khattab, after the outbreak of the second Chechen war in 1999, aligned ever more closely with the most radical Chechen elements around Shamil Basayev and Arbi Barayev, sidelining more moderate Chechen leader Aslan Maskhadov. Not only did significant funds and guns flow from al-Qaeda to Khattab; Chechens also received training in Afghanistan and an Islamic "learning center" preaching strict Wahhabism (and at one point counting 1,000 recruits to the Islamic jihad cause) was established in Chechnya.[16]

Indeed, Russian and US sources confirm that by 1999, al-Qaeda mujahideen from Afghanistan, Pakistan, Egypt, and Sudan, with heavy financing from bin Laden, were involved in Basayev's FSB-backed insurrection. According to Bodansky, the mujahideen force consisted of 10,000 fighters trained in al-Qaeda camps. Shortly before Basayev's invasion of Dagestan, Osama bin Laden himself "made a weeklong visit to a training camp in the village of Serzhen-Yurt in Chechnya."[17]

In other words, the 1999 invasion of Dagestan and Moscow apartment bombings were covert operations orchestrated by Russian intelligence agencies, which have for many years co-opted and manipulated the al-Qaeda leadership of the Wahabi Chechen guerrilla movement. The key Chechen commanders Shamil and Shirvani Basayev, who are al-Qaeda operatives personally connected to Osama bin Laden, are simultaneously agents of Russian military intelligence. Al-Qaeda's presence and activities in the Caucasus and its involvement in the 1999 insurrection and terror bombings are merely integral dimensions of a wider Russian strategy to fan the flames of war and legitimize the wholesale militarization of Russian policy in the region.

Ironically, the Russians are not the only ones who have co-opted the al-Qaeda guerrillas in Chechnya. US congressional intelligence and security analyst Yossef Bodansky reports that the US government was actively involved in "yet another anti-Russian jihad" in the "Summer of 2000." The end of the Cold War, it seems, did not mean the end of the US alliance with the mujahideen:

> As if reliving the "good ol' days" of Afghanistan of the 1980s, Washington is once again seeking to support and empower the most virulent anti-Western Islamist forces. The US crossed the line in mid-December 1999, when US officials participated in a formal meeting in Azerbaijan in which specific programs for the training and equipping of mujahedin from the Caucasus, Central/South Asia and the Arab world were discussed and agreed upon. This meeting led to Washington's tacit encouragement of both Muslim allies (mainly Turkey, Jordan and Saudi Arabia) and US "private security companies" (of the type which did the Clinton Administration's dirty job in the Balkans while skirting and violating the international embargo the US formally supported) to assist the Chechens and their Islamist allies to surge in the Spring of 2000 and sustain the ensuing jihad for a long time.

Thus, the al-Qaeda affiliated Chechen guerrillas have been jointly manipulated by both Russian and US intelligence services, although it seems that the two powers have varying interests for doing so. While Russia sees the war with Chechnya as an opportunity to militarize Russian foreign policy and forcefully maintain its military occupation of the region to protect strategic and oil pipeline routes, the US sees the ongoing conflict as a way to do the opposite by "depriv[ing] Russia of a viable pipeline route through spiraling violence and terrorism... US-assisted escalation and expansion of the war in Chechnya should deliver the desired debilitation of Russia." Thus, the US was "fanning the flames of the Islamist jihad in the Caucasus through covert assistance [and] tacit encouragement of allies to actively support the mujahedin."[18]

The Bush administration has apparently continued this policy. In January 23, 2002, State Department officials met with Chechen Foreign Minister Ilyas Akhmadov in Washington, DC, purportedly to discuss his "insights" into the conflict.[19] Russian officials, however, obviously aware of the extent of US involvement in the region, criticized the meeting as a public demonstration of support for the Chechen independence movement: "As we had warned the American side, such a contact, whatever the justifications for it, cannot but be seen as an unfriendly step in respect of Russia," stated the Russian Ministry of Foreign Affairs in a press statement. Such contact "essentially encourages Chechen separatists."[20] In other words, the US government is actively providing covert and other military and financial support to al-Qaeda fighters in the Caucasus in order to destabilize Russian power.

Algerian State-Terrorism and the Armed Islamic Group
In December 1991, the Islamic Salvation Front (FIS) won a landslide victory in Algeria's national democratic elections. But before the parliamentary seats could be taken in January 1992, the Algerian military violently overturned democracy. The elections were canceled while the army rounded up tens of thousands of Algerian FIS voters into concentration camps in the middle of the Sahara.[21] The army took power and forced the FIS to flee. As Lahouri Addi notes "the legalization of multipartism" in 1989 "mainly benefited the Islamists organized into the Islamic Salvation Front (FIS), which carried both the June 1990 local elections and the first round of the December 1991 national legislative races. The military suspended the process and nullified the first-round results in January 1992. Next, it forced President Chadli Benjedid to resign. Since then, Algeria has plunged into murderous strife that already has claimed more than 60,000 lives."[22]

This was a dark day for democracy. According to Ben Lombardi, who is with the Directorate of Strategic Analysis at the Department of National Defense in Ottawa, Canada: "In 1991, the West supported the coup in Algeria in an effort to prevent Islamic fundamentalists coming to power through the ballot box."[23] As noted by John Entelis, professor of political science and director of the Middle East Program at Fordham University in New York:

> The Arab world had never before experienced such a genuinely populist
> expression of democratic aspirations.... Yet when the army overturned the

whole democratic experiment in January 1992, the United States willingly accepted the results.... In short, a democratically elected Islamist government hostile to American hegemonic aspirations in the region... was considered unacceptable in Washington.

The new junta, in contrast, expressed "willingness to collaborate with American regional ambitions," which included "collaborating with Israel in establishing a Pax Americana in the Middle East and North Africa."[24]

Not long after the coup, hundreds of civilians were being mysteriously massacred by an unknown terrorist group shortly identified as a radical offshoot of the FIS. According to the new military regime, this band of terrorists calling itself the Armed Islamic Group (GIA) was composed of bitter former FIS members retaliating against the junta by murdering civilians. However, as the *Encyclopedia of the Orient* points out, the "GIA is not cooperating with FIS, and there is a strong political and ideological conflict between GIA and the militant part of FIS, the AIS." Moreover, the GIA's "core members are the thousands of 'Afghans,' men who have received their military training from Afghanistan."[25]

The formation of the GIA was rooted in al-Qaeda. The group was first "created in the house of the Muhajirin in 1989 in Peshawar." From here, on the border of Pakistan and Afghanistan, "the first hard core of 'Algerian Afghans' launched their terrorist campaign against Algeria." The al-Qaeda veterans of the Afghan war against the Soviets, "trained in the Afghan militias, returned to Algeria with the help of international networks, via Bosnia, Albania, Italy, France, Morocco or Sudan."[26] According to *Jane's Defense Weekly*, in the late 1980s between 400 and 1,000 Algerians who trained as bin Laden's mujahideen in Afghanistan joined various armed groups in Algeria. By January 1993, most of these groups united under the banner of the GIA.[27] The latter forged close links to al-Qaeda "in the early 1990s," reports the office of the Attorney-General in Australia, when the UK-based Abu Qatada "was designated by bin Laden as the spiritual adviser for Algerian groups including the GIA."[28] Afghan veteran Khamareddine Kherbane was close to both the GIA and al-Qaeda leaderships. Both the GIA and its sub-faction the Salafist Group for Preaching and Combat (GSPC) "developed ties with Al-Qaeda early on." From 1997 to 1998, al-Qaeda achieved further "large-scale penetration of Algerian groups."[29] So far the total civilian death toll from the GIA massacres in Algeria amounts to nearly 150,000.[30] The GIA is also implicated in terrorist atrocities outside Algeria and has been "linked to terrorist attacks in Europe."[31] According to Stephen Cook, an expert on Algeria at the Brookings Institute, "there are Algerian [terrorist] cells spread all over Europe, Canada, and the United States."[32]

In November 1997, Secretary-General of Amnesty International Pierre Sane observed that in that year alone "Algerians have been slain in their thousands with unspeakable brutality... decapitated, mutilated and burned alive in their homes," with torture, "disappearances" and extrajudicial executions becoming "part of the daily reality of Algerian life." He also noted, importantly, that "many of the massacres have been within shouting distance of army barracks, yet cries for help have gone unanswered, the killers allowed to walk away unscathed." Surprisingly, the majority of the massacres had "taken place in areas around the capital Algiers, in the most militarised region of the country." Massacres occurred "close to army barracks and security forces posts. Yet the army and security forces did not intervene, neither to stop the massacres nor to arrest the killers—who were able to leave undisturbed on each occasion." To convey the scale and brutality of the massacres, Sane cites several examples from 1997: "on the night of 11 July in Bou-Ismail, west of Algiers, a family of 12 were massacred"; "on the night of 28 August in Rais, south of Algiers, up to 300 people, many of them women and children, even small babies, were killed and more than 100 injured"; "on the night of 5 September in Sidi Youssef, on the outskirts of Algiers, more than 60 people were massacred"; "on the night of 22 September in Bentalha, south of Algiers, more than 200 men, women and children were massacred"; "in the past few weeks, hundreds more have been killed in a series of massacres of a dozen or more people at a time."[33]

Over the years, credible evidence has emerged pointing inescapably to the conclusion that the GIA is, in fact, a creature of the Algerian secret services. Dr. Hamoue Amirouche, a former fellow of the Institut National d'Etudes de Strategie Globale (Algiers), noted at the beginning of 1998 that

> ... the military regime is perpetuating itself by fabricating and nourishing a mysterious monster to fight, but it is demonstrating daily its failure to perform its most elementary duty: providing security for the population. In October 1997, troubling reports suggested that a faction of the army, dubbed the "land mafia," might actually be responsible for some of last summer's massacres, which... continued even after the Islamic Salvation Army, the armed wing of the FIS, called for a truce, in effect as of October 1, 1997.[34]

The French magazine *Paris Match* reported that this "land mafia," consisting of elements of the Algerian military regime, was cleansing premium lands of peasant occupants in anticipation of the privatization of all the land in 1998.[35]

A number of reports cast initial doubt over the conduct of the Algerian authorities vis-à-vis the massacres. Robert Fisk refers to "evidence that the massacred villagers were themselves Islamists, and increasing proof that the Algerian security forces remained—at best—incapable of coming to their rescue." This has "cast grave doubt on the government's role in Algeria's dirty war."[36] The *Sunday Times* similarly noted that the genocidal massacre of over 1,000 villagers in the first three weeks of 1998 occurred "within 500 yards of an army base that did not deploy a single soldier, despite the fact that the gunfire and screams would have been clearly audible. Villagers said that some of the attackers wore army uniforms."[37] Further questions were raised in light of the testimony of a 23-year-old Algerian army conscript who spoke of "watching officers torture suspected 'Islamist' prisoners by boring holes in their legs—and in one case, stomach—with electric drills in a dungeon called the 'killing room.'" Most pertinently, however, "he claimed that he found a false beard amid the clothing of soldiers who had returned from a raid on a village where 28 civilians were later found beheaded; the soldier suspects that his comrades had dressed up as Muslim rebels to carry out the atrocity."[38]

But these doubts were finally confirmed in multiple critical confessions from Algerian insiders defecting from positions in the regime's military intelligence agencies. In a detailed report, British journalists John Sweeney and Leonard Doyle interviewed "'Yussuf-Joseph' a career secret agent in Algeria's *securite militaire* until he defected to Britain." Algeria's secret police state, they conclude, "is indicted by one of its own members for crimes against humanity." "Joseph," who spent 14 years as an Algerian secret agent, told Sweeney and Doyle that: "The bombs that outraged Paris in 1995—blamed on Muslim fanatics—were the handiwork of the Algerian secret service. They were part of a propaganda war aimed at galvanising French public opinion against the Islamists."

The massacres in Algeria, blamed on the GIA, are in fact "the work of secret police and army death squads.... The killing of many foreigners was organised by the secret police, not Islamic extremists." GIA terror is, in fact, "orchestrated by two shadowy figures... Mohammed Mediane, codename 'Tewfik,' and General Smain Lamari, the most feared names in Algeria. They are, respectively, head of the Algerian secret service, the DRS, and its sub-department, the counter intelligence agency, the DCE." According to Joseph:

> The GIA is a pure product of Smain's secret service. I used to read all the secret telexes. I know that the GIA has been infiltrated and manipulated by the government. The GIA has been completely turned by the government.... In 1992 Smain created a special group, L'Escadron de la Mort [the Squadron of Death]. One of its main missions to begin with was to kill officers, colonels. The death squads organise the massacres. If anyone inside the killing machine hesitates to torture or kill, they are automatically killed.... The FIS aren't doing the massacres.

As for the Paris bombings, Joseph reveals that Algerian secret agents sent by Smain organized "at least" two of the bombs in Paris in summer 1995. "The operation was run by Colonel Souames Mahmoud, alias Habib, head of the secret service at the Algerian embassy in Paris."[39]

Another former Algerian secret service officer known as Captain "Haroune"—who was authenticated by the British Foreign Office—defected and sought asylum in London. He informed a British House of Commons all-party committee that his ex-colleagues carried out "dirty jobs, including killing of journalists, officers and children." The murder of seven Italians in Jenjen in July 1994 was, he disclosed, perpetrated by state military security death squads to blacken the name of "Islamic fundamentalists." Arrested suspects for the murder were merely scapegoats forced to sign confessions under torture.[40] In 1998, the former Algerian agent told Swiss TV that

> It's the army which is responsible for the massacres; it's the army which executes the massacres; not the regular soldiers, but a special unit under the orders of the generals. It should be remembered the lands are being privatized, and land is very important. One has first to chase people from their land so that land can be acquired cheaply. And then there must be a certain dose of terror in order to govern the Algerian people and remain in power. A Chinese saying tells that a picture is worth a thousand words. I could not stand the image of a young girl having her throat slit. I could not bear seeing what happened and not tell it. I have children, imagine what this girl had to suffer, the last 10 seconds of her life must have been horrible. I think it's our duty to speak up about this. I speak today in the hope that others would do the same, so that things change, and so that these killings cease.[41]

In November 1997, a serving officer with the Algerian military known as "Hakim" contacted the French newspaper Le Monde to express the feelings of a group of officers who were sickened by their work. According to the London Observer correspondent John Sweeney, Hakim claimed that the murder of seven monks by GIA terrorists "had been a hit staged by the secret police. He also said two bombs that killed eight and wounded 143 in Paris in 1995 were planted at the instigation of the Algerian junta." In his own words, Hakim stated

> We have become assassins, working for a caste of crooks who infest the military. They want everything: oil, control of imports, property...
>
> I confirm that the outrages of St. Michel (in which eight were killed and more than 130 people wounded on 25 July 1995) and that of Maison Blanche (when 13 were wounded on 6 October 1995) were committed at the instigation of the Infiltration and Manipulation Directorate (DIM) of the Directorate of the Intelligence Service (DRS), controlled by Mohammed Mediene, better known under the name "Toufik" and General Smain Lamari.

The objective of the operation had been to "win over public opinion in discrediting the Islamists." He also disclosed that the GIA's terrorist leader Djamel Zitouni, although presented as "public enemy number one" was in fact an agent of the Algerian regime. "He was recruited in 1991 in an internment camp in the south of Algeria, where thousands of Islamists had been imprisoned." According to Hakim, the junta had used Djamel to win control over the GIA in 1994. The GIA leader "had been under our control until the Tibehrine affair. The monks were to have been found in the village of an Islamic chief, who would be blamed. For reasons I do not know, he did not respect the contract. So he was liquidated." Hakim's courageous revelations soon led to his own liquidation. The *Observer* reports that

> Hakim was tracked down by the Algerian secret police shortly after he contacted *Le Monde*. They took away his diplomatic passport and sent him to the south—to the Sahara. His family were placed under close watch and were very frightened. (At no time have Hakim's family been in touch with the *Observer*.) Then they heard he had been killed in a helicopter accident.[42]

Further confirmation of the GIA's role as an instrument of governmental repression came from former Algerian Prime Minister (1984–1988) Dr. Abdel Hameed Al Ibrahimi, a member of Algeria's ruling party, the National Liberation Front, and Director of a London-based center for the study of North African affairs. "As for the Islamic armed groups," he discloses, "they are penetrated by the military intelligence service. It is known that most of the mass killings and bombings are made by the government itself whether through special forces or through the local militias (about 200,000 armed men), but the government accuses the Islamists of the violence." The vast majority of victims of the mass killings "are Islamists or ordinary citizens well-known for their support of the Islamic Salvation Front (FIS). Bombings always occur in quarters known to be affiliated with the FIS." As to the purpose of the killings, he argues that the regime is trying to "obtain additional financial, political, and diplomatic support from France and other Western countries," by posing as "the defender of the West against fundamentalism in Algeria and as an acclaimed partner in defending the French and Western interests in the region."[43]

The detailed testimony of a former Special Forces officer in the Algerian army, Second Lieutenant Habib Souaidia, further confirms that the GIA is a product of Algerian intelligence. In his landmark book *The Dirty War* Souaidia exposes how the GIA has been used to liquidate opposition to the regime. One example of his firsthand knowledge of army atrocities against civilians is particularly pertinent and is cited here in detail:

> It happened one night in March, 1993. After I finished my shift I was summoned to my commanding officer, Major Daoud. He ordered me to take my people to guard a truck on its way to one of the villages. I went outside and I saw the truck. I peeked inside and saw the silhouettes of dozens of commando fighters from one of the special units. They were carrying knives

and grenades. I was told that they were on their way to a "special mission."

I drove behind the truck until it stopped in the village of Dawar Azatariya where the inhabitants were suspected of supporting the FIS movement. I was asked to remain with my men outside the village. Two hours later the truck came back. One of the officers took a blood-stained knife that he held near his throat, making a sweeping side to side motion. I didn't need any additional signs to understand what had happened in the village. Two days later there were headlines in the Algerian press: "Islamic attack in Dawar Azatariya. Dozens killed in the massacre." I couldn't believe my eyes. I felt that I had been an accomplice to a terrible crime....

I wanted to write about the dirty war that was directed against innocent civilians, whose only crime was that they were well-disposed toward Islam. This war is still going on. Thus far more than 150,000 people have been killed, and those responsible for this crime are the generals who head the army. They are fighting to defend their rule and the enormous amount of property they have accumulated.... France has given me political asylum, but this cannot prevent me from declaring that it has abetted the murderous generals to protect its interests.[44]

Souaidia has further noted that Algerian government penetration of domestic Muslim terrorist networks was very thorough: "Several armed islamist groups... were created in the weeks that followed the stopping of the electoral process [in 1992]." These groups were in addition to already extant radical groups such as Takfir wal-Hijra. But even though "these groups were autonomous compared to the FIS... it was already being said at the time that they had been infiltrated or manipulated by the Securite Militaire (SM)."[45]

According to former Algerian colonel Mohammed Samraoui—a member of the post-coup Algerian junta, deputy director of Algerian counter-intelligence (DRS), and later top counter-intelligence officer in Europe based at the Algerian Embassy in Bonn—"the terror groups in the underground were bred and manipulated by the secret service of Algeria." In July 1991, the secret services established the first artificial Islamist terror base thirty miles from Algiers. After their arrest, Islamists from opposition groups were "turned" and used to run operations by the secret services. These operations were behind the endless series of GIA terror attacks in Algeria. Indeed, all key GIA emirs were operatives of the secret services.[46]

Algerian terror networks connected to the GIA—which in turn is interlinked with al-Qaeda—are in fact a product of the Algerian intelligence agencies that are manipulated and co-opted in the service of elite interests. The precise structure of this relationship is unclear. What is certain, however, is that while on a personnel-level the GIA interpenetrates with al-Qaeda, on an organizational level the network is manipulated by Algerian intelligence services, which, in turn, both interpenetrate the group and manipulate it through co-optation of key group members. Despite their avid denials, Western governments and intelligence agencies are fully cognizant—if not deeply complicit—in the Algerian state's subversion of the Algerian terror networks. After the publication of the confessions of Algerian defector "Joseph" in several European newspapers

> The Algerian ambassador to Italy was called in "for consultations." The next day, the Italian ambassador to Algeria was, in his turn, called in, "for consultations." The office of the Italian Prime Minister quoted British intelligence sources dismissing Joseph's story. The office of the French Interior Ministry dismissed the story. The Algerian ambassador to London, His Excellency Ahmed Benyamina, dismissed the story as "fanciful." All these dismissals had one thing in common: they were delivered at one remove.[47]

But the coordinated chorus of denial being sung by the West was a collective act of conscious deception. According to New Zealand lawyer and Algeria expert Richard McLeod: "When France withdrew from Algeria, it retained very close links with an elite group within Algerian society, namely the generals."[48] Gordon Campbell, correspondent for the *New Zealand Listener*, notes that "details of French/Algerian collusion with the GIA are even more disturbing." He cites the recent emergence of "firm evidence" from Algerian military sources and leading academics that "the dreaded GIA has been—perhaps from the outset... a dummy, or 'screen' organisation managed by French/Algerian counter-intelligence."[49] According to the *Observer*: "After the [summer 1995 Paris] bombings, the then French Interior Minister, Jean-Louis Debre, was asked at an off-the-record lunch whether it was possible the Algerian secret police had been behind the bombings. He said: 'The Algerian securite militaire would like us to go up the wrong trail so that we can eliminate people who annoy them.'"[50] Minister Debre's admission is a crucial revelation because his statement confirms French government knowledge that widespread adherence to the official narrative—the bomb plot was the work of the GIA—is "going up the wrong tail," and furthermore that the French government is complicit in the Algerian junta's program to "eliminate people who annoy" it, namely, the vast majority of the Algerian population. The French government, in other words, while maintaining close military intelligence ties with the Algerian generals behind the GIA, has failed to sanction them despite being aware that they are the root cause of the terror.

Indeed, Western intelligence agencies know far more about the crisis then they have publicly conceded. In a remarkable report in the *Guardian*, Richard Norton-Taylor recorded that "An unprecedented three-year terrorist case dramatically collapsed yesterday when an MI5 informant refused to appear in court after evidence which senior ministers tried to suppress revealed that

Algerian government forces were involved in atrocities against innocent civilians." The report further refers to "secret documents showing British intelligence believed the Algerian government was involved in atrocities, contradicting the view the government was claiming in public." Attempting to suppress the evidence, three British Cabinet ministers—Jack Straw, Geoffrey Hoon and Robin Cook—"signed public interest immunity certificates."[51]

The secret Foreign Office documents "were produced on the orders of the trial judge" 18 months late. But when they finally arrived, "they were in marked contrast to the government's publicly-stated view, expressed by the Foreign Office in 1998, that there was 'no credible, substantive evidence to confirm' allegations implicating Algerian government forces in atrocities." The documents, read out in open court, revealed that according to Whitehall's Joint Intelligence Committee: "responsibility for violence cannot be conclusively laid in one place.... There is no firm evidence to rule out government manipulation or involvement in terrorist violence." According to one document: "Sources had privately said some of the killings of civilians were the responsibility of the Algerian security services." Another document from January 1997 cites a British source as follows: "military security [in Algeria] would have... no scruples about killing innocent people.... My instincts remain that parts of the Algerian government would stop at nothing." Multiple documents, according to the *Guardian*, "referred to the 'manipulation' of the GIA being used as a cover to carry out their own operations." A US intelligence report similarly confirmed that "there was no evidence to link 1995 Paris bombings to Algerian militants." On the contrary, the US report indicates "that one killing at the time could have been ordered by the Algerian government." Crucially, a Whitehall document cites the danger to British government interests if this information becomes public—"if revealed," it warns, it "could open us to detailed questioning by NGOs and journalists."[52]

Why would the British government—or indeed any of the Western governments—fear public scrutiny of their Algerian policy, unless they were in some manner culpable? Perhaps a glimpse of an answer is provided by two French reports on the Algerian intelligence-backed GIA masterminds of the 1995 Paris bombings. According to the French daily *Le Figaro*: "The track of Boualem Bensaid, GIA leader in Paris, leads to Great Britain. The British capital has served as logistical and financial base for the terrorists."[53] *Le Parisien* further reported that the Algerian-backed organizer of the attacks was Abou Farres, a former leader of the Afghan mujahideen. Although he was already wanted for involvement in the Algiers airport bombing, Farres was granted a residence visa in London in 1992, where he recruits impoverished Muslim youngsters from Paris suburbs and sends them to al-Qaeda training camps in Afghanistan.[54]

The US government also appears to be connected. According to US historian James Ciment at the City College of New York, author of *Algeria: The*

Fundamentalist Challenge, there is reason to suspect "secret connections between the United States and the Islamists" in Algeria:

> A 1996 Rand study commissioned by the US Army, which was recently made public, added fuel to the fire. The report downplayed GIA atrocities and advised Washington to work with the Islamists, arguing that they were inevitably going to play a major role in Algerian affairs. It also noted that the Islamists were not necessarily enemies of the United States, since they have openly called for US investment to replace that of the hated French. In the hothouse atmosphere of Algerian politics, that sort of analysis constitutes tacit, if not direct, support.[55]

The US Army–Rand report is disquieting evidence of the pro-GIA sentiments of the US military policy establishment. But according to former Algerian secret service operative "Joseph," Western culpability in the subversion of the GIA and the consequent domestic and international terror threat extends far wider than London and Washington:

> Algerian intelligence agents routinely bribe European police, journalists and MPs. Joseph said he paid one French MP, who cannot be named for legal reasons, more than 500,000 francs (about $90,000) in bribes... Joseph said [Algerian military security chiefs] Tewfik and Smain spent some of Algeria's oil and gas billions to bribe politicians and security officials in Europe. Joseph said: "I personally delivered a suitcase containing 500,000 francs to one French MP with strong links to the French intelligence services." The MP, who lost his seat at the last election, is a noted apologist for the Algerian and Iraqi regimes.

"All the intelligence services in Europe know the government is doing it," Joseph continues, "but they are keeping quiet because they want to protect their supplies of oil."[56] The extent of this secret network of corruption extending throughout Europe is unknown. But as the London *Observer* notes, Algeria "squats on huge oil and gas deposits worth billions. It supplies the gas that warms Madrid and Rome. It has a 31.8 billion pounds contract with British Petroleum. No Western government wants to make trouble with the state of Algeria. Its wealth buys silence, buys complicity."[57]

Indeed, Western financial and military support for the Islamist terror-toting junta is extensive and entrenched. For example, British journalist Robert Fisk reported as early as 1994 that "France has been giving covert military support to the Algerian regime for months.... Helicopters, night sight technology for aerial surveillance of guerrilla hide outs and other equipment" were included in this support, having "been sent to the Algerian army, some aboard French military flights which reportedly make regular flights into Algiers airport." Fisk cites "well placed Algerian sources" confirming that "the son of a French government minister is involved. He is said to run a private security company outside Paris which has legally sold millions of francs worth of equipment to the Algerian security police." Additionally, Fisk reported that "French spy agencies monitor all Algerian radio traffic round the clock, much of it from a ship off the coast of France's former African colony," listening "day and night to the reports of Algerian commanders in the Lakhdaria mountains and the 'Bled,' the Algerian outback." This work is "supplemented by radio signals picked up aboard French air force planes flying along the Algerian coast, and by intelligence officers inside the heavily guarded French embassy in Algiers." France, in other words, is fully aware of the GIA's status as an instrument of Algerian statecraft. "France has acknowledged selling nine Ecureuil helicopters to the Algerian government" but claimed that they were "for 'civil' purposes—thereby avoiding statutory investigation by the French interministerial commission for the inspection of military exports. Military sources say helicopters have only to be equipped with rockets and night sight equipment, also provided by France, to become front line equipment in the anti guerrilla struggle."[58]

In the year 2000, the *Sunday Times* reported that the British government sold through the government of Qatar "almost £5m in military equipment to the Algerian army, despite a record of atrocities committed by its soldiers that contravenes the ethical foreign policy espoused by Robin Cook, the foreign secretary." The purchase was negotiated by BAe Systems, formerly British Aerospace, with the Qatar armed forces. The purchase order formally sent to BAe stated that Qatar was "to gift, free of charge, all of the items (as per the attached list) to the armed services of the state of Algeria." The purchase order went on to offer "an end-user certificate for Algeria, a document that details where the arms will end up. Last week BAe confirmed the May 31 order, which followed extensive consultations, and said it expected government approval." The order, worth £4.6 million, included: "20 Land Rover Defender 110 rapid deployment vehicles with hot climate specifications (at a total cost of £596,666); 50 Land Rover Defender 110 pickup trucks with hot climate specifications (£618,333), down to 500 Pilkington Optronics Kite night vision sights (£1.75m)."[59] Reuters subsequently confirmed the sale on July 19, 2000.[60] Such sales are routine. Foreign Office figures show that in 2000, Britain sold a total of £2 million directly to Algeria. In 1999, Britain had sold £5.5 million directly.[61]

In the same vein, US–Algerian military ties steadily deepened. While senior US naval officers have paid high profile visits to the country, US and Algerian navies have conducted joint marine rescue exercises in the Mediterranean Sea. In September 1999, US Sixth Fleet Admiral Daniel Murphy met President Bouteflika and army chief of staff Lieutenant-General Mohamed Lamari in Algiers. Admiral Charles Abbot, deputy commander of US armed forces in Europe, met with President Bouteflika and army chief of staff Maj. Gen.

Mohamed Lamari on April 24, 1999, and reportedly discussed setting up a permanent joint military program. Maj. Gen. Randall Schmidt, director of aerospace operations for the US Air Force in Europe, met with Algerian military and defense officials in Algiers late July 1999.[62] As Professor John Entelis observes, "such visits serve to advance diplomatic ties and strengthen military links between the two countries."[63] Indeed, by November 8, 2002, US Undersecretary of State for Political Affairs Marc Grossman went to Algiers and described joint "US–Algerian goals" as: "simultaneous work in anti-terrorism... and economic cooperation."[64]

The Algerian junta–GIA–al-Qaeda terror nexus has also received heavy Western financial assistance. In the late 1990s, for instance, the European Union released 60 million Euros—some $65 million—to the Algerian generals. The total loan package was worth 125 million Euros.[65] Algeria has the fifth largest reserves of natural gas in the world, and is the second largest gas exporter, with 130 trillion proven natural gas reserves. It ranks fourteenth for oil reserves, with official estimates at 9.2 billion barrels. Approximately 90 per cent of Algeria's crude oil exports go to Western Europe, including Britain, France, Italy, Germany, the Netherlands, and Spain. Algeria's major trading partners are Italy, France, the United States, Germany, and Spain.[66]

ABC News correspondent John Cooley, a specialist in North Africa and the Middle East, further reports the presence of "500 to 600 American engineers and technicians living and working behind barbed wire" in a collection of "protected gas and oil enclaves in Algeria." This little-publicized but heavy US commercial involvement in Algeria "began in earnest... in 1991." At the end of that year, the regime

> opened the energy sector on liberal terms to foreign investors and operators...
>
> About 30 oil and gas fields have been attributed to foreign companies since then. The main American firms involved, Arco, Exxon, Oryx, Anadarko, Mobil and Sun Oil received exploration permits, often in association with European firms like Agip, BP, Cepsa or the Korean group Daewoo.... The majority of oil and gas exports go to nearby Europe... the main clients in the late 1990s [being] France, Belgium, Spain and Italy.[67]

In June 2000, US-based international banks and investment houses such as Chase Manhattan visited Algiers, along with then Under-Secretary of the Treasury Stuart Eizenstat. US private investments in Algeria were estimated at between $3.5 and $4 billion—almost entirely in oil and gas exploration and production.[68]

In other words, the Algerian Islamist terror network under the wing of the GIA is a major player in the North African branch of al-Qaeda, implicated in not merely domestic massacres but international terrorist attacks, particularly in Europe. The GIA–al-Qaeda network, however, is a product and tool of the

Algerian military intelligence services. The Western powers, moreover, are fully cognizant of all this, and simultaneously are closely allied to the Algerian generals who pull significant GIA–al-Qaeda strings, providing the junta–GIA–al-Qaeda nexus with extensive financial and military support. Yet the same powers publicly lament the problem of terrorism emanating from the junta–GIA–al-Qaeda nexus, and actively propagate a false narrative of the Algerian conflict that is contrary to the facts. Essentially then, the Western powers are deeply involved in the financial and military support of the junta–GIA–al-Qaeda terrorist nexus in Algeria. By financing and arming the Algerian junta, they are consciously financing and arming the al-Qaeda affiliated GIA.

Abu Sayyaf and the CIA in the Philippines

The conflict in the Philippines is a legacy of Spanish and American colonialism. In the 1960s, the Muslim/Moro separatist movement in the Philippines emerged among a small number of students and intellectuals articulating widespread grievances concerned with "discrimination, poverty, and inequality, linked primarily to the displacement of Moro communities from their lands by Christian settlers." After the eruption of violence in Cotabato in 1969–1971 and in response to the declaration of martial law by President Ferdinand Marcos in 1972, the movement rapidly gained popular support, coalescing into an armed group, the Moro National Liberation Front (MNLF). With 30,000 fighters, the MNLF fought the Philippine military to a stalemate in the mid-1970s.[69]

In December 1976, the Philippine government and MNLF reached a settlement, the Tripoli Agreement, which included a ceasefire and the granting of autonomy to thirteen provinces where the majority of Muslims lived. But the Marcos regime never fulfilled its side of the agreement, leading to the outbreak of further fighting before the end of 1977. At the same time, factional infighting led to the founding of the Moro Islamic Liberation Front (MILF), which was later officially established in 1984. By the early 1980s, the Moro movement for self determination was largely non-violent. In 1986, the MNLF reached a ceasefire with President Corazon Aquino and in January 1987 signed an agreement relinquishing its goal of independence and accepting the government offer of autonomy. However, in 1987 negotiations reached a deadlock, and in February 1988 the MNLF officially resumed its armed insurrection while the government pressed ahead with its plans for Muslim autonomy. In 1991, the Abu Sayyaf group split from the MNLF under the leadership of Abdurajik Abubakar Janjalani, but is now nominally headed by Khadafi Janjalani.[70]

In 1996, the MNLF signed a peace agreement with the administration of Fidel Ramos and entered civilian politics, although the agreement was opposed by the MILF and Abu Sayyaf. Moreover, the government failed to properly implement the autonomy arrangement. Negotiations between the government and the MILF continued until early 2000 when the MILF came under attack from the Estrada administration. However, the main force of violence in the conflict, apart from the government, has been the Abu Sayyaf whose declared aim is the establishment of an Islamic state based on Islamic law (shariah) in the south. However, the group has no significant political support and has failed to espouse any meaningful policy statement. Its program of terrorism, including bombings and kidnappings, is condemned by both the MNLF and the MILF.[71]

The roots of the Abu Sayyaf lead us straight back to al-Qaeda. In the mid-1980s, Professor Abdul Rasul Sayyaf nominally headed an alliance of extremist armed groups financed by Osama bin Laden, among others, and influenced by Saudi Wahabism. He established a notorious but secretive "university"—Dawal al-Jihad—in the north of Peshawar, which functioned as a major terrorist training camp. Roughly 20,000 mujahideen from 40 countries—including the Philippines—were trained there by Pakistani military intelligence (ISI) with extensive CIA support in the form of expertise, weapons, and funds. Many of these fighters were in search of "other wars to fight," including in the Philippines, the Middle East, North Africa, and New York. It was not long before "a nucleus of Abu Sayyaf fighters had moved to the Philippines and were operating there under that name." The Philippines division of the Abu Sayyaf group conducted "kidnappings and bomb attacks on Christian and government targets" in the south. Among those coordinating operations in the Philippines with Afghan veterans of Abu Sayyaf was al-Qaeda operative Ramzi Yousef, the mastermind of the 1993 World Trade Center bombing plot and an author of Project Bojinka. The first half of Bojinka was implemented by Abu Sayyaf on December 11, 1994, in the bombing of a Philippines Airlines flight between Manila and Tokyo, and the targeting of 11 other American airliners over the Pacific on the same day. The latter plot failed due to the FAA's tighter security measures, but the plot was traced back by Philippine police and the FBI to Abu Sayyaf/al-Qaeda operative Yousef. The other half of Bojinka was eventually implemented on 9/11, involving a scheme to fly civilian planes into key US buildings.[72] Another member of the Abu Sayyaf terror cell in Manila was 9/11 mastermind Khalid Shaikh Mohammed, a key al-Qaeda leader who participated in Yousef's Bojinka operation. He lived only a few floors from Yousef.[73]

According to Washington, DC's Center for Defense Information "Abu Sayyaf–al Qaeda links are strong. Many of its fighters claim to have trained in Afghanistan, including as many as 20 who were in the graduating class of a Mazar-e Sharif camp in 2001... Zamboanga City, a Mindanao Islamic hotbed, was frequented by members of al Qaeda." Janjalani forged a close relationship with Saudi businessman Mohammed Jamal Khalifa, Osama bin Laden's brother-in-law, who set up a network of Islamic charities used to fund Abu Sayyaf fighters. Khalifa's "main organization, the International Islamic Relief Organization, has an office in Zamboanga, as does a bin Laden foundation. Abu

Sayyaf received training and money funneled through Khalifa's network."[74] According to the *National Review*, US investigators are convinced that Khalifa is "an important figure in al Qaeda. Khalifa has been linked to Ramzi Yousef, the mastermind of the 1993 World Trade Center bombing, as well as to the October 2000 bombing of the USS Cole. Khalifa is also thought to have provided crucial start-up money to Abu Sayyaf, the Philippine terrorist group."[75]

Khalifa had lived in the Philippines for several years before he visited the United States and was arrested in San Francisco in December 1994 for an immigration violation. He was of primary interest to the FBI, "which suspected him of assisting al Qaeda operatives Ramzi Yousef and Abdul Hakim Murad in a plot to bomb a dozen US airliners from their base in the Philippines." Indeed, he had already been formally named as an unindicted co-conspirator in the 1993 New York City Landmarks bombing plot. Furthermore, Philippines investigators charged that Khalifa had funded the Bojinka plot through a charity front in Manila. When detained by the INS in December, Khalifa was in possession of a phone number connected to the Manila terror cell responsible for the Bojinka plot, according to a 2002 indictment of Benevolence International Foundation and Bojinka trial records. The Abu Sayyaf/al-Qaeda cell was reportedly in frequent contact with Khalifa during November 1994. FBI affidavits and other trial testimony reveal that the FBI knew at the time that the al-Qaeda cell in Manila consisted of "Yousef, Murad, Khalid Shaikh Mohammed... and Wali Khan Amin Shah, a Malaysian al Qaeda operative who called Khalifa's cell phone several times during November." A known alias used by Khalifa was "found on one of several bomb-making manuals brought into the US" as early as 1992 "by an accomplice of Ramzi Yousef." The manuals contained "detailed instructions" on how to construct precisely the same explosives used in the 1993 World Trade Center attack and in the Oklahoma City bombing. Court records show that Philippines investigators found information connected to Khalifa when they raided Ramzi Yousef's apartment in January 1995. US authorities had also seized a number of highly incriminating items from his luggage in December, including "literature related to training terrorists in the Philippines, an address book and an electronic organizer listing Wali Khan Amin Shah's phone number in Manila, and immigration papers relating to his return to the Philippines."[76]

In other words, the FBI had sufficient evidence to suspect Khalifa of high-level terrorist activities on behalf of al-Qaeda. Indeed, as early as December 1994 "The Justice Department had wanted to hold Khalifa and investigate his alleged ties to terrorism." But the FBI investigation was ignored, and "Khalifa's deportation was ordered after direct intervention in the case by then-Secretary of State Warren Christopher in January 1995... [who] wrote a three-page letter to Attorney General Janet Reno in January urging that the deportation proceed." Moreover, the US attorney's office wrote that it had "no objection" to the return of the items seized from Khalifa's luggage, although they were relevant as evidence not only of Khalifa's terrorist activities, but also of that of his known colleagues Shah and Yousef—the former "was the subject of an ongoing international manhunt at the time" and the latter "was already under indictment in America." Additionally, the US government "not only agreed to Khalifa's request for deportation to Jordan, but in exchange for his cooperation it expunged terror-related charges from his INS record." In other words, despite incriminating evidence in Khalifa's own possession as well as extensive evidence from numerous credible sources demonstrating his longstanding terrorist connections and activities, the State Department blocked the FBI's attempt to detain and investigate him further, returned the incriminating evidence to him, erased all terrorist charges from his INS records, and allowed him to escape to Jordan.[77]

Clandestine official connivance in the activities of al-Qaeda's Abu Sayyaf group has also been documented by a leading member of the Philippine government, Senator Aquilino Q. Pimentel Jr. Pimentel, a former law professor, has been involved in Philippine politics for over 30 years, has been Senator of the Republic since 1998, and is a respected legislator. In a July 2000 speech before the Philippine Senate, he disclosed some startling evidence of joint US–Philippine government involvement in the emergence and activities of Abu Sayyaf:

> Because the Abu Sayyaf was operating on the fringe of the Muslim insurgency in the country, its partisans were enticed by certain officers of the armed forces to serve as informers on the activities of the Muslim insurgents in Southern Mindanao... at least, three military and police officers [were] coddlers or handlers of the Abu Sayyaf.

These officers hold very high posts. "One was the commanding general of the Marines at that time, Brig. Gen. Guillermo Ruiz; the other two were police officers, Chief Supt. Leandro Mendoza and Chief Supt. Rodolfo Mendoza," continued Senator Pimentel:

> My information is that the Abu Sayyaf partisans were given military intelligence services IDs, safe-houses, safe-conduct passes, firearms, cell phones and various sorts of financial support.
>
> Edwin Angeles, a leader of the Abu Sayyaf in Basilan, told me after the elections of 1995, that it was the Abu Sayyaf that was responsible for the raid and the razing down of the town of Ipil, Zamboanga del Sur in early 1995. In that raid, Angeles told me that the Abu Sayyaf raiders were reportedly provided with military vehicles, mortars and assorted firearms. All this time, Angeles was "handled"—by police officer, now chief superintendent, Rodolfo Mendoza.

Senator Pimentel also quoted one of Angeles' bodyguards:

> ... he told me the names of some other officers of the armed forces who 'handled' Abu Sayyaf matters. He is, however, deathly afraid of coming out into the open...
>
> The CIA has sired a monster.... What looks inexcusable to me is the involvement of a few officers of the armed forces—handlers of the Abu Sayyaf, my informants call them—in the training of the Abu Sayyaf partisans, the very same group of hooligans who are responsible for the kidnapping of foreigners and locals alike and the atrocities they had committed for several years now.

According to Senator Pimentel, these Philippine military and police "handlers" funneled CIA assistance in the form of both weapons and finances to Abu Sayyaf: "... these officers did not only 'handle' the Abu Sayyaf, they coddled them, trained them, protected them, passed on military equipment and funds from the CIA and its support network, and probably even from the intelligence funds of the armed forces to them." He also reported that "Gen. Alexander Aguirre was present at a meeting—perhaps organizational—of the Abu Sayyaf. Whatever the nature of Gen. Aguirre's involvement with the Abu Sayyaf has to be explained." He demanded that the chief of staff of the Philippine army in the 1990s, Gen. Renato de Villa, and the commander-in-chief of the army from 1992 to 1998, former President Fidel V. Ramos

> should likewise tell the people what he knows of the involvement of the CIA and our own military officers in the creation, handling and supervision of the Abu Sayyaf...
>
> The evidence is now overwhelming—unassailable in my mind—that the CIA was the procreator of the Abu Sayyaf and that some of our own military officers acted as midwives at its delivery and who have nursed the hooligans under illegal, if not, at least, questionable circumstances that enabled the latter to pursue their criminal activities to this very day...
>
> We have to find out what we can do as legislators to prevent a recurrence of the situation where certain military officers of our armed forces became willing tools of the CIA in the creation, funding, training and equipping of this bandit group.... The officers who have been identified as coddlers or handlers of the Abu Sayyaf in various studies and documents must be called to account.[78]

Despite Senator Pimentel's address, the Philippine authorities have failed to even investigate—let alone prosecute—these officials. However, his damning allegations are corroborated by testimonials from other leading observers. According to one MNLF commander, "the Abu Sayyaf had the protection of the Marines. They are provided high-powered guns, plenty of ammunition and

15,000 pesos to be recruited. Who else has this money except the military?" Another MNLF leader, Damming Hadjirul, is similarly convinced of a high-level military–Abu Sayyaf connection: "When there's no war, there's no business for the military, right?" Lt. Col. Ricardo Morales, a leading Philippine military analyst, noted in an army journal in 1995: "How can a band of criminals with no military training to speak of, withstand the full might of the armed forces, slip through troop cordons and conduct kidnapping right under the very noses of government troops?"

Former Army Captain Rene Jarque, a Philippine intelligence officer, similarly observed that "This small group has managed to evade the military operations for too long in a tiny island lends credence to reports that some military units have been ordered not to touch the Abu Sayyaf." Thus, as journalist Michael Bengwayan concludes:

> It is no surprise then that the Abu Sayyaf who earlier kidnapped 24 children, one priest, and five teachers were able to slip through a cordon sprang by 3,000 military men in Mount Puno Mahadji. Today, the Philippine government is faced with a terrorist problem it cannot handle because it has looked the other way when its military was coddling a growing extremist, fanatic and suicidal group.[79]

The manipulation of Abu Sayyaf by the Philippine military was thoroughly exposed in a joint investigative report by the *Boston Globe* and the Finnish daily *Helsingin Sanomat*, based on dozens of accounts from eyewitnesses, sworn testimony presented before Congress and the Senate, the Commission on Human Rights, as well as new admissions from military and local officials. In the *Globe*, US journalist Indira Lakshmanan wrote: "High-ranking members of the Philippine military, as well as members of local government, have colluded with the Islamic extremists that US troops are being sent here to combat, a *Globe* investigation has found." Finnish journalist Pekka Mykkanen wrote in the *Sanomat*: "An array of plausible military, eyewitness and documentary sources indicate that the ruthlessness and greed of some high-ranking Philippine Army officers may pose nearly as great a security concern for the US troops as the Islamic extremist Abu Sayyaf cadres they are seeking to eradicate." The investigation revealed, for instance, that the Arroyo administration was fully aware of—indeed complicit in—military–Abu Sayyaf collusion in the 2001 kidnapping of civilians at Dos Palmas and the occupation of a parish compound in Lamitan: "The sworn statements of witnesses who were inside and outside Jose Maria Torres Memorial Hospital—as well as the findings of an internal army inquiry and two government human rights reports—suggest that President Gloria Macapagal Arroyo knew about, but chose to whitewash, what went wrong." Government and military officers reportedly took substantial cuts in the ransom money paid to Abu Sayyaf to release its hostages and deliberately facilitated the group's escape.[80]

One pertinent illustration of the extent to which the Philippine military controls Abu Sayyaf is provided in the role of Edwin Angeles. With an outstanding track record of infiltrating urban opposition groups such as "the Moro National Liberation Front and the communist movement in Bataan as part of his work for a number of military intelligence agencies," Angeles was "the perfect government agent to infiltrate" the al-Qaeda terrorist group. He played a "pivotal role" in Abu Sayyaf's growth and policies. According to investigative journalist Arlyn de la Cruz, Angeles was "the first deep penetration agent of the military" to the group. He therefore "holds the key to the deep intricacies of how some government agencies manipulated the rawness of the Abu Sayyaf." It was, in fact, government agent Angeles who "introduced the idea of kidnapping as part of the fund-raising activities of the Abu Sayyaf." The group's first kidnapping occurred in 1992. As the group's Operations Officer, Angeles "planned the abduction and even initiated the plan himself." He was also active in the recruitment of Muslim converts to the group. Angeles later left the Abu Sayyaf to become an agent for the Intelligence Command of the Philippine National Police. In this capacity, he signed an affidavit revealing CIA involvement in the creation of Abu Sayyaf and exposed police corruption relating to the framing of Arabs as terrorists. Furious at his lack of loyalty to the authorities, they charged him with 54 counts of kidnapping with murder. But in the trial at Isabela, Basilan, the judge acquitted Angeles because he proved in court, using his original mission orders, that all the terrorist crimes attributed to him were committed as an integral function of his job as a government agent. As de la Cruz comments: "... at least two police officers from the PNP–IC and another from the Philippine Marines testified before the court attesting that indeed Edwin Angeles carried out a number of criminal acts in the performance of his duties as a DPA funded by legitimate agencies of government."[81]

There is good reason to believe that US intelligence agencies have played a surprisingly direct role in facilitating the Philippine military–Abu Sayyaf–al-Qaeda nexus. On May 2002, a sudden explosion wracked the room of an American citizen, Michael Meiring, in the Evergreen Hotel in Davao, mangling his lower limbs. The 65-year-old Californian was subsequently rushed to Davao Medical Mission Hospital. Four months later, after an official investigation by Philippine experts, the City Prosecution Office concluded that Meiring was a terrorist:

City Prosecutor Raul Bendico said findings from the investigation of the case indicated that Meiring apparently attempted to set up explosives intended to blow up Evergreen Hotel when the accidental explosion went off... Meiring was charged with illegal possession of explosives and reckless imprudence "for failing to practice proper attention and diligence regarding the handling of explosive materials."

But the most bizarre part of the story, as noted by Philippine's ABS-CBN News, "was that Meiring was reportedly whisked away by agents of the US Federal Bureau of Investigation and brought to the United States. Authorities want Meiring brought back to the country to face the criminal charges filed against him."[82] The Meiring explosion was only an early incident in a series of mysterious bomb attacks in Davao and elsewhere in the Philippines. Responsibility for the bombings was either claimed by Abu Sayyaf or blamed on the group by officials. In July 2003, the prominent Philippine civil society group, Interfaith for Peace in Mindanao (InPeace), cited the "claims of junior officers" in the Philippine army "that this terrorism is government-sponsored." A Magdelo "group of junior military officers" blamed Philippine Defense Secretary Angelo Reyes and Gen. Victor Corpus for orchestrating the bombings. InPeace also referred to the Meiring–CIA connection and called for a full independent investigation into the apparent role of both the Philippine military and US intelligence in the wave of terror.[83]

Citing Philippine intelligence sources, the *Philippine Star* subsequently reported that Meiring had been an active CIA agent: "Highly reliable sources told the *Star* Michael Terrence Meiring, 65, reportedly was deployed by the CIA, sometime in the early up to the mid 90s, on assignment here in Southern Mindanao," and had been flown back to California.[84] A detailed three-part investigation by the *Manila Times* uncovered further strange facts. Meiring first came to the Philippines in 1992, spending his time "with two agents of the National Bureau of Investigation (NBI)." He also had "close links with some well-placed government authorities in southern Mindanao as well as with national government officials." At the same time, however, Meiring had "connections with rebel leaders."[85] According to the *Manila Times*, Philippine's Immigration Deputy Commissioner Daniel Queto admitted that "no less than agents of the US National Security Council had brought Meiring from Davao to [a hospital in] Manila."[86]

Citing US intelligence sources, the *Times* reported that "The Americans have used treasure hunting as a cover for intelligence activities." One example is the case of "three Vietnamese terrorists arrested last year for plotting to blow up the Vietnamese Embassy." They were apparently "assets of the US intelligence community. They and their Japanese colleague were also involved in treasure hunting—and the export of marijuana." Intelligence officials gave the *Times* a list of names of agents, a.k.a. treasure hunters, operating in the 1990s, including that of "Nina North" from Fremont, California, whose "acquaintances claim she has connections to the Central Intelligence Agency." In 1990, 1991, and 1992, North "maintained contact with… high officials in the Mid-East, including representatives of Khadaffy and Bin Laden, with regard to transfer of gold bullion from the Philippines, through the 'back door.'"[87]

InPeace's allegations and the facts of the Meiring case—based on credible military and intelligence sources—provide a well-documented example of how the CIA continues to be active in the Philippines, working with Philippine police, military, and intelligence agencies, while simultaneously liaising with rebel groups ultimately leading to the outbreak of terrorist violence. It is certainly difficult, in this context, to avoid concluding that the collusion of Philippine military intelligence with al-Qaeda's Abu Sayyaf group occurs with significant US connivance.

Apart from the above documentation suggesting joint Philippine government–CIA involvement in Abu Sayyaf and recent terrorist violence, the US military works extremely closely with the Philippine military, providing weapons, advice, and extensive training. For instance, nearly 1,000 US combat troops were sent to the southern islands of Mindanao, Basilan, and Jolo in 2002 to join with thousands of Philippine troops supposedly hunting Abu Sayyaf. So closely are US military officers and soldiers liaising with their Philippine counterparts that Operation Balikatan ("shoulder to shoulder") commands US troops to accompany Philippine military patrols with permission to fight in self-defense. According to US Major Cynthia Teramae: "We are here as counterparts. We will be working alongside each other. We have two co-directors and two co-generals. It shows the kind of relationship that we have."[88]

It is not a surprise then that the key US objective in the Philippines is not the elimination of terror. On the contrary, US-backed Philippine state-sponsored terror appears to have provided a crucial justification within the "War on Terror" narrative for the expansion of US military power in the region and the consolidation of US economic control. "The important thing is to have a safe and stable security environment for domestic and foreign investors, including US entrepreneurs," remarked US Assistant Secretary of Commerce William Lash in a January 2002 visit to Manila. Indeed, according to former Philippine President Fidel Ramos, the US aim in the Philippines "is to maintain a viable presence in Asia-Pacific as a means to secure their own interests and their huge investments."[89]

Thus, Philippine military intelligence (AFP) has for more than the last decade manipulated and colluded with al-Qaeda's Abu Sayyaf terrorist network, establishing what amounts to a longstanding AFP–Abu Sayyaf-al-Qaeda nexus. In turn, US military intelligence, including the CIA, appears to have been deeply implicated in this process throughout the said period by literally operating side-by-side—"shoulder to shoulder"—with both its Philippine counterpart and Abu Sayyaf, as well as by providing extensive financial and military assistance to the former. In this manner, US military intelligence provides the overarching strategic directive within which the AFP–Abu Sayyaf-al-Qaeda nexus operates, constituting its most fundamental sponsor.

4.

THE ANGLO-AMERICAN AXIS: PROTECTING OSAMA

Both the United States and its lead ally the United Kingdom are conventionally believed to be at the forefront of fighting the global "War on Terror." An examination of the actual record of American and British policy toward Osama bin Laden and al-Qaeda, however, provides an entirely different picture. This contradiction is not so surprising, though, in light of the extent to which US and Western interests have systematically melded with the arteries of international terrorism. It is the underlying ties with terror penetrating Western institutions of power that are fundamentally responsible for the systematic failure of Western authorities to apprehend Osama bin Laden and his terrorist network.

Protecting Osama in Khartoum

According to *Jane's Intelligence Review*: "In February 1995, US authorities named bin Laden and his Saudi brother-in-law, Mohammed Jamal Khalifa, among 172 unindicted co-conspirators with the 11 Muslims charged for the World Trade Center bombing and the associated plot to blow up other New York landmarks."[1]

In March 1996, when Osama bin Laden was present in Sudan after leaving Saudi Arabia, United Nations Ambassador Major General Elfatih Erwa—then Sudanese Minister of State for Defense—offered to extradite bin Laden either to Saudi Arabia or the United States:

> The Sudanese security services, he said, would happily keep close watch on bin Laden for the United States. But if that would not suffice, the government was prepared to place him in custody and hand him over, though to whom was ambiguous. In one formulation, Erwa said Sudan would consider any legitimate proffer of criminal charges against the accused terrorist.[2]

Instead of accepting the offer of extradition, the US did the opposite:

> [US officials] said, "Just ask him to leave the country. Just don't let him go to Somalia," Erwa, the Sudanese general, said in an interview. "We said he will go to Afghanistan, and they [US officials] said, 'Let him.'" On May 15,

1996, Foreign Minister Taha sent a fax to Carney in Nairobi, giving up on the transfer of custody. His government had asked bin Laden to vacate the country, Taha wrote, and he would be free to go.[3]

Many US intelligence officials in the region have vociferously condemned the decision as a lost opportunity to capture or more closely monitor Osama bin Laden. One official said: "We kidnap minor drug czars and bring them back in burlap bags. Somebody didn't want this to happen." The official "added that the State Department may have blocked Bin Laden's arrest to placate a part of the Saudi Arabian government that supported Bin Laden." According to another US official involved in the secret negotiations, "the US could have used Khartoum's offer to keep an eye on Bin Laden, but... the efforts were blocked by another arm of the federal government. 'I've never seen a brick wall like that before. Somebody let this slip up,' the intelligence chief says. 'We could have dismantled his operations and put a cage on top. It was not a matter of arresting Bin Laden but of access to information. That's the story, and that's what could have prevented September 11. I knew it would come back to haunt us.'"[4]

But this was only one incident out of many in relation to Sudanese intelligence on the al-Qaeda network. The London *Observer*, for instance, reported that "Security chiefs on both sides of the Atlantic repeatedly turned down the chance to acquire a vast intelligence database on Osama bin Laden and more than 200 leading members of his al-Qaeda terrorist network in the years leading up to the 11 September attacks." US and British intelligence "were offered thick files, with photographs and detailed biographies" of Osama's principal cadres, along with "vital information about al-Qaeda's financial interests in many parts of the globe." Indeed, Western intelligence twice had the opportunity "to extradite or interview key bin Laden operatives who had been arrested in Africa because they appeared to be planning terrorist atrocities." Such offers, made regularly by the Sudanese administration since early 1995, were simply ignored.

A separate offer from Sudanese agents in Britain "to share intelligence with MI6" was also rejected, following "four years of similar rebuffs." A US source familiar with the files described them as "an inch and a half thick," including "photographs" and information on the "families, backgrounds and contacts" of al-Qaeda operatives. As one Sudanese source put it to the *Observer*: "We know them in detail. We know their leaders, how they implement their policies, how they plan for the future. We have tried to feed this information to American and British intelligence so they can learn how this thing can be tackled." Instead, by 1996 Sudan agreed to expel Osama bin Laden and 300 associates "following intense pressure from Saudi Arabia and the US... Sudanese intelligence believed this to be a great mistake." As the source put it, "There we could keep track of him, read his mail."

Indeed, rather than agreeing to bin Laden's extradition and indictment, two years later the US launched an attack on Sudan targeting the al-Shifa pharmaceutical plant, claiming that Sudan was harboring bin Laden-connected terrorists, in particular by allowing al-Shifa—alleged by the US to be developing chemical and biological weapons of mass destruction on bin Laden's behalf—to continue operation. Yet just before the US missile attack, Sudan had made further offers to hunt down members of bin Laden's network. According to "a copy of a personal memo sent from Sudan to Louis Freeh, former director of the FBI, after the murderous 1998 attacks on American embassies in Kenya and Tanzania," Sudan had arrested

> two named bin Laden operatives held the day after the bombings after they crossed the Sudanese border from Kenya...
>
> They had cited the manager of a Khartoum leather factory owned by bin Laden as a reference for their visas, and were held after they tried to rent a flat overlooking the US embassy in Khartoum, where they were thought to be planning an attack. US sources have confirmed that the FBI wished to arrange their immediate extradition. However, Clinton's Secretary of State, Madeleine Albright, forbade it. She had classed Sudan as a "terrorist state," and three days later US missiles blasted the al-Shifa medicine factory in Khartoum. The US wrongly claimed it was owned by bin Laden and making chemical weapons. In fact, it supplied 60 per cent of Sudan's medicines, and had contracts to make vaccines with the UN.

Despite the illegal bombing,[5] Sudan continued to hold the suspects for a further three weeks, "hoping the US would both perform their extradition and take up the offer to examine their bin Laden database. Finally, the two men were deported to Pakistan. Their present whereabouts are unknown." Furthermore, US indifference to intelligence information on bin Laden continued into the year 2000: "Last year the CIA and FBI, following four years of Sudanese entreaties, sent a joint investigative team to establish whether Sudan was in fact a sponsor of terrorism. Last May, it gave Sudan a clean bill of health. However, even then, it made no effort to examine the voluminous files on bin Laden."[6]

Ignoring Russian Intelligence

Sudanese intelligence on Osama bin Laden and al-Qaeda was not the only source of massive information spurned by the US government. *Jane's Intelligence Digest* reports that "Back in March [2001] Moscow's Permanent Mission at the UN submitted to the UN Security Council an unprecedentedly detailed report on Al-Qaeda's terrorist infrastructure in Afghanistan, but the US government opted not to act." The "extent of intelligence data tabled by the Russians" was "breathtaking." Also uncovered by the report was "the degree of Pakistani military and security involvement in Afghanistan."[7]

Indeed, in a detailed analysis of US government reluctance to act against Osama bin Laden and al-Qaeda, *Jane's Intelligence Digest* observed at the end of May 2002:

> The controversy raging in the US over whether warnings about potential terror attacks by Al-Qaeda were ignored before 11 September hardly comes as a surprise... As JID revealed last year, Russia's intelligence services had been extremely active in using their extensive operations in and around Afghanistan to build up a very detailed blueprint of the Taliban regime, its close links with the al-Qaeda organisation and the extent to which both were actively supported by the Pakistani military and the Inter-Service Intelligence agency (ISI). The Russian permanent mission to the United Nations provided a report on this subject to the UN Security Council on 9 March 2001 (see JID 5 October 2001).
>
> However, it is becoming clear that this was only the most high profile of a number of attempts by the Russians to alert the US and other members of the Security Council to the extent of the inter-dependence between the Taliban, al-Qaeda and the ISI. According to JID's Russian sources, there was a regular flow of information from Moscow to the US dating back to the last years of the Clinton presidency....
>
> However, given the detailed intelligence being provided by the Russians—and the fact that Bin Laden was making very clear threats to launch further strikes against US targets—it seems bizarre, to say the least, that no high-level political decision was taken to focus US intelligence efforts on Al-Qaeda and its international network, particularly following the bomb attack on the USS Cole in Aden harbor, Yemen, in October 2000.[8]

Protecting Osama from the CIA

In 1998, the CIA ignored warnings from Robert Baer, case officer in the CIA's directorate of operations, that the Saudi regime was harboring an al-Qaeda cell led by two known terrorists. US intelligence offered its Saudi counterpart a more detailed list of known terrorists in the country, but Saudi intelligence refused to accept it. According to the *Financial Times*, when the FBI "attempted to arrest them, the Gulf state's government provided the men with alias passports." Baer states that a military associate of a prince in a Gulf royal family also provided him with "a computer record of 'hundreds' of secret al-Qaeda operatives in the Gulf region, many in Saudi Arabia." Mr. Baer said that "in August 2001, at the military officer's request, he offered the list to the Saudi Arabian government. But an aide to the Saudi defense minister, Prince Sultan, refused to look at the list or to pass them (the names) on." Both Saudi and US intelligence simply sat on the information. "The information Mr. Baer gave to the CIA was not followed up, he said."[9] Baer explains the context of this obstructionism:

At a time when terrorist threats were compounding globally... Americans were making too much money to bother. Life was good. The White House and the National Security Council became cathedrals of commerce where the interests of big business outweighed the interests of protecting American citizens at home and abroad. Defanged and dispirited, the CIA went along for the ride.[10]

This was not an isolated incident. CIA obstructionism of al-Qaeda investigations was systematic. According to the conventional wisdom, for example, US officials had consistently been attempting to encourage the Taliban to hand over Osama bin Laden, but the regime consistently refused to do so. But according to Leili Helms, niece of former CIA Director Richard Helms and the unofficial US liaison to the Taliban in relation to clandestine oil pipeline negotiations, the US systematically turned down numerous offers by the Taliban to extradite—and even assassinate—bin Laden. The *Village Voice* reported that

Helms described one incident after another in which, she claimed, the Taliban agreed to give up bin Laden to the US, only to be rebuffed by the State Department. On one occasion, she said, the Taliban agreed to give the US coordinates for his campsite, leaving enough time so the Yanks could whack Al Qaeda's leader with a missile before he moved. The proposal, she claims, was nixed. The State Department denied receiving any such offer.[11]

In late 2000, National Security Council Chief of Counterterrorism Richard Clarke lobbied National Security Advisor Rice and other incoming Bush officials to resume Predator drone flights over Afghanistan to find and assassinate bin Laden. By February 16, 2001, the US Air Force successfully test fired a Hellfire missile from a Predator. In a test-case of an assassination attempt on bin Laden in early June, a replica of his brick house in Kandahar was constructed in Nevada and destroyed by a Predator missile. The missile, fired from miles away, would have killed anyone in the building. However, according to Clarke, the plan to use this method against bin Laden was foiled: "Every time we were ready to use it, the CIA would change its mind." By September 4, 2001, in a Bush Cabinet meeting to discuss terrorism, the Predator assassination plan was completely vetoed by CIA Director George Tenet, who said his agency would operate the armed Predator "over my dead body."[12]

There is also evidence of direct contact between the CIA and Osama bin Laden as late as the summer of 2001. The respected French daily *Le Figaro*, owned by the US defense contractor Carlyle Group that employs former President George Bush Sr., reported in October 2001 that Osama bin Laden underwent treatment in July at the American Hospital in Dubai, where he met a CIA official. Radio France International (RFI) also corroborated the report, which was based on French intelligence sources as well as "a witness, a professional partner of the administrative management of the hospital." The newspaper recorded:

> Dubai, one of the seven emirates of the Federation of the United Arab Emirates, North-East of Abu-Dhabi. This city, population 350,000, was the backdrop of a secret meeting between Osama bin Laden and the local CIA agent in July. A partner of the administration of the American Hospital in Dubai claims that public enemy number one stayed at this hospital between the 4th and 14th of July....
>
> Each floor of the hospital has two "VIP" suites and fifteen rooms. The Saudi billionaire was admitted to the well-respected urology department run by Terry Callaway, gallstone and infertility specialist. Dr. Callaway declined to respond to our questions despite several phone calls.... While he was hospitalised, bin Laden received visits from many members of his family as well as prominent Saudis and Emiratis. During the hospital stay, the local CIA agent, known to many in Dubai, was seen taking the main elevator of the hospital to go to bin Laden's hospital room. A few days later, the CIA man bragged to a few friends about having visited bin Laden. Authorised sources say that on July 15th, the day after bin Laden returned to Quetta, the CIA agent was called back to headquarters....
>
> Contacts between the CIA and bin Laden began in 1979 when, as a representative of his family's business, bin Laden began recruiting volunteers for the Afghan resistance against the Red Army. FBI investigators examining the embassy bombing sites in Nairobi and Dar es Salaam discovered that evidence led to military explosives from the US Army, and that these explosives had been delivered three years earlier to Afghan Arabs, the infamous international volunteer brigades involved side by side with bin Laden during the Afghan war against the Red Army. In the pursuit of its investigations, the FBI discovered "financing agreements" that the CIA had been developing with its "Arab friends" for years. The Dubai meeting is then within the logic of "a certain American policy."[13]

The London *Guardian* elaborated on the French report, noting that

> Two months before September 11 Osama bin Laden flew to Dubai for 10 days for treatment at the American hospital, where he was visited by the local CIA agent.... The disclosures are known to come from French intelligence.... Intelligence sources say that another CIA agent was also present; and that Bin Laden was also visited by Prince Turki al Faisal, then head of Saudi intelligence, who had long had links with the Taliban, and Bin Laden.[14]

Bin Laden's apparent stay at the American hospital in Dubai has also been commented on by the London *Times*.[15] These reports, while now denied by both the CIA and the hospital concerned, should nevertheless be investigated seriously due to the fact that they are based on credible sources, namely a partner of the hospital's administrative management along with disclosures from French intelligence—sources that both *Le Figaro* and Radio France International describe as "authoritative."

Arab specialist Antoine Sfeir commented that the ongoing CIA–bin Laden contacts indicated by these reports are not surprising: "The CIA maintained contacts with bin Laden until 1998. Those contacts didn't end after bin Laden moved to Afghanistan. Until the last minute, CIA agents hoped bin Laden would return to US command, as was the case before 1998." Sfeir further noted that the information on the ongoing CIA–bin Laden connection had been in circulation for 15 days before November 1, 2001.[16]

Radio France International followed up its first report with more specific information, identifying the CIA agent as Larry Mitchell, "a connoisseur of the Arab world and specialist of the (Arab) peninsula," whose business card identified him as a "consular agent." According to RFI, Mitchell is "a CIA agent and a prominent fixture in Dubai's expatriate community." RFI also reported that the precise date of the agent's encounter with bin Laden was July 12, two days before the head of Al-Qaeda left the hospital.[17] In the meantime, Dr Terry Callaway, who reportedly cared for bin Laden at the hospital, has declined to answer any questions on the matter, while one US diplomat in France refused to confirm or deny the meeting: "We're just not commenting on any of that stuff. We can't talk about meetings that may or may not have happened."[18]

Michel Chossudovsky, professor of economics at the University of Ottawa and director of the Centre for Research on Globalisation (CRG) based in Montreal, Canada, rightly observes that:

> While on the World's "most wanted list," no attempt was made to arrest him during his two week stay in the hospital, shedding doubt on the Administration's resolve to track down Osama bin Laden. Barely a few days ago Defense Secretary Rumsfeld stated that it would be difficult to find him and extradite him. It's like "searching for a needle in a stack of hay." But the US could have ordered his arrest and extradition in Dubai last July. But then they would not have had a pretext for waging a war. Meanwhile, innocent civilians are being killed by B-52 Bombers as means "to go after" Osama bin Laden. According to UN sources, the so-called "campaign against international terrorism" could lead to the death of several million people from an impending famine.[19]

Protecting Osama from the FBI

The testimony of the late John O'Neill, the Irish-American FBI agent who for several years led US investigations into Osama bin Laden's al-Qaeda network, is crucial in understanding the political context of the blocking of attempts to investigate, indict, and capture bin Laden. O'Neill, who was deputy director and director of anti-terrorism for the FBI, investigated the bombings of the World Trade Center in 1993, a US base in Saudi Arabia in 1996, the US embassies in Nairobi and Dar-Es-Salaam in 1998, and the USS Cole in 2000. According to his FBI associates, John O'Neill "has been regarded as a dedicated, relentless and hard-charging investigator who was one of the FBI's brightest stars." Barry W. Mawn, assistant director of the FBI in charge of the New York office described O'Neill as "a tireless worker" in whom he had "complete confidence."[20] The *Irish Times* reported that in interviews with French intelligence analyst Jean-Charles Brisard:

> He complained bitterly that the US State Department—and behind it the oil lobby who make up President Bush's entourage—blocked attempts to prove bin Laden's guilt. The US ambassador to Yemen, Ms Barbara Bodine, forbade O'Neill and his team of so-called Rambos (as the Yemeni authorities called them) from entering Yemen. In August 2001, O'Neill resigned in frustration and took up a new job as head of security at the World Trade Centre. He died in the September 11th attack.... The FBI agent had told Brisard: "All the answers, everything needed to dismantle Osama bin Laden's organisation, can be found in Saudi Arabia."
>
> But US diplomats shrank from offending the Saudi royal family. O'Neill went to Saudi Arabia after 19 US servicemen died in the bombing of a military installation in Dhahran in June 1996. Saudi officials interrogated the suspects, declared them guilty and executed them—without letting the FBI talk to them. "They were reduced to the role of forensic scientists, collecting material evidence on the bomb site," Brisard says. O'Neill said there was clear evidence in Yemen of bin Laden's guilt in the bombing of the USS Cole "in which 17 US servicemen died," but that the State Department prevented him from getting it.[21]

By blocking O'Neill's access to the "clear evidence" of bin Laden's guilt—which would have justified his indictment and arrest—the State Department allowed bin Laden to escape apprehension. This block on investigating salient leads to bin Laden became increasingly powerful with time. BBC *Newsnight*'s Greg Palast, for instance, recounts information he received "from a high-placed member of a US intelligence agency" who confirmed that "while there's always been constraints on investigating Saudis, under George Bush it's gotten much worse. After the elections, the agencies were told to 'back off' investigating the Bin Ladens and Saudi royals, and that angered agents... FBI headquarters told us they could not comment on our findings."[22]

Writing in the London *Guardian*, Palast cited "FBI and military intelligence officials in Washington" admitting that "they were prevented for political reasons from carrying out full investigations into members of the Bin Laden family in the US before the terrorist attacks of September 11." Intelligence agencies complained "that their hands were tied," and that there "were always constraints on investigating the Saudis." These restrictions worsened "after the Bush administration took over." The intelligence community was ordered "to 'back off' from investigations involving other members of the Bin Laden family, the Saudi royals, and possible Saudi links to the acquisition of nuclear weapons by Pakistan. 'There were particular investigations that were effectively killed.'"[23] Palast had

> obtained documents from inside the FBI showing that investigations had been shut down on the bin Laden family, the royal family of Saudi Arabia... and their connections to the financing of terrorism...
>
> Now there is one exception. The FBI, the CIA and all the rest of the agencies are allowed to investigate Osama, the so-called black sheep of the family. But what we were finding was that there was an awful lot of gray sheeps in this family—which is a family of billionaires which is tied in with the Saudi royal household which appears to be involved in the funding of terrorist organizations or organizations linked to terrorism.... Now the problem was the investigations were shut down. There were problems that go back to Father Bush—when he was head of the CIA, he tried to stop investigations of the Saudis, continued on under Reagan, Daddy Bush's president, and it continued under Clinton too... I have to add it was also CIA and all the other international agencies... I can say that the sources are not just FBI trying to get even with the other agencies, but in fact other agencies. The information was that they were absolutely prohibited, until Sept. 11, at looking at the Saudi funding of the Al-Qaeda network and other terrorist organizations. There is no question we had what looked like the biggest failure of the intelligence community since Pearl Harbor but what we are learning now is it wasn't a failure, it was a directive.[24]

A defecting Saudi diplomat offered the FBI 14,000 documents proving "Saudi royal involvement in everything from assassinations to terror funding." Although "low-level agents" were eager for the documentation which contained "tremendous leads," senior officials "did not want to touch this material."[25]

Protecting Osama from the US Military

Although President Bush announced that an integral objective of the "War on Terror" was to get Osama "dead or alive," the actual policy has continued the previous trend of doing the very opposite. Gen. Tommy Franks, head of the US Central Command and director of the post-9/11 military operation in Afghanistan, revealed that finding Osama bin Laden was not actually a mission objective. *USA Today* reported that: "The US combat commander in Afghanistan said Thursday that apprehending Osama bin Laden isn't one of the missions of Operation Enduring Storm." At his first Pentagon briefing in November 2001, Gen. Franks told reporters: "We have not said that Osama bin Laden is a target of this effort." Rather, he argued, the US military was interested in "the destruction of the al-Qa'eda network" and the Taliban—but Osama himself was irrelevant.[26]

The irrelevance of capturing bin Laden had actually come to light earlier on when, as London's *Daily Mirror* reported, "in late September and early October, leaders of Pakistan's two Islamic parties negotiated bin Laden's extradition to Pakistan to stand trial for the September 11 attacks."

> The deal was that he would be held under house arrest in Peshawar. According to reports in Pakistan (and the Daily Telegraph), this had both bin Laden's approval and that of Mullah Omah, the Taliban leader.... Later, a US official said that "casting our objectives too narrowly" risked "a premature collapse of the international effort if by some luck chance Mr. bin Laden was captured".... What the Afghani people got instead was "American justice"—imposed by a president who... has refused to sign up for an international court to try war criminals: the one place where bin Laden might be put on trial.[27]

These were perhaps early indications in the run-up to the post-9/11 war on Afghanistan that the Western powers were misrepresenting their real goals in the "War on Terror."

Harboring Osama's Financial Base

But the blocking of attempts to apprehend Osama bin Laden does not end there. The Washington, DC-based public interest law firm Judicial Watch notes that a number of organizations in the United States, some of which have even received government funding, reportedly fund Osama bin Laden: "Based on our analysis of publicly available documents, and other published reports, it is clear that this US-based network has also provided financial resources for Osama bin Laden and his terrorist operations." Judicial Watch accuses the US Internal Revenue Service (IRS) of looking "the other way when it came to investigating and taking action against radical Islamic front groups which reportedly launder money to fund terrorist operations on American soil." The Washington, DC law firm further reports that one particular group, the Islamic African Relief Agency (IARA)—which has continued to operate unhindered—"received 2 US State Department grants in 1998 worth $4.2 million dollars" and "transferred money to Mercy International... that purchased the vehicles used by Osama bin Laden to bomb the US embassies in both Kenya and Tanzania on August 8, 1998."[28]

The Agency also has reported ties to "an individual who supplied the cell phone Osama bin Laden used to orchestrate the bombing of two US embassies in Africa in 1998."[29] The conservative US news service, NewsMax, also cited Judicial Watch's concerns that more than 16 US-based non-profit entities financially linked to bin Laden have not been investigated by the IRS despite ample evidence of the connections on the public record, published for instance over three years in the New York Times.[30]

The Treasury Department began investigating only two of the alleged front organizations, including the IARA, but by November 2001 had still failed to take any action and had neglected all the other suspected organizations: "Though now under investigation by the Treasury Department, the organization, based in Columbia, Missouri, still operates freely."[31]

Jonathan Weiner, former US deputy assistant secretary of state for international law enforcement, confirmed in the same month that Bahrain, Kuwait, Saudi Arabia, and the United Arab Emirates have systematically failed to assist federal officials in the disclosure of known terrorist funds moving back and forth between those countries:

> Since September 11th, all those countries have frozen accounts or have looked in their banking systems for the money of people associated with terrorist finance, [and] have gone through the entire list provided by the United States… country after country has announced, "We've looked for funds. We've looked diligently. We've been ready to freeze some funds. We just haven't found anything." No money in the UAE, no money in Kuwait.… There is, I can tell, no money announced in Saudi Arabia, none announced in Bahrain. Well, given that we know [that terrorist] funds came out of there and we know [that terrorist] funds went back there, their inability to find funds is pretty astonishing.[32]

Successive US administrations have, however, consistently concealed the reality of this terror funding from public consumption. As the New Yorker reports, even in the aftermath of 9/11 the Saudi establishment has been "shielded from Washington's foreign-policy bureaucracy." According to one US government expert on Saudi affairs: "Only a tiny handful of people inside the government are familiar with US–Saudi relations. And that is purposeful." When confronted by press reports that substantial funds given by the Saudi monarchy to Islamic charities may have been funneled to al-Qaeda and other terrorist networks, the Saudis "denied any knowledge of such transfers. [National Security Agency] intercepts, however, have led many in the intelligence community to conclude otherwise." Yet, despite the government's longstanding knowledge of the Saudi establishment's financial support of Osama bin Laden and al-Qaeda, "The Bush administration has chosen not to confront the Saudi leadership over its financial support of terror organizations and its refusal to help in the investigation. 'As far as the Saudi Arabians go, they've been nothing but cooperative,' President Bush said at a news conference on September 24th."[33] Secretary of State Colin Powell similarly claimed that "every request we have put before the Saudis, they have responded to positively. They have taken action and they are going to do more as we give them more information to act upon."[34]

Two banks located in Bahrain and Kuwait—the Faysal Islamic Bank and the Kuwait Finance House—which had been listed in European reports as having terrorist ties, "were also excluded from Bush Jr.'s financial crackdown after September 11th." Worse still, both of these institutions are correspondent banks with Deutsche Bank, the German financial giant with links to insider trading in connection with 9/11. Reuters further reported on November 7, 2001 that the US Treasury Department had added 61 people and organizations to the President's original Executive Order of September 23, purportedly directed at cracking down on the financial arteries of Al-Qaeda—including banks in Somalia and Nassau, the Bahamas. "But mysteriously, no banks in Bahrain, Kuwait, or Saudi Arabia were named in either the original order or its expansion."

More curiously, according to the FBI, Osama bin Laden's personal bank—al Shamal Islamic Bank—which is headquartered in Khartoum, Sudan, and which bin Laden helped capitalize with $50 million in private funds, "is being investigated by US or overseas authorities." Yet the US News reported on October 8, 2001, that the FBI refuses to indicate exactly which authority, an event that is made all the more ominous by the fact that President Bush has also failed to include Osama bin Laden's al Shamal Islamic Bank in his Executive Order.[35] Yet it is a matter of record that bin Laden's personal bank is used through correspondent transactions with other banks to fund al-Qaeda projects.

For instance, according to the Washington Post, one of bin Laden's associates testified at the US trial on the 1998 African embassy bombings that: "$250,000 was wired from al Shamal Islamic Bank directly into the bin Laden cohort's Texas bank account—where he used it to buy a plane delivered to bin Laden... intended to transport Stinger missiles."

The Financial Times elaborated that: "The money was wired from the Wadi al Aqiq account at al Shamal bank via Bank of New York to a Bank of America account held in Dallas, Texas by Essam al Ridi. Al Ridi, an Egyptian flight instructor who met bin Laden in Pakistan in 1985, flew the plane to Khartoum."[36]

In an illuminating survey of this bizarre pattern of negligence, Intelligence Online observed in March 2000 that there is "some doubt on whether several intelligence and law enforcement agencies on the trail of suspected terrorist Ussama Bin Laden are really serious about catching him." The newsletter specified that Saudi Arabian agencies, as well as several US and European agencies, "seem to lack zeal." A prime example is the case of "five companies in the Sudanese capital of Khartoum and its suburbs which are managed directly or not by Bin Laden." Apart from the agricultural company Wadi al-Aqiq and the al-Shamal Bank discussed above, these include:

> ... al Timar al Mubarikah, a sugar concern; al Hijra, a building and public works company that was once an affiliate of the powerful Saudi group headed by Bin Laden's father and which is still officially managed by Ussama (al Hijra constructed the road between Khartoum and Port Sudan); Taba, a farming cooperative in Khartoum that belongs to Ussama but is in fact only the affiliate of a company in Jeddah.

The al-Hijra company, for instance, reportedly employed Mohamed Ould Salahi and Mahfud Ould al-Waled, who had been arrested in the US in December 1999 as suspected terrorists—but the company itself has faced no sanctions. Al-Qaeda also has a "strong financial network" in Kuwait and the UAE, known to investigators but, again, neglected. "Money from those countries pours into accounts at branch offices of the Taqwa Management Organization in Malta and in Lugano in Switzerland. The financial establishment in question is an affiliate of the Taqwa Bank whose headquarters are listed as being at 10 Devaux Street, Nassau, Bahamas." These and other organizations "openly back al Qaida" but continue to enjoy complete "freedom of action." Islamic Relief, for instance, is "a welfare organization linked to the Moslem Brotherhood" but based in Birmingham in the UK. Particularly active in Albania and the Caucasus, the organization also has an office in Montreuil, a Paris suburb. Worse still, the Islamic Renaissance Foundation is an association headed by bin Laden's top deputy, Ayman al-Zawahiri. Nevertheless, it operates "openly in Kuwait and has a branch in Albania." Another purported welfare association in London was al-Haramain, "known for its links with various Saudi dissidents, including Khaled al Fawaz," a leading al-Qaeda operative who was indicted for his role in the 1998 US embassy bombings. Despite its documented terrorist connections, authorities allowed al-Haramain to continue its operations long after 9/11. "This survey casts a new light on the world-wide hunt for Bin Laden," concludes *Intelligence Online*: "Recent anti-terrorism history has shown that when the authorities really want to crack down on an organization they cut off its financial and logistic roots. So why are Bin Laden's backers prospering when the world's most powerful anti-terrorist organizations are chasing him?"[37]

First-hand testimony on the existence of a block on investigating al-Qaeda comes from Chicago-based FBI special agent Robert Wright, who claims that FBI headquarters systemically obstructed his investigations into the financial arteries of al-Qaeda and Hamas terrorism. Wright charged that the FBI obstructed his efforts to investigate the funding of Middle Eastern terrorists in 1994 and 1995. The block "allowed foreign-born terrorist operatives, such as the perpetrators of the Sept. 11 attacks, to engage in illegal activities in the United States." In his lawsuit against the FBI filed in the US District Court in

Washington, Wright stated that the FBI's International Terrorism Unit "did not want terror suspects prosecuted and stymied his efforts to prepare cases of their involvement in 'well organized criminal activities.'" According to Wright, agents conducting counter-terrorism intelligence investigations made a "concerted effort to... insulate the subjects of their investigations from criminal investigation and prosecution." In effect, the FBI was "merely gathering intelligence so they would know who to arrest when a terrorist attack occurred." Wright subsequently initiated his own criminal investigation "against FBI management wishes," leading to a successful operation code-named "Vulgar Betrayal." On June 9, 1998, Wright's operation led "to the seizure of $1.4 million funds destined for terrorist activities. The 'seized funds' were linked directly to Saudi businessman Yassin Kadi." But it took the US government one month after 9/11 to designate Yassin Kadi, a.k.a. Yassin Al-Qadi, "a financial supporter of Osama bin Laden."[38]

This is disturbing precisely because federal authorities appear to have avoided sanctions against al-Qadi for as long as possible, although the information on his terrorist activity had been long established, as early as 1998. Rather than acting on the information to undercut a significant source of al-Qaeda's financial support, successive US governments simply sat on the information amidst escalating warnings of an impending terrorist attack. According to Wright's attorney, Judicial Watch counsel Larry Klayman, "these monies were moving through some powerful US banks" and affected "some very powerful interests in the US." Resistance to Wright's investigation stemmed from conflicts of interest among top officials who "are tight" with Saudi Arabia, where al-Qadi is based. If Wright's investigation had been pursued, "the money to fund terrorist operations, such as 9/11, would have been cut-off." According to Klayman, al-Qadi admits that he met bin Laden and ran a diamond business with the bin Laden family. But former President Bush Sr. was also close to the bin Laden family, having stayed with them during trips to Saudi Arabia. Such high-level "political and financial connections to Saudi interests could have played a role in the FBI's failure to support agent Wright's probe." Klayman remarked that the FBI ought to be concerned "when the rich and powerful in Washington, DC are doing business with some of these entities" connected to terrorism.[39]

As the *Toronto Star* comments: "What are we to make of all of this? One possible conclusion is that the bin Laden terror problem was allowed to get out of hand because bin Laden, himself, had powerful protectors in both Washington and Saudi Arabia."[40]

Perhaps this explains why even post-9/11 intelligence investigations have consistently ignored these connections, with the result that little real headway has been made. According to the London *Times*, for instance, the FBI has apparently "exhausted most of its leads" and acts as if "convinced that the key to al-Qaeda operations lay in Germany." But FBI arrests made with the assistance of German and European security services show that "in almost every case these cells knew nothing about the September 11 hijacks."[41]

Harboring al-Qaeda Cells in the United States

Even more extraordinary is the refusal to apprehend known al-Qaeda cells currently operating within the United States. According to the London *Telegraph*, al-Qaeda terrorist attacks against Western targets are largely conducted by "sleepers," who are "long-time residents of the countries they attacked, with ordinary jobs, identity papers and a social and family life."[42] Yet as the *Washington Post* reported a few weeks after 9/11, the FBI had known "for the last several years" of the existence of multiple al-Qaeda sleeper cells inside the US:

> The FBI has not made any arrests because the group members entered the country legally in recent years and have not been involved in illegal activities since they arrived, the officials said. Government officials say they do not know why the cells are here, what their purpose is or whether their members are planning attacks. One official even described their presence as "possibly benign," though others have a more sinister interpretation and give assurances that measures are in place to protect the public.[43]

Different government officials were clearly giving two explanations of this failure—one that the cells are "benign" and the other that they are "sinister." Why the inconsistency? In fact, the federal authorities' uncanny failure to apprehend known al-Qaeda operatives is in stark contrast to official post-9/11 US homeland security policy, initiated at the behest of Attorney-General John Ashcroft, where hundreds of Arab-Americans, Muslim-Americans, and immigrants have been indefinitely detained under the USA Patriot Act, based solely on their ethnicity and religion. The result has been that Arabs and other foreigners without any connection to terrorism at all are being detained indefinitely. Yet simultaneously, known members of Osama bin Laden's terrorist network are permitted to continue their activities freely on the absurd pretext that they may be "possibly benign."

London Saudis in Cohorts with Osama bin Laden

On the eve of 9/11, Prime Minister Tony Blair declared that Britain stood "shoulder to shoulder" with the United States against the "new evil of mass terrorism... we, the democracies of this world, are going to have to come together to fight it together and eradicate this evil completely from our world."[44] It is a declaration completely at odds to the reality of Anglo-American policy both prior to and after the 9/11 attacks. Indeed, Britain—America's key ally— has long served as a safe haven for bin Laden's terrorist networks where operations are extensively planned and financed. But even after 9/11, little if anything has been done about this problem.

Dr. Saad al-Fagih is a Saudi dissident based in London who heads the Saudi opposition group, Movement for Islamic Reform in Arabia (MIRA). Despite having a documented connection to al-Qaeda, both American and British authorities have neglected to charge or indict him, and the latter have failed to arrest him. Telephone records from the New York trial of four al-Qaeda operatives behind the 1998 bombing of US embassies in Kenya and Tanzania reveal that al-Fagih purchased Osama bin Laden's satellite phone, which was used by bin Laden and his military commander Muhammed Atef to direct al-Qaeda's operations from 1996 to 1998. Citing the records, BBC News notes that "On 30th July 1998 one of the suicide bombers who blew up the US embassy in Nairobi telephoned the satellite phone number: 00 873 682 505 331. Eight days later the suicide bombers struck in Nairobi and Dar-es-Salaam killing 247 people." Saad al-Fagih had bought the phone for bin Laden in November 1996.[45] The *Sunday Times* further reports that

> Bin Laden and his most senior lieutenants made more than 260 calls from their base in Afghanistan to 27 numbers in Britain. They included suspected terrorist agents, sympathisers and companies.... The records, obtained by The *Sunday Times*, show that the terrorist leader made more calls to Britain than any other country in the two years that he used the phone.
>
> ... According to trial documents, the satellite telephone was bought in 1996 with the help of Dr Saad al Fagih.... It was al Fagih's credit card which was used to help buy the £10,500 Compact-M satellite phone in the United States and it was shipped to his home in north London, according to American court documents. His credit card was also used to buy more than 3,000 minutes of pre-paid airtime... [He] has not been arrested or charged in connection with any of these actions.[46]

Moreover, court records show that al-Fagih's provision of the satellite telephone to bin Laden was conducted through the latter's key London lieutenant, Khalid al-Fawwaz, who has been indicted for complicity in the 1998 US embassy bombings.[47] Saad al-Fagih is closely associated with another London-based Saudi dissident, Dr Muhammed al-Masari, for whom al-Fagih campaigned to stop his deportation by then Conservative Home Secretary Michael Howard. Al-Masari, head of another Saudi opposition group, Committee for the Defense of Legitimate Rights (CDLR), has openly admitted both previous support of al-Qaeda and willingness to continue such support. BBC News reports that "Al-Masari admits he has talked with and helped Osama Bin Laden in the past and would do so again, telling [BBC Radio] Five Live Report: 'Yes, why not?' The program asked Al-Masari why he had helped Osama Bin Laden in the past, he said: 'It's the same cause.' When asked if he would still help him he replied:

'Yeah, if we can help anything, why not?'"[48] Al-Masari was also a close associate of Khalid al-Fawwaz, Osama bin Laden's European spokesman, who is now in a British prison awaiting extradition to the US for planning and supervising the 1998 embassy bombings. As the London *Telegraph* reports, al-Masari "helped Fawwaz establish bin Laden's London office."[49] Indeed, in an interview with journalist Nick Greenslade, he candidly confessed that "when Khalid al-Fawaz arrived here from Sudan, we helped him get set up with an office. Osama subsequently phoned to say thank you."[50]

This was a crucial form of logistical and financial assistance to al-Qaeda's terrorist activities. According to the official indictment for the 1998 US embassy bombings, bin Laden worked together "with KHALID AL FAWWAZ, ... [to] set up a media information office in London, England." The office was

> ... designed both to publicize the statements of USAMA BIN LADEN and to provide a cover for activity in support of al Qaeda's "military" activities, including the recruitment of military trainees, the disbursement of funds and the procurement of necessary equipment (including satellite telephones) and necessary services. In addition, the London office served as a conduit for messages, including reports on military and security matters from various al Qaeda cells, including the Kenyan cell, to al Qaeda's headquarters.[51]

Both Saad al-Fagih and Muhammed al-Masari are therefore unabashed al-Qaeda operatives based in London. Notwithstanding their confirmed financial, material, and logistical support of al-Qaeda and Osama bin Laden from the UK, directly facilitating the 1998 terrorist attacks on the US embassies in Kenya and Tanzania, American authorities have failed to indict them, and British authorities have failed to arrest or charge them. This dual failure has allowed them free reign to continue their dubious activities unhindered.

Al-Muhajiroun: Osama's UK Recruiters

Al-Fagih's and al-Masari's activities on the behalf of al-Qaeda are not isolated phenomena. Rather, the two men are leading elements of a prominent network of Islamic extremists connected to al-Qaeda in the UK, in relation to which appropriate British government sanctions have been decidedly lacking. Omar Bakri Mohammad, head of the marginal radical group al-Muhajiroun, is another London-based extremist whose pro-terror activities have been effectively condoned by British security agencies that have preferred to turn a blind eye to his connections to al-Qaeda. Al-Muhajiroun spokesmen, including Omar Bakri himself, have openly incited violence—even against Muslims who disagree with them—and incited acts of terrorism abroad. Reporting on an al-Muhajiroun meeting in Birmingham less than a week after 9/11, the *Telegraph* noted that: "…

a group of 50 young men and women was encouraged to travel to Afghanistan and give their lives in the defense of Islam. 'Martyrdom operatives will be rewarded in heaven,' one speaker declared." Another speaker said:

> I am a Muslim first and foremost. We will never be accepted by the Kufr [the West] so we should not pander to their whims or support their actions like some so-called Muslims have been doing. If they continue to do so, it is our duty to persuade them not to. But if they do not listen, they are Kufr too and so it is our duty to fight and even kill them.

Leaflets for the meeting contained brazenly pro-terror symbolism, stating, "The final hour will not come until the Muslims conquer the White House" upon a background with a picture of the Pentagon in flames.[52]

Omar Bakri himself has issued several fatwas (religious rulings) inciting international violence and terrorism. His "Jihad Fatwa Against Israel" dated October 2, 2000, reads:

> O' Muslims, this Fatwa is a call to fight against Israeli forces, their government, Israeli Embassies, military airports and jets etc.... as they are legitimate targets for Muslims wherever they may be... any aggression against any Muslim property or land by any Kuffar or non-Muslim forces whether American, British or the Jews of Israeli makes Jihad (i.e. fighting) against them an obligation upon all Muslims.... The Fatwa is therefore JIHAD against the Jewish occupiers, their government, army, interests, airports and institutions and it has been given by the most prominent scholars of Islam today because of the occupation of Muslim land and aggression against the Muslims of Palestine. The only Islamic Fatwa against this explicit aggression is Jihad.[53]

The fatwa contains only one qualification, that "it is prohibited to target any non-military or innocent Jews because this would be considered to be murder and therefore aggression against the sanctity of Human life." But as counterterrorism expert Ely Karmon rightly observes, the fatwa amounts to "a call to all Muslims to perpetrate acts of terrorism, not only in Palestine against Israelis, or against Israeli military forces, but also all over the world against 'Israeli embassies and companies... interests, airports and institutions.' This call to arms in fact contradicts the prohibition not 'to target any non-military or innocent Jews because this would be considered to be murder.'"[54]

A week later, al-Muhajiroun issued a press release titled "Advice and Warning to All Jews and Muslims in the UK," claiming that "it is an Islamic obligation upon Muslims everywhere to support the Jihad against those who fight Muslims anywhere in the world or who occupy Muslim land and that this support must be financial, physical, military or verbal." While adding a similar qualification, as above, that "civilians" should not be targeted, the document went on to describe all Jews who express even verbal support for Israel as legitimate targets: "We urge Jews in the UK and elsewhere not to show any support for the Israeli regime whether verbal, financial or physical or they may allow themselves to become targets for Muslims everywhere." The press release also quoted Omar Bakri inciting Muslims worldwide without exception to launch a violent uprising against all governments, including his own British government, and to ignore all national and international laws:

> I call upon Muslims around the world to march toward their government buildings, parliament and presidential palaces, to occupy them and to depose their leaders as a step forward and to take charge and send the Muslim armies to fight the aggressors and occupiers and to establish the Khilafah (i.e. the Islamic State)... I call the Muslims world-wide to resist all man made law wherever they are and to introduce Islamic law.[55]

In the same vein, al-Muhajiroun has published a variety of other fatwas issued by Omar Bakri, inciting acts of violence and terrorism against foreign governments, including, for example, a death threat against Pakistani military ruler Gen. Musharraf.[56] Omar Bakri also issued a similar wider death threat in December 1999 to Russian President Boris Yeltsin over the war in Chechnya. According to al-Muhajiroun spokesman Anjem Choudry: "Russian embassies... government buildings, ministers, [and] personnel" around the world, including in London, "are legitimate targets" of the fatwa. This broad category therefore would include a large number of civilians by definition. The key issue here is that such acts constitute violations of British anti-terrorism laws.[57]

In the aftermath of the beginning of the coalition invasion of Afghanistan, another al-Muhajiroun spokesman and leading member Abdel Rahman Saleem characterized the UK as a legitimate target of terrorist violence:

> Because the allies, the British and the Americans, have started bombing the Muslims of Afghanistan, for those people over there, the government buildings here, the military installations, including 10 Downing Street, become legitimate targets... if any Muslim wants to assassinate [the Prime Minister], wants to get rid of him, I am not going to shed any tears for him and from the Islamic point of view this person is not going to be chastised, this person is not going to be punished for that act, this person will be praised.[58]

Saleem has admitted to undergoing military training with al-Qaeda camps in Afghanistan and Pakistan, and has declared his intent to fight "on the front line."[59] He also admitted to be actively recruiting British Muslims to participate in such training abroad.[60] "My support for my brothers in the Taliban... will be verbal, financial and physical," he confirmed.[61]

Al-Muhajiroun has in fact been deeply involved in material support of al-Qaeda terrorism in the form of recruiting naive Britons to join the ranks of al-Qaeda abroad. Representative of the group's Pakistani wing, Briton Hassan Butt was in Lahore as the war on Afghanistan began. He "claims to have recruited hundreds of fellow Britons to the cause of Osama bin Laden," some of whom later died in the conflict.[62] Butt confirmed that 60 percent of foreigners fighting on behalf of al-Qaeda and the Taliban were from Britain, and that he was among 40 Britons in Lahore recruiting fighters: "I've been in contact with a thousand British Muslims who are going to the holy war. Hundreds have passed through here on their way."[63]

The al-Muhajiroun recruiter further noted that the British al-Qaeda volunteers "may return to Britain to launch terrorist attacks against government and military targets," a veritable "'new phase' of terrorism in their British homeland." In a BBC interview from Pakistan, he remarked: "If they do return, I do believe they will take military action within Britain," targeting "British military and government institutes, as well as British military and government individuals… I have always been in favour of this."[64] Butt's claims regarding al-Muhajiroun's extensive recruitment program were subsequently verified by British military intelligence in Afghanistan, which concluded that: "1,200 British Muslims trained with Osama bin Laden's al-Qa'eda terrorist network in Afghanistan.… The names, addresses and other details of the Britons were found by British military intelligence during searches of bin Laden's cave complex at Tora Bora in eastern Afghanistan." Apart from those who died in combat, the recruits "are now thought to have returned to Britain… Special Branch detectives fear that some of the men who cannot be traced could be plotting terrorist attacks in Britain." As for those who can be traced, it seems they have faced no sanctions at all from British authorities.[65] Butt was detained under the Terrorism Act 2000 toward the end of 2002 for his role in recruiting Britons to join al-Qaeda, but for unexplained reasons was almost immediately released.[66]

Based solely on such evidence from open sources, there is no doubt that al-Muhajiroun is inextricably involved in verbally inciting and physically supporting al-Qaeda's international terrorist network. According to one US government security and defense analyst, al-Muhajiroun's and Omar Bakri's connections to al-Qaeda are well-known in the intelligence community:

> Sure, [the Al Muhajiroun] are a major recruiter for terrorists. It is common knowledge among counterterrorism operatives and agents that they are a front for bin Laden. There are clear al Qaeda ties by way of religious, criminal and foreign mujahideen links. Al Muhajiroun, being the bin Laden front in the UK, essentially connects all the dots.[67]

In other words, contrary to British government denials, al-Muhajiroun's position as a UK-based front organization for al-Qaeda is well-documented and widely known in the international intelligence community. There is no possibility that the British government is in the dark about what is occurring on its own territory. As noted by Steve Atkins, spokesman for the British Embassy in Washington, DC:

> The police and security services are fully aware of this individual and his organization, Al-Muhajiroun. The home secretary has already made it clear that his and their activities are closely monitored. Anyone breaking the law, whether provisions of the Terrorism Act, the Race Relations Act or the Public Order Act, will be prosecuted.[68]

In reality however, despite the role of al-Muhajiroun in inciting and supporting international terrorism, the organization has faced no appropriate legal sanctions from British authorities, although its key leadership and membership have violated UK anti-terrorism (and other) laws with impunity. Indeed, if the British government were to apply its new anti-terrorist legislation to al-Fagih, al-Masari, and al-Muhajiroun, it would become evident that the latter have without doubt conducted terrorist activity on British soil with impunity. On the other hand, there is ample scope for the construction of a criminal case against them. Arguably, under the Terrorism Act 2000, the latter appear to have at least breached

- Part II, section 11(1), by "furthering the activities of" a proscribed terrorist group, al-Qaeda.
- Part II, section 12, by organizing or addressing a meeting with full knowledge of its aims to support or further the activities of a proscribed organization, al-Qaeda
- Part IV, section 59, by "inciting terrorist activity" overseas
- Part VI, Section 56, direct the activities of a terrorist organization, al-Qaeda "at any level"

Although British officials have repeatedly claimed that they simply do not have the legal power to pursue such individuals and groups for their documented involvement in the support of al-Qaeda, this claim is patently false. The UK government, in fact, has extremely strong, indeed draconian, powers. It should be noted that UK anti-terrorism legislation, as is the case with anti-terrorist legislation throughout the West, is intrinsically flawed and susceptible to unchecked government abuse. For example, under the Anti-Terrorism, Crime and Security Act 2001, the British government has the power to indefinitely detain without trial any asylum seeker on the pretext of a mere "suspicion" that they are involved in terrorist activity. But even taking the legislation at face value, the government has displayed a brazen double standard in its application. Thus, under the Prevention of Terrorism Act, the government has detained more than 7,000 people. The vast majority, however, were released without charge. Only a small fraction of this number has ever been charged with offenses related to terrorism. Indeed, rather than targeting genuine terrorists, "Current anti terror laws are being used to quell peaceful protest, to detain foreign nationals without trial, and are fostering discrimination against the Muslim community in Britain." Meanwhile, unscrupulous operatives connected to al-Qaeda, who certainly do fall under UK anti-terrorism legislation, are permitted to continue their activities unsanctioned.[69]

Abu Qatada and Abu Hamza: al-Qaeda's Finsbury Wing

The studious inaction on the part of British authorities, despite ample evidence of terrorist activity on UK soil, also pertains to one of Omar Bakri's associates, Abu Qatada, who is largely believed by the international intelligence community to be the leader of al-Qaeda's European networks. Linked to a large number of terror suspects throughout Europe, Spanish national High Court judge Baltasar Garzon accused him of masterminding al-Qaeda operations in Spain and described him as the "spiritual head of the mujahideen in Britain."[70] A US Executive Order identified Qatada as a "specially designated global terrorist" after 9/11,[71] while the British Treasury confirmed that he was "believed to have committed, or pose a significant risk of committing or providing material support for acts of terrorism."[72] Intelligence on Qatada's terrorist connections is, in other words, well-established. As the *Guardian* reports, he is "at the centre of a global web of terrorist conspiracies that runs from Washington to Amman and from London to Madrid. Police in America, Britain, Belgium, Spain, France, Germany, Italy, and Jordan want him."[73]

An extraordinary *Sunday Times* report two months after 9/11 revealed that British intelligence had been fully aware of Abu Qatada's terrorist activities at the notorious Finsbury Park mosque for several years, but had declined to take action against him. "MI5 was warned more than two years ago that an Islamic cleric said to be Osama Bin Laden's 'European ambassador' was using his mosque in London to raise money for a Muslim holy war in Afghanistan and to issue decrees justifying the murder of women and children," reported *Times* correspondent David Leppard. "A former MI5 agent claimed last week that intelligence chiefs failed to act after he told them that about 20 members of a group with links to Bin Laden's Al-Qaeda network were operating inside the mosque." The MI5 informer, Reda Hassnaine, had infiltrated Qatada's Finsbury network and witnessed firsthand how "several of the men were engaged in a counterfeit credit card ring that raised tens of thousands of pounds to fund terrorist activities abroad." Proceeds from the cards, sold by Qatada for £150 each to dozens of his supporters, were used to buy electrical goods, furniture, and clothes that he resold on the black market. Hassnaine found that Qatada's profits were invested in "communications equipment such as satellite telephones, computers and, it is believed, weapons in eastern Europe. The goods were then shipped to Islamic fighters in Algeria and Afghanistan."[74]

The former British intelligence informer recorded his findings in "a series of written reports to MI5," documenting that "Qatada was the 'spiritual leader' of a banned Algerian terror organisation called the Salafist Group for Call and Combat, known as GSPC," affiliated with al-Qaeda according to security officials. Hassaine recalled that when Qatada issued a fatwa, "he said that it was legitimate for fighters waging the holy war in Algeria and other Arab countries to kill the women and children of members of the security forces." Qatada was also linked with at least seven al-Qaeda operatives detained by Spanish authorities in connection with 9/11. The group's leader, Abu Dahdah, visited Qatada at least 20 times in the UK—the meetings were closely monitored by MI5.[75] Another of Hassnaine's findings while spying for MI5 was that Qatada was recruiting directly for al-Qaeda terrorist operations. The London *Times* reports that: "He saw a lot from the inside. Abu Qatada recruited the shoebomber Richard Reid and the '20th hijacker' Zacarias Moussaoui, Hassaine says. 'I saw them. Abu Qatada is the best brainwasher there is.'"[76] Yet still, the security services refused to prosecute Qatada and his associates.

In a number of other interviews, Hassnaine—an Algerian Muslim who infiltrated al-Qaeda networks for secret services in Algeria and France, for Scotland Yard's Special Branch and for M15—has disclosed further crucial details of his investigations into al-Qaeda's London network. Not only had he witnessed and documented for MI5 Abu Qatada's direct links with and material support to the al-Qaeda terrorist network, he also uncovered similar detailed information on Abu Qatada's Finsbury Park colleague, Abu Hamza.

At the beginning of 1999, Special Branch asked him to infiltrate the Finsbury Park mosque to "gather as much information as he could on Abu Hamza." He spent the next weeks at the mosque, every night writing a report for his handlers "detailing Abu Hamza's associates, his speeches and the attitudes of those around him." Later, under MI5 instructions, he burgled the offices of Abu Hamza and senior militant figures at the Finsbury Park mosque and elsewhere. For weeks, Hassnaine repeatedly "stole scores of documents" describing what police believed to be al-Qaeda cells in the UK planning terrorist attacks. The documents included communications from al-Qaeda affiliated terrorists in Algeria.[77]

As European law-enforcement officials confirm, reliable intelligence proves that the Finsbury Park mosque has "functioned openly as a center of recruitment, ideological incitement, and even support of terrorist acts." Investigators say that it constitutes "a crossroads connecting European ideologues to Afghan training camps and Islamic battlegrounds in Chechnya, Bosnia-Herzegovina, and the Middle East." Nevertheless, European experts have been alarmed that "British authorities were slow to move against Abu

Hamza or Abu Qatada."[78]

The extent of this failure is corroborated by a variety of other reports. A month after 9/11, Qatada himself told the London *Observer* that

> British security services offered him a chance to escape to Afghanistan. Abu Qatada, whose Bolton bank account was frozen last week when he was named on a US list of suspected terrorists, told the *Observer* that MI5 approached intermediaries to offer him a passport and an Iranian visa so he could leave the country.... The Home Office refused to comment on Abu Qatada's claim.[79]

Subsequently, amidst mounting international pressure from Europe and the United States demanding his arrest and interrogation, Abu Qatada disappeared, and British authorities claimed that they had no idea where he was hiding. Meanwhile, investigators were perplexed as to why British authorities had not arrested him sooner.[80] "But why hasn't he been caught?" asked the *Observer*. "The French secret service believe they know: he is a spy. That is also the view of many in Britain's Islamic community. In prayer halls and private houses, the opinions are the same: 'Qatada is an MI5 agent.'"[81]

Citing European intelligence sources, *Time* magazine elaborated on the evidence that Qatada was, in fact, being protected by British security services:

> ...senior European intelligence officials tell TIME that Abu Qatada is tucked away in a safe house in the north of England, where he and his family are being lodged, fed and clothed by British intelligence services. "The deal is that Abu Qatada is deprived of contact with extremists in London and Europe but can't be arrested or expelled because no one officially knows where he is," says the source, whose claims were corroborated by French authorities. "The British win because the last thing they want is a hot potato they can't extradite for fear of al-Qaeda reprisals but whose presence contradicts London's support of the war on terror."[82]

Time magazine's findings were corroborated by revelations in the London *Times* that Qatada was "a double agent working for MI5, raising criticism from European governments, which repeatedly called for his arrest." According to the *Times*, the British authorities

> ignored warnings—which began before the September 11 attacks—from half a dozen friendly governments about Abu Qatada's links with terrorist groups and refused to arrest him...
>
> Abu Qatada boasted to MI5 that he could prevent terrorist attacks and offered to expose dangerous extremists, while all along he was setting up a haven for his terror organisation in Britain.... Indignant French officials

accused MI5 of helping the cleric to abscond. While he remained on the run, one intelligence chief in Paris was quoted as saying: "British intelligence is saying they have no idea where he is, but we know where he is and, if we know, I'm quite sure they do." Almost a year later Abu Qatada was found hiding in a flat not far from Scotland Yard.[83]

A leaked judgment from the Special Immigration Appeals Commission (SIAC) on Qatada's case demonstrates that British security services had contacted him at least three times, in June and December 1996 and February 1997. The judgment records that in his conversations with one British intelligence official, Qatada

> ... claimed to "wield powerful, spiritual influence over the Algerian community in London and was confident that he could use this influence to prevent any terrorist repercussions..." He maintained that a decision had been taken in Algeria not to mount operations against the United Kingdom... The appellant said he did not want London to become a centre for settling Islamic scores... and apparently said that he would "report anyone damaging the interests of this country."

The unnamed British intelligence officer is cited in the judgment as confirming that Qatada "welded considerable 'spiritual, if not operational influence on an extensive number of Islamists of various nationalities and that, as a resident of the United Kingdom, I fully expected him to use that influence, wherever he could, to control the hotheads and ensure terrorism remained off the streets of London.'" The judgment continues to note that Qatada's interviews with British security services "show that he accepted and indeed asserted that he did have influence over some of the extremists who might be expected to become involved in violence and terrorism."[84]

A number of facts are apparent in light of all these authoritative revelations. Firstly, British intelligence was fully aware of Abu Qatada's prominent connections to al-Qaeda and involvement in incitement to and support of terrorism. Indeed, they believed that his control over al-Qaeda affiliated terrorists in the UK was sufficiently strong so as to prevent future terrorist attacks against British targets. Thus, despite his heavy involvement in the support of international terrorism (as opposed to domestic terrorism), British officials saw fit to recruit him to MI5, allow him to continue his involvement in terrorism abroad, and grant him protection from anti-terrorism laws.

As Qatada's legal representative, leading British lawyer Ben Emmerson QC, submitted in the preliminary SIAC hearing, according to the London *Guardian*: "Mr. Emmerson said his client had been monitored by security services since the mid-1990s and 'his actions had a large degree of tacit approval.'"[85] Terrorism expert Professor Gilles Kepel—research director of the Paris-based Center for International Studies and Research—supports this conclusion, arguing that there is an implicit agreement between British authorities and London terror networks allowing them to operate freely in the UK on condition that they refrain from targeting British interests:

> Britain was perceived mainly as a sanctuary and no terrorist activity took place in Britain, probably for that reason. Britain was even nicknamed by the militants "Londonistan," meaning that people from Afghanistan, Pakistan, what you call in English "The Stans," had gathered in London where they found, for many of them, political asylum, and they were able to organize their networks. Probably the condition for the deal, but this was never made explicit of course, was that they would not have any activity against British interests on British soil.[86]

Similarly, in an interview with Canadian journalist Terry McKenna, top Paris-based anti-terrorist expert Judge Jean-Louis Bruguiere was asked whether he was "surprised that a man like Abu Qatada has not yet been arrested." He responded: "I can say that if he was in France he would already have been arrested in this business. This was not the case because he was in Britain, and Britain apparently permits this sort of activity."[87] In other words, as long as al-Qaeda operatives in the UK avoided targeting British interests, they were permitted to do as they pleased. Abu Hamza and Abu Qatada were only belatedly arrested and detained under British anti-terrorism laws after years of facilitating international terrorism from the UK, when it became clear to authorities that they were planning domestic attacks on British targets—not years earlier when their complicity in international terrorism was well-established.[88]

Indeed, their detention in the UK appears to be only yet another bizarre strategy to keep them away from the scrutiny of the international intelligence community—and perhaps thereby to prevent further embarrassing or scandalous revelations about British intelligence and security policies. The *Times* noted, for instance, that

> foreign governments are also criticizing the Government…
>
> Their complaint is that they have been given no access to the detainees. Investigators from Spain, Germany and Italy are desperate to question Abu Qatada, who they claim is a pivotal figure in cells they have under arrest in their own countries.
>
> Their requests to question him and some of the other suspects directly have been rejected by the Government. Investigators in Spain who named Abu Qatada as "the spiritual leader of al-Qaeda in Europe," say their own terror trials are hindered by Britain's refusal to let them interrogate the cleric… In spite of holding most of the terror suspects for many months, the men are providing the security services and police with little intelligence on terrorist activity in the United Kingdom.89

Anas al-Liby: al-Qaeda Terrorist on MI6's Payroll

The remarkable case of leading al-Qaeda terrorist Anas al-Liby provides an explicit illustration of the implicit arrangement that was so convenient for both British security services and UK-based al-Qaeda terrorists. Anas al-Liby is on the FBI's list of "Most Wanted Terrorists" "in connection with the August 7, 1998, bombings of the United States Embassies in Dar es Salaam, Tanzania, and Nairobi, Kenya.... The Rewards For Justice Program, United States Department of State, is offering a reward of up to $25 million for information leading directly to the apprehension or conviction of Anas Al-Liby."[90]

The first inkling of how intelligence inquiries into al-Qaeda's role in the 1998 bombings were severely compromised came from the United States. In an interview with ABC News, Chicago-based FBI Special Agents Robert Wright and John Vincent complained that they

> were called off criminal investigations of suspected terrorists tied to the deadly bombings of two US embassies in Africa [1998]... the two Chicago-based agents were assigned to track a connection to Chicago, a suspected terrorist cell that would later lead them to a link with Osama bin Laden. Wright says that when he pressed for authorization to open a criminal investigation into the money trail, his supervisor stopped him... Wright, who remains with the FBI, says he soon discovered that all the FBI intelligence division wanted him to do was to follow suspected terrorists and file reports—but make no arrests. "The supervisor who was there from headquarters was right straight across from me and started yelling at me: 'You will not open criminal investigations. I forbid any of you. You will not open criminal investigations against any of these intelligence subjects,'" Wright said.[91]

Although Wright and Vincent were working as members of a terrorism task force and had gathered tangible proof of criminal activity, their investigations were blocked. The block remained in place even after al-Qaeda's bombing of the US embassies in 1998, although the financial trail for the attacks led back to the very same people they were monitoring in Chicago: "Yet, even after the bombings, Wright said FBI headquarters wanted no arrests. 'Two months after the embassies are hit in Africa, they wanted to shut down the criminal investigation,' said Wright. 'They wanted to kill it.'" Chicago federal prosecutor Mark Flessner who was assigned to the case noted that Wright and Vincent were contributing to a strong criminal case against the Chicago al-Qaeda operatives behind the 1998 embassy attacks. But, he said: "There were powers bigger than I was in the Justice Department and within the FBI that simply were not going to let it [the building of a criminal case] happen. And it didn't happen."[92]

The US block coincided with similar dubious developments in the UK, revealed by former leading MI5 counterterrorism agent David Shayler.

According to Shayler's revelations which were widely reported in the press, while US authorities were shutting down the criminal investigation into the al-Qaeda culprits behind the 1998 terror attacks, British authorities were cozying up to them to orchestrate a terrorist operation. Shayler worked for the international terrorism desk of MI5 for 6 years before resigning in 1997. In 1995, he obtained classified MI6 documents detailing a covert British intelligence plan to assassinate Libyan Head of State Col. Mu'ammar Gaddafi. Most surprisingly, Shayler disclosed that as part of the plot MI6 paid over £100,000 to the al-Qaeda network in Libya to conduct the assassination. The operation, however, failed. The al-Qaeda operatives working on the MI6 payroll placed a bomb under the wrong car, killing six innocent Libyan civilians.[93] In a press release on the subject, Shayler observed:

> We need a statement from the Prime Minister and the Foreign Secretary clarifying the facts of this matter. In particular, we need to know how around £100,000 of taxpayers' money was used to fund the sort of Islamic Extremists who have connections to Osama Bin Laden's Al Qaeda network. Did ministers give MI6 permission for this? By the time MI6 paid the group in late 1995 or early 1996, US investigators had already established that Bin Laden was implicated in the 1993 attack on the World Trade Centre. Given the timing and the close connections between Libyan and Egyptian Islamic Extremists, it may even have been used to fund the murder of British citizens in Luxor, Egypt in 1996.[94]

In a further comment piece for the *Observer*, Shayler elaborated on these concerns. The "real criminals," he argued, "are the British Government and the intelligence services. The Government has a duty to uphold the law. It cannot simply be ignored because crimes are carried out by friends of the Government." Noting his November 1999 dossier of evidence on the plot sent to Home Secretary Jack Straw, Shayler pointed out: "Although the assassination failed when attempted in 1996, innocent Libyan civilians were killed." In the face of such compelling evidence, "these very senior Ministers should, of course, have called in the police immediately.... The Government's failure to ensure that two MI6 officers are brought to justice for their part in planning a murder is what I would expect of despots and dictators."[95]

The British government's response was at first to completely deny the story. Then Foreign Secretary Robin Cook described Shayler's allegations as "pure fantasy." But Shayler's position was reinforced upon the leak of the original MI6 document on a US website, showing that "British intelligence knew of the murder plot two months in advance" and that "An Arab dissident was passing detailed information to his MI6 handler in anticipation of British assistance."[96] The government then accused Shayler of breaching the 1989 Official Secrets Act—his revelations, officials claimed, were a threat to British national security—and subsequently pursued legal action against him to prevent further publication of his information. Reporting on the upcoming trial in October 2002, the *Evening Standard* observed that

> Michael Tugendhat, QC, appearing for various national newspapers, is expected to argue that the Government has provided no evidence that national security will be threatened by the trial and will underline the importance of open justice... Shayler will be defending himself during the trial. He is expected to claim that British secret service agents paid up to £100,000 to al Qaeda terrorists for an assassination attempt on Libyan leader Colonel Gadaffy in 1996. He is seeking permission to plead a defense of "necessity"—that he acted for the greater good by revealing wrongdoing by the security service.[97]

In further startling revelations supporting Shayler's allegations, French intelligence experts journalist Guillaume Dasquié and Jean-Charles Brisard, adviser to President Jacques Chirac, documented that among the members of the Libyan al-Qaeda cell hired by MI6 to assassinate Col. Gaddafi was one of Osama bin Laden's most trusted lieutenants, Anas al-Liby, who as already noted was on the FBI's "Most Wanted Terrorist" list for his involvement in the 1998 terrorist attacks on US embassies in Africa. London *Observer* home affairs editor Martin Bright reported in detail on Dasquié's and Brisard's devastating findings:

> British intelligence paid large sums of money to an al-Qaeda cell in Libya in a doomed attempt to assassinate Colonel Gadaffi in 1996 and thwarted early attempts to bring Osama bin Laden to justice. The latest claims of MI6 involvement with Libya's fearsome Islamic Fighting Group, which is connected to one of bin Laden's trusted lieutenants, will be embarrassing to the Government...
>
> The allegations have emerged in the book *Forbidden Truth*, published in America by two French intelligence experts who reveal that the first Interpol arrest warrant for bin Laden was issued by Libya in March 1998... British and US intelligence agencies buried the fact that the arrest warrant had come from Libya and played down the threat. Five months after the warrant was issued, al-Qaeda killed more than 200 people in the truck bombings of US embassies in Kenya and Tanzania.

Libya's Interpol arrest warrant for Osama was issued in connection with the March 1994 murder of two German counterterrorism agents, Silvan and Vera Becker, in Africa. Bright points out that

> the resistance of Western intelligence agencies to the Libyan concerns can be explained by MI6's involvement with the al-Qaeda coup plot...

The Libyan al-Qaeda cell included Anas al-Liby, who remains on the US government's most wanted list with a reward of $25 million for his capture. He is wanted for his involvement in the African embassy bombings. Al-Liby was with bin Laden in Sudan before the al-Qaeda leader returned to Afghanistan in 1996. Astonishingly, despite suspicions that he was a high-level al-Qaeda operative, al-Liby was given political asylum in Britain and lived in Manchester until May of 2000.

A police raid at al-Liby's Manchester accommodation discovered a 180-page al-Qaeda "manual for jihad" containing instructions for terrorist attacks. According to Shayler, the plot came to his attention in formal meetings with his MI6 colleagues. The *Observer's* Bright revealed that the said officers involved in the plot were "Richard Bartlett, who has previously only been known under the codename PT16 and had overall responsibility for the operation; and David Watson, codename PT16B." The latter was the MI6 handler for Libyan al-Qaeda operative "Tunworth," who was providing information from within the cell. Eager to crush further damaging publicity on these issues emerging from the Shayler trial, Home Secretary David Blunkett and Foreign Secretary Jack Straw "signed Public Interest Immunity certificates to protect national security. Reporters were not able to report allegations about the Gadaffi plot during the course of the trial."[98]

The al-Liby affair provides a tangible—and shocking—illustration of the covert machinations behind the systematic negligence on the part of the American and British security services toward al-Qaeda terrorist operations. Clearly, Anglo-American intelligence agencies have compromised and, indeed, entirely blocked investigations to apprehend Osama bin Laden and al-Qaeda. The simple reason for this, it seems, is rooted in highly dubious policies entailing the utilization of al-Qaeda cells to pursue terrorist operations perceived to be within Anglo-American strategic interests. Indeed, the case of al-Liby clarifies one specific reason that British authorities have systematically granted free reign to known al-Qaeda terrorists on British soil: they are intelligence assets working within an overarching Anglo-American strategic framework. Although the security services are fully aware of the ramifications of this corrupt policy in terms of providing assistance to the al-Qaeda terrorist network, they clearly believe that the ends justify the means regardless of the fact that loss of innocent lives is an inevitable byproduct of this policy.

The al-Liby affair also brings to light a number of awkward questions regarding the relationship between the intelligence community and al-Qaeda's terrorist network. Al-Liby's complicity in the devastating 1998 US embassy bombings did not deter the security services from employing him as their agent for a British terrorist operation. The fact that al-Liby, described as one of Osama bin Laden's "most trusted lieutenants," could have been employed in this manner further calls into question the fundamental underpinnings of the "War on Terror" discourse. According to the conventional discourse, it would be impossible for al-Qaeda to ever work alongside or on behalf of Western intelligence agencies, simply because the West is al-Qaeda's enemy. To what extent, then, is al-Qaeda really an "enemy" of Western intelligence agencies to be investigated and apprehended, rather than a potential and oft-used asset of those agencies? Furthermore, how intricate and entrenched are such connections between Western intelligence agencies and the international al-Qaeda terrorist network?

Indeed, the unabashed conduct of British intelligence officers in pursuing this fraudulent policy of selectively employing al-Qaeda terrorists in the service of secretive Western strategic interests suggests the policy to be fairly routine. Moreover, there is little doubt that this policy of selectively supporting the al-Qaeda network has directly facilitated al-Qaeda's terrorist attacks on Western targets, while both hindering ongoing investigations and providing unchecked assistance to leading terrorists. Finally, British authorities are obviously pleased to allow known al-Qaeda terrorists to operate freely on UK soil, and to turn a blind eye to their activities despite the duty to apprehend them. Thus, while al-Liby was an MI6 double agent benefiting from political asylum in the UK, he was nevertheless involved in the planning of anti-Western terrorist attacks. In other words, the al-Liby affair establishes that Western intelligence agencies have intricate connections to high-level al-Qaeda operatives involved in large-scale terrorist atrocities, and rather than attempting to apprehend them and hold them to account, instead uses them to conduct specific covert operations in their interests. Terror, it seems, is not simply an unadulterated enemy to be fought in the New War—it is, on the contrary, an instrument of statecraft.

5.

SAUDI ARABIA: BIN LADEN'S FINANCIAL BASE

According to the conventional wisdom, due to his involvement in terrorism, Osama bin Laden is an outcast from both his own family and the Saudi establishment. There is, however, abundant evidence that Osama continues to maintain relations with both his family and the Saudi establishment—with tacit US connivance. Some of this evidence has already been discussed. Here, ongoing Saudi connections to al-Qaeda are explored in detail, along with their implications for the overall contours of Western policy.

Osama and the Bin Laden Clan

A wide number of credible reports indicate that Osama bin Laden never fundamentally broke away from his family. On the contrary, there is good reason to suspect that in some cases, intimate relations between the al-Qaeda terrorist and members of his family prevail. Former CIA counterterrorism chief Vincent Cannistraro comments: "There's obviously a lot of spin by the Saudi Binladin Group"—the family's corporate name—"to distinguish itself from Osama. I've been following the bin Ladens for years, and it's easy to say, 'We disown him.' Many in the family have. But blood is usually thicker than water." Although Cannistraro believes that many family members have ceased all contact with Osama, he also says that there remains "an interconnectedness" among others in the family. Indeed, according to journalist Jane Mayer reporting for *New Yorker* magazine: "He told me that as recently as nine months ago [February 2001] an allied intelligence agency had seen two of Osama's sisters apparently taking cash to an airport in Abu Dhabi, where they are suspected of handing it to a member of bin Laden's Al Qaeda organization." According to Cannistraro, Saudi sources also observed several of Osama's children traveling between Saudi Arabia and Afghanistan without restrictions. Mayer confirms that the intelligence community is well aware of such linkages:

> Some American and European intelligence officials told me that several members of the bin Laden family sympathize with Osama. These officials also acknowledged that with a family that large—it may number as many as six hundred, when one counts all the relatives—conflicts are inevitable... When bin Laden turned against the United States, his fortune

was still interwoven with the family's, which was invested in many American businesses.[1]

Mayer also interviewed the London-based alleged al-Qaeda operative Saad al-Fagih. As a Saudi dissident who participated in the Afghan war against the Soviets, al-Fagih is well acquainted with Osama bin Laden's modus operandi: "Some of the sisters are very religious and they believe that even if your brother is a real criminal he is your brother. He's got to live comfortably." Mayer relates:

Under Shariah, Islamic law, Al-Fagih said, it is unjust to deprive any member of a family of his rightful inheritance. Some of Osama's siblings are troubled by a decision that the Saudi government made, in 1994, to freeze his assets, including part of an inheritance, estimated at thirty million dollars, that Osama, like all the sons in the family, received. (The daughters, in accordance with Islamic law, each inherited half as much.) "Many of Osama's brothers and sisters think it is sinful if they keep any of his inheritance money," Al-Fagih said.

... Both Al-Fagih and Abdel Bari Atwan [editor of Al-Quds al-Arabi, an Arabic daily newspaper in Britain, who interviewed Osama bin Laden in November 1996, and is well acquainted with people close to bin Laden] claim that bin Laden's mother has twice met with her son since he moved to Afghanistan, in 1996. Atwan said that a trip in the spring of 1998 was arranged by Prince Turki al-Faisal, then the head of Saudi intelligence. Turki was in charge of the "Afghanistan file," and had long-standing ties to bin Laden and the Taliban. Indeed, Osama, before becoming an enemy of the state, had been something of a Turki protégé, according to his biographers. Prince Turki, Al-Fagih said, "made arrangements for Osama's mother and his stepfather to visit him and persuade him to stop what he was doing." When Al-Fagih was asked about bin Laden's response, he said, "He is very close to his mother, so he thought it was nice to see his mother. It's a free trip... They talk about health, and children. But he didn't promise anything."

The second trip, according to Al-Fagih, occurred last spring. "The royal family approved it... It was not just a family affair. It was to try to approach and influence him. They wanted to find out his intentions concerning the royal family. They gave him the impression that they wouldn't crack down on his followers in Saudi Arabia" as long as he set his sights on targets outside the desert kingdom. Last January, the Qatar-based news network Al-Jazeera broadcast footage of what was purported to be the wedding of bin Laden's son Muhammad. Three siblings from a later marriage of Osama's mother were in attendance.[2]

The New Yorker report also reveals that Osama bin Laden's half brother, Yeslam—Geneva-based head of the bin Laden family's European holding company, the Saudi Investment Company—sent funds to the notorious Huffman

Aviation in Venice, Florida, which trained several 9/11 al-Qaeda hijackers—including chief hijacker Mohamed Atta—for flying. Jane Mayer reports that despite issuing a statement denouncing Osama, "he has nonetheless attracted the scrutiny of Swiss and American investigators because of a financial stake he has in a Swiss aviation firm. By a seeming coincidence, he paid for flight instruction for an acquaintance at Huffman Aviation, the training school in Venice, Florida, that many of the suicide hijackers attended." Disavowing any contact with Osama for the last 20 years, Yeslam responded to the report with a fax claiming that although he "had subsidized the flying lessons, he was not involved in picking the flight school." But clearly, US and Swiss counterterrorist experts are concerned enough to be investigating the matter. The matter is, indeed, complicated by the testimony of "Yeslam's estranged wife, Carmen… that she never detected any distance between Osama and the rest of the family: 'In front of me, they never disowned Osama. They spoke of him as a brother.'"[3] Indeed, authorities have continued to investigate Yeslam. In March 2002, French police searched Yeslam bin Laden's villa in Cannes, reportedly searching "for evidence of terrorism-related money laundering involving the Saudi Investment Company. Swiss police also searched other properties connected to the firm."[4]

Several other bin Laden relatives are tied to a network of banks called al-Taqwa, suspected of laundering money to terrorist groups connected to al-Qaeda. The office of Switzerland's chief federal prosecutor has announced the receipt of new information indicating "links between Al Taqwa and the bin Laden network." The al-Taqwa network of companies was established in the 1980s by the Muslim Brotherhood. Documents verified by *Newsweek* magazine show that among the shareholders of the Nassau-based al-Taqwa bank are at least two relatives of Osama bin Laden. Furthermore, one of Osama's brothers, Ghalib Mohamed bin Laden, has an Islamic investment account—profitable at least until 1998—to the tune of several million dollars in the Bahamas-based Bank al-Taqwa.[5]

There are other corroborative reports in this regard. US national security expert James Bamford, for instances, cites declassified documents, newly released under the Freedom of Information Act, illustrating that: "In recent years, NSA has regularly listened to bin Laden's unencrypted telephone calls. [National Security] Agency officials have sometimes played tapes of bin Laden talking to his mother to impress members of Congress and select visitors to the agency."[6] In 1998, another report noted that although members of Osama's family publicly disown him: "Yossef Bodansky, director of the House Task Force on Terrorism and Unconventional Warfare, said 'Osama maintains connections' with some of his nearly two dozen brothers. He would not elaborate."[7] In October 2001, ABC News interviewed Osama's sister-in-law Carmen bin Laden concerning whether the family had given money to Osama. Although she emphasized that she could not be sure, she said, "but my opinion is yes… I think they would say, okay, this is — for Islam they would give. You know, for Islam they would give."[8]

Indeed, according to the *Wall Street Journal*, "the Federal Bureau of Investigation has issued subpoenas to banks used by the bin Laden family seeking records of family dealings."[9] The FBI's interest certainly seems justifiable. A report from French intelligence, for instance, uncovered "a web of bin Laden companies both good *and bad*." Meanwhile, the bin Laden family has remained "quite secretive… about how the financial network actually operates."[10]

Rescued from the FBI by the FBI

Although the intelligence community had for years been monitoring these reoccurring connections between Osama and his family, 24 members of his family "were urgently evacuated from the United States in the first days following the terrorist attacks on New York and Washington," according to CBS News citing the Saudi ambassador to Washington. "The young members of the bin Laden family were driven or flown under FBI supervision to a secret place in Texas and then to Washington."[11] Recently released documents from the Department of Homeland Security obtained by Judicial Watch further prove that in addition to "142 Saudis on six charter flights" that departed the US, another "160 Saudis left the United States on 55 flights immediately after 9/11—making a total of about 300 people who left with the apparent approval of the Bush administration."[12] These flights occurred on September 13, 2001— when the FAA's nationwide order grounding all planes was still in force.

A *National Review* investigation of the matter confirmed only that the urgent evacuation of the bin Laden family from the US had been arranged with high-level government approval. When the *Review* called an official at Logan Airport in Boston, he said: "You have to talk to the State Department. They're the ones who set it up." A State Department source, however, denied responsibility, claiming that it had "played no role" in the evacuation, instead pointing a finger at the White House. "This is not something we would have brokered. [Saudi Ambassador Prince] Bandar does not need Foggy Bottom to get a phone call returned by the White House." But the White House was similarly silent. As the *Review* observed: "That seemed a clear hint that the White House was involved, but the White House declined immediate comment… However it happened, the bin Ladens are long gone…. Now, a year after 9/11, should US law enforcement ever need them, investigators will know where they are—in Saudi Arabia, out of reach."

The government-approved FBI evacuation of the bin Laden family, despite the longstanding US intelligence investigations of members of the family due to suspected terrorist connections and activities, flew in the face of routine law enforcement procedures. Family members of suspects in murder cases are among the first people to face heavy questioning. Investigators "usually conduct an investigation to make sure the relatives can be eliminated as suspects or witnesses. While that is going on, the instincts of law enforcement are normally to freeze all potential suspects and witnesses in place until the investigation has reached some conclusions." Extraordinarily, in the case of 9/11, exactly the opposite of routine law enforcement procedure occurred: the very people who would normally be first on the list of suspects escaped to Saudi Arabia under FBI escort with US government clearance.[13]

BBC *Newsnight* has also investigated this issue, confirming that at least "11 members of Osama Bin Laden's family" had been whisked off to Saudi Arabia while other planes were grounded. Yet evidence obtained by *Newsnight* proved that

> the FBI was on the trail of other members of the Bin Laden family for links to terrorist organisations before and after September 11th…
>
> This document is marked "Secret." Case ID—199-Eye WF 213 589. 199 is FBI code for case type. 9 would be murder. 65 would be espionage. 199 means national security. WF indicates Washington field office special agents were investigating ABL—because its relationship with the World Assembly of Muslim Youth, WAMY—a suspected terrorist organisation. ABL is Abdullah Bin Laden, president and treasurer of WAMY.

The *Newsnight* investigation found that two brothers of Osama—Abdullah and Omar bin Laden—connected to WAMY were tracked by the FBI for suspected involvement in terrorism. They both lived at 3411 Silver Maple Place, "conveniently close" to WAMY, which is located at 5613 Leesburg Pike. "And here, just a couple blocks down the road at 5913 Leesburg, is where four of the hijackers that attacked New York and Washington are listed as having lived." Pakistani, Indian, and Philippine intelligence have cited evidence that WAMY is connected to al-Qaeda terrorist activities. Although the FBI was actively investigating these suspected terrorist connections, "for some reason, agents were pulled off the trail" and even now the US Treasury has refused to freeze WAMY's assets—"when we talked to them, they insisted they are a charity."[14]

US national security expert John Trento noted that although the FBI had "wanted to investigate these guys… they weren't permitted to," although WAMY have "had connections to Osama bin Laden's people" and other "groups that have terrorist connections." WAMY also fits "the pattern of groups that the Saudi royal family and Saudi community of princes—the 20,000 princes—have funded who've engaged in terrorist activity. Now, do I know that WAMY has done anything that's illegal? No, I don't know that. Do I know that as far back as 1996 the FBI was very concerned about this organisation? I do."[15] The London *Guardian* observed that the FBI had investigated "two of Osama bin Laden's relatives" as well as WAMY, but closed its files on them due to high-level constraints in 1996 "before any conclusions could be reached."[16] And according to the *Pittsburgh Tribune-Review*, both Abdullah and Omar bin Laden "have not been seen since the branch of the bin Laden family residing in the United States was flown home on a chartered jet."[17]

According to the *Tampa Tribune*—citing private investigators Dan Grossi and Manuel Perez, who were bodyguards on a Lear jet that flew three Saudis on September 13, 2001—the individuals on the flight included: the son of Prince Sultan bin Abdul Aziz, Saudi defense minister; the son of an unidentified Saudi military commander; and a third unidentified Saudi. Grossi and Perez are credible sources, the former being a retired Tampa police officer who worked in internal affairs and homicide and the latter being a retired 29-year FBI veteran with experience in counterterrorism.[18] Investigative journalist Craig Unger has also confirmed the flights based on interviews not only with Grossi and Perez, but also with sources who orchestrated the flights and even former counterterrorism czar Richard Clarke.[19]

Prince Sultan, whose son was on the Tampa flight, is also the target of a landmark lawsuit by 9/11 families seeking $1 trillion in damages for financing al-Qaeda. The Prince's own defense documents for the case revealed "highly detailed new evidence of the Saudi government's role in funnelling millions of dollars to a web of Islamic charities that are widely suspected by US officials of covertly financing the operations of Al Qaeda and other international terrorist groups," according to *Newsweek*. Stacks of "court affidavits and copies of cancelled checks" filed by the Prince's lawyers prove that for the past 16 years, he "approved regular payments of about $266,000 a year to the International Islamic Relief Organization—a large Saudi charity whose US offices were last year raided by federal agents." He also authorized "two additional grants totaling $52,000 to the World Assembly of Muslim Youth, another Saudi-based group that has drawn the scrutiny of US antiterrorism investigators."[20] Notably, the Saudi Defense Minister's legal representative is Baker Botts, which boasts James Baker—secretary of state in the first Bush administration—as a senior partner. "Its recent alumni include Robert Jordan, the former personal lawyer for President Bush who is now US ambassador to Saudi Arabia."[21]

Citing official passenger lists for four of the Saudi evacuation flights, Unger reports that another individual on the flight was Prince Ahmed bin Salman. In interrogations with the CIA in 2002, al-Qaeda operative Abu Zubayda—a member of Osama bin Laden's inner circle—reportedly confirmed that Prince Ahmed had ties to al-Qaeda, and also knew in advance of the 9/11 attacks. The Prince died of a heart attack not long after the interrogations.[22]

The Bin Laden Empire

While there is compelling evidence that Osama bin Laden has not broken away from his family, it is a matter of record that high-level elements on the right wing of the US political establishment, particularly in the Bush administration, are significantly tied to the same family. According to the *New Yorker*: "Over the years, there have been warm, substantial ties between members of the bin Laden family and leaders of the foreign-policy establishment in America and Britain."[23] Carlyle Group, the giant US defense contractor that employs former President George Bush Sr., has had long-standing financial ties to the bin Laden family. The Carlyle Group's investments include ownership in at least 164 companies worldwide, managing assets worth some $14 billion. As a leading defense contractor, Carlyle has profited immensely from the war on Afghanistan and the corresponding militarization of US foreign policy after 9/11. According to the *Wall Street Journal* shortly after 9/11, "there may be one unexpected beneficiary" of the US boost in defense spending in the post-9/11 "War on Terror": "Mr. bin Laden's family...

> Among its far-flung business interests, the well-heeled Saudi Arabian clan—which says it is estranged from Osama—is an investor in a fund established by Carlyle Group, a well-connected Washington merchant bank specializing in buyouts of defense and aerospace companies. Through this investment and its ties to Saudi royalty, the bin Laden family has become acquainted with some of the biggest names in the Republican Party. In recent years, former President Bush, ex-Secretary of State James Baker and ex-Secretary of Defense Frank Carlucci have made the pilgrimage to the bin Laden family's headquarters in Jeddah, Saudi Arabia. Mr. Bush makes speeches on behalf of Carlyle Group and is senior adviser to its Asian Partners fund, while Mr. Baker is its senior counselor. Mr. Carlucci is the group's chairman. Osama is one of more than 50 children of Mohammed bin Laden, who built the family's $5 billion business, Saudi Binladin Group, largely with construction contracts from the Saudi government.[24]

Other individuals involved in Carlyle include former British Prime Minister John Major, an "adviser" to the Group, as well as former Philippine President Fidel Ramos, former Thai Premier Anand Panyarachun, a former president of Germany's Bundesbank and a former head of the US Securities and Exchange Commission.[25] The extent to which the Carlyle Group is connected to the US government only exacerbates these concerns. According to Department of Defense documents obtained by Judicial Watch under the Freedom of Information Act, "the Carlyle Group has high-level access to the US government." The documents include: a February 15, 2001 a letter on Carlyle Group letterhead to Defense Secretary Donald Rumsfeld, signed by Carlyle Group members former Defense Secretaries Frank Carlucci and William Perry; and a April 3 response from Secretary Rumsfeld. "The letters seemingly discuss the restructuring of the Defense Department. The Carlyle Group is listed in the documents as Defense Department contractor."[26] Carlyle, in other words, is so wired into the government that it has a direct impact on US defense policies.

According to one Carlyle executive, the bin Laden family "committed $2 million through a London investment arm in 1995 in Carlyle Partners II Fund," raising a total of $1.3 billion. Among 29 deals, the fund has "purchased several aerospace companies." The bin Laden family "has received $1.3 million back in completed investments and should ultimately realize a 40% annualized rate of return." Other sources confirmed that the family investment in Carlyle is "considerably larger." A foreign financier "with ties to the bin Laden family" stated that the $2 million "was merely an initial contribution: 'It's like plowing a field. You seed it once. You plow it, and then you reseed it again.'"[27]

The *Wall Street Journal* also notes that there is a history here. US government officials have always been keenly interested in the bin Laden family's views of the US, particularly in relation to investment:

> During the past several years, the [bin Laden] family's close ties to the Saudi royal family prompted executives and staff from closely held New York publisher Forbes, Inc. to make two trips to the family headquarters, according to Forbes Chairman Caspar Weinberger, a former US Secretary of Defense in the Reagan administration. "We would call on them to get their view of the country and what would be of interest to investors."[28]

Weinberger has close links to President Bush Sr., who pardoned him for his criminal conduct in the Iran–Contra scandal in 1989. But most pertinently, through Carlyle, both George Bush Sr. and the bin Laden family were set to profit from the post-9/11 "War on Terror." "As America's military involvement abroad deepens, profits are increasing for the Carlyle Group—and, it turns out, for thousands of California civil servants," observed the *San Francisco Chronicle*, which neglected to mention two other key beneficiaries: the Bush and bin Laden families. "Critics of the Carlyle Group have grown increasingly vocal in recent weeks, particularly over the perception that a private organization with unmistakable links to the White House is benefiting from America's military action in Afghanistan."[29]

President George W. Bush also has links to the Carlyle Group. In the years preceding his 1994 bid for Texas governor, "Bush owned stock in and sat on the board of directors of Caterair, a service company that provided airplane food and was also a component of Carlyle." A Texas insider revealed that Bush was paid $15,000 a year for his consulting position, and a bonus of $1,000 for every meeting he attended—amounting to a total of around $75,000. "Reports show Carlyle was also a major contributor to his electoral fund."[30]

Given that there are credible reports that Osama bin Laden has not broken away from his family and that he maintains ties with them—and financial ties at that—the revelations that the Bush family has long-standing financial ties to the bin Laden family in the defense industry, among other business connections, is a startling indication of the complex web of interests surrounding 9/11. Carlyle, however, is only the tip of the iceberg in the bin Laden family's vast financial empire. According to the *New Yorker*:

> The [bin Laden] family continues to have a stake, estimated by one source at about ten million dollars, in the Fremont Group, a private investment company, on whose board of directors sits another former Secretary of State, George Shultz...
>
> Much of the family's private banking is handled by Citigroup, which is chaired by former Treasury Secretary Robert Rubin. The family has equity investments with Merrill Lynch and Goldman, Sachs. Among the family's business partners is General Electric. A spokesman for Jack Welch, the chairman of G.E., says that the family threw a party for him in the nineteen-nineties in Saudi Arabia, and that Welch "considers them good business partners." One American diplomat says, "You talk about your global investors, it's them. They own part of Microsoft, Boeing, and who knows what else." Others note that the family has been awarded contracts to help rebuild American military installations, including the Khobar Towers, which were damaged in a terrorist attack that killed nineteen servicemen in 1996.[31]

Notably, that terrorist attack, from which the bin Laden family indirectly profited, was also allegedly masterminded by Osama. The possible implications are alarming, especially when we note that: "When bin Laden turned against the United States, his fortune was still interwoven with the family's, which was invested in many American businesses."[32] Indeed, the list of US–bin Laden enterprises is voluminous. For instance, among the multiple projects for the establishment of oil pipelines through Afghanistan is a joint venture between the construction firm H. P. Price and the bin Laden family. H. P. Price changed its name to Bredero Shaw, Inc., and now happens to be owned by a subsidiary of the giant Halliburton Corporation of which Vice President Dick Cheney was CEO until the 2000 elections.[33]

Increasing press scrutiny of these matters, leading to embarrassing revelations for both the Bush and bin Laden families, appears to have been behind the latter's sudden decision to withdraw their stake in Carlyle in the aftermath of 9/11.[34] The timing of this action only raises further questions about the nature of this Carlyle–bin Laden financial affair and whether it really was as innocent as is claimed. If so, why the need for the bin Laden family to pull out, thus preempting further investigations and inquiries?

Whatever the implications of this complex web of terror, money, and government activity, the basic facts are potentially scandalous. The US political and financial establishment, including the Bush family, maintains long-standing ties to the bin Laden family, senior members of which in turn reportedly remain closely tied to Osama, and have therefore been under investigation by US intelligence. In the post-9/11 "War on Terror," this network of ties remains fundamentally unchanged.

The Saudi–Bin Laden Connection

The curious connections of the bin Laden family are representative of a wider set of policies implemented by the Saudi regime. According to former senior US State Department official Martin S. Indyk,[35] "the Clinton administration indulged Riyadh's penchant for buying off trouble as long as the regime also paid its huge arms bills, purchased Boeing aircraft, kept the price of oil within reasonable bounds, and allowed the United States to use Saudi air bases." Buying off trouble meant siphoning millions of dollars to al-Qaeda. "The Saudis had protected themselves by co-opting and accommodating the Islamist extremists in their midst, a move they felt was necessary in the uncertain aftermath of the Gulf War," observes Indyk. "And once Crown Prince Abdullah assumed the regency in 1996, the ruling family set about the determined business of buying off its opposition...

> The vulnerabilities exposed by the Gulf War, however, created a greater need for shoring up Wahhabi support. The regime accordingly financed the export of Wahhabism through the building of hundreds of mosques and madrassas (religious schools) abroad. The activity was particularly intense in areas affected by the collapse of the Soviet Union—the Balkans, Central Asia, Afghanistan, and Pakistan—where the Saudis engaged in competition with Iranian mullahs for the hearts and minds of local Muslim populations. A public-private partnership was also created in which rich Saudi families would help to fund the enterprise.

Meanwhile "charitable organizations" were "subverted" to provide conduits for this funding. Although bin Laden had officially been stripped of his Saudi citizenship, he took ample advantage of this system "to raise funds and establish his network." Ultimately then, Saudi-backed institutions with royal connivance "were used as covers for financing al Qaeda's nefarious activities. And the Sunni fundamentalist Taliban regime in Afghanistan, providers of sanctuary to bin Laden and his cohort, also found itself the direct and indirect beneficiary of Saudi largess."[36] Investigative journalist Palast observes that, like the Clinton administration, the Bush administration is also "trying very hard to cover-up" these payments.[37] Indeed, the US intelligence community has been aware of the Saudi policy for several years. The *New Yorker* reports that:

> Since 1994 or earlier, the National Security Agency has been collecting electronic intercepts of conversations between members of the Saudi Arabian royal family, which is headed by King Fahd.... The intercepts

depict a regime increasingly corrupt, alienated from the country's religious rank and file, and so weakened and frightened that it has brokered its future by channelling hundreds of millions of dollars in what amounts to protection money to fundamentalist groups that wish to overthrow it.

The NSA intercepts prove that by 1996, "Saudi money was supporting Osama bin Laden's Al Qaeda and other extremist groups in Afghanistan, Lebanon, Yemen, and Central Asia, and throughout the Persian Gulf region."[38] But as the Toronto-based newsmagazine *NOW Magazine* reports, "US officials were unwilling to make an issue of al Qaeda's connections to wealthy Saudis," although Osama bin Laden continued to maintain "close contact with key Saudi figures including Prince Turki al-Faisal, the powerful intelligence chief and brother of King Fahd."[38]

According to the *Los Angeles Times*, throughout the 1990s the Taliban routinely hosted "high-ranking Persian Gulf state officials" who flew in "for lavish hunting parties." The dignitaries included officials from Saudi Arabia and the Emirates—and were sometimes joined by Osama bin Laden and other Taliban leaders. They left "money, vehicles and equipment with their hosts." US and former Afghan civil air officials confirm that among Osama's guests was "Prince Turki al Faisal, son of the late Saudi King Faisal." Another guest, officials confirm, was "Sheik Mohammed ibn Rashid al Maktum, the Dubai crown prince and Emirates defense minister."[40] Labeviere records that Prince Turki is "a constrained friend of the CIA [who] made abundant use of bin Laden's networks."[41] The Prince resigned from his position a few days before 9/11, to become Saudi Ambassador to London.[42]

According to former CIA counterterrorism chief Cannistraro, "on one of the trips the Saudis made 'a large monetary offer' to bin Laden, consisting of tens of millions of dollars, if he would agree to end his murderous political rebellion" against the kingdom. In other words, as long as Osama refrained from destabilizing the reign of the Saudi royal family, instead setting "his sights on targets outside the desert kingdom"[43]—inevitably, American and other Western targets—he would continue to receive millions of dollars in funding from the kingdom.

The Flourishing Business of US–Saudi Terror Ties
While significant elements of the Saudi royal establishment support Osama bin Laden, in turn, the United States has always protected the Saudi royal establishment. In the words of Tariq Ali in the *New Statesman*, "Bin Laden and his gang are just the tentacles; the head lies safely in Saudi Arabia, protected by US forces." The bulk of Osama bin Laden's "real cadres (as opposed to foot soldiers) are located in Egypt or Saudi Arabia—America's two principal allies in the region, barring Israel." The state religion in Saudi Arabia is "not an everyday

version of Sunni or Shi'a Islam, but a peculiarly virulent, ultra-puritanical strain known as Wahhabism." Wahhabism is followed by "the Saudi royal family, the state bureaucracy, the army, the air force and Bin Laden—the best-known Saudi citizen in the world." The head of the Wahhabi octopus "is safe and sound in Saudi Arabia, guarding the oil wells, growing new arms, and protected by US soldiers and the US air-force base in Dhahran. Washington's failure to disengage its vital interests from the fate of the Saudi monarchy could well lead to further blow-back."[44]

There is an important context to this longstanding political and military alliance between Saudi Arabia and the United States. The *Washington Post* observes that the "good fortune" of "a small group of Saudi citizens" who have "accumulated vast personal wealth… has spilled over to the benefit of American and European money managers, investment banks and the companies in which the money is invested." The members of the royal family number about 40,000, including 8,000 princes. The Saudi government has never reported the share of oil profits accruing to the royal family, "whose senior princes accumulated fantastic fortunes" deposited safely in Western banks. One credible account, for instance, indicates that "members of the royal family have billions of dollars on deposit in the Banque Pictet in Geneva."

After three decades, "high net worth Saudi individuals" hold together between $500 billion and $1 trillion abroad, "most of it in European and American investments." Brad Bourland, chief economist of the Saudi American Bank (one-quarter owned by Citibank), confirmed in June 2001 his bank's best estimate of the total "is about $700 billion, with the possibility that it is as much as $1 trillion." A similar estimate was made by Raymond Seitz, Vice-Chairman of Lehman Brothers in London and a former US ambassador to Britain. It is normal, he notes, for Saudis to place "three-quarters of their money into the United States" and the "rest in Europe and Asia," meaning that $500 billion to $700 billion of the US economy constitutes Saudi investments. "This is a huge sea of fungible assets supporting the American economy and belonging to a relatively small group of people—about 85,000 Saudis, Seitz said, is the estimate of bankers. Managing these hundreds of billions can be a lucrative business for brokers and bankers in London, Geneva and New York."[45]

Indeed, a more in-depth inquiry demonstrates that there are very specific, long-standing financial connections between the White House and leading Saudi figures who reportedly support Osama bin Laden. One report by the investigative journalist Wayne Madsen—a former National Security Agency communications security analyst who has been called to testify as an expert witness in Congressional hearings on covert US foreign policy—is worth noting. Madsen finds that: "George W. [Bush's] own businesses were once tied to financial figures in Saudi Arabia who currently support bin Laden." His first business, Arbusto Energy, was financed in 1979 by James Bath, "a Houstonian and close family friend." Among other investors, "Bath gave Bush $50,000 for a 5 percent stake in Arbusto." Bath, however, was at that time "the sole US business representative for Salem bin Laden, head of the wealthy Saudi Arabian family and a brother (one of seventeen) to Osama bin Laden." Although there is no direct proof, it has long been suspected that Bath's investment "came directly from Salem bin Laden." Not long after 9/11 "the White House vehemently denied the connection, insisting that Bath invested his own money" in Arbusto. Then Bush entirely "denied ever knowing Bath." He then reneged on his own denial, acknowledging Bath's stake in Arbusto "and that he was aware Bath represented Saudi interests." But as Madsen points out

> Bath has extensive ties, both to the bin Laden family and major players in the scandal-ridden Bank of Commerce and Credit International (BCCI) who have gone on to fund Osama bin Laden...
>
> BCCI defrauded depositors of $10 billion in the '80s in what has been called the "largest bank fraud in world financial history" by former Manhattan District Attorney Robert Morgenthau. During the '80s, BCCI also acted as a main conduit for laundering money intended for clandestine CIA activities, ranging from financial support to the Afghan mujahedin to paying intermediaries in the Iran-Contra affair.
>
> When Salem bin Laden died in 1988, powerful Saudi Arabian banker and BCCI principal Khalid bin Mahfouz inherited his interests in Houston. Bath ran a business for bin Mahfouz in Houston and joined a partnership with bin Mahfouz and Gaith Pharaon, BCCI's frontman in Houston's Main Bank.

In 1986, Bush Jr.'s company Arbusto reemerged as Harken Energy Corporation. After facing problems a year later, Arbusto received aid from Saudi Sheik Abdullah Taha Bakhsh who "purchased a 17.6 percent stake in the company. Bakhsh was a business partner with Pharaon in Saudi Arabia; his banker there just happened to be bin Mahfouz."

Bush claims that he had "no idea" of the BCCI's involvement in Harken's financial dealings, but as the *Wall Street Journal* noted: "The number of BCCI-connected people who had dealings with Harken—all since George W. Bush came on board—raises the question of whether they mask an effort to cozy up to a presidential son."

"Worst of all," observes Madsen,

> bin Mahfouz allegedly has been financing the bin Laden terrorist network—making Bush a US citizen who has done business with those who finance and support terrorists...
>
> According to *USA Today*, bin Mahfouz and other Saudis attempted to transfer $3 million to various bin Laden front operations in Saudi Arabia in 1999. ABC News reported the same year that Saudi officials stopped bin

Mahfouz from contributing money directly to bin Laden. (Bin Mahfouz's sister is also a wife of Osama bin Laden, a fact that former CIA Director James Woolsey revealed in 1998 Senate testimony.)

When President Bush announced he is hot on the trail of the money used over the years to finance terrorism, he must realize that trail ultimately leads not only to Saudi Arabia, but to some of the same financiers who originally helped propel him into the oil business and later the White House. The ties between bin Laden and the White House may be much closer than he is willing to acknowledge.[46]

And this state of affairs largely continues, even now. Indeed, another *Boston Herald* report records a particularly disconcerting example related to Khalid bin Mahfouz: "Two billionaire Saudi families scrutinized by authorities for possible financial ties to Osama bin Laden's terrorist network continue to engage in major oil deals with leading US corporations," to the unnerving silence of the Bush administration. "The bin Mahfouz and Al-Amoudi clans, who control three private Saudi Arabian oil companies, are partners with US firms in a series of ambitious oil development and pipeline projects in central and south Asia, records show." The bin Mahfouz and al-Amoudi families, working through their companies—Delta Oil, Nimir Petroleum, and Corral Petroleum—have formed international consortiums "with US oil giants Texaco, Unocal, Amerada Hess, and Frontera Resources." Such financial ties have not been damaged by "evidence that members of the two Saudi families—headed by patriarchs Khalid bin Mahfouz and Mohammed Hussein Al-Amoudi—have had ties to Islamic charities and companies linked financially to bin Laden's al-Qaeda organization."

Indeed, both bin Mahfouz and al-Amoudi "have been left untouched by the US Treasury Department." A May 1999 report by the US Embassy in Saudi Arabia records that Delta Oil was created by 50 prominent Saudi investors in the early 1990s, the prime force behind which "appears to be Mohammed Hussein Al-Amoudi, who is based in Ethiopia and oversees a vast network of companies involved in construction, mining, banking and oil." The al-Amoudis' business interests, however, are inextricably entwined with the bin Mahfouz family, who own "the third privately held Saudi oil company, Nimir Petroleum" established in Bermuda in 1991. The two families are closely allied, as is clear from their joint oil venture, Delta-Nimir, as well as by "their partnership in the Saudi firm The Marei Bin Mahfouz & Ahmed Al Amoudi Group of Companies & Factories." A 1999 audit conducted by the Saudi government allegedly discovered that the bin Mahfouz family's National Commercial Bank "had transferred at least $3 million to charitable organizations believed to be fronts for bin Laden's terror network." One of the charities was "Blessed Relief, whose board members included bin Mahfouz's son, Abdul Rahman bin Mahfouz." Blessed Relief was named as a front organization providing funds to bin Laden in

October 2001 by the US Treasury Department as follows: "Saudi businessmen have been transferring millions of dollars to bin Laden through Blessed Relief." As the *Herald* further notes: "Despite officials' suspicions, the bin Mahfouz and Al-Amoudi oil companies continue to profit from their working relationship with America's own oil elite."[47]

Thus, while the Saudi regime—including alleged members of the bin Laden family—continues to funnel millions of dollars to the al-Qaeda terrorist network, the United States and the West maintain interlocking financial ties to the regime, and actively attempt to protect the Saudi–al-Qaeda relationship from intelligence inquiries—despite having been aware of the relationship for more than a decade.

6.

Pakistan: Bin Laden's Power Base

The US–Pakistan Alliance and the ISI

The missing link in this dubious web of relationships is the role of Pakistan as another principal supporter of al-Qaeda, once more with apparent US and Western connivance. As Selig Harrison has noted: "The Taliban are a creation of America's Central Intelligence Agency (CIA) in cooperation with Pakistan's Inter-Services Intelligence Directorate (ISI)." But in March 2001, he also observed that the ISI's role as a regional instrument of the CIA has not ended. The "old association between the intelligence agencies continues." Harrison observes that "the CIA still has close links with the ISI."[1]

Simultaneously, however, the ISI retains extremely close ties to al-Qaeda, even after 9/11. The *New York Times* reports, for example, that the ISI, despite being "a crucial American ally in the war on terrorism," has had a "longstanding relationship with Al Qaeda, turning a blind eye for years to the growing ties between Osama bin Laden and the Taliban, according to American officials." The ISI used al-Qaeda camps in Afghanistan "to train covert operatives for use in a war of terror against India."[2]

But the problem goes deeper. As noted in previous chapters, official government sources confirm that the US provided support to the Taliban throughout much of 1990s through Pakistani military intelligence. The State Department's *Patterns of Global Terrorism* noted in 2000 "reports of continued Pakistani support for the Taliban's military operations in Afghanistan." The support consisted of "materiel, fuel, funding, technical assistance, and military advisers," as well as the influx of "large numbers of Pakistani nationals" into Afghanistan to fight for the Taliban. "Islamabad also failed to take effective steps to curb the activities of certain madrassas, or religious schools, that serve as recruiting grounds for terrorism."[3]

But behind the public front of concern, Pakistan's support of the Taliban was actively supported by the United States, as proven in the testimony of US Representative Rohrabacher for instance. So institutionally intertwined is the ISI with al-Qaeda and the Taliban that according to the *National Post*, an estimated "10,000 officers and staff" of the agency have become "thoroughly contaminated with Islamic radicalism." The US government is by no means unaware of this fact, since the ISI has long been "under [its] close scrutiny."[4]

Ahmed Rashid, for example, refers to "the ISI's close contacts with bin

Laden, and the fact that he was helping fund and train Kashmiri militants who were using the Khost camps... in December 1998." Rashid quotes a statement from bin Laden himself indicating the extent of his official Pakistani support:

> As for Pakistan there are some governmental departments, which, by the Grace of God, respond to the Islamic sentiments of the masses in Pakistan. This is reflected in sympathy and co-operation. However, some other governmental departments fell into the trap of the infidels. We pray to God to return them to the right path.

But at the same time, Rashid observes, "The US was Pakistan's closest ally, with deep links to the military and the ISI."[5]

Indeed, a CBS Evening News report by anchorman Dan Rather and foreign correspondent Barry Peterson, citing "Pakistani intelligence sources," reported that "the night before the September 11 terrorist attack, Osama bin Laden was in Pakistan" receiving "medical treatment with the support of the very military that days later pledged its backing for the US war on terror in Afghanistan." Bin Laden was "spirited into this military hospital in Rawalpindi for kidney dialysis treatment. On that night, says this medical worker who wanted her identity protected, they moved out all the regular staff in the urology department and sent in a secret team to replace them." Another hospital employee said: "The military had him surrounded... and I saw the mysterious patient helped out of a car. Since that time, I have seen many pictures of the man. He is the man we know as Osama bin Laden. I also heard two army officers talking to each other. They were saying that Osama bin Laden had to be watched carefully and looked after."[6]

Indian sources earlier reported in July 2001 that "bin Laden, who suffers from renal deficiency, has been periodically undergoing dialysis in a Peshawar military hospital with the knowledge and approval of the Inter-Services Intelligence (ISI), if not of [Pakistani President] Musharraf himself."[7] Confirming this report, *Jane's Intelligence Digest* adds that US intelligence has been long aware of Pakistan's support to bin Laden:

> According to local intelligence sources, the Pakistani authorities have provided medical facilities for the ailing Bin Laden, including renal dialysis, at a military hospital in Peshawar. None of this will be unfamiliar to US intelligence operatives who have been compiling extensive reports on these alleged activities.... Both the Taliban and al-Qa'eda would have found it difficult to have continued functioning—including the latter group's terrorist activities—without substantial aid and support from Islamabad. This would, logically, place Pakistan in the category of "states which support terrorism," according to the US government's definition.[8]

All this is merely part of a much wider context of Pakistani sponsorship and harboring of al-Qaeda, which continues with what amounts to the tacit consent of US authorities. The pattern is described well by leading 9/11 investigator Paul Thompson of the Center for Cooperative Research:

> A UPI editorial stated, "Al-Qaeda terrorists have long since scattered deep inside Pakistan and in Pakistani-controlled Kashmir where they enjoy the protection of the [ISI].... The unspeakable is that Pakistan is the new Afghanistan, a privileged sanctuary for hundreds of al-Qaeda fighters and Taliban operatives. Some estimates go as high as 5,000.... The Pakistani-al-Qaeda connection is visible to all but the geopolitically challenged." [UPI, 8/28/02] Prominent Taliban leaders wanted by the US have been living openly in Pakistani cities and yet the US does nothing about them. [Guardian, 12/24/01, Time, 5/6/02] It is now widely reported that Osama bin Laden, Khalid Shaikh Mohammed and most other prominent al-Qaeda leaders are believed to be living in Pakistan, some of them living in the open and in luxury, with the protection of the ISI. It is frequently pointed out that Pakistan's efforts to find them are mostly a charade. [Los Angeles Times, 4/6/02, Christian Science Monitor, 7/2/02, Los Angeles Times, 6/16/02, Time 7/29/02, Washington Post, 8/4/02, New York Times, 9/15/02, AP, 11/12/02, Los Angeles Times, 11/17/02] But still, the situation doesn't change. As an example of Bush's seemingly inexplicable response to terrorism in Pakistan, Azhar's group Jaish-e-Mohammed had its assets frozen shortly after 9/11, but the group simply changed its name and over a year later the US has not frozen the assets of this "new" group. [Financial Times, 2/8/03, Washington Post, 2/8/03].[9]

But the US involvement apparently goes far beyond simple tacit consent. Doggedly following the intriguing trail of the Pakistani/ISI connection to al-Qaeda, Canadian economist Professor Michel Chossudovsky was among the first to expose in detail the curious connections between the ISI, 9/11, and the US government.[10]

The ISI and the 9/11 Money Trail

A delegation led by the Director-General of the ISI, Lt. Gen. Mahmoud Ahmad, "was in the US for consultations with the CIA and the Pentagon when the attacks occurred, having arrived on Sept. 4."[11] Lt. Gen. Mahmoud Ahmad, described by Time magazine as a "trusted friend" of the Pakistani President Gen. Pervez Musharraf, was also "widely regarded as the country's invisible government [and] a staunch patron of pro-Taliban policies."[12] Pakistan's daily News, reported that during his "week-long presence in Washington," the ISI chief had a number of "mysterious meetings" at the Pentagon, the National Security Council, the White House and the CIA. Touted as a routine visit in return to CIA Director George Tenet's earlier visit to Islamabad, *The News* observed on September 10, 2001 that "the history of such visits" suggests otherwise: "Last time Ziauddin Butt, Mahmood's predecessor, was here during Nawaz Sharif's government domestic politics turned topsy-turvy within days. That this is not the first visit by Mahmood in the last three months shows the urgency of the ongoing parleys."[13]

By late September 2001, ABC News reported that the FBI had "tracked more than $100,000 from banks in Pakistan to two banks in Florida, to accounts held by suspected hijack ringleader, Mohammed Atta." FBI files describe Atta as "the lead hijacker of the first jet airliner to slam into the World Trade Center and, apparently, the lead conspirator."[14] Citing a *Time* magazine report, ABC News added that "some of that money came in the days just before the attack and can be traced directly to people connected with Osama bin Laden."[15]

Then in early October—as the Anglo-American invasion of Afghanistan was about to begin—Lt. Gen. Mahmoud Ahmad suddenly disappeared from the ISI. According to ISI Public Relations, he had "sought retirement after being superseded" by another officer on October 8 in a routine reshuffling of staff. However, an investigative report by the *Times of India* found that Lt. Gen. Ahmad was in fact secretly shifted from his position on orders from the US government, after the FBI had proven his role in sending finances directly to the chief 9/11 al-Qaeda hijacker, Mohamed Atta:

> Top sources confirmed here on Tuesday, that the general lost his job because of the "evidence" India produced to show his links to one of the suicide bombers that wrecked the World Trade Centre. The US authorities sought his removal after confirming the fact that $100,000 were wired to WTC hijacker Mohammed Atta from Pakistan by Ahmad Umar Sheikh at the instance of Gen Mahmud.
>
> Senior government sources have confirmed that India contributed significantly to establishing the link between the money transfer and the role played by the dismissed ISI chief... Indian inputs, including Sheikh's mobile phone number, helped the FBI in tracing and establishing the link.
>
> A direct link between the ISI and the WTC attack could have enormous repercussions. The US cannot but suspect whether or not there were other senior Pakistani Army commanders who were in the know of things. Evidence of a larger conspiracy could shake US confidence in Pakistan's ability to participate in the anti-terrorism coalition.
>
> Indian officials say they are vitally interested in the unravelling of the case since it could link the ISI directly to the hijacking of the Indian Airlines Kathmandu–Delhi flight to Kandahar last December. Ahmad Umar Sayeed Sheikh is a British national and a London School of Economics graduate who was arrested by the police in Delhi following a bungled 1994 kidnapping of four westerners, including an American citizen.[16]

The revelations were also reported by Agence France Press, which received information from a "highly-placed [Indian] government source" that "the evidence we have supplied to the US is of a much wider range and depth than just one piece of paper linking a rogue general to some misplaced act of terrorism."[17] The revelations were soon reported in the Pakistani and American press. The Pakistani newspaper *Dawn* cited "informed sources" in Pakistan confirming that "Director General of Pakistan's Inter-Services Intelligence (ISI) Lt Gen Mahmud Ahmed has been replaced after the FBI investigators established credible links between him and Umar Sheikh." When the FBI traced calls made between Gen. Mahmoud Ahmad and Ahmed Omar Sheikh Saeed's cellular phone, a pattern linking the ISI chief with Sheikh clearly emerged. The US intelligence community believed that "it was at Gen Mahmud's instruction that Sheikh had transferred 100,000 US dollars into the account of Mohammed Atta."[18] The *Wall Street Journal* also cited "senior government sources" in the United States who confirmed that Gen. Mahmoud was ordered to resign due to the evidence of his wiring $100,000 to chief hijacker Atta.[19]

German intelligence has also confirmed the transaction.[20] Given that the ISI has received considerable military and financial aid from the US to support the Taliban—al-Qaeda's state headquarters in Afghanistan—these connections are disturbing. Further details are provided by a CNN report based on information from US law enforcement officials, who reveal that "Pakistan is a common conduit for money going in and out of Afghanistan." The wire transfers from Pakistan totaling $100,000 "were sent to Atta through two banks in Florida. Then, Atta allegedly would obtain money orders—a few thousand dollars at a time—to distribute to others involved in the plot in the months before the hijackings." Those funds paid for the hijackers' flight-school tuition, airfare, and living expenses. Sources in the Middle East confirm that

> Atta and two other men wired more than $15,000 back to the United Arab Emirates just before the attacks—what may have been leftover cash from the terrorism funds.... The money went to a man who flew out of Dubai for Karachi, Pakistan, on September 11—the day of the attack.... Officials in the United Arab Emirates have identified the recipient of those wire transfers as Mustapha Ahmad Al-Hawsawi. They are investigating whether he may have any ties to Al Qaeda, the terror network headed by bin Laden.[21]

Ahmed Omar Sheikh Saeed: the CIA–MI6–ISI–al-Qaeda Link

Who is Mustapha Ahmad al-Hawsawi? An inspection of several other reliable reports indicates that this figure is, in fact, the same person who originally wired the $100,000 to Atta from Pakistan: Ahmed Omar Sheikh Saeed. According to Paul Sperry, Washington bureau chief of *WorldNetDaily*, Sheikh is "one of

Osama bin Laden's chief money men." He wired $100,000 "from Pakistan to Atta from an account in the United Arab Emirates capital of Dubai." Furthermore, "Sheikh picked up an unspent residual of more than $25,000 from Atta and three other hijackers in Dubai right before the attacks, then fled back to Karachi, Pakistan."[22] Sperry's account suggests that the person who received the residual funds in Dubai, identified as al-Hawsawi, was in fact Sheikh.

Sheikh's transfer of $100,000 to Mohamed Atta under the direction of then ISI chief Gen. Ahmad—which occurred in the year 2000—seems to have specifically occurred during or just prior to June 2000, since between June 29 and September 18, a total of $109,910 was received in installments by Mohamed Atta and his right-hand-man Marwan al-Shehhi via the United Arab Emirates.[23] According to the *Washington Post*, a figure identified as "Mustafa Ahmed al-Hawsawi… played a central role in the financial mechanics of the Sept. 11 plot." US officials believe that "he may be the same man as Mustafa Muhammad Ahmad, alias Shaykh Saiid, who is a top bin Laden financial lieutenant included on the list of alleged terrorists whose assets have been frozen by the United States."[24] The *Post* elsewhere notes that US investigators believe al-Hawsawi is "the central financial figure" of the 9/11 plot, as well as "al Qaeda's finance chief." According to law enforcement officials, he uses numerous aliases and "disappeared in Karachi, Pakistan, just before the attacks" after transferring "most of the money used to pay for the hijackers' pilot training, living expenses and airline tickets in the United States."[25]

CNN cites a top US government source confirming that investigators have verified beyond doubt that Mustafa Ahmad al-Hawsawi is precisely the same man whose real name is Ahmed Omar Sheikh Saeed:

A man suspected of playing a key role in bankrolling the September 11 terrorist attacks in the United States was released from prison in India less than two years ago after hijackers of an Indian Airlines flight demanded his freedom, a senior-level US government source told CNN…. This source said US investigators now believe Sheik Syed, using the alias Mustafa Muhammad Ahmad, sent more than $100,000 from Pakistan to Mohammed Atta, the suspected hijacking ringleader who piloted one of the jetliners into the World Trade Center.

Investigators said Atta then distributed the funds to conspirators in Florida in the weeks before the deadliest act of terrorism on US soil that destroyed the World Trade Center, heavily damaged the Pentagon and left thousands dead. In addition, sources have said Atta sent thousands of dollars—believed to be excess funds from the operation—back to Syed in the United Arab Emirates in the days before September 11. Syed also is described as a key figure in the funding operation of al Qaeda, the network headed by suspected terrorist mastermind Osama bin Laden.[26]

By the assessment of terrorism expert Magnus Ranstorp—deputy director of the Center for Study of Terrorism and Political Violence at the University of St. Andrews—Sheikh's role in al-Qaeda is well-known in the intelligence community: "He [Sheikh] is also linked to the financial network feeding bin Laden's assets, so therefore he's quite an important person... because he transfers money between various operatives, and he's a node between al Qaeda and foot soldiers on the ground."[27]

But as the *Financial Times* points out, Sheikh sent a total of far more than $100,000: "US investigators believe about *half the $500,000* that the hijackers spent on the September 11 plot was sent by Mustafa Ahmad [al-Hawsawi], who is today regarded by investigators as bin Laden's finance chief, via Dubai money exchanges through Citibank in New York and on to Florida."[28] The *New York Times* puts the figure at $325,000 moving through 14 Florida accounts at SunTrust Banks.[29] Sheikh's involvement in al-Qaeda and 9/11, however, apparently went much further. British police officials, for example, believe that Sheikh "trained the [9/11] terrorists in hijacking techniques."[30]

South Asian Outlook notes that "Ahmed Omar Saeed Sheikh is a man with many names but one purpose: waging a war of terror against Indian and American targets." His other aliases include: "Sheikh Syed, Mustafa Muhammad Ahmed, Chaudhry Bashir Ahmed Shabir and Imtiaz Siddique."[31] Sheikh's simultaneous high-level connections to Osama bin Laden and the ISI have been further corroborated by other reports. The *New York Times*, for instance, confirms that Sheikh "is a leader of Jaish-e-Mohammad," or Army of Muhammad, a militant Muslim group based in Pakistan that was officially banned by Pakistani President Musharraf in December 2001, as part of his crackdown on extremist groups.[32] But simultaneously the *Times* notes reports that [Sheikh] has links to Pakistan's main intelligence agency [the ISI]."[33]

> During his years of international crime and terrorism Mr. Sheikh was a member of a militant Islamic group, Army of Muhammad, that until recently had the support of the Pakistani Inter-Services Intelligence agency...
>
> Mr. Sheikh could presumably shed more light on the agency's involvement with militant groups.... Five years [after his arrest in 1994 in India], still in jail awaiting trial, he was released, in exchange for the release of passengers aboard an Indian airlines jet that had been hijacked from Katmandu, a hijacking in which Pakistani intelligence officials had a hand, American officials have said.[34]

Indeed, citing US intelligence sources, *Newsweek* observes that Sheikh "did little to hide his connections to terrorist organizations, and even attended swanky parties attended by senior Pakistani government officials." US law enforcement and intelligence officials believe that "Sheikh has been a 'protected asset,' of Pakistan's shadowy spy service, the Inter-Services Intelligence, or ISI."[35] In other words, US intelligence has long been aware of the contemporaneous links between Ahmed Omar Sheikh Saeed, al-Qaeda, and Pakistani intelligence. Indeed, Sheikh's role as key financial controller within al-Qaeda was revealed in court hearings concerning the US embassy bombings of 1998, which revealed "an al Qaeda operative known as 'Sheik Sayid'... controlled the group's finances... Sheik Sayid is now reported to be the finance chairman of al Qaeda and the man suspected of wiring money from Pakistan to Mohamed Atta."[36]

According to the *Pittsburgh Tribune Review*: "Saeed Sheikh has acted as a 'go between' for the 'tall man'—as bin-Laden is known—and the Inter Services Intelligence (ISI)." Sheikh's entrenched ISI–al-Qaeda connections have always been known to Washington: "Many and varied sources have told Washington officials that in all these attacks, Saeed Sheikh had logistical and operational support from the ISI in Karachi and Islamabad. ISI also helped him form and operate the Jaish-e-Muhammed—Muhammed's Army—for his terrorist campaigns in Kashmir."[37] Osama bin Laden's relationship to Sheikh is so close that within a few years of joining al-Qaeda, bin Laden described him as his "favoured son."[38]

But despite his close connections to al-Qaeda, and despite President Musharraf's avowal to crackdown on extremist groups, it seems to have been agreed upon by both the American and Pakistani administrations that Ahmed Omar Sheikh—leader of the banned "Jaish-e-Mohammad" connected to al-Qaeda; responsible for terrorism against British and American citizens as well as in Kashmir and India; and Osama's financial chief and al-Qaeda paymaster for Mohamed Atta—would be allowed to operate freely, without his activities even being monitored: "Despite face-to-face meetings between President Musharraf and President Bush, US Ambassador to Pakistan Wendy Chamberlain and FBI Director Robert Mueller, Saeed Sheik was neither arrested nor placed under surveillance." This mutual US–Pakistani agreement rendered Musharraf's crackdown on Jaish-e-Mohammad rather hollow, given that the group's militant leader was left untouched.[39]

There is a long history here—both American and British governments have studiously avoided taking any action against Sheikh despite the fact that he is a known terrorist who has targeted US and UK citizens. As observed by *Frontline* in October 2001: "Last month, the UK served a letters rogatory on India, asking for information on Sheikh in relation to the 1994 kidnapping of its nationals. It is unclear why it has taken that country so long to initiate the legal proceedings, and why the US has chosen not to act so far."[40] Indeed, the *New York Times* reports that Sheikh "was secretly indicted by a grand jury in Washington last November [2001] for his role in the 1994 kidnapping."[41] Noting the "secret" nature of the indictment, CNN reported that: "Justice Department officials won't say what prompted that indictment, which came more than six years after the incident."[42] In other words, both countries only chose to indict Sheikh for his role in the 1994 terrorist act after the 9/11 attacks.

Why did American and British law enforcement authorities do nothing for so long in relation to Sheikh, despite the responsibility to do so? This basic US–UK government negligence granted free reign to Osama's financial chief to fund the 9/11 hijackers, although Sheikh, who did little to conceal his terrorist connections, could easily have been apprehended by the Pakistani authorities at the request of the US and UK governments. What is certainly clear is that the Bush administration does not want information on Sheikh's background and high-level intelligence connections to be disclosed to the public. On March 3, 2002, US Secretary of State Colin Powell appeared on CNN to categorically deny that there are any links at all between "elements of the ISI" and those who murdered *Wall Street Journal* correspondent Daniel Pearl, including al-Qaeda 9/11 financier Sheikh Saeed. The London *Guardian* aptly described Powell's denial "shocking" in light of the abundant evidence (confirmed by US intelligence officials) of Sheikh's ISI connections. Why does the US government wish to cover-up information on Sheikh's ISI connections?

The answer may lie partially in the UK. According to the London *Times*, "British-born terrorist Ahmed Omar Saeed Sheikh was secretly offered an amnesty by British officials in 1999 if he would betray his links with al-Qaeda."[43] The *Daily Mail* similarly confirmed that "Britain offered Sheikh a deal that would allow him to live in London a free man if he told them all he knew."[44] Both reports claim that Sheikh refused the offer. However, by the beginning of the next year, the British Foreign Office decided "to allow him to enter Britain," without even being investigated. The three Britons who had been kidnapped, held hostage, and threatened with death by Sheikh in 1994—Rhys Partridge, Miles Croston, and Paul Rideout—were "appalled to learn that Sheikh, a British passport holder, would be allowed to return to Britain without fear of charge."[45] Sheikh subsequently "proceeded to London, where he reunited with family" in "early January 2000."[46] He again visited his London home in "early 2001" where he was spotted by a neighbor.[47]

Amazingly, a Foreign Office spokesman justified the decision to allow him into the country without charge and lacking even a police investigation: "He has not been convicted of any offences. He has not even been brought to trial."[48] But this explanation was simply misleading. The British government had ample evidence—including the firsthand testimonials of the three kidnapped British citizens—necessitating that Sheikh be immediately charged and investigated (certainly, a trial and conviction are supposed to come *after* being charged and investigated, not before) upon his arrival on UK soil. Indeed, the spuriousness of this position was evident when the US government later indicted Sheikh, and when the British government began pursuing a legal investigation with the Indian government, for his role in the 1994 kidnapping. Why were these measures postponed for so long?

The earlier reports on this matter provide an explanation. In 1999, the British security services—despite being fully cognizant of Sheikh's involvement in al-Qaeda terrorism, including the 1991 hijacking—offered Sheikh free reign inside the UK on condition that he act as an informant on al-Qaeda. The offer indicates firstly that the government had sufficient intelligence on Sheikh's activities to know of his terrorist activities as an al-Qaeda operative; secondly that his track record would normally necessitate his immediate arrest upon entry into the UK; and thirdly that the government was willing to bypass the normal requirements of law if he merely provided information. In this context, there can be no doubt that the claim that Sheikh refused the offer of amnesty is false, since Sheikh was only to be permitted amnesty in the UK if he accepted the British offer to be an MI6 informant. In other words, the British government had granted free reign to Osama bin Laden's financial chief to do as he liked on British soil, and had recruited him to MI6 at least as late as 1999 (and perhaps even earlier). Crucially, this implies that at least after his release in 1999, Sheikh was used and tracked by British intelligence as an MI6 asset.

But Sheikh's connections do not end there. According to the *Pittsburgh Tribune-Review*, high-level Pakistani government officials believe that Ahmed Omar Sheikh is not only an ISI agent but also an active CIA operative:

> There are many in Musharraf's government who believe that Saeed Sheikh's power comes not from the ISI, but from his connections with our own CIA. The theory is that with such intense pressure to locate bin Laden, Saeed Sheikh was bought and paid for.... It would be logical for the CIA to recruit an intelligent, young political criminal with contacts in both India and Pakistan.[49]

Pakistani government officials would obviously only hold this opinion about Sheikh on the basis of actual evidence available to them. Notably, this report does not refer to one, but rather "many" informed insiders within the Pakistani administration confirming that Sheikh is a CIA informant as well as an ISI operative.

Together these reports indicate that the consistent pattern of Anglo-American inaction toward Ahmed Omar Sheikh Saeed and terrorists connected to him was not merely the product of random indifference occurring without rhyme or reason. Rather, this systemic inaction was the product of a longstanding Anglo-American policy rooted in Sheikh's connections to the ISI—and more pertinently his apparent connections to MI6 and the CIA—which are further embedded in the complex relationship of co-optation between al-Qaeda and the United States.

Al-Qaeda Financier Meets US Officials on 9/11

That this co-optation may have been active on the very day of the 9/11 terrorist attacks is suggested by the fact that US government and intelligence officials were meeting with Sheikh's chief, then ISI Director-General Mahmoud Ahmad in the week of the attacks—and even on the same day. On the morning of September 11, 2001, as Professor Chossudovsky records, the ISI chief and 9/11 "money man" was meeting on Capitol Hill with Chairman of the Senate Intelligence Committee Bob Graham and Chairman of the House Intelligence Committee Porter Goss. Other members of these intelligence committees were also present. The *Stuart News Company Press Journal* reported:

> When the news [of the WTC attacks] came, the two Florida lawmakers who lead the House and Senate intelligence committees were having breakfast with the head of the Pakistani intelligence service. Rep. Porter Goss, R-Sanibel, Sen. Bob Graham and other members of the House Intelligence Committee were talking about terrorism issues with the Pakistani official when a member of Goss' staff handed a note to Goss, who handed it to Graham. "We were talking about terrorism, specifically terrorism generated from Afghanistan," Graham said.[50]

Exactly what issues related to "terrorism generated from Afghanistan" were discussed between these officials, on the very day of al-Qaeda's unprecedented attack on the World Trade Center and the Pentagon, has not been disclosed to the public in any meaningful detail. Neither have the contents of Mahmoud Ahmad's other meetings with various top government officials. In context with the previous documentation, the meeting is certainly yet another indication of the disturbingly close liaisons US government officials have had with the 9/11 "money men" prior to—and on—September 11, 2001. To paraphrase the ironic observations of Professor Chossudovsky, from a "sociological perspective" if the 9/11 money man is "buddy-buddy" with the administration at the same time that he is "buddy-buddy" with the 9/11 hijackers, the issue must at the very least be the subject of an official inquiry.[51] As is discussed in further detail later on in this study, Senator Bob Graham was well aware of the ISI's connections to al-Qaeda prior to 9/11. His office received an urgent warning of an imminent terrorist attack on the World Trade Center being planned by ISI agents connected to al-Qaeda, from FBI informant Randy Glass, three months prior to 9/11.[52] In this context, Graham's meeting with the ISI chief on the morning of 9/11 is an exceedingly curious coincidence—and certainly begs an official inquiry.

Protecting the ISI "Money Men"

As the Associated Press points out, "US officials have repeatedly said that capturing or killing bin Laden's cadre of lieutenants... is a key goal in the war on terrorism."[53] But the roles of both Mahmoud Ahmad and Omar Sheikh have been completely ignored by US authorities. As former US intelligence official Wayne Madsen observes, Lt. Gen. Ahmad's involvement "in the Sheik–Atta money transfer was more than enough for a nervous and embarrassed Bush administration," which "pressed Musharraf to dump General Ahmed"—but refused to arrange for his charging, arrest, prosecution, and extradition to the US.[54]

Indeed, this measure served to obstruct a more in-depth inquiry into the ISI's role in 9/11. By pressuring the former ISI Director-General to resign without scandal on the pretext of routine reshuffling, the entire issue was effectively closed, allowing the ISI—which was clearly complicit in the 9/11 terrorist attacks—to continue operating freely. The studious non-response to Ahmad and Sheikh on the part of US authorities should be compared to their response to other terror suspects in Germany. "Warrants have been issued for four people" by the FBI, according to Associated Press, "and one of those has been arrested. Still at large are Said Bahaji, Ramsi Binalshibh and Zakariya Essabar. A fourth suspect, Mounir El Motassadeq, was arrested at his Hamburg apartment Nov. 28 on charges he controlled an account used to bankroll several of the hijackers."[55]

Yet no warrant for the arrest of either Ahmad or Sheikh for their role in financing the 9/11 terrorist attacks has ever been issued. Even after Sheikh was detained, put on trial, and sentenced to death for the murder of US citizen Daniel Pearl, the US government refused to act in relation to his far more devastating role in financing the murder of 3,000 American citizens. His crucial function as Osama bin Laden's financial chief is being neglected, as is former ISI chief Mahmoud Ahmad's role in instructing Sheikh.

Why the deafening silence on Ahmad and Sheikh? Pakistan's role as a strategic asset in the bombing campaign against Afghanistan that began in October 2001 might explain the obstructionism to some extent. But even this is a shallow explanation. An in-depth investigation into ISI complicity in 9/11 could at least have been postponed until after the bombing campaign. But although that campaign is largely over, the US has refused to launch an investigation of wider ISI complicity that might bring into clear light the state-intelligence supporters of the al-Qaeda 9/11 operation—which would of course be an essential component of any meaningful attempt to de-radicalize the Pakistani regime and purge al-Qaeda's ISI support base. But it seems the US is not interested in pursuing any sort of strategy—diplomatic, intelligence, or otherwise—to secure this outcome. Perhaps there is, indeed, something to hide. And it is plausible that this is directly related to the intimate ties that both Sheikh and Ahmad have had with Western intelligence agencies.

US–Pakistan Strategy Saves al-Qaeda

Gen. Pervez Musharraf's Pakistan played an integral role in US regional strategy. The US government needed Pakistani airspace and extensive assistance from Pakistani military intelligence to conduct the post-9/11 war on Afghanistan. The result was that the US teamed up with a government tied institutionally to the very terrorist network it was supposed to be fighting. Given the latter's ongoing ties with al-Qaeda, the idea that the US would be able to target and destroy al-Qaeda effectively with the latter's assistance was highly unlikely by the most obvious standards.

But this was not a serious concern. Throughout the military operation, US authorities maintained a bizarre indifference to information that could have led to al-Qaeda's destruction. For instance, to date the CIA has refused to question a former Taliban Deputy Interior Minister possessing detailed information on al-Qaeda's locations in Afghanistan and the network's institutionalized linkages to the Pakistani state-apparatus. "Has the CIA ignored a potentially useful Taliban informant?" asked *Time* magazine.

> Mullah Haji Abdul Samat Khaksar, the No 2 Taliban official in US custody, has been waiting months for the CIA to talk to him. The former Taliban official says he has valuable information for the US—and may be able to help locate former Taliban leader Mullah Omar…. But until TIME recently alerted the US military in Kabul to Khaksar's desire to talk, American officials had not spoken with him….
>
> Two weeks later Khaksar met with a US general, but no senior intelligence official has come for a full interview. The CIA will not comment. When the Taliban abandoned Kabul, Khaksar stayed behind, giving himself up to the Northern Alliance. Since then, he says he has sent five letters to the US embassy in Kabul offering to pass on information about al-Qaeda hideouts in Afghanistan…. He claims to have information about al-Qaeda links to ISI, the Pakistani intelligence agency that has been a key partner in the US war on terror. In exchange for his information, Khaksar wants safe passage for his family to a location of his choice. Though he has had trouble getting US intelligence officials to listen, Khaksar fears his former comrades are playing close attention and want him silenced.[56]

It is not surprising that Pakistan's role in the US war in Afghanistan served— quite predictably—to actually aid al-Qaeda, often with an astonishing degree of US connivance. "Pakistan continues to give help to Afghanistan's ruling Taleban despite supporting the US war against the militia, according to the anti-Taleban Northern Alliance," reported the Indo-Asian News Service in mid-October 2001:

In an interview with World Report TV, Northern Alliance envoy to Uzbekistan Muhammad Hasham Saad said: "The regular Pakistani army, the officers, are still inside Afghanistan with the Taleban." Saad added: "Last week we had information that a lot of trucks were coming (to Afghanistan) from Chaman, which is in the side of Quetta in Pakistan, to help the Taleban." The Northern Alliance estimates that about 100 trucks entered Afghanistan the week before the US began bombing Afghanistan, carrying ammunition and other military supplies.[57]

The US military, monitoring the region both from the air and on the ground, was obviously aware of Pakistan's aid to al-Qaeda. By November, however, the US military began actively participating in the covert Pakistani policy. As the London *Times* reported:

> [Northern Alliance commander] General Dawood said that Alliance intelligence sources in the city had reported that at least two large Pakistani planes had landed at Konduz airfield to extricate "military personnel" on Tuesday night, followed by at least two more flights on Wednesday night. Asked why the US, which controls the skies over Afghanistan, should have allowed such flights, he replied: "That is a question that you will have to put to the Americans."[58]

Fortunately, that is exactly what one US investigative journalist did. In November 2001, the Northern Alliance—backed by US Special Forces and a devastating US bombing campaign—"forced thousands of Taliban and Al Qaeda fighters to retreat inside the northern hill town of Kunduz." The Taliban and al-Qaeda fighters were accompanied by "Pakistani Army officers, intelligence advisers, and volunteers" who were fighting with them. At this point, the road to Kabul, "a potential point of retreat, was blocked and was targeted by American bombers. Kunduz offered safety from the bombs and a chance to negotiate painless surrender terms." The negotiations were opposed by the US government. By November 25, the Northern Alliance had moved in, "capturing some four thousand of the Taliban and Al Qaeda fighters," leading President Bush to comment the next day: "We're smoking them out. They're running, and now we're going to bring them to justice."

What happened subsequently amounted not to bringing al-Qaeda to justice, but on the contrary to letting the terrorists off the hook. "Even before the siege ended," observes Seymour Hersh in *New Yorker* magazine, "a puzzling series of reports appeared in the *Times* and in other publications, quoting Northern Alliance officials who claimed that Pakistani airplanes had flown into Kunduz to evacuate the Pakistanis there. American and Pakistani officials refused to confirm the reports." But Hersh's interviews with US officials behind-the-scenes showed that the airlifts had been arranged by the Pentagon:

American intelligence officials and high-ranking military officers said that Pakistanis were indeed flown to safety, in a series of nighttime airlifts that were approved by the Bush Administration. The Americans also said that what was supposed to be a limited evacuation apparently slipped out of control... [A]n unknown number of Taliban and Al Qaeda fighters managed to join in the exodus. "Dirt got through the screen," a senior intelligence official told me....

A CIA analyst said that it was his understanding that the decision to permit the airlift was made by the White House.... The airlift "made sense at the time," the CIA analyst said. "Many of the people they spirited away were the Taliban leadership."... According to a former high-level American defense official, the airlift was approved because of representations by the Pakistanis that "there were guys—intelligence agents and underground guys—who needed to get out."...

The Bush Administration may have done more than simply acquiesce in the rescue effort: at the height of the standoff, according to both a CIA official and a military analyst who has worked with the Delta Force, the American commando unit that was destroying Taliban units on the ground, the Administration ordered the United States Central Command to set up a special air corridor to help insure the safety of the Pakistani rescue flights from Kunduz to the northwest corner of Pakistan, about two hundred miles away....

None of the American intelligence officials I spoke with were able to say with certainty how many Taliban and Al Qaeda fighters were flown to safety, or may have escaped from Kunduz by other means.... Some CIA analysts believe that bin Laden eluded American capture inside Afghanistan with help from elements of the Pakistani intelligence service. "The game against bin Laden is not over," one analyst told me in early January.[59]

The covert operation mirrored previous similar operations such as the mujahideen air corridor in Bosnia-Herzegovina organized by the Pentagon and the CIA. And it is hardly credible that the outcome surprised US military intelligence planners. As Marin Strmecki observed in *Commentary*:

Over the past decade, it was the ISI that forged the link between bin Laden and the Taliban leader Mullah Muhammad Omar, and it also played a central role in developing the al Qaeda infrastructure in Afghanistan and integrating its fighting forces with the Taliban military. The agency's involvement raises profound questions about our alliance with Pakistan in the war against terrorism, particularly as long as the Pakistani intelligence service remains unpurged of its pro-Taliban, pro-al Qaeda elements.[60]

Therefore, the US government had asked al-Qaeda's principal state-intelligence supporter to help destroy the very Afghanistan-based terrorist infrastructure with which it is ideologically and institutionally intertwined. As a senior US defense adviser familiar with the US airlifts observed: "Everyone brought their friends with them"—their "friends" constituting the al-Qaeda and Taliban fighters "with whom the Pakistanis had worked, and whom they had trained or had used to run intelligence operations." Citing the US evacuation at the climax of the Vietnam War as an example, he pointed out the obvious: "You're not going to leave them behind to get their throats cut. When we came out of Saigon, we brought our boys [South Vietnamese nationals] with us. How many does that helicopter hold? Ten? We're bringing fourteen." In other words, such results were entirely predictable. US military planners, aware of the extent to which Pakistani military intelligence and al-Qaeda absorb one another, envisaged the consequences of arranging the airlift.

The government meanwhile has strenuously denied that any such airlifts occurred at all. The Musharraf administration in Pakistan, following the US lead, has also pretended that the US-approved airlifts never happened:

> On November 16th, when journalists asked Secretary of Defense Donald Rumsfeld about the reports of rescue aircraft, he was dismissive. "Well, if we see them, we shoot them down," he said. Five days later, Rumsfeld declared, "Any idea that those people should be let loose on any basis at all to leave that country and to go bring terror to other countries and destabilize other countries is unacceptable." At a Pentagon news conference on Monday, November 26th, the day after Kunduz fell, General Richard B. Myers, of the Air Force, who is the chairman of the Joint Chiefs of Staff, was asked about the reports. The General did not directly answer the question but stated, "The runway there is not usable. I mean, there are segments of it that are usable. They're too short for your standard transport aircraft. So we're not sure where the reports are coming from." Pakistani officials also debunked the rescue reports, and continued to insist, as they had throughout the Afghanistan war, that no Pakistani military personnel were in the country. Anwar Mehmood, the government spokesman, told newsmen at the time that reports of a Pakistani airlift were "total rubbish. Hogwash."[61]

Obviously, the existence of the US-approved airlifts was not meant for public consumption. Perhaps the most damning testimonial is the above admission of US Secretary of Defense Rumsfeld, who appears to be quite conscious of the fact that the airlifts entailed saving the terrorists and granting them free reign to wreak havoc outside Afghanistan. It is hard to deny, then, that the US government was fully aware that the airlifts would "let loose" al-Qaeda operatives "to go bring terror" and "destabilize" other countries—clearly, this outcome was "unacceptable" only for the public, but otherwise perfectly acceptable to the political elite. The attempt to misrepresent the reality of the matter raises legitimate suspicions about the real motives behind the secret joint operation which flew al-Qaeda terrorists to safety.

The *New Yorker's* revelations should be understood in context with the fact that US military strategy had from the outset established a scenario from which al-Qaeda would easily be able to escape. Even a local Afghan tribal chief was able to observe how strange it was that US strategy had carefully left open "exit routes" by which al-Qaeda fighters were able to—predictably given the circumstances—flee for their lives. According to the *Telegraph*

> US generals made it clear by the end of November that they believed senior al-Qa'eda operatives were inside Tora Bora...
>
> A convoy of several hundred Arab fighters, including bin Laden and his close associates, entered it [i.e. the Tora Bora cave complex] from Jalalabad on the night of Nov 12, and the US bombing around the base intensified three days later. The US strategy bore little logic for those suffering the brunt of the attacks. "When we round up a pack of stray sheep, we send in shepherds from four sides, not just one," said Malik Osman Khan, a one-eyed tribal chief whose 16-year-old son Wahid Ullah was one of more than 100 Afghan civilians killed in the intense US bombing. "At first, we thought that the US military was trying to frighten the Arabs out, since they were only bombing on one side."... Bin Laden had left some days previously, and even as the US military's proxy war got under way, the rush of his fighters out of Tora Bora, which had been a trickle and then a stream, now became a mad dash for freedom.
>
> The eastern Afghanistan intelligence chief for the country's new government, Pir Baksh Bardiwal, was astounded that the Pentagon planners of the battle for Tora Bora had failed to even consider the most obvious exit routes. He said: "The border with Pakistan was the key, but no one paid any attention to it. And there were plenty of landing areas for helicopters had the Americans acted decisively. Al-Qa'eda escaped right out from under their feet."[62]

The picture only worsens. The London *Times* has revealed how ongoing US inaction allowed a massive truck convoy carrying the al-Qaeda leadership to trundle comfortably into neighboring Pakistan:

> Afghans still marvel that 1,000 cars and lorries escaped in the night.... Locals still talk of the night-time escape, past the Bala Hissar fortress and south through the Logar Valley, when the advisers escaped US airstrikes...
>
> Mohammed Rahim, a local businessman, said that the al-Qaeda convoy arrived between November 1 and 15. "'We don't understand how they weren't all killed the night before because they came in a convoy of at least 1,000 cars and trucks," he said. "It was a very dark night, but it must have been easy for the American pilots to see the headlights." The next evening the convoy moved on. "The main road was jammed from eight in the evening until three in the morning."[63]

As *Newsmax* rightly asked: "How—with every satellite, overflight, radio intercept and on-the-ground agent imaginable—could these criminals have crossed into a country that's a supposed ally? Especially an ally whom we have plied with money and debt relief since September 11?"[64] A reasonable explanation, particularly in context with other facts documented here, is that this escape was permitted to happen.

These were only key elements of a wider military strategy in Afghanistan that had been systemically avoided significant action to eliminate al-Qaeda. The London *Times* noted in late November 2002, for instance, that: "American warplanes have had al-Qaeda and Taleban leaders in their sights as many as ten times over the past six weeks, but have been unable to attack because they did not receive permission quickly enough, US Air Force officials complained yesterday."[65]

Yet another bizarre coincidence? Perhaps not. According to John Arquilla and David Ronfeldt, two US military-strategic experts who "codified the strategy that helped the United States overthrow the Taliban regime in Afghanistan," the military strategy employed in Afghanistan was not designed to destroy al-Qaeda. On the contrary, the large-scale air bombardment was designed only to smash Afghanistan's ad hoc state-structure, the Taliban regime, and was unsuitable to target the al-Qaeda network, which it directly and inevitably flushed out of the country. John Arquilla, a former US Marine, is a professor at the Naval Postgraduate College in Monterey, California, working closely with top Pentagon officials; David Ronfeldt is a networks specialist and researcher at the RAND Corporation in Los Angeles. According to the French journal *Le Monde Diplomatique*:

> Arquilla estimates that 90% of the current US military effort is invested in dealing with "state actors." This reflects archaic military thinking, dating from the days of the Soviet threat, but it does not meet the needs of a war against a network...
>
> That prompts the question of whether the US won the wrong war in Afghanistan, crushing the Taliban nation state, but allowing the al-Qaida network to slip through its grasp. It would be all the more serious for Washington if it turned out that by destroying one of al-Qaida's main sanctuaries, it had in fact created more problems for itself. "When I think of an all-channel network operating in a sanctuary I want to leave it right there," says Arquilla. "If I take the sanctuary, then it is going to hide in places I may never find. Simply, we must be looking around the world." Some members of al-Qaida may have taken refuge, for example, in west Africa (Guinea, Mali, Senegal) where no-one seems to be looking for them.

Thus, far from damaging Osama bin Laden's terrorist network, the US bombing campaign in Afghanistan demolished the Taliban regime while allowing the al-Qaeda network along with the Taliban leadership to escape and regroup elsewhere. Arquilla and Ronfeldt explain this result by noting that a network can continue functioning with twice as many losses, "in part because in a distributed network some nodes are not even aware of the damage. They don't feel, they don't see the loss to others. And so the psychological effect of attrition is not the same."[66]

A plausible conclusion from all this is that the US military campaign in Afghanistan, assisted by Pakistani military intelligence, was not really designed to destroy al-Qaeda at all. Rather, it was designed to crush the Taliban regime, in the knowledge that al-Qaeda would be displaced elsewhere to safety. Fighting a "War on Terror" against al-Qaeda had never been the real goal of the plans for a military invasion of Afghanistan, which had been formulated years before 9/11. Those plans were motivated by other strategic and economic interests. But the 9/11 terrorist attacks happened to provide a convenient and powerful pretext to implement those plans, as well as other geostrategic imperatives.

PART TWO
THE 9/11 INTELLIGENCE FAILURE

Here we aim to develop a coherent picture of the nature and scope of intelligence received by the US intelligence community about the 9/11 attacks in the months and years preceding them. A key concern of this subject is to discover how the community responded to intelligence data received, and why this response failed to foil 9/11. An explanation of the 9/11 intelligence failure will be constructed based on an informed grasp of the structure, capabilities, and deficiencies of the intelligence community, as well as on the nature of intelligence received.

7.

WHAT THEY KNEW, WHEN

W e've been focusing on this perpetrator Osama bin Laden for 3 years, and yet we didn't see this one coming," said Vincent Cannistraro, former chief of CIA counter-terrorism operations. A US Air Force General described the attack as "something we had never seen before, something we had never even thought of." FBI Director Robert Mueller further declared that "there were no warning signs that I'm aware of." Senior FBI officials insisted that: "The notion of flying a plane into a building or using it as a bomb never came up."[1] Notoriously, National Security Adviser Condoleeza Rice asserted: "I don't think that anybody could have predicted that these people would take an airplane and slam it into the World Trade Center, take another one and slam it into the Pentagon."[2]

According to the conventional wisdom, then, no one in the Bush administration had the slightest idea of the identities of those who orchestrated the 9/11 attacks, the nature of their plans, or their targets. This, indeed, is the assessment of the 9/11 Commission which concludes in its Staff Statement No. 11 that:

> ... the Intelligence Community [was] struggling to collect on and analyze the phenomena of transnational terrorism through the mid- to late 1990s. While many dedicated officers worked day and night for years to piece together the growing body of evidence on al Qaeda and to understand the threats, in the end it was not enough to gain the advantage before the 9/11 attacks.[3]

This conclusion, however, is contradicted by a vast amount of data on the public record based largely on official intelligence sources. An analysis of this declassified information alone indicates that the intelligence community and the US government received extensive advanced warning of the 9/11 terrorist attacks, but nevertheless failed to act, in a manner replicating the same patterns documented in the previous chapters.

The 9/11 Plot: 1993–1994

The Pentagon commissioned an expert panel in 1993 to investigate the possibility of an airplane being used to bomb national landmarks. Retired Air

Force Col. Doug Menarchik, who organized the $150,000 study for the Defense Department's Office of Special Operations and Low-Intensity Conflict, recalled: "It was considered radical thinking, a little too scary for the times. After I left, it met a quiet death." Other participants have noted that the decision not to publish detailed scenarios issued from fear that doing so might give terrorists ideas. Although senior officials decided against a public release, a draft document detailing the results of the investigation circulated throughout the Pentagon, the Justice Department, and the Federal Emergency Management Agency.[4]

The particular vulnerability of New York City's Twin Towers to just such an attack was, in fact, specifically noted. In 1994, one year after the first World Trade Center bombing, one of the experts on the aforementioned Pentagon panel wrote in *Futurist* magazine that the World Trade Center was an extremely likely target of such an "airplanes as weapons" terrorist attack:

> Targets such as the World Trade Center not only provide the requisite casualties but, because of their symbolic nature, provide more bang for the buck. In order to maximize their odds for success, terrorist groups will likely consider mounting multiple, simultaneous operations with the aim of overtaxing a government's ability to respond, as well as demonstrating their professionalism and reach.[5]

In other words, as early as 1994, the Pentagon was acutely aware not only of the threat to the World Trade Center from an "airplanes as weapons" plot, but was specifically concerned about the possibility of such a plot being implemented in the form of "multiple, simultaneous operations."

The Pentagon's concerns were confirmed in 1994 when there occurred three attempted attacks on buildings using airplanes. The first, in April of that year, involved a Federal Express flight engineer facing dismissal. Having boarded a DC-10 as a passenger, he invaded the cockpit, planning to crash the plane into a company building in Memphis. Fortunately, he was overpowered by the crew. The second attempt occurred in September. A lone pilot crashed a small plane into a tree on the White House grounds, just short of the President's bedroom. The third incident occurred in December. An Air France flight in Algiers was hijacked by members of the Armed Islamic Group (GIA)—which is linked to al-Qaeda—aiming to crash it into the Eiffel Tower. French Special Forces stormed the plane on the ground.[6]

Indeed, the US intelligence community was long aware that al-Qaeda saw the 1993 World Trade Center bombing plot as a failure, and therefore planned to target the Twin Towers again. According to the Associated Press:

> After the 1993 attack on the World Trade Center, investigators discovered that conspirator Nidal Ayyad had left behind a chilling computer message: "Next time, it will be very precise." The note along with evidence from past

cases of terrorism gives insight into a more than decade-long learning curve that culminated in the devastating Sept. 11 attack.[7]

In other words, US investigators knew with certainty there would be another al-Qaeda attempted terrorist attack on the World Trade Center. Simultaneously, the intelligence community was well aware that a future plot against the Twin Towers was likely to involve a multiple, simultaneous "airplanes as weapons" operation. Therefore, as early as 1993/94, the Pentagon had clearly anticipated the fundamental scenario that actually unfolded on the morning of September 11, 2001.

The 9/11 Plot: 1995

By 1995, the US intelligence community became aware that al-Qaeda was planning exactly such an operation to target not only the World Trade Center, but a wide number of other key US buildings. As the *Chicago Sun-Times* reported: "The FBI had advance indications of plans to hijack US airliners and use them as weapons, but neither acted on them nor distributed the intelligence to local police agencies."[8]

Federal investigative sources confirmed that Abdul Hakim Murad—"a close confidant and right-hand man" to Ramzi Yousef, "who was convicted of crimes relating to the 1993 bombing of the World Trade Center"—"detailed an entire plot to dive bomb aircraft in the headquarters of the Central Intelligence Agency in Langley, VA" along with other US buildings. "Yousef independently boasted of the plot to US Secret Service agent Brian Parr and FBI agent Charles Stern on an extradition flight from Pakistan to the United States in February 1995," according to Washington, DC's Public Education Center. "The agents later testified to that fact in court... [T]he plan targeted not only the CIA but other US government buildings in Washington, including the Pentagon."[9]

Western intelligence sources confirm that plan was discovered in January 1995 by Philippine police investigating a possible attack against Pope John Paul II on a visit to Manila. The details were found on a computer seized in an apartment used by three al-Qaeda operatives, providing for "11 planes to be exploded simultaneously by bombs placed on board, but also in an alternative form for several planes flying to the United States to be hijacked and flown into civilian targets." The first half of the plan had been attempted and failed—but the other alternative lay in waiting. "Among targets mentioned was the World Trade Center in New York." The plot became a matter of public record in 1997 during Yousef's New York trial.[10]

Rafael M. Garcia III, Chairman/CEO of the Mega Group of Computer Companies in the Philippines, who often works with the National Bureau of Investigation (NBI) in his field of expertise, was involved in the intelligence operation that uncovered Project Bojinka. Garcia was responsible for the decoding of Yousef's computer: "... we discovered a second, even more sinister plot: Project Bojinka." Project Bojinka aimed to crash "planes into selected targets in the United States" including "the CIA headquarters in Langley, Virginia; the World Trade Center in New York; the Sears Tower in Chicago; the TransAmerica Tower in San Francisco; and the White House in Washington, DC." These findings were submitted to NBI officials, "who most certainly turned over the report (and the computer) either to then Senior Superintendent Avelino Razon of the PNP [the Philippine National Police] or to Bob Heafner of the FBI.... I have since had meetings with certain US authorities and they have confirmed to me that indeed, many things were done in response to my report."[11]

Professor Paul Monk of the Australian Defense University cites "confidential sources" in Manila and Washington further detailing that: "The flights to be hijacked were specified. They were all United Airlines, Northwest Airlines and Delta flights." Evidence surrounding Project Bojinka and its planners further indicated a probable date for the implementation of the plot. "The date of Yousef's conviction was 11 September 1996. From that point, given the fascination terrorists have with anniversaries, 11 September should surely have become a watch date."[12] Reinforcing this perspective, Philippine Chief Superintendent Avelino Razon said:

> US federal officials were aware of Project Bojinka and... the Philippines' crack terrorist team was continuing to work closely with them.... "I remember that after the first World Trade Center bombing Osama bin Laden made a statement that on the second attempt they would be successful," Razon stressed. He said they could have chosen to carry out the attack on September 11, to mark the anniversary of Yousef's conviction for the first attack several years ago.[13]

Insight On The News magazine managed to obtain "copies of the original Philippines-police interrogation of Murad (a report code-named Blue Marlin)" and has cited the relevant portions of the latter. Murad had

> detailed his own training as a pilot at more than a half-dozen US flight schools, along with other Middle Eastern and Pakistani men...
>
> He began at the Alfa-Tango Flying School in San Antonio in 1990, then transferred to Richmore Aviation in Schenectady, N.Y., and subsequently to Coast Aviation Flying School in New Bern, N.C. Ultimately, he was certified by the FAA to fly small propeller aircraft. As Murad's interrogation continued into February and early March 1995, he began telling police more about Project Bojinka. "With regards in [sic] their plan to dive-crash a commercial aircraft at the CIA headquarters in Virginia, subject alleged that the idea of doing more came out during his casual conversation with Abdul Basit [Yousef] and there is no specific plan

yet for its execution," according to Blue Marlin. "What the subject have [sic] in his mind is that he will board any American commercial aircraft pretending to be an ordinary passenger. Then he will hijack said aircraft, control its cockpit and dive it at the CIA headquarters. There will be no bomb or any explosive that he will use in its execution. It is simply a suicidal mission that he is very much willing to execute. That all he need is to be able to board the aircraft with a pistol so that he could execute the hijacking." There in a nutshell was the Sept. 11 plot, laid out in detail in the Blue Marlin file fully seven years earlier.[14]

Project Bojinka was extremely well-known among the highest echelons of the US intelligence community. According to Professor John Arquilla, an information warfare and Special Operations expert at the Naval Postgraduate School: "The idea of such an attack (like 9-11) was well known. It had been wargamed as a possibility in exercises before Sept. 11, 2001."[15]

A Rising Tide of Terrorist Alerts: 1996-2000

As Washington, DC's *Accuracy in Media* observes, the "most obvious indicator, and one that should have been watched most carefully" that Project Bojinka was being prepared "was the recruitment of young, dedicated followers to learn to fly American airliners. That would require keeping a close watch on flight schools where that training is given."[16]

As *Insight* magazine reports: "FBI officials took Blue Marlin and ran with it, visiting each of the flight schools Murad had mentioned and interrogating all the Middle Eastern men he had named." *Insight*, however, quotes unnamed US officials claiming that they "did not find evidence that any Middle Easterners other than Murad were plotting anything. With no other evidence to go on, they took no further action."[17] But this claim is false. In fact, a wide number of credible reports from intelligence sources confirm that the FBI—prompted by Project Bojinka—found ample evidence of al-Qaeda terrorist activity at flight schools across the United States.

The *San Francisco Chronicle*, for example, reports that in response to the revelations about Project Bojinka, "FBI agents descended upon flying schools in 1995," and discovered that Murad had actually been in contact with at least 10 other Middle Eastern men training in US flight schools.[18] Similarly, the *Washington Post* cited intelligence officials confirming that: "A foiled plot in Manila to blow up US airliners and later court testimony by an associate of bin Laden"—i.e. Project Bojinka—"had touched off FBI inquiries at several schools." Through those investigations, "[s]ince 1996, the FBI had been developing evidence that international terrorists were using flight schools to learn to fly jumbo jets."[19]

Another *Post* report describes in detail the findings of some of these inquiries. According to two flight school operators at Coastal Aviation of New Bern, NC, and Richmor Aviation of Schenectady, NY, in 1996 "FBI agents visited them to obtain information about several Arab pilots connected to a Pakistani terrorist eventually convicted of plotting to bomb US airliners"—i.e. Murad. "In 1998, FBI agents questioned officials from Airman Flight School in Norman, Okla., about a graduate later identified in court testimony as a pilot for bin Laden, according to Dale Davis, the school's director of operations." A government witness in the 1998 embassy bombing trial, Essam al-Ridi, testified that he had trained and taught at the Ed Boardman Aviation School in Fort Worth, and "purchased a used Saber-40 aircraft on bin Laden's behalf for $210,000 in Tucson."[20]

A clear pattern of al-Qaeda activity at US flight schools was evident. Simultaneously, concerns for an "airplanes as weapons" terrorist attack were prevalent. In early 1996, for example, US officials identified crop-dusters and suicide flights as potential terrorist weapons. Elaborate steps were adopted to prevent a suicide air attack during the Summer Olympic Games in Atlanta. US military jets were deployed to intercept suspicious aircraft in the skies over Olympic venues, while agents monitored crop-duster flights within hundreds of miles of downtown Atlanta. According to Woody Johnson, head of the FBI's Atlanta office at the time, law enforcement agents fanned out to regional airports throughout northern Georgia "to make sure nobody hijacked a small aircraft and tried to attack one of the venues." From July 6 to August 11, when the Games ended, the FAA had banned all aviation within a one-mile radius of the Olympic Village where athletes were resident. Aircraft were also ordered to stay at least three miles away for three hours before and after each event.[21]

By this time, the intelligence community's awareness of al-Qaeda's intent to target key US buildings—specifically in Washington, DC and New York City—was undoubtedly well-developed. The *Washington Times* notes for instance that: "In late 1998, US intelligence reports said Osama bin Laden was planning strikes on Washington or New York to avenge a US missile strike on his headquarters in Afghanistan."[22] Director of the House/Senate Joint Inquiry Staff Eleanor Hill has described a large body of related 1998 reports on al-Qaeda's plans to launch an attack on US soil that "were disseminated throughout the Intelligence Community and to senior US policy-makers." These reports "clearly reiterated a consistent and critically important theme: Usama Bin Laden's intent to launch terrorist attacks inside the United States," specifically against symbolic targets in Washington and New York.[23]

In 1999, an extensive report prepared by the National Intelligence Council (NIC) highlighted the likelihood of a Project Bojinka operation. It "warned that terrorists associated with bin Laden might hijack an airplane and crash it into the Pentagon, White House or CIA headquarters." In support of its conclusions, the NIC report

... recounts well-known case studies of similar plots, including a 1995 plan by al Qaeda operatives to hijack and crash a dozen US airliners in the South Pacific and pilot a light aircraft into Langley. "Suicide bomber(s) belonging to al-Qaida's Martyrdom Battalion could crash-land an aircraft packed with high explosives (C-4 and semtex) into the Pentagon, the headquarters of the Central Intelligence Agency (CIA), or the White House," the September 1999 report said.[24]

"Whatever form an attack may take," the report concludes, "bin Laden will most likely retaliate in a spectacular way for the cruise missile attack against his Afghan camp in August 1998."[25] This report was highly significant because the NIC is the US government's "center of strategic thinking... reporting to the Director of Central Intelligence (DCI) and providing coordinated analyses of foreign policy issues for the President and other senior policymakers."[26] Moreover, the NIC's products are:

> ... the DCI's most authoritative written judgments concerning national security issues. They contain the coordinated judgments of the Intelligence Community regarding the likely course of future events. The NIC's goal is to provide policymakers with the best, unvarnished, and unbiased information—regardless of whether analytic judgments conform to US policy.[27]

The NIC report—which was "widely shared within the government"[28]— therefore clarifies beyond doubt that in September 1999, the US intelligence community, senior government officials, and the President were aware that a Project Bojinka operation was the most probable method of a future al-Qaeda terrorist attack.

A month after the dissemination of the NIC report, US intelligence agencies were alerted to signs of al-Qaeda preparations for a major attack on US soil. Citing London's *Terrorism and Security Monitor*, *NewsMax* reported that US intelligence sources are "particularly concerned about some kind of attack on New York, and they have recommended stepped-up security at the New York Stock Exchange and the Federal Reserve." Yossef Bodansky of the Congressional Task Force on Terrorism and Unconventional Warfare stated: "There are rumblings throughout the Islamic community right now. There's a lot of movement and talk. It's like a volcano just before the explosion."[29] Indeed, as revealed in Eleanor Hill's Joint Inquiry Staff statement, the US intelligence community throughout that year received evidence of ongoing preparations for an attack against US government facilities and specific landmarks in Washington, DC and New York City.[30]

The Federal Aviation Administration's annual report on Criminal Acts Against Aviation noted in 1999 the threat posed by bin Laden, recalling that a radical Muslim leader living in British exile had warned in August 1998 that bin Laden "would bring down an airliner, or hijack an airliner to humiliate the United States." The 2000 edition of the annual report, published early in 2001, reiterated concerns that although bin Laden "is not known to have attacked civil aviation, he has both the motivation and the wherewithal to do so.... Bin Laden's anti-Western and anti-American attitudes make him and his followers a significant threat to civil aviation, particularly to US civil aviation."[31]

By the year 2000, Pentagon policy clearly indicated that military intelligence officials anticipated an "airplanes as weapons" attack. The London Mirror reports that in October that year: "Military chiefs were so convinced terrorists could fly a plane into the Pentagon that they planned for an attack." Only 11 months prior to 9/11, the Pentagon "carried out a detailed emergency exercise." The Mirror cites a report in "an internal Pentagon newspaper" showing that between the 24th and 26th of that month, "military planners held an exercise to prepare for 'incidents including a passenger plane crashing into the Pentagon.'" The report "reads like an account of what actually happened." A Pentagon emergency planning spokesman, Glen Flood, told the Mirror: "We had been aware there could be possible aeroplane accidents and we have had various tabletop exercises."[32]

FBI Whistleblower: Sibel Edmonds and "Airplanes as Weapons"

Other sources give an inkling not only of the precise degree of advanced warning available to the government, but also of the corrupt policy machinery behind the government's failure to act on the warnings. One such source is Sibel Edmonds, a former FBI translator with top security clearance who worked part-time for the Bureau's Washington Field Office Translation Department for 6 months starting September 20, 2001. According to Edmonds, a 10-year US citizen who has passed a polygraph examination, she was asked by the Justice Department to "retranslate and adjust the translations of (terrorist) subject intercepts that had been received before September 11, 2001 by the FBI and CIA." To prevent her from going public about the extent of advanced warning revealed by this material, she was "offered a substantial raise and a full time job." Edmonds testified several times before the Justice Department's Inspector General, the Senate Judiciary Committee, and the 9/11 Commission in closed sessions. When these efforts failed to bring the government to account, Edmonds attempted to publicize the information she had gleaned during her tenure at the FBI. In response, Attorney General John Ashcroft invoked "State Secret Privilege and National Security" to prevent her from giving subpoenaed testimony in a US court. The substance of her allegations is as follows:

> My translations of the pre 9-11 intercepts included [terrorist] money laundering, detailed and date specific information enough to alert the

American people, and other issues dating back to 1999 which I won't go into right now.... The Senate Judiciary Committee and the 9/11 Commission have heard me testify for lengthy periods of time (3 hours) about very specific plots, dates, airplanes used as weapons, and specific individuals and activities... translators before me had ongoing personal relationships with the subjects or targets of the FBI and DOJ pre 9-11 investigations—linked to intercepts and other intelligence—in June—July—August, just prior to the attacks.... This whole situation is outrageous and I am going public.[33]

In her previous interview with CBS's 60 *Minutes*, Edmonds emphasized that the Justice Department ordered her and other translators not only to re-translate hundreds of already accurately translated intercepts, but further to indefinitely delay the translation of hundreds of other intercepts, especially those highly relevant and immediately required for ongoing FBI/CIA terrorist investigations:

> Ms. EDMONDS: We were told by our supervisors that this was the great opportunity for asking for increased budget and asking for more translators. And in order to do that, don't do the work and let the documents pile up so we can show it and say that we need more translators and expand the department.
>
> BRADLEY: So you—you have FBI agents who in the field relying on your translation work in order to move their cases forward, and your supervisor is saying, "Slow down. Let the cases pile up"?
>
> Ms. EDMONDS: Correct.
>
> BRADLEY: I mean, how is it possible that the focus wasn't on terrorism, particularly after 9/11?
>
> Ms. EDMONDS: It was not. At least in that department, it was not.
>
> (Footage of Bradley and Edmonds)
>
> BRADLEY: (Voiceover) Edmonds says that the supervisor, in an effort to slow her down, went so far as to erase completed translations from her FBI computer after she'd left work for the day.
>
> Ms. EDMONDS: The next day, I would come to work, turn on my computer and the work would be gone. The translation would be gone. Then I had to start all over again and retranslate the same document. And I went to my supervisor and he said, "Consider it a lesson and don't talk about it to anyone else and don't mention it."

BRADLEY: What's the lesson?

Ms. EDMONDS: The lesson was don't work, don't do the translations. Go out and spend two hours lunch breaks, you know. Go and—don't go and get coffee downstairs. Go eight blocks away. Just chat with your friends. But don't do the work because—and this is our chance to increase the number of people here in this department.[34]

Even more shockingly, Edmonds revealed that one of her colleagues, Turkish translator Jan Dickerson, worked for "a Turkish organization being investigated by the FBI's own counterintelligence unit" and had a relationship with "a Turkish intelligence officer stationed in Washington who was the target of that investigation." After reviewing Dickerson's translations, "she found that Dickerson had left out information crucial to the FBI's investigation"— information proving that "the Turkish intelligence officer had spies working for him inside the US State Department and at the Pentagon."

When Edmonds reported this misconduct both in writing and verbally to her immediate superiors and a top FBI official, she received no response. After complaining repeatedly to her bosses, it became clear that "nobody at the FBI wanted to hear about it... not even the assistant special agent in charge." The latter reportedly told Edmonds: "Do you realize what you are saying here in your allegations? Are you telling me that our security people are not doing their jobs? Is that what you're telling me? If you insist on this investigation, I'll make sure in no time it will turn around and become an investigation about you." Edmonds was subsequently fired in March 2002 with no explanation except that it was "for the government's convenience."[35]

Edmonds also points out that from the material that was already translated, there was significant and precise information on the impending attacks—but this information was ignored. In an interview with US journalist Amy Goodman, she noted:

I became aware of several investigations that were ongoing dating back to a year or—some of them actually years before 9/11 that contained significant amount of information about various activities... we are talking about money laundering activities directed toward these terrorist activities.... in fact there were [sic] information that were translated very precisely and accurately before. And somehow having that information did not achieve anything.... How about the information we had before that were pretty specific and they were pretty accurate, and they came from real reliable sources assets. What happened to that information?[36]

Perhaps the most significant piece of information disclosed by Edmonds for our purposes is the fact that the government had extremely "specific information" including dates, plots, perpetrators, and most crucially the method—"airplanes used as weapons"—yet another clear indication that the intelligence community was well-aware of the impending Bojinka plan.

Urgent Warnings of an Imminent Attack: 2001

By 2000, the US intelligence community had no doubt about Osama bin Laden's plans to conduct a terrorist attack on US soil. Between 2000 and 2001, the CIA made the FBI aware of the names of about 100 suspected members of bin Laden's terrorist network thought to be headed to, or already in, the United States.[37]

Between February and July 2001, the New York trial which eventually convicted the 1998 embassy bombers also revealed ongoing terrorist activity at US flight schools. The trial proved, for instance, that two bin Laden operatives received pilot training in Texas and Oklahoma, while another had been asked to take lessons. One bin Laden aide became a government witness, giving the FBI detailed information on the al-Qaeda pilot training scheme.[38]

In the following months, glaring indications of an underground terrorist training operation being pursued inside the United States continued to arise. Eleanor Hill's Joint Inquiry statement refers to several reports "widely disseminated within the Intelligence Community" in every month between March and August 2001 that were considered credible warnings of al-Qaeda preparations for an attack.[39] As the Los Angeles Times noted:

> American intelligence agencies, as well as other governments' spy services, were picking up a crescendo of threats of possible terrorist strikes last summer. "The chatter level went way off the charts," Rep. Porter J. Goss (R-Fla.), chairman of the House Intelligence Committee, recalled recently, "and had been for several months."[40]

These escalating alerts of an impending al-Qaeda attack during this entire period were almost all viewed with utmost seriousness. Two US counterterrorism officials have described the warnings received by the intelligence community in early and mid-summer 2001 as "the most urgent in decades."[41]

German intelligence officials have revealed that some of this information warned specifically of a Project Bojinka operation. Six months before 9/11 (May 2001), they report, US agencies became aware that Osama bin Laden was planning to implement an "airplanes as weapons" attack. Then three months prior to 9/11 (July 2001), these warnings were repeated, and the US intelligence community considered them reliable. These revelations were carried by Newsbytes, an online division of the Washington Post, a few days after 9/11:

> US and Israeli intelligence agencies received warning signals at least three months ago that Middle Eastern terrorists were planning to hijack

commercial aircraft to use as weapons to attack important symbols of American and Israeli culture, according to a story in Germany's daily *Frankfurter Allgemeine Zeitung* (FAZ).

The FAZ, quoting unnamed German intelligence sources, said that the Echelon spy network was being used to collect information about the terrorist threats, and that UK intelligence services apparently also had advance warning. The FAZ, one of Germany's most respected dailies, said that even as far back as six months ago western and near-east press services were receiving information that such attacks were being planned. Within the American intelligence community, the warnings were taken seriously and surveillance intensified, the FAZ said.[42]

The last comment—"Within the American intelligence community, the warnings were taken seriously"—is highly significant. It demonstrates that due to the ECHELON warnings, the entire US intelligence community was alerted to an imminent Project Bojinka operation and consequently intensified surveillance. This is important for one key reason—it means that in the months preceding 9/11, the intelligence community was fully aware of an impending al-Qaeda attack and was actively escalating intelligence efforts to discern its nature. All new intelligence on al-Qaeda would have been collected and assessed against this background of awareness. A CIA intelligence briefing for senior government officials cited by Eleanor Hill suggests that this information was speedily passed on to the White House. Only the following excerpt has been declassified:

A briefing prepared for senior government officials at the beginning of July 2001 contained the following language, "Based on a review of all-source reporting over the last five months, we believe that UBL [Usama Bin Laden] will launch a significant terrorist attack against US and/or Israeli interests in the coming weeks. The attack will be spectacular and designed to inflict mass casualties against US facilities or interests. Attack preparations have been made. Attack will occur with little or no warning."[43]

This depiction of the impending attack as "spectacular" has also been used by the National Intelligence Council report describing the distinct possibility of a Project Bojinka operation. There can be no doubt in this context that the information summarized in July 2001 concerned exactly this.

Additionally, the *New Yorker* cites Richard A. Clarke—former US National Coordinator for Counterterrorism in the White House—confirming that about 10 weeks before 9/11, the US intelligence community was convinced that an al-Qaeda terrorist attack on US soil was imminent. Seven to eight weeks prior to 9/11—coinciding with the second ECHELON warning cited above—Clarke issued an urgent warning to all internal US security agencies. "Meanwhile, intelligence had been streaming in concerning a likely Al Qaeda attack," reported the *New Yorker*. "'It all came together in the third week in June,' Clarke said. 'The CIA's view was that a major terrorist attack was coming in the next several weeks.'" Then on July 5, just as an all-source intelligence briefing warned the government of a spectacular imminent attack, "Clarke summoned all the domestic security agencies—the Federal Aviation Administration, the Coast Guard, Customs, the Immigration and Naturalization Service, and the FBI—and told them to increase their security in light of an impending attack."[44] According to the *Washington Post*, on the same day Clarke stated that "something really spectacular is going to happen here, and it's going to happen soon."[45] Indeed, Clarke's Counterterrorism Security Group "issued no fewer than five separate Federal Aviation Administration (FAA) Information Circulars to alert private air carriers to various potential terrorist threats" in the months leading up to the September 11 attacks, on June 22, July 2, July 18, July 31, and August 16.[46]

Therefore, the intelligence community fully anticipated an impending attack by al-Qaeda by the beginning of July 2001, and knew that "terrorists were planning to hijack commercial aircraft to use as weapons to attack important symbols of American... culture." Among the buildings identified by al-Qaeda as "symbolic of American culture" were the World Trade Center, the Pentagon, and the White House. Out of these, the World Trade Center was a foremost priority for al-Qaeda, which had vowed to coordinate a successful attack on the Twin Towers.

Warnings of the impending attack continued to be received thereafter. Approximately four weeks prior to 9/11, the CIA received specific information of an attack on US soil. The Associated Press reports that: "Officials also said the CIA had developed general information a month before the attacks that heightened concerns that bin Laden and his followers were increasingly determined to strike on US soil." A CIA official affirmed that: "There was something specific in early August that said to us that he was determined in striking on US soil." AP elaborates "The information prompted the CIA to issue a warning to federal agencies."[47] In hindsight, it's clear that this report concerns the August 6, 2001, Presidential Daily Brief, discussed in the next section.

Collating the above data, it is apparent that six months prior to 9/11—May 2001—the US intelligence community was alerted to al-Qaeda's intention to conduct a terrorist attack from the air against symbolic US buildings, as in Project Bojinka. That information was "taken seriously" by the community, and subsequently reconfirmed three months prior to the attacks—June/July 2001. The intelligence community acted upon this information each time by intensifying surveillance.

By early July 2001, the credible information "streaming in" continued to confirm an impending domestic attack, and prompted the White House

National Coordinator for Counterterrorism to issue an urgent alert to all federal domestic security agencies. By early August 2001, further confirmation that al-Qaeda was about to implement the attacks was received.

FBI Whistleblower: Randy Glass and the World Trade Center

Randy Glass, a con artist convicted of 13 felonies, was due a 20-month prison sentence before the government offered him the chance to reduce his prison time by working as an undercover informant for the FBI. Despite his undoubtedly shady criminal past, Glass swiftly proved himself to be an extraordinarily capable and credible government agent. According to Glass' prosecutor, assistant US Attorney Neil Karadbil, Glass

- Provided information for the FBI, the ATF, the Secret Service, Florida Department of Law Enforcement, and the Palm Beach County Sheriff's Office.
- Helped recover a 30-plus carat diamond stolen in the armed robbery of $2.5 million in jewels from a Palm Beach jewelry store. The FBI was then able to arrest the robbers and their fence.
- Worked with the New York City FBI regarding forged Picasso and Reubens paintings and the recovery of two burial masks, said to be more than 30 centuries old, stolen from Egyptian museums.
- Helped the Secret Service expose a counterfeit operation of fake $100 bills supplied through Guyana

But Glass was also involved with operations relevant to US national security and was a member of an FBI terrorism task force. "He has met with individuals in Pakistan, Egypt, Lebanon, Syria, Republic of Congo, in South America and West Africa, as well," Karadbil told a judge on May 19, 2000. "The individuals that Mr. Glass has dealt with are essentially terrorists. They are without question dangerous individuals."[48]

In late 1998, Glass was deployed as an informant in a government sting operation in which Pakistani government agents attempted to buy missiles and nuclear weapons components for use by terrorists, namely Osama bin Laden and al-Qaeda. Glass led federal agents to Diaa Mohsen. "Wired for sound by agents, Glass listened as Mohsen said he knew people eager to buy US weapons, including officials of a government and 'terrorists' who would pay in heroin." Mohsen also introduced Glass to his friend "Mohammed 'Mike' Malik,... Mohsen said Malik, in turn, could connect them to the ultimate buyers, who Mohsen identified as 'the intelligence of Pakistan' and as people close to Afghanistan's Taliban regime and al Qaeda founder Osama bin Laden."

Subsequently, Pakistani representatives of the buyers in Islamabad flew to Florida several times to negotiate the arms deal. They said that "they represented Pakistan's spy agency, the Inter-Services Intelligence (ISI). The ISI... was seeking weapons for the Pakistani military and for terrorist groups Islamabad has sponsored." As US officials confirmed, "elements of ISI and Pakistan's military worked closely with bin Laden, the Taliban."[49]

On July 14, 1999, Glass had dinner with illegal arms dealers Mohsen and Malik, former Egyptian judge Shireen Shawky, and ISI agent Rajaa Gulum Abbas, at a restaurant within view of the World Trade Center. The entire meeting was secretly recorded and filmed while FBI agents eavesdropped from neighboring tables, posing as restaurant customers. Excerpts of the filming have been aired by various US news shows, including MSNBC.[50] According to Cox News Service:

> Glass, wearing a wire, met with a man referred to in court documents as Abbas, believed to be a Pakistani government agent brought in by Malik. Glass was informed that they wanted to buy a whole shipload of weapons and they said it was for bin Laden.... Glass said, "As we leave the restaurant, Abbas turns and says, 'those towers (the World Trade Center) are coming down.'"[51]

According to Glass, this was not the only reference to an imminent al-Qaeda attack on the World Trade Center. The *Palm Beach Post* reports that "a Pakistani operative working for the Taliban known as R.G. Abbas made three references to imminent plans to attack the World Trade Center during the probe, which ended in June 2001."[52] In one meeting, as NBC records, "Diaa Mohsen, the arms broker on the left whispers across the desk to agent Stoltz. Abbas, he says, has direct connections to Osama bin Laden himself.... 'He gets in with dignitaries, bin Laden, bin Laden who blew that embassy.'"[53]

FBI informant Glass relayed the warnings of the impending al-Qaeda terrorist attack on the World Trade Center to high-level US government officials. But, he says, "The complaints were ordered sanitized by the highest levels of government." Instead of acting on the warnings and investigating further, that a Florida TV news show reported "The complaints were sealed, but Glass pointed out that his sentencing document June 15 [2001] listed threats against the World Trade Center and Americans. The towers came down three months later."[54] Glass, whose record as an intelligence informant is described by US government agents as "heroic," summarized the case as follows:

> The government knows about those involved in my case who were never charged, never deported, who actively took part in bringing terrorists into our country to meet with me and undercover agents.... They wanted to purchase sophisticated weapons systems up to and including nuclear material and radioactive isotopes to make dirty bombs to be used by terrorists to hurt Americans.[55]

Indeed, FBI agents involved in the case, including Glass himself, were perplexed at the lack of high-level government interest in pursuing such a serious investigation revealing Pakistani state-sponsorship of al-Qaeda terrorists planning on collapsing the World Trade Center and attempting to purchase nuclear weapons. According to William Wechsler—Director for Transnational Threats on the US National Security Council during the Clinton administration and head of a commission investigating bin Laden's finances—in an interview with NBC:

> Mr. WECHSLER: Any time you have an individual who is talking about getting serious weapons, getting weapons of mass destruction, especially in the United States, you have to take that exceedingly seriously. And you have to take action immediately....
>
> HANSEN: Based upon what you know about this case, did federal investigators go far enough?
>
> Mr. WECHSLER: Based on what I've been told about this case, federal investigators certainly did not go far enough. Certainly not quickly enough.[56]

The lack of action continued despite the fact noted by veteran FBI agent Stolz that Glass' contacts were "checked out by US intelligence experts and found to have real connections." Various sources confirmed to US intelligence "that Abbas and Malik did have links to weapons trafficking groups—and militant operations."[57] In other words, normal mandatory intelligence protocols entailed that immediate action was required with respect to these individuals, both in terms of their attempts to transfer weapons to al-Qaeda and in terms of their declaration of a terrorist plot on US soil. But instead, the FBI sat on it. According to the *Washington Post*:

> Some federal officials were frustrated that the FBI, while allowing a Florida agent to work on the probe, did not declare the case a counterterrorism matter. That would have given ATF officials better access to FBI information and US intelligence from around the world, and would have drawn bureaucratic backing from people all the way to the White House, officials said.
>
> "Had more attention been paid to this inside the government, the case agents in the trenches would have had more information on who these Pakistani people on US soil were," said Stoltz, who is now retired. "It would have steered us in other directions, and possibly justified continuing the investigation.... We couldn't understand why this wasn't treated as a national security matter."[58]

Noting the significance of bin Laden-affiliated ISI agent Abbas' warning of a terrorist plot to collapse the WTC, Glass asks: "Wouldn't you think that there should have been a wire tap on [Abbas' US contacts] Diaa's phone and Malik's phone?"[59] The shocking failure to tap the two al-Qaeda affiliated arms dealers was not for lack of asking. Cox News Service noted, for instance, that not only did the government refuse to support the FBI team's operation, it undermined it:

> Repeatedly, the team found itself running into a lack of support. They could not get prosecutors to approve wiretaps. A FBI supervisor in Miami for that agency's terrorist task force refused to front money for the sting, forcing federal agents to use money from US Customs and even from Glass to help keep the sting going.[60]

In summer 2001, Glass also sent the WTC warning to Senators Bob Graham (Chairman of the Senate Select Committee on Intelligence), US Representative Robert Wexler (senior Member of the House International Relations Committee), and Senator Ron Klein—Member of the Committee on Home Defense, Public Security and Ports. As a member of the US intelligence community, Senator Graham in particular would have been well aware that the information needed to be acted on. The *Palm Beach Post* noted that: "Graham acknowledged at a news conference in Boca Raton last month that Glass had contact with his office before Sept. 11, 2001, about an attack on the World Trade Center. 'I was concerned about that and a dozen other pieces of information which emanated from the summer of 2001,' the senator said."[61] In an NBC interview, both Senator Graham and Senator Klein admitted to receiving the warning from Glass before 9/11 and passing it on to an appropriate (albeit unnamed) federal intelligence agency. Relevant excerpts from the transcript of the interview are as follows:

> [KATHLEEN WALTER]: ... According to Graham spokesperson Jill Greenberg, case worker Charlie Yonts spoke with Glass last summer, prior to September 11th, Glass claiming he had at least six conversations with the case worker. And while we've been unable to corroborate the nature of those conversations, Greenberg confirms some of that information was passed along to the Senate Intelligence Committee.
>
> [REPORTER INTERVIEWING GRAHAM]: A few months before September 11th, your office received information from A.T.F. informant Randy Glass who also worked on the terrorism task force. And, he also advised your office of terrorist intentions to bring down the World Trade Center. This was before September 11th. Your office tells me it forwarded information from Mr. Glass to the Intelligence Committee. And my question is, why did no one from the Committee follow up with Mr. Glass to pursue this?

[BOB GRAHAM]: Because we in turn gave that information to the appropriate intelligence agency. Uh, we are an oversight and legislative agency. The actual operations of collection of information, interviewing possible sources, is the responsibility of the F.B.I. if it's a domestic matter or the C.I.A. if it's foreign.

[KATHLEEN WALTER]: And according to State Senator Klein, three weeks after he made the initial contact with Senator Graham's office, staffers there confirmed to him Glass's information had been passed on to the intelligence community.

[REPORTER]: So they confirmed to you that they sent it along.

[RON KLEIN]: Um hm. They said—they said to me that they had spoken, uh, they had processed it through their office, um, and um, spoken to Randy I believe is what they said and they had processed it.

[BOB GRAHAM]: I had a concern about that and a dozen other pieces of information, uh, which were emanating in the summer of 2001.

[REPORTER]: So you did forward Mr. Glass's information...

[BOB GRAHAM]: Yeah.

[REPORTER]: Along to ... to whom?

[BOB GRAHAM]: I, I cannot say what agency but the agency that we felt was the most appropriate for the nature of the information that he was providing.[62]

Graham's and Klein's statements confirmed clearly that Glass' WTC warnings had been considered credible and taken seriously by the "intelligence community," which had "processed" the data and followed it up with Glass. Later however, in a bizarre and self-contradictory turnaround, Senator Graham backtracked on these initial admissions and issued a strong statement avidly denying that he had ever had any communications from Glass prior to 9/11. The NBC transcript continues:

And since our interview with Senator Graham in Boca Raton last month his office offered this clarification. That:

"Mister Glass didn't provide any information to our office prior to Sept. 11, 2001, that needed to be pursued by intelligence agencies. When I was interviewed in Boca Raton, I said I did know of this individual and that he had been in touch with the Intelligence Committee, but I didn't indicate when that contact had taken place. It was earlier this year, not prior to Sept. 11, 2001."

[KATHLEEN WALTER]: Even though Graham's press aide Jill Greenberg and State Senator Klein says Glass's information did go before the intelligence community prior to September 11th, 2001, the senator still maintains that's not the case, even though that's what he initially told us.[63]

There can be little doubt, given the credible testimony of four individuals—Senator Klein, two of Senator Graham's own staffers, and Senator Graham himself—that Graham's subsequent denial of his own lucid and detailed admission is false, indeed, a deliberate attempt to mislead the public. The question, of course, is why the Senator would be dishonest about the Glass warning. A plausible answer is that this was a highly embarrassing and potentially damaging admission for the US government. Randy Glass may have been a con man in his past, but he is nevertheless recognized universally by federal officials as a highly capable, professional, and credible government agent—moreover court records reveal that he has a documented track record of success in this capacity because his warnings and findings as an informer were routinely taken seriously by authorities and acted on to arrest and prosecute several major criminal cases.

Moreover, the Glass warning of an imminent plot to collapse the World Trade Center was derived reliably from a source known by the FBI to be an ISI agent connected to al-Qaeda, and documented by the FBI in the form of both official reports and audiovisual recordings. That credible warning, emerging from a significant FBI undercover sting operation, was passed on to the US intelligence community though a relevant federal agency via Graham, Klein, and the Select Intelligence Committee. Thus, Glass' warning was certainly received by the US intelligence community about three months prior to 9/11. Furthermore, Graham and the Select Intelligence Committee—the body with powerful oversight powers over the US intelligence community—clearly took this warning very seriously. Neither Graham himself nor the intelligence community's very own oversight body would have relayed the Glass warning on if they had believed it to be without credibility. Moreover, according to Graham, the Glass warning was only one of a dozen similar warnings in summer 2001 known to him, about which he had very real "concern." Additionally, according to Klein, the data was "processed" and followed up on. In other words, contrary to the government's repeated denials that they never had any precise warning of the 9/11 plot, Senator Graham's televised admission indicates that the intelligence community received the Glass warning prior to 9/11, and believed it to be credible. In the months prior to 9/11 then, the US intelligence community had received credible advanced warning that the World Trade

Center was to be the predominant target of an impending al-Qaeda attack.

But the US government response was shocking. Rather than acting on this information by pursuing the relevant suspects connected to Glass' operation, the government simply canceled the entire operation: "Despite that information, available to the government two years before the World Trade Center attack, the FBI's terrorism task force didn't appear to take the threat seriously, Glass said."[64] The apparent attempt to conceal the facts surrounding this case did not end there. Mohsen and Malik were arrested by US authorities and faced "two counts of trying to illegally export military weaponry. Mohsen also faces additional money-laundering charges."[65] However, in the words of NBC correspondent Hansen, "After 9/11, both men pled guilty to violating arms laws. But remarkably, even though they were apparently willing to supply America's enemies"—including, by their own recorded admission, al-Qaeda and Osama bin Laden—"with sophisticated weapons, even nuclear weapons technology, Mohsen was sentenced to just 30 months in prison. And Malik? Mysteriously, his sentence remains under seal. And he appears to be a free man, as we saw recently when we visited him at his New Jersey convenience store."[66] While Malik's court files remain sealed, prosecutors "removed references to Pakistan" from Mohsen's court files "because of diplomatic concerns."[67] Furthermore, in June 2002, ISI–al-Qaeda operatives Abbas and Malik were secretly indicted. "The latest indictment," notes the *Palm Beach Post*, "makes no reference to where the weapons were heading, stating only that Abbas and Abdul Malik were exporting the arms to 'a foreign country'"—the indictment thus successfully bypassed the inevitable terrorism charges entailed in the recognition that Abbas and Malik intended the arms to be "funneled to Osama bin Laden and used against American targets." Despite the indictment, no mention of Abbas' connection to 9/11 has been made, nor has any effort been made to extradite him.[68]

In other words, federal officials were actively attempting to conceal the facts of the Glass case from public consumption, simultaneously allowing key operatives connected to al-Qaeda to now conduct their dealings freely on US soil. Why would the government wish to conceal the fact that these individuals were terrorist operatives actively involved in the financial and military support of al-Qaeda, thus protecting them from appropriate counterterrorist sanctions, although they had clearly been linked to the 9/11 plot and were the source of a precise advanced warning that the World Trade Center was soon to be attacked?

The Presidential Daily Brief

Curiously, for years the White House refused to publicly release the CIA briefing, "Bin Laden determined to strike in the US," that had been handed to the president at his Texas ranch on August 6, 2001. That brief had been prepared at President Bush's request after he was notified of credible warnings of "an impending attack in the summer of 2001." Bush was reportedly concerned about "domestic targets."[69] Both the July "threat assessment" and the August briefing requested by Bush in response to that assessment remained classified at the insistence of the White House. According to Daniel Schorr, senior news analyst at National Public Radio: "Vice President Dick Cheney said the CIA paper was just a 'rehash,' containing nothing new. But as to why Congress should not see it, Mr. Cheney said, 'Because it contains the most sensitive sources and methods. It's the family jewels.' A rehash is the family jewels?"[70]

Prior to the September 11 attacks, CIA Director George Tenet delivered to President Bush an oral briefing for about half an hour almost every morning at 8:00 AM.[71] According to the *Washington Post*, the President's Daily Briefing (PDB) "is prepared at Langley by the CIA's analytical directorate, and a draft goes home with Tenet each night. Tenet edits it personally and delivers it orally during his early morning meeting with Bush."[72] It is noteworthy that such CIA oral briefings are quite unprecedented—previous presidents received only a written briefing. According to the *Post*, a consequence of this unprecedented procedure was a very close relationship between the President and the head of the CIA: "With Bush, who liked oral briefings and the CIA director in attendance, a strong relationship had developed. Tenet could be direct, even irreverent and earthy."[73]

Under pressure from certain members of the 9/11 Commission, the White House was forced to declassify the August 6 Presidential Daily Brief. As the *New York Times* noted: "In a single 17-sentence document, the intelligence briefing delivered to President Bush in August 2001 spells out the who, hints at the what and points toward the where of the terrorist attacks on New York and Washington that followed 36 days later."[74]

Despite the brief's partial declassification, few commentators have taken note of its extremely damaging implications. Relevant excerpts from the brief are as follows:

> Clandestine, foreign government, and media reports indicate Bin Ladin since 1997 has wanted to conduct terrorist attacks in the US. Bin Ladin implied in US television interviews in 1997 and 1998 that his followers would follow the example of World Trade Center bomber Ramzi Yousef and "bring the fighting to America."
>
> After US missile strikes on his base in Afghanistan in 1998, Bin Ladin told followers he wanted to retaliate in Washington, according to a ...(redacted portion) ... service.
>
> An Egyptian Islamic Jihad (EIJ) operative told an ... (redacted portion) ... service at the same time that Bin Ladin was planning to exploit the operative's access to the US to mount a terrorist strike.
>
> ... Al-Qa'ida members—including some who are US citizens—have resided in or traveled to the US for years, and the group apparently

maintains a support structure that could aid attacks.... A clandestine source said in 1998 that a Bin Ladin cell in New York was recruiting Muslim-American youth for attacks.

... FBI information since that time indicates patterns of suspicious activity in this country consistent with preparations for hijackings or other types of attacks, including recent surveillance of federal buildings in New York.

The FBI is conducting approximately 70 full field investigations throughout the US that it considers Bin Ladin-related.[75]

A simple examination of the brief reveals the following critical facts: The US intelligence community and the President were fully aware that firstly, al-Qaeda was deeply active inside the United States and planning attacks, so much so that the FBI had about *70 ongoing investigations* in al-Qaeda operations *in the US alone*; secondly, al-Qaeda had a powerful support structure engaging vigorously in preparations to carry out *hijackings*; thirdly, Osama bin Laden was particularly keen to carry out attacks on *key targets in Washington, DC and New York*, such that US intelligence was aware of al-Qaeda surveillance of various *federal buildings in New York*; fourthly, bin Laden was particularly keen to *follow the example of Ramzi Yousef*, the mastermind of the 1993 *World Trade Center* bombing. The brief, in other words, outlined in a few paragraphs the entire 9/11 plot—only one perpetrator was mentioned, al-Qaeda; only two areas in the US were indicated, Washington, DC and New York; only one method was indicated, hijacking; and only one key building was referred to as a potential target, the World Trade Center. In other words, al-Qaeda terrorists were planning to hijack aircraft on US soil and target key US buildings in Washington, DC and New York, particularly the World Trade Center—even at face value, an unambiguous depiction of the Bojinka scheme to hurl hijacked civilian planes into key US buildings. In context with the crescendo of other warnings—both over the years and in 2001 alone—referring specifically to an "airplanes as weapons" scenario, it is difficult to avoid the conclusion that the government did indeed have a fairly precise understanding of what al-Qaeda was about to do.

If this is only a sample of a single simplified intelligence briefing given to the President on one day, we may legitimately ponder what is contained in the classified portion of the brief, what is elaborated on in numerous other CIA Presidential Briefs, and indeed what other specific details were available to the intelligence community as such, which was conducting at least 70 investigations into al-Qaeda operations in the US. The significance of this question is heightened in light of the ongoing refusal of the Bush administration to release information on intelligence assessments provided to the President and the White House. UPI reported that: "The administration has denied lawmakers investigating the Sept. 11 attacks permission to reveal whether the president or other White House staff received warning of potential terrorist attacks against the United States, including plans by al Qaida linked terrorists to use hijacked planes as weapons."[76] Eleanor Hill, Director of the Joint Inquiry Staff into the 9/11 intelligence failure, noted in an official statement before the Chairmen of the Inquiry:

> Over the last two months, we have been working with the Intelligence Community in a long and arduous process to declassify information we believe is important to the public's understanding... By late last night, we were able to resolve all but two issues... The Director of Central Intelligence has declined to declassify two issues of particular importance to this Inquiry:
> Any references to the Intelligence Community providing information to the President or White House; and
> The identity of and information on a key al-Qa'ida leader involved in the September 11 attacks.
> According to the DCI, the President's knowledge of intelligence information relevant to this Inquiry remains classified even when the substance of that intelligence information has been declassified....
> The Joint Inquiry Staff disagrees with the DCI's position... We believe the American public has a compelling interest in this information and that public disclosure would not harm national security.[77]

The administration's staunch refusal to declassify information related to what the White House knew about the 9/11 plot is an indication of the fact that the US political establishment certainly had received more advanced warning of the attacks than officially admitted. Indeed, according to the findings of the Joint Congressional Inquiry: "The US government had received repeated warnings of impending attacks—and attacks using planes directed at New York and Washington—for several years.... The report lists 36 different summaries of warnings dating back to 1997." So compelling were these findings that John Dean, former White House counsel to President Nixon, observed: "In sum, the 9-11 Report of the Congressional Inquiry indicates that the intelligence community was very aware that Bin Laden might fly an airplane into an American skyscraper."[78] In that context, the implications of the August 6 brief are absolutely clear and disturbingly precise. And the question remains as to what else was known through other briefs that the Bush administration refused to declassify. None of the official inquiries have dared press this question any further.

Foreign Government Warnings
Against the background of multiple warnings of an impending attack by al-Qaeda, numerous urgent alerts from foreign governments and allies of the United States streamed in, reinforcing the incoming danger. These reports

discussed various dimensions of the plot, some highlighting "airplanes as weapons," some highlighting general or particular targets on US soil, some providing insight into a probable date, many of them discussing all of these, and all of them confirming an imminent al-Qaeda attack. The convergence of these warnings, against the background of escalating alerts on an imminent Bojinka operation, provided a clear and urgent picture of what was to happen.

As *USA Today* observed: "The Bush administration received what Secretary of State Colin Powell describes as a 'lot of signs' throughout the summer that terrorists were plotting US attacks. Among them: al-Qa'eda mentions of an impending 'Hiroshima' on US soil."[79] The truth is that at no time in the history of the United States had the government received so many urgent credible warnings of a terrorist attack within the country in such a short space of time.

According to the London *Telegraph*, for instance, Israeli intelligence services provided detailed advanced warning of an imminent al-Qaeda attack:

> Israeli intelligence officials say that they warned their counterparts in the United States last month [August 2001] that large-scale terrorist attacks on highly visible targets on the American mainland were imminent.... The Telegraph has learnt that two senior experts with Mossad, the Israeli military intelligence service, were sent to Washington in August to alert the CIA and FBI to the existence of a cell of as many of 200 terrorists said to be preparing a big operation... [They] linked the plot to Osama bin Laden.[80]

Russian President Vladimir Putin informed interviewers on MSNBC that the Russian government had warned the US of imminent attacks on airports and government buildings in the strongest possible terms for several weeks prior to the September 11 attacks. "I ordered my intelligence to warn President Bush in the strongest terms that 25 terrorists were getting ready to attack the US, including important government buildings like the Pentagon," said Putin. "Washington's reaction at the time really amazed me. They shrugged their shoulders and said matter-of-factly: 'We can't do anything because the Taliban does not want to turn him over.'"[81] Notably, Putin reveals that the US did not reject the warnings due to lack of credibility—rather they claimed that nothing could be done in response to them. But the information was extraordinarily precise. According to the Russian press, Russia had warned of the hijacking of civilian airliners to be used as missiles against key US buildings and confirmed that 25 pilots had been trained for the suicide mission. The Russian *Izvestia* reported that: "Russian Intelligence agents know the organizers and executors of these terrorist attacks. More than that, Moscow warned Washington about preparation to these actions a couple of weeks before they happened."[82] According to the head of Russian intelligence, "We had clearly warned them [i.e. the Americans]" on several occasions about imminent attacks on US soil.[83]

Other credible warnings came from British intelligence. According to the London *Times*

> MI6 warned the American intelligence services about a plot to hijack aircraft and crash them into buildings two years before the September 11 attacks...
>
> Liaison staff at the American embassy in Grosvenor Square in London were passed a secret report by MI6 in 1999 after the intelligence service picked up indications from human intelligence sources (Humint) that Osama Bin Laden's followers were planning attacks in which civilian aircraft could be used in "unconventional ways"....
>
> MI6 had information as early as 1998 that Al-Qaeda was plotting fresh attacks. A series of warnings was passed to Washington, some concerning threats to American interests in Europe, including the US embassy in Paris. One message detailed heightened activity by suspected Al-Qaeda terror cells. "The Americans knew of plans to use commercial aircraft in unconventional ways, possibly as flying bombs," said a senior Foreign Office source.[84]

The *Times* also noted that US intelligence received urgent warnings from their British counterparts that al-Qaeda was planning to attack US targets two months prior to 9/11

> Britain's spy chiefs warned the Prime Minister less than two months before September 11 that Osama bin Laden's al-Qaeda group was in 'the final stages' of preparing a terrorist attack in the West...
>
> The heads of MI6, MI5 and GCHQ, the signals eavesdropping centre, suggested that while the most likely targets were American or Israeli, there could be British casualties. Their warning was included in a report sent to Tony Blair and other senior Cabinet Ministers on July 16....
>
> The July 16 warning to ministers was included in the weekly precis of intelligence assessments made by the Cabinet Office Joint Intelligence Committee (JIC), on which the heads of the intelligence agencies sit. The JIC prediction of an al-Qaeda attack was based on intelligence gleaned not just from MI6 and GCHQ but also from US agencies, including the CIA and the National Security Agency, which has staff working jointly with GCHQ....
>
> The contents of the July 16 warning would have been passed to the Americans, Whitehall sources confirmed.... However, the July 2001 JIC assessment, warning that "organised attacks were in their final stages of preparation," predicted that "UK interests were at risk, including from collateral damage in attacks on US targets." Seventy-eight Britons died in the attack on the World Trade Centre.[85]

French intelligence also issued urgent warnings to their US counterparts of an impending attack, days before 9/11. The respected French daily *Le Figaro* reported that:

According to Arab diplomatic sources as well as French intelligence, very specific information was transmitted to the CIA with respect to terrorist attacks against American interests around the world, including on US soil. A DST [French intelligence] report dated 7 September enumerates all the intelligence, and specifies that the order to attack was to come from Afghanistan.[86]

According to the London *Independent*, the US government "was warned repeatedly that a devastating attack on the United States was on its way" in a late August interview given by Osama bin Laden to a London-based Arabic-language newspaper, *al-Quds al-Arabi*, warning of a planned attack. At about the same time, tighter security measures were ordered at the World Trade Center, for unexplained reasons.[87] Indeed, three days after the terrorist attacks, Senator Dianne Feinstein pointed out that: "Bin Laden's people had made statements three weeks ago carried in the Arab press in Great Britain that they were preparing to carry out unprecedented attacks in the US."[88]

The Bush administration also received urgent credible alerts from two Arab allies, Jordan and Morocco, just weeks before the September 11 attacks. Former ABC News correspondent John K. Cooley reports in connection to the Jordan warning, mentioning the exemplary record of that country's intelligence services in tracking al-Qaeda, that the kingdom's "well-organized and efficient intelligence service, called the GID (General Intelligence Division), reporting directly to the king, carefully tracked CIA- and Pakistani-trained Arab guerrillas both in and outside of Jordan" since the early 1990s. Jordan's GID captured some of these guerrillas who had become active terrorists, and kept a watch on those who did not. In doing so, Jordanian intelligence "aided the United States government in countless ways." The GID cooperated with the US to foil "multiple attacks on Jordanian tourist sites planned for New Year's Eve 1999. It helped US law enforcement apprehend Al Qaeda and other operatives who had reached the US or Canada and had formed active or 'sleeper' cells there." The GID was thus a crucial and highly reliable US ally in the pre-9/11 war on terror. Cooly continues:

> Sometime in the late summer of 2001, GID headquarters in Jordan intercepted a crucial Al Qaeda communication. This probably took place after the July 5 warning by a Phoenix, AZ, FBI agent that Arab terrorists could be sending men to flight schools, and either before or shortly after Aug. 6, when President Bush received a CIA briefing about possible hijackings.
>
> The intercept's content was deemed so important that Jordanian King Abdallah's men relayed it to Washington, probably through the CIA station at the US Embassy in Amman. To be sure that the message got through, it was also passed to a German intelligence agent who was visiting Amman at the time.

The message showed clearly that a major attack was planned inside the continental US. It said aircraft would be used.... When it became clear that the information about the intercept was embarrassing to the Bush administration and to congressmen who at first denied there had been any advance warnings of 9/11, senior Jordan officials backed off their earlier confirmations.

Cooley also refers to yet another urgent and credible warning from Moroccan intelligence, based on reports in "a French magazine and a Moroccan newspaper," citing French and Moroccan intelligence sources. "A Moroccan secret agent named Hassan Dabou had infiltrated Al Qaeda. Several weeks before Sept. 11," Dabou informed his supervisors in King Muhammed VI's royal intelligence service that "Mr. bin Laden's men were preparing 'large-scale operations in New York in the summer or autumn of 2001.'" The warning was "passed from the Moroccan capital of Rabat to Washington." Dabou reported that "bin Laden was 'very disappointed' by the failure of the 1993 bombing of the World Trade Center to topple the towers."[89]

The US also received an authoritative warning from Egyptian intelligence. According to the Associated Press, the warning was passed on personally by Egyptian president Hosni Mubarak, a close US ally and friend of the Bush family, who "says he warned the United States that 'something would happen' 12 days before the Sept. 11 terror attacks on New York and Washington.... 'We expected that something was going to happen and informed the Americans. We told them,' Mubarak said. He did not mention a US response."[90] It should be noted that the Egyptian president was also among several other sources that had previously warned the US of the danger of a hijacked airplane filled with explosives crashing into the conference buildings at the G-8 conference in Genoa, Italy (July 20-22, 2001). In response, the Italian authorities deployed anti-aircraft guns around the site and banned local flights—meanwhile President Bush confined himself to a US Navy warship in the harbor due to these security concerns.

Another credible warning came from Garth L. Nicolson, chief scientific officer and research professor at the Institute for Molecular Medicine in Huntington Beach, California. Nicolson has been called to testify as an expert before the US Senate in relation to Department of Defense investigations of Gulf War chemical and biological incidents[91]—so his credibility is verified by the government. Professor Nicolson issued the following statement to this author:

My wife, Dr. Nancy Nicolson, and I received at least three warnings of the attack on the Pentagon on Sept. 11, 2001. The nature of these warnings (the specific site, date and source) indicated to us that they were credible. We have many contacts in the retired intelligence community, including Special Forces, and domestic and foreign intelligence services. Mostly these were individuals that we assisted with their health problems from the Gulf War, Vietnam or other conflicts.

The most dramatic source was a Head of State of a North African country. This occurred during a visit to Tunisia in July 2001. This head of state was travelling under cover and met with us at our hotel. He warned us as to the correct date and one of the targets, the Pentagon. We were not given any information as to the method or any other targets.

The information was passed on to the Director of Policy, DoD [Department of Defense], the National Security Council, the leadership in the House of Representatives and the Inspector General of the US Army Medical Corps, who happened to be visiting us a month or so before Sept. 11.

To our knowledge no action was ever taken on this information. There has been some mention in the press that others also warned the US Government that on Sept. 11, 2001 there would be a terrorist attack on US soil. I do not know if any of the information from our sources or other sources was ever taken seriously by the National Security Council.[92]

Yet another warning from multiple intelligence agencies just before 9/11 put the US intelligence community on alert for an impending attack. The *New York Times* reported:

One intercept [of bin Laden's communications] before the Sept. 11 attack was, according to two senior intelligence officials, the first early warning of the assault and it set off a scramble by American and other intelligence agencies.... That message, which was intercepted by the intelligence services of more than one country, was passed on to the United States, officials from three countries said. "... [W]e assumed it would be soon," a senior intelligence official said.[93]

On September 7, 2001, the State Department issued a worldwide alert warning that "American citizens may be the target of a terrorist threat from extremist groups with links to [Osama bin Laden's] al-Qaeda organization." According to ABC News, the "report cited information gathered in May that suggested an attack somewhere was imminent."[94] These reports indicate without doubt that the US intelligence community was on alert for an imminent al-Qaeda attack literally days before 9/11.

Just before the attacks, US intelligence intercepted information from Osama bin Laden himself that something "big" would happen on September 11. NBC News reported on October 4 that Osama bin Laden had phoned his mother two days before the World Trade Center attacks and told her: "In two days you're going to hear big news, and you're not going to hear from me for a while." According to NBC, a foreign intelligence service had recorded the call and relayed the information to US intelligence.[95]

MI6 and CIA Pinpoint 9/11

After 9/11, one of the frequently touted explanations for why the intelligence community failed to anticipate the attacks was that since 1998 Osama bin Laden and al-Qaeda had consistently avoided the use of all electronic communications in order to escape US technological eavesdropping capabilities. The National Security Agency uses the ECHELON international satellite surveillance system to monitor electronic communications around the world, including "over the Internet and of databases, faxes, phone calls and e-mails connected with it" as well as "money transfers, airline destinations, stock information, data on demonstrations or international conferences" and much more.

ECHELON's effectiveness against bin Laden's network was further revealed in relation to a case against him in a US District Court in Manhattan, illustrating that the National Security Agency was able to penetrate bin Laden's most secure communications. "The US case unfolding against him in United States District Court in Manhattan is based mainly on National Security Agency intercepts of phone calls between bin Laden and his operatives around the world—Afghanistan to London, from Kenya to the United States."

Bin Laden has attempted to use encryption technology to counter ECHELON surveillance of his electronic communications since at least 1995— but to no avail:

> Since 1995, bin Laden has tried to protect his communications with a "full suite of tools," according to Ben Venzke, director of intelligence, special projects, for iDefense, a Virginia information warfare firm.... Since Bin Laden started to encrypt certain calls in 1995, why would they now be part of a court record? "Codes were broken," US officials said, and Venzke added that you don't use your highest level of secure communications all the time. "It's too burdensome, and it exposes it to other types of exploitation."

The UPI report clarifies that much of the evidence in the case had been obtained in ECHELON intercepts subsequent to the 1998 bombings of US embassies in East Africa.[96] For instance, the NSA had recorded almost every minute of conversations on a satellite telephone Osama bin Laden was using in Afghanistan. Bin Laden had used all of its more than 2,000 prepaid minutes phoning supporters in dozens of countries.[97] Given that US officials "believe the planning for the Sept. 11 attacks probably began two years" before they occurred, detailed information on preparations for the attacks should have been available to, and picked up by, ECHELON.[98]

But some officials insist that access was blocked in 1998, with al-Qaeda ceasing the use of electronic communications entirely. According to the *Baltimore Sun*, citing US officials: "Since the East Africa bombings, however, the NSA has had far less success in picking up bin Laden's communications, according to people knowledgeable about US intelligence." US interception capability of al-Qaeda "has narrowed considerably since 1998, though it might not have closed completely."[99]

That claim, however, appears to be disinformation designed to absolve US intelligence of failing to thwart the 9/11 plot. Confirmation that US intelligence had been successfully monitoring ongoing electronic al-Qaeda communications by al-Qaeda operatives right through to the aftermath of 9/11 came from Utah Senator Orrin Hatch, a conservative Republican with wide contacts in the national security establishment. On the day of the attacks, Hatch stated that the government had been monitoring al-Qaeda's communications electronically, and had thus intercepted two bin Laden aides celebrating the attacks: "They have an intercept of some information that included people associated with bin Laden who acknowledged a couple of targets were hit."[100]

In an interview with ABC News the same day, Hatch elaborated that his information originated from CIA and FBI officials. The US government was clearly unhappy with the revelation. In response, US Defense Secretary Donald Rumsfeld angrily denounced the report as an unauthorized release of classified information. The White House later cited the leak as good reason to withhold information concerning US counterterrorist actions from Congress. ABC News further reported that shortly before 9/11, the US National Security Agency intercepted "multiple phone calls from Abu Zubaida, bin Laden's chief of operations, to the United States." The information contained in these intercepted phone calls has not been disclosed.[101] Indeed, according to USA Today, recently released CIA documents reveal the existence of "Electronic intercepts as late as Sept. 10 of al-Qaeda members speaking cryptically of a major attack. Two US intelligence officials, paraphrasing highly classified intercepts, say they include such remarks as, 'Good things are coming,' 'Watch the news' and 'Tomorrow will be a great day for us.'"[102]

The NSA had also recorded "September 10 intercepts" of other "conversations in Arabic between individuals in Afghanistan and Saudi Arabia that US officials believe were connected to al Qaeda.... Congressional and other sources said that in one communication intercepted by the NSA, a person said, 'The match begins tomorrow.' In another intercept that same day, a different person said, 'Tomorrow is zero hour.'"[103] These leaks also greatly angered the Bush administration. According to White House sources, President Bush had "deep concerns" about the public release of this "alarmingly specific" information.[104]

The official explanation of the failure to act on such revealing intercepts is the notion that they were never translated in time, due to the lack of qualified analysts. No specific evidence for this claim has been presented, while reports indicate that US intelligence had successfully established over several years a routine round-the-clock system of monitoring bin Laden's and al-Qaeda's communications and activities. Indeed, that explanation does not square with the fact that intercepts "are sent immediately to the headquarters of the listening organization—in the NSA's case, the vast complex of buildings and computers at Fort Meade that houses 20,000 employees."[105] Additionally, according to James W. Harris, former head of the CIA's Strategic Assessment Group, "the task of intercepting electronic information from overseas sources was generally the purview of the National Security Agency. The CIA would certainly be given access to the intercepts, Harris said, as would the counterterrorism unit of the FBI."[106]

The available evidence also indicates that the NSA did, indeed, have qualified translators available to process the intercepted communications and disseminate them to other agencies such as the CIA and FBI. Senator Orrin Hatch's report of a celebration of the attack by bin Laden's aides, based on an intercept on the very day of 9/11, is a specific instance demonstrating this capability. That information—picked up by the NSA, which was clearly monitoring al-Qaeda's electronic communications extensively—was immediately translated, disseminated to the CIA, FBI, and probably other relevant agencies, which then informed Senator Hatch, who released the data to the public on the same day. If the NSA were suffering from structural, bureaucratic, and logistical deficiencies, such as lack of translators and so on, such rapid communication would never have been possible. Evidently, the NSA easily had the capabilities to intercept, translate, and disseminate information to the intelligence community *in a matter of hours*. And indeed, in the months and weeks prior to 9/11, the intelligence community was evidently on high alert for an impending al-Qaeda attack.

Indeed, the evidence cited by the British government to demonstrate bin Laden's guilt is in fact based directly on intercepts of electronic communications pertaining to al-Qaeda planners, including bin Laden himself—indicating that British intelligence had the terrorist plotters behind 9/11 under extensive surveillance before 9/11. The *Sunday Times* cites "an informed Whitehall source" revealing that among the proof of al-Qaeda's planning of the attacks collected before 9/11 "were intercepted exchanges between Bin Laden and his lieutenants, made shortly before September 11…

> Two are of overriding significance. In one exchange, Bin Laden is said to have contacted an associate thought to be in Pakistan. The conversation referred to an incident that would take place in America on, or around, September 11 and discussed possible repercussions. In a separate instance Bin Laden contacted another associate, thought to have been in Afghanistan. They discussed the scale and effect of a forthcoming operation; Bin Laden praised his colleague for his part in the planning.

Importantly, this information was not collected directly. Elements of the evidence "were obtained not by British or US intelligence, but by a Middle

Eastern country whose identity is not revealed for security reasons." That country's intelligence services passed on the information to both the CIA and MI6. Sources "at both MI6 and the CIA independently revealed to The *Sunday Times* that 'technical intelligence'—believed to be intercepted telephone conversations and electronic bank transfers" implicated one of bin Laden's top military planners in the 9/11 attacks.[107]

The British government has refused to make the intercepts public on the pretext of protecting sources and methods from being compromised. This, however, was the same dubious reason cited by the US government for failing to declassify the August 6 Presidential Daily Brief—when it was finally partially declassified under intense public pressure, it was demonstrated that declassification of even sensitive memos was easily achievable by erasing the said sources and methods from the declassified text. As with that brief, it seems that the British government recognizes that revealing the full extent of information available to Western intelligence agencies prior to 9/11 through electronic surveillance would also highlight the degree to which those agencies were privy to al-Qaeda's 9/11 planning but failed to act accordingly. In a statement before the House of Commons, British Prime Minister Tony Blair referred to a British intelligence dossier based on telephone intercepts and other sources showing that:

> Shortly before the September 11 bin Laden told associates that he had a major operation against America under preparation, a range of people were warned to return back to Afghanistan because of action on or around September 11, and, most importantly, one of bin Laden's closest lieutenants has said clearly that he helped with the planning of the September 11 attacks and admitted the involvement of the al Qaida organisation.[108]

According to *Time* magazine: "The British document... also reveals that orders were sent to a number of the network's key operatives to return to Afghanistan by September 10."[109] Officials have incoherently claimed that this information was only gleaned after 9/11—but clearly, the evidence cited by British authorities as evidence of bin Laden's guilt is based on intensive round-the-clock surveillance by a network of Western and allied intelligence services prior to 9/11, not only of Osama bin Laden himself, but of the principal planners of the 9/11 attacks. As already documented, al-Qaeda communications were monitored extensively by US intelligence agencies all the way through the 9/11 attacks—and even afterwards.

For example, 350,000 pages of documents turned over by the CIA to US investigators working with the Joint Congressional Inquiry into 9/11 reveal that "US intelligence overheard al-Qaeda operatives discussing a major pending terrorist attack in the weeks prior to Sept. 11 and had agents inside the terror group." The agents and electronic intercepts discovered crucial data leading them to transcribe "[r]eports discussing the possibility of suicide bombings, plots to fly planes into buildings and strikes against the Pentagon, World Trade Center and other high-profile targets" well in advance of the attacks. On September 10, 2001, the same US intelligence officers intercepted al-Qaeda members speaking of a major attack with the words, "Tomorrow will be a great day for us," among others.[110] According to *Newsweek*, shortly before 9/11, the FBI interceptedsimilar communications from al-Qaeda associates of the hijackers: "There is a big thing coming," "They're going to pay the price," "We're ready to go."[111]

This demonstrates again not only that the CIA received exact advanced warning of the most likely date of the impending attack, but also that they had intercepted credible information from al-Qaeda sources involved in the planning for the operation indicating the method would follow the Bojinka scheme. Intercepts and information gleaned by undercover US intelligence officers specifically mentioned flying planes into key buildings, including the World Trade Center and the Pentagon. Overall then, this pre-9/11 monitoring of the key al-Qaeda plotters behind the 9/11 attacks by Western intelligence agencies disclosed information specifying that a terrorist attack on US soil was being prepared for on or around September 11, 2001. Despite this precise indication of the date of an impending attack—as well as its method and targets—the security services failed to act.

9/11 Warnings: Heeded, Not Ignored

Indeed, there is evidence that the threat was not ignored, at least not in certain selected respects. There have been several alarming accounts of activities that indicate the government officials' precise foreknowledge of an unprecedented crisis on September 11, 2001. As veteran journalist Randalph Holnut observed in the May 2002 edition of the *Albion Monitor*:

> The G8 economic summit in Genoa, Italy, last July—which President Bush attended—featured extraordinary security, including ground-to-air missile batteries. According to a report in the the *Times of London* that month, "the Italian Defense Ministry ha(d) taken the precaution after a tip by 'a friendly foreign intelligence service' [i.e. Egypt's] that Islamic suicide bombers might try to attack the summit in a small aircraft or helicopter." During that same month, Attorney General John Ashcroft stopped taking commercial flights. CBS News reported at the time the reason Ashcroft started flying exclusively in private aircraft was because of a "threat assessment" by the FBI.[112]

Another veteran American journalist, Harley Soronson, wrote in the *San Francisco Chronicle* that "Ashcroft used to fly commercial, just as Janet Reno did.

So why, two months before Sept. 11, did he start taking chartered government planes?" Although the Justice Department cited the FBI threat assessment as reason, according to CBS News "neither the FBI nor the Justice Department... would identify what the threat was, when it was detected or who made it." Soronson comments:

> The FBI did advise Ashcroft to stay off commercial aircraft. The rest of us just had to take our chances. The FBI obviously knew something was in the wind. Why else would it have Ashcroft use a $1,600-plus per hour G-3 Gulfstream when he could have flown commercial, as he always did before, for a fraction of the cost?
>
> Ashcroft demonstrated an amazing lack of curiosity when asked if he knew anything about the threat. "Frankly, I don't," he told reporters. So our nation's chief law enforcement officer was told that flying commercial was hazardous to his health, and yet he appeared not to care what the threat was, who made it, how, or why?
>
> Note that it was the FBI that warned Ashcroft before Sept. 11. That's the same FBI now claiming it didn't "connect the dots" before Sept. 11... [I]f flying commercial posed a threat to John Ashcroft, it also posed a threat to the population at large.[113]

There were other curious developments elsewhere around the same time. A former member of the 1/118th Infantry Battalion of the South Carolina National Guard in the District of Columbia (DC) told US attorney Tom Turnipseed:

> My unit reported for drill in July 2001 and we were suddenly and unexpectedly informed that all activities planned for the next two months would be suspended in order to prepare for a mobilization exercise to be held on September 14, 2001. We worked diligently for two weekends and even came in on an unscheduled day in August to prepare for the exercise. By the end of August all we needed was a phone call, which we were told to expect, and we could hop into a fully prepared convoy with our bags and equipment packed.[114]

This account undoubtedly suggests that DC's emergency National Guard activities were inexplicably placed on hold in anticipation of a crisis that they "were told to expect" would occur mid-September 2001. This precise information was available as early as July 2001. Similar intriguing preparations were made elsewhere. As journalist William Rivers Pitt reported:

> Governor Jeb Bush of Florida signed Executive Order No. 01-261 on September 7th, 2001, renewing an order signed six months earlier that

allowed the National Guard to be called out in case of emergency. On September 11th, he used this order to command members of the National Guard into active service and essentially declared martial law in Florida.[115]

Elaborating, the *Idaho Observer* reported that:

> The governor, in his EO, delegated to, "...the Adjutant General of the state of Florida all necessary authority....to order members of the Florida National Guard into Active Service." Immediately after the second WTC tower fell, Governor Bush signed EO 01-262 to make Florida the first state to declare a state of emergency though his state did not experience any terrorist events that day.
>
> ...The text of the little reported declared state of emergency that exists in Florida leaves little doubt that the state is currently functioning under martial law. The Florida National Guard, like the national guard units in the several states, is operated under the authority of the state government.... Jeb Bush, the son of former President Bush and the brother of current President Bush, has signed an EO that will keep Florida in a perpetual state of martial law until the EO has been revoked.[116]

Why was Governor Jeb Bush preparing for the implementation of martial law due to a state of emergency just four days prior to the unprecedented emergency that constituted the 9/11 attacks? What information prompted him to act as if he was anticipating those attacks?

The plot only thickens. The *San Francisco Chronicle* reported one day after the attacks that Mayor Willie Brown received a phone call eight hours before the hijackings from what he described as his air security staff, warning him not to travel by air:

> For Mayor Willie Brown, the first signs that something was amiss came late Monday when he got a call from what he described as his airport security— a full eight hours before yesterday's string of terrorist attacks—advising him that Americans should be cautious about their air travel.... Exactly where the call came from is a bit of a mystery. The mayor would say only that it came from "my security people at the airport."[117]

San Francisco Mayor Willie Brown was booked to fly from the Bay area to New York City on the morning of 9/11.[118] It seems that certain US security authorities anticipated some sort of grave danger, and believed it to be urgent, threatening and certainly real enough to inform a US city mayor about to catch a flight to New York—but not the general public.

The London *Times* reported that the famous novelist, Salman Rushdie, received a similar warning to avoid US and Canadian airlines. According to

Rushdie's own testimony, the warning came directly from the Federal Aviation Administration (FAA). The *Times* reports:

> The author Salman Rushdie believes that US authorities knew of an imminent terrorist strike when they banned him from taking internal flights in Canada and the US only a week before the attacks. On September 3 the Federal Aviation Authority made an emergency ruling to prevent Mr. Rushdie from flying.[119]

Another news report records that "the FAA has confirmed it stepped up security levels relating to Rushdie," but "the airlines weren't willing to upgrade their security" in relation to the wider public.[120] It is public knowledge that due to the Ayatullah Khomeini's death *fatwa* against him, Rushdie is under 24-hour protection of UK Scotland Yard's Special Branch, and that all his travel plans are approved by the MI5 for domestic travel within the UK and by the MI6 for international travel. Clearly, it appears that US and British authorities anticipated an imminent threat, and believed it to be urgent, threatening, and real enough to inform Rushdie—but once again not the general public.

Another report points to the Pentagon's role. *Newsweek* reported that on September 10, 2001, the day before the attacks, "a group of top Pentagon officials suddenly canceled travel plans for the next morning, apparently because of security concerns."[121] An earlier report by *Newsweek*, published two days after the attacks, referred to the same event in more detail:

> ... the state of alert had been high during the past two weeks, and a particularly urgent warning may have been received the night before the attacks, causing some top Pentagon brass to cancel a trip. Why that same information was not available to the 266 people who died aboard the four hijacked commercial aircraft may become a hot topic on the Hill.[122]

Apparently, top officials in the US Department of Defense had known not only of an imminent threat to "security" in relation to their "travel plans," but had even anticipated its exact data—the morning of 9/11—and taken measures to protect themselves, but yet again not the general public. In other words, the US government pursued preventive emergency security measures to protect top US government officials from the threat of terrorism, based on credible intelligence warnings—but did nothing of the sort in relation to US citizens, contrary to its public responsibility. Overall, these reports strongly suggest that senior elements of the US national security apparatus had precise information on a terror threat on or around 9/11 and took it seriously enough to implement selective preventive measures. As *WorldNetDaily* editor and veteran American journalist Joseph Farah rightly observes: "Now, you're probably wondering why Willie Brown and Salman Rushdie [and senior Pentagon officials] are more important to the US government than you and me and Barbara Olson. I'm wondering the same thing...

> These selective warnings—and I have no doubt there were many more we have not yet heard about—suggest strongly that the FBI, CIA and other federal agencies had the information, knew something big was up, something that involved terrorist attacks on airliners, but failed to disclose the information to the airlines and the flying public in general. I think heads should roll at the FBI and CIA. I think there ought to be an investigation into what the FAA knew and when it knew it. I think, once again, the federal government has neglected its main responsibility under the Constitution—protecting the American people from attack.[123]

Who Profited from 9/11 Foreknowledge?

Not only is it apparent that officials took measures only to protect themselves, there is convincing evidence that unknown individuals exploited their advanced knowledge of the attacks to reap huge profits. It is a matter of record that some of these individuals are connected to the US intelligence community, providing yet another indication of the degree of advanced warning available. One of the first researchers to investigate this phenomenon, 9/11 insider trading, was journalist Michael C. Ruppert—a former Los Angeles Police Department narcotics detective who famously exposed CIA drug-trafficking.[124]

Ruppert reports that only three trading days before 9/11, shares of United Airlines—whose planes were hijacked in the attacks—were massively "sold short" by as yet unknown investors. This was done by buying dirt-cheap "put" options, giving the owner a short-term right to sell specific shares at a price well below the current market—"a long-shot bet." When the stock prices dropped even lower in response to the 9/11 terrorist attacks, the options multiplied a hundredfold in value, making millions of dollars in profit. These "short" options purchases proved beyond doubt that certain investors had advanced warning of a calamity that would occur within a few days and drastically reduce the market price of those shares. As the *San Francisco Chronicle* reported:

> Investors have yet to collect more than $2.5 million in profits they made trading options in the stock of United Airlines before the Sept. 11 terrorist attacks, according to a source familiar with the trades and market data. The uncollected money raises suspicions that the investors—whose identities and nationalities have not been made public—had advance knowledge of the strikes.
>
> ... October series options for UAL Corp. were purchased in highly unusual volumes three trading days before the terrorist attacks for a total outlay of $2,070; investors bought the option contracts, each representing 100 shares, for 90 cents each [a price of less than one cent per share, on a

total of 230,000 options]. Those options are now selling at more than $12 each. There are still 2,313 so-called "put" options outstanding [representing 231,300 shares and a profit of $2.77 million] according to the Options Clearinghouse Corp.

...The source familiar with the United trades identified Deutsche Bank Alex. Brown, the American investment banking arm of German giant Deutsche Bank, as the investment bank used to purchase at least some of these options...[125]

But the United Airlines case was not the only dubious financial transaction indicating advanced warning of the attacks. The Israeli Herzliyya International Policy Institute for Counterterrorism documented the following transactions related to 9/11 involving American Airlines—whose planes were also used in the attacks—and other companies with large offices in the Twin Towers:

Between September 6 and 7, the Chicago Board Options Exchange saw purchases of 4,744 put options on United Airlines, but only 396 call options... Assuming that 4,000 of the options were bought by people with advance knowledge of the imminent attacks, these "insiders" would have profited by almost $5 million.

On September 10, 4,516 put options on American Airlines were bought on the Chicago exchange, compared to only 748 calls. Again, there was no news at that point to justify this imbalance;... Again, assuming that 4,000 of these options trades represent "insiders," they would represent a gain of about $4 million [the above levels of put options were more than six times higher than normal].

No similar trading in other airlines occurred on the Chicago exchange in the days immediately preceding Black Tuesday.

Morgan Stanley Dean Witter & Co., which occupied 22 floors of the World Trade Center, saw 2,157 of its October $45 put options bought in the three trading days before Black Tuesday; this compares to an average of 27 contracts per day before September 6. Morgan Stanley's share price fell from $48.90 to $42.50 in the aftermath of the attacks. Assuming that 2,000 of these options contracts were bought based upon knowledge of the approaching attacks, their purchasers could have profited by at least $1.2 million.

Merrill Lynch & Co., with headquarters near the Twin Towers, saw 12,215 October $45 put options bought in the four trading days before the attacks; the previous average volume in those shares had been 252 contracts per day [a dramatic increase of 1200%]. When trading resumed, Merrill's shares fell from $46.88 to $41.50; assuming that 11,000 option contracts were bought by "insiders," their profit would have been about $5.5 million.

European regulators are examining trades in Germany's Munich Re,

Switzerland's Swiss Re, and AXA of France, all major reinsurers with exposure to the Black Tuesday disaster [AXA also owns more than 25% of American Airlines stock].[126]

These multiple, massive, and unprecedented financial transactions pointed unequivocally to the fact that the investors behind these trades were speculating in anticipation of a mid-September 2001 catastrophe that would involve United Airlines and American Airlines and offices in the Twin Towers. But as noted by Ruppert, who has submitted testimony to the Senate Select Committee on Intelligence on CIA covert operations related to narcotics: "It is well documented that the CIA has long monitored such trades—in real time—as potential warnings of terrorist attacks and other economic moves contrary to US interests."[127] According to Ruppert: "It has been documented that the CIA, the Israeli Mossad and many other intelligence agencies monitor stock trading in real time using highly advanced programs reported to be descended from Promis software." In the wake of several news stories on PROMIS by FOX News, "both the FBI and the Justice Department have confirmed its use for US intelligence gathering through at least this summer. This would confirm that CIA had additional advance warning of imminent attacks."[128]

Indeed, Ruppert reports that a "primary function" of the CIA is "to track, monitor, all financial markets worldwide, to look for anomalous trades, indicative of either economic warfare, or insider currency trading or speculation which might affect the US Treasury, or… which indicated foreknowledge of attacks like we saw." PROMIS software, originally developed in 1979 by Bill Hamilton and a Washington, DC firm, INSLAW, "had the ability to integrate a wide range of databases using different computer languages and to make them all into one readable format." Since then, PROMIS was "mated with artificial intelligence to even predict moves in markets and to detect trades that are anomalous, as a result of those projections."[129] The CIA has in fact confirmed its ongoing use of PROMIS software from abroad to monitor worldwide stock option trading activity. Investigative journalist Tom Flocco reports that:

> In a returned phone call from the Central Intelligence Agency, press spokesman Tom Crispell denied that the CIA was monitoring "real-time," pre-September 11, stock option trading activity within United States borders using such software as the Prosecutor's Management Information System (PROMIS). "That would be illegal. We only operate outside the United States," the intelligence official said.[130]

The CIA confirmation shows that although the software is not being used on US soil, it is being used from outside the US to monitor real-time stock trading around the world. However, there are also other monitoring systems that perform the same function. The UPI reported that ECHELON closely monitors stock trading.[131] The London *Times* further notes that the UK Financial Services Authority (FSA) is a "stock market watchdog" possessing a "transaction monitoring department that checks suspicious share movements." The FSA, however, has not issued any informative statement on the investigation into the share movements before 9/11: "The FSA would not comment on its instructions from the CIA."[132] In any case, there are clearly both intelligence and civilian monitoring systems that monitor share transactions for the express purpose of tracking suspicious movements, and which would have received warning.

Kyle Hence, Director of the New York-based 9/11 Citizens Watch, further reports "the movement of unusually large sums of money through the computers of the WTC in the hours before the attack." According to one expert, "not only the volume, but the size of the transactions was far higher than usual for a day like that." Richard Wagner, a data retrieval expert "estimated that more than $100 million in illegal transactions appeared to have rushed through the WTC computers before and during the disaster." The evidence indicated "a carefully planned and sophisticated effort of massive profiteering from the precipitous fall of stocks that occurred when trading opened following the attack."[133]

Ernest Welteke, President of the German Bundesbank, concluded that a group of speculators must have known of the attacks: "There have been fundamental movements in these markets [i.e. the airlines], and the oil price rise just ahead of the attacks is otherwise inexplicable."[134] Toward the end of September, he explained that "a study by his bank strongly points to 'terrorism insider trading' not only in shares of heavily affected industries such as airlines and insurance companies, but also in gold and oil."[135] Admitting that there has been a great deal of "speculation and rumours," Welteke also stated that "there are ever clearer signs that there were activities on international financial markets which must have been carried out with the necessary expert knowledge."[136]

The London *Times* reports that the US government has a similar perspective: "American authorities are investigating unusually large numbers of shares in airlines, insurance companies and arms manufacturers that were sold off in the days and weeks before the attacks. They believe that the sales were by people who knew about the impending disaster."[137] Similarly, *USA Today* cited co-founder of PTI Securities Jon Najarian, described as an "active player" on the Chicago Board Options Exchange, confirming that the volumes were exceptional versus the norm."[138] Principal of Broadband Research John Kinnucan commented: "I saw put-call numbers higher than I've ever seen in 10 years of following the markets, particularly the options markets."[139] As CBS *60 Minutes* reported: "Sources tell CBS News that the afternoon before the attack, alarm bells were sounding over unusual trading in the US stock options market."[140]

Given that there are both intelligence and civilian systems that monitor share transactions for the express purpose of tracking suspicious movements, and given further that the transactions just prior to 9/11 were so unprecedented, massive, and specific, these monitoring systems would have received precise advance warning. These systems would also have clearly pointed to a specified time for the attacks as occurring between early and mid-September. The intelligence community would have been alerted by September 7, 2001 that American and United Airlines, along with the World Trade Center, were potential targets.

In an interview with journalist Tom Flocco, when asked about alleged terrorist ties to Deutsche Bank and potential pre-attack CIA trade monitoring via PROMIS, Treasury Department spokesman Rob Nichols said: "This is clearly an interesting line of questioning regarding conflicts of interest."[141] That this line of question is likely to bear fruit is alarmingly illustrated in a report in the London *Independent*: "To the embarrassment of investigators, it has also emerged that the firm used to buy many of the 'put' options—where a trader, in effect, bets on a share price fall—on United Airlines stock was headed until 1998 by 'Buzzy' Krongard, now executive director of the CIA."[142]

There is abundant evidence discussed by Ruppert that the relationship between Wall Street and the CIA is akin to a "revolving door." For instance, Ruppert notes that until 1997, A. B. "Buzzy" Krongard was Chairman of the investment bank AB Brown, acquired by Banker's Trust in 1997. As part of the merger he became Vice-Chairman of Banker's Trust–AB Brown—but Banker's Trust was criticized by the Senate and regulators for money laundering. Krongard went on to join the CIA in 1998 as counsel to CIA Director George Tenet. Banker's Trust was acquired by Deutsche Bank in 1999, forming the single largest bank in Europe. Meanwhile, Krongard was later promoted to CIA Executive Director by President Bush in March 2001.[143] Curiously, CIA spokesman Tom Crispell "declined comment" when asked by journalist Flocco "whether the Treasury Department or FBI had questioned CIA Executive Director and former Deutsche Bank–Alex Brown CEO, A.B. 'Buzzy' Krongard, about CIA monitoring of financial markets using PROMIS and his former position as overseer of Brown's 'private client' relations."[144]

Far more direct evidence of insider trading by elements of the US intelligence community was disclosed by the *New York Times* in late May 2002. A San Diego stock adviser was accused by a US government investigator of "bribing an FBI agent to give him confidential government information," and exploiting his prior knowledge of the 9/11 attacks to profit from related share trades. In the court hearings, Kenneth Breen—an assistant United States attorney and coordinator of the stock market unit of a government task force set up to investigate financing for terrorist groups—alleged that stock adviser Amr Ibrahim Elgindy "tried to sell $300,000 in stock on the afternoon of Sept. 10 and told his broker that the stock market would soon plunge." Elgindy told his Salomon Smith Barney broker during "the Sept. 10 conversation" that he "predicted that the Dow Jones industrial average, which at the time stood at about 9,600, would soon crash to below 3,000"—which subsequently occurred. As it happens, he was unable to sell the stock before markets closed on September 10 and only managed to sell them a week later when markets reopened. In court, Breen stated: "Perhaps Mr. Elgindy had preknowledge of Sept. 11, and rather than report it he attempted to profit from it." Most disturbing of all, however, is the fact that Elgindy was allegedly conducting his fraudulent dealings in liaison with several FBI agents, from whom he was constantly receiving sensitive government data:

> ...Mr. Elgindy and four other people, including one current and one former
> F.B.I. agent, were charged Wednesday with using confidential government
> information to manipulate stock prices and extort money from companies.
> Jeffrey A. Royer, who was an F.B.I. agent before joining Mr. Elgindy's stock
> advisory firm in December, accepted $30,000 from a partner of Mr.
> Elgindy's in exchange for providing Mr. Elgindy with information about
> current criminal investigations of companies, prosecutors allege.
>
> Mr. Elgindy and his partner, Derrick W. Cleveland, sold short the
> shares of companies that they learned were under investigation, according
> to the indictment. (Short sellers borrow shares and sell them, hoping to buy
> them back later at a lower price and pocket the difference.) Then Mr.
> Elgindy publicized the negative information on two Web sites he ran,
> hoping that the companies' stocks would fall, prosecutors say.
>
> ...When F.B.I. agents raided Mr. Elgindy's home outside San Diego on
> Wednesday, Mr. Breen said, they found $43,000 in cash, as well as a loose
> diamond and faxes indicating that Mr. Elgindy had been tipped about the
> raid and had given his wife a power of attorney to liquidate his assets.[145]

The *New York Times* account shows that, according to government prosecutors, US stock adviser Amr Elgindy established a corrupt relationship with several active and former FBI agents, using them regularly to obtain "confidential government information to manipulate stock prices and extort money from companies" as well as to engage in related share trading to make profits. It appears that Elgindy's reported September 10 attempt to sell $300,000 in stock was rooted in advanced knowledge that Dow Jones would soon crash to an unprecedented degree—an event which subsequently occurred as a consequence of 9/11. Whether or not Elgindy had foreknowledge of the attacks themselves, the government prosecutors' case indicates that he had foreknowledge of the imminent devastating financial impact of the attacks. Given that Elgindy allegedly conducted such stock trades based on "confidential government information" obtained from several well-placed FBI connections—and given also that those connections seem to have continued in the aftermath of the attacks (in relation to the tip-off regarding the FBI raid)—this further indicates that the information allegedly used by him on September 10 was obtained from the same FBI connections. This would only be possible if elements in the FBI had received precise advanced warning of a terrible calamity on 9/11. In other words, the *New York Times* account strongly suggests that elements of the FBI had significant information predicting a cataclysmic event on September 11, 2001.

But in the context of this analysis, such foreknowledge is not surprising. As noted above, both intelligence and civilian systems monitor stock trading for the express purpose of tracking anomalous trades. Both would have homed in on the extremely prominent indicators from insider trading just prior to 9/11, pointing unequivocally to an imminent terrorist attack on the World Trade Center from the air. The *New York Times* report corroborates this analysis, suggesting that certain active and former FBI officials had specific information pertaining to the 9/11 attacks—and used it to make a profit. It is possible that this activity is linked to CIA Executive Director "Buzzy" Krongard's connections, as former head of the firm used to purchase many of the 9/11 put options.

The *Wall Street Journal* reported some other disturbing developments in the investigation into this suspicious share trading. The ongoing investigation by the Security and Exchange Commission (SEC) had by October 2001 been joined by a Secret Service probe into purchases of an exceptionally large number of five-year US Treasury notes, shortly before 9/11. Among the Treasury note transactions was a single $5 billion trade. The *Journal* points out that: "Five-year Treasury notes are among the best investments in the event of a world crisis, especially one that hits the US. The notes are prized for their safety and their backing by the US government, and usually rally when investors flee riskier investments, such as stocks."[146] No one can purchase US government Treasury bonds of this quantity without the Treasury Department knowing the identity of the purchaser(s).

To date, both the SEC and the FBI have been tightlipped about their investigation of the trades.[147] Indeed, the FBI appears to have taken measures to block public knowledge of the progress of the investigation. On October 3, 2001, chief of the FBI's financial crimes unit Dennis Lormel attempted to downplay the significance of the trades. Despite all the evidence to the contrary, Lormel claimed in testimony before a Congressional committee that "there are no flags or indicators" showing that terrorists used strategies such as "short selling" to profit from the attacks.[148]

"Why then were investigations launched by over a dozen nations and 8 or 9 US government agencies, exchanges and commissions?" asks Kyle Hence.

How does one account for supporting comments of the traders and analysts with years of hands-on experience in the markets?...

Lormel's testimony, coming from an official charged with tracking down and starving terrorists of funding to protect Americans does little to inspire confidence; especially in the wake of the worst intelligence failure in US history. On the contrary, such remarks only raise very uncomfortable suspicions and legitimate concern that the forces behind walls of financial secrecy are so powerful as to thwart or intimidate the highest echelon of those responsible for executing our nation's war on terrorism.[149]

Another example of the block on publicizing the outcome of the investigation is the fact that information has been removed on high-level orders. The Investment Dealers Association (IDA), a trade association for the Canadian securities industry, posted on its website an SEC list of 38 stocks. The SEC had requested Canadian security firms to investigate suspicious trading in these stocks between August 27 and September 11, 2001. But as soon as US officials became aware that the full list of stocks had been posted online, they demanded the removal of the list from the Investment Dealers Association's site. The IDA complied, but reporters were able to copy the list before its removal.[150]

The list of stocks includes the parent companies of American, Continental, Delta, Northwest, Southwest, United, and US Airways, as well as Carnival and Royal Caribbean cruise lines, aircraft maker Boeing and defense contractor Lockheed Martin. Several insurance companies are on the list—American International Group, Axa, Chubb, Cigna, CNA Financial, John Hancock, and MetLife. Several giant companies that were former tenants in the World Trade Center were also on the list: the largest tenant, investment firms Morgan Stanley; Lehman Brothers; Bank of America; and the financial firm Marsh & McLennan. Other major companies on the list were General Motors, Raytheon, LTV, WR Grace, Lone Star Technologies, American Express, Bank of New York, Bank One, Citigroup, and Bear Stearns.[151]

A probe of suspicious stock trading in these companies would attempt to successively isolate the investors, or group of investors, involved in them, following the chain until it leads back to those who initiated the trades and therefore had advanced warning of the attacks. Bloomberg News reported that according to William McLucas, former SEC Chief of Enforcement, financial regulators would "certainly be able to track down every trade, where the trade cleared, where the trade was directed from."[152] Why did US officials object to publication of a list of stocks in which suspicious trading occurred? Moreover, why have the results of the investigation so far, and any progress being made, not been made public? Are the answers to these questions, perhaps, linked with embarrassing connections to insider trading from within elements of the CIA and FBI?

8.

Tracking the Terrorists

Zacarias Moussaoui

The vast extent of the intelligence community's advanced warning of the 9/11 attacks is further revealed by the degree to which the 9/11 hijackers were being monitored by US intelligence agencies. *WorldNetDaily*, the Internet news service of the US-based non-profit Western Journalism Center, reports some pertinent revelations in this respect:

> Zacarias Moussaoui was arrested after flight trainers tipped off the feds that he wanted to learn how to fly a 747 but wasn't interested in takeoffs or landings. Zacarias was traveling on a French passport. When contacted, the French government reported that he was a suspected terrorist [linked to Osama Bin Laden].[1]

Reuters reported in relation to Zacarias that: "The FBI arrested an Islamic militant in Boston last month and received French intelligence reports linking him to Saudi-born dissident Osama bin Laden but apparently did not act on them." According to French *Europe 1* radio, Zacarias had "dual French and Algerian nationality," and when arrested was in possession of "several passports, technical information on Boeing aircraft and flight manuals." He had been taking flying lessons. "Asked for information by the Federal Bureau of Investigation, French security services provided a dossier clearly identifying him as an Islamic militant working with bin Laden."[2]

CBS's *60 Minutes II* elaborated that the information provided in the French intelligence report depicted Zacarias as "a dangerous Islamic extremist." Some of the information came from Judge Jean-Louis Bruguiere, France's leading legal-terrorism expert, who said that the French had given the FBI "everything we had."[3] Damien Cave further reported in *Salon* that: "French authorities alerted the FBI in August that the '20th hijacker' had trained in al-Qaida camps in Afghanistan, according to an intelligence expert—but the US did nothing." Al-Qaeda expert Jean-Charles Brisard, a former French intelligence official who authored the first intelligence report on al-Qaeda's financial networks, asserted "that French intelligence officials warned their US counterparts in considerable detail about al-Qaida's ties to Zacarias Moussaoui, the alleged 20th hijacker, but the US failed to act on the information."[4]

FBI headquarters had received the French intelligence information on Zacarias' extensive ties to al-Qaeda on August 26, 2001. But the Minnesota flight school, Pan Am International Flight Academy, where Zacarias had been training, was the first to warn the FBI in no uncertain terms. As the *Minneapolis Star-Tribune* reported: "Moussaoui raised suspicions at the Pan Am International Flight Academy in Egan [Minnesota]" when he attended the Academy in August 2001 to learn how to fly jumbo jets. He "first raised eyebrows when, during a simple introductory exchange, he said he was from France, but then didn't seem to understand when the instructor spoke French to him.... In addition, he seemed inept in basic flying procedures, while seeking expensive training on an advanced commercial jet simulator."[5]

Even the flight school's own employees "began whispering that he could be a hijacker." The director of operations at the academy, John Rosengren, recounts how Zacarias' instructor was "concerned and wondered why someone who was not a pilot and had so little experience was trying to pack so much training into such a short time.... 'The more he was able to talk to him, the more he decided he was not pilot material.... There was discussion about how much fuel was on board a 747-400 and how much damage that could cause if it hit anything.'"[6] So the instructor contacted the FBI, as the *San Francisco Chronicle* reported:

> An instructor at a Minnesota flight school warned the FBI in August of his suspicion that a student who was later identified as a part of Osama bin Laden's terror network might be planning to use a commercial plane loaded with fuel as a weapon, a member of Congress and other officials said yesterday. The officials, who were briefed by the school, said the instructor warned the FBI in urgent tones about the terrorist threat posed by the student, Zacarias Moussaoui.
>
> According to US Representative James L. Oberstar of Minnesota, the instructor called the bureau several times to find someone in authority who seemed willing to act on the information. His warnings could not have been more blunt. Oberstar noted that: "He told them, 'Do you realize that a 747 loaded with fuel can be used as a bomb?'"
>
> Congressional officials said the account by the school, the Pan Am International Flight Academy in Eagan, outside Minneapolis, raised new questions about why the FBI and other agencies did not prevent the hijackings... [The flight instructor] was a former military pilot who grew suspicious after encounters in which Moussaoui was belligerent and evasive about his background and because he was so adamant about learning to fly a 747 jumbo jet despite his clear incompetence as a pilot. Moussaoui, 33, was arrested in August on immigration charges. But despite the urging of the school and federal agents in Minnesota and despite a warning from the French that Moussaoui was linked to Muslim extremists, FBI headquarters resisted opening a broader investigation until after Sept. 11.[7]

A few hours after Zacarias Moussaoui's arrest by the FBI, Mr. Atlas, a student who had driven Moussaoui from Oklahoma to the Minnesota flight school, told the FBI's Minnesota office that Moussaoui believed it was "acceptable to kill civilians who harm Muslims and that he approved of Muslims who died as 'martyrs' in such attacks."[8]

But the US government actively prevented a further investigation from being conducted. Local FBI investigators in Minneapolis had immediately viewed Zacarias as a suspected terrorist and sought authorization for a special counterintelligence surveillance warrant in order to search the hard drive of his home computer. The Justice Department and top FBI officials blocked the FBI request for a national security warrant to search Zacarias' computer, claiming that FBI agents lacked sufficient information to meet the legal requirements to justify the warrant. The block remained in place even after the notification from French intelligence that Zacarias was linked to bin Laden.[9]

A special counterterrorism panel of the FBI and CIA reviewed the information against him and claimed there was insufficient evidence that he represented a threat: "Moussaoui was taken into custody on August 16, but to the outrage of FBI agents in the field, headquarters was slow to react and said he could not be connected to any known terror group."[10] The decision was particularly bizarre in light of the detailed documentation from French intelligence clearly demonstrating his al-Qaeda ties. Indeed, many law enforcement officials believe that the decision was unlawful. "That decision is being questioned by some FISA experts, who say it's possible a warrant would have been granted," reported Greg Gordon. "The special court that reviews FISA requests has approved more than 12,000 Justice Department applications for covert search warrants and wiretaps and rejected only one since the act was passed in 1978, according to government reports."[11] In that context, the rejection of the FBI–Zacarias FISA application clearly constituted an unprecedented violation of normal protocols. MSNBC has similarly reported that:

> ...other law enforcement officials are equally insistent that a more aggressive probe of Moussaoui—when combined with other intelligence in the possession of US agencies—might have yielded sufficient clues about the impending plot. "The question being asked here is if they put two and two together, they could have gotten a lot more information about the guy—if not stopped the hijacking," said one investigator.[12]

Indeed, Zacarias's notoriety as an al-Qaeda operative was well-known to the international intelligence community. For example, the *Observer* reports that the British MI5 was monitoring him in 2000, including "intercepted phone calls" between him and al-Qaeda shoe-bomber Richard Reid:

The calls, made between the pair in Britain and monitored by MI5, ended abruptly when Moussaoui left Britain for Pakistan on 9 December last year to attend an al-Qaeda training camp in Afghanistan.... MI5 had had Moussaoui under surveillance in the UK in the months before he left for Pakistan. He was then arrested by US authorities in August.[13]

Thus, the US intelligence community not only had access to information from French intelligence, but also from British intelligence. Curiously, according to motions from Moussaoui unsealed in Federal court, he wished to testify before both a grand jury and the US Congress about the 9/11 attacks, claiming to possess information that the US government permitted the attacks to happen. That request has so far been refused.[14]

Mohamed Atta

The US response to Mohamed Atta, the lead 9/11 hijacker, was even more extraordinary. The German public TV channel, ARD, reported on November 23, 2001, that Mohamed Atta was subject to telephone monitoring by the Egyptian secret service, thus discovering that Atta had made at least one recent visit to Afghanistan from his home in Hamburg, Germany. The FBI had also been monitoring Atta's movements for several months in 2000, when he traveled several times from Hamburg to Frankfurt and bought large quantities of chemicals potentially usable for building explosives. Atta's name had also been mentioned in a Hamburg phone call between Islamic fundamentalists monitored by the German police in 1999.[15]

In January 2001, Atta was permitted reentry into the United States after a trip to Germany, despite being in violation of his visa status. He had landed in Miami on January 10 on a flight from Madrid on a tourist visa—yet he had told immigration inspectors that he was taking flying lessons in the US, for which an M-1 student visa is strictly required. Jeanne Butterfield, executive director of the American Immigration Lawyers Association, points out that: "Nine times out of 10, they would have told him to go back and file [for that status] overseas. You're not supposed to come in as a visitor for pleasure and go to work or school."[16] PBS's *Frontline* also takes note of "The failure of the INS to stop the attack's ringleader, Mohamed Atta, from entering the US three times on a tourist visa in 2001, even though officials knew the visa had expired in 2000 and Atta had violated its terms by taking flight lessons."[17]

This failure should be evaluated in context with the fact that Atta had been under FBI surveillance for stockpiling bomb-making materials. Furthermore, Canadian TV reported that Atta had already been implicated in a terrorist bombing in Israel, with the information passed on to the United States before he was first issued his tourist visa.[18] As Ken Garcia of the *San Francisco Chronicle* notes:

I realize that many people can fly under the radar of the nation's security network, but I didn't really think that they would include a number of international terrorists who were known to the FBI, the CIA, the State Department, the Immigration and Naturalization Service as well as numerous police agencies in the ballot-challenged state of Florida... at least one of the suicidal hijackers, Mohamed Atta, managed to travel in and out of the United States on an expired visa. *This despite the fact that Atta was on the government's watch list of suspected terrorists and had been since 1986 when he was implicated in a bus bombing attack in Israel.*

Since Atta apparently flew under his own name on his many jaunts to Spain and Germany and back to the United States, you'd presumably think that someone in the FBI, CIA, State Department or the INS might have noticed his comings and goings.[19]

Yet despite his terrorist connections—and despite being on a US government terrorist watch list since 1986—Atta was still allowed into the United States freely, and made repeated trips to Europe, each time returning to the US to be admitted by US customs and immigration without obstruction—not because visa regulations were lax, but because they were simply repeatedly violated. The London *Observer* notes in surprise that Atta

> ... was under surveillance between January and May last year after he was reportedly observed buying large quantities of chemicals in Frankfurt, apparently for the production of explosives and for biological warfare.... The US agents reported to have trailed Atta are said to have failed to inform the German authorities about their investigation. The disclosure that Atta was being trailed by police long before 11 September raises the question why the attacks could not have been prevented with the man's arrest.[20]

In summary, despite being well known to authorities, Mohamed Atta seems to have led a rather charmed life. Although listed since 1986 on the State Department's terrorist watch list, he was repeatedly permitted to enter, leave, and return to the US freely. He had been under surveillance by US agents between January and May 2000 due to his suspicious purchase of large amounts of chemicals, which might be used to make explosives. In January 2001 he was detained by INS agents at Miami International Airport for 57 minutes due to previously overstaying a visa and failing to produce a proper visa to enter the US to train at a Florida flight school. But that did not stop him. Despite the FBI's longstanding concern that terrorists might be attending flight schools in the US, Atta was allowed to enroll in the Florida flight school. By April 2001, he was stopped by police for driving without a license. He failed to show up in court in May and a bench warrant was issued for his arrest. But that did not stop him either, because the warrant was never executed—although he was subsequently arrested for drunk driving on two more occasions. Throughout this period in the US, Atta never made any attempt to operate under an alias, traveling, living, and studying at the flight school under his real name.[21] Stranger still, Atta was in regular email contact with current and former employees of major US defense contractors, as revealed by a regular email list of some 40 individuals he maintained, discovered by the FBI in September 2001. One of the defense contractors is "a Canadian company called Virtual Prototypes, whose website touts the fact that the firm helped prototype the avionics instruments in the F-15 jet fighter, the F-22 Raptor, the B2 bomber and the Apache Longbow, among others."[22]

It is hard to interpret this sequence of events in a benign light. In short, it seems to be an unavoidable—if inexplicable—conclusion that the US government knowingly and repeatedly granted free passage to a confirmed terrorist to enter the United States and undergo flight training. As the BBC observed: "The evidence... reinforces concerns that the international intelligence community may have known more about Atta before September 11 than was previously thought, but had failed to act."[23] The BBC's conclusion is buttressed by revelations that US intelligence had *not* ceased monitoring Mohamed Atta's activities when he entered the United States. According to the *Miami Herald*: "A secretive US eavesdropping agency monitored telephone conversations before Sept. 11 between the suspected commander of the World Trade Center and Pentagon attacks and the alleged chief hijacker." According to anonymous US officials

> the conversations between Khalid Shaikh Mohammed and Mohamed Atta were intercepted by the National Security Agency, or NSA, an intelligence agency that monitors and decodes foreign communications...
>
> The officials declined to disclose the nature of the discussions between Mohammed, a known leader of Osama bin Laden's al Qaeda network who is on the FBI's Most Wanted Terrorists list, and Atta, who is believed to have piloted one of the planes that hit the World Trade Center after honing his flying skills at a Venice, FL, aviation school. Khalid Shaikh Mohammed is believed to be hiding in Pakistan.... The senior intelligence official said that when the NSA monitored their conversations, Mohammed was overseas and Atta was in the United States.
>
> Mohammed was included on the FBI's Most Wanted Terrorist List when it was published in October because he had been indicted on charges of being involved in a failed 1995 plot [i.e. Project Bojinka] to bomb 11 US airliners flying over the Pacific Ocean on a single day. The US Justice Department has offered a $25 million reward for him.[24]

Notably, the *Herald* also points out that: "The NSA is prohibited by law from monitoring calls to and from the United States without special court orders."[25] In other words, the monitoring of Atta's communications could only occur with special high-level legal approval sought by either the CIA or the FBI.

It should be noted that according to US counterterrorism officials, Khalid Sheikh Mohammed—on the most wanted list—was the key operational planner behind the 9/11 attacks. His conversations with Atta, monitored by the NSA, presumably would have revealed extensive details of the unfolding terror plot. Indeed, the London *Independent* reports that: "Officials say that Mr. Mohammed received a telephone call from Mohammed Atta, the hijackers' ringleader, on 10 September. Intelligence officials who monitored and then translated that conversation believe that using coded language, Mr. Mohammed gave Mr. Atta the final approval to launch the strikes."[26]

Khalid Sheikh Mohammed

The Bush administration certainly has a great deal to hide concerning its knowledge of the 9/11 plot gleaned from the Atta–Khalid communications— which perhaps explains why information on Khalid remains classified.[27] As one UPI report notes, the "key al-Qaida" leader thought to have masterminded the 9/11 attacks, although officially undisclosed, "is widely believed to be [Khalid Sheikh] Mohammed." It seems that US intelligence has known about Khalid Sheikh Mohammed for some time. Yossef Bodansky, director of the Congressional Task Force on Terrorism and Unconventional Warfare, has revealed that "Mohammed also has ties to Pakistan's Inter-Service Intelligence agency, which he said had acted to shield him in the past. 'Mohammed was running operations right in Karachi,' said Bodansky. Bodansky would not reveal his sources of information."[28] Bodansky's admission is critical evidence that US intelligence has for long been aware of Khalid Sheikh Mohammed's activities as an al-Qaeda operative working in close liaison with Pakistani military intelligence. In that context, the testimony of Robert Baer—former veteran case officer in the CIA's Directorate of Operations—is potentially damning. Baer "was first informed of Mohammed's role as a key aide to terrorist mastermind bin Laden as early as December 1997 when he met a former police chief from Doha, Qatar, at a dinner in Damascus."

> In 1997, Baer had left the agency to become a consultant in Beirut. Terrorism was Baer's field and Baer began to meet the ex-Doha police chief from time to time. The ex-Doha police chief, who Baer declined to identify by name, told Baer that during the course of his work he found that there was a bin Laden cell in Qatar, being sheltered by the Qatari government.
>
> The two main members of the cell were Khalid Shaikh Mohammed and Shawqui Islambuli, the brother of the Egyptian who had killed Anwar

Sadat. They also were linked to terrorist Ramzi Yousef, but what worried the former police chief was the fact that Mohammed and Islambuli were experts in hijacking commercial planes. The ex-police chief told Baer that Mohammed "is going to hijack some planes." The ex-police chief said his basis for this was evidence developed by police and Qatari intelligence.

The ex-police chief told Baer that Mohammed was being shielded by the Qatar government and told how, in 1996, the FBI sent in a team to arrest Mohammed and Islambuli. While pretending to help, elements in the Qatari government stalled US agents and supplied the two suspects, Mohammed and Islambuli, with passports in fake names and spirited them out of the country.... Mohammed also traveled to Germany to meet bin Laden associates, Baer said. Baer sent this information to a friend in the CIA Counter-terrorist Center who forwarded the information to his superiors. Baer heard nothing. "There was no interest," he said.[29]

The apparent lack of response, of course, is hard to square with the fact revealed by Bodansky—as well as by the FBI's 1996 attempt to apprehend Mohammed—that US intelligence seems to have been monitoring Mohammed for a significant period, having gathered information on his al-Qaeda terrorist operations for several years. Further revelations on the surveillance of Mohammed came to light in the July 2003 testimony of Rohan Gunaratna of the Centre for the Study of Terrorism and Political Violence, University of St. Andrews—one the world's foremost experts on al-Qaeda—before the 9/11 Commission. Citing CIA sources and official transcripts of the interrogation of Mohammed and other high-level al-Qaeda operatives such as Abu Zubaydah, Gunaratna revealed that: "The Sept. 11 attacks were given the code name 'Operation Holy Tuesday' and precisely planned at an al Qaeda meeting in Malaysia chaired by terror mastermind Khalid Sheikh Mohammed in January 2000." The 3-day conference "was monitored by the Malaysian secret police at the CIA's request," and hosted 12 terrorists at an apartment in Kuala Lumpur, including "two hijackers, Khalid al-Mihdhar and Nawaf al-Hazmi, who flew from there to Bangkok, Thailand and to the United States without interference, as well as Tawfiq Attash, a key planner in the October 2000 bombing of the USS Cole in Yemen." The conference consisted of detailed discussions on "how the hijackers should train and hide in the United States and how the attacks should be carried out." Khalid Sheikh Mohammed, who was "in charge of the Malaysia meeting," told some of the participants that "the targets would include the World Trade Center and the date of the attacks would be Sept. 11, 2001, Gunaratna said."[30] Although officials have claimed that this January 2000 9/11 planning meeting was not recorded, this claim is untrue—the entire conference was recorded on video with "surveillance tape" by Malaysian security services on behalf of the CIA.[31]

When asked about Gunaratna's revelations, US intelligence officials vehemently denied that Mohammed had attended the meeting: "We have no information to suggest that Khalid Sheikh Mohammed was at the meeting in Kuala Lumpur. We don't believe it to be true."[32] But even CNN, citing intelligence sources, confirms Mohammed's attendance.[33] The official denial is understandable, however, since Gunaratna's testimony demonstrates that as early as January 2000, the CIA had precise advanced warning of al-Qaeda's plan to target the World Trade Center on September 11, 2001. It is no surprise then that the Bush administration blocked the declassification of all intelligence data on Khalid Shaikh Mohammed—including his name.[34]

Alhamzi and Almihdhar

Nawaf Alhazmi and Khalid Almihdhar (the latter being among those who had perpetrated the bombing of the USS Cole in October 2000), had been tracked for more than a year by the CIA—but somehow they were neither barred from entry into the US nor apprehended after their arrival. Citing the findings of an investigation by *Newsweek*, Reuters noted that "the CIA became aware of one of the terrorists, Nawaf Alhazmi, a few days after he attended a secret planning meeting of Osama bin Laden's al Qaeda in Malaysia in January 2000." The CIA was also aware that "another of the men, Khalid Almihdhar"—who had also attended the Kuala Lumpur 9/11 planning meeting—"had already obtained a multiple-entry visa that allowed him to enter and leave the United States at will." But amazingly, the CIA "did nothing with the information, neither notifying the FBI, which could have tracked the two men, or the Immigration and Naturalization Service, which could have turned them away at the border." Instead, for a year and nine months after the CIA identified them as terrorists, "Alhazmi and Almihdhar lived openly in the United States, using their real names, obtaining driver's licenses, opening bank accounts and enrolling in flight schools."[35]

Indeed, a whole "two years before the attacks," the CIA "knew of and tracked" Alhamzi and Alhmidhar "to and from the US." The surveillance continued an intelligence operation that had begun much earlier, since the CIA "knew in advance of a 'summit meeting' of al-Qaeda in January 2000 and of the attendance there of two men then living in the US, Nawaf Alhazmi and Khalid Almihdhar." Although Alhazmi was tracked by the CIA "as he flew back to Los Angeles," he had no problems re-entering the country—like his colleague Almidhar who "flew with him on a multiple-entry visa" which was renewed by the State Department in June 2001, "despite the fact that the CIA had linked him to the bombing of the USS Cole in October 2000."[36]

The CIA's discovery that at least one of the two al-Qaeda operatives was entering and leaving the US at will did not prompt the agency to action. Why were domestic intelligence agencies not informed? The CIA's previous claim that it had no knowledge of Almidhar's activities "until a month before the hijackings" was contradicted by its own "classified chronology submitted to Congress," documenting that the CIA knew about Almidhar at least as early as between late 2000 and early 2001. In fact, since the January 2000 meeting in Malaysia, the CIA had identified the two as al-Qaeda operatives, and in the same year "learned that both men had visited the United States... on several occasions."[37]

The CIA's extraordinary failure to disseminate crucial information about these two al-Qaeda terrorists leads to some awkward questions. As Paul Thompson observes, the CIA had admitted that their names should have been placed on a terrorist watch list according to normal protocols:

> The watch list, a database known as TIPOFF, currently consists of over 80,000 names, with about 2,000 new names being added every month. [Los Angeles Times, 9/22/02] Regulations require that the list is checked for visa applications or whenever someone enters or leaves the US (note that it is not checked for domestic flights). Officials are liable to be subject to criminal penalties if they fail to consult TIPOFF when required. The Congressional inquiry noted that "the threshold for adding a name to TIPOFF is low," explaining that even a "reasonable suspicion" that a person is connected with a terrorist group, warrants the addition of the person's name to the database. [Congressional Intelligence Committee, 9/20/02] Why were Almihdhar and Alhazmi, whose names were reportedly important enough to have been mentioned to the CIA Director several times that January [Congressional Intelligence Committee, 9/20/02], not added to the watch list?[38]

While the CIA's failure to add the two to the watch list is inexplicable, the FBI's insistence that it had no knowledge of the two terrorists—supported by CIA claims—is questionable. According to Eleanor Hill, staff director of the Congressional Joint Inquiry:

> A CIA communication in early January 2000 states that Almihdhar's travel documents, including his multiple entry visa for the United States, were shared with the FBI for further investigation. No one at the FBI recalls having received such documents at the time. No confirmatory record of the transmittal of the travel documents has yet been located at either the CIA or the FBI.[39]

The existence of the CIA memo to the FBI demonstrates that information was sent along. What happened to it thereafter, however, remains a mystery. Again, this short-stopping of the normal flow of critical intelligence is difficult to understand. But other information throws some light on the matter. Another CIA document indicates that the CIA had actually made a conscious policy decision—not an unfathomable mistake—to allow the two terrorists to continue their activities on US soil. A March 2000 cable sent to CIA headquarters concerning Alhazmi's presence in the US was marked as follows: "Action Required: None." An overseas CIA station noted that the cable had been "read with interest" the next day, "particularly the information that a member of this [terrorist] group traveled to the US"— but action was purportedly "not required," hence none was taken.[40]

But the short-stopping of the flow of critical intelligence did not end there. When the FBI belatedly received information about the two terrorists from the CIA—assuming of course that the FBI was not informed earlier—it was still by no means too late to apprehend them. But the FBI sat on the information, and refused to disseminate the intelligence to airlines. Yet again, the FBI's failure is difficult to understand because this is a routine procedure in criminal investigations, let alone real emergencies. As *Human Events* reported:

> The FBI and other federal law enforcement agencies knew about the presence of at least two of the terrorists in the United States, but failed to get the information to airlines. Khalid Al-Midhar and Nawaq Alhamzi, who were on Flight 77 that hit the Pentagon, were already on the so-called watch list. But federal officials failed to notify airline officials who might have been able to stop at least one of the terror attacks.[41]

The *Los Angeles Times*, quoting officials directly acquainted with the matter, also concludes that: "Federal law enforcement authorities did not notify American Airlines that two men with links to terrorist Osama bin Laden were on a 'watch list' before they helped hijack a flight from Dulles International Airport." The FBI knew about Almidhar and Alhamzi even "before they had reserved their tickets for the Los Angeles-bound flight that crashed into the Pentagon." But although the FBI had them placed them on a watch list, neither they nor other authorities

> signaled any concern about the two men to the airline...
> Watch lists are intended to allow a number of federal law enforcement agencies to run names of people entering the US with the aim of questioning or detaining potential terrorists or other criminals.... The Federal Aviation Administration, prior to Sept. 11, had procedures for law enforcement agencies to share information from various watch lists with airlines and airports, said FAA spokeswoman Rebecca Trexler.
> But this was not done with Flight 77, according to those familiar with the matter.... When less significant crimes were suspected in recent years—including drug smuggling and theft—federal authorities have often tipped the airlines or sought their cooperation. Indeed, authorities have alerted American Airlines on numerous occasions to drug or theft suspects appearing on passenger lists, sources said. In at least a dozen

instances, the airline has allowed the FBI to place agents within its work force to conduct undercover operations. [42]

Why did the intelligence community repeatedly breach standard protocols, allowing the two al-Qaeda terrorists to continue their activities without sanction? The gravity of this question is heightened given that these failures are only the tip of the iceberg. *Newsweek* has summarized other revelations contained in the Report of the Congressional Joint Inquiry into 9/11, demonstrating that the FBI had in fact known about Almidhar and Alhamzi for at least nearly two years—as had the CIA. The two had lived in San Diego "with one of the bureau's own informants." The FBI was also aware of a Saudi connection, Omar al-Bayoumi, who was "a key associate of two of the hijackers" and believed to be "a Saudi-government agent" according to intelligence sources. The Joint Inquiry report "documents extensive ties between al-Bayoumi and the hijackers.... In January 2000, al-Bayoumi had a meeting at the Saudi Consulate in Los Angeles—and then went directly to a restaurant where he met future hijackers Khalid Almihdhar and Nawaf Alhazmi, whom he took back with him to San Diego." Al-Bayoumi also arranged an apartment for them next to his own, and gave them their first two months' rent. Nevertheless, the FBI was disinterested in al-Bayoumi. But the most significant revelation is that "a few months after al-Bayoumi took them to San Diego"—in early 2000—"Almihdhar and Alhazmi moved into the house of a local professor who was a longtime FBI 'asset.' The prof also had earlier contact with another hijacker, Hani Hanjour... [T]he informant was in regular touch with his FBI handler." [43]

Officials, recognizing the damaging implications of these reports, have denied that the FBI informant provided them any significant information on the two. According to *Newsweek*, for instance, although the FBI informant was "a 'tested' undercover 'asset' who had been working closely with the FBI office in San Diego on terrorism cases," he had "never provided the bureau with the names of his two houseguests from Saudi Arabia." At face value, this claim is incredulous—the first thing a "tested" informant would do is provide the names of whom he is monitoring. Indeed, in the same report, *Newsweek* cites information demonstrating that the informant did provide the FBI his name: "On one occasion, a source says, the case agent called up the informant and was told he couldn't talk because 'Khalid'—a reference to Almihdhar—was in the room." [44] As Thompson pointedly asked, citing a *New York Times* report of October 5, 2002: "Wouldn't that imply that the FBI knew whom this Khalid being referred to was? Interestingly, the FBI has refused to allow the 9/11 Congressional inquiry to interview either Shaikh [the FBI informant] or his FBI contact. They say he would have nothing interesting to say, but the inquiry doesn't agree." [45]

In this context, the entire official narrative for the failure of the intelligence community to apprehend Almihdhar and Alhazmi collapses. Both the CIA and the FBI had been monitoring the two for at least two years and were well aware of their al-Qaeda connections. They were even aware of their involvement in the 9/11 plot, which was revealed in the January 2000 Malaysia planning conference. Their concerns were so great that the FBI had an informant providing information on their activities. The question remains as to why both the CIA and the FBI systematically neglected to act on the information available to them, in violation of their own routine procedures.

Ziad Samir Jarrah

Al-Qaeda hijacker Ziad Samir Jarrah was on board the United Airlines jet that crashed in Pennsylvania. Two days before 9/11, Jarrah was stopped for speeding on Interstate 95 in Maryland, ticketed, and released. The Maryland state police reportedly ran his name through their computers and found nothing untoward or suspicious. FBI and CIA officials explain this anomaly by claiming that the US intelligence community was completely clueless about Jarrah prior to the 9/11 attacks, and therefore had never placed him on a terrorist watch list.

But the official account is highly questionable. United Arab Emirates (UAE) officials acknowledge that Jarrah arrived in the UAE on January 30, 2001, after spending two months in Afghanistan and Pakistan. The officials confirm that he was questioned for several hours at Dubai International Airport, at the explicit instruction of the US government. Clearly, to have been aware of his arrival in the UAE, US intelligence services must have been monitoring his prior activities for a significant time—and it is a rational inference that such monitoring would only have occurred due to highly suspicious behavior connected to criminal or terrorist activities.

Jarrah was then permitted to leave, whereupon he traveled to Hamburg via Amsterdam, and later flew to the United States. Despite the US government's urgent interest in Jarrah eight months earlier, enough to have him detained in the UAE, he permitted to enter the country and then enroll in a flight school. US intelligence officials claiming to have never known of Jarrah's existence at all prior to 9/11 are clearly being economical with the truth. The question, of course, is: Why? The answer perhaps lies in the following detailed testimony of a UAE official cited in the *Chicago Tribune*:

> Jarrah, who with Mohamed Atta and Marwan Al-Shehhi is considered one of the hijacking plot's three main instigators, was detained, the source said, because his name previously had been placed on an Emirati *"watch list" of terrorist suspects at the request of the US....* "The Americans told us that he was a *supporter of terrorist organizations,* that he had connections with terrorist organizations," the source said. "His name was given to us as someone to check. The US said he should be questioned. He was questioned at the request of the US."

During questioning by Emiratis, Jarrah, 26, divulged that he had spent the previous "two months and five days" in Pakistan and Afghanistan—the only known acknowledgment of an Afghan visit by any of the hijackers—and that he was returning to Florida, where he had been living and taking flying lessons for more than six months. "He had a visa to the US, so he was allowed to proceed," the source said.[46]

A CNN investigation of these reports provided further corroboration and some specific details. "One of the September 11 hijackers was stopped and questioned in the United Arab Emirates in January 2001 at the request of the CIA," CNN concluded, "nearly nine months before the attacks," according to "sources in the government of the UAE, and other Middle Eastern and European sources.... The CIA suspected Ziad Jarrah had been in Afghanistan and wanted him questioned because of 'his suspected involvement in terrorist activities,' UAE sources said." Both US and UAE officials revealed that he was stopped "after the CIA notified UAE officials that he would be arriving from Pakistan on his way back to Europe. UAE sources say the CIA wanted to know where he had been in Afghanistan and how long he had been there." The CIA was also informed of the results of the interrogation "while Jarrah was still at the airport," said a senior UAE source.

> Both US and UAE officials acknowledge the relationship between the two country's intelligence services is extremely close. But the CIA says that the first time it learned that Jarrah had been stopped was in a cable from CIA officers in the UAE after September 11. Told of the CIA's denial, UAE government officials repeated to CNN that Jarrah was questioned at the request of the United States. Senior UAE sources said they had no reason to question him for their own purposes because he was in transit....
>
> Jarrah was questioned after he had already spent six months in the United States learning to fly. He had a valid US multiple-entry visa in his passport, a fragment of which was found at the Flight 93 crash site. Investigators have confirmed that Jarrah had spent at least three weeks in January 2001 at an al Qaeda training camp in Afghanistan. He was released because US officials were satisfied, according to sources.[47]

This sequence of events is quite extraordinary. American, UAE, and European intelligence sources confirm that the CIA had been monitoring Ziad Jarrah for nearly a year (at least) prior to the 9/11 terrorist attacks. Indeed, he had apparently been on a CIA terrorist watch list, since the agency had requested that the UAE place him on a watch list, considered him a "supporter of terrorist organizations," and believed he "had connections with terrorist organizations."

Most significantly, according to US investigators, Jarrah had already spent three weeks training at an al-Qaeda terrorist camp while in Afghanistan prior to his arrival at Dubai. But as CNN noted citing official sources, it was the CIA that had informed UAE officials of Jarrah's arrival "from Pakistan," and asked officials to interrogate him on "where he had been in Afghanistan." The CIA had therefore been monitoring Jarrah's activities since January 2001, including his stay with al-Qaeda in Afghanistan, and was cognizant of his terrorist connections. The unnerving implication is that the CIA knowingly allowed an al-Qaeda operative, already on a terrorist watch list and under surveillance for terrorist activities, into the United States.

Intelligence sources disclose that the CIA's surveillance of Jarrah was part of a long-established surveillance policy:

> UAE and European intelligence sources told CNN that the questioning of Jarrah fits a pattern of a CIA operation begun in 1999 to track suspected al Qaeda operatives who were traveling through the United Arab Emirates. These sources told CNN that UAE officials were often told in advance by US officials which persons were coming through the country and whom they wanted questioned.
>
> One source provided CNN a drawing of the Dubai airport and described how people wanted for questioning were intercepted, most often at a transit desk. US officials declined to comment on whether the CIA operated this way at the Dubai airport.[48]

The plot only thickens. CNN throws further light on what happened to Jarrah on September 9, 2001, when a Maryland state trooper stopped Jarrah "for speeding on Interstate 95 in Cecil County, near the Delaware state line." After 9/11, Jarrah's car was found at the airport with the speeding citation still in the glove box. "Baltimore Mayor Martin O'Malley has said local law enforcement officials should have been told by the FBI that Jarrah was on a CIA watch list… [H]is criticism… came during O'Malley's testimony at a Senate Judiciary Committee hearing last fall."[49] Even after the FBI's official denial, Mayor O'Malley firmly repeated his allegation "during remarks at a US Conference of Mayors meeting in Washington."[50] The Mayor's criticism suggests specifically that this was also an FBI failure—the FBI had been privy to the CIA's information on Jarrah, but failed to disseminate the information.

Why was Ziad Jarrah, despite being under CIA surveillance on a CIA terrorist watch list, permitted to move in and out of the United States without problems on a multiple-entry US visa? And worse still, why was his inclusion on a CIA–FBI watch list not disseminated to local law enforcement? The CIA is undoubtedly aware of the damaging import of these questions, which is why a CIA spokesman "vigorously denied that the CIA knew anything about Jarrah before September 11 or had anything do with his questioning in Dubai. 'That is flatly untrue,' the spokesman said."[51]

Hani Hanjour

The case of 9/11 hijacker Hani Hanjour is very similar. According to ABC News, an FBI informant—Aukai Collins—had given extensive information on Hanjour's activities to the FBI for several years up to 9/11. "A paid FBI informant" revealed that "three years before Sept. 11, he began providing the FBI with information about a young Saudi who later flew a hijacked passenger plane into the Pentagon." Collins apparently told the FBI about Hanjour while he "was in flight training in Phoenix." According to Collins, "the FBI knew Hanjour lived in Phoenix, knew his exact address, his phone number and even what car he drove. 'They knew everything about the guy,' said Collins."

As long ago as 1996, "the FBI asked Collins to focus on a group of young Arab men, many of whom were taking flying lessons, including Hanjour," Collins reported. "They drank alcohol, messed around with girls and stuff like that," he told ABC News. "They all lived in an apartment together, Hani and the others." Although FBI officials and "various FBI sources… acknowledge they paid Collins for four years to monitor the Islamic and Arab communities of Phoenix" in relation to "terrorist activity in Phoenix," FBI spokesmen issued an "emphatic denial" that Collins had passed on any information at all about Hani Hanjour.[52]

Further details on FBI surveillance of Hanjour and his colleagues is available in the Joint Inquiry report, drawing on FBI data, which concludes that an unidentified individual who "was known to the FBI and is discussed in the Phoenix Communication" (the latter warned of an al-Qaeda presence at US flight schools) "may have assisted hijacker pilot Hani Hanjour." Beginning in 1997, the FBI—who already had Hanjour under close surveillance—was aware that

> Hanjour and this individual trained together at a flight school in Arizona. Several instructors at the school told the FBI that the two were associates and one instructor thought they might have carpooled together. The FBI has confirmed five occasions when this individual and Hanjour were at the school on the same day. On one occasion in 1999, logs show that Hanjour and this individual used the same plane. According to a flight instructor, the individual was an observer and school rules require that Hanjour approve the individual's presence in the aircraft.

For undisclosed reasons, the FBI was prompted to investigate Hanjour's associate in May 2001, "but decided not to open a formal investigation after determining that the individual was out of the country." Furthermore, the FBI "did not place the individual's name on a watchlist," although the FBI clearly believed he was an al-Qaeda operative and knew that he was associated with fellow al-Qaeda operative Hanjour.[53]

Indeed, neither Hanjour nor his colleagues faced any impediments from US authorities and were permitted to travel freely in and out of the US, mingling with other al-Qaeda operatives and engaging in al-Qaeda terrorist training in preparation for an attack. There is obviously an alarming pattern here of extensive US intelligence surveillance of al-Qaeda operatives with confirmed records of terrorist activity, on various watch lists, deeply involved in preparations for an impending terrorist attack, nonetheless being able to freely pass in and out of the United States without restrictions. As the *Washington Post* has concluded:

> More than 50 people were likely involved, Justice Department officials have said, and the plot required extensive communications and planning to pull off. The group's size—not to mention the complexity of its endeavor—should have offered many opportunities for intelligence infiltration. Yet the conspirators proceeded unmolested. What is striking is how safe these people apparently felt, how unthreatened by law enforcement. Some of the terrorists were here for long periods. They left and entered the country unimpeded. Some were reportedly on the so-called "watch list," a government catalogue of people who ostensibly are not permitted to enter the country. Yet this apparently caused them no problems.[54]

The State Department's Green Light for Terrorists

Al-Qaeda operatives were able to repeatedly leave and enter the United States despite being known terrorists. But according to journalist Joel Mowbray, they should have been fully barred from the country on the basis of their suspicious visa applications alone:

> … expert analyses of the visa-application forms of 15 of the 9/11 terrorists (the other four applications could not be obtained), [show] all the applicants among the 15 reviewed should have been denied visas under then-existing law. Six separate experts who analyzed the simple, two-page forms came to the same conclusion: All of the visa applications they reviewed should have been denied on their face.

Among the experts who independently examined the terrorist visa applications of 14 Saudis and one from the UAE were four former consular officers, a current consular officer stationed in Latin America, and a senior official at the State Department's office of Consular Affairs (CA). All six experts "strongly agreed that even allowing for human error" the visa lapses were "inexplicable," and all the more so because "the State Department claims that at least 11 of the 15 were interviewed by consular officers." According to former consular officer Nikolai Wenzel, the State Department's issuance of the visas "amounts to criminal negligence." The terrorists' applications were "littered with red flags" and "significant amounts of missing information"—all of which were simply ignored. "Even to the untrained eye, it is easy to see why many of the visas should have been denied," observes Mowbray. "If the US State Department had followed the law, at least 15 of the 19 'dots' should have been denied visas — and they likely wouldn't have been in the United States on September 11, 2001."[55]

How to explain this pattern of State Department law-breaking? Michael Springmann—former head of the Visa Bureau at the US Consulate in Jeddah, Saudi Arabia, between 1987 and 1989—has thrown significant light on this phenomenon. Springmann, who has had 20 years of experience in the US government and is now a practicing lawyer in Washington, DC, told BBC's *Newsnight* that: "In Saudi Arabia I was repeatedly ordered by high level State Dept officials to issue visas to unqualified applicants. These were, essentially, people who had no ties either to Saudi Arabia or to their own country."[56]

In another interview with CBC's Radio One, he stated that CIA officials had consistently violated State Department regulations to issue visas to terrorists recruited to "fight against the then Soviets." There were "as many as a hundred" recruits, people "with no ties to any place in particular... Afghanistan was the end user of their facilities. They were coming to the US for training as terrorists. The countries that had supplied them did not want them back."

CBC: Does this demonstrate a relationship between the CIA and Osama Bin Laden dating back as far as 1987?

SPRINGMANN: That's right, and as you recall, they believe that this fellow Sheikh Abdurrahman who was tied to the first New York World Trade Center bombing had gotten his visa from a CIA case officer in the Sudan. And that the 15 or so people who came from Saudi Arabia to participate in the attacks on the WTC and the Pentagon had gotten visas through the American consulate general in Jeddah.

CBC: So what does that suggest, that this pipeline was never rolled up, that it's still operating?

SPRINGMANN: Exactly. I thought that it had been, because I'd raised sufficient hell that I thought that they'd done it. I had complained to the Embassy in Riyadh, I had complained to diplomatic security in Washington, I had complained to the General Accounting Office, I had complained to the State Department Inspector-General's Office, I had complained to the Bureau of Consular Affairs at the State Department and apparently the reverberations from this were heard all over the State Department.

CBC: If what you say may be true, many of the terrorists who allegedly flew those planes into those targets, got their US visas through the CIA and your US consulate in Jeddah. That suggests a relationship ongoing as recently as obviously September. But what was the CIA presumably recruiting these people for as recently as September 11th?

SPRINGMANN: That I don't know. And that's one of the things that I tried to find out through a series of Freedom of Information Act requests starting ten years ago. At the time the State Department and the CIA stonewalled my requests. They're still doing so.

CBC: If the CIA had a relationship with the people responsible for September 11th, are you suggesting therein that they are somehow complicit?

SPRINGMANN: Yes, either through omission or through failure to act.... By the attempts to cover me up and shut me down, this convinced me more and more that this was not a pipedream, this was not imagination.

(...)

CBC: But you're quite sure that Mohamed Atta and others had their visas issued in Jeddah?

SPRINGMANN: Well this is what I was told by reading an article in the *Los Angeles Times*.[57]

Indeed, between April 23 and June 29, 2001, thirteen of the hijackers obtained visas to come to United States based on identities they presented at the US Consulate in Jeddah, Saudi Arabia.[58] But as noted by the former chief of the US Visa Bureau in Jeddah:

> I had not been protesting fraud. What I was protesting was, in reality, an effort to bring recruits, rounded up by Osama bin Laden, to the US for terrorist training by the CIA.... The State Department did not run the Consulate in Jeddah. The CIA did. Of the roughly 20 Washington-dispatched staff there, I know for a certainty that only three people (including myself) had no ties, either professional or familial, to any of the US intelligence services.[59]

It appears that the US government responded to Springmann's complaints not by rolling up the pipeline, but by widening it, despite increasing evidence of a Saudi connection to al-Qaeda. The *St. Petersburg Times* reports that although "FBI agents complained that their Saudi counterparts hampered investigations into terror attacks, including a 1996 bombing on Dhahran that killed 19 US servicemen," rather than "tightening visa requirements, the US government made it easier for Saudi visitors to come to America." Only four months prior to

9/11 a new program "called US Visa Express" was introduced allowing Saudis "to arrange visas through 10 travel agencies—often without coming to the US Embassy or consulate for interviews."[60]

These preposterous and illegal measures were instituted the same time that the intelligence community was on alert for an imminent al-Qaeda attack. Indeed, as Mowbray reports, at least 3 Saudis who were "among the last of the Sept. 11 homicide hijackers to enter this country didn't visit a US embassy or consulate to get their visas; they went to a *travel agent*, where they only submitted a short, two-page form and a photo," a method made possible by "Visa Express." One senior Consular Affairs official described the program as "an open-door policy for terrorists," since "Saudi Arabia… is the only country with such special visa privileges whose citizens pose a known terrorist risk."[61]

While the government has exploited this phenomenon to argue for the necessity of pushing through draconian legislation to tighten borders, in fact existing law was perfectly capable of protecting the United States—but was violated with impunity by the State Department. The continuation of such policies is hard to understand given that Springmann himself had warned the State Department repeatedly that unqualified applicants were being issued US visas by the CIA.

US Military Training: Atta, Abdulaziz Alomari, Saeed Alghamdi, and Others

Not only did the State Department seem to go out of its way to allow the hijackers to enter the United States, many of them went on to gain access to secure US military installations, where they received various forms of training. According to reports in *Newsweek*, the *Washington Post*, and the *New York Times*, US military officials confirmed to the FBI "that five of the alleged hijackers received training in the 1990s at secure US military installations."[62] *Newsweek* further notes that US military training of foreign students is routine, but occurs with the authorization of both the US military and the respective government, as well as on condition of the latter's payment:

> US military sources have given the FBI information that suggests five of the alleged hijackers of the planes that were used in Tuesday's terror attacks received training at secure US military installations in the 1990s. Another of the alleged hijackers may have been trained in strategy and tactics at the Air War College in Montgomery, Ala., said another high-ranking Pentagon official. The fifth man may have received language instruction at Lackland Air Force Base in San Antonio, Tex. Both were former Saudi Air Force pilots who had come to the United States, according to the Pentagon source…. *Newsweek* visited the base early Saturday morning, where military police confirmed that the address housed foreign military flight

trainees…. It is not unusual for foreign nationals to train at US military facilities. A former Navy pilot told *Newsweek* that during his years on the base, "we always, always, always trained other countries' pilots. When I was there two decades ago, it was Iranians. The shah was in power. Whoever the country du jour is, that's whose pilots we train."

Candidates begin with "an officer's equivalent of boot camp," he said. "Then they would put them through flight training." The US has a long-standing agreement with Saudi Arabia—a key ally in the 1990-91 gulf war—to train pilots for its National Guard. Candidates are trained in air combat on several Army and Navy bases. Training is paid for by Saudi Arabia.[63]

Knight Ridder news service provided more specific details of the findings. Mohamed Atta had attended International Officers School at Maxwell Air Force Base in Montgomery, Alabama; Abdulaziz Alomari had attended Aerospace Medical School at Brooks Air Force base in Texas; and Saeed Alghamdi had been to the Defense Language Institute in Monterey, California. Citing sources in the US Defense Department, the *New York Times* confirmed the same.[64] A *Washington Post* report further revealed that as many as "four of 19 suspected hijackers may have participated during the 1990s" in a "flight training program for foreign military trainees" at Pensacola Naval Air Station. "Two of 19 suspects named by the FBI, Saeed Alghamdi and Ahmed Alghamdi, have the same names as men listed at a housing facility for foreign military trainees at Pensacola. Two others, Hamza Alghamdi and Ahmed Alnami, have names similar to individuals listed in public records as using the same address inside the base."[65]

The key problem here is that the hijackers would have required a certain degree of high-level security clearance to train at these military installations, and would have had their backgrounds thoroughly checked. But Mohamed Atta, for example, was on a terrorist watch list since 1986. How could this lapse have occurred?

Not long after these embarrassing reports of US military ties to al-Qaeda terrorists, the US Air Force issued an official statement of denial, arguing that "the name matches may not necessarily mean the students were the hijackers because of discrepancies in ages and other personal data." Although some terrorists "had similar names to foreign alumni of US military courses," these biographical discrepancies "indicate we are probably not talking about the same people." But the government has refused to substantiate the denial, by preventing the publication of the relevant biographical data that would actually prove the discrepancies. On September 16, 2001, news reports asserted that "Officials would not release ages, country of origin or any other specific details of the three individuals"—and have refused to do so to date.

The most pertinent illustration of the duplicity of official explanations, however, is that even Senate inquiries were simultaneously stonewalled by government officials from three agencies and departments—the Department of Justice, the Department of Defense, and the FBI. When *Newsweek* reported that three of the hijackers were trained at the secure Pensacola Naval Station in Florida, Senator Bill Nelson faxed Attorney-General John Ashcroft demanding to know if it was true. On September 17, 2001, Senator Nelson also "asked the Pentagon to confirm or refute reports that two of the terrorists were listed at a housing facility for foreign military officers at a Pensacola Florida Air Base."[66] By September 21, Senator Nelson "was informed that the FBI could neither say 'yes' or 'no,'" according to Nelson's press office. Apparently, the bureau was still "investigating any connection to the military facility."[67] By October 30, 2001, journalist Daniel Hopsicker—who has been a producer at PBS's *Wall Street Week*, an executive producer of NBC TV's *Global Business*, and an investigative reporter for NBC News—contacted Senator Nelson's office and was told that "In the wake of those reports we asked about the Pensacola Naval Air Station but we never got a definitive answer from the Justice Department. So we asked the FBI for an answer 'if and when' they could provide us one. Their response to date has been that they are trying to sort through something complicated and difficult."[68] What was so complicated and difficult about confirming the identity of the military trainees?

Curiously, in complete contradiction to the stance of other federal agencies, the US Air Force's public position was that the matter was in fact solved, case closed. Hopsicker subsequently queried a major in the US Air Force's public affairs office who "was familiar with the question." She explained "Biographically, they're not the same people. Some of the ages are 20 years off." But when questioned to substantiate the specific discrepancy, she was forced to admit that *there was no discrepancy*. According to Hopsicker: "'Some' of the ages? We told her we were only interested in Atta. Was she saying that the age of the Mohamed Atta who attended the Air Force's International Officer's School at Maxwell Air Force Base was different from the terrorist Atta's age as reported? Um, er, no, the major admitted." Hopsicker asked if he could contact the other alleged "Mohamed Atta" at the International Officer's School at Maxwell Air Force Base, who was purportedly confused with the chief 9/11 hijacker, so that he could confirm that they were indeed two different individuals. The major declined without explanation, stating that she did not "think you're going to get that information."[69]

But Hopsicker was not finished. In an interview with the Pentagon, Hopsicker was told by a spokesman for the US Defense Department that some terrorists did attend US military installations, but declined to release any further details:

> Despite earlier denials, terrorists in the Sept. 11 attacks received training at secure US military bases, a Defense Department spokesman

admitted.... In an interview with a reporter questioning the vaguely-worded Sept 16 Pentagon denial, the Defense Department spokesman was asked to explain the particulars of fuzzy statements in which officials said "name matches *may not necessarily* mean the students were the hijackers," and that discrepancies in biographical data indicate "we are *probably* not talking about the same people."

Pressed repeatedly to provide specifics, the spokesperson finally admitted, "I do not have the authority to tell you who (which terrorists) attended which schools." So it appears certain that at least some of the previous denials have been rendered inoperative, and that a list exists in the Defense Department which names Sept 11 terrorists who received training at US military facilities, a list the Pentagon is in no hurry to make public.[70]

How did al-Qaeda terrorists receive clearance for training at secure US military facilities and for what purpose?

The Drug Enforcement Administration's "Green Light" for Flight Training

Three days after 9/11, FBI Director Robert S. Mueller III claimed that the FBI had no idea that al-Qaeda operatives were training at US flight schools before the attacks. According to the *Washington Post*, he had "described reports that several of the hijackers had received flight training in the United States as 'news, quite obviously,' adding, 'If we had understood that to be the case, we would have—perhaps one could have averted this.'" But astonishingly, the same *Post* article illustrated that Mueller had misled the public about the FBI's lack of knowledge—because the FBI had been aware of such domestic terrorist activity for far longer: "Federal authorities have been aware for years that suspected terrorists with ties to Osama bin Laden were receiving flight training at schools in the United States and abroad, according to interviews and court testimony." A senior government official acknowledged the FBI knew of nearly "a dozen people with links to bin Laden had attended US flight schools."[71]

In the aftermath of 9/11, authorities were probing the European business associations of a Venice flight school owner, "whose school at the Venice airport trained the nucleus of foreign national terrorist pilots." Three of the airliners involved in 9/11 "were piloted by terrorists who had trained at two flight schools at the Venice, Florida airport."[72]

Indeed, almost all of them trained at either of two flight schools owned by Arne Kruithof and Rudi Dekkers. Convincing circumstantial data indicates that the FBI knew about the al-Qaeda flight training long before 9/11. "The FBI was swarming Huffman Aviation by 2 AM, just 18 hours following the attack. They removed student files from two schools at the Venice airport: Huffman Aviation and the Florida Flight Training Center just down the street."[73] According to one

Huffman Aviation official interviewed by Hopsicker: "How do you think the FBI got here [Huffman Aviation] so fast after the attack? They knew what was going on here. Hell, they were parked in a white van outside my house less than *four* hours after the buildings collapsed."[74] One federal investigator from the FBI Joint Terrorism Task Force in South Florida, an elite squad assigned to track possible espionage and terrorism cases, agreed that the speed at which the FBI furnished the names of the hijackers and located their flight schools proved that they were being monitored:

> Right after the hijackings we knew the government had a problem. Within hours of the attack we had names of the hijackers and that we needed to focus on flight schools. It was clear how the information quickly flowed down that someone in Washington must have had previous knowledge. They sat on this and they blew it and it's finally coming out.[75]

If within *hours* of the attack, the FBI knew where to look—which particular flight schools and which terrorists—then both were undoubtedly already being investigated. In that case, the failure to pursue preemptive action against them is disturbing. A related issue concerns the man who runs Huffman Aviation where most of the 9/11 terrorists were trained: Rudi Dekkers, who has not been investigated by authorities. At face value, Dekkers is a suspicious character. For instance, his chronology of the flight training of hijackers Atta and Al-Shehhi contradicts the independent testimony of several other flight instructors at Jones Aviation Flying Instructors, Inc. Therefore, his honesty is questionable. Additionally, "Dekkers had purchased his aviation school at just about the time the terrorist pilots moved into town and began their lessons," according to an aviation employee at Venice Airport. Another observer at the Airport admitted: "I've always had some suspicions about the way he breezed into town out of nowhere. Just too many odd little things. For example, he has absolutely no aviation background as far as anyone can tell. And he evidently had no use for, nor knowledge of, FAA rules and regs." A Special Operations Commando leader from the nearby McDill Air Force Base observed: "Rudi's greedy, and when you're greedy you can be used for something."[76]

Hopsicker reports that according to law enforcement officials, Dekkers has even been officially indicted in his native country, Holland, on financial charges including fraud and money laundering.[77] Yet despite his dubious background and connections, in addition to the fact that he trained most of the terrorists behind 9/11, 48 hours after the attacks, "Dekkers, known to have trained virtually the entire terrorist pilot cadre… seemed impervious to suspicion."[78]

Evidence that Dekkers' activities were known by elements of the federal government was revealed by a Venice Airport executive who told Hopsicker that Britannia Aviation—which operates from a hangar at Rudi Dekker's Huffman

Aviation in Venice Airport—had a "green light" from the Justice Department's Drugs Enforcement Administration (DEA). The executive also confirmed that the Venice Police Department "had been warned to leave them alone." Britannia Aviation had been awarded a five-year contract to run a large regional maintenance facility at the Lynchburg, Virginia, regional airport. At the time of the award, virtually nothing was known about the company. When Britannia was chosen over a respected and successful Lynchburg company boasting a multi-million dollar balance sheet and more than 40 employees, aviation executives there began voicing concerns to reporters at the local newspaper:

> ... it was discovered that Britannia Aviation is a company with virtually no assets, employees, or corporate history. Moreover, the company did not even possess the necessary FAA license to perform the aircraft maintenance services for which it had just been contracted by the city of Lynchburg.... When Britannia Aviation's financial statements were released after prodding by the local aviation community, they revealed Britannia to be a "company" worth less than $750.

"Why did a transparent dummy front company like Paul Marten's Britannia Aviation have a 'green light' from the DEA?" asks Hopsicker. "A green light for what?" It also emerged that the company had, according to one of its executives Paul Marten, "for some time been successfully providing aviation maintenance services for Caribe Air, a Caribbean carrier." Hopsicker reports that Caribe Air is:

> ... a notorious CIA proprietary air carrier which, even by the standards of a CIA proprietary, has had a particularly checkered past.... Caribe Air's history includes "blemishes" like having its aircraft seized by federal officials at the infamous Mena, Arkansas, airport a decade ago, after the company was accused by government prosecutors of having used as many as 20 planes to ship drugs worth billions of dollars into this country.

Why does Britannia—a company reportedly with CIA connections that is operating illegally out of the same flight school which trained al-Qaeda hijackers—have a "green light" from the Justice Department's DEA and effective immunity from local police inquiries? In Hopsicker's view: "The new evidence adds to existing indications that Mohamed Atta and his terrorist cadre's flight training in this country was part of a so-far unacknowledged US government intelligence operation."[79]

Especially in the context of the previous documentation in this study, it is difficult to avoid the conclusion that, somehow, as yet undisclosed US covert operations conducted jointly with various allies systematically intersected with the activities of al-Qaeda operatives facilitating their plans. The above account certainly suggests that while US intelligence was well aware of al-Qaeda terrorists training at US flight schools and had monitored them for years, no effort was made to apprehend them. On the contrary, they evidently were given a "green light" from some federal agencies—despite the escalating warnings of an imminent al-Qaeda attack.

Islamic Fundamentalists?

A variety of reports based on journalistic investigations and eye-witness testimonials provide a bizarre picture at odds with the conventional portrayal of the 9/11 hijackers as Islamic fundamentalists. Two key hijackers, Mohamed Atta and Marwan al-Shehhi, visited the popular Woodland Park Resort Hotel in the Philippines several times between 1998 and 2000 according to numerous local residents and hotel workers who recognized them from news photographs. They reportedly "drank whiskey with Philippine bargirls, dined at a restaurant that specializes in Middle Eastern cuisine and visited at least one of the local flight schools." Al-Shehhi threw a party with six or seven Arab friends in December 2000 at the Hotel according to former waitress Gina Marcelo. "They rented the open area by the swimming pool for 1,000 pesos," she recounts. "They drank Johnnie Walker Black Label whiskey and mineral water. They barbecued shrimp and onions. They came in big vehicles, and they had a lot of money. They all had girlfriends." But one big mistake they made was that unlike most foreign visitors, "[t]hey never tipped. If they did, I would not remember them so well." Victoria Brocoy, a chambermaid at the Woodland, recalls: "Many times I saw him let a girl go at the gate in the morning. It was always a different girl."[80]

According to US investigators, five of the hijackers including Atta, Al-Shehhi, Nawaq Alhamzi, Ziad Jarrah, and Hani Hanjour visited Las Vegas at least six times between May and August 2001. The *San Francisco Chronicle* reports that here they "engaged in some decidedly un-Islamic sampling of prohibited pleasures in America's reputed capital of moral corrosion," including drinking alcohol, gambling, and visiting strip-clubs.[81] As the *South Florida Sun Sentinel* observed, the hijackers' frequent debauchery was at odds with the most basic tenets of Islam:

> Three guys cavorting with lap dancers at the Pink Pony Nude Theater. Two others knocking back glasses of Stolichnaya and rum and Coke at a fish joint in Hollywood the weekend before committing suicide and mass murder. That might describe the behavior of several men who are suspects in Tuesday's terrorist attack, but it is not a picture of devout Muslims, experts say. Let alone that of religious zealots in their final days on Earth.

For instance, specialist in Islamic and Middle East studies Mahmoud Mustafa Ayoub, professor of religion at Temple University in Philadelphia, noted that the prohibition of alcohol, gambling, and sex outside marriage are Islam's most fundamental precepts: "It is incomprehensible that a person could drink and go to a strip bar one night, then kill themselves the next day in the name of Islam. People who would kill themselves for their faith would come from very strict Islamic ideology. Something here does not add up."[82]

Similar reports abound regarding other al-Qaeda terrorists connected to 9/11. Even alleged 9/11 mastermind Khalid Sheikh Mohammad reportedly "met associates in karaoke bars and giant go-go clubs filled with mirrors, flashing lights and bikini-clad dancers," according to evidence collected by Philippine investigators:

> He held meetings at four-star hotels. He took scuba-diving lessons at a coastal resort. When he wasn't engaged with the go-go dancers, he courted a Philippine dentist. Once, to impress her, he rented a helicopter and flew it over her office, then called her on his cell phone and told her to look up and wave.

Mohammad's al-Qaeda associates engaged in much the same behavior. They had local girlfriends and held a drinking party "to celebrate the anniversary of the 1988 Pan Am Flight 103 explosion over Lockerbie, Scotland."[83]

Clearly, this pattern of debauchery is not by any standard commensurate with the strict requirements of al-Qaeda's brand of Islamic fundamentalism. As Professors Quintan Wiktorowicz and John Kaltner point out, al-Qaeda is

> a radical tendency within a broader Islamic movement known as the Salafi movement...
>
> The term Salafi is derived from the Arabic salaf, which means "to precede" and refers to the companions of the Prophet Muhammed. Because the salaf learned about Islam directly from the messenger of God, their example is an important illustration of piety and unadulterated religious practice. Salafis argue that centuries of syncretic cultural and popular religious rituals and interpretations distorted the purity of the message of God and that only by returning to the example of the prophet and his companions can Muslims achieve salvation. The label "Salafi" is thus used to connote "proper" religious adherence and moral legitimacy, implying that alternative understandings are corrupt deviations from the straight path of Islam.

Thus, although there are various schools of thought within Salafism—including al-Qaeda's violent jihadist interpretation—they all emphasize and indeed attempt to derive their legitimacy from the Salafist goal of "piety and unadulterated religious practice" based directly on the piety and practice of the Prophet.[84] In this context, the depraved conduct of the 9/11 hijackers in terms of their routine violation of the most basic Islamic precepts contradicts al-Qaeda's strictly puritan Salafist philosophy.

The Takfir Paradigm

How to explain this anomaly? Western intelligence agencies have come up with one attempt at an answer. *Time* magazine reports that intelligence officials claim that many al-Qaeda terrorists are "followers of an extremist Islamic ideology called Takfir wal Hijra (Anathema and Exile). That's bad news: by blending into host communities, Takfiris attempt to avoid suspicion. A French official says they come across as 'regular, fun-loving guys—but they'd slit your throat or bomb your building in a second.'" Another French official says that the goal of Takfir "is to blend into corrupt societies in order to plot attacks against them better. Members live together, will drink alcohol, eat during Ramadan, become smart dressers and ladies' men to show just how integrated they are."[85]

However, this depiction of al-Qaeda and Takfir wal Hijra is thoroughly inaccurate. Takfir wal Hijra was the title given to a radical Islamic movement known as the Society of Muslims. The latter was founded in Egypt by Muslim Brotherhood member Shukri Mustafa after his release from prison in 1971. The group disintegrated after Mustafa was arrested and executed by the Egyptian government, but some of its followers went on to join other radical groups such as al-Jihad and/or fled to North Africa. Rather than attempting to integrate into modern society to carry out attacks, as intelligence officials now claim, Takfiri ideology advocated the very opposite: "As contemporary society was infidel, he argued, Takfir would set up its own alternative community that would work, study and pray together.... Takfir declared that not only the regime but the society itself was infidel and under excommunication. This entailed... a personal withdrawal from society." Even Takfir's rival radical Islamic group in Egypt, Jama'at al-Jihad, known as the Society of Struggle, espoused such a harsh perspective of Islamic practice that it advocated as Islam's top priority "jihad against unbelievers—including 'Muslims' who did not observe the religion's requirements properly"—far from endorsing in any manner a violation of those requirements.[86]

Indeed, according to the *South Asia Analysis Group (SAAG)*, the fact that "some analysts treat the Takfirees as no different from the Al-Qaeda" is a mistake. Citing religious sources in Pakistan, *SAAG* observes that Takfir wal Hijra as it exists now

> is one of the very few jihadi groups in the Pakistan-Afghanistan region which has refused to accept the leadership and the modus operandi of Osama bin Laden and his Al-Qaeda...
>
> According to them, it had unsuccessfully tried to assassinate him when he was living in the Sudan before the middle of 1996 when he shifted to Afghanistan. It had also reportedly issued a fatwa in 1999 calling for his assassination. Even though it's religious ideology is as extreme as that of bin Laden, if not more, its modus operandi differs in the sense it believes that before getting involved in a head-on confrontation with the US one should get rid of all US surrogates in the Islamic countries through targeted

assassinations. It feels that bin Laden weakened the cause of the jihad against the US by prematurely taking the US head-on on 9/11 without first eliminating its surrogates in Pakistan and other countries of the Islamic world.[87]

The *Sunday Times* similarly reported a month after 9/11 that Takfir "regards Osama bin Laden as an infidel who has sold out." The group's fundamentalism is so extreme that its members "have embarked on killing sprees in mosques against fellow Muslims in the belief that a pure Islamic state can be built only if the corrupt elements of the last one are wiped out." Takfir's enmity toward al-Qaeda is based on the perception that Osama bin Laden is "excessively liberal." In 1995, four Takfir members attempted to assassinate bin Laden at his home in Khartoum. Takfiris continue to be "angered" at bin Laden's leadership of a "compromised jihad." According to the *Times*, "Takfir denounces all but those who copy the behaviour of the prophet Muhammad as infidels and promises to kill them." One senior Sudanese government source confirmed that Takfir "regard [bin Laden] as a sellout... the Takfir think that everything in contemporary Muslim society is corrupt and should be destroyed." Both Abu Hamza and Omar Bakri Mohammed, London-based clerics allegedly linked to al-Qaeda, have condemned Takfir and distanced al-Qaeda from the former.[88]

Djamel Beghal and Kamel Daoudi—alleged UK-based terrorists arrested in September 2001 for plotting a series of spectacular terrorist assaults on Europe—were both supposed to be members of Takfir wal Hijra. But according to one Algerian in London who knew Beghal, integrating into Western culture by engaging in various acts of debauchery in violation of Islamic tenets was the last thing this alleged Takfiri would ever do: "Believe me, you do not want these people in your country... they will kill anybody, including their own family, if they are caught smoking or drinking."[89]

Thus, the new scenario being proposed by Western intelligence officials to explain the patently un-Islamic behavior of the 9/11 hijackers is largely incoherent. Despite claims to the contrary, Takfir wal Hijra is aggressively opposed to al-Qaeda and its strict ideology is fundamentally incommensurate with the prospect of permitting defiance of Islamic rules under any circumstances. Furthermore, al-Qaeda is in turn staunchly opposed to Takfir. Therefore, the anomaly of the 9/11 hijackers persists: They clearly did not possess the conduct of hardened Islamic fundamentalists connected to al-Qaeda. So, who were they?

San Francisco lawyer Stanley Hilton has offered one explanation. Hilton, former US Senate Attorney and senior counsel to Republican Senator Bob Dole, filed a $7 billion lawsuit in US district court on June 3, 2002.[90] Citing official documents, sources, and depositions under oath for his case, Hilton explained that one of his key witnesses is a woman married to one of the 9/11 hijackers. He describes how he had deposed, obtained certified marriage certificates, and even photographic evidence, proving her relationship to the hijacker, and corroborated her testimony under oath with interviews and depositions under oath from other individuals connected to the hijackers. The picture that emerges from his work is truly alarming. In his own words, quoted below:

> I do have a witness who was married, she's an American woman, but she was married to one of the hijackers and she knew about seven of them. She met seven of them. Essentially these Arab hijackers were double agents. That is, they were operating inside the US for ten to fifteen years in "cells." Some of them used the term al Qaeda, they've used other terms. Al Qaeda is just a word. That means nothing. You could call them the Muslim Brotherhood, the Army of God, they go by all sorts of names. But what they are is a series of cells that have been aided and abetted by the US Government. This woman was involved also, married to him at the time of the 1993 World Trade Center first bombing.... And they were involved, apparently, in that.
>
> But what we have here is double agents. In that they nominally appear to be Arab fanatics. But one of the points that she stressed is they are really not Muslims. They are more interested in *Playboy* than in the Koran. I mean these people drink. They are very secular. They are not the fanatical Muslim zealots that the Bush criminals would lead us to believe is what's operating here. What they are is they receive regular payments from the US Government. They have been recruited by the CIA, FBI, counter-intelligence, and so-forth and paid money and allowed to exchange information with US government agents about various activities going on and....
>
> ... [T]hese people operated in cells. The cells are from six to twelve individuals. And the cells move around, for instance, from Portland, Oregon to San Diego. It's just one example. But they didn't move all six to twelve of them by chance. They were instructed to do it. They were at locations or schools or apartments, etc., that were bought here. Again, this is from a direct eyewitness. This has been verified with marriage certificates, documents, photographs—photographs with bin Laden and his brothers.[91]

Hilton's extraordinary information, of course, is impossible to corroborate independently at this stage. But given his credentials as a lawyer and the fact that he represents 400 plaintiffs nationwide who are 9/11 families, his work—however unconventional—deserves attention, particularly in view of its explanatory power. Hilton's evidence makes sense of the bizarre pattern of Western–al-Qaeda connections across the globe. If the hijackers were paid informants connected to foreign governments, it is conceivable that they received a degree of immunity and security clearance. Were 9/11 and other terrorist attacks on US soil forms of "blowback" from concurrent US military intelligence operations?

9.

Intelligence Breakdown or Political Fiasco?

As early as 1995, the US had information relating to the plans to launch air attacks on the World Trade Center—information that was repeatedly confirmed by the American intelligence community since then, all the way to the year 2001. Yet these agencies almost entirely neglected to do anything to prevent or prepare for these attacks as far as the general public was concerned.[1] Indeed, all such possible measures of prevention were cut short. Such was the case with the investigations by FBI agents confirming the impending attacks, whose leads were severed by the FBI command without explanation—a situation apparently maintained with the complicity of the Attorney General, a presidential appointee. The US government's leading law enforcement agency thus deliberately ignored its own findings and blocked these findings from being publicized.

We should particularly consider ECHELON's warnings of a Project Bojinka operation by al-Qaeda on US soil, targeting "symbols of American culture," first 6 months and then 3 months prior to September. According to the *Newsbytes* division of the *Washington Post*, "the warnings" that terrorists planned to hijack civilian airplanes and use them as bombs "were taken seriously" by "the American intelligence community," as a consequence of which "surveillance intensified." Furthermore, White House counterterrorism chief Richard A. Clarke confirms that the CIA fully anticipated an impending al-Qaeda attack on US soil in June 2001, and that the entire intelligence community was alerted by the beginning of July, just over six weeks prior to September 11, 2001.

The term "intelligence community" refers to all the official government agencies that have an "intelligence" role. The official line has been that intelligence agencies had no reason to believe that operatives linked to bin Laden were about to use their training to perform a terrorist act—but the documentation presented here shows that this is entirely false: the intelligence community already knew what al-Qaeda was planning—it was just a matter of who and when.

Indeed, as a direct consequence of the intensification of surveillance, US intelligence began finding out who. And as a direct consequence of the convergence of urgent warnings from multiple credible sources, including the interception of communications by Osama bin Laden himself, the probable date of the attacks also grew increasingly evident. Yet when FBI agents began finding out who (i.e. al-Qaeda operatives training at US military and flight facilities), the investigations were blocked by the FBI command and Justice Department. When multiple warnings together pointed clearly to the probability of an imminent attack by bin Laden, likely to occur on 9/11, these warnings were ignored. In summary, the data evaluated heretofore demonstrates without doubt that the US intelligence community had developed fairly extensive information on the probable time of the attacks (the week of September 11, 2001, with circumstantial evidence suggesting specific warning of the exact data of 9/11, e.g. the cancelation of the next day's travel plans by senior Pentagon officials on September 10, 2001, "over security concerns"); had repeated and credible warnings that the World Trade Center and other key symbolic structures on the US mainland were the most probable targets of an impending attack on US soil, with repeated warnings of attacks on Washington and New York; had ample warning that the World Trade Center was on the top of the list of targets; and had precise and credible information on the exact method and nature of the attacks (i.e. hijacked commercial planes being used as bombs).

In summary, the material examined here demonstrates that the intelligence community, in advance of the 9/11 attacks, was fully cognizant that: 1) the principal terrorist threat to the United States came from al-Qaeda and Osama bin Laden; 2) the specific method of the planned attack was to hijack civilian planes and fly them into key US buildings; 3) the primary targets of the plans were key buildings in Washington and New York, including the White House, the Pentagon, and the World Trade Center, the latter being a top priority; 4) high-level al-Qaeda planners monitored by the intelligence community as well as the intelligence community itself expected the attack to occur on or around September 11, 2001. This data is entirely at odds with the picture disseminated by officials, including the findings of the 9/11 Commission. In this context, the US government's failure to act is inexplicable. This seems to lead the chain of responsibility for the failure to act right to the top echelons of government.

Structural Fragmentation?: A Critique

The idea that the failure to act was a result of institutionalized incompetence resulting from unintentional bureaucratic problems within the American intelligence community—leading to the failure to disseminate and analyze relevant information—does not address the nature of the multiple warnings received, nor the intelligence community's capabilities and activities prior to 9/11.

That assumption has been uncritically adopted even by the private US intelligence firm Stratfor (Strategic Forecasting), which employs former US intelligence officers who produce independent intelligence analysis on world affairs. In a report on the 9/11 intelligence failure, Stratfor stated:

We have no doubt that, after the databases have been searched, it will be found that US intelligence had plenty of information in some highly secure computer. The newspapers will trumpet, "CIA knew identity of attackers." That will be only technically true. Buried in the huge mounds of information perhaps once having passed across an overworked analyst's desk, some bit of information might have made its circuit of the agencies. But saying that US intelligence actually "knew" about the attackers' plots would be overstating it. Owning a book and knowing what's in it are two vastly different things.[2]

In another report, Stratfor elaborated on this perspective in some detail, arguing that the colossal 9/11 intelligence failure was a consequence of the structural fragmentation of the US intelligence community:

The Central Intelligence Agency, as the name suggests, was founded to centralize the intelligence function of the United States.... Unfortunately, [this] is an idea that has never been truly implemented and from which, over time, the government has moved intractably away. A centralized intelligence capability is essential if the United States is to have a single, integrated, coherent picture of what is happening in the world. A bureaucratically fragmented intelligence community will generate a fragmented picture of the world. That is currently what we have.[3]

While it is clear that a generally "fragmented picture of the world" is a likely consequence of a "bureaucratically fragmented intelligence community," in itself this does not demonstrate that the capabilities of that community in developing specific intelligence on various aspects of the world is completely dysfunctional. Rather it suggests something very specific: that the US intelligence community will find it hard to develop an integrated, coherent understanding of world affairs and their interrelationships.

What is likely to be developed instead are somewhat uncorrelated and/or disconnected pockets of intelligence on various aspects of world affairs. This, however, does not entail that the intelligence produced will be inaccurate with respect to those *particular* aspects. On the contrary, it indicates that while the US intelligence community is capable of developing accurate intelligence on *specific* disparate aspects of world affairs, due to the structural fragmentation among the various agencies that constitute the intelligence community, a coherent overall intelligence picture of the world based on comprehension of the complex influences and interconnections between these disparate aspects will be extremely difficult to construct. Indeed, Stratfor itself grasps this implication: "It is unclear whether any of these agencies completely understand their own internal vision, let alone that they are able to transmit a comprehensive picture to the CIA (which is supposed to integrate all this into a coherent world view and serve it up to the president and other senior officials for action)."

Clearly, the problem here does not relate to the task of focusing and gathering intelligence on, for instance, a *particular threat to US national security* or *the specific field of counterterrorism*—rather it relates to the integration of disparate intelligence into "a single, integrated, coherent picture" of world affairs. Structural stumbling blocks principally affect the coordination of the US intelligence community in developing "a coherent worldview." Attempting to account for an intelligence failure on an extremely specific aspect of world affairs—namely, a particular terrorist threat to US national security—on the basis of such structural stumbling blocks is wholly unwarranted.

In other words, while it is certainly possible that structural deficiencies may have played some role in any intelligence failure, to simply pre-suppose that this provides an adequate explanation for the failure in the absence of an in-depth factual analysis of the failure itself is nothing but gratuitous speculation. Indeed, given that such structural fragmentation principally affects the integration of intelligence into a "a single, integrated, coherent picture of what is happening in the world," at face value it is highly unlikely that this fragmentation alone would be sufficient to result in a wholesale intelligence failure on any isolated *aspect* of world affairs.

Stratfor, however, mistakenly extends the scope of its analysis of structural fragmentation to the 9/11 intelligence failure—which of course was a very specific threat to US national security. But Stratfor's own definitions preclude this extension. Stratfor goes on to observe that

> ... [T]he US intelligence system is overwhelmingly geared toward the collection, rather than the analysis, of information. The result is inevitable: a huge amount of information is gathered, but it is never turned into intelligence.... The collection capacity of the United States, both technical and human, is vast. But it is deliberately and institutionally compartmentalized in such a way that prevents a coherent perspective from emerging.[4]

As is documented later on in this study, this statement is factually incorrect—in recent years, the intelligence community has invested hugely in the expansion of its analytical capabilities, which prior to 9/11 became quite formidable. Furthermore, it is the coordination of intelligence on *different* aspects of world affairs into *an integrated whole* that is institutionally problematic as a consequence of the intelligence community's compartmentalization. Intelligence on specific issues is not implicated here.

It is, therefore, incorrect for Stratfor to claim that "Given this incredible tangle of capabilities, jurisdictions and competencies, it is a marvel that a finished intelligence product is ever delivered to decision makers." Indeed, according to John Deutch, former Director of Central Intelligence, and Jeffrey

H. Smith, former CIA General Counsel: "Over the past two decades, despite organizational handicaps and conflicting authorities, the intelligence community has built up a considerable counterterrorism capability that has resulted in many successes."[5] Whatever the structural deficiencies of the intelligence community, then, those have not fundamentally impeded the community's counterterrorism operations.

Military intelligence expert Professor Richard K. Betts of the Institute of War and Peace Studies at Columbia University—a former staff member of the National Security Council, Senate Intelligence Committee, and National Commission on Terrorism—observes in *Foreign Affairs* that prior to 9/11, the intelligence community's counterterrorism programs had a high degree of success. "[T]he intelligence community has worked much better" than its critics assumed, he argues. "Contrary to the image left by the destruction of September 11, US intelligence and associated services have generally done very well at protecting the country." Many great successes in "thwarting previous terrorist attacks are too easily forgotten." Betts' analysis clarifies that it is unwarranted to presume that institutionalized structural deficiencies were solely responsible for the 9/11 intelligence failure.[6]

According to a 1998 report by the International Policy Institute for Counter-Terrorism (ICT) based in Herzliya, the past decade has featured a wide array of US intelligence successes due to a vast improvement in capabilities. "Many terrorist attacks have been prevented or foiled, but successes of intelligence services generally are not published," the ICT points out.

> From the organizational point of view, the security and intelligence agencies have taken serious steps to improve their capabilities. The FBI has tripled its counter-terrorism force after the World Trade Center attack and the CIA has created a Terrorism Warning Group to deal with the threat at the highest civilian and military level.[7]

By November 2000, Washington Director of RAND Bruce Hoffman cited the findings of a RAND report, *Foreign Policy and National Security Transition 2001*, authored by a bipartisan group of more than 40 distinguished national security experts. The report was commissioned to explore whether the "fundamental architecture" of the US intelligence community, "created more than 50 years ago to counter the communist threat... is relevant to contemporary security challenges." Hoffman argues that the intelligence community "must resist the temptation to fix wheels that aren't broken," and highlights the community's

> highly commendable track record in thwarting a succession of anti-American terrorist acts here and abroad...
>
> These include repeated attempts made against US embassies following the East Africa bombings, the apprehension last December of a terrorist in

Washington state and the disruption of a related plot to kill US tourists in Jordan that month. Indeed, this appears to be the one key area of US counterterrorism policy that functions admirably.[8]

In this context, if structural deficiencies are not the principal cause of past intelligence failures, what is the cause? A well-documented answer to this question is provided by US intelligence expert Loch K. Johnson—former assistant to Defense Secretary Les Aspin and Regents Professor of political science at the University of Georgia—in his Yale University study, *Secret Agencies*. Johnson studies how, and how well, intelligence efforts have guarded and advanced perceived US interests, based on a detailed analysis of a series of intelligence successes and failures. His key finding is that common simplistic charges of ineptitude following embarrassing intelligence failures such as the Aldrich Ames case are fundamentally flawed. Rather, he argues convincingly that the successes of the CIA and the intelligence community far outweigh such setbacks. Most significantly, he garners meticulous evidence that responsibility for past intelligence failures have largely been laid at the wrong door. The vast majority of intelligence failures occur, Johnson concludes, because perfectly good intelligence has been ignored by the upper political echelons of the Washington bureaucracy. He attributes the causes of these failures not to the quality of the intelligence product itself, but rather to inappropriate decisions on the part of the political leadership.[9]

Although, to its credit, Stratfor concedes that the US government "had collected much of the information that would have been necessary to prevent Sept. 11," the organization then presumes—without having even examined the data itself and what was done with it—that this information "wasn't collated, integrated, or analyzed and therefore could not be disseminated." But in the context of the above analysis, there is simply no good reason to make this presumption. On the contrary, historic precedent suggests that to understand the principal causes of any intelligence failure, one should begin by examining the decisions of the political establishment.

Pre-9/11 Intelligence Collection and Analysis

Washington editor of the *Nation* David Corn argues that "anyone with the most basic understanding of how government functions (or, does not function) realizes that the various bureaucracies of Washington—particularly those of the national security 'community'—do not work well together."[10] Unfortunately, Corn fails to specify in what respect this is the case. Unlike Stratfor, he fails to even offer a tangible argument on the structural discontinuities between different bureaucratic and intelligence agencies that might justify his conclusion.

Consequently, his blanket statement about the national security community "not working well together" fails to communicate anything significant. The assertion is devoid of even a minimal attempt to specify factually what this implies. As has been discussed, while the intelligence community suffers from institutional compartmentalization, this does not automatically entail that the community is completely incompetent and dysfunctional. Rather, as Stratfor admits, it impairs the functioning of the community in the preparation of integrated intelligence to develop "a coherent worldview." Corn's attempt to apply this specific problem in an extended and general manner is vacuous.

As noted by one State Department official, there exists a long-established and clearly defined standard procedure for dealing with any notice of a potential or alleged terrorist act, adopted by the US government and intelligence community at least as early as the 1980s. The US State Department acts as the lead coordinator in this regard, with other intelligence agencies participating in the overall process. This State Department working group was thus set up to share the same task as the CIA. Information on a potential or alleged terrorist act, according to standard procedure, is circulated and disseminated to other agencies in the intelligence community so that protective measures can be considered if necessary. Individual intelligence agencies subsequently evaluate the information in connection with other information received to determine whether such measures are required and to inform further intelligence investigations if justified.[11]

Indeed, David Corn's extreme portrayal is contradicted by a report in the *Washington Post* in May 2001, which observed that the two specialized US intelligence agencies, the FBI and the CIA, have "in recent years" developed a very close "working relationship" with respect to the specific field of counterterrorism. Former FBI Director Louis Freeh has been "credited with greatly improving the FBI's ability to counter terrorist threats," as well as "for altering the FBI's working relationship with the CIA, which long had been strained." As noted by CIA Director George J. Tenet, "Director Freeh's vision, leadership and commitment have been directly responsible for the unprecedented strategic partnership between the FBI and the CIA," a partnership that in the past few years has borne fruit in a verifiable record of intelligence successes. Tenet commented, for instance, that "Very significant successes in the counterterrorism and counterintelligence areas... are evidence of the remarkable cooperation that has existed between our two agencies in recent years."[12]

Such cooperation is corroborated by a *Washington Post* report at the beginning of the year 2000, documenting the highly successful combination of the intelligence community's comprehensive infiltration of al-Qaeda, extensive interception of al-Qaeda's electronic communications, and intensive ongoing internal and international cooperation with foreign intelligence services, leading to ongoing arrests of terrorist plotters. This provided the US with detailed round-the-clock information on al-Qaeda operations, allowing the US to prevent and pre-empt innumerable al-Qaeda terrorist attacks.

Saudi fugitive Osama bin Laden's terrorist network has been seriously weakened by arrests on three continents, infiltration by confidential informants and electronic eavesdropping by intelligence services, according to US and foreign government officials, law enforcement sources and terrorism experts...

Since the deadly bombings of US embassies in Tanzania and Kenya in 1998 that killed 224 people, bin Laden's attempts to carry out terrorist acts aimed at the United States, Jordan, Albania and elsewhere have been foiled by the cooperative efforts of intelligence officials around the world, sources said. While no one is declaring victory over bin Laden, who is living in Afghanistan, the round-the-clock focus on his movements and methods has proven effective at combating terrorist acts.

Dozens of terrorists allegedly trained in Afghanistan and connected to bin Laden have been arrested in Britain, Germany, Canada, the United States, Jordan and Pakistan, sources said. Thirteen were arrested after allegedly conspiring to bomb the Radisson Hotel in Jordan and nearby holy sites frequented by US and Israeli tourists; 12 others were arrested as they attempted to carry out a bomb plot in the United States by ferrying explosives into the country from Canada.

Informants in the Middle East and elsewhere have provided intelligence and law enforcement officials with valuable information about bin Laden's movements and plans, sources said, after infiltrating his al Qaeda terrorist network and training camps in Afghanistan. The net result of the arrests, the increased surveillance, cooperation among intelligence services and infiltration has been to weaken bin Laden's terrorist infrastructure and limit his freedom of movement.[13]

The above account significantly challenges the conventional wisdom that the 9/11 attacks were able to proceed solely because US intelligence agencies had failed to connect the dots adequately due to serious institutional deficiencies. As noted by Senator Bob Graham (D-Fla.), chairman of the Senate Intelligence Committee, any sentient individual with access to the information on the impending al-Qaeda attack should have been able to connect it to form a precise picture of what would occur: "Had one human being or a common group of human beings sat down with all that information, we could have gotten to the hijackers before they flew those four airplanes either into the World Trade Center, the Pentagon, or the ground of Pennsylvania."[14]

But federal agencies had been working together very well indeed on the issue of counterterrorism. A common group of intelligence experts, known as the Counterterrorism Security Group (CSG), was regularly assessing all reliable information received on the al-Qaeda attacks prior to 9/11. The CSG was chaired by Richard Clarke, White House National Coordinator for Infrastructure Protection and Counterterrorism. As the *Washington Post* reports:

While Clarke does not have direct authority over agencies such as the FBI or CIA, his position puts him at the center of the action when there is a terrorist alert. He chairs half a dozen agency groups including the powerful Counterterrorism Sub-Group (CSG), which coordinates the US government response to terrorist incidents... [H]e also wins high marks for effectiveness. "He is a pivotal figure," says Jonathan Winer, who previously fought international crime at the State Department and now works for the law firm of Alston & Bird. "There are times when he irritates people because he takes on institutional inertia. But he is thinking outside the box every single day, rather than just processing the paper."[15]

The inter-agency CSG constitutes a "highly effective" connecting point for "all federal agencies," whose members are "drawn mainly from the CIA, the National Security Council, and the upper tiers of the Defense Department, the Justice Department, and the State Department," and who meet "every week in the White House Situation Room." The CSG assesses "all reliable intelligence" related to counterterrorism received by the intelligence community. The CSG was working incessantly on the specific threat of the impending al-Qaeda plot prior to 9/11.[16] Indeed, according to *Insight On The News*: "[T]he White House now has revealed that its Counterterrorism Security Group (CSG), which brought together White House officials with those from all relevant federal agencies, began meeting several times a week within months after Bush took office."[17]

Through the CSG, in other words, officials from the major agencies of the US intelligence community—including high-level officials—were collectively assessing intelligence on al-Qaeda on a regular basis prior to 9/11. Thus, from both a statutory and an organizational standpoint, the argument of institutional incompetence is extremely weak. Even to argue that elements of the Bush administration had significant knowledge of what would happen, but not enough detail to take measures to prevent the attacks, is based on a very shallow appraisal of the nature of the intelligence warnings received. As evidenced on public records, these warnings were not only extremely detailed, but also extremely specific as to probable perpetrators, methods, targets, and dates.[18] As the *Intelligence Note Book* of the Canadian Forces Intelligence Branch Association clarifies in relation to methods of intelligence gathering:

> ... one always wants to have as many different sources as possible confirming one's intelligence assessment. When many different sources are combined in this way to produce one final assessment, this is known as "fused," "multi-source" or even "all-source" intelligence. Really, the sources used are a technicality, of more concern to the intelligence personnel producing the assessment than to the end-user. The end-users' primary interest in the sources used will simply be to reflect how certain the

conclusions are. The more different sources there are indicating a conclusion, the more certain we can be about that conclusion.[19]

Indeed, the numerous warnings received and intercepted by the US intelligence community in regard to 9/11 certainly met the four established criteria of what constitutes an intelligence success in strategic warning. Robert Betts refers to these criteria as follows:

- Intercepted information about the location and timing of attack was so rich as to make the deduction of warning obvious.
- The event involved was truly vital to US security rather than just one among many important problems, so leaders had no reason to avoid focusing on the warning.
- There was no problem of estimating the enemy's political intent to resort to force, as in pre-war crises.
- There was nothing to be lost from prompt and vigorous military reaction to warning...[20]

When the ECHELON warnings of a Project Bojinka operation were followed by warning after warning to the US intelligence community from Israel, Russia, France, Egypt, along with numerous leads and warnings within the US itself, according to the established procedures of intelligence gathering, the intelligence community should have grown increasingly certain of what was about to occur, by whom, and when. This is particularly clear given that the ECHELON warnings were taken seriously by the US intelligence community—thus providing the backdrop of credibility against which subsequent reliable warnings could be assessed. Yet, we find that despite this backdrop of credibility, the very opposite happened: legitimate and critical intelligence investigations were cut short.

The FBI's Blind Eye?

The 9/11 Commission has offered nothing new by way of explanation for the failure to act on these warnings. Rather, it has largely parroted the claims of senior government officials in their testimony before the Commission panel: that no credible, explicit, and sufficiently precise information on the attacks was ever received by the US intelligence community, and that the community was unable to react to information that was received due to structural interagency communication problems. Indeed, if the Commission is to be believed, the FBI was fundamentally lacking in funding, staff, and competence for the entire decade before 9/11 occurred—and somehow only 9/11 spurred the government to take notice and transform the Bureau in a matter of years.

In Staff Statement No. 9, for example, the Commission argues that "the FBI did not have a process in place to effectively manage its intelligence collection efforts. It did not identify intelligence gaps." Moreover, it suffered from a "wall" between "criminal and intelligence investigations" that apparently "caused agents to be less aggressive than they might otherwise have been in pursuing Foreign Intelligence Surveillance Act (FISA) surveillance powers in counterterrorism investigations."[21] That claim is incommensurate with the actual record which demonstrates not that FBI agents were "less aggressive" in pursuing FISA applications, but that the government was "less aggressive" in granting leave even though the evidence of a serious terrorist threat/connection was overwhelming. The prime example of this is the Moussaoui case, discussed in greater detail later on in this study, where the Justice Department rejected a FISA request in a decision that has been criticized as unjustifiable by FISA experts. Given that since 1978, 12,000 FISA applications for covert search warrants have been approved and only one (presumably Moussaoui's) rejected, it is absolutely clear that the Commission's narrative of "the wall" is demonstrably false.[22]

Nevertheless, the FBI, claims the Commission, was so impotent that it "did not have an adequate ability to know what it knew. In other words, the FBI did not have an effective mechanism for capturing or sharing its institutional knowledge." The Bureau had a sorely limited ability "to share its information internally and externally." Amazingly, it even "lacked an effective system for storing, searching, or retrieving information of intelligence value contained in its investigative files."[23] By this estimate, the FBI was supposedly virtually incapable of accessing its own intelligence files. But if that were the case, how would the FBI have been able to conduct a series of successful counterterrorist intelligence investigations resulting in prosecutions throughout the last decade? According to the Commission itself, these included: the World Trade Center bombing; the Landmarks plot; the Manila Airlines plot; the Khobar Towers bombing; the East Africa Embassy bombings; the Millennium plot; and the USS Cole bombing. And these are only "a few of the major episodes," excluding a large number of unpublished successes.[24] By this standard, the FBI had a verifiable record of success. Moreover, the evidence on record discussed previously shows that problems faced by the FBI in such investigations had little to do with "inadequate resources" and other inherent bureaucratic problems, but rather resulted directly from high-level political obstruction.

The Commission also contradicts itself. Despite acknowledging that "information sharing between the FBI and CIA improved greatly when the agencies began exchanging senior counterterrorism officials in 1996," the FBI was supposedly chronically unable to actually share information, to the point that the National Security Council never received any "relevant information" from the FBI at all—except once during the Millenium crisis.[25] Simultaneously, the Commission acknowledges that

The Justice Department representative on Clarke's interagency group, the Counterterrorism and Security Group, has told us, however, that—to his knowledge—neither Clarke nor anyone else at the NSC raised any systemic issue of FBI information sharing as a policy issue or a matter to be considered by the Attorney General.[26]

If a systemic FBI failure to share information was really a significant problem, senior government and intelligence officials working with the FBI from a variety of agencies and departments—not merely the NSC—would no doubt have raised the matter. But none of them did for over a decade. This is simply unbelievable. The implications here are critical—if the Commission's narrative is correct, then it in no way absolves senior government officials of responsibility. By failing to do anything about this alleged problem for more than a decade, they tacitly consented to it and in fact demonstrated their approval that this is how they wished the FBI to function: as a chronically "hobbled," inefficient, under-resourced agency. The question would then arise as to why the government connived in the emasculation of its own domestic law enforcement arm. And in that case, government officials are guilty of criminal negligence. However, given the resounding silence of so many officials from so many different agencies for so long, it is far more plausible to conclude that no such problem existed on such an absurd scale.

Indeed, even the Commission's claim that the FBI did not receive sufficient funding is questionable. While noting, for instance, that in 2001 the government did not include specific "counterterrorism enhancements" in that year's budget proposal, it did "include an enhancement for the FBI's information technology program intended to support the collection, analysis, and rapid dissemination of information pertinent to FBI investigations." Most crucial is the Commission's admission that "the FBI's counterterrorism budget tripled during the mid-1990s." Thus, the FBI had received a massive increase in funding. But the Commission complains that "FBI counterterrorism spending remained fairly constant between fiscal years 1998 and 2001" despite the tripling of its budget. This fact demonstrates clearly that funding itself has never been a problem—the FBI counterterrorism budget was so huge *it was not even being spent.* At the same time, the Commission insists that the FBI did not receive all the funds it requested from the Justice Department[27] and that then FBI Director Louis Freeh was "begging and screaming" for funds to spend on counterterrorist information technology.[28]

Indeed, the Commission is significantly incoherent on this point. While citing then-Attorney General Janet Reno opining that FBI Director Freeh was "unwilling to shift resources to terrorism from other areas such as violent crime," the Commission seems to not recognize that by its own admission, the FBI counterterrorism unit had tripled its budget but was still not utilizing its own funds to the full. Obviously, with that amount of resources at its disposal, the FBI's terrorism departments had no need to take resources from other departments. And anyhow, if Director Freeh had such powerful, unchecked discretion to resist the Justice Department's instructions on resource allocation, why did he not use that power to ignore his bosses by spending the considerable unused excess in his counterterrorism budget on the counterterrorist information technology he supposedly required so urgently? With these inconsistencies, the credibility of the Commission's narrative collapses. Based as it clearly is on endless "interviews"[29] with various "officials," rather than on an in-depth critical analysis of FBI records, the Commission ends up simply parroting an inconsistent, politically-motivated picture constructed to legitimize an ever increasing influx of funds.

Another motive of the Commission's unsubstantiated portrayal is with regard to the FBI's investigations of terrorist financing on US soil:

> FBI offices had been able to gain a basic understanding of some of the largest and most problematic terrorist financing conspiracies that have since been identified. The agents understood that there was a network of extremist organizations operating within the United States supporting a global Islamic jihad movement.

On the one hand, the Commission says that the FBI "did not know the degree to which these extremist groups were associated with al Qaeda. It was also unclear whether any of these groups were sending money to al Qaeda." On the other hand, the Commission firmly concludes that field offices in "New York, Chicago, Detroit, San Diego, and Minneapolis, had significant intelligence investigations into groups that appeared to be raising money for Islamic extremist groups" many of whom "appeared to the FBI to have some connection to either al Qaeda or Usama Bin Ladin." The Commission cannot have it both ways. Either the FBI had significant intelligence on al-Qaeda fundraising in the US, or it did not. As documented in previous chapters, it is a matter of public record that the FBI and wider intelligence community had extensive detailed intelligence on al-Qaeda's fundraising activities, both in the US and abroad— but these investigations were inexplicably ignored and/or blocked by senior officials. That is why, in the Commission's words: "FBI agents simply kept tabs on these fundraisers, even as millions of dollars flowed to foreign Islamic extremists."[30]

The Intelligence Community's Blind Eye?

In its transparent efforts to depict the US intelligence community as a collection of unremittingly constrained, frustrated, under-funded, and structurally impaired organizations incapable of developing integrated, all-source, and strategic analysis for government policymakers, the Commission has no qualms about brazenly lying. For example, the Commission goes so far as to claim that "While we now know that al Qaeda was formed in 1988, at the end of the Soviet occupation of Afghanistan, the Intelligence Community did not describe this organization, at least in documents we have seen, until 1999."[31] At face value, this statement is absurd. Ironically, the dishonesty of this claim is confirmed by the Commission itself in its earlier Staff Statement No. 5, as follows:

> By early 1997 intelligence and law enforcement officials in the US government had finally received reliable information disclosing the existence of al Qaeda as a worldwide terrorist organization. That information elaborated a command-and-control structure headed by Bin Ladin and various lieutenants, described a network of training camps to process recruits, discussed efforts to acquire weapons of mass destruction, and placed al Qaeda at the center among other groups affiliated with them in its "Islamic Army."[32]

The Commission's penchant for being distinctly economical with the truth is so flagrant that serious contradictions are rife within and among its own Staff Statements. This incoherence clarifies the extent to which the Commission's narrative as a whole has little credibility. Thus, the Commission says that the intelligence community simply "lacked a common information architecture that would help to ensure the integration of counterterrorism data across CIA, NSA, DIA, the FBI, and other agencies." The community consisted of "loosely associated agencies and departmental offices that lacked the incentives to cooperate, collaborate, and share information."[33] If this image of a thoroughly blind, incapable, and fundamentally fragmented intelligence community were true, the community would never be able to produce any meaningful intelligence on any threat whatsoever. But the Commission's claims do not fit with testimonials from the intelligence community itself. In his 1998 Congressional testimony, quoted below extensively, FBI Director Freeh confirmed that the US intelligence community was distinctly conscious of the domestic threat posed by international terrorism; had already developed highly sophisticated legal, investigative, and interagency information sharing structures and mechanisms; and was in the process of actively pursuing several new programs to upgrade these mechanisms and introduce new ones. Overall, this picture is in flat contradiction to the one offered by the Commission:

> [T]he trend toward more large-scale incidents designed for maximum destruction, terror, and media impact actually places an increasing proportion of our population at risk... this threat confronts Americans both here and abroad.... And as the trend toward more destructive terrorist plots continues, the threat to Americans will increase.... Today, Americans

engaged in activities as routine as working in an office building or commuting home during the evening rush hour can become innocent victims to the aims of international terrorists....

The FBI counterterrorism center [established in 1995] represents a new direction in the FBI's response to terrorism. Eighteen federal agencies maintain a regular presence in the center and participate in its daily operations. These agencies include the Central Intelligence Agency, the Defense Intelligence Agency, and the United States Secret Service, among others. This multi-agency arrangement provides an unprecedented opportunity for information sharing, warning, and real-time intelligence analysis.

... This sense of cooperation also has led to other important changes. During the past several years, the FBI and CIA have developed a closer working relationship that has strengthened the ability of each agency to respond to terrorist threats and has improved the ability of the US Government to respond to terrorist attacks that do occur. An element of this cooperation is an ongoing exchange of personnel between the two agencies. Included among the CIA employees detailed to the FBI's national security division is a veteran CIA case officer who serves as the deputy section chief for international terrorism. Likewise, FBI agents are detailed to the CIA, and several serve in comparable positions.

... Because warning is critical to the prevention of terrorist acts, the FBI also has expanded the terrorist threat warning system first implemented in 1989. The system now reaches all aspects of the law enforcement and intelligence communities. Currently, more than 45 federal agencies involved in the US Government's counterterrorism effort receive information via secure teletype through this system. The messages also are transmitted to all 56 FBI field offices and 32 foreign liaison posts.

If threat information requires nationwide unclassified dissemination to all federal, state, and local law enforcement agencies, the FBI transmits messages via the national law enforcement telecommunications system. In addition, the FBI disseminates threat information to security managers of thousands of US Commercial interests around the country through the awareness of national security issues and response (ANSIR) program....

The FBI's counterterrorism capabilities also have been enhanced by the expansion of our legal attaché—or LEGAT offices—around the world. These small offices can have a significant impact on the FBI's ability to track terrorist threats and bring investigative resources to bear on cases where quick response is critical. As I've mentioned, the FBI currently has 32 such LEGAT offices....

[Interagency] cooperation assumes its most tangible operational form in the joint terrorism task forces that exist in 16 cities across the nation. These task forces are particularly well-suited to responding to international terrorism because they combine the international investigative resources of the FBI with the street-level expertise of local law enforcement agencies.

This cop-to-cop cooperation has proven highly successful in preventing several potential terrorist attacks.... Due to the measures I've discussed and several other initiatives, we are much better prepared to address the international terrorist threat than we were just a few years ago.... The United States must continue to move toward strengthening its capabilities to confront this threat.[34]

So extensive was the FBI's interagency mechanisms by the following year that in his 1999 testimony before the Senate, Director Freeh noted that the Bureau had "identified as our highest priority foreign intelligence, terrorist, and criminal activities that directly threaten the national or economic security of the United States." He noted that the FBI Counterterrorism Center by then encompassed "nineteen other federal agencies," including

... the Diplomatic Security Service... the Air Force Office of Special Investigations, the Bureau of Alcohol, Tobacco, and Firearms, the Federal Bureau of Prisons, the Central Intelligence Agency, the Defense Intelligence Agency, the Department of Commerce, the Department of Defense, the Department of Energy, the Department of Transportation, the Environmental Protection Agency, the Federal Aviation Administration, the Federal Emergency Management Agency, the Immigration and Naturalization Service, the Internal Revenue Service, the National Security Agency, the Naval Criminal Investigative Service, the United States Customs Service, the United States Marshals Service, and the United States Secret Service.

The FBI had also set up a new "mechanism for promoting coordination"—the Strategic Information and Operations Center:

Congress provided funding for this project beginning in 1995. The new Strategic Information and Operations Center allows us to handle multiple incidents simultaneously. It also provides us with greatly enhanced communications capabilities between FBI Headquarters and field offices, as well as between the FBI and other federal agencies.

Freeh also notes the Senate's

extraordinary support for the FBI's counterterrorism programs and initiatives...
Over the past several years, you have generously provided us with additional agents, technicians, and analysts, as well as the technical and forensic tools, that allow us to respond quickly and effectively to acts of terrorism against the United States and its citizens wherever they occur.... Annual funding for the FBI's Counterterrorism program has grown from

$78.5 million in 1993 to $301.2 million in 1999. The number of agents funded for counterterrorism investigations has grown from 550 in 1993 to 1,383 in 1999.[35]

In other words, contrary to what the Commission has claimed, the intelligence community did not suffer from funding shortages, fatal interagency deficiencies, the logistical and technological inability to collect and share information, or unwillingness to coordinate investigations. Rather, wide-ranging structures and mechanisms for these purposes, including the introduction of advanced information technologies, had long been established and were actively being reviewed and improved. The Commission's narrative, therefore, not only completely ignores overwhelming evidence of the obstruction of successful legitimate counterterrorist investigations by Washington, but fails entirely to account for how such high-level politicized obstructionism systematically undermined the operations of a capable intelligence community.

A Failure of State Policy—Not Intelligence

Indeed, the authoritative British intelligence analysis newsletter *Jane's Intelligence Digest* argues that the 9/11 "intelligence failure" was not in reality the result of mere structural incompetence among US intelligence agencies, but rather of explicit political decisions made by the political echelons of Washington, i.e. the highest levels of the Bush administration:

> ... as more evidence emerges about the type of intelligence which was available—and those who had access to this material, but failed to make use of it—the politicians are going to have to answer some very awkward questions.... It seems apparent, however, that although this intelligence was being received by the CIA and other US agencies, there was a distinct lack of enthusiasm within political—as opposed to military—circles for the launch of pre-emptive strikes against either the Taliban or Al-Qaeda.
>
> However, given the detailed intelligence [available]... and the fact that Bin Laden was making very clear threats to launch further strikes against US targets—it seems bizarre, to say the least, that no high-level political decision was taken to focus US intelligence efforts on Al-Qaeda and its international network.[36]

This problem, moreover, prevailed during both Democrat and Republican administrations. Further clarification on how the problem developed in the Bush administration comes in the form of a National Security Presidential Directive (NSPD) issued on February 13, 2001—President Bush's first official White House document pertaining to national security—which fundamentally reorganized the National Security Council. University of Maryland Professor

Margie Burns, a journalist who writes for the *Legal Times*, notes that the NSPD memorandum was "addressed to all members of the Cabinet, several economic advisors, White House personnel, the Joint Chiefs of Staff, and some officials concerned with security—41 people in all with the Vice President at the top of the list." The NSPD states that it replaced

> ... both Presidential Decision Directives and Presidential Review Directives as an instrument for communicating presidential decisions about the national security policies of the United States.... The NSC shall advise and assist me in integrating all aspects of national security policy as it affects the United States—domestic, foreign, military, intelligence, and economics (in conjunction with the National Economic Council (NEC)).

Regular attendees for NSC meetings, according to the Directive, continued to be included in regular meetings—namely the president, the vice president, the secretary of state, the secretary of the treasury, the secretary of defense, and the assistant to the president for national security affairs, as well as the CIA director and the chairman of the joint chiefs of staff. However, other officials such as the attorney general, the "heads of other executive departments and agencies, as well as other senior officials"—meaning almost the entirety of the US intelligence community other than the CIA—were excluded from the automatic right to attend NSC meetings. Rather, they "shall be invited to attend meetings of the NSC [only] when appropriate." In contrast, the White House Chief of Staff Andrew Card and the assistant to the president for economic policy "are invited to attend any NSC meeting."

Significantly, National Security Advisor Condoleezza Rice was to play a key role in representing the president. As Burns observes, she was "slated to attend all NSC meetings, per the above," and was also to be "responsible, at my direction and in consultation with the other regular attendees of the NSC, for determining the agenda, ensuring that necessary papers are prepared, and recording NSC actions and Presidential decisions."

While consolidating control over and information concerning US national security in the higher political echelons of the Bush administration, the NSPD simultaneously undercut the mechanisms by which federal agencies communicate and coordinate on national security issues. Concentrating the production of US national security policy in the hands of the White House political establishment, the Directive stated:

> Management of the development and implementation of national security policies by multiple agencies of the United States Government shall usually be accomplished by the NSC Policy Coordination Committees (NSC/PCCs). The NSC/PCCs shall be the main day-to-day for interagency coordination of national security policy.

Thus, the White House political establishment would, through the NSC, be primarily responsible for coordination and communication between federal agencies on issues of national security. To this end, eleven separate interagency coordination committees within the NSC were established to deal with "functional topics" including "Counter-Terrorism and National Preparedness," a committee chaired by Condoleeza Rice (along with "Intelligence and Counter-Intelligence" and "Records Access and Information Security," among others). Rice was also entasked with appointing the executive secretary of each NSC committee. Thus, in summary, responsibility for interagency coordination and communication on national security was placed by the NSPD primarily on the White House political establishment through the NSC, especially Condoleeza Rice.

Meanwhile, the NSPD went so far as to render dysfunctional the normal institutional system of NSC interagency coordination with a single sentence: "The existing system of Interagency Working Groups is abolished." As Margie Burns comments, this statement means that "the chief existing structural mechanism for coordinating information among federal agencies including the intelligence agencies, transportation, and immigration" was removed. In the words of the Directive: "Except for those established by statute, other existing NSC interagency groups, ad hoc bodies, and executive committees are also abolished as of March 1, 2001, unless they are specifically reestablished as subordinate working groups within the new NSC system as of that date." Continuing operation of any such NSC interagency working groups would be at Rice's sole discretion:

> Cabinet officers, the heads of other executive agencies, and the directors of offices within the Executive Office of the President shall advise the Assistant to the President for National Security Affairs of those specific NSC interagency groups chaired by their respective departments or agencies that are either mandated by statute or are otherwise of sufficient importance and vitality as to warrant being reestablished. In each case the Cabinet officer, agency head, or office director should describe the scope of the activities proposed for or now carried out by the interagency group, the relevant statutory mandate if any, and the particular NSC/PCC that should coordinate this work.

Indeed, all other interagency coordination was to be replaced by the new form of organization: "As to those committees expressly established in the National Security Act, the NSC/PC and/or NSC/DC shall serve as those committees and perform the functions assigned to those committees by the Act." The Directive thus raises some important questions, as noted by Margie Burns:

> How could the White House ever have thought that abolishing the inter-agency work groups was a good idea if security was the objective? Why was

so much responsibility placed on the shoulders of one person, Condoleezza Rice, whose previous experience had been at Stanford University and Chevron Oil? Why was national security blended with commerce? Above all, why was virtually total control of national security taken over by a politically-preoccupied White House?[37]

But perhaps most relevant to our examination here of the 9/11 intelligence failure is the title of Burn's report on the Directive, which appears in the form of a burning question: *"Why did Bush abolish information sharing and route all national security information to him, via Condoleezza Rice?"*

The implications of President Bush's February 13, 2001, NSPD are devastating. Firstly, it indicates that the normal operation of the US national security apparatus was fundamentally hampered and rendered dysfunctional due to a high-level Bush administration policy that obstructed interagency coordination on specific issues of national security. Secondly, it indicates that the new mechanism of interagency coordination and communication on national security matters was pivoted on a select few senior government officials in the National Security Council, and specifically in the office of the President's National Security Adviser. As such, a key source of interagency "failures" related to 9/11 trace back to the new interagency committees of the NSC in which Rice was heavily involved. Thirdly, while this goes some way in providing a general explanation of some of the bizarre communication blockages between agencies on national security matters pertaining to the pre-9/11 al-Qaeda threat, it lays fundamental responsibility for these blockages on the White House political establishment. According to new procedures set out in the February NSPD, senior White House officials were not only in receipt of all information relevant to national security obtained by the US intelligence community, but furthermore bear fundamental responsibility for the systematic obstruction of the normal circulation of information throughout the US intelligence community. In other words, the White House political establishment via the National Security Council played two roles that facilitated the 9/11 intelligence failure: firstly, routing all national security information to a small group of administration officials in the White House including specifically the President; secondly, obstructing normal mechanisms for the sharing of that information among intelligence agencies.

Not only does this situation strongly suggest that the White House was privy to all information available to the US intelligence community regarding 9/11, thus granting the administration fairly precise advanced warning of the terrorist attacks, it indicates that significant cases of the obstruction of legitimate counterterrorist investigations and information sharing, were direct consequences of White House decisions made through NSC policy committees. As noted by former 26-year veteran CIA analyst Ray McGovern, who regularly reported to the vice president and senior policymakers on the president's daily brief: "No one wants to believe that the attacks of Sept. 11 could have been prevented, but we do a disservice to our country if we stay in denial. No one wants to believe that President Bush had more forewarning than he acknowledges, but there is strong circumstantial evidence that he did."[38]

Connecting the Dots—a Case Study: The Moussaoui Failure

A memo from Minneapolis-based FBI Special Agent and Chief Division Counsel Coleen M. Rowley, sent on May 22 to FBI Director Robert Mueller and to the Senate Intelligence Committee, provides clear evidence that the 9/11 attacks did not constitute an intelligence failure due to a simple failure to integrate extant information. This memo documents how high-level US officials deliberately obstructed legitimate counterterrorist investigations while ignoring credible intelligence warnings of the attacks.

Rowley names specific individuals at FBI headquarters whose systemic obstructions created a veritable "blockade" against the investigation into Zacarias Moussaoui, charged as a co-conspirator in the 9/11 attacks. After Moussaoui was detained by the INS in tandem with the FBI joint terrorism task force, local Minneapolis FBI officials sought authorization from Washington for a search warrant to conduct a wider probe, particularly to search his computer. Rowley reports that officials at FBI headquarters rebuffed several urgent requests from the Minneapolis office, claiming a lack of sufficient evidence that Moussaoui was connected to a foreign terrorist organization. That stance was maintained even after French intelligence confirmed Moussaoui's connections to Osama bin Laden's al-Qaeda. Rowley writes:

> While reasonable minds may differ as to whether probable cause existed prior to receipt of the French intelligence information, it was certainly established after that point and became even greater with successive, more detailed information from the French and other intelligence sources.... Notably also, the actual search warrant obtained on September 11th did not include the French intelligence information.

Rowley also refers to

> ... statements made on September 11th, after the first attacks on the World Trade Center had already occurred, made telephonically by the FBI Supervisory Special Agent (SSA) who was the one most involved in the Moussaoui matter and who, up to that point, seemed to have been consistently, almost deliberately thwarting the Minneapolis FBI agents' efforts. Even after the attacks had begun, the SSA in question was still attempting to block the search of Moussaoui's computer, characterizing the World Trade Center attacks as a mere coincidence with Minneapolis' prior suspicions about Moussaoui.

In order to prevent a proper investigation of Moussaoui, a supervisory official at FBI headquarters deliberately altered the text of the formal request filed by the Minneapolis office for authorization to begin an investigation into Moussaoui under the Foreign Intelligence Surveillance Act (FISA). This official changed the warrant application in such a way that FBI lawyers would probably reject it. Rowley continues:

> The fact is that key FBIHQ [FBI headquarters] personnel whose jobs it was to assist and coordinate with field division agents on terrorism investigations and the obtaining and use of FISA searches (and who theoretically were privy to many more sources of intelligence information than field division agents), continued to, almost inexplicably, throw up roadblocks and undermine Minneapolis' by-now desperate efforts to obtain a FISA search warrant, long after the French intelligence service provided its information and probable cause became clear. HQ personnel brought up almost ridiculous questions in their apparent efforts to undermine the probable cause. In all of their conversations and correspondence, HQ personnel never disclosed to the Minneapolis agents that the Phoenix Division had, only approximately three weeks earlier, warned of Al Qaeda operatives in flight schools seeking flight training for terrorist purposes.... Eventually on August 28, 2001, after a series of e-mails between Minneapolis and FBIHQ, which suggest that the FBIHQ SSA deliberately further undercut the FISA effort by not adding the further intelligence information which he had promised to add that supported Moussaoui's foreign power connection and making several changes in the wording of the information that had been provided by the Minneapolis Agent, the Minneapolis agents were notified that the NSLU Unit Chief did not think there was sufficient evidence of Moussaoui's connection to a foreign power.... The e-mail communications between Minneapolis and FBIHQ, however, speak for themselves and there are far better witnesses than me who can provide their first hand knowledge of these events characterized in one Minneapolis agent's e-mail as FBIHQ is "setting this up for failure." My only comment is that the process of allowing the FBI supervisors to make changes in affidavits is itself fundamentally wrong.... In the Moussaoui case... the process allowed the Headquarters Supervisor to downplay the significance of the information thus far collected.[39]

Rowley's memo significantly undermines the official explanation of the 9/11 intelligence failure: that no one in the US intelligence community "connected the dots." On the contrary, her memo clearly demonstrates that the intelligence breakdown did not amount to a failure to integratively analyze fragmentary data to draw the right conclusion, but rather constituted a deliberate, orchestrated refusal to follow through with legitimate counterterrorism investigations, coupled with the willful suppression of credible intelligence—on the part of Washington officials.

For instance, as noted above, Rowley observed that: "In all of their conversations and correspondence, headquarters personnel never disclosed to the Minneapolis agents that the Phoenix Division had only three weeks earlier warned of al Qaeda operatives in flight schools seeking flight training for terrorist purposes." That information, if made available, would have provided even more support for a search warrant for Moussaoui's computer.

It has now come to light in the wake of the public release of Rowley's memo that both the Minneapolis information on Moussaoui collected in August and the July 10 Phoenix memo urging a systematic review of Middle Eastern students at US flight schools were received by the same official: David Frasca, head of the Radical Fundamentalist Unit at FBI headquarters in Washington, DC. Frasca had in other words possessed two vital pieces of data: a memo documenting that Muslim militants linked to al-Qaeda were seeking training at US flight schools; and a report that one such militant had been arrested after seeking training to fly a Boeing 747 without taking off or landing and with confirmed connections to al-Qaeda. One does not need special intelligence skills to perceive the obvious connection between the two reports—certainly, a highly trained FBI counterterrorism specialist whose job is to make exactly such connections would note the potential threat immediately. Rowley, a 21-year veteran of the FBI, records that the combination of the Moussaoui arrest and the Phoenix memo's focus on flight schools was more than sufficient to lead to preventive action that could have prevented the 9/11 attacks.

On July 10, 2001, the FBI office in Phoenix had alerted FBI headquarters to an unusual influx of al-Qaeda connected Arab students into local flight schools. The warning was ignored by FBI supervisors.[40] The Phoenix memo recommended checking flight schools around the country: "The FBI sent the intelligence to its terrorism experts in Washington and New York for analysis and had begun discussing conducting a nationwide canvass of flight schools." According to FBI Assistant Director John Collingwood: "The Phoenix communication went to appropriate operational agents and analysts but it did not lead to uncovering the impending attacks."[41] *Insight On The News* attempts to explain this lack of action by citing "midlevel managers" in the FBI who "claimed they lacked the resources to implement the agent's far-reaching recommendations."[42] The memo, written by FBI Special Agent Kenneth Williams "was copied to John O'Neill in New York." The memo focused on one student, "Zakaria Mustapha Soubra who was linked to al-Qa'ida and who had been under investigation by the Bureau for 12 months already."[43]

Vice President Dick Cheney claimed that the memo was merely the result of a "hunch." Other officials, such as FBI Assistant Director John Collingwood, claimed that the memo did not point specifically to suspected terrorists linked to the 9/11 attacks. Most media reports characterized the Phoenix memo as largely speculative. However, a detailed account in the *Los Angeles Times* demonstrates that such assertions are misleading. Special Agent William's memorandum was the product of a painstaking 7-year long counterterrorism investigation that had focused on several Muslim militants with confirmed al-Qaeda connections training at Phoenix flight schools. As early as 1994, the FBI's counterterrorism unit in Phoenix was investigating an informant recruited as a suicide bomber by al-Qaeda. FBI counterterrorist officials even videotaped the informant being escorted into the desert to undergo terrorist training, including how to set off bombs. In 1996, after a tip-off from another informant, Special Agent Williams turned to local flight schools. Among those who were at that time enrolled at one flight school in Phoenix was 9/11 hijacker Hani Hanjour. By 1998, the FBI's Phoenix office was investigating a flight school student from the Middle East with ties to several terrorist groups. Early in 2000, officials were so concerned that they had placed students at several Phoenix flight schools—including Embry-Riddle Aeronautical University in Prescott, Arizona—under surveillance. This was, in other words, an investigation that had confirmed an al-Qaeda presence at Phoenix flight schools. Special Agent Williams' memo summarized these investigations and their findings. Unsurprisingly, FBI headquarters has kept the memo classified.[44]

Williams urged FBI headquarters to conduct a systematic canvass of all US flight schools to investigate students from the Middle East. FBI headquarters not only rejected wholesale the idea of such a sweep—despite being in receipt of urgent multiple warnings of an impending al-Qaeda attack from the air, widely known and considered credible in the intelligence community—they even rejected the idea of investigating flight schools in Phoenix. The official pretext was that the measures were impracticable and too much of a burden on Bureau resources. In reality, a list of US flight schools can be obtained easily on the Internet. Indeed, according to the Los Angeles Times, an associate of Hani Hanjour's was enrolled at Sawyer School of Aviation at Sky Harbor Airport in Phoenix when Williams' memo reached FBI headquarters in Washington. If his recommendations had been followed, a routine canvass lasting only a few hours or days would have led directly to one of the 9/11 hijackers.[45] Kenneth Williams was the most senior member of a joint terrorist task force. Ronald Myers, a 31-year FBI veteran and a former colleague of Williams, described him as "one of the strongest agents I have ever met. Anyone in FBI management who wouldn't take what Williams said seriously is a fool."[46]

But FBI headquarters are not staffed by fools. Retired FBI Special Agent James H. Hauswirth, who was based in the Phoenix office where Williams works, sent a two-page letter to FBI Director Robert Mueller in December 2001, charging that high-level "micromanaging, constant indecision and stonewalling" had consistently obstructed ongoing attempts to apprehend suspected terrorists, thus facilitating the 9/11 attacks.[47]

Both the Phoenix memo and Moussaoui data pointed clearly to multiple attempts by al-Qaeda to infiltrate flight schools in preparation for attacks. Indeed, FBI investigators working on these cases precisely anticipated the 9/11 plot only a few days before the attacks: "US lawmakers remain astounded that the Phoenix memo and Moussaoui's arrest failed to set alarm bells ringing at FBI headquarters, even after one agent speculated at a high-level meeting that Moussaoui might have been taking lessons to enable him to crash an aircraft into the World Trade Centre in New York."[48]

The revelation that FBI headquarters were warned by a counterterrorism official of a plot to attack the World Trade Center by plane came when FBI Director Mueller referred to an internal FBI document in May 2002 Congressional hearings. According to *Newsweek*:

> The FBI has insisted it had no advance warning about the 9-11 attacks. But internal documents suggest there were more concerns inside the bureau's field offices than Washington has acknowledged...
>
> Last week, in little-noticed testimony before a Senate panel, FBI Director Robert Mueller referred to another internal document that may prove more explosive: notes by a Minneapolis agent worrying that French Moroccan flight student Zacarias Moussaoui might be planning to "fly something into the World Trade Center."... Sources say the notes Mueller referred to were written in early September 2001—days before the attack. The author was part of a counterterrorism team desperately trying to figure out what Moussaoui was up to.[49]

However, the *New York Post* reports that the agent's "red-flag warnings" to "FBI headquarters" arrived as long as "a month before 9/11" according to FBI Director Robert Mueller. "Mueller's revelation at a congressional hearing showed... that an FBI investigator... actually considered the scenario that occurred Sept. 11" but was "ignored" by FBI superiors.[50] In the context of the documentation discussed previously, it is clear that this conclusion was not drawn randomly in an information vacuum. On the contrary, there was very precise information available to the FBI and other intelligence agencies on al-Qaeda's plans, providing reasonable grounds to believe that the World Trade Center was the most probable target of an imminent al-Qaeda attack.

FBI officials initially confirmed reports that supervisor David Frasca had received both the Phoenix memo and the information about Moussaoui from Minnesota. The *New York Times* reported that: "The FBI clearinghouse for Al Qaeda intelligence was the bin Laden and radical fundamentalist units in its counterterrorism division. The units had complete access to the Phoenix memorandum, the Moussaoui case and the Ressam debriefings."[51] *Newsweek* confirmed that "Frasca was the agent in charge of the Moussaoui case and his office also received the Phoenix memo."[52] As already noted, FBI Assistant Director John Collingwood also indicated that the Phoenix memo was circulated and disseminated within FBI headquarters, reaching "midlevel managers." Nevertheless, according to the *Washington Post:* "The [Phoenix] request was formally closed within a few weeks, and it was never acted on."[53]

In response to these revelations "A bipartisan group of senators has demanded that the FBI explain why a senior agent who had access to two important strands of counterterrorism information never put the information together in a way that might have helped thwart the Sept. 11 attacks."[54] Later, as the damning implications of having admitted Frasca's access to both memos became clear, the FBI backtracked, claiming that the Phoenix memo had not even been read by Frasca until after the 9/11 attacks—despite the fact that it had been sent weeks prior to the Moussaoui report, which *was* read (and "sabotaged" according to one senator). Meanwhile Frasca himself has refused to make any comment on the subject: "Frasca, who works at the bureau's headquarters in Washington, DC, would not return a telephone call from the *Eagle-Tribune* yesterday and has not commented publicly on the matter so far."[55]

Indeed, Special Agent Rowley commented that the facts discussed in her memo, including the Phoenix memo, were fully known by the FBI leadership:

> Despite FBI leaders' full knowledge of all the items mentioned herein (and probably more that I'm unaware of), the SSA, his unit chief, and other involved HQ personnel were allowed to stay in their positions and, what's worse, occupy critical positions in the FBI's SIOC Command Center post September 11th. (The SSA in question actually received a promotion some months afterward!)

According to the *Washington Post*, citing Rowley's memo: "FBI supervisors in Washington seemed so intent on ignoring the threat posed by Moussaoui, Rowley wrote, that some field agents speculated that key officials at FBI headquarters 'had to be spies or moles... who were actually working for Osama bin Laden to have so undercut Minneapolis' effort.'"[56] As Steve Moore of the Canadian Centre for Research on Globalisation (CRG) observes in an extensive review of the role of FBI supervisor David Frasca in sabotaging al-Qaeda terrorist investigations:

> [W]hen Rowley talked to other FBI agents in other parts of the country, the first question was Why?—'Why would an FBI agent(s) deliberately sabotage a case?'...
>
> Agent Rowley reports that jokes were made that FBI Headquarters personnel were "spies" or "moles" who were actually "working for Osama Bin Laden." (Rowley Report p. 7) Apparently no one mentioned that it could be the other way around.... The notion that Bush cabinet members were urging the CIA/FBI chiefs to keep a lid on local FBI investigative actions to arrest or curtail terrorist plots was, at the time, an unthinkable

thought. That after all, would not be a joke. It would be one of the most murderous, diabolical cover ups committed against American citizens by an American President and cabinet.... FBI agents don't get promoted for messing up; they get promoted for a job well done. The key areas for further research are connecting the dots in the chain of command from Dave Frasca to his Unit Chief to the Director of the FBI to John Ashcroft, the Attorney General and President George Bush.[57]

Indeed, in that respect, Rowley accused FBI Director Robert Mueller, along with the FBI leadership as such, of deliberately obfuscating the facts around these intelligence inquiries for what might be "improper political reasons":

> I have deep concerns that a delicate and subtle shading/skewing of facts by you and others at the highest levels of FBI management has occurred and is occurring.... I feel that certain facts... have, up to now, been omitted, downplayed, glossed over and/or mis-characterized in an effort to avoid or minimize personal and/or institutional embarrassment on the part of the FBI and/or perhaps even for improper political reasons.[58]

Rowley's memo was considered revealing and damaging enough by the FBI for Director Robert Mueller to initially attempt a cover-up by keeping the memo classified, refusing to disclose it to the Senate Judiciary Committee. The Rowley and Williams memos, and FBI headquarters' unconscionable response to them—designed to obstruct legitimate if not routine counterterrorist investigations into al-Qaeda preparations for terrorism within the United States—clearly show that the 9/11 intelligence failure did not result from a failure to "connect the dots." On the contrary, it appears that the dots were connected, but that preventive action based on accurate intelligence received was deliberately blocked by Washington "for improper political reasons."

It must be emphasized that at the time FBI headquarters received the July and August memos from Phoenix and Minneapolis, the entire US intelligence community was simultaneously in receipt of credible urgent warnings of an al-Qaeda terrorist attack on US soil from the air. Such information was widely circulated and well-known to high-level US intelligence officials. These two FBI memos are only two publicly revealed pieces of information that had pointed unambiguously to *how* al-Qaeda was proceeding with its preparations for an attack within the US. Despite being aware that preparations for an air attack on US soil were underway, Washington blocked investigations uncovering those preparations—while simultaneously taking measures to protect high-level administration officials.

This case study based principally on the Rowley memo demonstrates without doubt—in tandem with our previous analysis—that US intelligence agencies had collected sufficiently precise information on the impending al-Qaeda attack to take appropriate preventive and preemptive measures. It is hard to avoid the conclusion that the 9/11 intelligence failure occurred because officials in Washington who received all relevant intelligence on the attacks refused to disseminate crucial selected pieces of information to other agencies; willfully ignored and actively altered evidence of al-Qaeda operations; and carefully obstructed legitimate preventive measures and inquiries. The flow of detailed and precise information on the 9/11 attacks, in other words, was centrally manipulated from Washington. This manipulation meant that while high-level US officials seem to have had access to ample information on the attacks, mid- and lower-level officials only had access to snippets of data.

There is ample reason, therefore, to conclude that the FBI's failure to apprehend suspected terrorists linked to al-Qaeda was the result of high-level blocks from the FBI command and the Justice Department. Further evidence for this connection comes from the authoritative testimony of US attorney David Philip Schippers, former chief investigative counsel for the US House Judiciary Committee, and head prosecutor responsible for conducting the impeachment against former President Bill Clinton. His long record of impeccable expertise and extensive experience makes him a highly credible source.[59]

Two days after the attacks, Schippers went public in an interview with WRRK in Pittsburgh, PA, stating that he had attempted to warn US Attorney General John Ashcroft, along with other federal officials, about the terrorist attacks weeks before they occurred. He stated that he had received information from US intelligence sources, including FBI agents, that a massive attack was being planned by terrorists targeting the financial arteries of lower Manhattan. Schippers had attempted to bring this information to the attention of John Ashcroft, six weeks before the tragedy of Black Tuesday.[60] Schippers went public again in October 2001, reiterating that, several months prior to September, impeccable sources in the US intelligence community, including FBI agents, had approached him with information about the impending attacks.

According to Schippers, these agents knew, months before the 9/11 attacks, the names of the hijackers, the targets of their attacks, the proposed dates, and the sources of their funding, along with other information. At least two weeks prior to 9/11, the agents again confirmed that an attack on lower Manhattan, orchestrated by Osama bin Laden, was imminent. However, the FBI command cut short their investigations into the impending terrorist attacks and those involved, threatening the agents with prosecution under the National Security Act if they publicized information pertaining to their investigations.

The agents subsequently sought the council of David Schippers in order to pressure elements in the US government to take action to prevent the attacks. Schippers warned many congressmen and senators and also attempted to contact Attorney General John Ashcroft without success, managing only to explain the situation to a lower-ranking Justice Department official who promised a return call from Ashcroft the next day. The attorney general did not return the call despite the gravity of the situation. In an interview with Geoff Metcalf on *WorldNetDaily*, Schippers stated:

> I [had] information indicating there was going to be a massive attack in lower Manhattan [from FBI sources]. I couldn't get anybody to listen to me… about a month-and-a-half before Sept. 11. The original thing that I heard—and you might ask Mr. Bodansky about that…. He was one of the people behind the warning that came out Feb. 19, 1995, and this was the [original] warning that I saw: that there was going to be an attack on the United States by bin Laden's people, that the original target—and this is the way it reads—the original target was supposed to be the White House and the Capitol building, and they were going to use commercial airliners as bombs.[61]

In another interview with talk radio host Alex Jones, Schippers specifically confirmed that "FBI agents in Chicago and Minnesota" informed him "that there was going to be an attack on lower Manhattan." Notably, no official attempt has been made to investigate FBI inquiries relating to 9/11 in these cities. Schippers recalls

> that's what started me calling…
> First of all, I tried to see if I could get a Congressman to go to bat for me and at least bring these people out there and listen to them. I sent them information and nobody cared. It was always, "We'll get back to you," "we'll get back to you," "we'll get back to you." Then I reached out and tried to get to the Attorney General, when finally we got an attorney general in there that I would be willing to talk to. And, again, I used people who were personal friends of John Ashcroft to try to get him. One of them called me back and said, "Alright I have talked to him. He will call you tomorrow morning." This was like a month before the bombing…[62]

The call never came. In an interview with the *Eagle Forum of Illinois* concerning the evidence of a terrorist attack "on the financial district in south Manhattan," Schippers stated: "Five weeks before the September 11 tragedy, I did my best to get a hold of Attorney General John Ashcroft with my concerns. The best that I could do was get in touch with an underling in that office who told me that all investigations start out at lower levels such as his."[63]

Schippers elaborated on these matters in an interview with this author. He confirmed that US intelligence had "established the sources of the money flow of bin Laden" as early as 1996, but by 1999 intelligence officers were facing fundamental high-level obstructions to their investigations into these matters. Schippers maintained the anonymity of his sources to avoid undue pressure on them from elements in government and intelligence agencies.

The earliest warning of attacks was issued by the Congressional Task Force on Terrorism and Unconventional Warfare in February 1995, which specified in general terms that al-Qaeda was planning a terrorist attack on lower Manhattan, through the use of hijacked civilian planes as bombs. According to Schippers, the same individuals who issued this warning had been working ever since on uncovering further information on the same threat. He stated that the warning "had started out just a general threat, but they narrowed it and narrowed it, more and more with time," until the "same people who came out with the first warning" informed him in May 2001 that "an attack on lower Manhattan is imminent." Schippers elaborates that these US intelligence officers had approached him as a result of "growing frustration" at the higher echelons of the intelligence community, who were refusing to take action in response to the imminent threat to US national security.[64]

In addition to the several FBI agents who had spoken to Schippers directly, other US intelligence sources told him "there are others all over the country who are frustrated, and just waiting to come out." The frustration of these intelligence officers, Schippers explained, was because of the obstructions of a "bureaucratic elite in Washington short-stopping information," with the consequence that they have granted "terrorism a free reign in the United States."

Schippers was also able to confirm the specific nature of some of the FBI investigations, which had been cut short under high-level orders, noting for instance that the agents who had approached him claimed that "they had Atta [the chief hijacker] in their sights." The agents also claimed to have been aware of the names and activities of "very strange characters training at flight schools," which they had attempted to "check out."

Such investigations were blocked from above, to the fury of agents on the trail of individuals who appear to have gone on to perpetrate the 9/11 atrocities—including chief hijacker Atta himself. There was simply no adequate justification for these blocks, legal or otherwise, the agents argue, adding that the obstructions came down for no apparent reason. Accordingly, one of them remarked to Schippers that "if they had been permitted to follow through with their investigations, 9-11 would never have happened."[65]

Other investigators have articulated similar conclusions that the intelligence failure was not due to a lack of information, nor even necessarily due to an inability to integrate disparate data, but was rather the result of inexplicable inaction by Washington. Senate Judiciary Chairman Patrick J. Leahy (D-Vt.), in an interview with CNN, commented: "There was plenty of information available before September 11. I think historians are going to find, tragically, that, had it been acted upon, the hijackers could have been stopped." Former Chairman of the Senate Intelligence Committee Arlen Specter (R-Pa.) further observed: "I don't believe any longer this is a matter of connecting the dots. I think they had a veritable road map. And we want to know why they didn't act on it."[66]

Schippers' general thesis, that the intelligence community had precise advanced warning of the 9/11 attacks but was prevented by a Washington political elite from acting on them, is corroborated by the statements of several other FBI officials interviewed by the conservative *New American* magazine. In a March 2002 report, the magazine reported that:

> Three veteran federal law enforcement agents confirmed to the *New American* that the information provided to Schippers was widely known within the Bureau before September 11th. Because these individuals face possible personal or professional retaliation, they agreed to speak with us on condition of anonymity. Two of them, however, have expressed a willingness to testify before Congress regarding the views they have shared with us.

A former FBI official with extensive counterterrorism experience told the magazine: "I don't buy the idea that we didn't know what was coming." He referred to the extraordinary speed with which the FBI had produced detailed information on the attack and the hijackers responsible: "Within 24 hours [of the attack] the Bureau had about 20 people identified, and photos were sent out to the news media. Obviously this information was available in the files and somebody was sitting on it."

Another active FBI counterterrorism investigator stated that it was widely known

> all over the Bureau, how these [warnings] were ignored by Washington...
>
> All indications are that this information came from some of [the FBI's] most experienced guys, people who have devoted their lives to this kind of work. But their warnings were placed in a pile in someone's office in Washington.... In some cases, these field agents predicted, almost precisely, what happened on September 11th. So we were all holding our breath... hoping that the situation would be remedied.

The first former FBI agent's further damning comments to the *New American* are particularly worth noting:

> This is pretty appalling. The FBI has had access to this information since at least 1997. We're obviously not doing our job. I never expected to see something like this happen in our country, but in a way I wasn't shocked when it did. There's got to be more to this than we can see—high-level people whose careers are at stake, and don't want the truth coming out.... What agenda is someone following? Obviously, people had to know—there had to be people who knew this information was being circulated. People

like [al-Qaeda terrorists] don't just move in and out of the country undetected. If somebody in DC is taking this information and burying it— and it's very easy to control things from DC—then this problem goes much, much deeper.... It's terrible to think this, but this must have been allowed to happen as part of some other agenda.[67]

Other well-informed intelligence experts who have studied the subject concur with this analysis, going even further in their conclusions. Tyrone Powers, a 10-year veteran former FBI special agent specializing in terrorism and counter-intelligence—now professor of law enforcement and criminal justice at Anne Arundel County Community College and director of the Institute for Criminal Justice, Legal Studies and Public Service—points out that there was "credible information from the FBI, CIA and foreign intelligence services that an attack was imminent." The information indicated that an al-Qaeda hijacking attempt was probable. Powers puts this idea in context with what he describes as the "consequentialism" inherent to the decision-making process, which he has witnessed firsthand in his intelligence and counter-intelligence background: "...on occasion, [damaging] acts are allowed if in the minds of the decision-makers, they will lead to 'greater good,'" and as long as the damage is contained within certain limits. Powers further refers to pressure on intelligence agencies to vastly reduce their powers; concern over the "blowback" from the controversies of the presidential election; the desire on the part of elements of the intelligence community to "reconstitute the CIA" after its perceived "emasculation by the Clinton administration;" their belief that such a reconstitution required "a need, a demand and a free hand that would be given by a democratic Congress [only] if there was a National outcry."

He states: "My experience tells me that these incidents would have reached the level at which the 'consequentialism' thought process would have been made a real option"—in other words, that elements of the intelligence community and the administration may have deliberately failed to act in the belief that the resultant damage would contribute to a "greater good," providing a pretext for such policies as the reconstitution of the CIA. However, Powers emphasizes that this policy would have been the result of a "miscalculation"—a failure to anticipate the extent of this damage: "But the amount of destruction wrought on a civilian population shocked even the advocates of this policy."[68]

The US intelligence community clearly had sufficient information of an impending al-Qaeda attack, but was unable to undertake preventive action. This data strongly suggests at the very least that a deliberate decision had been taken by the higher political echelons in Washington to turn a blind eye to accurate intelligence on the impending al-Qaeda terrorist attack. In other words, the intelligence failure was the inevitable culmination of carefully imposed blocks that restrained agencies from acting on the very clear intelligence received. Those blocks were issued for improper political reasons. The intelligence failure did not pertain to a blinded bureaucracy as such. Indeed, the intelligence community had been struggling against awkward, bizarre, and inexplicable obstructionism originating from the highest levels of government. The failure was therefore a consequence of US government policy. While administration officials had access to abundant intelligence on the attacks, they withheld and manipulated the internal flow of information within the intelligence community, facilitating the "intelligence failure." There is no doubt that the complex web of political, military, and financial connections tying US elites to al-Qaeda, discussed in previous chapters, substantially explains why this manipulation might have happened.

PART THREE
THE 9/11 AIR DEFENSE FAILURE

Here, we aim to develop, firstly, an understanding of the framework of relevant domestic security procedures established by the US national security apparatus to deter and prevent terrorism on US soil; secondly, an understanding of how and why these procedures failed to actually deter and prevent the 9/11 terrorist attacks. The focus of this chapter is to study the failure of US air defense, which operates on the basis of standard operating procedures designed to immediately scramble military aircraft in the event of even mundane emergencies (e.g. a commercial aircraft deviating from its established flight path). Discovering how and why these procedures failed to deter and/or prevent the attacks is a crucial motive for the following analysis.

10.

DECONSTRUCTING THE COMMISSION'S CHRONOLOGY

Standard Operating Procedures for Air Emergencies

Before examining the actual events of 9/11, it is necessary to establish the context in which they occurred, namely, the mandatory rules of emergency response employed by air authorities in various kinds of emergency. Although what occurred on 9/11—planes flown as missiles into key buildings—is of course unusual, the fact is that the constituents of the crisis were quite routine emergencies. Commercial and private airliners flying off their flight paths, loss of radio contact with pilots, transponder failures as well as possible and actual hijackings, are handled on a day-to-day basis by air authorities with expert efficiency.[1]

As noted by former Assistant Attorney Mary Schiavo—formerly Inspector-General at the US Department of Transportation and currently lawyer for 32 families of victims families who perished in the 9/11 attacks—in the last 30 years there have been 682 hijackings in the United States which have been responded to in accordance with the appropriate FAA procedures.[2] Indeed, in the calendar year prior to 9/11, fighter aircraft were successfully scrambled on 56 occasions in response to such emergencies, within minutes.[3] The Associated Press refers to "67 scrambles" between September 2000 and June 2001.[4]

Air traffic controllers routinely request fighter craft to intercept commercial planes for various reasons when problems faced cannot be solved through radio contact, for instance, to inform commercial pilots when their plane is off course or simply to assess the situation directly. The deviation of commercial planes from their designated flight paths is a common problem solved via interception. As a matter of mandatory Standard Operating Procedures, no approval from the White House is required for interception. On the contrary, interception occurs on the basis of established flight and emergency response rules.

Military interceptors do not need instructions from the White House to carry out emergency response procedures and other such services—they already have clear "instructions to act," which are followed automatically in relation to varying situations. Detailed FAA and Department of Defense manuals clarify that these instructions are exceedingly comprehensive, including issues from minor emergencies to full-blown hijackings. According to these instructions, serious problems are immediately handed over to the National Military

Command Center in the Pentagon, if necessary.

Commercial flights must adhere to Instrument Flight Rules (IFR). According to the IFR, before takeoff pilots must file a flight plan with the FAA:

> Commercial flights fly according to predefined flight plans. These flight plans are intended to provide quick routes that take advantage of favorable winds while avoiding the routes traveled by other aircraft. The usual flight plan is a series of three connected routes: a standard instrument departure (SID) route, an en route path, and a standard instrument arrival (STAR). Each route consists of a sequence of geographic points, or fixes, which, when connected, form a trajectory from the point of departure to the point of arrival.[5]

As soon as a plane deviates from its flight plan—for instance, by making a wrong turn at a "fix"—an air traffic controller contacts the pilot. If the controller fails to make contact or routine communication becomes impossible, established rules dictate that an aircraft will be requested to scramble and assess the situation by "interception."

A clear example of this routine procedure is the FAA's response when the Lear jet chartered by golf professional Payne Stewart deviated from its flight path while the pilot failed to reply by radio. MSNBC reported that:

> Pilots are supposed to hit each fix with pinpoint accuracy. If a plane deviates by 15 degrees, or two miles from that course, the flight controllers will hit the panic button. They'll call the plane, saying "American 11, you're deviating from course." It's considered a real emergency, like a police car screeching down a highway at 100 miles an hour. When golfer Payne Stewart's incapacitated Learjet missed a turn at a fix, heading north instead of west to Texas, F-16 interceptors were quickly dispatched.[6]

The FAA, in other words, contacted the military when it was confirmed that the plane was off course, and communication with the plane was blocked. As CNN reported: "Several Air Force and Air National Guard fighter jets, plus an AWACS radar control plane, helped the Federal Aviation Administration track the runaway Learjet and estimate when it would run out of fuel."[7]

Once a plane is intercepted by military jets, daytime communications with a commercial plane that fails to respond properly to radio contact are described by the FAA manual as follows: "… [The interceptor military craft communicates by] Rocking wings from a position slightly above and ahead of, and normally to the left of, the intercepted aircraft…" This action conveys the message: "You have been intercepted." The commercial jet is then supposed to respond by rocking its wings to indicate compliance, upon which the interceptor performs a "slow level turn, normally to the left, on to the desired heading [direction]." The commercial plane then responds by following the escort.[8]

The deviation of a plane from its designated flight path obviously creates a hazard in the form of a potential collision with another plane. The FAA thus has a clear definition of what constitutes an emergency situation: "Consider that an aircraft emergency exists... when:... There is unexpected loss of radar contact and radio communications with any... aircraft."[9] Elsewhere, the FAA states: "EMERGENCY DETERMINATIONS: If... you are in doubt that a situation constitutes an emergency or potential emergency, handle it as though it were an emergency."[10]

An FAA air defense liaison officer stationed in the headquarters of the North American Aerospace Defense Command (NORAD) plays the role of coordinating the FAA with the US military to handle emergencies as efficiently as possible.[11] While NORAD normally scrambles fighter jets from specified NORAD bases, if necessary military jets from non-NORAD bases can easily be scrambled as well: "Normally, NORAD escort aircraft will take the required action. However, for the purpose of these procedures, the term 'escort aircraft' applies to any military aircraft assigned to the escort mission."[12] Again, the response to the deviation of Payne Stuart's jet from its flight path provides an example. ABC News reported that: "First, a fighter jet from Tyndall, FL, was diverted from a routine training flight to check out the Learjet. Two F-16s from another Florida base then picked up the chase, later handing it over to two Air National Guard F-16s from Oklahoma, which handed it over to two F-16s from Fargo, North Dakota."[13]

As a matter of mandatory routine, the established instructions for a serious emergency are followed, and this includes emergencies involving the possibility of a hijacking:

> The FAA hijack coordinator (the Director or his designate of the FAA Office of Civil Aviation Security) on duty at Washington headquarters will request the military to provide an escort aircraft for a confirmed hijacked aircraft to:
> a. Assure positive flight following.
> b. Report unusual observances.
> c. Aid search and rescue in the event of an emergency...
> ... The escort service will be requested by the FAA hijack coordinator by direct contact with the National Military Command Center (NMCC).... When the military can provide escort aircraft, the NMCC will advise the FAA hijack coordinator the identification and location of the squadron tasked to provide escort aircraft. NMCC will then authorize direct coordination between FAA and the designated military unit. When a NORAD resource is tasked, FAA will coordinate through the appropriate SOCC/ROCC.[14]

Once military planes are scrambled in accordance with immediate responses, the

Department of Defense will be contacted for approval of further special measures: "In the event of a hijacking, the NMCC will be notified by the most expeditious means by the FAA. The NMCC will, with the exception of immediate responses... forward requests for DoD [Department of Defense] assistance to the Secretary of Defense for approval."[15]

With regards to the definition of "immediate responses," a 1997 DoD directive dictates that they do not require the highest levels of approval:

> Requests for an immediate response (i.e., any form of immediate action taken by a DoD Component or military commander to save lives, prevent human suffering, or mitigate great property damage under imminently serious conditions) may be made to any Component or Command. The DoD Components that receive verbal requests from civil authorities for support in an exigent emergency may initiate informal planning and, if required, immediately respond as authorized in DoD Directive 3025.1.[16]

Nevertheless, high-level officials such as the secretary of defense and the chairman of the joint chiefs of staff are to be kept fully informed:

> As soon as practical, the Component or Command rendering assistance shall report the fact of the request, the nature of the response, and any other pertinent information through the chain of command to the DoD Executive Secretary, who shall notify the Secretary of Defense, the Chairman of the Joint Chiefs of Staff, and any other appropriate officials.[17]

This directive elaborates on an earlier DoD Directive which confirms as follows that:

> Imminently serious conditions resulting from any civil emergency or attack may require immediate action by military commanders, or by responsible officials of other DoD Agencies, to save lives, prevent human suffering, or mitigate great property damage. When such conditions exist and time does not permit prior approval from higher headquarters, local military commanders and responsible officials of other DoD Components are authorized by this Directive, subject to any supplemental direction that may be provided by their DoD Component, to take necessary action to respond to requests of civil authorities. All such necessary action is referred to in this Directive as "Immediate Response."
>
> 4.5.2. While Immediate Response should be provided to civil agencies on a cost-reimbursable basis if possible, it should not be delayed or denied because of the inability or unwillingness of the requester to make a commitment to reimburse the Department of Defense.
>
> 4.5.3. Any commander or official acting under the Immediate

Response authority of this Directive shall advise the DoD Executive Agent through command channels, by the most expeditious means available, and shall seek approval or additional authorizations as needed.[18]

It should be reiterated that procedures require controllers to immediately alert the military to scramble fighter craft, simply if a plane deviates from its flight path and communication between the plane and controllers is blocked. This alert occurs whether or not the situation consists of a potential hijacking, as was the case with Payne Stuart's Lear jet, which was intercepted by military planes almost immediately and while communication with the jet was blocked.

Indeed, "The US military has their own radar network …. (NORAD). *They are tied into the FAA computer in order to get information on incoming flights.*" If a target is discovered "without flight plan information," or in violation of the same, "they will call on the 'shout' line to the appropriate [Air Traffic Control] Center sector for an ID." If the Center sector "has no datablock or other information on it, the military will usually scramble an intercept flight. Essentially always they turn out to be private pilots… not talking to anybody, who stray too far outside the boundary, then get picked up on their way back in. But, procedures are procedures, and they will likely find two F-18s on their tail within 10 or so minutes."[19] The NMCC thus routinely taps into FAA radar to monitor emergencies and hijackings, as occurred during Payne Stewart's flight when "officers on the Joint Chiefs were monitoring the Learjet on radar screens inside the Pentagon's National Military Command Center."[20]

A lucid and concise description of these procedures is provided by a US air traffic control expert interviewed by the New York-based Institute of Electrical and Electronic Engineers:

> Losing transponder contact with an airliner would prompt a controller to ask the pilot to reset the device. When all communication with an aircraft breaks off, procedures are in place that allow controllers to alert the military to a developing situation and to track the plane using primary radar. Primary radar is tied into the perimeter air defense radar for joint use by air traffic controllers and the military. It paints the skin of the aircraft to give controllers an idea of where the plane is…. Procedures dictate that controllers alert the US military when a hijacking is known to be under way. The typical response is for the Air Force to scramble intercept jets.[21]

Indeed, according to NORAD spokesman Marine Corps Major Mike Snyder, "its fighters routinely intercept aircraft": "When planes are intercepted, they typically are handled with a graduated response. The approaching fighter may rock its wingtips to attract the pilot's attention, or make a pass in front of the aircraft. Eventually, it can fire tracer rounds in the airplane's path, or, under certain circumstances, down it with a missile."[22]

Although time periods for routine air responses of this kind vary from case to case, depending on the particular nature of the emergency, they are always relatively swift. One pertinent criteria affecting response times is the type of airspace in which the emergency occurs and the potential impact of the emergency on civilian life. In this connection, it is worth examining further the response to the Payne Stewart case.

Stewart's Lear jet was a small business jet—a private plane—flying autopilot toward a low-population area, and was not a commercial airliner with hundreds of passengers on board. It was also heading off course at high speed away from the Florida base at a very high altitude. Consequently, it was an altogether different kind of emergency—far less dangerous in scale and potential impact than what happened on 9/11. A senior US defense official commented that: "The [Federal Aviation Administration] said this thing was headed to a sparsely populated part of the country, so let it go."[23] In other words, the air response to the Lear jet was significantly tempered by the lesser scale of the emergency.

Nevertheless, the response of air authorities was relatively swift. At 9:33 AM (EDT), the air traffic controller attempted unsuccessfully to make radio contact with Stewart's Lear jet. Over the next four and a half minutes the controller attempted to contact the flight five more times without response.[24] By 9:44, the FAA had concluded that radio contact with the Lear jet was lost.[25] The FAA contacted the military to intercept the Lear with fighter craft about 24 minutes later according to a US Air Force chronology cited by the Associated Press, which confirmed that "FAA requested emergency escort" at 10:08 AM[26] Immediately upon request, fighters from Tyndall Air Force Base were scrambled to intercept the Lear jet. The Washington Post notes that: "Pentagon officials said the military began its pursuit of the ghostly civilian aircraft at 10:08 AM, when two Air Force F-16 fighters from Tyndall Air Force Base in Florida that were on a routine training mission were asked by the FAA to intercept it."[27] Citing a US Air Force report, ABC News confirms the same: "According to an Air Force summary, after contact was initially lost, two F-15s from Tyndall Air Force Base, Fla., were sent to track the Learjet...

> The F-15s pulled back and two F-16s in the air from Elgin Air Force Base, Fla., moved in to track the aircraft. After the Learjet reached the Midwest, the Eglin F-16s pulled off and four F-16s and a midair refueling tanker from the Tulsa National Guard followed it. Eventually, two F-16s from Fargo, N.D., moved in close to look into the windows to see if the pilot was slumped over and to help clear air space.[28]

In other words, after the FAA contacted the military, interceptors were immediately made available to track the Lear jet. Furthermore, fighter craft were scrambled from several air force bases in order to sustain the ongoing monitoring of the situation. This illustrates the capabilities of US air authorities very well—if this was the relatively speedy military response to a lesser emergency, the routine military response to a potentially more catastrophic emergency such as the hijacking of a commercial airliner occurring in restricted airspace over a heavily populated district would be of the highest speed, due to the sheer urgency of the crisis.

Jerry Quickley—a 25-year veteran US commercial pilot—in an interview with this author confirmed that the response times of the US military and FAA to air emergencies can vary from situation to situation, particularly depending on the degree to which the airspace in which the crisis occurs is restricted: the greater the restriction the faster the response time of US fighter craft. Thus, Quickley pointed out that the airspace over Washington, DC and New York—unlike the airspace over which Payne Stewart's Learjet had flown—is "prohibited airspace" (the highest level of restriction), and consequently if a plane flies off course into this airspace while losing radio contact, it will be routinely intercepted by US fighter craft "within minutes."[29]

Using the chronology of events compiled by ABC News just after the 9/11 attacks (timelines vary according to the source), all four commercial planes involved in the attacks took to the air between 7:59 AM and 8:14 AM, September 11, 2001—American Airlines Flight 11, United Airlines Flight 93, American Airlines Flight 77, and United Airlines Flight 175. Although each of these flights was successfully hijacked, as the *New York Press* records: "Initial reports suggested that no aircraft were scrambled to intercept or shoot down the hijacked jets."[30]

On September 13, Acting Chairman of the Joint Chiefs of Staff and Air Force General Richard B. Myers stated before the Senate Armed Services Committee: "When it became clear what the threat was, we did scramble fighter aircraft, AWACS, radar aircraft and tanker aircraft to begin to establish orbits in case other aircraft showed up in the FAA system that were hijacked." Myers was then asked: "Was that order that you just described given before or after the Pentagon was struck? Do you know?" The Air Force General admitted that he did know, replying: "That order, to the best of my knowledge, was after the Pentagon was struck."[31] Myers was asked three times before the Committee about the failure to scramble planes, and each time confirmed the same. At no time in this testimony did Myers indicate that he did not know, had not been in a position to know, or might be mistaken.

A spokesman for NORAD, Marine Corps Major Mike Snyder, corroborated Myers' testimony, explaining that no US fighter jets had been scrambled at all until after the Pentagon crash. Reporting on the NORAD statement, the *Boston Globe* reported on September 15 that: "[T]he command did not immediately scramble any fighters even though it was alerted to a hijacking 10 minutes before the first plane... slammed into the first World Trade Center tower.... The spokesman said the fighters remained on the ground until after the Pentagon was hit…." The failure to act was particularly surprising since Snyder had also admitted that "fighters routinely intercept aircraft."[32]

The same was admitted by Vice President Dick Cheney on September 16 in a "Meet the Press" session with NBC News correspondent Tim Russert, who observed that: "The first hijacking was confirmed at 8:20, the Pentagon was struck at 9:40, and yet, it seems we were not able to scramble fighter jets in time to protect the Pentagon and perhaps even more than that." Cheney did not dispute Russert's assertion, and further suggested that it was the President who made the decision to allow planes to scramble after the Pentagon crash.[33]

Suddenly, the official story changed. US Air Force and government officials reneged on their own multiple testimonies, attempting to explain away the failure to respond to the attacks. In the weeks after the attacks, new official timelines and reports were issued denying these early admissions which indicated that the US military had waited until after the attacks had been completed— nearly one and a half hours after the beginning of the crisis when the first airliner had been hijacked—to scramble fighter craft. This new narrative—which claims that fighters were indeed scrambled from Otis and Langley Air Force Bases— unfortunately suffers from deep-seated inconsistencies. Having been revised by government officials several times, this new narrative is now finalized in the reports of the 9/11 Commission. Therefore, the ensuing analysis focuses on the finalized narrative of the 9/11 Commission. In this discussion, the Commission's narrative is not simply accepted at face value but subjected to a detailed critique as to its internal consistency, its substantiation on the basis of external reliable sources, and the shocking implications of its own findings.

8:14 AM *Multiple Hijackings Confirmed*

At 8:00 AM on September 11, 2001, American Airlines Flight 11 began to takeoff at Logan Airport in Boston. According to the 9/11 Commission's Staff Statement No. 17, at 8:13 air traffic control instructed the flight to "turn twenty degrees right." The instruction, which was acknowledged by the flight, was the last transmission to which the flight responded. When the controller instructed the flight to climb to 35,000 feet 16 seconds later, "there was no response," reports the 9/11 Commission in its Staff Statement No. 17:

> … the controller repeated the command seconds later, and then tried repeatedly to raise the flight. He used the emergency frequency to try to reach the pilot. Though there was no response, he kept trying to contact the aircraft. At 8:21, American 11 turned off its transponder, immediately degrading the available information about the aircraft. The controller told his supervisor that he thought something was seriously wrong with the plane. At this point, neither the controller nor his supervisor suspected a hijacking. The supervisor instructed the controller to follow standard

operating procedures for handling a "no radio" aircraft.[34]

However, those procedures—which entailed the immediate scrambling of military jets to intercept the flight—were ignored. According to the Commission's narrative, although Flight 11 had already begun moving into another sector's airspace, controllers merely instructed other craft to stay out of its way and repeatedly attempted to establish radio contact. Purportedly, at 8:24:38, Flight 11 transmitted: "We have some planes. Just stay quiet, and you'll be OK. We are returning to the airport." But, claims Staff Statement No. 17: "The controller only heard something unintelligible; he did not hear the specific words '[w]e have some planes.'" Only after the next transmission—"Nobody move. Everything will be OK. If you try to make any moves, you'll endanger yourself and the airplane. Just stay quiet"—did the controller realize that Flight 11 had been hijacked, says the Commission. Even then, at 8:24 AM, no military planes were scrambled. Indeed, according to the Commission's narrative, although regional controllers knew this was a hijacking over a heavily populated civilian area, they literally waited a crucial 10 minutes before even attempting to contact the military. During this time, the Commission claims that controllers attempted to notify the FAA chain of command that a hijacking was in progress—but failed to request military assistance:

> Boston Center did not follow the routine protocol in seeking military assistance through the prescribed chain of command. In addition to making notifications within the FAA, Boston Center took the initiative, at 8:34, to contact the military through the FAA's Cape Cod facility. They also tried to obtain assistance from a former alert site in Atlantic City, unaware it had been phased out. At 8:37:52, Boston Center reached NEADS. This was the first notification received by the military—at any level—that American 11 had been hijacked.[35]

It is a matter of record, however, that the Commission's narrative of events has been falsified. Official tape recordings of events on Flight 11 conducted by American Airlines at its Fort Worth, Texas, headquarters demonstrate that air authorities knew of multiple hijackings long before they have officially admitted. The tapes, whose contents have been heard and reported by relatives of the 9/11 victims, reveal that:

> Flight 11 had missed its first mark at 8:13 AM when, shortly after controllers asked the pilot to climb to 35,000 feet, the transponder stopped transmitting the electronic signal that identifies exact location and altitude. Air traffic manager Glenn Michael later said, "We considered it at that time to be a possible hijacking."[36]

In other words, contrary to the Commission narrative, Flight 11 was suspected of being hijacked as early as 8:13 AM.

> At 8:14 AM, FAA flight controllers in Boston began hearing an extraordinary radio transmission from the cockpit of Flight 11 that should have set off alarm bells. Before their FAA superiors forbade them to talk to anyone, two of the controllers told the CSM [manager at Systems Operation Control (SOC)] on Sept. 11 that the captain of Flight 11, John Ogonowski, was surreptitiously triggering a "push-to-talk" button on the aircraft's yoke most of the way to NY. When controllers picked up the voices of men speaking in Arabic and heavily accented English, they knew something was terribly wrong. More than one FAA controller heard an ominous statement by a terrorist in the background saying, "We have more planes. We have other planes."[37]

In other words, at 8:13 AM the FAA suspected that Flight 11 had been hijacked, and at 8:14 AM, the FAA knew not only that Flight 11 had certainly been hijacked, but moreover that other planes had been simultaneously hijacked by operatives connected to those who had taken over Flight 11—once more, contradicting the Commission's narrative. As *New York Observer* correspondent Gail Sheehy notes: "... the FAA, which was in contact with American Airlines and other traffic-control centers, heard the tip-off from terrorists in Flight 11's cockpit—'We have planes, more planes'—and thus knew before the first crash of a possible multiple hijacking and the use of planes as weapons." But what was the FAA's response? Rather than attempting to notify all relevant personnel of the hijacking at 8:14 AM, the FAA supervisors did the very opposite. "Apparently, none of this crucial information was transmitted to other American pilots already airborne," reports Sheehy, "—notably Flight 77 out of Dulles, which took off at 8:20 AM only to be redirected to its target, the Pentagon—or to other airlines with planes in harm's way: United's Flight 173, which took off at 8:14 AM from Boston, or United's Flight 93, whose 'wheels-up' was recorded at 8:42 AM." As noted by Rosemary Dillard—American Airlines base manager at Reagan National Airport on 9/11 responsible for three DC-area airports including Dulles: "You would have thought American's SOC would have grounded everything. They were in the lead spot, they're in Texas—they had control over the whole system. They could have stopped it. Everybody should have been grounded."[38]

But instead, there was no reaction even though flight attendants Madeline (Amy) Sweeney and Betty Ong on Flight 11 "were calmly and bravely transmitting the most illuminating details anyone has yet heard" of the hijacking as it proceeded: "This is Amy Sweeney. I'm on Flight 11—this plane has been hijacked." Sweeney's words were being relayed to FAA supervisors at Logan and to the airline's Fort Worth headquarters. According to one former American

Airlines employee who heard the recording: "In Ft. Worth, two managers in SOC were sitting beside each other and hearing it. They were both saying, 'Do not pass this along. Let's keep it right here. Keep it among the five of us.'" This was despite the fact that by latest 8:25 AM, Sweeney had informed officials that one of the passengers "had been stabbed, possibly fatally." Then president and chief executive of American Airlines Gerard Arpey has testified that at this time:

> We were also receiving information from the FAA that, instead of heading west on its intended flight path, Flight 11 was headed south. We believed that Flight 11 might be headed for the NY area. Our pilots were not responding to air traffic control or company radio calls, and the aircraft transponder had been turned off.

Sheehy thus points out that in this context: "The failure to trumpet vital news from calls placed from the first hijacked flight throughout the system and into the highest circles of government leaves families wondering whether military jets could have intercepted American Airlines Flight 77 in time to keep it from diving into the Pentagon and killing 184 more people."[39]

When the FAA finally made contact with the military according to the Commission narrative, it was supposedly at 8:37 AM—23 minutes after a multiple hijacking had in fact been confirmed. But this account is doubtful. According to NORAD's original official timeline, the FAA's notification to NORAD that Flight 11 had been hijacked occurred at 8:40 AM.[40] By this timeline, FAA superiors had inexplicably waited 26 minutes after a multiple hijacking had been confirmed before notifying NORAD. Moreover, it seems, they neglected entirely to inform any other agencies that multiple planes had been hijacked.

8:46 AM: F-15s Scrambled

Staff Statement No. 17 continues, stating that "F-15 fighters were ordered scrambled at 8:46 from Otis Air Force Base." But NEADS supposedly did not know where to send the fighters. The Commission quotes an alleged official complaining: "I don't know where I'm scrambling these guys to. I need a direction, a destination." Because Flight 11's transponder had been turned off, the FAA had allegedly lost sight of the plane while NEADS personnel frantically "spent the next minutes searching their radar scopes for the elusive primary radar return."[41] In reality, this attempt to explain the delay in sending the fighters to intercept Flight 11 is also false—FAA radar was seamlessly tracking the plane throughout the hijacking, even though the transponder signal had been canceled. Citing some of the controllers who had worked that morning, the *Christian Science Monitor* reported that: "At about 8:28 AM, the controller handling the plane and back-up support watched the jet's radar signal turn over eastern New York and head south along the Hudson River."[42] The *Wall Street Journal* similarly reported that: "The FAA had tagged the radar blip that Flight 11 had become, and it was now isolated on an Aircraft Situation Display, a big radar-tracking screen. All eyes watched as the plane headed south. On the screen, the plane showed a squiggly line after its turn near Albany, then it straightened."[43] Simultaneously, NEADS purportedly could not find Flight 11 on NORAD radars, although NORAD can tap into FAA radar and routinely does so in emergencies.

But according to NORAD official Lt. Col. Dawne Deskins of Air National Guard, who was on duty on the morning of 9/11, NORAD received notification of the Flight 11 hijacking at 8:31 AM.[44] Citing a number of NORAD officials on duty that morning—including Lt. Col. Deskins, Air Force Col. Robert Marr, and Air Force Maj. Gen. Larry Arnold—ABC News similarly confirmed that "shortly after 8:30 AM EST, behind the scenes, word of a possible hijacking reached various stations of NORAD."[45] Former FAA administrator Jane Garvey similarly "testified that the notification took place... at 8:34."[46]

Although all these accounts are conflicting, the NORAD timeline's claim that notification occurred at 8:40 AM is contradicted by some of NORAD's own employees and by the FAA. The majority of accounts—two based on NORAD employees and one from the FAA—suggest that notification occurred just after 8:30 AM. The Commission's account, however—that NORAD was notified at 8:37 AM—seems to have been merely conjured out of thin air, and cannot be tracked to any particular NORAD or FAA source. Rather, the Commission seems to have simply arrived at the figure by averaging 8:40 AM (NORAD's official testimony) and 8:34 AM (the FAA's official testimony). Although the Commission has failed to substantiate the 8:37 AM figure, here it will be assumed to be accurate to avoid further complications.

8:46 AM: *Air-Threat Conference Call*

Flight 11 hit the World Trade Center's north tower at 8:46:40—seconds after fighters from Otis reportedly received NORAD scramble orders. Almost immediately after the impact, senior US government officials became involved, having "initiated an 'air-threat conference call'" between all relevant government, military, and civilian agencies:

> Through the course of the day, participants included Vice President Dick Cheney, Defense Secretary Donald Rumsfeld, and senior officials from the National Security Council (NSC), the Federal Aviation Administration (FAA), and the North American Aerospace Defense Command (NORAD). Pentagon officials familiar with the events say the conference call was broadcast over a loudspeaker inside the National Military Command Center at the Pentagon, which Rumsfeld and Gen. Richard Myers, chairman of the

Joint Chiefs of Staff, were using as an emergency command post.[47]

And "several minutes" after the crash, the FAA informed NORAD that "Flight 11 had hit the World Trade Center."[48] As the Commission points out in Staff Statement No. 17, on 9/11 "[t]he White House Situation Room initiated a video teleconference, chaired by Richard Clarke," who was then White House National Coordinator for Counterterrorism. Former counterterrorism czar Clarke played an extremely prominent role in the government response on 9/11, having overseen the US government and military response to 9/11 attacks from the Secure Video Conferencing Center next to the White House Situation Room. In his best-selling book *Against All Enemies*, Clarke confirms that as of around 9:10 AM, senior officials linked up on video included Defense Secretary Rumsfeld, CIA Director Tenet, FBI Director Mueller, FAA Administrator Jane Garvey, Deputy Attorney General Larry Thompson, Deputy Secretary of State Richard Armitage, Acting Chairman of the Joint Chiefs of Staff Richard Myers, and National Security Advisor Condoleeza Rice. NORAD was also connected—"We're on the line with NORAD, on an air threat conference call," an aide told Clarke.[49]

8:53 AM: *F-15s Stood Down*

According to the Commission, the progress of the F-15 fighter jets ordered to scramble at 8:46 AM was decidedly inadequate:

> Radar data show the Otis fighters were airborne at 8:53. Lacking a target, they were vectored toward military controlled airspace off the Long Island coast. To avoid New York area air traffic and uncertain about what to do, the fighters were brought down to military air space to "hold as needed." From 9:08 to 9:13, the Otis fighters were in this holding pattern.[50]

If this is, indeed, what happened, it is damning. It means that NORAD waited an excruciating 9 minutes after receiving notification of a hijacking at 8:37 AM before giving the order to scramble at 8:46 AM. If the FAA account that notification was given at 8:34 AM is correct, then this delay was actually 12 minutes. If other NORAD accounts that notification was received at 8:31 AM are correct, then the delay lasted 15 minutes. Either way, this is a delay lasting between 9 and 15 minutes—a delay that remains inexplicable, indefensible, and in breach of standard procedures. By the time fighters actually left the ground, the fighters had no particular target to intercept according to the Commission because NORAD still could not locate Flight 11 on its radars—so instead of being sent to New York, the fighters were sent "off the Long Island coast" and by 9:08 were placed on "hold" in military airspace.

A report from Newhouse News Service flatly contradicts the Commission's claim that NORAD had no idea where to send its fighters, justifying keeping them on hold. Citing other FAA and NORAD officials on duty that morning, Newhouse News reports that at 8:43 AM, NORAD official Master Sgt. Maureen Dooley had swiftly calculated that Flight 11 would be in "a sector northeast of New York... Dooley's technicians centered in on a radar blip that might be Flight 11. They watched it close on New York City." Thus, the latest NORAD had pinpointed the location of Flight 11 was 8:43 AM. At the same time: "At 8:43 AM, Dooley's technicians, their headsets linked to Boston Center, heard of a second plane, United Flight 175, that also was not responding. It, too, was moving to New York."[51] Simultaneously, according to NORAD's own timeline, NORAD received separate notification from the FAA that Flight 175 was hijacked (at exactly 8:43 AM).[52]

The Commission report ignores these facts as documented on the basis of official NORAD sources, claiming instead that: "The first indication that the NORAD air defenders had of the second hijacked aircraft, United 175, came in a phone call from New York Center to NEADS at 9:03. The notice came in at about the time the plane was hitting the South Tower."[53] But this narrative, as the previous NORAD sources confirm, is completely disconnected from reality. NORAD knew Flight 175 was hijacked at 8:43 AM.

Despite NORAD having precisely pinpointed the location of Flight 11 moving toward New York City at 8:43 AM before the scramble order was given, by the Commission's account Otis fighters becoming airborne at 8:53 AM were still confused as to where they ought to fly. Taking these accounts together suggests that the fighters were not given the appropriate orders. On the contrary, rather than being instructed swiftly toward New York City, according to the Commission they were not given any particular target to intercept, were "vectored toward military controlled airspace off the Long Island coast," and most shocking of all were ordered explicitly "to avoid the New York area" and subsequently placed on hold—effectively, to stand down. These bizarre orders seem to have prevailed even though firstly, Flight 11 crashed into the first World Trade Center tower at 8:46 AM and secondly, Flight 175 was known to have been hijacked and heading in the same direction toward New York City.

The Commission report thus challenges earlier news accounts claiming that the Otis fighters were sent directly to New York City as a matter of urgency. According to this narrative, when Flight 11 disappeared off the radar (after it crashed into the north WTC tower), the Otis fighters attempted to reach Flight 175 instead, but failed to reach it in time to divert the hijacked craft from the World Trade Center. But this account is incoherent. According to Air Force News, the F-15 has a top speed of 1,875 mph.[54] Otis is 188 miles from New York. At top speed, the fighters could have reached New York City in approximately 6 minutes, arriving at 8:59 AM—4 minutes *before* the second hijacked craft Flight 175 crashed into the World Trade Center's south tower at

9:03:02. Four minutes would have provided ample opportunity for the Otis fighters to divert Flight 175 from its suicidal flight path into a safer airspace, or shoot it down. But according to NORAD's timeline, at the time of Flight 175's crash into the south tower the Otis F-15s were still 71 miles away. In other words, they had covered only 117 miles in the 10 minutes since they had been airborne. *This means that they were flying at 702 mph—less than half of their maximum speed.*

US Air Force spokesmen have given contradictory estimates of the speed of the Otis fighters. Maj. Gen. Paul Weaver, director of the Air National Guard, described the F-15s as flying "like a scalded ape," topping at 500 mph. But this speed is even worse—less than a third of an F-15's maximum speed. ABC News claimed that the fighters traveled "nearly 900 miles per hour," while one NORAD commander Maj. Gen. Larry Arnold said that the fighters headed straight toward New York City "at about 1100 to 1200 mph."[55]

All of these off-hand estimates are clearly false, since they contradict the above calculation based on official timelines. However, they do corroborate the conclusion that in reality the F-15s certainly were not flying with extreme urgency at supersonic speed in an attempt to respond to the crisis at hand as fast as possible. On the contrary, the Otis fighters were flying at a decidedly leisurely pace. This, however, is perfectly consistent with the Commission's on-the-record confirmation that the fighters scrambled from Otis Air Force base were never intended to reach New York City, were never given any particular target, and were in fact ordered to keep "away" from New York.

Senior government officials oversaw this effective stand down of the Otis fighters throughout this period, through their participation in the National Military Command Center interagency air-threat conference call, which had been initiated almost immediately after Flight 11 hit the north WTC tower. There is therefore little doubt that ultimate responsibility for the US Air Force's failure to prevent the hijacked flights from successively hitting the World Trade Center lies with those officials who supervised the obstruction and diversion of the Otis fighters away from New York.

8:56 AM: *The Disappearing Plane?*

American Airlines 77 began its takeoff roll from Dulles International Airport at 8:20 AM. According to Staff Report 17, the last transmission received from Flight 77 was at 8:50 AM when the pilot acknowledged an instruction to climb. At 8:54 AM, the Commission reports, the flight deviated from its flight path with a "slight turn toward the south." The Commission cites the controller saying he saw the aircraft "turning to the southwest, and then saw the data disappear" from the radar at 8:56 AM. According to this narrative, the controller had no inkling that Flight 77 had been hijacked. However, the Commission concedes that despite the fact that all radio contact had been lost, and the plane had not only deviated from its flight path but purportedly disappeared completely, no fighters were scrambled to intercept the plane in accordance with standard procedures. The controller, rather, "believed American 77 had experienced serious electrical and/or mechanical failure, and was gone." Despite the fact that the FAA notified its other internal agencies of the problem, the Commission claims that NORAD was not informed in the same manner. Instead, controllers apparently waited until 9:09 AM—13 to 15 minutes—before informing the FAA regional center, which in turn waited another 15 minutes before informing FAA headquarters at 9:24 AM. Both these delays in themselves are inexplicable.[56]

The Commission also forwards a rather curious explanation of why the FAA had failed to continue tracking Flight 77 on primary radar after its transponder was turned off. "Radar reconstructions performed after 9/11 reveal that FAA radar equipment tracked the flight from the moment its transponder was turned off at 8:56," the Commission concedes. "But for eight minutes and thirteen seconds, between 8:56 and 9:05, this primary radar information… was not displayed to controllers." The Commission provides a vague story of mysterious "technical" problems "arising from the way the software processed radar information, as well as from poor primary radar coverage where American 77 was flying." Without even taking into account authoritative reports from other credible sources conflicting with this claim, at face value the Commission's story is incoherent. On the one hand, the Commission concedes that FAA radar continued to track the flight after the transponder was turned off. On the other hand, the Commission says that there was poor primary radar in that area—but if the regional radar was poor and therefore unable to track the flight, then the Commission's initial admission that FAA radar had indeed tracked the flight loses value. The Commission also blames problems due to the software's processing of the information—but if such problems are indeed inherent to the functioning of the software itself and its processing of radar data, then it would follow that the software itself is fundamentally flawed. In that case, the ensuing problem of primary radar not being displayed to controllers would be endemic, such that this problem would continually arise as long as the software was being used.[57]

The Commission claims that due to this unfathomable failure of FAA radar—an incoherent narrative that is clearly therefore untrue—controllers "never saw Flight 77 turn around" toward Washington, DC. "By the time it reappeared in primary radar coverage, controllers had either stopped looking for the aircraft because they thought it had crashed or were looking toward the west," hence failing to find it. At the same time, the FAA failed to issue a bulletin to surrounding centers "to search for primary radar targets. American 77 traveled undetected for 36 minutes on a course heading due east for Washington, DC." In the meantime, NORAD was purportedly not contacted or notified by the FAA of the threat posed by this missing commercial airliner.[58] Instead, at

9:21 AM the FAA informed NORAD—according to the Commission—that a "hijacked" Flight 11 (not Flight 77) was "heading into Washington," prompting NORAD to send scramble orders at 9:24 AM to Langley Air Force Base. The Commission is "unable to identify the source of this mistaken FAA information." Langley fighters were then reportedly airborne at 9:30 AM. Moreover, NORAD was not informed by the FAA at all about the purportedly lost Flight 77 until 9:34 AM—4 minutes before it crashed into the Pentagon.[59]

This entire narrative is not only internally incoherent, but in contradiction to other authoritative accounts. For instance, the FAA clearly knew that a third aircraft was hurtling toward Washington, DC. But if controllers were not able to find Flight 77 on their primary radar such that the flight was effectively "lost," what radar data was being monitored by the FAA proving that a phantom "Flight 11" was speeding toward Washington, DC? Clearly, the FAA must have been monitoring the hijacked flight headed toward Washington, DC—Flight 77. Furthermore, given that the FAA was well aware that Flight 11 had *already* crashed into the north tower of the World Trade Center, how could it have been presumed to have been the same flight now heading toward Washington, DC? Although the Commission alleges that the phantom "Flight 11" narrative is based on official records, those alleged records have not been released to the public. Indeed, the Commission provides no explanation whatsoever for its assertion that "NEADS, multiple FAA centers, Continental Region headquarters, NORAD," and other agencies all began simultaneously hallucinating that a phantom "Flight 11" had extricated itself from the north WTC tower to head southward to Washington—nor is the Commission interested in understanding how such a monumental dysfunction of multiple agencies could occur simultaneously such that a phantom flight is tracked on multiple radar screens. At the same time, the Commission concedes that "this response to a phantom aircraft, American 11, is not recounted in a single public timeline or statement issued by FAA or DOD."[60]

In fact, according to testimony under oath before the Commission of a NORAD official on duty on 9/11, Col. Alan Scott: "At 9:24, the FAA reports a possible hijack of 77. That's some time after they had been tracking its primary target. And at that moment as well is when the Langley F-16s were scrambled out of Langley." A minute later, according to Col. Scott, "American 77 is reported heading toward Washington, D.C."[61]

Thus, the Commission's account is unsubstantiated and contradictory—clearly the FAA and NORAD were aware that Flight 77 was heading toward Washington, DC. Notably, even assuming that the Commission's account of the phantom flight is correct, it does not demonstrate that the FAA and NORAD were unaware of the real Flight 77. The evidence produced repeatedly and independently by various FAA and NORAD officials shows that Flight 77 was being closely tracked since takeoff for at least the vast majority of its winding course toward Washington, DC. Indeed, as is demonstrated below, the phantom flight narrative proves to be irrelevant—regardless of its alleged accuracy—in explaining the failure to respond to Flight 77.

8:56 AM: Hijack Confirmed—Plane Lost?

In fact, a number of reports based on FAA and NORAD sources provide a different picture to that being constructed by the Commission. As early as 8:46 AM—exactly the same as the first WTC crash—Flight 77 deviated severely off course, heading first due north, then turning due south again before returning to its assigned course. USA Today flight path maps show that it went off course for approximately 15 miles for 5 minutes.[62] During this time, FAA officials realized that this was another hijack. According to the New York Times "within a few minutes" after 8:48 AM when the first news reports of the first WTC attack emerged, controllers knew that "both United 175 (the second plane to hit the World Trade Center) and American 77 (which hit the Pentagon) had probably been hijacked."[63]

According to Newsday, which cited "government records" and "interviews with military and civilian officials," "About 8:55 AM Flight 77 was flying west over southern Ohio when it abruptly turned and headed back toward Washington." The flight disappeared off the radar at 8:56 AM, which means the FAA would have been fully aware that the flight had turned toward Washington, DC, before its transponder was turned off. Moreover even after reportedly "losing track of Flight 77 for about 10 minutes, the FAA rediscovered the plane heading east over West Virginia."[64] Similarly, a Washington Post timeline based on "witnesses" and "authorities" records that at "8:55 AM: Flight 77 began turning east, away from its intended course," and again at "9:10 AM: Flight 77 was detected by radar in West Virginia, heading east."[65] According to these accounts, based on FAA sources, the Commission's claim—that at 8:56 AM the FAA saw Flight 77 turn toward "the southwest" before its transponder was turned off—is inaccurate. In reality, the FAA had watched Flight 77 on the radar as it turned east toward Washington. Moreover, whether or not it is plausible to believe that the FAA had subsequently lost track of the flight, between 9:05 and 9:10 AM the FAA had undoubtedly recommenced tracking the flight as it headed east toward Washington, DC. The Commission's claim, therefore, that the FAA had lost track of Flight 77 all the way until 9:32 AM,[66] is untrue.

The Commission also claims that NORAD was not informed by the FAA of Flight 77's path to DC until 4 minutes before the Pentagon crash (9:34 AM)—that is, at least 24 minutes after Flight 77 is picked up on FAA radar in West Virginia. If true, the FAA's failure to do so is yet another inexplicable violation of standard procedures. However, authoritative testimony indicates that the Commission's claim is incorrect. In an official memo to the Commission read out after the testimony of FAA Administrator Jane Garvey, the FAA pointed out firstly that

NORAD was specifically informed of the hijacked Flight 77 heading toward Washington at 9:24 AM—10 minutes earlier than the Commission claims—and secondly that open lines between the FAA and NORAD had kept NORAD fully informed of Flight 77's activities long before 9:24 AM:

> The FAA shared real-time information on the phone bridges about the unfolding events, including information about loss of communication with aircraft, loss of transponder signals, unauthorized changes in course, and other actions being taken by all the flights of interest, including Flight 77. Other parties on the phone bridges, in turn, shared information about actions they were taking.
>
> NORAD logs indicate that the FAA made formal notification about American Flight 77 at 9:24 AM, but information about the flight was conveyed continuously during the phone bridges before the formal notification.[67]

Moreover, the FAA memo also reveals that NORAD was thereby privy to all FAA information at least as early as the first World Trade Center crash, through the phone bridges which were part of the previously mentioned air-threat conference call:

> Within minutes after the first aircraft hit the World Trade Center, the FAA immediately established several phone bridges that included FAA field facilities, the FAA Command Center, FAA headquarters, DOD, the Secret Service, and other government agencies. The US Air Force liaison to the FAA immediately joined the FAA headquarters phone bridge and established contact with NORAD on a separate line.[68]

This information implies that like the FAA, NORAD was aware of Flight 77's hijacking and course toward Washington "within minutes" after 8:48 AM— approximately 8:51 AM by investigator Paul Thompson's calculation.[69] Indeed, their awareness of the danger to DC would have been reinforced at 9:10 AM at the latest when Flight 77 was picked up by the FAA in West Virginia. Furthermore, given the inherent incoherence of the claim that the FAA's primary radar monitoring Flight 77 when it first flew off course was faulty, the very narrative that the FAA and NORAD had lost track of Flight 77 at all collapses. Nevertheless, no orders to scramble aircraft were issued by NORAD until 9:23 AM. This is a delay of approximately 32 minutes.

9:30 AM: F-16s Scrambled, Stood Down

When the F-16s from Langley were finally airborne at 9:30 AM, however, they were not ordered to fly full-throttle toward Washington, DC, where Flight 77 was headed—instead, they were ordered to the nearby city of Baltimore where they were supposed to wait for several minutes for the imaginary southbound Flight 11 to arrive on its way to DC:

> NEADS decided to keep the Otis fighters over New York. The heading of the Langley fighters was adjusted to send them to the Baltimore area. The Mission Crew Commander explained to us that the purpose was to position the Langley fighters between the reported southbound American 11 and the nation's capital.[70]

But as has already been documented above, the Commission's claim that both the FAA and NORAD believed that an imaginary Flight 11 was traveling southbound from another location is internally incoherent as well as contradictory to official FAA and NORAD data. On the contrary, the FAA and NORAD were well aware of Flight 77's eastward course toward Washington, DC, which they had been monitoring all along. Thus, although the Commission's revelation—that the Langley fighters were misdirected toward Baltimore where they were intended to be held in position—is useful, the depiction of FAA/NORAD officials convinced that the target of engagement was a completely different imaginary "Flight 11" somewhere else, designed to justify that misdirection, is false. Despite knowing full well Flight 77's course toward Washington, DC, the Langley fighters were ordered to position over Baltimore.

It is in this context that the Commission's narrative of ensuing events entirely falls apart. Despite the fact, as documented here, that the FAA and NORAD had been well aware of hijacked Flight 77's course toward Washington, DC, the Commission claims that at 9:34, the FAA informs NORAD that "we also lost American 77," and argues that this "was the first notice to the military that American 77 was missing." The Commission further claims that as late as 9:36 AM, the FAA and NORAD had suddenly discovered an unknown aircraft about to impact in DC, and were completely clueless that this was Flight 77: "At 9:36, the FAA's Boston Center called NEADS and relayed the discovery about the aircraft closing in on Washington, an aircraft that still had not been linked with the missing American 77." This purportedly prompted NORAD to instruct the Langley fighters to fly immediately toward Washington, DC. Worse still, Staff Report 17 reveals that—like the Otis fighters—the Langley F-16s had been given vague and incorrect orders from the outset. At this time, the Langley fighters were found not heading toward Baltimore, but "east over the ocean."[71] The Commission provides three inadequate explanations of this bizarre misdirection:

> First, unlike a normal scramble order, this order did not include a distance to the target, or the target's location. Second, a "generic" flight plan incorrectly led the Langley fighters to believe they were ordered to fly due

east (090) for 60 miles. The purpose of the generic flight plan was to quickly get the aircraft airborne and out of local airspace. Third, the lead pilot and local FAA controller incorrectly assumed the flight plan instruction to go "090 for 60" was newer guidance that superseded the original scramble order.[72]

Each of these reasons is either nonsensical or incriminating. If the scramble order was to head immediately to a precise position in Baltimore between an imaginary Flight 11 and the nation's capital, then the target of the scramble orders was exactly this position. Hence, the scramble orders—if they were to have any meaning at all—should have included not only the distance to this position, but also the position's location. The Commission's disclosure that the scramble order lacked both the "target's location" and the "distance to the target" indicates that, in reality, the Langley fighters had not been given *any* instructions at all, let alone instructions to go to Baltimore—or in simpler terms: *they had no target.* This inexplicable fact has been independently confirmed by NORAD officer Maj. James Fox, who "dispatched the jets without targets. That would come later."[73] It should be noted that the phantom "Flight 11" narrative does not resolve this problem, nor lessen its magnitude—whether or not the Langley fighters were supposed to have been scrambled to Baltimore to intercept the phantom flight, the evidence on record demonstrates that their actual scramble orders did not even direct them to Baltimore. Why such useless "targetless" scramble orders, then, in the midst of a clear crisis in or around Washington?

In this context, the Commission's second and third explanations are damning. Lacking any orders at all, therefore, Langley fighters were provided nothing except "a 'generic' flight plan" ordering them "to fly due east (090) for 60 miles." The third explanation—that this generic order to fly east was incorrectly assumed to have superseded "the original scramble order"—collapses simply because according to the admissions of both the Commission and NORAD officer Maj. Fox, there was no original scramble order designating any particular target in the first instance. Finally, and perhaps most obviously, NORAD obviously tracks its own fighters—if a fighter does not follow its orders, then NORAD is in a position to monitor and correct the problem by immediately contacting the pilot and re-issuing the appropriate order. However, such contact did not occur in the case of the Langley fighters, signifying that their flight paths were in fact not erroneous at all, but were consistent with NORAD instructions.

The implications of this information, once again, are damning and alarming. Despite the fact that the FAA and NORAD were cognizant of Flight 77's quickening approach toward Washington, DC, Langley F-16s were scrambled without specific instructions, lacking any particular target, and ordered instead to fly 60 miles east over the ocean—in other words, in precisely the wrong direction away from Washington, DC. In this manner, again, they were effectively stood down. This process, again, occurred under the auspices and careful decisions of the most senior government and military officials overseeing the air-threat conference call that connected the FAA, NORAD, and all other relevant agencies. It is no surprise then to learn from the Commission that by the time the Pentagon had been struck at 9:38 AM, "The Langley fighters were approximately 150 miles away."[74]

9:26 AM: *National Military Stand Down*

At 9:27 AM, Vice President Cheney and National Security Advisor Rice were in their bunker below the White House monitoring the progress of Flight 77. An aide told them that an unidentified aircraft was 50 miles outside Washington, DC and headed toward it. Transportation Secretary Norman Mineta asked Federal Aviation Deputy Chief Monty Belger for further clarification. Belger responded: "Well we're watching this target on the radar, but the transponder's been turned off. So we have no identification." The aide gave Cheney and Rice further notices on the flight's suicidal course into Washington, DC. "Mr. Vice President, the airplane's 30 miles out"; "it's 10 miles out"; "uh-oh, we just lost the bogey." At the last point, the plane disappeared off the radar—just as it hit the Pentagon.[75] Throughout this period, no effort was made to evacuate any key government buildings in DC, including the White House, the Capitol Building, State Department, and the Pentagon.[76] Thompson asks pointedly: "Why did Cheney and others track Flight 77 getting closer and closer to Washington, and fail to give any evacuation orders? How many of the 125 people killed inside the Pentagon could have been saved?"[77]

However, in his testimony before the Commission, Norman Mineta related the following crucial sequence of events occurring in the White House bunker during this time:

> During the time that the airplane was coming in to the Pentagon, there was a young man who would come in and say to the Vice President, "The plane is 50 miles out." "The plane is 30 miles out." And when it got down to "the plane is 10 miles out," the young man also said to the Vice President, "Do the orders still stand?" And the Vice President turned and whipped his neck around and said, "Of course the orders still stand. Have you heard anything to the contrary?" Well at the time, I didn't know what all of that meant.[78]

Transportation Secretary Mineta inferred that Cheney must have been referring to an order to permit fighters to shoot down rogue commercial airliners. But Mineta's inference was wrong—as the *Washington Post* reported, citing a Commission staff report: "Vice President Cheney did not issue orders to shoot down hostile aircraft on Sept. 11, 2001, until long after the last hijacked airliner had already crashed, and that the order was never passed along to military fighter pilots searching for errant aircraft that morning."[79] As Staff Statement No. 17 confirms, some time between 10:10 and 10:15 AM, President Bush communicated to the Vice President Cheney the order to shoot down any hostile aircraft, including commercial planes.[80]

Therefore, Cheney's reference to "orders" that had to be sustained a few minutes after 9:27 AM, had nothing to do with shooting down planes. On the contrary, Cheney's orders were concerned with the very opposite—a comprehensive stand down of all planes: including US military fighters. In an extraordinary report, *Time* magazine revealed that a few minutes earlier at 9:25 AM, FAA Administrator Jane Garvey

> ... almost certainly after getting an okay from the White House, initiated a national ground stop, which forbids takeoffs and requires planes in the air to get down as soon as reasonable. The order, which has never been implemented since flying was invented in 1903, applied to virtually every single kind of machine that can takeoff—civilian, military, or law enforcement.

Thus, military and law enforcement flights were also comprehensively grounded, even as Flight 77 was closing in on Washington, DC and the Pentagon at about 500 mph. The ban on military fighters was only lifted at 10:31 AM.[81]

In other words, while Vice President Cheney was monitoring Flight 77's course toward Washington, DC, about 8 minutes prior to the Pentagon crash he had explicitly emphasized that the White House's comprehensive stand down of planes nationwide—including military fighters that might have intercepted the last two hijacked aircraft including Flight 93—be rigorously maintained without exceptions. It is not surprising in that context to note that although calls to NORAD from multiple US fighter units nationwide poured in after the second WTC crash offering to launch armed jets to protect the skies in a matter of minutes, nothing happened. A particularly disturbing example is that of the Air National Guard commander in Syracuse, New York, who told NORAD Col. Robert Marr, in charge of the Northeastern [NEADS] sector: "Give me 10 min. and I can give you hot guns. Give me 30 min. and I'll have heat-seeker [missiles]. Give me an hour and I can give you slammers [Amraams]."[82] But in fact, Syracuse fighters were only airborne by 10:44 AM. Why the delay? As Thompson observes: "Syracuse could have had planes with some weapons in the sky in ten minutes. Even if fighters didn't take off from Syracuse until 9:20, that still would have been enough time for those fighters to reach Washington before Flight 77 did, if they had been ordered to protect that city."[83]

The White House stand-down order, apparently executed by Vice President Cheney, was the last crucial senior government decision that prevented military fighters from intercepting Flight 77, allowing it to plough into a Pentagon that senior officials refused to have evacuated.

10:03 AM: *Abandoned Flight Crashes*

The plight of Flight 93, which had taken off at 8:42 AM, was similarly ignored. According to the Commission narrative, NORAD was first notified by the FAA that the aircraft was hijacked at 10:07 AM—although as early as 9:30 AM, the controller knew that the plane had been hijacked—another unexplained delay of 37 minutes.[84] But Flight 93 had already crashed at 10:03 AM. Supposedly, the FAA was unaware of this fact despite having tracked the plane all along, contacting NORAD for military assistance five minutes after it had crashed.[85] Therefore, claims the Commission, "NEADS was never able to locate United 93 on radar because it was already in the ground."[86]

This bizarre version of events is contradicted by multiple testimonials and accounts from FAA and NORAD sources. Citing "informed senior Department of Defense officials," CNN reported that at: "9:16 AM: FAA informs NORAD that United Airlines flight 93 may have been hijacked."[87] Even the Commission concedes that: "In May 2003 public testimony before this Commission, NORAD officials stated that, at 9:16, NEADS received hijack notification of United 93 from the FAA."[88]

Although it is not clear what prompted the FAA to do so, something seems to have occurred in the cockpit that alerted the FAA to a hijacking situation. This tallies with reports that a hijacker may have been in one of the flight's cockpit even before takeoff. Thus, FOX News "learned that investigators believe that on at least one flight, one of the hijackers was already inside the cockpit before takeoff." According to law enforcement sources, evidence from "cockpit voice recordings" suggests that "at least one of the hijackers was posing as a pilot and was thereby extended the typical airline courtesy of allowing any pilot from any airline to join a flight by sitting in the jump seat, the fold-over extra seat, located inside the cockpit."[89] It should be noted that edited transcripts of cockpit voice recordings have been released for every flight except Flight 93.[90]

The Commission, however, simply dismisses the FAA–NORAD–9:16 AM hijacking alert as "incorrect," although it has been independently confirmed by several NORAD and Defense Department officials. This alert demonstrates that the two agencies were tracking the hijacked Flight 93 since 9:16 AM, but completely failed for at least 47 minutes to intercept the flight in time. Indeed, according to Deputy Secretary of Defense Paul Wolfowitz, "the Air Force was tracking the hijacked plane that crashed in Pennsylvania."[91] Yet standard procedures were, again, breached with unnerving impunity.

Citing NORAD's original timeline, Thompson observes that "a fighter was

100 miles or 11 minutes away when Flight 93 crashed in the Pennsylvania countryside. That means the fighter was traveling about 550 mph"—again, less than half its maximum speed. In other words, "the fighters had only gone about 80 miles from Washington when Flight 93 crashed...

> If we assume the slow 550 mph speed was correct and constant, that means the fighters left Washington about eight minutes before the crash, or 9:58. Think about the implications of that. Even before Flight 93 was hijacked at 9:16, the nations' defenses were in an uproar, with base commanders all over the country calling in, asking to help. Yet, incredibly, about 42 minutes passed before even anyone sent any fighters toward the hijacked Flight 93![92]

Throughout the 9/11 terrorist attacks, then, the US national security apparatus systematically facilitated the attacks by implementing policies that either inexplicably delayed the response of US air defense or methodically diverted it. Both the FAA and NORAD inexplicably delayed their responses for unconscionably prolonged periods, in breach of standard procedures. Repeatedly, fighter craft were indefinitely postponed, continuously misdirected, and ultimately stood down, in such a manner that permitted the attacks to occur entirely unhindered for over one and a half hours in the most restricted airspace in the world.

11.

THE PARALYSIS OF THE NATIONAL SECURITY SYSTEM ON 9/11

Washington, DC's Air Defense

The US Department of Defense initially issued reports that there were simply no local fighter jets available to intercept Flight 77. According to USA Today, attempting to provide an explanation based on US Department of Defense sources: "Andrews Air Force Base, home to Air Force One, is only 15 miles [sic] away from the Pentagon, but it had no fighters assigned to it. Defense officials won't say whether that has changed."

Yet in a report on the same day, USA Today stated in contradiction to its other story that Andrews Air Force Base did actually have fighters present there—but supposedly they were not on alert: "The District of Columbia National Guard maintained fighter planes at Andrews Air Force Base, only about 15 miles [sic] from the Pentagon, but those planes were not on alert and not deployed."[1]

Both these reports amounted to disinformation, as is suggested by their mutual inconsistency. Quoting directly from US National Guard sources, the San Diego Union-Tribune clarified the reality of the matter:

> Air defense around Washington is provided mainly by fighter planes from Andrews Air Force Base in Maryland near the District of Columbia border. The DC Air National Guard is also based there and equipped with F-16 fighter planes, a National Guard spokesman said. "But the fighters took to the skies over Washington only after the devastating attack on the Pentagon."[2]

It is thus clear that combat-ready fighters assigned to the protection of Washington, DC did not do anything at all for almost one and a half hours, although it was known that Flight 77 was heading toward DC as early as 8:55 AM. Even when NORAD was, according to Gen. Eberhart in his testimony before the Senate Armed Services Committee (September 13, 2001), notified by the FAA at 9:24 of the danger posed by Flight 77, rather than scrambling Andrews fighter craft 10 miles away from Washington, DC, craft from the more distant Langley Air Force base were scrambled instead.

Indeed, Andrews Air Force Base houses two combat-ready squadrons served by hundreds of full-time personnel: the 121st Fighter Squadron (FS-121) of the

113th Fighter Wing (FW-113), equipped with F-16 fighters; and the 321st Marine Fighter Attack Squadron (VMFA-321) of the 49th Marine Air Group, Detachment A (MAG-49 Det-A), equipped with F/A-18 fighters:

> ... as part of its dual mission, the 113th provides capable and ready response forces for the District of Columbia in the event of a natural disaster or civil emergency. Members also assist local and federal law enforcement agencies in combating drug trafficking in the District of Colombia. At Andrews, the 113th Wing, its associated DCANG units, and their people are full partners with the active Air Force.... In the best tradition of the Marine Corps, a "few good men and women" support two combat-ready reserve units at Andrews AFB. Marine Fighter Attack Squadron (VMFA) 321, a Marine Corps Reserve squadron, flies the sophisticated F/A-18 Hornet. Marine Aviation Logistics Squadron 49, Detachment A, provides maintenance and supply functions necessary to maintain a force in readiness.[3]

Indeed, the official mission of the DC Air National Guard (DCANG) is: "To provide combat units in the *highest possible state of readiness*. We will support the Air Force and other DoD agencies."[4] This is a clear indication that specifically assigned fighter craft in the DCANG units at Andrews are constantly in the highest possible state of combat readiness, available to be immediately scrambled to respond to a "civil emergency."

Other reports confirm that Andrews aircraft were available to be alerted and activated in response to the Pentagon attack. For example, the *Sunday Telegraph* observed that: "Within minutes of the attack American forces around the world were put on one of their highest states of alert—Defcon 3, just two notches short of all-out war—and F-16s from Andrews Air Force Base were in the air over Washington, DC."[5]

The *Denver Post* similarly reported that

> There was a slight murmur in the audience at the Postal Service headquarters when the board chairman announced that two planes had hit the World Trade Center in New York. A few moments later an audible gasp went up from the rear of the audience as a large black plume of smoke arose from the Pentagon. Terrorism suddenly was at the doorstep and clearly visible through the big glass windows overlooking the Potomac River. Overhead, fighter jets scrambled from Andrews Air Force Base and other installations and criss-crossed the skies amid reports that more hijacked planes were bound for the Capitol on suicide missions. 'My God, it's like we're at war,' said a woman as the jets streaked overhead.[6]

NBC News similarly reported that "It was after the attack on the Pentagon that the Air Force then decided to scramble F-16s out of the DC National Guard

Andrews Air Force Base to fly cover, a protective cover over Washington, DC."[7]

Scramble Orders: The President's Decision

The official US government explanation of the calamitous failure to protect Washington, DC can be found in excerpts from an NBC press conference with US Vice President Dick Cheney:

> JOURNALIST TIM RUSSERT: What's the most important decision you think he [President Bush] made during the course of the day?
>
> DICK CHENEY: Well, the—I suppose the toughest decision was this question of whether or not we would intercept incoming commercial aircraft…. We decided to do it. We'd, in effect, put a flying combat air patrol up over the city; F16s with an AWACS, which is an airborne radar system, and tanker support so they could stay up a long time…. It doesn't do any good to put up a combat air patrol if you don't give them instructions to act, if, in fact, they feel it's appropriate.[8]

Cheney had created the impression that the military required presidential authorization to scramble fighter jets to intercept American Airlines Flight 77 before it hit the Pentagon. He seems to have done so on the basis of witnessing actual discussions within the White House related to this issue. He also avoided any discussion of the ominous failure to intercept this flight. Both these actions on his part amounted to disinformation. In fact, the idea that intercepting the hijacked airliners by fighter jets was "the toughest decision" to be made exclusively on presidential authority, contradicts Standard Operating Procedures as outlined in FAA and Defense Department documents. As documented at the beginning of this chapter, fighter jets routinely intercept commercial aircraft under designated circumstances without White House approval, in response to the most mundane emergencies, let alone hijackings.

But Cheney's statements on NBC confirmed that on the morning of 9/11, regardless of existing regulations, the decision to "put a flying combat air patrol up over the city" was a presidential-level decision. The idea inadvertently suggested by Cheney, apparently based on the occurrence of White House discussions in which he was involved, is that the White House had somehow intervened in standard procedures, leading to their disruption—Cheney implied that it was the President who decided to allow planes to scramble one and a half hours too late, thus bearing principal responsibility for the sabotage of systems designed to protect civilians.

Cheney also incorrectly implied that interception of the commercial flight automatically implied shooting it down. "It doesn't do any good to put up a combat air patrol if you don't give them instructions to act, if, in fact, they feel it's appropriate," he stated.

TIM RUSSERT: So if the United States government became aware that a hijacked commercial airline was destined for the White House or the Capitol, we would take the plane down?

DICK CHENEY: Yes. The president made the decision... that if the plane would not divert... as a last resort, our pilots were authorized to take them out. Now, people say, you know, that's a horrendous decision to make. Well, it is. You've got an airplane full of American citizens, civilians, captured by... terrorists, headed and are you going to, in fact, shoot it down, obviously, and kill all those Americans on board?... It's a presidential-level decision, and the president made, I think, exactly the right call in this case, to say, "I wished we'd had combat air patrol up over New York."[9]

Cheney therefore claimed not only that White House approval is necessary to approve the scrambling of fighter jets—when in fact this occurs automatically according to clear military and FAA regulations—but that this approval is necessary because detailed instructions are required from the White House as to what the craft should perform. Otherwise, Cheney asserted, there is no point in putting up "combat air patrol." But as Jared Israel points out, the *American Heritage Dictionary* defines "intercept" as follows: "to stop, deflect or interrupt the progress or intended course of." Interception of a plane is thus aimed at changing its course and does not in itself imply violence. Moreover, FAA and military regulations mandate the immediate interception of commercial airliners in such circumstances. The option of shooting the plane down only comes into consideration after fighter jets are scrambled in accordance with standard procedures. The question as to why no fighter craft were scrambled to intercept Flight 77, as would happen in any routine emergency, therefore remains as pertinent as ever. But Cheney's statement also provides an answer to this question, since as noted already, the Vice President clearly confirmed that scramble orders on 9/11 were a White House decision. Since, as extensively documented heretofore, scramble orders on 9/11 were invariably delayed and/or misdirected, this claim implies that the White House was principally responsible for the failure of combat aircraft to scramble and therefore responsible for the violation of standard procedures.[10] Whichever narrative of the 9/11 air response one chooses to accept (whether it be the initial narrative from multiple high-level testimonials confirming that no fighter jets were scrambled at all until after the Pentagon was hit, or whether it be subsequent narratives that fighters were scrambled but clearly obstructed, misdirected, and delayed), standard air force response procedures on 9/11 were systematically violated, and by the Vice President's account, the White House bears ultimate responsibility.

Two particular dimensions of the violations can be discerned. Firstly, the FAA systematically failed to immediately contact the military in accordance with standard procedures. Secondly, NORAD systematically failed to immediately scramble fighter jets and swiftly intercept the hijacked airliners in accordance with standard procedures. According to Vice President Cheney, the FAA had "open lines" with the US Secret Service—at least as soon as the first WTC Tower was hit.[11] This again raises the question of presidential responsibility, since his Secret Service would have been kept him fully informed of the unfolding crisis through its contact with the FAA.

Government Officials on 9/11: Orchestrated Negligence

Most surprisingly, an examination of the actions of some of the most prominent government and military officials on the morning of 9/11 further suggests that the collapse of standard procedures is directly connected to high-level government inaction.

On 9/11, Gen. Richard B. Myers—a former Commander of NORAD—was Acting Chairman of the Joint Chiefs of Staff. According to the *Washington Post*, Gen. Richard Myers "was deeply involved in the military's response [on September 11th] this week from the outset."[12] That morning, the *New York Press* reports, Chairman of the Joint Chiefs of Staff Gen. Myers, was having a routine meeting on Capitol Hill with then Senator Max Cleland.[13] According to the American Forces Press Service (AFPS), just before the meeting began: "While in an outer office, he said, he saw a television report that a plane had hit the World Trade Center. 'They thought it was a small plane or something like that,' Myers said. So the two men went ahead with the office call."[14]

In other words, having been notified of an unprecedented emergency in New York—with a plane for the first time in history ploughing into the World Trade Center—the response of Gen. Myers, who has specific responsibility to oversee military policies and advise the government on the same, was to ignore it. This constituted a direct and apparently quite deliberate neglect of the responsibility of his post during this obviously unprecedented crisis. Alarmingly, while Myers and Cleland chatted away, a "hijacked jet plowed into the World Trade Center's north tower, another one plowed into the south tower and a third one into the Pentagon. And still they went on with their meeting."[15] According to the AFPS:

> Meanwhile, the second World Trade Center tower was hit by another jet. "Nobody informed us of that," Myers said. "But when we came out, that was obvious. Then, right at that time, somebody said the Pentagon had been hit." Somebody thrust a cell phone in Myers' hand. Gen. Ralph Eberhart, commander of US Space Command and the North American Aerospace Defense Command [NORAD] was on the other end of the line "talking about what was happening and the actions he was going to take."[16]

In his testimony before the Senate Armed Services Committee, Myers additionally confirmed that the decision to scramble fighter craft was made during his conversation with NORAD Commander Gen. Eberhart: "I spoke to the commander of NORAD, General Eberhart. And at that point, I think the decision was at that point to start launching aircraft." This statement is particularly disturbing given that in the same testimony, Myers also confirmed that the Pentagon had been overseeing the crisis at least as soon as the first of the Twin Towers was hit:

> SENATOR LEVIN: The time that we don't have is when the Pentagon was notified, if they were, by the FAA or the FBI or any other agency, relative to any potential threat or any planes having changed direction or anything like that. And that's the same which you will give us because that's...
>
> MYERS: I can answer that. At the time of the first impact on the World Trade Center, we stood up our crisis action team. That was done immediately. So we stood it up. And we started talking to the federal agencies.[17]

These reports indicate, apart from Myers' inexplicable indifference to notification of an air attack on the WTC, that the US military had been monitoring the crisis at least as soon as the first tower had been hit (although the previous documentation proves that it had been monitoring the crisis far earlier). Yet Myers also testified that the military only began to consider actions to be taken in response to the attacks after the Pentagon was hit. Acting Chairman of the Joint Chiefs Myers was apparently contacted by NORAD Commander Gen. Eberhart about "the actions he was going to take," *after* three hijacked civilian planes had already hit the World Trade Center and the Pentagon, at which time it was finally decided between them to scramble aircraft. Notably, this testimony by Myers about his actions on 9/11 is at odds with Richard Clarke's claim that he was in fact actively involved in the interagency phone bridges during this period, as discussed on page 279.

Myers' confirmation that high-level officials (including himself) were directly responsible for the decision to scramble aircraft is bizarre, given that the latter normally occurs routinely and automatically on the basis of Standard Operating Procedures without higher authorization being required. This again suggests firstly that mandatory standard procedures were inexplicably inoperable on 9/11, and secondly that both Gen. Myers and Gen. Eberhart violated these procedures by deciding a response to the hijackings almost one and a half hours later than should have been the case. Military aircraft should have been scrambled immediately and automatically, as soon as the hijackings were confirmed—indeed, as soon as the planes had deviated from their flight paths, and communication between them and air traffic control was blocked.

While routine procedures dictate that high-level military approval is not required for "immediate responses" to save lives and avoid substantial destruction, it appears that both Myers and Eberhart waited until after the Pentagon was attacked before allowing fighter craft to be scrambled.

The actions of President George W. Bush on 9/11 suggest a similar astonishing degree of indifference to the attacks. The *New York Press* reports, for example, that in Florida, "just as President Bush was about to leave his hotel he was told about the attack on the first WTC tower. He was asked by a reporter if he knew what was going on in New York."[18] This was, indeed, confirmed by an ABC News television report broadcast on the very morning of 9/11. ABC News correspondent John Cochran, who was covering the President's trip, informed Peter Jennings on ABC TV at 8:53 AM:

> He [the President] got out of his hotel suite this morning, was about to leave, reporters saw the White House chief of staff, Andy Card, whisper into his ear. The reporter said to the president, "Do you know what's going on in New York?" He said he did, and he said he will have something about it [i.e. a statement] later.[19]

As the *Press* reports, "He said he did, and then went to an elementary school in Sarasota to read to children."[20] President Bush knew because by that time the FAA was connected to the President's Secret Service. And at this time, not only had the WTC been already hit once, the FAA—and therefore the Secret Service—were well aware that other planes had been hijacked. But only the president, commander in chief of the US military, had the authority to give the order to shoot down a civilian airliner. As noted by Professor Francisco J. Gil-White of the University of Pennsylvania, a fellow in the Solomon Asch Center for Study of Ethnopolitical Conflict:

> As soon as President Bush was aware that a plane had been deliberately flown into the World Trade Center, he had two positive obligations.... Bush's first obligation was to protect the government and military chains of command. Since Bush was both head of state and commander in chief of the US military, this meant protecting himself and his closest advisers.
>
> Bush's second obligation was to protect the people by immediately conferring with his top military commanders. This included Donald Rumsfeld, the secretary of defense, who is second in the military chain of command and also has special responsibilities in case of a hijacking, General Richard B. Myers, who was acting chairperson of the Joint Chiefs of Staff, and various officers at the Pentagon's National Military Command Center (NMCC), the military nerve center for dealing with hijackings.[21]

But rather than immediately holding an emergency meeting to ensure his own protection, to oversee the scrambling of fighter craft, and to consider special instructions to them, President Bush instead continued on to the elementary school. On arrival at the school, President Bush emphasized that the event would go ahead as scheduled. Citing the account of the school's principal, Mrs. Rigell, MSNBC reported:

> "The limousine stops and the president comes out," says Rigell. "He walks toward me. I'm standing here in a lineup; there are about five people. He walks over and says he has to make a phone call, and he'll be right back."
>
> That phone call was to National Security Advisor Condoleezza Rice. It was the first inkling the president would get about what was to unfold [sic]. But the people at Emma E. Booker School cleared by security and cut off from the world, still had no clue anything was wrong.
>
> "I actually heard the first plane had hit from the president, and he said that a plane had hit the World Trade Center and that it was a commercial plane," says Rigell. "He said but we're going to go on, and in my mind I had created this picture of a plane knocking off some bricks on the corner of the World Trade Center."
>
> So as planned, President Bush walked into the classroom, and as planned, live television crews prepared to bring the country details of the president's reading initiative.[22]

When President Bush was informed that the second hijacked commercial airliner had hit the south tower of the World Trade Center, President Bush still refrained from exiting the classroom to hold an emergency meeting with senior military officials. Instead, he remained in the classroom for at least 10—and up to 20—minutes, before issuing a public statement about the terrorist attacks from the school's podium:

> The man was White House Chief of Staff Andy Card, and the words he whispered to the president, "There's been a second plane crash. America is under attack."
>
> "To think of the information that you would be given and the human side of you, how you'd respond," says Rigell. "I mean just to think of what any of us could have done with our faith at that particular time and to see that there was just a slight hesitancy in him, just a slight pause and then he continued..."
>
> The next time the president would speak to the principal, it was to tell her he was heading back to DC. "Something has happened, and we are not going to be able to proceed," says Rigell. "And I'm thinking OK, something has happened, but still not to the magnitude and they went on to say that there was a second plane that had hit the World Trade Center, and it was terrorists. It was a commercial plane, yes, but we think that the country is

under a terrorist attack at this time, and he apologized for having to leave."[23]

In a public speech at a Florida town hall, President Bush himself confirmed that he did not attempt to take any action in relation to the attacks as commander in chief until after the attacks had been successfully completed:

> And I was sitting in the classroom, and Andy Card, my chief of staff, who is sitting over here, walked in and said, "A second plane has hit the tower. America's under attack." ... And I started thinking hard, in that very brief period of time, about what it meant to be under attack. I knew that when I got all the facts, if we were under attack, there would be hell to pay for attacking America.... I tried to get as many facts as I could... to make sure I knew... exactly what I was basing my decisions on.... And so I got on the phone from Air Force One asking to find out the facts.... There were all kinds of rumors floating around. Some of them were erroneous... I needed to know what the facts were. But I knew I needed to act. I knew that if the nation's under attack, the role of the commander in chief is to respond forcefully to prevent other attacks from happening. And so I talked to the secretary of defense, and one of the first acts I did was put our military on alert.[24]

This is an extraordinary confession for several reasons. The President's traveling entourage, which included the Secret Service and other key officials were fully informed of the course of the events of 9/11, since the Secret Service had established open lines with the FAA at about 8:46 AM, according to Vice President Dick Cheney. The US government's knowledge of 9/11 was obviously not based on second-hand news sources, but on first-hand reporting by the FAA, the Pentagon, and so on. President Bush therefore was apparently being kept fully informed of the course of events. Nevertheless, having admitted his key role as commander in chief of the US military along with his consequent pinnacle responsibility to act, Bush also confirms that he failed to even bother "finding out the facts" on which to "base his decisions" until he had "got on the phone from Air Force One." Yet Bush already had ample access to the facts. Furthermore, it was only after having boarded Air Force One that he began discussing action to be taken, when he "talked to the secretary of defense" and ordered the "military on alert" in "one of the first acts" he took.

Bush could only have been "on the phone from Air Force One" at approximately 10:00 AM EST, which is when Air Force One departed Sarasota-Brandenton International Airport—this was almost an hour after Bush was reportedly told of the second WTC attack, or in other words, one hour and 15 minutes after the Secret Service had opened emergency lines with the FAA and one hour and 40 minutes after the FAA reportedly confirmed the hijacking of Flight 11 from Boston.[25] By this time, the terrorist attacks were already successfully completed.

Defense Secretary Donald Rumsfeld conducted himself in a similarly bizarre fashion that morning. Rumsfeld, like Bush and Myers, despite being aware of a crisis, had decided to completely ignore it. Co-chair of September 11 Advocates and member of the Family Steering Committee for the 9/11 Independent Commission, Mindy Kleinberg—whose husband had died in the terrorist attacks—"pieced together the actions of Secretary of Defense Donald Rumsfeld," reports the *New York Observer*:

> He had been in his Washington office engaged in his "usual intelligence briefing." After being informed of the two attacks on the World Trade Center, he proceeded with his briefing until the third hijacked plane struck the Pentagon. Mindy relayed the information to [her colleague] Kristen [Breitweiser]: "Can you believe this? Two planes hitting the Twin Towers in New York City did not rise to the level of Rumsfeld's leaving his office and going to the war room to check out just what the hell went wrong." Mindy sounded scared. "This is my President. This is my Secretary of Defense. You mean to tell me Rumsfeld had to get up from his desk and look out his window at the burning Pentagon before he knew anything was wrong? How can that be?"
>
> "It can't be," said Kristen ominously.[26]

Indeed, Secretary Rumsfeld knew full well what was happening. According to Assistant Secretary of Defense Torie Clarke, at about "8:45... we realized a plane and then a second plane had hit the World Trade Center...

> And immediately the crisis management process started up. A couple of us had gone into the secretary's office, Secretary Rumsfeld's office, to alert him to that, tell him that the crisis management process was starting up. He wanted to make a few phone calls. So a few of us headed across the hallway to an area called the National Military Command Center. He stayed in his office.[27]

By the time of the Pentagon crash, Rumsfeld was still "in his office inside the Pentagon," whereupon rather than rushing to the National Military Command Center, he "rushed to the area of the blast and for 15 minutes helped load the wounded onto stretchers. He then retreated to the National Military Command Center where senior military leaders pondered the question: What Now."[28] The inexcusable nature of Rumsfeld's studious indifference to the attacks is particularly clear from a previously cited instruction issued by the Chairman of the Joint Chiefs of Staff on June 1, 2001. The instruction highlights the pivotal role played by the defense department and the secretary of defense in defining a military response to a hijacking: "When notified that military assistance is needed in conjunction with an aircraft piracy (hijacking) emergency, the DoD, NMCC, will

> (1) Determine whether or not the assistance needed is reasonably available from police or commercial sources. If not, the DoD, NMCC, will notify the appropriate unified command or NORAD to determine if suitable assets are available and will forward the request to the Secretary of Defense for approval...
>
> When notified that military escort aircraft are needed in conjunction with an aircraft piracy (hijacking) emergency, the DoD, NMCC, will notify the appropriate unified command or USELEMNORAD to determine if suitable aircraft are available and forward the request to the Secretary of Defense for approval.[29]

In other words, with the exception of immediate responses, which may be pursued at the discretion of military commanders and other appropriate officials in the relevant lines of command, Rumsfeld was primarily responsible for approving and overseeing any military response to a hijacking. Yet despite this basic function of his office, Defense Secretary Rumsfeld, like Myers and Bush, was totally unresponsive to the attacks.

If these individuals had acted sooner, they might have averted the attacks on the World Trade Center and the Pentagon, saving thousands of lives. Yet by refusing to respond at all and by deliberately continuing with their comparatively mundane activities, they shirked their specific duties to the American people, permitting the attacks to proceed unhindered. Their inaction was a function of a wider, systematic negligence among government agencies. Despite the president's own critical responsibility as commander in chief, with the sole authority to shoot down a civilian plane, President Bush was able to continue on his way to the elementary school in Sarasota, without any apparent protest from his advisory officials from the Secret Service, the Pentagon, the department of defense, and so on, who should have called him for an emergency meeting immediately after the first WTC attack at the latest. Exactly the same principle applies also to Myers and Rumsfeld.

This circle of systematic official negligence continued despite the fact that the Pentagon was monitoring the flight paths of all the hijacked airliners and their course toward key targets in key cities. There is no doubt that this orchestrated negligence was responsible for the unprecedented collapse of standard procedures on 9/11. Key government agencies and officials therefore bear enormous culpability in the failure of a perfectly capable US air defense system.

This inference is supported by Cheney's previously discussed testimonial on NBC's *Meet the Press*. Cheney stated that the entire issue of scrambling planes for interception on 9/11 was a "presidential-level decision." He explicitly indicated that the decision to scramble planes was discussed by members of the White House cabinet, who eventually "decided to do it" with presidential authorization. This places direct responsibility for the behavior of the US Air Force on 9/11 on the president and his cabinet. Furthermore, according to Cheney, this decision resulted in planes being scrambled over New York and Washington, DC nearly one and a half hours later than what is required by the mandatory FAA and department of defense procedures. At face value, Cheney's testimony suggests that the blame for the obstruction of mandatory standard procedures and the failure of the US Air Force to respond on 9/11 that followed lies squarely on the White House. Unfortunately, the official inquiries have failed to even begin exploring this conundrum, no doubt due to fear that doing so may lead to some embarrassing, perhaps politically fatal, revelations.

Unexplained War Games

During the final Commission hearing when families of the 9/11 victims were played FAA tape recordings of the events of that terrible day, one member of the audience shouted: "Tell us about the 9/11 war games!" He was subsequently dragged out of the hearing by security staff.[30] The demand was perfectly valid— but it is one that has been completely ignored by the Commission.

It is a matter of record that on the morning of 9/11, US military and intelligence agencies were engaged in multiple simultaneous war games related to terrorism, fighter craft, and hijackings. According to *Aviation Week & Space Technology*, when NORAD commander Col. Robert K. Marr was first notified by the FAA at around 8:40 AM of a hijacking, he wondered: "Part of the exercise?"

> No; this is a real-world event, he was told. Several days into a semiannual exercise known as Vigilant Guardian, NEADS was fully staffed, its key officers and enlisted supervisors already manning the operations center "battle cab."
>
> In retrospect, the exercise would prove to be a serendipitous enabler of a rapid military response to terrorist attacks on Sept. 11. Senior officers involved in Vigilant Guardian were manning NORAD command centers throughout the US and Canada, available to make immediate decisions.[31]

Newhouse News Service disclosed that "Sept. 11 was Day II of 'Vigilant Guardian,' an exercise that would pose an imaginary crisis to North American Air Defense outposts nationwide."[32] US intelligence expert James Bamford notes that Vigilant Guardian "was designed to create a fictional crisis affecting the United States and test the network of radar watch stations around the country...

> ... the scenario involved Russian bombers flying over the North Pole in attack formation. The Rome command center was responsible for monitoring more than half a million square miles of airspace, from the

Montana-North Dakota border to the coast of Maine down through South Carolina. Included were the skies over New York City and Washington, DC. Should a crisis develop, the radar specialists could pick up the phone and alert fighter pilots at National Guard units at Burlington, Vermont; Atlantic City, New Jersey; Cape Cod, Massachusetts; and Duluth, Minnesota.[33]

As a consequence of this exercise, NORAD's North East Air Defense Sector was—at least from a logistical perspective—extraordinarily prepared on 9/11, with "key officers... manning the operation battle center," and "fighter jets... cocked, loaded, and carrying extra gas on board."[34]

At the same time, on 9/11 in a mountain in Colorado, NORAD's Command Center was apparently a few days into a separate war game, "Northern Vigilance," that had begun on September 9, 2001. Like "Vigilant Guardian," this exercise was designed to keep "a close eye on the Russians" who had "dispatched long-range bombers to their own high north on a similar exercise... Operation Northern Vigilance, planned months in advance, involves deploying fighter jets to locations in Alaska and northern Canada." The *Toronto Star* continues to describe what occurred next:

> An hour into his shift, something unscripted happens. NORAD's Northeast Air Defense Sector (NEADS), based in Rome, N.Y., contacts the mountain. The Federal Aviation Administration has evidence of a hijacking and is asking for NORAD support. This is not part of the exercise....
>
> Operation Northern Vigilance is called off. Any simulated information, what's known as an "inject," is purged from the screens. Someone shouted to look at the monitor displaying CNN. "At that point, we saw the World Trade Center, one of the towers, smoke coming out of it. And a minute later, we watched the live feed as the second aircraft swung around into the second tower," says [Capt. Mike] Jellinek.
>
> ... He had one question for the people on the line from NEADS: "Was that the hijacked aircraft you were dealing with?" he asked. Yes, it was, came the reply. And then, Jellinek says, "it got really, really busy."[35]

This report is disturbing, primarily because it suggests that although NORAD's Rome headquarters (NEADS) were contacted by the FAA far earlier, NORAD's Command Center was only notified of the hijackings just as Flight 175 went hurtling into the World Trade Center's south tower—at roughly 9:03 AM. Although this correlates with the Commission's general claim that NORAD was only notified of the hijacking at this time, in reality—as revealed by NORAD's own timeline and NORAD officials on duty that morning—NORAD knew that Flight 175 was hijacked at 8:43 AM.[36] Why the Command Center was reportedly not informed for so long, however, is hard to explain. The Commission has simply ignored the entire discrepancy. This is one of the few credible reports directly indicating that the simultaneous NORAD simulations may have had some role in obstructing the standard response of the US Air Force to the hijackings, by creating an internal dysfunction.

NORAD was also involved in a third exercise on the morning of 9/11. Citing "an on-the-record statement from someone in NORAD," US journalist and former LAPD investigator Michael Ruppert reports that "on the day of 9/11 the Joint Chiefs (Myers) and NORAD were conducting a joint, live-fly, hijack Field Training Exercise (FTX) which involved at least one (and almost certainly many more) aircraft under US control that was posing as a hijacked airliner."[37] It should be noted that this NORAD hijack exercise run by Gen. Richard Myers—Acting Chairman of the Joint Chiefs of Staff on 9/11—may have had pre-planned overlaps with the other NEADS (Rome) war game first discussed here. Several NORAD officers involved in the NEADS war game including Gen. Larry Arnold responded with the initial conviction that the FAA's hijack notification was part of the planned exercise. At face value, this confusion would only be possible if the NEADS war game itself had included a hijack scenario—otherwise NORAD officers would have known from the outset that the FAA notification was not part of the exercise. As if to illustrate this point, the *Star* report concerning the NORAD Command Center exercise specifically points out that as soon as the Colorado mountain-based center was informed that the FAA had evidence of a hijacking, NORAD officials knew that "something unscripted" had happened. "This is not part of the exercise."[38] In that context, if NEADS officials did not know whether the Boston Flight 11 hijacking was part of their exercise, clearly the "scripting" for their exercise did not preclude hijacking scenarios—and on the contrary probably did include them.

In any case, further insight into the configuration of Gen. Myer's NORAD hijack exercise can be derived from hijack exercises and plans for future hijack exercises completed by NORAD in earlier years, as well as in 2001 only a few months prior to 9/11. "In the two years before the Sept. 11 attacks," reported *USA Today*, "the North American Aerospace Defense Command conducted exercises simulating what the White House says was unimaginable at the time: hijacked airliners used as weapons to crash into targets and cause mass casualties." Most remarkably, "One of the imagined targets was the World Trade Center. In another exercise, jets performed a mock shootdown over the Atlantic Ocean of a jet supposedly laden with chemical poisons headed toward a target in the United States." In a written statement, NORAD confirmed the occurrence of such "airplane as weapons" hijacking exercises: "Numerous types of civilian and military aircraft were used as mock hijacked aircraft. These exercises tested track detection and identification; scramble and interception; hijack procedures; internal and external agency coordination and operational security and communications security procedures."[39]

According to USA Today "in the early drills, including one operation, planned in July 2001 and conducted later," scenarios "involved planes from airports in Utah and Washington state that were 'hijacked.' Those planes were escorted by US and Canadian aircraft to airfields in British Columbia and Alaska." Indeed, "NORAD officials have acknowledged that 'scriptwriters' for the drills included the idea of hijacked aircraft being used as weapons." NORAD official Maj. Gen. Craig McKinley told the Commission that: "Threats of killing hostages or crashing were left to the scriptwriters to invoke creativity and broaden the required response."[40] Indeed, a June 2001 National Defense Industrial Association report proposing counterterrorism scenarios for NORAD's Amalgam Virgo 01 exercise titled "Combined (Joint) Training for Unconventional Threat," has a picture of Osama bin Laden on the front cover. On page 34 of the report is a large photographic diagram titled "Hijack Scenario," depicting an American Airlines plane flying across the North American continent and converging on the Capitol building in Washington, DC.[41]

It is perhaps fitting at this point to consider the Commission's narrative concerning a phantom "Flight 11" being monitored by multiple divisions of the FAA and NORAD. It has of course been demonstrated previously that the Commission's discussion of the phantom flight in an effort to explain the failure to respond to Flight 77 is incoherent, contradictory to FAA and NORAD data, and largely irrelevant to the actual nature of the response itself. If indeed as the Commission claims it is true that a phantom aircraft was tracked by FAA and NORAD radars identifying itself clearly as the hijacked "Flight 11," then the question remains as to how multiple radars could undergo the same bizarre technical glitch by simultaneously displaying this particular non-existent aircraft. If this were really a solely technical problem related to FAA/NORAD technology, then surely one would find many other such instances of similar glaring mistakes. On the contrary, however, no such incidents have occurred before—it is absolutely unprecedented in itself. What is more perplexing is that such a uniquely bizarre phenomenon occurred on the very day that the FAA and NORAD were faced with an unprecedented air defense crisis. This is a burning question that the Commission has studiously ignored, and that most commentators have completely missed. The fact of the matter is that the only conceivable way that multiple radars could track a non-existent aircraft is through a pre-planned simulation, which of course leads directly to the issue of the manifold NORAD simulations and war games being conducted on the morning of 9/11. Although the Commission's own discussion of the phantom "Flight 11" therefore points to the pertinence of understanding the role of 9/11 war games, the Commission has refused to investigate the matter any further.

Without attempting to provide any sort of final answer to this question, the documentation on NORAD war games discussed here does provide a glimpse of a coherent explanation. On the morning of 9/11 there were at least three simultaneous NORAD exercises being conducted—including a live-fly hijack exercise that may have featured the "airplanes as weapons" scheme—which entailed that "simulated information"[42] would be fed into radar screens. Credible reports suggest that the overlap of these simultaneous NORAD exercises with the 9/11 crisis occurred contemporaneously with several types of internal dysfunction, one between NORAD Command and NEADS, and the other producing at least one simulated phantom "Flight 11" on FAA and NORAD radars. What is perhaps most perturbing is that the 9/11 live-fly hijack exercise was overseen by the Joint Chiefs of Staff and Acting Chairman Gen. Myers, principal military adviser to the President, Secretary of Defense, and the National Security Council (NSC). Given this superimposition of NORAD war games and internal dysfunctions on 9/11 under the Joint Chiefs Chairman's auspices, it is hard to deny that the contemporaneous exercises and dysfunctions were somehow connected.

Indeed, it should be noted that the Joint Chiefs have no executive authority to command combatant forces. Their role in these exercises, therefore, points directly to the White House: Because the Chairman of the Joint Chiefs of Staff "does not exercise military command over any combatant forces," he may only "transmit communications to the commanders of the combatant commands from the President and Secretary of Defense." The implication, of course, is that any Joint Chiefs–NORAD exercise on 9/11 would have been conducted solely on specific instructions from the president and/or the secretary of defense.[43]

Remarkably, however, these were not the only pre-planned military exercises that day. On the same fateful morning, yet another Air Force exercise was being conducted by F-16 fighters at Andrews Air Force Base with the District of Columbia Air National Guard (DCANG) unit. Andrews hosted two "combat ready" squadrons constituting "capable and ready response forces for the District of Columbia in the event of a natural disaster or civil emergency." The mission of the DCANG unit, 10 miles from the center of Washington, was "to provide combat units in the highest possible state of readiness."[44] Despite the explicit role of DCANG fighters in defending Washington, DC against emergencies with combat fighters in the "highest" readiness, they were curiously absent on the very day that Washington, DC was attacked. According to *Aviation Week*, when Flight 11 and 175 were crashing into the World Trade Center, rather than being in the "highest possible state of readiness" in accordance with their assigned mission, three DCANG fighters were involved in training exercises. They continued the exercises even while Flight 77 was circling around to head toward Washington and eventually slam into the Pentagon:

> Three F-16s were flying an air-to-ground training mission on a range in North Carolina, 180 naut. mi. away. At Andrews, several officers were in a scheduling meeting when they received word that the World Trade Center

had been hit by an aircraft. Minutes later, after United Airlines Flight 175 slammed into the second WTC tower, a squadron pilot called a friend in the Secret Service "to see what was going on. He was told some bad things were happening. At that time, we weren't thinking about defending anything. Our primary concern was what would happen to the air traffic system," said Lt. Col. Marc H. (Sass) Sasseville [who] was the director of operations and air operations officer—the acting operations group commander under the 113th Wing.[45]

The fighters engaged in training exercises in North Carolina had not been recalled throughout this episode. Only after the Pentagon was hit did Lt. Col. Sasseville specifically give the order to scramble three fighters to defend DC, on a Secret Service request which came, again, after the Pentagon crash. Then:

> Maj. Billy Hutchison and his wingmen had just landed after being recalled from a training mission in North Carolina. When Hutchison checked in via radio, Thompson [chief of safety for the 113th Wing] told him to take off immediately.... According to now-official accounts, an armed Norad-alert F-16 from Langley AFB, flown by Maj. Dean Eckmann of the 119th Fighter Wing Alert Detachment 1, was the first defender to overfly the Pentagon.[46]

In other words, due to the delay caused by a training exercise that clearly interfered with DCANG's assigned mission status to remain in the "highest possible state of readiness," Andrews pilots were only scrambled after the F-16s from Langley finally arrived in Washington, DC—roughly after 9:49 AM.[47] The DCANG unit was inattentive on 9/11 because its aforesaid mission was interfered with via an order to conduct training exercises, an order which remained in place seemingly until after the Pentagon was hit.

Kyle Hence—director of the New York-based oversight group 9/11 Citizen's Watch—was informed by one prominent member of the Commission panel that due to the training exercise, at the time of attacks the Andrews fighters were lacking sufficient fuel to intercept Flight 77 in time.[48] Hence asked Commissioner Jamie Gorelick about the Andrews exercises and their role in the failure of US air defense on 9/11 at the last Commission hearing (16–17 June 2004):

> At the last hearing during a break outside the hearing room this was confirmed to me privately off the record by a senior member of the Commission staff. When I confronted Gorelick on camera with this information asking how would Andrews conduct exercises that morning but leave D.C. undefended she was instantly defensive and wouldn't comment...

Hence noted that "that these planes were not tasked to intercept any of the hijacked planes because by the time they occurred the planes did not have adequate fuel. According to this source, they were flying over Cape Hatteras, North Carolina."[49]

Yet another exercise was planned on the morning of 9/11 by the National Reconnaissance Office (NRO), a secretive US intelligence agency which "designs, builds and operates the nation's reconnaissance satellites" in order to "help plan military operations" and "monitor the environment" for the "Central Intelligence Agency (CIA) and the Department of Defense (DoD).... As part of the 13-member Intelligence Community, the NRO plays a primary role in achieving information superiority for the US Government and Armed Forces." The NRO also "conducts intelligence-related activities essential for US National Security."[50] According to the Associated Press:

> ... one US intelligence agency was planning an exercise last Sept. 11 in which an errant aircraft would crash into one of its buildings... National Reconnaissance Office had scheduled an exercise that morning in which a small corporate jet would crash into one of the four towers at the agency's headquarters building after experiencing a mechanical failure. The agency is about four miles from the runways of Washington Dulles International Airport.

An NRO official insisted that: "As soon as the real world events began, we canceled the exercise." The exercise was first publicly revealed in an announcement for a homeland security conference in Chicago:

> In a promotion for speaker John Fulton, a CIA officer assigned as chief of NRO's strategic gaming division, the announcement says, "On the morning of September 11th 2001, Mr. Fulton and his team... were running a pre-planned simulation to explore the emergency response issues that would be created if a plane were to strike a building. Little did they know that the scenario would come true in a dramatic way that day."[51]

Although officials promptly denied that the simulation was a counterterrorism and/or security exercise, claiming that it was to simulate a mere accident, this is hard to believe given Fulton's specific credentials—serving as Chief of the Strategic War Gaming Division of the National Reconnaissance Office, a member of the US Joint Forces Command's Project Alpha, and an adviser on counterterrorism and homeland defense to the Director Central Intelligence Staff.[52] Fulton's expertise as chief NRO war gamer is therefore fundamentally concerned with exploring scenarios in the event of some form of conflict. The US Joint Forces Command (USJFCOM) is the Department of Defense's "transformation laboratory" of the US military, tasked among other things to develop concepts, test these concepts through live experimentation, and implement joint training exercises involving the "choreographing" of multiple military commands.[53] Indeed, USJFCOM's Project Alpha specifically pursues programs concerned with utilizing advanced space-based satellite, surveillance, and communication technologies for military operations. Intriguingly, many of these programs have significant aerial connotations, including the use of "unmanned, autonomous airborne vehicles" in war.[54] Project Alpha—which is subordinate to the Department of Defense—also conducts military experiments that bring live field exercises and computer simulations together.[55] Fulton's job, in other words, is not to simulate accidents—it is to wargame complex joint military operations involving space-based and aerial technologies. Whatever the "plane into building" simulation that Fulton was exercising on the morning of 9/11, it was almost certainly a highly complex wargame.

And in yet another bizarre coincidence, USJFCOM's Air Force component consists of the Air Combat Command (ACC) unit which essentially provides the groundwork for US air defense. The ACC "organizes, trains, equips and maintains combat-ready air forces for rapid deployment and employment" and thus provides "air defense forces to the North American Aerospace Defense Command [NORAD] and theater air forces to the five geographical unified commands [around the world]." The UNSJFCOM's ACC, moreover, is headquartered at Langley Air Force Base, where UNSJFCOM's Aerospace Command and Control, Intelligence, Surveillance and Reconnaissance Center is also located[56]—the same base from which F-16s were belatedly scrambled and purportedly misdirected on 9/11 by a phantom "Flight 11," when responding to Flight 77—a phantom flight that can only have been produced by a simulation.

Curiously, according to the Associated Press, Fulton's exercise began at approximately 9:00 AM.[57]—around the same time of Flight 77's sudden deviation from its flight path at 8:54 AM. A further bizarre coincidence is that according to the *Washington Post*, the pilot of Flight 77—which eventually crashed into the Pentagon—was an F-4 pilot, Charles Burlingame, who used to develop anti-terror strategies before retiring to fly for American Airlines. Burlingame, according to the *Post*, drafted emergency response plans for the scenario of a hijacked commercial airliner hitting the Pentagon.[58] Given this intriguing web of coincidences, it is hard to believe that the CIA-NRO "plane into building" war game had no connection at all to the other wargames and exercises being pursued that morning.

Another significant exercise focusing on emergency preparedness for a bioterrorism attack was planned to occur in New York City on September 12, 2001. The exercise, known as Operation Tripod, was disclosed by former New York City Mayor Rudy Giuliani in his testimony before the Commission (18-19 May 2004):

... the reason Pier 92 was selected as a command center was because on the next day, on September 12, Pier 92 was going to have a drill, it had hundreds of people here, from FEMA, from the Federal Government, from the State, from the State Emergency Management Office, and they were getting ready for a drill for biochemical attack. So that was gonna be the place they were going to have the drill....

The equipment was already there, so we were able to establish a command center there, within three days, that was two and a half to three times bigger than the command center that we had lost at 7 World Trade Center. And it was from there that the rest of the search and rescue effort was completed.[59]

According to the New York City's Office of Emergency Management, Operation Tripod was successfully conducted on May 22, 2002: "Tripod had originally been scheduled to take place on September 12th, 2001, at Pier 92—which ironically had served as the temporary home of OEM shortly after the terrorist attacks on 9/11." Moreover, Tripod was administered "in cooperation with the United States Department of Justice (USDOJ)." The latter's "Office of Justice Programs, through its Office for Domestic Preparedness, [was] pleased to support the New York City Tripod Exercise."[60]

The Office for Domestic Preparedness is the successor to the Office of National Preparedness established by President Bush and directed by Vice President Cheney as of May 8, 2001, "to coordinate development of US government initiatives to combat terrorist attacks on the United States." The new Cheney taskforce on terrorism was linked to the creation within the Federal Emergency Management Agency (FEMA) of "an Office of National Preparedness that will coordinate an integrated and comprehensive federal response to weapons of mass destruction (WMD)—biological, chemical or nuclear—used in an attack on the United States." At that time, Cheney commented that: "The threat to the continental United States and our infrastructure is changing and evolving and we need to look at this whole area oftentimes referred to as homeland defense." Through his new task force and the Office of National Preparedness, Cheney was thus to "oversee domestic counterterrorist efforts" including working with state and local government agencies "to ensure their planning, training, and equipment needs are addressed."[61]

It is worth noting then that the Office's objectives were to oversee all planning, training, and coordination relevant to US counterterrorism and crisis management. Although the Office was never—at least publicly—fully formalized until after 9/11, many of the other war games and exercises discussed here (not merely Tripod) would might fall under the Office's purview. Although the exact implications of these multiple simultaneous war games and exercises implemented and/or planned on or around September 11, 2001 is certainly unclear, there is sufficient evidence from these sources alone demonstrating that some of these exercises may have substantially interfered with US air defense and emergency preparedness on 9/11. Despite that, the Commission has simply pretended that these war games and exercises never existed and/or are irrelevant to understanding the events of 9/11. This analysis, of course, unambiguously suggests otherwise.

Indeed, it is hard to see how such a large number of war games and exercises involving key US agencies—including the CIA, the NRO, NORAD, the Joint Chiefs of Staff, FEMA, and the DCANG unit at Andrews Air Force Base—could all have been planned and/or implemented on or around September 11, 2001 by complete coincidence. It is far more plausible that on some level, the simultaneous overlap of these multiple exercises—clearly utilizing significant assets and resources of the US national security, military, and intelligence apparatus—on or around 9/11, was coordinated at a senior level in the Pentagon.

Given that, as has already been documented, the US intelligence community was cognizant that a terrorist attack on the US was imminent on or around 9/11, the continuance of these war games and exercises regardless is alarming. So urgent was one warning discussed in the previous chapters that as Newsweek correspondents Evan Thomas and Mark Hosenball reported on September 24, 2001, "top Pentagon officials" on September 10, 2001, canceled travel plans for the next morning "over security concerns." This vital piece of data establishes beyond doubt that the "headquarters of the United States Department of Defense and the nerve center for command and control"[62] had specific advanced warning of a threat to US national security on the morning of September 11, 2001. Yet despite top US Defense Department officials being aware of the threat on 9/11, they allowed a variety of overlapping war games and exercises to occupy the assets and resources of various US national security agencies on the same fateful day, to the point that even the nation's capital was left completely undefended on a morning whose crisis was anticipated by the government.

The Ptech Connection

The role of a little-known but extremely powerful software company based in Boston—known as Ptech—is perhaps highly pertinent in beginning to understand the overlapping 9/11 wargames. Before and after 9/11, Ptech provided advanced software and information technology services for the US government's most sensitive agencies, including for instance the US Air Force, Federal Aviation Administration, Pentagon, Naval Air Systems Command, NATO, Department of Energy, Internal Revenue Service, House of Representatives, among others.[63]

According to General Services Administration records, Ptech attained government approval in 1997 under the Clinton administration. Government filings obtained by the Washington terror research group—the Investigative Project—state that since December of that year, the company enjoys security clearance to work on highly sensitive projects. Among its high-level projects is "the Military Information Architecture Framework [MIAF], a software tool used by the Department of Defense to link data networks from various military computer systems and databases." Ptech's contract for the MIAF was renewed in September 2002.[64]

The problem here is that Ptech appears to have close ties to well-known suspected terrorists. Among the company's financial backers, for instance, are Yassin Qadi and M. Yaqub Mirza, both of whom have been investigated by the US government for terrorist financing. Qadi, a character discussed earlier in this study, has been listed as a leading financial supporter of al-Qaeda by the US Treasury. Qadi invested at least $5 million in the Ptech in the mid-1990s—although according to his lawyer his stake was sold in 1999. As for Mirza, he is currently a Ptech board member. Yet court records and Justice Department documents show that he and several associates "are suspected of funding the Palestinian Islamic Jihad, which targets Israeli civilians with suicide bombers. US officials privately say Mr. Mirza and his associates also have connections to al-Qaeda and to other entities officially listed by the US as sponsors of terrorism."[65]

Ptech also received financial backing from BMI, Inc., a now defunct firm based in New Jersey under FBI investigation for financing al-Qaeda and other terrorists, including for instance the 1998 US embassy bombings. In 1994, BMI reportedly made loans to, and invested in, Ptech when the company was founded. Coincidentally, Qadi also invested in BMI. Worse still, Ptech's current vice president and chief scientist—Hussein Ibrahim—was originally vice president of BMI from 1989 to 1995, after which he joined the Boston software firm. Two other Ptech officials—Muhammed Mubayyid and Suheil Laheir—currently being investigated by the US government formerly worked for a Boston-based Muslim charity, Care International, which has in turn been the subject of serious government terrorism probes since 9/11. One compelling piece of evidence lies in Care's 1993 incorporation documents, which list its location as the same suite used by the Boston branch of the blind sheik's Al-Kifah Refugee Center. State records also reveal that two of Ptech's founding directors were former BMI officials.[66]

Ptech's software is used to broadly assess strengths and weaknesses across organizations. According to Indira Singh, a risk management and computer systems consultant who came into contact with Ptech while working on a project at JP Morgan Chase, Ptech employees she spoke to were gravely concerned about the Yassin Qadi connection and even believed that he currently owned the company. Several Ptech officials were targets of Operation Greenquest, a US Treasury terrorism probe.[67] Indeed, according to CNN, citing US government sources, "company employees contacted the FBI last fall when the state department put Yasin al-Qadi, a Saudi businessman, on a watch list of individuals and organizations whose US assets were frozen because of suspected ties to terrorists. The employees told the FBI that they had been introduced to al-Qadi in Saudi Arabia as 'the owner' of Ptech." CNN's sources further allege that "Ptech executives are believed to have been aware of al-Qadi's suspected connections but did not sever their relationship with him."[68]

Whistleblower Indira Singh had originally intended to explore the prospect of using Ptech to help develop risk architecture software for JP Morgan Chase. In the process of checking on the company through current and former Ptech employees, she became aware of its dubious terrorist connections. In October 2001, the FBI had already been contacted by an ex-employee of Ptech warning them of the company's connections.[69] However, when she contacted the FBI herself much later in May 2002, she discovered to her chagrin that "absolutely no investigation was going on, that it was totally at a standstill, at which point my hair stood on end."[70] When she disclosed this startling information to her superiors at JP Morgan Chase, she was reportedly told by the bank's "general auditor" to turn a blind eye—if she wanted to keep her job. To date, Ptech continues to perform as a prominent contractor for the most sensitive agencies of the US government.

So why has the FBI stalled yet another investigation into al-Qaeda terrorism? The answer is probably linked to the fact noted by Singh that Ptech had:

> ... worked on a project that revealed all information processes and issues that the FAA had with the National Airspace Systems Agency, NAS. The project included incident investigation, law enforcement, military aviation systems, highly sensitive information, especially if you wanted to exploit the FAA's current capabilities and holes... to jam or slow down US military response to a domestic hijacking, for example.[71]

It is plausible, then, that Ptech is one of the most pivotal links in this increasingly ominous picture. Ptech and its sprawling web of connections to the apparent financial architects of al-Qaeda terrorism is at once a provider of critical information technologies to US government agencies—dealing with classified databases used by the Air Force, FAA, NAS, Pentagon, among others—and also a key financial-corporate nexus in the al-Qaeda terrorist network. This Ptech–US–al-Qaeda nexus has existed in both Democratic and Republican administrations. Moreover, US intelligence appears well aware of the nexus, but extremely reluctant to actually pursue urgent measures to guarantee the security of sensitive government data by severing Ptech's connections with the government.

This response is certainly odd. Given the sensitivity of the data accessed by Ptech, encompassing the highest levels of the US government, it would seem to be most prudent to do everything necessary to protect government information security based on even a reasonable suspicion of potential unwarranted and/or dangerous access to such data. Clearly, Ptech's terrorist connections were sufficiently strong to necessitate an FBI and US Customs raid on the company's premises in December 2002.[72] But Ptech's continued strong relationship to the government indicates that the Ptech–US–al-Qaeda nexus is far from a mere unfortunate coincidence. Rather, it appears to be a manifestation of the degree to which the financial arteries of international terrorism have melded into the interests and institutions of US and Western power. Ptech, it seems, is perhaps the most plausible candidate for an explanation of at least one mechanism by which the 9/11 wargames, along with the contemporaneous dysfunctions of the US air defense system, were facilitated by al-Qaeda from within the US government itself.

PART FOUR
THE INFINITE WAR

9/11 was the trigger for the escalation of the projection of US military might internationally and the expansion of domestic state-power, resulting in some drastic developments in world order as a whole. Here we attempt to provide a brief outline of the geostrategic imperatives behind the "War on Terror" and their ramifications.

12.

A Two-Pronged Military Strategy

In the aftermath of 9/11, the US government employed a global military strategy with both overt and covert dimensions. The most immediately obvious overt military overtures consisted of the 2001 war on Afghanistan as a means to establish an unprecedented US military presence in Central Asia. As for the covert aspect of US military operations, some indications of what was in store for the world came about from a classified report for the Pentagon.

The Takeover of Central Asia

In October 2001, as soon as the bombing campaign in Afghanistan commenced, the Bush administration began pursuing the principal interests that had motivated its pre-9/11 regional war plans. Pakistan's *Frontier Post* reported that:

> The US ambassador to Pakistan Wendy Chamberlain paid a courtesy call on the Federal Minister for Petroleum and Natural Resources, Usman Aminuddin, here Tuesday and discussed with him matters pertaining to Pak–US cooperation in the oil and gas sector.... Usman Aminuddin also briefed the Ambassador on the proposed Turkmenistan–Afghanistan–Pakistan gas pipeline project and said that this project opens up new avenues of multi-dimensional regional cooperation particularly in view of the recent geo-political developments in the region.[1]

With the removal of the Taliban from power, the US was ready to establish a regime friendlier to regional US requirements. The new federal administration of Northern Alliance warlords signaled a return to the pre-Taliban era of barbarism and brutality—although this time with factional war and rivalry limited under the terms of the US–UN-brokered agreements. Former Canadian diplomat Professor Peter Dale Scott, a political scientist at the University of California, Berkeley, noted in January 2002 that:

> [O]ne has a clear sense that warlordism is returning to Afghanistan. We are seeing a return of the worst features of the pre-Taliban 1990s: unrestricted banditry, looting of food supplies meant for civilians, widespread smuggling of all forms and above all extensive production of opium and heroin.[2]

But the problems of the Afghan people were irrelevant. What was relevant was obtaining security for regional US interests. Commenting on the disconcerting prominence of the oil and gas issue, the *San Francisco Chronicle* observed a few weeks after 9/11 that:

> The hidden stakes in the war against terrorism can be summed up in a single word: oil. The map of terrorist sanctuaries and targets in the Middle East and Central Asia is also, to an extraordinary degree, a map of the world's principal energy sources in the 21st century.... It is inevitable that the war against terrorism will be seen by many as a war on behalf of America's Chevron, Exxon, and Arco; France's TotalFinaElf; British Petroleum; Royal Dutch Shell and other multinational giants, which have hundreds of billions of dollars of investment in the region.[3]

The *Chronicle*'s concerns were confirmed by the end of November when the White House released a statement from Bush on the opening of the first new pipeline by the Caspian Pipeline Consortium: "The CPC project also advances my Administration's National Energy Policy by developing a network of multiple Caspian pipelines that also includes the Baku–Tbilisi–Ceyhan, Baku–Supsa, and Baku–Novorossiysk oil pipelines and the Baku–Tbilisi–Erzurum gas pipeline."[4]

The pipeline is a joint venture of Russia, Kazakhstan, Oman, ChevronTexaco, ExxonMobil and several other oil companies, connecting the Tengiz oilfield in northwestern Kazakhstan to the Russian Black Sea port of Novorossiysk. American companies had put up $1 billion of the $2.65 billion construction cost. The pipeline consortium involved in the Baku–Ceyhan plan, led by British oil company BP, is represented by the law firm of Baker & Botts, whose principal attorney is James Baker III. Baker III was secretary of state under the first Bush administration. He was also the chief spokesman for the second Bush's 2000 campaign, during its successful attempt to block the vote recount in Florida.

The *New York Times* reported further developments in December 2001:

> There is no oil in Afghanistan, but there are oil politics, and Washington is subtly tending to them, using the promise of energy investments in Central Asia to nurture a budding set of political alliances in the region with Russia, Kazakhstan and, to some extent, Uzbekistan...
>
> Since the Sept. 11 attacks, the United States has lauded the region as a stable oil supplier, in a tacit comparison with the Persian Gulf states that have been viewed lately as less cooperative. The State Department is exploring the potential for post-Taliban energy projects in the region, which has more than 6 percent of the world's proven oil reserves and almost 40 percent of its gas reserves.... Better ties between Russia and the United States, for example, have accelerated a thaw that began more than a year ago over pipeline routes from the Caspian Sea to the West.[5]

By New Year's Eve, nine days after the US-backed interim government of Hamid Karzai took office in Kabul, President Bush appointed a former aide to the American oil company UNOCAL, Zalmay Khalilzad, as special envoy to Afghanistan. Khalilzad drew up a risk analysis of a proposed gas pipeline from the former Soviet republic of Turkmenistan across Afghanistan and Pakistan to the Indian Ocean and also participated in talks between UNOCAL and Taliban officials in 1997, aimed at implementing a 1995 agreement to build the pipeline across western Afghanistan. It turns out that the newly appointed Afghani Prime Minister Hamid Karzai is also a former paid consultant for UNOCAL, according to reports in the French *Le Monde* and the Saudi *Al-Watan*.[6] These nominations illustrate the fundamental interests behind US military intervention in Afghanistan,[7] which have been articulated aptly by S. Rob Sobhani, professor of foreign relations at Georgetown University and director of Caspian Energy Consulting: "It is absolutely essential that the US make the pipeline the centerpiece of rebuilding Afghanistan."[8]

UNOCAL has publicly denied its Karzai connection, but as investigative journalist and former National Security Agency official Wayne Madsen observes: "According to Afghan, Iranian, and Turkish government sources, Hamid Karzai, the interim Prime Minister of Afghanistan, was a top adviser to the... UNOCAL Corporation which was negotiating with the Taliban to construct a Central Asia Gas (CentGas) pipeline from Turkmenistan through western Afghanistan to Pakistan." Madsen's sources indicate that Karzai "maintained close relations with CIA Director William Casey, Vice President George Bush, and their Pakistani Inter Service Intelligence (ISI) interlocutors" during the Afghan war with the Soviets...

> Later, Karzai and a number of his brothers moved to the United States under the auspices of the CIA. Karzai continued to serve the agency's interests, as well as those of the Bush family and their oil friends in negotiating the CentGas deal, according to Middle East and South Asian sources.... Karzai's ties with UNOCAL and the Bush administration are the main reason why the CIA pushed him for Afghan leader over rival Abdul Haq, the assassinated former mujaheddin leader from Jalalabad, and the leadership of the Northern Alliance, seen by Langley as being too close to the Russians and Iranians.[9]

Thus, by mid-February, the *Irish Times* reported that:

> Pakistani President Gen Pervez Musharraf, and the Afghan interim leader Mr. Hamid Karzai, agreed yesterday that their two countries should develop "mutual brotherly relations" and co-operate "in all spheres of activity"—including a proposed gas pipeline from Central Asia to Pakistan via Afghanistan... Mr. Karzai, who arrived in Islamabad earlier

yesterday for a one-day visit, said he and Gen Musharraf discussed the proposed Central Asian gas pipeline project "and agreed that it was in the interest of both countries."[10]

By mid-April 2002, the head of the World Bank James Wolfensohn gave an address at the opening of the World Bank's offices in Kabul. He stated that he had held high-level discussions about financing the trans-Afghan gas pipeline. While confirming $100 million in new grants for the interim Afghan government, Wolfensohn also confirmed that several companies had already privately expressed their interest in the project.[11] Although UNOCAL continues to publicly deny involvement—and no corporations are yet firmly committed—credible Pakistani sources reported significant progress on both oil and gas pipelines through Afghanistan, suggesting specifically that UNOCAL is likely to re-emerge as a pipeline contender.[12]

Alim Razi, the Afghan minister for mines and industries, also stated that UNOCAL is likely to play a lead role in the pipeline project once conditions in the country make it viable. According to BBC News: "Mr. Razim said US energy company Unocal was the 'lead company' among those that would build the pipeline, which would bring 30 billion cubic meters of Turkmen gas to market annually."[13] The *Asia Times* further reported that

Unocal also has a project to build the so-called Central Asian Oil Pipeline, almost 1,700 km long, linking Chardzhou in Turkmenistan to Russian's existing Siberian oil pipelines and also to the Pakistani Arabian Sea coast. This pipeline will carry 1 mm bpd of oil from different areas of former Soviet republics, and it will run parallel to the gas pipeline route through Afghanistan.[14]

Regional sources indicate that the trans-Afghan

pipeline has full backing of the Bush administration and some more US companies were expected to join the consortium in a bid to block entry of Argentinean Bridas or Russian Gazprom in the mega oil and gas pipeline projects...

Energy experts have been indicating US eyes on Caspian Sea reserves of $5 t with companies owned by Bush senior and Vice President Dick Cheny showing keen interest. The United States is also expecting investment from US-based energy firms through Overseas Private Investment Corporation (OPIC) to reactivate over $2 billion Turkmenistan to Pakistan gas pipeline.[15]

The US military intervention in Afghanistan also allowed the US to counter its Russian rival and establish dominance over the Central Asian republics on the country's border. Reuters reported near the end of September that:

> The ex-Soviet republics used the crisis to assert their independence from Moscow, quickly agreeing to open air corridors and possibly airports to the United States, something that was unthinkable only two weeks ago. Once the region's unquestioned master, Moscow found it had little choice but to agree with the Central Asian states and let US forces into the region for the first time.[16]

Thus, new economic programs have been accompanied by the establishment of a permanent military presence in the region, even while the war on Afghanistan was drawing to a close. The *Los Angeles Times* reported that: "Behind a veil of secret agreements, the United States is creating a ring of new and expanded military bases that encircle Afghanistan and enhance the armed forces' ability to strike targets throughout much of the Muslim world...

> Since Sept. 11, according to Pentagon sources, military tent cities have sprung up at 13 locations in nine countries neighboring Afghanistan, substantially extending the network of bases in the region. All together, from Bulgaria and Uzbekistan to Turkey, Kuwait and beyond, more than 60,000 US military personnel now live and work at these forward bases. Hundreds of aircraft fly in and out of so-called "expeditionary airfields."[17]

There can be no doubt that this presence is intended to be permanent. Radio Free Europe/Liberty further reported developments in the region indicating that the US military has been making itself at home in Central Asia:

> Even though the US-led campaign in Afghanistan appears to be drawing to a close, Washington is building up its military presence in Central Asia to protect what it describes as its long-term interests, in an area Russia and China consider part of their sphere of influence.... The United States, which has gained a foothold in Central Asia over the course of its antiterrorism campaign in Afghanistan, is now considering ways to consolidate its military buildup there in a bid to raise its political profile in the region.

"[T]he Pentagon and its allies" have already established a foothold in Uzbekistan and Kyrgyzstan as a "rear base for military operations and as a corridor for humanitarian aid." Kazakhstan and Tajikistan "have offered their respective airspaces and airfields to US planes for operations in Afghanistan." Meanwhile, "some 2,000 US soldiers are already deployed in former Soviet Central Asia, mainly on Uzbekistan's southern Khanabad airfield, near the Afghan border," and according to the Uzbek President speaking on December 28, 2001, there is "no deadline for US troops to pull out of the base." Despite the cessation of the "US-led anti-Taliban operation... the Pentagon is building military facilities at Manas international airport—some 30 kilometers outside the Kyrgyz capital Bishkek—which could house up to 3,000 troops." The Kyrgyz parliament had also agreed to allow the US military to install a base at Manas. The *New York Times* further reported on January 10, 2002 that "US military planners are also considering rotating troops in the region every six months, increasing technical support for and conducting training exercises with Central Asian countries." US officials have generally confirmed the permanent nature of the expanding US military occupation of the region.

> In comments last month to the US Congress's Foreign Affairs Committee, Elizabeth Jones—the assistant secretary of state for European and Eurasian affairs—notably said President George W. Bush's administration hopes a permanent US presence in Central Asia will boost regional economic development.... US Deputy Defense Secretary James Wolfowitz said that, by upgrading its military presence in Central Asia, the US wishes to send a clear message to regional countries—especially to Uzbekistan—that it will not forget about them and that it "has a capacity to come back and will come back in" whenever needed.... A report published on 6 January in the *Washington Post* said that, in addition, the Bush administration is planning to abrogate a Cold War-era bill that places conditions on a number of former Soviet republics' trade relations with the US based on their human rights records.... The planned move has already stirred controversy among regional analysts, who believe it could send the message that the US is ready to condone human rights abuses in some of these countries in return for their loyalty.[18]

The expansion of US hegemony is thus to be accompanied by the legitimization of regional human rights abuses. The instrumental role played by 9/11 in providing a justification for the anti-humanitarian expansion and consolidation of US hegemony in Central Asia was specifically indicated by US Senator Joseph Lieberman. Speaking on January 7, 2002, at Bagram air base near Kabul, he observed: "We learned at a very high and painful price the cost of a lack of involvement in Central Asia on 11 September, and we're not going to let it happen again."[19]

The Post-9/11 Terror-Security Apparatus

In a little noted but important article for the *Los Angeles Times*, US defense analyst William Arkin referred to a classified "outbrief" compiled by US Defense Secretary Donald Rumsfeld's Defense Science Board 2002 Summer Study on Special Operations and Joint Forces in Support of Countering Terrorism. The secret study—drafted to guide other Pentagon agencies—recommended the implementation of "new strategies, postures and organization" in fighting the "War on Terror." The principal vehicle of these new methods is:

... a super-Intelligence Support Activity, an organization it dubs the Proactive, Preemptive Operations Group, (P2OG), to bring together CIA and military covert action, information warfare, intelligence, and cover and deception.

Among other things, this body would launch secret operations aimed at "stimulating reactions" among terrorists and states possessing weapons of mass destruction—that is, for instance, prodding terrorist cells into action and exposing themselves to "quick-response" attacks by US forces.

Military intervention would be justified because such actions "would hold 'states/sub-state actors accountable' and 'signal to harboring states that their sovereignty will be at risk.'" The Proactive, Preemptive Operations Group (P2OG) is not an entirely unprecedented structure. Rather, its roots go back to the Intelligence Support Activity (ISA) established in 1981, which "fought in drug wars and counter-terror operations from the Middle East to South America," building a reputation for lawlessness. Throughout the 1990s, the ISA operated under different guises, and today is active under the code name Gray Fox:

Gray Fox's low-profile eavesdropping planes also fly without military markings. Working closely with Special Forces and the CIA, Gray Fox also places operatives inside hostile territory. In and around Afghanistan, Gray Fox was part of a secret sphere that included the CIA's paramilitary Special Activities Division and the Pentagon's Joint Special Operations Command. These commands and "white" Special Forces like the Green Berets, as well as Air Force combat controllers and commandos of eight different nations report to a mind-boggling array of new command cells and coordination units set up after Sept. 11.[20]

In other words, the P2OG merely expands an already existing apparatus for covert operations connected to terrorism. However, the language of the Defense Science Board clarifies that P2OG's primary purpose is to provoke terrorist groups into actually conducting anti-US operations in order permit a US military response. The Board additionally proposes "tagging key terrorist figures with special chemicals so they can be tracked by laser anywhere on Earth" and "creating a 'red team' of particularly diabolical thinkers to plot imaginary terror attacks on the United States so the government can plan to thwart them." A key role for "an elite group of counter-terror operatives" would be "duping al Qaeda into undertaking operations" and attempting to "stimulate terrorists into responding or moving operations." This will be facilitated by dramatic increases in urban warfare capabilities through "the development of a detailed database of most of the cities in the world... with GPS coordinates marking key structures and roads." This constantly updated database would "come together in a three-dimensional display showing buildings, including windows and doors, streets and alleys and underground passages, obstacles like power lines and key infrastructure like water and communications lines."[21]

The new Pentagon strategy then is ultimately "aimed at luring terrorists into committing acts of terrorism" as an integral part of fighting terrorism.[22] As journalist Chris Floyd wryly observes:

> Once they have sparked terrorists into action—by killing their family members? luring them with loot? fueling them with drugs? plying them with jihad propaganda? messing with their mamas? or with agents provocateurs, perhaps, who infiltrate groups then plan and direct the attacks themselves?—they can then take measures against the "states/sub-state actors accountable" for "harboring" the Rumsfeld-roused gangs.[23]

P2OG raises a number of critical issues. Most pertinently, P2OG undoubtedly demonstrates the overarching trends that characterize the fundamental framework of thinking behind some of the most influential US policymakers involved in planning for the "War on Terror." This in turn raises the issue of whether P2OG is really an entirely novel and unprecedented proposal, or in fact a one-off public revelation of a particular program of policies that has a much deeper ancestry in the US policymaking establishment. In light of the previous documentation concerning the interlocking web of US–al-Qaeda connections across the globe, one may reasonably conclude that this notion provides the most plausible explanation of the facilitation of international terrorism systematically generated by the US national security apparatus over the last decade or so. Unfortunately, further information on P2OG has not been forthcoming. Nevertheless, credible circumstantial evidence exists confirming that in the post-9/11 era, the same pattern of Western–al-Qaeda connections discerned in the pre-9/11 era continues to prevail. A prime example of this is al-Qaeda's Moroccan network.

The Terror-Security Apparatus in Action: Moroccan Terrorists, Spanish Security Services, and the Madrid Bombings

On the morning of March 11, 2004, a series of ten coordinated terrorist bombings against the commuter train system of Madrid, Spain, occurred, killing 191 people and wounding more than 1,800. These were the worst terrorist attacks in Europe since the 1988 Lockerbie bombing. It was not long before, after having jumped to blame the bombings on ETA, the Spanish Interior Minister disclosed that a video had been obtained on which a man identifying himself as an al-Qaeda military spokesman claimed responsibility for the attacks.[24] Soon Spanish police identified twenty Moroccans who they believed to have "planned and carried out" the bombings, based on "a trail of evidence that began with a pre-paid cell phone card, found inside a backpack along with an unexploded bomb and a cell phone wired as a detonator." Three Moroccans were arrested, including "Jamal Zougam... a key suspect in their investigation." Zougam is apparently among a list of figures in a Spanish indictment of "alleged Al Qaeda members accused of helping plan the Sept. 11 attacks." He is also tied to the 2003 Casablanca suicide bombing that killed 40 people and was conducted by a "Moroccan al Qaeda faction. Many of the group's radical Islamist followers studied in Saudi-financed schools that sprang up in Casablanca's poor neighborhoods in the 1970s."[25]

Indeed, citing counterterrorism sources, the Jerusalem-based intelligence news service DEBKAFile, reported that: "Like the attacks in the United States, they were conceived, planned, orchestrated and directed by Osama bin Laden and his top lieutenant, Ayman Zuwahiri, in person."[26] Several intelligence sources report that the Moroccan group is known as Salafia Jihad—the same al-Qaeda affiliate that bombed Casablanca in 2003.[27]

Apart from the alarming implications of the Zawahiri connection, DEBKAFile raises some other pertinent facts concerning the extent of advanced warning available to both US and European intelligence agencies about the impending Madrid attacks:

> Bin Laden's "success" owes less to his superior craft than to the laxness of US and European counter-terror authorities. The names and descriptions of all the members of the Moroccan network which perpetrated the worst terrorist outrage since 9/11 were in their possession, handed over by Ramzi bin al Shaiba after he reached US custody in September 2002. All that time, none of the Moroccan terrorists named were detained, although their network is directly controlled by bin Laden himself and despite the fact that they lived mostly in Madrid or Tangiers.[28]

The barely reported revelation that US and European intelligence services had in their possession a detailed list of the entire structure and membership of al-Qaeda Moroccan network is startling—why was it not acted upon? In another report, DEBKAFile stated citing counterterrorism sources that US and European intelligence services had also received detailed, repeated, and explicit warnings of an impending attack on Europe in general and particularly in Spain:

> According to data gathered by our experts, from December 2002, three months before the US invasion of Iraq, al Qaeda began issuing a stream of fatwas designating its main operating theatres in Europe. Spain was on the list, but not the first.
> 1. Turkey was first. Islamic fundamentalists were constrained to recover

the honor and glory of the Ottoman caliphates which were trampled by Christian forces in 1917 in the last days of World War I.
2. Spain followed. There, al Qaeda set Muslims the goal of recovering their lost kingdom in Andalusia.
3. Italy and its capital were third. Muslim fundamentalists view Rome as a world center of heresy because of the Vatican and the Pope.
4. Vienna came next because the advancing Muslim armies were defeated there in 1683 before they could engulf the heart of Europe.[29]

These warnings were born out in the first wave of attacks that occurred in late 2003 in the suicide bombing of two synagogues, the British consulate, and a London-based bank in Istanbul, attributed to al-Qaeda operatives.[30] Spain was clearly next on the list. Yet astonishingly, despite having anticipated an al-Qaeda terrorist operation in Spain and despite having detailed intelligence on the operatives planning the attack, neither US nor European intelligence agencies lifted a finger to shut down al-Qaeda's Moroccan terrorist network in Spain.

Even more remarkably, further official investigations confirmed ties between key al-Qaeda Moroccan operatives involved in the Madrid attack and Spanish security services. The London *Times* reported that:

The man accused of supplying the dynamite used in the al-Qaeda train bombings in Madrid was in possession of the private telephone number of the head of Spain's Civil Guard bomb squad… Emilio Suárez Trashorras, who is alleged to have supplied 200kg of dynamite used in the bombs, had obtained the number of Juan Jesús Sánchez Manzano, the head of Tedax.

The revelation has raised fresh concerns in Madrid about links between those held responsible for the March bombings, which killed 190 people, and Spain's security services, and shortcomings in the police investigation. Señor Suárez Trashorras and two other men implicated in the bombings have already been identified as police informers. Other members of the group had evaded police surveillance, despite concerns within the security services about their activities and evidence of their association with al-Qaeda.[31]

BBC News provides some further crucial context to these disclosures, noting that the Spanish Interior Ministry was investigating evidence that two of the suspects "were police informants." The Spanish daily *El Mundo* reported that "Moroccan Rafa Zuher and Spaniard Jose Emilio Suarez had been in contact with police before the attacks." Both men are believed to have provided dynamite for the attacks. Zuher was "an informant for the National Police, providing information about trafficking in weapons, drugs and explosives." Citing security sources, *El Mundo* noted that Zuher "was believed to be the link between Mr. Suarez, who allegedly supplied the explosives, and the cell that carried out the attacks."[32]

There are also reported French connections to this Moroccan network. In Casablanca, five simultaneous bombings on May 16, 2003, killed 45 people. The al-Qaeda affiliated Salafia Jihad was found to have organized the attacks. One of the defendants in the trial, however, was Frenchman Robert Richard Antoine-Pierre, otherwise known as Pierre Robert. Robert, who also used the names Lhaj and Abou Abderrahmane, was detained in Tangiers where he had lived for several years as a convert to Islam.[33] In controversial court testimony, Robert—who was charged with "criminal conspiracy, conspiracy to undermine state security, premeditated murder and possession of arms and explosives in connection with the attacks in Casablanca"[34]—claimed that he has "worked for French intelligence" and "had been paid to infiltrate Muslim groups…

> Mr. Robert, 31, said a French secret service agent known as "Mr. Luc" first approached him to recruit him five years ago, and paid him for his services. "I was contacted at the time of the [soccer] World Cup in 1998 by the DST to conduct inquiries into Algerian Islamist networks in France, and I did that," Mr. Robert told the court in Rabat. After successfully completing the mission, Mr. Robert was asked by Mr. Luc to investigate "Islamist activities in Belgium"—which he also carried out, he said.

The French government has apparently denied the allegations—albeit in a rather peculiar way, with one French Interior Ministry official insisting "that the department had 'never had contact with this person.'"[35] This bizarre statement, in fact, only denies that Robert ever had direct contact with the French Interior Ministry, not that he had contact with a French intelligence agency. In any case, what is certain is that the covert pattern of Western–al-Qaeda connections is evident again: Spanish and European security services interpenetrate with a Moroccan terrorist network, which in turn is interpenetrated with al-Qaeda. Against this background, studious Western inaction, despite urgent advanced warnings of the attacks and detailed intelligence on their planners, facilitated terrorism.

Next in Line: Bin Laden in China?

According to the Israeli intelligence news service DEBKAFile, a large number of Western intelligence services as of October 2004 believe that Osama bin Laden was headed toward China. American, Indian, Pakistani, and Russian intelligence agencies are reportedly "convinced that… he headed out to his winter hideout in the Himalayas or Little Pamir and will stay there until the spring thaw." However, between October 17 and 19, an Indian Air Force reconnaissance plane spotted bin Laden "in the Tibet-Laddakh region close to the northeastern corner of Pakistan bordering India and China…

Additional surveillance aircraft were called in and identified the al Qaeda leader on the move with a 10-vehicle convoy of black Japanese minivans. Four of the vehicles turned up again on October 22 heading east towards the Chinese border. Our sources maintain that the rumored sightings of bin Laden on the Lingzi Thang Plain on the Tibetan border in June may have been true then but are now outdated.[36]

Bizarrely, the US government responded by sending a single FBI agent from Islamabad to New Delhi to examine the aerial photographs of the bin Laden convoy and requested the Indian government to comb the area "before the snowfall." Why, however, did the US government not take the opportunity to immediately order the US military into action to liquidate the convoy, thus assassinating bin Laden? Rather, the government belatedly decided to delegate a "response" to India, requesting its security forces in the northwest to go on "red alert"—but no mention here of any force undertaking a swift and specific military action against the convoy. This is simply another example of the inexplicable disinterest with which the US government approaches—in real terms—the task of taking real measures against international terrorism in accordance with the declared principles of the "War on Terror," foremost of which is allegedly to get Osama—"dead or alive," in President Bush's infamous words.

13.

THE GRAND DESIGN

The previous documentation demonstrates unambiguously that the new "War on Terror" under US leadership is not, in reality, fundamentally concerned with the elimination of international terrorism. On the contrary, not only does the strategy employed in the new "War on Terror" seem to provoke international terrorism, but an integral dimension of the strategy is the protection of key actors culpable in the financial, logistical, and military-intelligence support of international terrorism. Indeed, there is ample evidence from the historical and contemporary record of wider geostrategic imperatives behind the "War on Terror."

Contemplating Central Asia

The US military industrial complex has been contemplating a prolonged intervention in Central Asia for at least a decade. As early as 1991, in the aftermath of the Persian Gulf War, *Newsweek* reported in an article titled "Operation Steppe Shield?" that the US military was preparing an operation in Kazakhstan. Planning for the operation was modeled on the Operation Desert Shield deployment in Saudi Arabia, Kuwait, and Iraq, which successfully resulted in the establishment of a network of permanent US military bases in the region.

More specifically, the US war plan to invade Afghanistan has roots in strategic and economic concerns in Central Asia, stretching as far back as 1989. Afghanistan has been widely recognized by US officials as the gateway to Central Asia and the Caspian, and thus to global primacy. Former Department of Defense official Elie Krakowski, who worked on the Afghan issue in the 1980s, records that:

> With the collapse of the Soviet Union, [Afghanistan] has become an important potential opening to the sea for the landlocked new states of Central Asia. The presence of large oil and gas deposits in that area has attracted countries and multinational corporations.... Because Afghanistan is a major strategic pivot what happens there affects the rest of the world.[1]

Afghanistan is thus the primary gateway to Central Asia and the immense energy deposits therein. A September 2001 report on the results of a May 2001 Brookings Institution conference shows clearly that the exploitation of Caspian and Asian energy markets was an urgent priority for the Bush administration:

[T]he administration's report warned that "growth in international oil demand will exert increasing pressure on global oil availability" and that developing Asian economies and populations—particularly in China and India—will be major contributors to this increased demand... options for constructing gas pipelines east to Asia from the Caspian have been discussed for the last decade.

Access to Central Asian and Caspian resources has thus been the centerpiece of the Bush energy policy.[2] Indeed, experts agree that both the Caspian Basin and Central Asia are the keys to energy in the 21st century. James Dorian, for instance, observes in the *Oil & Gas Journal*: "Those who control the oil routes out of Central Asia will impact all future direction and quantities of flow and the distribution of revenues from new production."[3] *Oil & Gas International* further clarifies the uniquely pivotal role of Afghanistan in access to Central Asian energy deposits: "Afghanistan's significance from an energy standpoint stems from its geographical position as a potential transit route for oil and natural gas exports from Central Asia to the Arabian Sea. This potential includes the possible construction of oil and natural gas export pipelines through Afghanistan."[4]

A 1999 study edited by the leading Central Asian experts Michael Croissant and Bulant Aras, *Oil and Geopolitics in the Caspian Sea Region*, provides further insight. In the book's forward, Pat Clawson of the National Defense University describes the Caspian Sea as a crucial oil region, the target of ongoing and conflicting interests of surrounding states, as well as the Western powers. The economic and geostrategic issues relate particularly to potential pipeline routes and attempts by the United States to monopolize them by creating an appropriate international oil regime in the region.[5]

The establishment of such a regime, by nature, requires a combination of economic, political, and military arrangements to support and protect oil production and transportation to markets.[6] US policies, geared toward the creation of an appropriate climate within the region, in accordance with US interests, have thus consisted of a three-pronged program of economic, political, and military penetration into the region. This program has included persistent efforts to sideline the intrusion of other powers, particularly Russia and Europe, in attempts to control access to regional resources.[7]

As noted in 1997 by an energy expert at the National Security Council on US policy in Central Asia: "US policy was to promote the rapid development of Caspian energy.... We did so specifically to promote the independence of these oil-rich countries, to in essence break Russia's monopoly control over the transportation of oil from that region, and frankly, to promote Western energy security through diversification of supply."[8]

Former US Energy Secretary Bill Richardson observed in 1998 in relation to the republics of Central Asia: "We would like these newly independent countries reliant on Western commercial and political interests rather than going another way. We've made a substantial political investment in the Caspian, and it's very important to us that both the pipeline map and the politics come out right."[9]

One year later, the 106th Congress passed the Silk Road Strategy Act of 1999, "…to amend the Foreign Assistance Act of 1961 to target assistance to support the economic and political independence of the countries of the South Caucasus and Central Asia." The US Congress noted that: "The region of the South Caucasus and Central Asia could produce oil and gas in sufficient quantities to reduce the dependence of the United States on energy from the volatile Persian Gulf region." Accordingly, one of the principal objectives of US policy, it was agreed, is "to support United States business interests and investments in the region."[10]

US policy plans in Central Asia are thus rooted in a broad imperialistic context. A 46-page Pentagon draft document, leaked by Pentagon officials in March 1992, clearly reflects the internal planning and strategies produced by the US military in the post-Cold War era. The Pentagon document states that the United States' "first objective is to prevent the re-emergence of a new rival" who may threaten America's domination of global resources in the post-Cold War era. This would naturally involve the US endeavor "to establish and protect a new order that holds the promise of convincing potential competitors that they need not aspire to a greater role or pursue a more aggressive posture to protect their legitimate interests." This world order must "account sufficiently for the interests of the advanced industrial nations to discourage them from seeking to overturn the established political and economic order" under US hegemony. US military dominance must be maintained as "the mechanism for deterring potential competitors from even aspiring to a larger regional or global role."

Such military dominance implicates the preservation of "NATO as the primary instrument of Western defense and security," because NATO extends US hegemony over Western Europe. Thus, the US "must seek to prevent the emergence of European-only security arrangements which would undermine NATO" and thereby US hegemony over Europe. A "dominant consideration underlying the new regional defense strategy" is the necessity for the US to "endeavor to prevent any hostile power from dominating a region whose resources would, under consolidated control, be sufficient to generate global power." These regions include Western Europe, East Asia, the former Soviet Union, and the Middle East, which should, therefore, be integrated into the US-dominated global economic system, and thereby brought under American world domination. What is therefore paramount to maintain is "the sense that the world order is ultimately backed by the US…. The US should be postured to act independently when collective action cannot be orchestrated." There is no doubt that this Pentagon draft document reflects the fundamental motivations and concerns of US policy planners today.[11]

For these reasons, tension between the United States and Russia still exists in the post-Cold War era, although not with the same degree of intensity and conflict of earlier years. This change is primarily due to Russia's weakening since the collapse of the USSR. This weakening has contributed significantly to Russia's willingness to join the US in an alliance dominated by the latter, while attempting to pursue its own goals within a US-dominated framework, challenging that framework only marginally.

As noted by Douglas MacArthur and Professor Stephen Blank, the principal expert on Russia, the Commonwealth of Independent States, and Eastern Europe at the US Army War College's Strategic Studies Institute, "the Transcaspian has become perhaps the most important area of direct Western-Russian contention today."[12] However, Russia is not the only rival to US interests in the Caspian. US policy, with British complicity, also appears to be designed to eventually distance the Balkan and Central Asian countries from German–EU influence, as well as weaken competing Franco–Belgian–Italian oil interests.[13] Stephen Blank suggests that an ingenious method of imposing US hegemony is now being pursued in the form of peacekeeping missions. Because an open military-backed diplomatic confrontation with US rivals, such as Russia, China and others, remains dangerous and therefore inappropriate, US policy is to find ways of implementing the "functional equivalent... [i.e.] peace operations."[14] Thus, there is good reason to argue that US involvement in Central Asia, undertaken ostensibly as humanitarian peace/security operations, are in fact designed to secure economic and strategic interests.

Indeed, there can be no real disputing the fact that, as matter of policy, military intervention is concerned fundamentally with the protection of Western interests as opposed to human rights or even domestic security. Although NATO military expansion is publicly touted as a means of legitimately strengthening the security of NATO members from conflict, and more recently the human rights of peoples around the world thereby, the reality is rather different. The actual objective of NATO, along with NATO's regional programs, such as Partnership for Peace, can be discerned from NATO's definition of "security" as *any event or entity that challenges the "collective interests" of NATO members*. For example, former US secretaries of state and defense, Christopher and Perry, stated in 1997 that "the danger to security... is not primarily potential aggression to their collective [NATO] territory, but threats to their collective interests beyond their territory.... To deal with such threats alliance members need to have a way to rapidly form military coalitions that can accomplish goals beyond NATO territory."[15]

NATO is, therefore, to play the role of military enforcer and protector of regional Western interests. References to "security," therefore, relate to these interests, which are primarily economic in nature. That these interests are primarily orientated around strategic and economic issues, such as access to regional resources and the countering of US rivals, is clear from several examples, such as the fact that US Central Asia experts met at NATO headquarters to discuss not the threat of conflict, but rather major US interests in Caspian basin energy deposits. It is in this context that Javier Solana, who became NATO Secretary-General during the intervention in Kosovo and later EU Security Affairs chief, stated at a Washington conference on NATO enlargement that Europe cannot be fully secure without bringing the Caucasus into its security zone.[16]

US Ambassador Nathan Nimitz elaborated on how US policy should hence be directed, in no uncertain terms: He concluded that the entirety of Eurasia must be brought under US military-economic hegemony:

> Pax NATO is the only logical regime to maintain security in the traditional sense... [and] must recognize a need for expansion of its stabilizing influence in adjacent areas, particularly in Southeastern Europe, the Black Sea region (in concert of course with the regional powers...) and in the Arabian/Persian Gulf. The United States must continue to play the major role in this security system.[17]

As Stephen Blank thus reports, regional military exercises held in 1997 were designed to demonstrate to the world that "US and NATO forces could be deployed anywhere.... The obvious implication of current policy is that NATO, under US leadership, will become an international policeman and hegemon in the Transcaspian and define the limits of Russian participation in the region's expected oil boom."[18] Perhaps no better and more authoritative depiction of the current projection of US power in the aftermath of 9/11 exists than that of Stephen Peter Rose, Kaneb Professor of national security and military affairs at Harvard University and director of the Olin Institute of Strategic Studies:

> A political unit that has overwhelming superiority in military power, and uses that power to influence the internal behavior of other states, is called an empire. The United States [is] an indirect empire, to be sure, but an empire nonetheless...
>
> If this is correct, our goal is not combating a rival, but maintaining our imperial position, and maintaining imperial order. Imperial wars are not so constrained [from escalation as when still confronted by the Soviet Union]. The maximum amount of force can and should be used as quickly as possible for psychological impact—to demonstrate that the empire cannot be challenged with impunity. Now we are in the business of bringing down hostile governments and creating governments favorable to us. Imperial wars end, but imperial garrisons must be left in place for decades to ensure order and stability. This is, in fact, what we are beginning to see, first in the Balkans and now in Central Asia [and] requires a lightly armed ground

force for garrison purposes. Finally, imperial strategy focuses on preventing the emergence of powerful, hostile challengers to empire: by war if necessary, but by imperial assimilation if possible. China will be a major economic and military power in a generation but is not yet powerful enough to be a challenger to American empire, and the goal of the United States is to prevent that challenge from emerging. The United States could do what it does now: reassure its friends in Asia that we will not allow Chinese military intimidation to succeed. We may also want unconventional weapons with which to remind China.[19]

The New Geostrategy for "American Primacy"

In other words, the Great Game of the nineteenth century, which consisted of competition among the powers for control of Central Eurasia, has continued into the 21st century with the United States leading the way. While Afghanistan thus constitutes the essential vehicle of control of Central Asia, Central Asia is in turn an essential instrument of global control.

This fact, along with extensive strategic planning for future US intervention in the region, was discussed in a 1997 Council on Foreign Relations (CFR) study, *The Grand Chessboard: American Primacy and its Geostrategic Imperatives*. Authored by longtime US geostrategist and former national security adviser under the Carter Administration, Zbigniew Brzezinski, the CFR study goes into great detail about US interests in "Eurasia" and the need for a "sustained and directed" US involvement in the Central Asian region to secure these interests.[20] "Ever since the continents started interacting politically, some five hundred years ago, Eurasia has been the center of world power," he observes.[21] Eurasia consists of all the territory east of Germany and Poland, all the way through Russia and China to the Pacific Ocean, including the Middle East and most of the Indian subcontinent. Brzezinski notes that the key to controlling Eurasia lies in establishing control over the republics of Central Asia.

He further describes Russia and China, both of which border Central Asia, as the two main powers that might threaten US interests in the region, Russia being the more prominent threat. The US must accordingly manage and manipulate the "lesser" surrounding powers, such as Ukraine, Azerbaijan, Iran, and Kazakhstan, as counter-actions to Russian and Chinese moves to control the oil, gas, and minerals of the republics of Central Asia, namely Turkmenistan, Uzbekistan, Tajikistan, and Kyrgyzstan. He also notes that any nation becoming predominant in Central Asia would thus pose a direct threat to US control of oil resources both within the region and in the Persian Gulf. The Central Asian republics, he records,

> are of importance from the standpoint of security and historical ambitions to at least three of their most immediate and more powerful neighbors,

namely Russia, Turkey and Iran, with China also signaling an increasing political interest in the region...

But the Eurasian Balkans are infinitely more important as a potential economic prize: an enormous concentration of natural gas and oil reserves is located in the region, in addition to important minerals, including gold.... The world's energy consumption is bound to vastly increase over the next two or three decades. Estimates by the US Department of Energy anticipate that world demand will rise by more than 50 percent between 1993 and 2015, with the most significant increase in consumption occurring in the Far East. The momentum of Asia's economic development is already generating massive pressures for the exploration and exploitation of new sources of energy, and the Central Asian region and the Caspian Sea basin are known to contain reserves of natural gas and oil that dwarf those of Kuwait, the Gulf of Mexico, or the North Sea[22].... Kazakhstan is the shield and Uzbekistan is the soul for the region's diverse national awakenings.... Uzbekistan is, in fact, the prime candidate for regional leadership in Central Asia.[23]... Once pipelines to the area have been developed, Turkmenistan's truly vast natural gas reserves augur a prosperous future for the country's people.... In fact, an Islamic revival—already abetted from the outside not only by Iran but also by Saudi Arabia—is likely to become the mobilizing impulse for the increasingly pervasive new nationalisms, determined to oppose any reintegration under Russian—and hence infidel—control[24]

.... For Pakistan, the primary interest is to gain Geostrategic depth through political influence in Afghanistan—and to deny to Iran the exercise of such influence in Afghanistan and Tajikistan—and to benefit eventually from any pipeline construction linking Central Asia with the Arabian Sea[25]

.... Moreover, sensible Russian leaders realize that the demographic explosion underway in the new states means that their failure to sustain economic growth will eventually create an explosive situation along Russia's entire southern frontier.[26]

Turkmenistan... has been actively exploring the construction of a new pipeline through Afghanistan and Pakistan to the Arabian Sea.[27]

He then pointed out from the above that: "It follows that America's primary interest is to help ensure that no single power comes to control this geopolitical space and that the global community has unhindered financial and economic access to it."[28]

...China's growing economic presence in the region and its political stake in the area's independence are also congruent with America's interests... America is now the only global superpower, and Eurasia is the globe's central arena. Hence, what happens to the distribution of power on the Eurasian continent will be of decisive importance to America's global primacy and to America's historical legacy… the Eurasian Balkans threaten to become a cauldron of ethnic conflict and great-power rivalry.[29]

Brzezinski then comes to the crucial conclusion that: "Without sustained and directed American involvement, before long the forces of global disorder could come to dominate the world scene. And the possibility of such a fragmentation is inherent in the geopolitical tensions not only of today's Eurasia but of the world more generally."[30] These observations are rooted indelibly in the Council on Foreign Relations' principal concern—the maintenance of global US dominance:

The last decade of the twentieth century has witnessed a tectonic shift in world affairs. For the first time ever, a non-Eurasian power has emerged not only as a key arbiter of Eurasian power relations but also as the world's paramount power. The defeat and collapse of the Soviet Union was the final step in the rapid ascendance of a Western Hemisphere power, the United States, as the sole and, indeed, the first truly global power[31]….

But in the meantime, it is imperative that no Eurasian challenger emerges, capable of dominating Eurasia and thus of also challenging America. The formulation of a comprehensive and integrated Eurasian geostrategy is therefore the purpose of this book.[32] … For America, the chief geopolitical prize is Eurasia…. Now a non-Eurasian power is preeminent in Eurasia—and America's global primacy is directly dependent on how long and how effectively its preponderance on the Eurasian continent is sustained.[33]

… In that context, how America "manages" Eurasia is critical. Eurasia is the globe's largest continent and is geopolitically axial. A power that dominates Eurasia would control two of the world's three most advanced and economically productive regions. A mere glance at the map also suggests that control over Eurasia would almost automatically entail Africa's subordination, rendering the Western Hemisphere and Oceania geopolitically peripheral to the world's central continent. About 75 percent of the world's people live in Eurasia, and most of the world's physical wealth is there as well, both in its enterprises and underneath its soil. Eurasia accounts for 60 percent of the world's GNP and about three-fourths of the world's known energy resources.[34]

… Two basic steps are thus required: first, to identify the geostrategically dynamic Eurasian states that have the power to cause a potentially important shift in the international distribution of power and to decipher the central external goals of their respective political elites and the likely consequences of their seeking to attain them;… second, to formulate specific US policies to offset, co-opt, and/or control the above….

To put it in a terminology that harkens back to the more brutal age of ancient empires, the three grand imperatives of imperial geostrategy are to prevent collusion and maintain security dependence among the vassals, to keep tributaries pliant and protected, and to keep the barbarians from coming together.[35]

... Henceforth, the United States may have to determine how to cope with regional coalitions that seek to push America out of Eurasia, thereby threatening America's status as a global power[36].... Hence, support for the new post-Soviet states—for geopolitical pluralism in the space of the former Soviet empire—has to be an integral part of a policy designed to induce Russia to exercise unambiguously its European option. Among these states, three are geopolitically especially important: Azerbaijan, Uzbekistan, and Ukraine.... Uzbekistan, nationally the most vital and the most populous of the central Asian states, represents the major obstacle to any renewed Russian control over the region. Its independence is critical to the survival of the other Central Asian states, and it is the least vulnerable to Russian pressures.[37]

Elaborating, Brzezinski observes that:

With warning signs on the horizon across Europe and Asia, any successful American policy must focus on Eurasia as a whole and be guided by a geostrategic design.... That puts a premium on maneuver and manipulation in order to prevent the emergence of a hostile coalition that could eventually seek to challenge America's primacy.... The most immediate task is to make certain that no state or combination of states gains the capacity to expel the United States from Eurasia or even to diminish significantly its decisive arbitration role.[38]...

In the long run, global politics are bound to become increasingly uncongenial to the concentration of hegemonic power in the hands of a single state. Hence, America is not only the first, as well as the only, truly global superpower, but it is also likely to be the very last.[39]

The next point made by Brzezinski is crucial: "Moreover, as America becomes an increasingly multicultural society, it may find it more difficult to fashion a consensus on foreign policy issues, except in the circumstance of a truly massive and widely perceived direct external threat."[40] Long-standing US aims to establish hegemony—the "decisive arbitration role" of "America's primacy"—over "Eurasia" through control of Central Asia thus entailed the use of "sustained and directed American involvement," justified through the manufacture of "a truly massive and widely perceived direct external threat." This should also be understood in context with his earlier assertion that: "The attitude of the American public toward the external projection of American power has been much more ambivalent. The public supported America's engagement in World War II largely because of the shock effect of the Japanese attack on Pearl Harbor."[41]

Brzezinski clearly envisaged that the establishment, consolidation, and expansion of US military hegemony over Eurasia through Central Asia would require the unprecedented, open-ended militarization of foreign policy coupled with an unprecedented manufacture of domestic support and consensus on this militarization campaign. He also recognized that this would require the perception of an external threat of hitherto unprecedented proportions. The comparison to Pearl Harbor is particularly unnerving, in that Brzezinski seems to suggest that only a Pearl Harbor-style attack on the United States would be sufficient to generate the required domestic support for the implementation of his grand strategy.

Given that Afghanistan constitutes the principal opening into Central Asia, it is clear that the CFR's strategic planning for the expansion and consolidation of US global hegemony via control of Eurasia—itself secured through control of Central Asia—would of necessity be initiated through the establishment of US hegemony in Afghanistan. In other words, the strategy for US global dominance begins in Afghanistan, extends to Central Asia, and moves forward to Eurasia.

Energy, Conflict, and "Global US Pre-eminence"

The strategic and military considerations described previously are inextricably linked to the predicted peak in world oil production, an occurrence that has extreme ramifications for the global economy and for Western industrial civilization as such. Gerald Leach, former director of the energy program at the International Institute for Environment & Development in London and currently a senior research fellow at the Stockholm Environment Institute studying energy, environment, and development—concisely elucidates the problem posed by "the probability that world oil production will reach a peak sometime during this decade and then start to fall, never to rise again...

> An abundant and growing supply of cheap oil has been one of the fundamental drivers of increasing prosperity during the past century. At the same time, supply failure—or the fear of its failure—has been a principal source of economic hardship, geopolitical manoeuvring, and war. Equally, an imminent peak and decline of this industrial lifeblood promises severe economic difficulties and political tensions across the planet that will leave few untouched.
>
> These world-wide upheavals may outweigh in scale and gravity any impacts on climate-related questions such as greenhouse gas mitigation strategies and emissions reduction targets. But they will nevertheless upset these considerably....
>
> To start with the obvious, the planet has a finite endowment of oil. Petroleum experts call this quantity the "ultimately recoverable reserve," or simply the "Ultimate." At any time, the Ultimate equals Cumulative

Production + Reserves (proved, probable, possible) + Yet-to-Find. One set of estimates for conventional oil at the end of 1999 was, in billions of barrels (Bb): Cumulative Production 820, Reserves 827, Yet-to-Find 153, with an Ultimate of 1800.

On these estimates, cumulative production will be around 900, or half way to the Ultimate, in the year 2003. Ominously, in view of events since 11th September 2001, about half the Yet-to-Find lies in just five Middle East countries: Iran, Iraq, Kuwait, Saudi Arabia and the United Arab Emirates.

The halfway point to the Ultimate is a crucial milestone. Strong historical evidence for many oil basins shows that oil production peaks and starts to decline when about half the recoverable resource has been consumed. This is a matter of oil reservoir physics rather than production technology or economics.

The idea was first proposed by the United States oil geologist M King Hubbert who predicted, in 1956, using two estimates of that country's oil Ultimate, that United States oil production would peak in the early 1970s. Hubbert was widely ridiculed by the oil industry, but was proved right when United States oil production peaked and began to fall in 1971.

Hubbert's model was taken up in the 1970s and early 1980s by competent authorities including Esso, Shell and the World Bank. Using a global Ultimate of around 2000 Bb they all independently predicted a conventional oil peak close to the year 2000. However, the forecasts overlooked the slowdown in global oil demand growth following the 1970s oil price shocks. Correcting for this postpones their predicted peak to about 2010.

In the mid-1990s, several independent analysts applied the same method to improved reserve data and broadly agreed that non-OPEC (Organization of Petroleum-Exporting Countries) oil production would peak about now, while global production would peak around 2005–2010.

Once oil production does peak, the analyses suggest that production will fall each year by about two million barrels per day. Daily production is now about 74 million barrels, so the fall will be some 2.7 per cent annually. That means a huge and highly disruptive shift from present-day growth in oil use.[42]

As documented by international oil industry expert Colin J. Campbell—associate of the government/industry advisory group the Geneva-based Petroconsultants and Trustee of the London-based Oil Depletion Analysis Centre—conventional oil production appears to have already peaked in the year 2000. Campbell demonstrates that almost half the oil that is available has already been consumed, leaving only an estimated 150 Gb (billion barrels) still be to be found. Oil reserves are now being depleted at the rate of about 2 percent each year, and thus it seems clear that conventional oil production has peaked.

However, the actual consequent decline of production will probably take a few more years to sink in.[43] Structural geologist Dave Allen Pfieffer describes the potential impact of the coming decline of oil production:

> As oil and natural gas production decline, so will the economy and our technological civilization. Without oil and natural gas modern agriculture will fail, and people will starve. Without oil and natural gas, industry will grind to a halt, transportation will be grounded, and people in northern climes will freeze in the winter.
>
> Scientist Richard Duncan has created a model that has so far gone unrefuted. His model states that technological civilization cannot outlast its resource base, particularly its energy resource base. Once this resource base is exhausted, technological civilization will be forever beyond the grasp of life on a particular planet. Duncan makes his model readily available to anyone who wishes to test it in the hope that someone will be able to successfully refute the model. To date, no one has done so.[44]

The scientific model produced by Richard Duncan, director of the Institute on Energy and Man, was presented to the Summit 2000 of the Geological Society of America. It elaborates in detail on the alarming implications of the peak of world oil production for the fate of industrial civilization without urgent appropriate measures to reduce oil-dependency and transfer to renewable energy resources.[45] Unfortunately, Western governments do not seem to be interested in implementing such measures, perhaps due to the corresponding consequence in terms of the decentralization of power, since control over renewable resources such as solar energy and so on is harder to concentrate in the hands of a few by their very nature. US/Western elites appear to be more concerned with maintaining their immediate investments and profits, while establishing grand plans to consolidate their control over the world's remaining energy reserves. Colin Campbell observes that as a result, US foreign policy seems to be fundamentally directed at racing to grab these reserves:

> We may look back and find that the year 2000 was the peak: a turning point when the prosperity of the past, driven by an abundant supply of cheap oil-based energy, gave way to decline in the future. A discontinuity of this magnitude is hard to grasp. The poor countries of the world will bear most of the burden. But the United States will be in serious difficulties. There is a danger of some ill-considered military intervention to try to secure oil.[46]

It should not be surprising then that the new "War on Terror" is based on military plans that were formulated long before 9/11 in order to target key strategic regions heavily laden with energy reserves. Scotland's *Sunday Herald* refers to "a secret blueprint for US global domination" revealing extensive military plans endorsed by "President Bush and his cabinet... even before he took power in January 2001...

> The blueprint, uncovered by the *Sunday Herald*, for the creation of a "global Pax Americana" was drawn up for Dick Cheney (now vice- president), Donald Rumsfeld (defense secretary), Paul Wolfowitz (Rumsfeld's deputy), George W Bush's younger brother Jeb and Lewis Libby (Cheney's chief of staff). The document, entitled *Rebuilding America's Defences: Strategies, Forces And Resources For A New Century*, was written in September 2000 by the neo-conservative think-tank Project for the New American Century (PNAC).[47]

Other members of the Bush administration who contributed to the report include John Bolton, undersecretary of state; Stephen Cambone, head of the Pentagon's Office of Program, Analysis, and Evaluation; Eliot Cohen and Devon Cross, members of the Defense Policy Board, the powerful Pentagon advisory group; and Dov Zakheim, defense department comptroller.[48] The plan outlined in the PNAC document, representing the essential sentiments of Bush's cabinet, is therefore worth exploring here in some detail. Principally, the document supports a "blueprint for maintaining global US pre-eminence, precluding the rise of a great power rival, and shaping the international security order in line with American principles and interests." It also cites approvingly an earlier 1992 Pentagon document authored by Wolfowitz and Libby advocating that the US must "discourage advanced industrial nations from challenging our leadership or even aspiring to a larger regional or global role."

In this vein, US armed forces operating abroad are described as "the cavalry on the new American frontier." A "core mission" for the "cavalry" is to "fight and decisively win multiple, simultaneous major theatre wars." To thus preserve the "global Pax Americana," the report concludes that US forces must perform "constabulary duties"—in other words, act as policeman of the world thus undermining the United Nations. Peacekeeping missions, for instance, "demand American political leadership rather than that of the United Nations." Instead of the UN, the United Kingdom is pinpointed as a convenient instrument of the American Empire, or in the words of the PNAC: "the most effective and efficient means of exercising American global leadership." Moreover, this overall imperial blueprint amounts to an "American grand strategy" that must be advanced for "as far into the future as possible."

To secure this state of affairs and to prevent any state from challenging the US, a much larger US military presence must be spread throughout the world in addition to the approximately 130 nations where US forces are already stationed. To that end, permanent military bases must be installed in the Middle East, in southeast Europe, in Latin America, and in southeast Asia, where no such bases previously existed. Even further, the report endorses the creation of "US Space Forces" to dominate space, as well as absolute control of cyberspace to counter "enemies" attempting to use the internet to thwart US interests.

Most pertinent to this study, the PNAC blueprint shows that Bush's cabinet had planned to establish military control over the Persian Gulf regardless of Saddam Hussein and any threat his regime may or may not have posed to the world, or to his own people. "The United States has for decades sought to play a more permanent role in Gulf regional security," the document notes. "While the unresolved conflict with Iraq provides the immediate justification, the need for a substantial American force presence in the Gulf transcends the issue of the regime of Saddam Hussein." In one fell-swoop, the document dispels the myth that the Bush plan to invade Iraq was fundamentally motivated by concerns regarding Saddam's regime such as weapons of mass destruction and so on. Such "unresolved" issues were only useful in providing "immediate justification" for an intervention designed to expand "the new American frontier" in order to maintain "global US pre-eminence."

But Iraq is only the beginning. Among the other pertinent points raised by the PNAC report is the fact that "even should Saddam pass from the scene," the US intends to maintain bases in Saudi Arabia and Kuwait permanently, despite domestic opposition. The document further lists several other states as dangerous rogues representing a threat to US designs, namely, North Korea, Libya, Syria, and Iran. The existence of such regimes requires the establishment of a "world-wide command-and-control system" under US tutelage. Iran in particular, the report observes "may well prove as large a threat to US interests as Iraq has," raising the specter of another US intervention. Worse still, the document advocates "regime change" in China, to be supported by increasing "the presence of American forces in southeast Asia" in order that "American and allied power" provide "the spur to the process of democratization in China." Europe is also targeted as potentially rivaling the US.[49]

Labor MP Tam Dalyell, the highly-regarded father of the House of Commons, described the PNAC report as "a blueprint for US world domination—a new world order of their making. These are the thought processes of fantasist Americans who want to control the world. I am appalled that a British Labor Prime Minister should have got into bed with a crew which has this moral standing."[50]

The "American grand strategy" outlined by the PNAC in 2000, however, was in the making for at least almost a decade. As noted by David Armstrong, an investigative reporter for the Washington, DC-based National Security News Service, unclassified documents from the Office of the Secretary of Defense, authored principally by current Vice President Dick Cheney as well as by other key government officials such as Paul Wolfowitz, Colin Powell, and Donald Rumsfield, reveal continually updated planning "for global dominance."[51] The series of documents outlines a consistent direction for US foreign policy that Armstrong characterizes as "the Plan." The Plan was published in unclassified form most recently as Defense Strategy for the 1990s, when Cheney was ending his term as Secretary of Defense under the Presidency of George Bush Sr. in 1993. The Plan, "a perpetually evolving work" again surfaced in June 2002 as "a presidential lecture in the form of a commencement address at West Point," and was "leaked to the press as yet another Defense Planning Guidance...

> It will take its ultimate form, though, as America's new national security strategy.... The Plan is for the United States to rule the world. The overt theme is unilateralism, but it is ultimately a story of domination. It calls for the United States to maintain its overwhelming superiority and prevent new rivals from rising up to challenge it on the world stage. It calls for dominion over friends and enemies alike. It says not that the United States must be more powerful, or most powerful, but that it must be absolutely powerful.[52]

Perhaps the most disturbing element of the PNAC blueprint for global domination is its recognition that the blueprint could not be implemented without the United States suffering some sort of sudden unprecedented crisis. Echoing the observations of US arch-geostrategist Zbigniew Brzezinski in 1997, the September 2000 PNAC document notes:

> Any serious effort at transformation must occur within the larger framework of US national security strategy, military missions and defense budgets.... Further, the process of transformation, even if it brings revolutionary change, is likely to be a long one, absent some catastrophic and catalyzing event—like a new Pearl Harbor.[53]

As ABC News reports: "That event came on Sept. 11, 2001."[54] The international terrorist threat, following on from the 9/11 terrorist attacks, is being used to justify the US drive "to rule the world," implementing plans and strategies that were formulated quite independently (i.e. long before), those attacks. Under the guise of fighting international terrorism on a crusade for justice, the US-led "War on Terror" in reality continues a far more familiar tradition of Western crusading for the expansion of power and profit. International terrorism, it seems, plays a decidedly functional role in the international system under US/Western hegemony. Without al-Qaeda, the "War on Terror" would lack a permanent worldwide target, eroding the legitimacy of the drive for a new Pax Americana.

These historic developments are unprecedented in scale. The virtually unhindered expansion of the American Empire is simultaneously and systematically eroding the very values that America claims to stand for.

Throughout the West and beyond, civil liberties, basic freedoms, and human rights are being curtailed in the name of fighting terrorism, while military interventions with nuclear implications are being planned to pursue brute strategic and economic interests, at the expense of indigenous populations—and for the benefit of corporate elites. Under US leadership, it seems that the entire world is moving toward a situation of global apartheid governed by the Western-based international institutions of what is fast becoming a global police state administered by the powerful for their own profit.

The Death of Democracy

In certain quarters, there has been an important series of attempts to investigate anomalies demonstrating the fraudulence of the elections that made Bush president, both in the 2000[55] and 2004 elections.

Shocking evidence of voting irregularities engineered by Republican officials in key states in the 2004 elections has been documented by members of the House of Representatives Committee on the Judiciary. Allegations of irregularities form "a troubled portrait of a one-two punch that may well have altered and suppressed votes, particularly minority and Democratic votes. First, it appears there were substantial irregularities in vote tallies...

> Second, it appears that a series of actions of government and non-government officials may have worked to frustrate minority voters. Consistent and widespread reports indicate a lack of voting machines in urban, minority, and Democratic areas, and a surplus of such machines in Republican, white and rural areas. As a result, minority voters were discouraged from voting by lines that were in excess of eight hours long. Many of these voters were also apparently victims of a campaign of deception, where flyers and calls would direct them to the wrong polling place. Once at that polling place, after waiting for hours in line, many of these voters were provided provisional ballots after learning they were at the wrong location. These ballots were not counted in many jurisdictions because of a directive issued by some election officials, such as yourself.[56]

An authoritative study by the Quantitative Methods Research Team at the University of California, Berkeley—led by Sociology Professor Michael Hout—concluded that "irregularities associated with electronic voting machines may have awarded 130,000–260,000 or more excess votes to President George W. Bush in Florida in the 2004 presidential election." The probability of such a discrepancy between votes for President Bush in counties where electronic voting machines were used versus counties using traditional voting methods arising by chance "is less than 0.1 percent." In the words of Professor Hout:

No matter how many factors and variables we took into consideration [e.g. differences in income between counties; number of voters; change in voter turnout; size of Hispanic/Latino population], the significant correlation in the votes for President Bush and electronic voting cannot be explained. The study shows that a county's use of electronic voting resulted in a disproportionate increase in votes for President Bush. There is just a trivial probability of evidence like this appearing in a population where the true difference is zero—less than once in a thousand chances.[57]

Indeed, as reported by Greg Palast on the morning of November 3, 2004 at 1:05 AM, CNN exit polls showed Democrat candidate John Kerry ahead of Bush by 53 percent to 47 percent. Among Ohio's male votes, Kerry was ahead of Bush by 51 percent to 49 percent. "Unless a third gender voted in Ohio, Kerry took the state," observes Palast. The exit polls, he argues, were quite accurate, but were "later combined with—and therefore contaminated by—the tabulated results.... Although the exit polls show that most voters in Ohio punched cards for Kerry-Edwards, thousands of these votes were simply not recorded." The phenomenon is known as "spoilage"—when approximately 3 percent of the actual vote is simply discarded or voided.[58] According to a detailed study by Harvard University's Civil Rights Project, the vast majority of spoiled votes pertain to counties with high concentrations of minority voters—"as the black population in a county increases, the uncounted ballot rate correspondingly increases."[59]

As Palast observes, the 2004 elections mirrored irregularities that occurred during the 2000 elections, when exit polls "showed Gore with a plurality of at least 50,000, but it didn't match the official count. That's because the official, Secretary of State Katherine Harris, excluded 179,855 spoiled votes." These votes were uncounted only because "the hole wasn't punched through completely—leaving a 'hanging chad,'—or was punched extra times.... Expert statisticians investigating spoilage for the government calculated that 54 percent of the ballots thrown in the dumpster were cast by black folks." In 2004, there were an additional 175,000 minimum "provisional" ballots handed out to minority voters—"a kind of voting placebo—which may or may not be counted." In Ohio alone there are a total of uncounted 247,672 votes consisting of 92,672 discarded votes plus 155,000 provisional ballots.[60]

The story of 2000 and 2004's "disappeared voters" has barely been heard in the mainstream media, although clearly the significance of the relatively new phenomenon of electoral fraud in American politics is unparalleled. However, while the far-reaching implications of this phenomenon should not be understated, it is essential to maintain a degree of historical perspective in viewing its emergence from the context of escalating counter-democratic trends during the last few decades. The rise to power of the conglomerate of neo-conservative factions represented in the Bush administration and its web of political, financial, and religious connections was, perhaps, merely the inevitable outcome of the very logic of the interests and operations of US and Western power in the post-Cold War period.

As this study has demonstrated in detail, US/Western military-intelligence policy has consistently been conducted in a manner that is fundamentally unaccountable to meaningful democratic influence. The root of this problem clearly lies in the structure of Western power itself, which—although conventionally believed to be the epitome of democracy—is in reality conjoined to a sprawling network of overarching criminal and financial interests. It is this network of unaccountable military, corporate, and financial interests that tends to drive US/Western foreign policies and which in the post-Cold War period has driven the West and international terrorism into an increasingly dynamic (and unstable) interconnected continuum of power.

The criminalization of Western power and the corruption of Western democracy is therefore not a new phenomenon exclusively linked to the rise of the Bush administration. On the contrary, the Bush administration has merely followed through with the inner logic of the historical trajectory of the policies of previous US administrations. The rise of the Bush administration simply demonstrates the extreme degree to which the criminalization of power has come to penetrate so deeply into the structure of society. It is therefore crucial to recognize that the cause of the problem here is not a particular group of individuals, or a particular set of ideologies, or a particular party's political program, linked to the Bush—or any other—administration. The problem, which has plagued both Democratic and Republican administrations to varying degrees and has only grown increasingly entrenched with time, relates fundamentally to the structure of Western power itself, from an internal domestic standpoint, and the structure of the international system, which Western power dominates. It is these structures that generate the individuals, ideologies, and political programs that promote the climate in which international terrorism flourishes.

PART FIVE
Concluding Analysis

Here, the author conducts a systematic critique of the structure and role of the 9/11 Commission and its ability to undertake a genuinely independent and credible investigation likely to hold officials appropriately accountable. An attempt is also made to summarize the factual findings of the previous chapters into a single coherent set of propositions. These in turn are subjected to further analysis in order to concisely clarify some of their implications with respect to a number of critical issues, namely, the trajectories of US power projection, the undermining of national security, the root causes of international terrorism, and the extent to which international terrorism has come to penetrate Western institutions of power.

14.

THE FAILURE OF THE 9/11 NATIONAL COMMISSION

A s this study has made clear, the National Commission on Terrorist Attacks Upon the United States has failed dismally to investigate the 9/11 terrorist attacks in an appropriately credible and critical manner. Huge amounts of relevant historical and contemporary data have been ignored; irrelevant data and narratives have been used to construct an inaccurate chronology of 9/11 and its historical context; the embarrassing and damaging implications of ample evidence, including testimony presented to the Commission, have been overlooked; blatantly dishonest testimony contradicting well-documented facts has been uncritically accepted. The end-result has been the erection of a fundamentally inconsistent story designed to absolve successive governments of responsibility for implementing a broad range of policies that cumulatively facilitated not only the 9/11 terrorist attacks, but also previous terrorist attacks since the end of the Cold War. Ultimately, the Commission has served to veil the underlying truth behind the phenomenon of international terrorism in the post-Cold War period, of which 9/11 was a most terrifying manifestation: that terrorism is symbiotically intertwined with the structure of the post-Cold War international system under US/Western hegemony.

The failure of the Commission, in this respect, is due to its architecture as a pure product of the Bush administration. The notion that the Commission benefits from even a modicum of independence is untrue. On the contrary, it is riddled with conflicts of interest arising from the fact that the most prominent members of the Commission have documented ties to the very subjects they have been appointed to investigate: not only government, military, and intelligence agencies, but more specifically, to individuals suspected of al-Qaeda terrorist activity. The preliminary appointment of such figures as Henry Kissinger and George Mitchell—who both resigned due to widely reported controversy over conflicts of interest arising over their financial ties to key Saudis—were only warning signs that far worse was to come.

The Leadership

It is prudent to begin this analysis with the chair of the Commission, Thomas H. Kean, former governor of New Jersey. Kean's appointment received no controversial coverage in the media, despite glaring conflicts of interest.[1] Kean sits on the board of directors and is a shareholder of one of the world's largest international oil corporations, Amerada Hess, based in New York. Kean's company has been involved in a secretive joint venture with a giant Saudi oil company, Delta Oil, owned by the powerful bin Mahfouz and al-Amoudi clans believed to finance al-Qaeda and Osama bin Laden to the tune of millions of dollars. The joint venture, known as the Delta–Hess Alliance, "was established in 1998 for the development and exploration of oil fields in the Caspian region."[2] According to the leading energy intelligence newsletter, *Energy Compass*, the terms of the joint venture between the Kean and bin Mahfouz/al-Amoudi companies are sealed from public scrutiny: "An air of mystery hangs over Delta-Hess, which... is registered in the Cayman Islands. Hess is in no hurry to reveal the terms of the alliance, which it says are subject to confidentiality clauses. 'There's no reason why this should be public information,' a Hess spokesman says."[3]

Khalid bin Mahfouz, one of the owners of Delta Oil, is reportedly Osama bin Laden's brother-in-law, a relationship confirmed by the 1998 testimony of former CIA director James Woolsey before the Senate. According to Woolsey, Khalid bin Mahfouz's younger sister is married to Osama bin Laden.[4] Khalid bin Mahfouz was also reportedly "placed under house arrest by the Saudi government after his National Commercial Bank allegedly funneled millions of dollars to front organizations for Osama bin Laden, including Blessed Relief."[5] Both Khalid bin Mahfouz and Mohammed Hussein al-Amoudi are named as alleged "financiers" of al-Qaeda in a $1 trillion lawsuit filed in August 2002 by the families of the victims of the 9/11 attacks. "Now you would think that being a business partner of the brother in law and alleged financier of 'Enemy No. 1' would also be considered a bona fide 'conflict of interest,'" observes Professor Chossudovsky, "particularly when your mandate—as part of the 9/11 Commission's work—is to investigate 'Enemy No. 1.'"[6] Kean's business partnership with the two alleged al-Qaeda financiers continued for 15 months after the 9/11 terrorist attacks. But a mere 21 days before President Bush appointed Kean to the Commission, the joint venture was ended.[7]

Kean is also co-chair of the Homeland Security Project, an organization that had significant input in the drafting of legislation for the Bush administration's Office of Homeland Security and which continues to play a prominent role in the latter.[8]

The Commission's vice chair, Lee Hamilton, holds a variety of key advisory positions to the Bush administration, including in "the President's Homeland Security Advisory Council, the Secretary of Defense's National Security Study Group, and the CIA Economic Intelligence Advisory Panel." He also serves on an advisory board to the Association of the US Army.[9] Hamilton also has a background of whitewashing government investigations. As chairman of the Select Committee to Investigate Covert Arms Transactions with Iran, he was involved in limiting the damage to the Reagan administration from the Iran–Contra scandal—as Chossudovsky points out, he "failed to investigate the roles of other Reagan officials," especially President Reagan, Vice President Bush, Colin Powell, and Richard Armitage—the last two being members of the latest Bush administration. "In other words, Lee H. Hamilton brings to the Commission the 'damage control' procedures followed during the Iran Contra investigation."[10]

The Staff

The Commission's executive director, Philip Zelikow, is a former member of President Bush's Foreign Intelligence Advisory Board (PFIAB), to which he was appointed just after the 2001 invasion of Afghanistan began. The PFIAB's mandate is to "provide advice to the President concerning the quality and adequacy of intelligence collection, of analysis and estimates, of counter-intelligence, and of other intelligence activities." Zelikow also appears to have a close personal relationship to President Bush's National Security Adviser Condaleeza Rice, with whom he authored a book called *Germany Unified and Europe Transformed.*[11]

Commission Deputy Executive Director Christopher Kojm has held a senior intelligence position in both the Clinton and Bush administrations, serving as deputy assistant secretary for Intelligence Policy and Coordination in the State Department's Bureau of Intelligence and Research from 1998 until February 2003. It is clear that he is a close colleague and student of "damage control" specialist Lee Hamilton, having worked under his supervision in previous posts. For example, in the House International Relations Committee Kojm served "under Ranking Member Lee Hamilton as Deputy Director of the Democratic staff (1997–98), as Coordinator for Regional Issues (1993–1997) and under Chairman Hamilton on the Europe and Middle East subcommittee staff (1984–92)."[12] Although this is not a straightforward conflict of interest, it is an indication of Kojm's sympathies.

The Commission's general counsel, Daniel Marcus, was for many years a partner in the Washington law firm Wilmer, Cutler & Pickering. He also served on the firm's management committee from 1995 to 1998. This is the same firm whose clients included—during Marcus' tenure there—Prince Mohammed al-Faisal, who is also identified as one of the top three alleged financiers of al-Qaeda in the 9/11 families' $1 trillion lawsuit cited above.[13]

The Panel Members

As for Commissioner Richard Ben-Veniste, he has, according to Daniel Hopsicker, "made a career of defending political crooks, specializing in cases that involve drugs and politics." Ben-Veniste was, for instance, attorney for the notorious convicted drug dealer Barry Seal, a man alleged to have had CIA connections, and who after serving his sentence went on to become a government informant "embraced by [then] Vice President Bush," working against the Sandinistas in Nicaragua.[14] Ben-Veniste was also majority counsel to the Senate Whitewater probe where he was supposed to be inquiring into the scandalous fund-raising schemes of Truman Arnold, chief Democrat fundraiser in 1995 and friend of then President Clinton. That was before he went on to defend Arnold as his lawyer before Ken Starr's Whitewater grand jury. Curiously, FAA documents prove that the same Arnold "loaned"—for only a dollar—a Beechcraft King Air 200 worth over $2 million to Willy Hilliard, the owner of a flight school in Venice, Florida, which trained four leading 9/11 al-Qaeda hijackers.[15] Finally, Ben-Veniste's law firm, Mayer Brown, is representing Boeing—the company that built all the planes that were destroyed on 9/11— and United Airlines,[16] as well as Deutsche Bank, which holds many accounts suspected of being linked to terrorists.[17]

Commissioner Fred Fielding was clearance counsel in the Bush–Cheney Presidential Transition Team in 2001. He is currently senior partner and head of Wiley, Rein, & Fielding's Government Affairs, Business & Finance, Litigation and Crisis Management/White Collar Crime Practices.[18] Fielding's law firm is lobbying for Spirit Airlines and United Airlines.[19] Among Fielding's other legal clients are Peter Terpeluk Jr., "one of President Bush's leading 'Pioneer' fund-raisers, and Berman Enterprises, which is owned by another Bush 'Pioneer,' Wayne Berman."[20]

Commissioner Jamie Gorelick currently serves on the Central Intelligence Agency's National Security Advisory Panel as well as the President's Review of Intelligence—two key advisory positions to the Bush administration related directly to the government's policy vis-à-vis the CIA and national security.[21] She is also on the board of directors of United Technologies, "one of the Pentagon's biggest defense contractors and a supplier of engines to airline manufacturers." She earned up to $100,000 from this post.[22]

Commissioner Slade Gorton has close ties to the airline industry. He earned $274,000 from Preston Gates & Ellis, the Seattle-based law firm whose clients include major airlines. He provided advisory and lobbying services to the Air Transport Association and helped Evergreen International Airlines seek federal loan guarantees. More directly, Gorton was a senator from Washington— Boeing's home state—and Gorton has frequently made deals to benefit Boeing, which contributed over $23,000 to Gorton in 1996.[23] Additionally, his law firm represents several major airlines, including Delta Airlines.[24]

Commissioner Max Cleland, the former senator, was paid $300,000 from the airline industry. However, he soon resigned from the Commission, apparently furious about what he felt was a whitewash. In an interview with the *New York Times*, he said "Bush is scamming America. As each day goes by, we learn that this government knew a whole lot more about these terrorists before Sept. 11 than it has ever admitted."[25] In an interview with *Salon*, he said "Let's chase this rabbit into the ground here. They had a plan to go to war, and when 9/11 happened that's what they did. They went to war." He then compared the Kean Commission to the Warren Commission, which, he argued, "blew it. I'm not going to be part of that. I'm not going to be part of looking at information only partially. I'm not going to be part of just coming to quick conclusions. I'm not going to be part of political pressure to do this or not do that."[26]

After Cleland's resignation, former senator and vice-chairman of the Senate Intelligence Committee Bob Kerrey was appointed to replace him. Kerrey, according to the *Washington Post*, was "an influential figure in intelligence circles who has also been a strong supporter of CIA Director George J. Tenet." He was in fact a member of a CIA advisory science panel just before he joined the Commission.[27] Kerrey was also on the advisory panel to a group called the Committee for the Liberation on Iraq, a pro-war lobby front for the neoconservative Project for the New American Century, in turn a think tank sponsored by senior members of the Bush administration.[28]

Most disturbingly, Kerrey is a war criminal who has yet to face prosecution for his 1969 involvement in the massacre of 21 Vietnamese civilians. The operation, carried out by a SEAL unit under his command as a Navy lieutenant, was purportedly aimed at assassinating a local Vietcong official as part of the CIA's Operation Phoenix. After one massacre, Kerrey's troops discovered a cluster of thatched hut dwellings, and rounded up another 15 or more unarmed civilians—including women, children, and the elderly. Kerrey ordered them all to be killed. The testimony by Gerhard Klann—a former Navy Seal and member of Kerrey's contingent—has confirmed the details:

> Klann says that Kerrey gave the order and the team, standing between 6 and 10 feet away, started shooting—raking the group with automatic-weapons fire for about 30 seconds. They heard moans, Klann says, and began firing again, for another 30 seconds. There was one final cry, from a baby. "The baby was the last one alive," Klann says, fighting back tears. "There were blood and guts splattering everywhere." Klann does not recall the men firing at the people who, in Kerrey's memory and the after-action reports, tried to run away after the initial massacre.[29]

Kerrey received a bronze medal for his military service. The fact that a war criminal responsible for the mass murder of a total of 21 civilians has been appointed to investigate the largest single mass murder of US civilians in the country's history is yet another illustration of the Commission's lack of integrity.

Commissioner John Lehman is former secretary of the Navy under the Reagan administration and served as special counsel and senior staff member to Henry Kissinger under the National Security Council.[30] Since 1987, he has been on the board of directors of the Ball Corporation, in which he has a stake of $1 million to $5 million and stock options worth $500,000 to $1 million.

Ball Corp. is a major contributor to the aerospace industry and particularly the US military. Among its "extensive defense contracts" is a laser program for the US government's Strategic Defense Initiative—Reagan's "Star Wars" missile defense system—resurrected by the Bush administration after 9/11 as part of the "War on Terror."[31]

Commissioner Timothy Roemer has served on the Permanent Select Committee on Intelligence and is a former member of the Intelligence Committee's Task Force on Homeland Security and Terrorism, as well as of the House and Senate Joint Inquiry into 9/11.[32] Chossudovsky observes that he amounts to "a go-between the Commission, Homeland Security and the members of the intelligence committees of the House and Senate."[33] Moreover, his law firm represents Boeing and Lockheed Martin, which both have major links to the airline and defense industries.[34]

Commissioner James Thompson is chairman of the law firm, Winston & Strawn, headquartered in Chicago, which he first joined in 1975 and then rejoined as a partner in 1991. Thompson's law firm routinely defends the interest of giant corporations, many with strong government and defense connections, including, for instance, General Electric, Philip Morris USA, Motorola, Inc. and Deutsche Bank, which was the locus of 9/11 insider trading.[35] Thompson himself has previously represented United Airlines, and his law firm is currently representing American Airlines.[36] His law firm was paid $1.66 million by American Airlines for federal lobbying efforts from January 1997 through June 2002.[37]

Damage Control

A number of observers have become perturbed at the implications of this vast array of conflicts of interest and interconnections with the very industries and government, military, and intelligence agencies that are purportedly being investigated. Terry Brunner, a former federal prosecutor who now runs the Aviation Integrity Project in Chicago, put it mildly when he declared: "Here we've got the most important event in America in the past 50 years, the most horrible thing that's happened to Americans, and yet we pick a bunch of people who are connected to the very people who are at the center of the question of who's at fault."[38]

Perhaps the most startling indication of the Commission's agenda occurred when an agreement was negotiated with the White House over access to classified Oval Office intelligence reports—Presidential Daily Briefs. Under the agreement, Commission panel members would be barred from accessing the briefs. Instead: "Commission officials have said that under the agreement the panel will be able to designate four members to read the reports. They will be allowed to take notes on the documents, and the White House will be allowed to review and edit the notes to remove especially sensitive information." This agreement fundamentally compromised the integrity of the investigation and prompted former Senator Cleland to resign. Despite possessing subpoena power, the Commission refused to use that power to obtain all relevant intelligence material that would disclose the extent of the intelligence community's and the White House's advanced warning of the 9/11 attacks. Instead, the Commission granted the White House a freehand to censor information it unilaterally deemed to be unsuitable for public consumption.

"Administration officials have acknowledged that they are concerned that intelligence reports received by Mr. Bush in the weeks before 9/11 might be construed to suggest that the White House failed to respond to evidence suggesting that Al Qaeda was planning a catastrophic attack."[39] This admission is revealing in that it points directly to the prime motive of the White House censorship agreement—to obscure the embarrassing fact that the White House did indeed receive precise advanced warning of the attacks.

This documentation illustrates that the Commission is utterly co-opted by a significant network of powerful, vested political, military, and economic interests connected not only to the US government, but also to those suspected of supporting international terrorism. Not only, therefore, does the Commission lack genuine independence, as a consequence its primary role is inevitably to support the vested interests represented by its membership. It was entirely predictable, in this context, that the Commission would fail to pursue a meaningful investigation that might expose the alarming extent to which powerful political, military, and economic interests connected to the government are reciprocally conjoined to the vital arteries of terrorism, in the form of the international al-Qaeda terrorist network. On the contrary, in accordance with the same interests, the Commission has instead produced a compilation of disjointed, illogical, and unsubstantiated narratives with the aim of burying the truth.

15.

SUMMARY OF FINDINGS

There is no doubt that there are a myriad of officially undisclosed connections between various elements of the US establishment and key figures involved in the financing and logistical facilitation of the 9/11 attacks and the network behind it. These connections indicate that the operation of various US agencies has inadvertently (or perhaps otherwise) contributed to the development of an international infrastructure of terrorist networks, both prior to and after the 9/11 attacks. In some cases, there is evidence that other states considered close US allies have also played central roles, often with US knowledge, in the development of this infrastructure. The conclusion that the 9/11 attacks were state-sponsored by several US allies as discussed is a plausible and compelling inference from the available data.

We may begin, for instance, by reminding ourselves of the *Times of India* comment in relation to revelations that the former ISI director-general ordered Omar Sheikh's money transfer to Mohamed Atta: "A direct link between the ISI and the WTC attack could have enormous repercussions. The US cannot but suspect whether or not there were other senior Pakistani Army commanders who were in the know of things. Evidence of a larger conspiracy could shake US confidence in Pakistan's ability to participate in the anti-terrorism coalition."[1]

This statement should be understood in the context of the observations of Middle East specialist Mohamed Heikal, former Egyptian foreign minister and "the Arab world's most respected political commentator." The London *Guardian* reports that Heikal questions whether Osama bin Laden and his al-Qaeda network were solely responsible for the September 11 attacks. He pointed out in October that

> Bin Laden does not have the capabilities for an operation of this magnitude. When I hear Bush talking about al-Qaida as if it was Nazi Germany or the communist party of the Soviet Union, I laugh because I know what is there. Bin Laden has been under surveillance for years: every telephone call was monitored and al-Qaida has been penetrated by American intelligence, Pakistani intelligence, Saudi intelligence, Egyptian intelligence. They could not have kept secret an operation that required such a degree of organisation and sophistication.[2]

Military veteran Stan Goff, a retired US Army Special Forces master sergeant and an expert in military science and doctrine, similarly observes that

> One, there is the premise that what this de facto administration is doing now is a 'response' to September 11th. Two, there is the premise that this attack on the World Trade Center and the Pentagon was done by people based in Afghanistan. In my opinion, neither of these is sound...
>
> This cartoon heavy they've turned bin Laden into makes no sense, when you begin to appreciate the complexity and synchronicity of the attacks. As a former military person who's been involved in the development of countless operations orders over the years, I can tell you that this was a very sophisticated and costly enterprise that would have left what we call a huge "signature." In other words, it would be very hard to effectively conceal.[3]

The testimony of Milton Bearden, the former director of CIA operations in Afghanistan, is also worth noting. In a CBS interview after the 9/11 attacks with Dan Rather, Bearden was asked if he thought Osama bin Laden was responsible for the attacks. Bearden observed that on his evaluation of the scale of the attacks, blame should not be automatically laid on bin Laden. Instead, he elaborated that it was more likely that a far more "sophisticated" intelligence operation was behind these precise coordinated attacks. Indeed, when pressed by Rather on the possibility of bin Laden's involvement, Bearden responded: "Look, if they didn't have an Osama bin Laden, they would invent one."[4]

Other intelligence experts have been even more forthright in deriding the idea that al-Qaeda could perform the 9/11 operation alone. According to one CIA official, "This guy [Osama bin Laden] sits in a cave in Afghanistan and he's running this operation? It's so huge. He couldn't have done it alone."[5] Former CIA official Robert Baer, who was case officer in the Directorate of Operations for the CIA from 1976 to 1997, and who received the Career Intelligence Medal in 1997, observes: "Did bin Laden act alone, through his own al-Qaida network, in launching the attacks? About that I'm far more certain and emphatic: no."[6]

US military intelligence expert Professor Anthony Cordesman—senior fellow in strategic assessment at the Washington-based Center for Strategic and International Studies (CSIS) and former senior official in the Office of the Secretary of Defense, the State Department, the Department of Energy, the Defense Advanced Research Projects Agency, and the NATO International Staff—strongly warned against assuming that Osama bin Laden's al-Qaeda was to blame. He emphasized the fact that no known terrorist network, including al-Qaeda, has the capability to carry out the sophisticated 9/11 attacks alone: "There is a level of sophistication and co-ordination that no counterterrorism expert had ever previously anticipated, and we don't have a group that we can immediately identify that has this kind of capability."[7]

Eckehardt Werthebach, former president of Germany's domestic intelligence service, Verfassungsschutz, notes that "the deathly precision" and "the magnitude of planning" behind the September 11th attacks would have required "years of planning." An operation of this level of sophistication, would need the "fixed frame" of a state intelligence organization, something not found in a "loose group" of terrorists like the one allegedly led by Mohammed Atta while he studied in Hamburg, Germany. Werthebach thus argues that the scale of the attacks indicates that they were a product of "state organized actions."[8]

Another former German official has similarly dismissed the conventional explanation. German intelligence expert Herr von Buelow, who was state secretary in the German Defense Ministry in the 1970s and Social Democratic Party speaker in the Schalk–Golodkowski investigation committee in 1993, observed that "[T]he planning of the attacks was technically and organizationally a master achievement. To hijack four huge airplanes within a few minutes and within one hour, to drive them into their targets, with complicated flight maneuvers! This is unthinkable, without years-long support from secret apparatuses of the state and industry."[9]

Military-strategic analyst and retired Major General Dr. Mahmoud Khalaf— member of the Royal College of Defense Studies (RCDS) London and honorary member of the Association of the United States Army, Fort Benning, Georgia— agrees with this analysis. In a presentation at the Center for Asian Studies in the University of Cairo, he observed:

> Military-strategic analysis is an independent branch of science within the strategic sciences, and not mere predictions and speculations. But, it has complete rules that are identical to 'post-mortem tests,' an autopsy process used to find out the causes of the death…
>
> First, [regarding the September 11 attacks] we are confronted with a technical operation of extremely great dimensions. We estimate that the planning organ for this operation must have consisted of at least 100 specialized technicians, who needed one year for planning…. The high level of the operation does not match the level of the evidence presented…. Now, the puzzling question is the preparation and training of these people who had the capability to follow up and execute…. There is, actually, one question, which is posed here. That is that there is no proportionality between the performance of the operation and the performance of bin Laden and his followers.[10]

In a December 2002 interview with PBS's *NewsHour*, co-chair of the Congressional Joint Inquiry Senator Bob Graham eliminated any ambiguity around this issue, confirming that he had been "surprised at the evidence that there were foreign governments involved in facilitating the activities of at least some of the terrorists [responsible for 9/11] in the United States…. To me that is an extremely significant issue and most of that information is classified, I think overly-classified. I believe the American people should know the extent of the challenge that we face in terms of foreign government involvement."[11]

It is a documented fact that the government systematically blocked investigations of terrorists involved or strongly suspected of being involved—including Osama bin Laden, his family, and Saudi royals suspected of supporting him—prior to 9/11. Even after 9/11, the government has continued to misdirect investigations and block pertinent inquiries, with the FBI concentrating futile efforts on Germany rather than Saudi Arabia, where according to late former FBI Deputy Director John O'Neill the real source of bin Laden's network lies.

In particular, it is a documented fact that the government has sealed any inquiry into the complicity of the ISI in 9/11. Indeed, there is reason to believe that through the ISI, which has "close links" to the CIA and plays the role of a regional instrument of US interests, there may be decidedly sinister reasons behind this policy. The government has, however, not only obstructed legitimate investigations of terrorists, but has maintained a covert financial, political, and even military alliance with their governmental and institutional supporters. The objective of US policy has, furthermore, been focused principally on securing elite strategic and economic interests abroad, while deterring public understanding at home.

A summary of the findings of this study follows:

Both the US and the USSR are responsible for the rise of religious extremism, terrorism, and civil war within Afghanistan since the 1980s. The US, however, is directly responsible for the cultivation of a distorted "jihadi" ideology that fueled, along with US arms and training, the ongoing war and acts of terrorism within the country after the withdrawal of Soviet forces.

The US approved of the rise of the Taliban and went on to at least tacitly support the movement, despite its egregious human rights abuses against Afghan civilians and its institutional ties to al-Qaeda, to secure regional strategic and economic interests.

The US government and military planned a war on Afghanistan, Iraq, and other potential targets in accordance with the planned unlimited militarization of foreign policy at least a year prior to 9/11, a plan rooted in broad strategic and economic considerations related to control of Eurasia, and thus the consolidation of unrivaled global US hegemony.

The US government has consistently blocked investigations and inquiries into the Saudi government, Saudi royals, Saudi businessmen, members of the bin Laden family, Pakistani military intelligence, and operatives connected thereto, who are implicated in supporting Osama bin Laden and terrorist operatives linked to him. These acts amount in effect to protecting leading figures residing in Saudi Arabia who possess ties with Osama bin Laden.

The US government has consistently blocked attempts to indict and apprehend Osama bin Laden, thus effectively protecting him directly.

The US government has allowed suspected terrorists linked to Osama bin Laden to train at US military facilities, financed by Saudi Arabia, as well as at US flight schools, for years.

High-level elements of the US government, military, intelligence, and law enforcement agencies received numerous credible and urgent warnings of the 9/11 attacks, which were of such a nature as to successively reinforce one another in providing a precise advanced picture thereof. This investigation suggests that the failure was ultimately one belonging to the political establishment, as opposed to the intelligence agencies, whose activities faced systematic obstructions due to administration decisions.

In spite of extensive forewarnings, the US Air Force emergency response systems collapsed systematically on 9/11, in violation of the clear rules that are normally and routinely followed on a strict basis. This investigation suggests that, like the intelligence failure, this failure was ultimately the responsibility of the political establishment, the reckless and irrational behavior of which seems to have been directly connected to the systematic obstructions to the functioning of standard operating procedures.

President Bush, Chairman of the Joint Chiefs of Staff Myers, and Defense Secretary Rumsfeld for instance, displayed sheer indifference to the 9/11 attacks as they were occurring, providing three clear examples of negligence in action.

The events of 9/11 have in fact been of crucial benefit to the US state, justifying the consolidation of elite power and profit both within the US and throughout the world. The tragic events that involved the murder of thousands of innocent civilians were exploited by the government to crackdown on domestic freedoms, while launching a ruthless series of military operations in Afghanistan, Iraq, and elsewhere.

There are a variety of possible scenarios regarding the role of the US government that explain these facts. All of these possibilities, however, strongly suggest a significant degree of US state responsibility for the failures that made the terrorist attacks possible. Surprisingly, US government policy was conducted in such a reckless and bizarre manner for so many years that it effectively facilitated the attacks, protected those responsible, blocked attempts to prevent/pre-empt the attacks, and maintained close political, financial, military, and intelligence ties to key figures who supported those responsible.

The role that successive US administrations have played both historically and currently in key events both before and after 9/11, points concretely to high-level state policies that fundamentally hampered the US national security apparatus in such a way as to render the multiple investigations and operations of its agencies dysfunctional. The blame for this dysfunction, however, quite categorically does not belong to the agencies or the agents themselves (generally speaking), but rather to the intersecting circle of bureaucratic and political superiors in Washington, DC, who, acting on behalf of government policy, made decisions which tragically facilitated the 9/11 attacks. Government policy, moreover, was without doubt motivated less by any concern for American lives and safety and more by the concern to further and protect a host of vested elite interests. The aforementioned superiors, including those holding the highest offices of government and the military/corporate interests they effectively represented, have yet to be held account for these gross acts of negligence and/or omission. These policies continue to be implemented even in the aftermath of 9/11.

Simultaneously, it is also clear that US intelligence agencies had largely successfully anticipated many of al-Qaeda's major terrorist operations—including 9/11—but were prevented from following through with legitimate investigations and counterterrorist operations. At the same time, US government policy had permitted its regional allies to facilitate and support the establishment of a terrorist infrastructure within the US. Meanwhile, preventive measures were completely lacking despite urgent recommendations from relevant agencies.

Coincidentally, the 9/11 attacks were ultimately fortuitous for the Bush administration, which was facing both a domestic and an international crisis of legitimacy prior to 9/11. Under the mantle of the new "War on Terror" that followed the attacks, the government was able to significantly divert and reverse these trends. The domestic crackdown on basic civil rights, combined with the demonization of dissent, has arrived part and parcel with the granting of unlimited war powers—lending the US state a free hand to embark on a new unlimited war against any regime that challenges US interests.

Meanwhile, the scattered existence of al-Qaeda plays into the hands of government planners eager to justify the continual projection of US military power internationally. As the London *Guardian* reports:

> If Osama bin Laden did not exist, it would be necessary to invent him. For the past four years, his name has been invoked whenever a US president has sought to increase the defense budget or wriggle out of arms control treaties. He has been used to justify even President Bush's missile defense program, though neither he nor his associates are known to possess anything approaching ballistic missile technology. Now he has become the personification of evil required to launch a crusade for good: the face behind the faceless terror... [H]is usefulness to western governments lies in his power to terrify. When billions of pounds of military spending are at stake, rogue states and terrorist warlords become assets precisely because they are liabilities.[12]

A massive external threat is an ideally convenient excuse to consolidate and expand US hegemony, fully counter Russian, Chinese, and European rivals, and to drum up the domestic consensus required to legitimize the unrelentingly interventionist character of US foreign policy in the new and unlimited "War on Terror."

Could it be that the bogeyman of Osama bin Laden's international terrorist network thus plays, in the view of certain senior factions in the highest echelons of Western government, a nominally functional role within the matrix of longstanding plans to increasingly subject world order to US/Western military, political, strategic, and economic influence? Perhaps this notion explains the West's systematic failure to investigate known supporters of al-Qaeda in Saudi Arabia and Pakistan—and even al-Qaeda cells operating within the West itself. Certainly, this idea is consistent with the wistful statements concerning the potential benefits of a new Pearl Harbor-style attack on US soil from the Council on Foreign Relations and the Project for the New American Century.

While the answer to this question may be speculative, it is obvious that the US government has adopted this array of policies on the basis of a cold, but meticulous "cost-benefit" analysis, weighing up the potential gains and losses of the following possible policies:

- Taking meaningful action against al-Qaeda, while damaging US regional interests tied to allies who support bin Laden
- Allowing allies to continue their support of al-Qaeda and refraining from action against it in order to protect perceived US interests

It is plausible that the second policy has been currently adopted by the US state, for the reasons discussed above. This is a reckless and irrational policy that endangers American lives, as well as domestic and international security—for the US government is fully aware that its regional allies, Saudi Arabia, Pakistan, and many others, have funded and supported al-Qaeda for years. Despite the dangers, Western governments have permitted this support to continue, actively obstructing intelligence investigations into the matter and funneling US aid to the same allies. This policy has continued with the objective of maintaining these lucrative alliances, through which regional US economic and strategic interests are secured.

Nevertheless, the US government has long been aware of the threat posed by al-Qaeda to US national security, and in particular was certainly aware that some sort of devastating attack by al-Qaeda on US soil was imminent in the later half of 2001. Despite this knowledge, the US government refused to reverse its policy of maintaining regional alliances with the principal supporters of al-Qaeda, including the funneling of financial and military aid—and continues to do the same, even after 9/11. This ongoing US policy of willful and reckless indifference to American lives does seem to be motivated fundamentally by powerful elite interests. 9/11, it seems, was a direct product of US/Western policy and the international system nurtured by that policy.

Various countries around the world that are of strategic value to the US find themselves falling victim to its new war for hegemony—on the pretext that it is targeting scattered terrorist cells. The escalating and contrived "clash of civilizations" that is fast resulting from this cynical policy bears ominous implications for the future of humanity. President Bush virtually declared war on any country deemed by the US to be a threat in his State of the Union address on Tuesday, January 29, 2002. Bush warned of "thousands of dangerous killers, schooled in the methods of murder, often supported by outlaw regimes," and openly threatened an attack on Iran, Iraq, and North Korea in particular. Both the US government and media have made concerted efforts to allege some sort of connection between al-Qaeda and the countries of Iran and Iraq. "By seeking weapons of mass destruction, these regimes pose a grave and growing danger. States like these and their terrorist allies constitute an axis of evil, arming to threaten the peace of the world," Bush claimed. "The United States of America will not permit the world's most dangerous regimes to threaten us with the world's most destructive weapons." It was not long before the second country on that list, Iraq, was subjected to an illegitimate US invasion designed to secure the same brand of economic and strategic interests discussed previously.[13]

The horrid irony of these statements is clear in light of the documentation presented here concerning the US state's dubious role in the events of 9/11 and the accompanying policies of imperialism at home and abroad—not to mention the dubious role of the Clinton administration in the 1993 WTC bombing and 1998 embassy bombings, as well as its associated foreign policies.

The Middle East and Central Asia together hold over two-thirds of the world's reserves of oil and natural gas. After Saudi Arabia, Iran and Iraq are respectively the second and third largest oil-producers in the region. Both Iran and Iraq, in accordance with their local interests, are fundamentally opposed to the US drive to secure unimpeded access to regional resources. Iran, for instance, has been attempting to secure its own interests in Afghanistan and Central Asia, thus coming into direct conflict with regional US interests. Iraq was tolerated for so long only because the US has been unable to replace Saddam Hussein's regime with a viable alternative. In light of the results of the "test case" provided by the 2001 war on Afghanistan, the US was intent on attempting a replay in Iraq by eliminating Saddam and enlisting the opposition to establish a compliant new regime. After the relative short-term success of the 2003 Gulf War, similar plans may be in the pipeline for Iran, Syria, and other countries deemed to be threats.[14]

As for North Korea, its border with China makes it strategically located in terms of longstanding US policy planning. China has long been viewed by US policy planners as its principal rival in north and east Asia. The military network being installed by the United States in the wake of September 11, 2001, systematically encircles China—Uzbekistan, Tajikistan, Kyrgyzstan, Pakistan, India, the Philippines, and now Korea. The *Guardian* has also commented on these developments and their military-strategic context: "Every twist in the war on terrorism seems to leave a new Pentagon outpost in the Asia-Pacific region, from the former USSR to the Philippines. One of the lasting consequences of the war could be what amounts to a military encirclement of China." In explanation, the London daily cites the Pentagon's *Quadrennial Defense Review* warning of the danger that "a military competitor with a formidable resource base will emerge in the region." The journal recommended a US policy that "places a premium on securing additional access and infrastructure agreements."[15] The expansion of the misnamed "war on terror" is thus specifically tailored to target regions of strategic and economic interest to the United States and thus to consolidate unrivaled US hegemony in these regions.

The facts documented and analyzed in this study have simply not been addressed in an adequate fashion by the official inquiries. The conventional version of events officially espoused by the US state and slavishly repeated by the media and academia fails to account for or explain them. The publication of the findings of the Joint Congressional Inquiry into 9/11[16] and the Staff Statements and final report of the National Commission has only served to whitewash and ignore many of the salient anomalies discussed in this study, while avoiding the placement of blame on high-level administration policies.

Indeed, one of the notable conclusions of the report of the joint House and Senate inquiry—seconded by the 9/11 Commission—is the lack of a so-called "smoking gun," i.e. no single piece of evidence that provided advance warning of the entire 9/11 plot. The report concludes that the US intelligence community had no information indicating the "time, place and specific nature" of the 9/11 attacks. Such a conclusion, of course—parroted in greatest detail by the 9/11 Commission—is patently irrelevant, misleading, and untruthful, since the US intelligence community had received abundant and precise advance warning of the 9/11 plot from the collation of multiple credible reports. The failure to act, therefore, is all the more inexplicable, especially in consideration of the real capabilities and normal operation of the US intelligence community, which are by no means perfect, but certainly not absurdly and intrinsically incompetent.

Thus, while the Joint Inquiry and 9/11 Commission outline a number of the inexplicable occurrences of systematic unwarranted interagency short-stopping of information that should have been widely circulated; systematic and irrational reluctance to investigate obvious evidence of terrorist activity; systematic and incomprehensible lethargy on the part of the US government to pursue concrete measures to crackdown on al-Qaeda and its supporters; and so on, it makes no attempt to account for authoritative and credible evidence that such an almost endless series of failures occurred systematically *as a direct consequence of high-level US government policy, policy that has been conducted in the same manner for decades.* In the words of Judicial Watch, the Congressional inquiry "failed to hold any individuals accountable, or specifically identify any US government officials for failing to perform their duty in protecting the United States."[17] The 9/11 Commission has only served to deepen this unconscionable failure.

As we have already noted, for instance, *Jane's Intelligence Digest* reports that the so-called intelligence failure had less to do with the US intelligence community and more to do with the political decisions of successive US administrations and their impact upon the entire US national security apparatus. As "more evidence emerges about the type of intelligence which was available—and those who had access to this material, but failed to make use of it—the politicians are going to have to answer some very awkward questions," questions, it seems, that no official inquiry to date is willing to ask.[18]

US—and wider Western—government policy bears monumental responsibility for what happened on 9/11, through the implementation of policies that contributed systematically to the malfunction of the US national security apparatus, leading to multiple extraordinary failures of government agencies in flagrant violation of the duties of government office. Such state policies were pursued to protect a variety of powerful strategic and economic interests that are historically deeply entrenched in the very core structures of US/Western institutions of power.

Most commentators, including supposed critics of US policy, are content to arbitrarily dismiss any discussion of high-level US government policy vis-à-vis 9/11 as irrelevant, or even overtly "conspiratorial." This idea is simply not warranted, and merely deflects public attention from facts that fundamentally challenge vacuous governmental justifications for negligent, irrational, self-interested, and ultimately disastrous policies. As this study demonstrates, the facts on record are far too important in their implications to be dismissed by anyone who is serious about understanding the events of 9/11. The facts on record strongly suggest that the US government could easily have averted the 9/11 attacks and other terrorist attacks. It only failed to do so because it systematically and recklessly neglected to fulfill its most important official duties.

A Web of Terror

Although the conventional discourse posits the Western fight against terrorism as a fundamental geopolitical and geostrategic framework defining the broad trajectory of Western foreign policy and international relations throughout the post-Cold War period, it is clear that this discourse is fatally incoherent. In fact, Western intelligence agencies have both maintained connections with and actively/tacitly supported al-Qaeda throughout the post-Cold War period, in the following diverse countries across the globe: Bosnia, Kosovo, Macedonia, Chechnya, Algeria, Libya, Egypt, Saudi Arabia, Pakistan, Afghanistan, and the Philippines. These countries span several key regions: the Balkans, the Caucasus, North Africa, the Middle East, Central Asia, and the Asia-Pacific, all of which are strategically connected to the Eurasian continent—the latter being at once a depository of vast economic resources and a lever of global pre-eminence.

Essentially the same pattern of intersecting relationships surfaces consistently: a domestic terrorist group is financially and militarily interpenetrated with Osama bin Laden's al-Qaeda; the domestic terrorist group is financially and militarily interpenetrated with state government, military, and intelligence agencies; the state is heavily financially and militarily sponsored by Western governments who maintain extremely close interpenetrative financial, military, and intelligence ties to these states. This interlocking web of connections between the West and al-Qaeda systematically repeats itself across the globe in the five key regions described above. In most cases, regional states constitute a focal point or nexus through which various forms of concrete Western assistance connect to al-Qaeda. These states and regions, therefore, effectively constitute central conduits for the covert Western sponsorship of terrorism.

This situation has important implications for a number of misconceptions about the phenomenon of international terrorism, of which al-Qaeda is an archetypal example. Firstly, the widely held distinction between state-sponsored terrorism and international non-state terrorism, as represented in the form of al-Qaeda, is non-existent. Al-Qaeda is well and truly a state-sponsored terrorist network. Secondly, in this sense, al-Qaeda does constitute a particularly unique terrorist model, but not in the conventional sense of an international non-state network. Al-Qaeda is, in fact, sponsored by a multiplicity of states strategically connected to the Eurasian continent, all of which are closely allied to the West, which we have good reason to believe is fully aware of this sponsorship, avid denials notwithstanding. A close inspection reveals that underlying this interlocking web of international state-sponsorship of al-Qaeda are the military intelligence services of the leading Western powers, particularly (but not exclusively) the United States and United Kingdom. Thirdly, given this international web of Western–al-Qaeda connections, the supposed global conflict between us (the West), and them (the terrorists), turns out to be less of a reality and more of a convenient narrative, a façade, concealing a core system of reciprocal interests and policies binding the West to its solemn enemies. Fourthly, this means that *al-Qaeda terrorism is itself a system,* or more precisely, *an integral function of the world system under Western hegemony in the post-Cold War era.* In the words of former Secretary of State Colin Powell: "Terrorism is a part of the dark side of globalization. It is a part of doing business in the world, business we as Americans are not going to stop doing." Presumably then, terrorism is not going to go away at all, because "we" will continue doing "business."[19]

Given the consistency with which this interlocking web of effective Western–al-Qaeda collaboration has occurred throughout the post-Cold War period, as well as its prevalence across several key regions of extreme economic and strategic interest to the Western powers (and their rivals), it is hard to conclude that there is anything accidental about it. On the contrary, the sheer pervasiveness of this pattern—not to mention the alarming attributes of specific regional collaborative Western–al-Qaeda relationships—is sufficient to plausibly conclude that the Western "War on Terror" is at best fundamentally flawed and at worst completely non-existent. To the extent that Western intelligence agencies and operatives may be sincere in attempting to fight terror, clearly Western governments and policymakers have manipulated intelligence agencies and suppressed the publication of critical information in order to pursue a program of elite interests that is ultimately of systematic detriment to Western national security.

On the one hand, it seems, national security has been quite deliberately sacrificed by Western governments, especially the United States and the United Kingdom, throughout the post-Cold War period to secure not the nation but rather the interests of the corporate-military-industrial complex. On the other hand, the very national insecurity systematically generated by the same unconscionable policy is exploited as a convenient mechanism by which to consolidate the power of both the state and the corporate-military-industrial complex, and the latter's interests, under the guise of fighting the "War on Terror." The consequence is an ever-deepening vicious circle of escalating insecurity and intensifying police-state powers on a national and international scale: a guaranteed recipe for the emergence of a new form of postmodern fascism. This pattern impacted detrimentally vis-à-vis a variety of anti-Western terrorist attacks, including the 1993 World Trade Center bombing, the 1998 US embassy bombings, and the 9/11 terrorist attacks—as well as post-9/11 attacks in Spain and elsewhere.

In the final analysis, then, this study points to a host of unanswered questions and blatant anomalies that US government, military, and intelligence agencies must be forced to answer through a genuinely independent public inquiry. Moreover, it should be recognized that such an inquiry cannot be limited in its scope solely to the events of 9/11—9/11 was merely one of the latest and worst manifestations of the symbiotic financial, military, and intelligence connections between the Western powers and al-Qaeda, connections that have grown increasingly entrenched in the post-Cold War period despite their deadly ramifications for Western and non-Western citizens alike.

Our governments' actions should be transparent, justifiable, and reasonable. And in the event of a failure to meet these criteria, our governments should be accountable to their people. This accountability is a public right and an elementary aspect of democracy. Whether key Western figures and institutions have been guilty of the worst forms of negligence or the lowest forms of incompetence, the public has a right to know, and those responsible must be removed from their office and held to account. Thus, a full-scale public inquiry—or series of inquiries—endowed with legal and judicial authority entirely independent of potentially adverse government influence must be launched as soon as possible to discern and rout out this entrenched international network of corruption that systematically generates terrorism. In the absence of such an inquiry, global citizens should organize and gather together resources and experts to establish the rudimentary beginnings of a public inquiry into the global "War on Terror" and its roots—this is the least that should be done in memory of those who died on 9/11.

PART SIX
Postscript

This final section provides a brief overview of a wealth of historical documentation on the strategic pattern that has been adopted by the United States, and other powers, in relation to war and military intervention. The principal concern here is simply to examine each case in isolation, in order to discern precisely how the use of propaganda and provocation has always been integral to the domestic legitimization of an expansionist or interventionist military policy. This historical background is relevant in terms of contextualizing the "War on Terror," both before and after 9/11.

16.

TERRORISM AS
HISTORICAL GEOSTRATEGY

While many would consider the findings of this study to be contrary to the general course of US policy, there is in fact long-standing historical precedent for this policy. Indeed, it is a matter of public record that the US government and military intelligence apparatus has in the past deliberately provoked or permitted attacks on US symbols of power in order to justify US military action. As noted in detail by Canadian social philosopher Professor John McMurtry at the University of Guelph, a fellow at the Royal Society of Canada:

> Shocking attacks on symbols of American power as a pretext for aggressive war is, in fact, an old and familiar pattern of the American corporate state. Even the sacrifice of thousands of ordinary Americans is not new, although so many people have never died so very fast.... The basic point is that the U.S. "secret government" (Bill Moyers' phrase) has a very long record of contriving attacks on its symbols of power as a pretext for the declaration of wars, with an attendant corporate media frenzy focussing all public attention on the Enemy to justify the next transnational mass murder. This pattern is as old as the U.S. corporate state....
>
> Throughout there is one constant to this long record of hoodwinking the American public into bankrolling ever rising military expenditures and periodic wars for corporate treasure. This decision structure ruled before and through 9/11, and has escalated after it—to fabricate or construct shocking attacks on U.S. symbols of power to provide the pretext and the public rage to launch wars of aggression against convenient and weaker enemies by which very major and many-levelled gains are achieved for the U.S. corporate–military complex.[1]

The essential implication of McMurtry's point is as follows: The possibility that the Bush administration had ample warning of the 9/11 attacks but deliberately refused to act in order to generate a pretext for the consolidation of the US corporate–military complex should not be discounted, in light of the well-documented historical record, which illustrates that such a policy is nothing new. On the contrary, McMurtry rightly notes that it is systematic. Given that the same essential decision-making structure responsible for that history continues to exist today, it is hardly reasonable to dismiss the need to discern whether the latest terrorist atrocity against the US was not merely another element of the same underlying pattern.

Such "conspiratorial" behavior is thus a direct consequence of a wider framework of institutional dynamics. Political, social, and economic forms in the United States have frequently led to such behavior. The existence of such a systematic historical pattern is evidence of a deeply-entrenched web of institutionalized decision-making structures at the helm of the US military-intelligence community.

Indeed, there are enough other examples from the historical record, some mentioned by Professor McMurtry, demonstrating decisively that certain US decision-making structures are morally capable of generally allowing US citizens to be killed to serve geostrategic interests and specifically provoking attacks on symbols of US power to justify the projection of US military force.

A number of American researchers have attempted to explore this subject, especially radio journalist Ed Rippy and journalist Richard Sanders, whose work is drawn on here (Rippy's in particular). Citing several academic historical studies, Rippy analyzes a series of examples to uncover the pattern of how the US government has entered into wars over time. He finds that early US history is littered with examples demonstrating the formation of a particular structure of geostrategic thinking that envisaged provocation as a convenient policy tool.

The Boston Massacre

As Rippy observes, the Boston Massacre, in which British soldiers fatally shot five colonists in Boston, "was pivotal in the events leading up to the War of Independence between England and the colonies which later became the US." However, although the Boston revolutionaries under the leadership of Sam Adams described the event as a "cold-blooded slaughter of defenseless colonists revealing England as irremediably murderous and oppressive," historical data suggests that this was an overly simplistic picture. The Boston Massacre was cited by Adams as "proof that there was no alternative to war"—but such a conclusion was incorrect.[2] A Stanford University study by historian John C. Miller reveals that the incident was consciously contrived by certain individuals to generate a pretext for war:

> One morning shortly before that day [March 5, 1770], the citizens of Boston awoke to find the streets plastered with notices, signed by many of the soldiers garrisoned in the town, that the troops intended to attack the townspeople. This startling news threw the town into a ferment, for apparently few citizens doubted the genuineness of these papers. It is singular, nevertheless, that the soldiers should have given their plans away in this manner if they really contemplated an attack and that they signed their names to documents that might be used as damning evidence against

them. These notices were doubtless forgeries made by Adams and his followers and posted during the night by the "Loyal Nine" [a secret group of revolutionary ringleaders] to produce an explosion that would sweep Boston clear of redcoats; for during the Massacre trials it is significant that the prosecution did not enter them as evidence of the soldiers' guilt. The events of the night of March 5 bear out this explanation of their origin.

Public rage escalated in response to the posters, increasing the prospect of an impending clash. When a group of British guards chased away some small boys who had been pelting them with snowballs, the situation reached boiling point—the guards were soon confronted by a crowd of angry, armed thugs:

> The square before the courthouse was soon filled with a swearing, turbulent mass of men, many of whom were armed with clubs, staves, and formidable pieces of jagged ice…. These stout cudgel-boys had beaten up so many redcoats that the sentry hastily summoned the main guard, which, led by Captain Preston of the Twenty-ninth Regiment, tumbled out eagerly for a fight… pellets of ice, sticks, and cudgels flew fast…. Thus far, the soldiers had used their bayonets to keep the mob at bay and no patriot had suffered worse casualty than a smart rap on the shins. In spite of the hail of missiles the soldiers withheld their fire until the mob screamed that the "bloody-backed rascals" did not dare to shoot. The troops restrained themselves with difficulty from giving Adams's "Mohawks" a taste of powder and ball, but when one of them was knocked sprawling by a Patriot brickbat he recovered his gun and fired directly into the mob. Most of the soldiers likewise opened fire—at Captain Preston's order, many of the town's witnesses later testified—and after they had emptied their guns five civilians had been killed or mortally wounded.

It was common knowledge, however, that one of those killed "had led an army of thirty sailors armed with clubs in Cornhill [a district in Boston] on the night of March 5 and… it was chiefly his violent assault upon the troops that had caused bloodshed."[3] Perhaps most significant is the fact recorded by Miller that even

> John Adams was convinced that the Massacre was an 'explosion which had been intentionally wrought up by designing men, who knew what they were aiming at better than the instruments employed'…
>
> Evidence was brought out at the trial which raised serious doubt in New England whether the Boston Massacre had not been precipitated by Sam Adams and the Sons of Liberty in a desperate effort to turn the troops out of the metropolis. Thirty-eight witnesses testified that there had been a civilian plot to attack the soldiers, and the defense put forward evidence proving the townspeople were the aggressors….
>
> Presiding Judge Lynde told the jury, "I feel myself deeply affected…

that this affair turns out so much to the disgrace of every person concerned against him [Preston], and so much to the shame of the town in general." Preston was promptly acquitted on the ground that there was not sufficient evidence that he had given the order to fire. Of the soldiers who had fired upon the mob, only two were found guilty of manslaughter, and their punishment was mitigated to burning on the hand....

Although a Commissioner of Customs had been accused of firing on the crowd from the customhouse windows, all the Commissioners could prove they were miles away at the time, and the defense exposed the patriots' star witness to the alleged plot to murder civilians as a perjurer "whose falsehood had been encouraged by divers high Whigs...."

...On his deathbed, one of the victims confessed "that the townspeople had been the aggressors and that the soldiers had fired in self-defense."... Like other Whig leaders after the Boston Massacre, Sam Adams painted war as glorious and fostered those "generous and manly Sentiments, which usually attend a true military Spirit." He was overjoyed to see how eagerly New Englanders cleaned their muskets and drilled in militia companies to prepare for the day when they should be compelled to fight for their liberties. Boston led the movement to build up a militia capable of holding its own against British regulars, and plans were laid to give the next army of British "invaders" a warm reception.[4]

Thus, Miller showed how the Boston Massacre was produced by provocation and exploited to legitimize the build-up to war.

The Mexican–American War

Similarly, the 1846 annexation of Mexico by the United States was only able to proceed after the manufacture of a pretext. Despite intensive lobbying for a US war with Mexico by Texans, Northerners disagreed with the idea and actively opposed it. But carefully planned US policies had provoked Mexico into aggressive action, thus tipping the balance in favor of a war. Thirteen-year CIA veteran John Stockwell recalls how

> ... they offered two dollars-a-head to every soldier who would enlist. They didn't get enough takers, so they offered 100 acres to anyone who would be a veteran of that war. They still didn't get enough takers, so [Gen.] Zachary Taylor was sent down to parade up and down the border—the disputed border—until the Mexicans fired on him... and the nation rose up, and we fought the war.[5]

As noted by the Washington, DC-based White House Historical Association, President Polk had intended from the outset to go to war, hoping that a pretext would be provided by a Mexican attack—but he was even willing to wage war without a pretext:

Polk sent General Zachary Taylor and 3,500 men down to the Rio Grande River. On May 8, 1846, Polk met with his Cabinet at the White House and told them that if the Mexican army attacked the U.S. forces, he was going to send a message to Congress asking for a declaration of war. It was decided that war should be declared in three days even if there was no attack. When Polk went downstairs, members of Congress were waiting. They told the president the news that fighting had begun between Mexico and the United States. Polk closed the doors of the White House and carefully wrote his war message. It was delivered to Congress on May 11 and two days later Congress declared war against Mexico. As soldiers headed south, some stopped at the White House, where Polk greeted them and wished them luck. Eventually, the United States would add Texas, New Mexico and California as a result of the Mexican War.[6]

In an exhibit for the Texas-based Brazoria County Historical Museum, US historian Dr. Betsy Powers—drawing from her University of Houston doctoral dissertation—argued that Mexico had

> warned the United States that annexation of Texas would be seen as a declaration of war and did indeed, issue that declaration when Texas was annexed in 1845. Mexico did not, however, provoke war. The United States did...
>
> Now in the most aggressively expansionist phase of its history—commonly known as the period of "Manifest Destiny"—the United States fully intended to secure the region between the Nueces and Rio Grande for itself. It did not intend to stop there. President Polk and the Democratic Party had designs on Mexican territory all the way to the Pacific. Frustrated in his efforts to purchase Mexican territory, Polk dispatched General Zachary Taylor and US Army troops to the Rio Grande. When informed of a skirmish between US and Mexican forces on the northern bank of the Rio Grande—Polk sent a message to Congress that "Mexico has passed the boundary of the United States and shed American blood on American soil." Congress declared war against Mexico....
>
> Northern opposition leaders denounced the war as an immoral land grab against a weak neighbor. The critics claimed that President Polk deliberately provoked Mexico into war by ordering American troops into disputed territory. They also argued that the conflict was an expansionist plan by southern slave owners intent on acquiring more land for cotton cultivation and more slave states.[7]

Remember the Maine

The sinking of the Maine provides another example of this pattern. The Spanish–American War was sparked when the US military stationed a navy vessel, the Maine, in Havana harbor. The Maine exploded, resulting in the deaths of 266 crew members. The incident was blamed on Spain, generating a pretext for military action resulting in the expansion of the US empire. "Although the US government was negotiating for a settlement, the sinking of the Maine in Havana Harbor led to an outcry which swept the nation to war."[8] Historian Jerald A. Combs records that

> Although some of the more lurid newspapers and excitable politicians of the time implied that the Spanish had sunk the Maine, neither the naval board [which believed that the explosion had an external not an internal cause] nor most American leaders accused the Spanish of deliberate sabotage. Yet Spain was responsible for the safety of ships in its harbors, and the Maine incident convinced almost all Americans of Spain's impotence to control the colony over which it claimed sovereignty.[9]

The Spanish–American War included an attack on the fleet at the Spanish naval base in the Philippines, ultimately leading to US occupation of the islands. Combs refers to the work of another historian, Philip S. Foner, who concluded that the entire purpose of the war was to expand the empire, with the Maine being sent to Spanish waters as a deliberate provocation toward this end:

> Using Cuban documents… Foner claimed that the rebels had actually opposed American intervention and had wanted only arms and munitions. McKinley intervened not to help them, but to expand the American empire. Thus, Foner said, McKinley had purposely omitted a demand for Cuban independence in his ultimatum, refused to recognize the rebel government, and meant from the outset to use the war to take the Philippines. He intended his delays merely to provide time for military preparations. When he was ready, he sent the Maine to Havana to create an incident that would justify war.[10]

As noted by historian Patrick McSherry, the weight of the evidence suggests that if the ship was destroyed by an external source such as a mine, it was most plausibly planted by Cuban revolutionaries who "were supported and supplied by the Americans. Arms and equipment were run through the Spanish blockade into Cuba by independent parties, unmolested by the US government. Basically, it was a covert operation by pro-Cuban groups in the US."[11] However, it should be noted that, as *Smithsonian* magazine records, a 1976 expert inquiry concluded that the explosion came from within the vessel:

> The American press was quick to point to an external explosion—a mine or torpedo—as the cause of the tragedy. An official US investigation agreed. On April 25, 1898, Congress formally declared war on Spain. By summer's end, Spain had ceded Cuba, along with the Philippines, Puerto

Rico and Guam, to the United States. In 1976, Adm. Hyman Rickover of the US Navy mounted yet another investigation into the cause of the Maine disaster. His team of experts found that the ship's demise was self-inflicted—likely the result of a coal bunker fire.[12]

In other words, whether the explosion was external or internal, there was never any evidence of Spanish responsibility for the blast—but that did not stop the Maine incident from being exploited to seal public support for war.

The Sinking of the Lusitania

Even with the sinking of the Lusitania, which was instrumental in turning the tide toward US entry into the First World War, there is evidence of a degree of executive connivance in the atrocity. On May 7, 1915, a German submarine (U-boat) fired upon a British passenger ship, the Lusitania, killing 1,198 civilians—including 128 Americans. Rippy notes that: "It was clear that the liner might be a target and that President Wilson [nevertheless] dissuaded Congress from officially warning US citizens from traveling aboard British ships. Although the US did not immediately enter the war, the sinking of the Lusitania turned the tide."[13]

The US government's decision to avoid protecting its own citizens was the final step in a process that had been largely inspired by the United Kingdom. Prime Minister Winston Churchill had previously commissioned "a study to determine the political impact if an ocean liner were sunk with Americans on board."[14] Only a week before the Lusitania was sunk, he wrote to the President of the Board of Trade that: "[It is] most important to attract neutral shipping to our shores, in the hopes especially of embroiling the US with Germany." Ralph Raico, professor of history at Buffalo State College, further observes that: "Many highly-placed persons in Britain and America believed that the German sinking of the Lusitania would bring the United States into the war."[15] Raico also cites the work of historian Patrick Beesly in *Room 40: British Naval Intelligence, 1914–18*:

> The most recent student of the subject is Patrick Beesly, whose *Room 40* is a history of British Naval Intelligence in World War I. Beesly's careful account is all the more persuasive for going against the grain of his own sentiments. He points out that the British Admiralty was aware that German U-boat Command had informed U-boat captains at sea of the sailings of the Lusitania, and that the U-boat responsible for the sinking of two ships in recent days was present in the vicinity of Queenstown, off the southern coast of Ireland, in the path the Lusitania was scheduled to take. There is no surviving record of any specific warning to the Lusitania. No destroyer escort was sent to accompany the ship to port, nor were any of the readily available destroyers instructed to hunt for the submarine. In fact,

"no effective steps were taken to protect the Lusitania." Beesly concludes: "… unless and until fresh information comes to light, I am reluctantly driven to the conclusion that there was a conspiracy deliberately to put the Lusitania at risk in the hope that even an abortive attack on her would bring the United States into the war. Such a conspiracy could not have been put into effect without Winston Churchill's express permission and approval."[16]

In this case, then, both the American and British governments cooperated to allow a catastrophe to occur, killing and injuring US citizens, with the specific goal of pulling the US into the conflict.

Pearl Harbor

Another outstanding example is Pearl Harbor. "There is no reasonable doubt that the Japanese attack on Pearl Harbor in 1941 was deliberately provoked and allowed to happen in order to generate US public support for entry into World War II," observes Rippy. "There is no conclusive proof that President Roosevelt knew or approved of this plan, although there is proof that his top naval advisors did, and plenty of evidence which is difficult to interpret in any way other than that FDR did too."[17] The History Channel recently aired a BBC-produced documentary, *Betrayal at Pearl Harbor*, which demonstrated—using declassified top secret US documents and other historical records—that President Franklin Roosevelt and his chief military advisers anticipated a Japanese surprise attack on the US.[18]

Detailed documentation has been provided by Robert Stinnett in his authoritative study, *Day of Deceit: The Truth About FDR and Pearl Harbor*. Stinnett served in the US Navy from 1942–46 where he earned 10 battle stars and a Presidential Unit Citation. Examining recently declassified US documents, he concludes that far more than merely knowing of the Japanese plan to bomb Pearl Harbor, Roosevelt deliberately steered Japan into war with America. Stinnet's work is based on 17 years of archival research along with interviews with US Navy cryptographers, gathering a total of over 200,000 documents and interviews.[19]

By the summer of 1940, although Roosevelt's advisors had concluded that a German victory over England would threaten the United States, Canada, and much of South America, polls showed that "a majority of Americans did not want the country involved in Europe's wars."[20] Many sources indicate that Roosevelt wanted to transform public opinion in favor of entry into the Second World War. According to T. North Whitehead, British Prime Minister Winston Churchill's advisor on US affairs, writing in the late 1940s: "America is not in the bag. However, the President is engaged in carefully calculated steps to give us full assistance."[21] Then Commander in Chief of the US Fleet

Admiral James O. Richardson, after an extensive discussion with Roosevelt in the Oval Office, later quoted him as saying that "sooner or later the Japanese would commit an overt act against the Unites States and the nation would be willing to enter the war."[22]

Stinnet further summarizes his case as follows:

> Lieutenant Commander Arthur McCollum, a US Naval officer in the Office of Naval Intelligence, saw an opportunity to counter the US anti-war movement by provoking Japan into a state of war with the US, and triggering the mutual assistance provisions of the Tripartite Pact. Memorialized in a secret memo dated October 7, 1940, McCollum's proposal called for eight provocations aimed at Japan. President Roosevelt acted swiftly, and throughout 1941, implemented the remaining seven provocations. The island nation's militarists used the provocations to seize control of Japan and organize their military forces for war against the US, Great Britain, and the Netherlands. During the next 11 months, the White House followed the Japanese war plans through the intercepted and decoded diplomatic and military communications intelligence. At least 1,000 Japanese radio messages per day were intercepted by monitoring stations operated by the US and her Allies, and the message contents were summarized for the White House. The intercept summaries from Station CAST on Corregidor Island were current—contrary to the assertions of some who claim that the messages were not decoded and translated until years later—and they were clear: Pearl Harbor would be attacked on December 7, 1941, by Japanese forces advancing through the Central and North Pacific Oceans.[23]

Lieutenant Commander Arthur H. McCollum was head of the Far East desk of the Office of Naval Intelligence (ONI) and also one of the nation's top experts on Japan. He prepared his eight-step plan for provoking war with Japan in a memo for two of Roosevelt's most trusted military advisors, reading as follows:

> A. Make an arrangement with Britain for the use of British bases in the Pacific, particularly Singapore.
> B. Make an arrangement with Holland for use of base facilities and acquisition of supplies in the Dutch East Indies [now Indonesia].
> C. Give all possible aid to the Chinese government of Chiang Kai-shek.
> D. Send a division of long-range heavy cruisers to the Orient, Philippines, or Singapore.
> E. Send two divisions of submarines to the Orient.
> F. Keep the main strength of the US Fleet, now in the Pacific, in the vicinity of the Hawaiian Islands.
> G. Insist that the Dutch refuse to grant Japanese demands for undue economic concessions, particularly oil.

H. Completely embargo all trade with Japan, in collaboration with a similar embargo imposed by the British Empire.[24]

Captain Dudley Knox, chief of the ONI library, also received the memo, forwarding it to Captain Walter Anderson, director of ONI, with the comment to McCollum: "I concur in your courses of action."[25] It is a matter of historical record, well documented by Stinnet, that almost every detail of these steps was subsequently carried out by the Roosevelt administration.

The case has also been put well from another perspective by Daryl S. Borgquist, a US Naval Reserve public affairs officer and a media affairs officer for the community relations service headquarters at the Justice Department:

> President Franklin D. Roosevelt requested the national office of the American Red Cross to send medical supplies secretly to Pearl Harbor in advance of the 7 December 1941 Japanese attack.... Don C. Smith, who directed the War Service for the Red Cross before World War II and was deputy administrator of services to the armed forces from 1942 to 1946, when he became administrator, apparently knew about the timing of the Pearl Harbor attack in advance. Unfortunately, Smith died in 1990 at age 98. But when his daughter, Helen E. Hamman, saw news coverage of efforts by the families of Husband Kimmel and Walter Short to restore the two Pearl Harbor commanders posthumously to what the families contend to be their deserved ranks, she wrote a letter to President Bill Clinton on 5 September 1995. Recalling a conversation with her father, Hamman wrote:
>
> > ... Shortly before the attack in 1941 President Roosevelt called him [Smith] to the White House for a meeting concerning a Top Secret matter. At this meeting the President advised my father that his intelligence staff had informed him of a pending attack on Pearl Harbor, by the Japanese. He anticipated many casualties and much loss, he instructed my father to send workers and supplies to a holding area at a P.O.E. [port of entry] on the West Coast where they would await further orders to ship out, no destination was to be revealed. He left no doubt in my father's mind that none of the Naval and Military officials in Hawaii were to be informed and he was not to advise the Red Cross officers who were already stationed in the area. When he protested to the President, President Roosevelt told him that the American people would never agree to enter the war in Europe unless they were attack [sic] within their own borders....
> >
> > He [Smith] was privy to Top Secret operations and worked directly with all of our outstanding leaders. He followed the orders of his President and spent many later years contemplating this action which he considered ethically and morally wrong. I do not

know the Kimmel family, therefore would gain nothing by fabricating this situation, however, I do feel the time has come for this conspiracy to be exposed and Admiral Kimmel be vindicated of all charges. In this manner perhaps both he and my father may rest in peace.

In a detailed historical account published by the respected *Naval History* journal of the US Naval Institute, Borgquist documents the US government's foreknowledge and provocation of Japan's attack on Pearl Harbor through analysis of the relationship between the government and the Red Cross alone.[26]

Operation Northwoods

The last example discussed here is Operation Northwoods. Declassified secret documents reveal that top levels of the US military proposed carrying out acts of terrorism within US cities in the early 1960s in order to drag the United States into a war against Cuba. These revelations have been extensively documented in a study by US national security expert James Bamford, a former investigative reporter for ABC News. In his book, *Body of Secrets: Anatomy of the Ultra-Secret National Security Agency*, Bamford records that the Joint Chiefs of Staff "proposed launching a secret and bloody war of terrorism against their own country in order to trick the American public into supporting an ill-conceived war they intended to launch against Cuba.... [T]he Joint Chiefs of Staff drew up and approved plans for what may be the most corrupt plan ever created by the US government." This account is based on documents that were ordered declassified by the Assassination Records Review Board, and subsequently released by the National Archives within the past few years.

The terrorism plan, called Operation Northwoods, is laid out in documents signed by the five Joint Chiefs but never carried out. Citing a White House document, Bamford notes that the idea of creating a pretext for the invasion of Cuba appears to have begun with President Dwight D. Eisenhower in the last weeks of his administration. The plans were drawn up after President John F. Kennedy had shifted responsibility for dealing with Cuba, in late 1961, from the CIA to the Department of Defense (DoD), in the aftermath of the Bay of Pigs. The overall Pentagon project was known as Operation Mongoose, and was the responsibility of Edward Lansdale, deputy director of the Pentagon's Office of Special Operations, and the Chairman of the Joint Chiefs of Staff US Army General Lyman Lemnitzer.

Gen. Lyman L. Lemnitzer presented the Operation Northwoods plan to Kennedy early in 1962. Bamford records that the President rejected the plan that March because he wanted no overt US military action against Cuba. Lemnitzer then sought unsuccessfully to destroy all evidence of the plan. US military planners under Lemnitzer's leadership had aimed to launch a full-scale invasion of Cuba to overthrow Castro. The planning culminated in a series of memoranda and recommendations addressed in their final form from Lemnitzer to then Secretary of Defense Robert McNamara on March 13, 1962. It is, however, not certain that McNamara ever received them, since he now denies any knowledge of the plan.

Lemnitzer's covering memorandum states that the Joint Chiefs of Staff "have considered" an attached memorandum constituting a "description of pretexts which would provide justification for military intervention in Cuba." The attached memorandum, entitled "Justification for US Military Intervention in Cuba," asserts that a political decision for a US military intervention "will result from a period of heightened US–Cuban tensions which place the United States in the position of suffering justifiable grievances." World opinion and the United Nations "should be favorably affected by developing the image of the Cuban government as rash and irresponsible, and as an alarming and unpredictable threat to the peace of the Western Hemisphere."

"We could develop a Communist Cuban terror campaign in the Miami area, in other Florida cities and even in Washington," said one document prepared by the Joint Chiefs of Staff. "We could blow up a US ship in Guantanamo Bay and blame Cuba," it continues. "Casualty lists in US newspapers would cause a helpful wave of indignation." Other measures were also recommended: "Exploding a few plastic bombs in carefully chosen spots, the arrests of Cuban agents and the release of prepared documents also would be helpful.... We could sink a boatload of Cubans en route to Florida (real or simulated).... We could foster attempts on lives of Cubans in the United States, even to the extent of wounding in instances to be widely publicized." Other proposals included the idea of using fake Soviet MiG aircraft to harass civil aircraft, to attack surface shipping, and to destroy US military drone aircraft. "Hijacking attempts against civil air and surface craft" were recommended, along with the idea of shooting down a CIA plane designed to simulate a passenger flight and announce that Cuban forces shot it down. The Northwoods plan even proposed that if the 1962 launch of astronaut John Glenn into orbit failed, resulting in his death, the US government would publicize fabricated evidence that Cuba had used electronic interference to sabotage the flight.[27]

Many analysts mistake the primary value of an analysis of the Operations Northwoods document to be that the US decision-making structure is capable of arranging the killing of its own citizens. One does not need Northwoods to know, however, that the US decision-making structure views US citizens as expendable. The willingness of the US decision-making structure to send ever larger numbers of young soldiers to their death in the Vietnam War is a single obvious illustration of that expendability. Other examples are numerous, such as how the US government has many times knowingly subjected its citizenry to a dangerous—and potentially lethal—test of biological weapons. Former US intelligence analyst at the National Security Agency Wayne Madsen asks whether "the US Government [would] knowingly subject its citizenry to a dangerous test of biological weapons." Citing biologist Malcolm Dando, professor of international security at the department of peace studies in Bradford University, Madsen reports that:

> In the 1950s, the military released uninfected female mosquitoes in a residential area of Savannah, Georgia. It then checked on how many entered houses and how many people were bitten. In 1956, 600,000 mosquitoes were released from an airplane on a bombing range. Within one day, the mosquitoes had traveled as far as two miles and had bitten a number of people. In 1957, at the Dugway Proving Grounds in Utah, the Q-Fever toxin was discharged by an airborne F-100A plane. If a more potent dose had been used, the Army concluded 99 per cent of the humans in the area would have been infected. In the 1960s, conscientious objecting Seventh Day Adventists, serving in non-combat positions in the Army, were exposed to airborne tularemia. In addition to Dando's revelations, a retired high-ranking US Army civilian official reported that the Army used aerosol forms of influenza to infect the subway systems of New York, Chicago, and Philadelphia in the early 1960s.[28]

The primary value of analyzing the plan hatched by the Joint Chiefs outlined in the Northwoods document is in providing direct proof of the US military-intelligence infrastructure's willingness to resort to the long-standing method of, in McMurtry's words, provoking or constructing "shocking attacks on US symbols of power to provide the pretext and the public rage to launch wars of aggression against convenient and weaker enemies by which very major and many-levelled gains are achieved for the US corporate-military complex."

The Gulf of Tonkin

The 1964 Gulf of Tonkin incident which occurred during the Vietnam War provides yet another illustration of the oft-used strategy. The US bombing of North Vietnam officially began in response to North Vietnamese aggression. The official story was that North Vietnamese torpedo boats had launched an "unprovoked attack" against a US destroyer on "routine patrol" in the Tonkin Gulf on August 2 and that North Vietnamese PT boats followed up with a "deliberate attack" on a pair of US ships two days later.[29] As noted by historian Professor Mark P. Bradley at the University of Wisconsin, however, the official story was a lie that generated a pretext for US expansion of the war:

> The Gulf of Tonkin, near the northern Vietnamese coast, was the site of one of the key incidents that deepened American involvement in the war in Vietnam.... In what is known as the Gulf of Tonkin Incident, the American government claimed that Vietnamese patrol boats fired on the

US destroyer Maddox... on two separate occasions in early August 1964 in the waters of the Gulf of Tonkin. Although later serious questions were raised about the nature and even the existence of one of the attacks, President Lyndon Johnson seized the opportunity to secure a Congressional resolution authorizing him to take "all necessary measures to repel any armed attacks against the forces of the United States and to prevent further aggression" in Vietnam. This authorization, often called the "Gulf of Tonkin Resolution," essentially provided the Johnson Administration with a blank check for further expansion of the war without having to seek additional Congressional approval.[30]

Indeed, as noted by investigative journalists Jeff Cohen and Normon Solomon of the New York-based media watchdog Fairness & Accuracy In Reporting (FAIR):

Rather than being on a routine patrol Aug. 2, the US destroyer Maddox was actually engaged in aggressive intelligence-gathering maneuvers—in sync with coordinated attacks on North Vietnam by the South Vietnamese navy and the Laotian air force.... "The day before, two attacks on North Vietnam... had taken place," writes scholar Daniel C. Hallin. Those assaults were "part of a campaign of increasing military pressure on the North that the United States had been pursuing since early 1964."

On the night of Aug. 4, the Pentagon proclaimed that a second attack by North Vietnamese PT boats had occurred earlier that day in the Tonkin Gulf—a report cited by President Johnson as he went on national TV that evening to announce a momentous escalation in the war: air strikes against North Vietnam. But Johnson ordered US bombers to "retaliate" for a North Vietnamese torpedo attack that never happened.

Prior to the US air strikes, top officials in Washington had reason to doubt that any Aug. 4 attack by North Vietnam had occurred.... One of the Navy pilots flying overhead that night was squadron commander James Stockdale, who gained fame later as a POW and then Ross Perot's vice presidential candidate. "I had the best seat in the house to watch that event," recalled Stockdale a few years ago, "and our destroyers were just shooting at phantom targets—there were no PT boats there.... There was nothing there but black water and American fire power." In 1965, Lyndon Johnson commented: "For all I know, our Navy was shooting at whales out there."[31]

That the Tonkin Gulf incident was a US provocation to generate a pretext to widen the Vietnam War is further confirmed by declassified official documents. Jerald Combs records that

The Pentagon Papers [a secret US government study leaked to the press by State Department consultant Daniel Ellsberg] revealed, among other things, the covert operations that had provoked the Tonkin Gulf incident and the contingency planning for bombing the North that Johnson had ordered even while he was running against Barry Goldwater in 1964 on a campaign of restraint in Vietnam.[32]

At a Washington, DC conference of American veterans, historians, and scholars sponsored by the Vietnam Veterans Institute, former Johnson administration official Ellsberg revealed that the administration had indeed lied to Congress about the incident:

> Did McNamara lie to Congress in 1964? I can answer that question. Yes, he did lie, and I knew it at the time. I was working for John McNaughton... I was his special assistant. He was Assistant Secretary of Defense for International Security Affairs. He knew McNamara had lied. McNamara knew he had lied. He is still lying. [Former Secretary of State Dean] Rusk and McNamara testified to Congress... prior to their vote... Congress was being lied into... what was to be used as a formal declaration of war. I knew that... I don't look back on that situation with pride.[33]

Other former government officials have also exposed the strategy of provocation. In a 1977 interview with the BBC, former Under Secretary of State George Ball confirmed: "Many of the people associated with the war... were looking for any excuse to initiate bombing. The DeSoto Patrols were primarily for provocation.... There was a feeling that if the destroyer got into trouble, that would provide the provocation needed."[34]

The Pattern of War

This brief review demonstrates that many of the wars in which the US has been involved have been justified on the basis of either provocations or fabrications of attacks on US symbols of power. The systematic use of this strategy when it is deemed to be effective indicates that it is, indeed, intrinsic to the structure of US decision-making institutions.

It is certainly plausible that as a consequence of this institutional dynamic, the system itself develops in a manner that is not necessarily the same as before, but institutionalizes novel and perhaps unpredictable features. On a merely theoretical basis, therefore, one cannot fully predict the future (otherwise we would all be political astrologists) or assume that events will remain stuck within a particular institutional trajectory. But there is good reason to believe that the very institutional trajectory of the US decision-making structure over history has operated in such a manner as to develop and consolidate its power in progressively new, and even worse, features than before. A close analysis of the cabinet members of the current Bush administration, for instance, discloses therein the unprecedented conjuncture of officials representing the most powerful elements of the US military, intelligence, and corporate complex. Never before has an administration been so directly wired into the ruthless US military-industrial complex.[35]

In that context, it is perfectly reasonable to consider the possibility that the 9/11 terrorist attacks were the outcome of the same sort of geostrategic thinking—rooted in long-standing political, social, and economic forms—that gave rise to previous US operations along a similar framework.

NOTES

Preface

[1] In my opinion, the only other published works of academic merit on this subject are Michel Chosudovsky's *War and Globalisation: The Truth Behind September 11*, Global Outlook, 2002, and especially David Ray Griffin's *The New Pearl Harbor: Disturbing Questions about the Bush Administration and 9/11*, Olive Branch Press, 2004. The latter is based substantially on my earlier work *The War on Freedom: How & Why America Was Attacked*, September 11, 2001, Tree of Life, Joshua Tree, CA, 2002. Published half a year after 9/11, this was the first book to comprehensively examine the inconsistencies in the official narrative.

Chapter 1: Afghanistan and "International Terrorism"

[1] Paull, Philip, *"International Terrorism": The Propaganda War*, San Francisco State University, California, June 1982 (Thesis submitted in partial fulfilment of the requirements for the degree Masters of Arts in International Relations), p. 9–10. I would like to thank the Arab American Institute for kindly sending me this thesis within a matter of days, and Roger Trilling for alerting me to it in the first place.

[2] Ibid., p. 18–20.

[3] Ibid., p. 48–52.

[4] Ibid., p. 59–91.

[5] Ibid., p. 95, 99–100.

[6] Ibid., p. 96–98.

[7] Cited in Ruth Blakely, 'Rhetoric and Reality: US Foreign Military Training Since 1945', Network of Activist Scholars of Politics and International Relations (NASPIR), www.naspir.org/members/ruth_blakeley/rhetoricandreality1.htm. viewed 19 February 2004.

[8] Paull, *"International Terrorism"*, op. cit., p. 8.

[9] Ibid., p. 9–17.

[10] Donner, Frank J., *The Age of Surveillance: The Aims and Methods of America's Political Intelligence System*, Vintage, New York, 1981, p. 455.

[11] *Newsweek*, 16 April 1979. Cited in Blum, William, *Killing Hope: US Military and CIA Interventions Since World War II*, Common Courage Press, Monroe, Maine, 1995, p. 341.

[12] *New York Times*, 13 April 1979. Cited in Blum, ibid.

[13] *Economist*, 11 September 1979. Ibid.

[14] Agence France Presse (AFP), 12 December 2000.

[15] Cited by Agence France Presse, 14 January 1998. Also see Greg Guma, 'Cracks in the Covert Iceberg,' *Toward Freedom*, May 1998, p. 2; Feinberg, Leslie, 'Brezezinski brags, blows cover: US intervened in Afghanistan first,' *Workers World*, 12 March 1998.

[16] *Le Nouvel Observateur*, 15–21 January 1998, p. 76.

[17] Cited in Blum, op. cit.

[18] Rubin, Barnett R., 'Afghanistan: The Forgotten Crisis,' Writenet (UK), Feb. 1996; Rubin, Barnett R., 'In Focus: Afghanistan,' *Foreign Policy In Focus*, Dec. 1996, Vol. 1, No. 25, www.foreignpolicy-infocus.org; Catalinotto, John, 'Afghan feudal reaction: Washington reaps what it has sown,' Workers World News Service, 3 Sept. 1998; Pentagon report, *Afghanistan: A Country Study*, 1986, cited in ibid.; Rubin, Barnett R., 'The Political Economy of War and Peace in Afghanistan,' paper presented at Afghan Support Group, Stockholm, Sweden, 21 June 1999, Institute for Afghan Studies. For more detail on the contemporary history of the crisis in Afghanistan see Roy, Oliver, *Islam and Resistance in Afghanistan*, Cambridge University Press, Cambridge, 1990; Rubin, Barnett R., *The Fragmentation of Afghanistan: State Formation and Collapse in the International System*, Yale University Press, New Haven, 1995; Rubin, *The Search for Peace in Afghanistan: From Buffer State to Failed State*, Yale University Press, New Haven, 1995. For further information online, see www.institute-for-afghan-studies.org.

[19] Ali, Nour, *US–UN Conspiracy Against the People of Afghanistan*, Online Center for Afghan Studies, now the Institute for Afghan Studies (www.institute-for-afghan-studies.org), 21 February 1998.

[20] Hiro, Dilip, 'Fallout from the Afghan Jihad,' Inter Press Services, 21 November 1995.

[21] 'From US, the ABC's Of Jihad; Violent Soviet-Era Textbooks Complicate Afghan Education Efforts', *Washington Post*, 23 March 2002.

[22] Suri, Sanjay, 'CIA worked with Pak to create the Taliban,' India Abroad News Service, 6 March 2001.

[23] Silverstein, Ken, 'Blasts From the Past,' *Salon*, 22 Sept. 2001, www.salon.com.

[24] Cooley, John K., *Unholy Wars: Afghanistan, American and International Terrorism*, Pluto Press, London, 1999, p. 117–118.

[25] Rashid, Ahmed, 'How a Holy War Against the Soviets Turned on US,' *Pittsburgh Post-Gazette*, 23 September 2001.

[26] Cooley, John K., *Unholy Wars: Afghanistan, American and International Terrorism*, op. cit., p. 120.

[27] Rashid, Ahmed, 'How a Holy War Against the Soviets Turned on US,' op. cit.

[28] Cooley, John K., *Unholy Wars: Afghanistan, American and International Terrorism*, op. cit., p. 119.

[29] Ibid., p. 222.

[30] BBC *Newsnight*, 'Has Someone Been Sitting On The FBI?', BBC 2, 6 Nov. 2001, news.bbc.co.uk/hi/english/events/newsnight/newsid_1645000/1645527.stm.

[31] Rashid, Ahmed, *Taliban: Militant Islam, Oil, and Fundamentalism in Central Asia*, Yale University Press, 2000, p. 91; Leupp, Gary, 'Meet Mr. Blowback: Gulbuddin Hekmatyar, CIA Op and Homicidal Thug', *Counterpunch*, 14 February 2003, www.counterpunch.org/leupp02142003.html.

[32] Coll, Steve, *Washington Post*, 19 July 1992. Cited in Chossudovsky, Michel, 'Who is Osama bin Laden', Centre for Research on Globalisation, Montreal, 12 September 2001, www.globalresearch.ca/articles/CHO109C.html.

[33] Banerjee, Dipankar, 'Possible Connection of ISI With Drug Industry,' *India Abroad*, 2 December 1994. Cited in Chossudovsky, 'Who is Osama', op. cit.

[34] Bedi, Rahul, 'Why? An Attempt to Explain the Unexplainable,' *Jane's Defence Weekly*, 14 September 2001. Cited in Chossudovsky, 'Who is Osama', op. cit.

[35] Labeviere, *Dollars For Terror: The United States and Islam*, Algora Publishing, New York, 2000; Weiner, David, 'Tangled History Set Up Arab "Blowback"', *Progressive Populist*, December 2002, www.populist.com/02.12.dweiner.arab.html.

[36] Labeviere, *Dollars For Terror: The United States and Islam*, Algora Publishing, New York, 2000, p. 104f.

[37] Cooley, John K., *Unholy Wars: Afghanistan, American and International Terrorism*, op. cit., p. 120.

[38] Rashid, Ahmed, 'How a Holy War Against the Soviets Turned on US,' op. cit.

[39] Posner, Gerald, *Why America Slept: The Failure to Prevent 9/11*, Random House, New York, 2003, p. 40–42. Also see Thompson, Paul, *Update [Complete 911 Timeline]*, Center for Cooperative Research, 8 April 2004, (sections December 1991, April 1991) www.cooperativeresearch.org/timeline/updates/update19.html.

[40] Rubin, Barnett, 'In Focus: Afghanistan,' *Foreign Policy In Focus*, Vol. 1, No. 25., December 1996.

[41] Human Rights Watch, New York, December 1992; *Economist*, 24 July 1993.

[42] Fisk, Robert, 'Just Who Are Our Allies in Afghanistan?', *Independent*, 3 October 2001.

[43] Fisk, Robert, 'What Will the Northern Alliance Do in Our Name Now?', *Independent*, 14 November 2001.

[44] HRW Backgrounder, 'Afghanistan: Poor Rights Record of Opposition Commanders,' Human Rights Watch, New York, 6 October 2001, www.hrw.org/press/2001/10/afghan1005.htm. Also see HRW Backgrounder, 'Military Assistance to the Afghan Opposition,' Human Rights Watch, October 2001, www.hrw.org/backgrounder/asia/afghan-bck1005.htm.

[45] Scott, Peter Dale, 'Afghanistan, Turkmenistan Oil and Gas, and the Projected Pipeline,' Online Resource on Al-Qaeda and Osama Bin Laden, 21 October 2001, socrates.berkeley.edu/~pdscott/q.html.

[46] Posner, *Why America Slept*, op. cit., p. 105–6. Thompson, *Update [Complete 911 Timeline]*, op. cit. (section June 1996).

[47] Naji, Kasra, 'UN: Taliban Forcing Thousands From Homes in Afghanistan,' CNN, 15 August 1999.

[48] Rubin, Barnett, 'In Focus: Afghanistan,' *Foreign Policy In Focus*, Vol. 1, No. 25., December 1996.

[49] Krakowski, Elie, 'The Afghan Vortex,' *IASPS Research Papers in Strategy*, Institute for Advanced Strategic and Political Studies, Jerusalem, No. 9, April 2000.

[50] AI report, *Afghanistan: Grave Abuses in the Name of Religion*, Amnesty International, London, November 1996; *Guardian*, 9 October 1996. Also see *Financial Times*, 9 October 1996.

[51] Agence France Presse, 'US Gave Silent Blessing to Taliban Rise to Power: Analysis,' 7 October 2001.

[52] AI report, *Afghanistan: Grave Abuses in the Name of Religion*, op. cit.

[53] Cited in Suri, Sanjay, 'CIA worked with Pakistan to help create Taliban,' India Abroad News Service, 6 March 2001.

[54] Cited in Rashid, Ahmed, *Taliban: Militant Islam, Oil and Fundamentalism in Central Asia*, Yale University Press, New Haven, CT., 2000, p. 166.

[55] Ibid., p. 201.

[56] Agence France-Presse, 'US Gave Silent Blessing to Taliban Rise to Power: analysis,' 7 October 2001.

[57] Beeman, William O., 'Follow the Oil Trail—Mess in Afghanistan Partly Our Government's Fault,' *Jinn* (online magazine), Pacific News Service, San Francisco, 24 August 1998, website at www.pacificnews.org/jinn. The importance of Pakistan to the US, as Brzezinski alluded to, is in its effect on neighboring countries such as Iran, Afghanistan, and India. Pakistan can play a powerful tool of the United States in this respect.

[58] Ibid.

[59] Cited in Rashid, Ahmed, *Taliban*, op. cit., p. 179.

[60] BBC News, 'Taliban in Texas for Talks on Gas Pipeline,' 4 Dec. 1997.

[61] CNN, 'US in a Diplomatic Hard Place in Dealing with Afghanistan's Taliban,' 8 October 1996.

[62] Intra Press Service (IPS), 'Politics: UN Considers Arms Embargo on Afghanistan,' IPS, 16 December 1997, website at www.oneworld.org/ips2/dec/afghan.html.

[63] Godoy, Julio, 'US Taliban Policy Influenced by Oil,' Inter Press Service, 16 November 2001.

[64] *Frankfurter Rundschau*, October 1996. Also see Catalinotto, John, 'Afghanistan: Battle Deepens for Central Asian Oil,' Workers World News Service, 24 October 1996.

[65] Goltz, Thomas, 'The Caspian Oil Sweepstakes—A Great Game Replayed,' *Jinn* (online magazine), Pacific News Service, San Francisco, 15 October 1997, www.pacificnews.org/jinn.

[66] Schurmann, Franz, 'US Changes Flow of History with New Pipeline Deal,' *Jinn* (online magazine), Pacific News Service, San Francisco, 1 August 1997, www.pacificnews.org/jinn.

[67] *Wall Street Journal*, 23 May 1997.

[68] *New York Times*, 26 May 1997.

[69] Fitchett, Joseph, 'Worries Rise that Taleban May Try to Export Unrest,' *International Herald Tribune*, 26 September 1998; also see Gall, Carlotta, 'Dagestan Skirmish is a Big Russian Risk,' *New York Times*, 13 Aug. 1999.

[70] Stobdan, P., 'The Afghan Conflict and Regional Security,' *Strategic Analysis* (journal of the Institute for Defence & Strategic Analysis [ISDA]), August 1999, Vol. XXIII, No. 5, p. 719–747.

[71] Ahmad, Ishtiaq, 'How America Courted the Taliban,' *Pakistan Observer*, 20 October 2001.

[72] 'UNOCAL Trying to Re-enter Turkmen Gas Pipeline Project', *Business Recorder*, Karachi, 24 March 2000. Available online at users.otenet.gr/a/adgeki/afg/p006.htm.

[73] Info-Prod Research [Middle East] Ltd., *Middle East News Items*, 22 November 1998.

[74] 'Enron Gave Taliban $Millions', *National Enquirer*, 4 March 2002.

[75] Press Release, 'What Congress Does Not Know About Enron,' Attorney John J. Loftus, St. Petersburg, 31 May 2002, www.john-loftus.com/enron3.htm#congress.

[76] Turnipseed, Tom, 'A Creeping Collapse in Credibility at the White House', *Counterpunch*, 10 January 2002.

[77] Statement of Congressman Dana Rohrabacher, 'US Policy Toward Afghanistan,' Senate Foreign Relations Subcommittee on South Asia, 14 April 1999. Rohrabacher includes the following reasons in his analysis:

"[1] In 1996, the Taliban first emerged as a mysterious force that swept out of so-called religious schools in Pakistan to a blitzkrieg type of conquest of most of Afghanistan against some very seasoned former-mujahideen fighters. As a so-called 'student militia,' the Taliban could not have succeeded without the support, organization and logistics of military professionals, who would not have been faculty in religious schools.

[2] The US has a very close relationship with Saudi Arabia and Pakistan, in matters concerning Afghanistan, but unfortunately, instead of providing leadership, we are letting them lead our policy. This began during the Afghan war against the Soviets. I witnessed this in the White House when US officials in charge of the military aid program to the mujahideen permitted a large percentage of our assistance to be channeled to the most anti-western non-democratic elements of the mujahideen, such as Golbodin Hekmatayar. This was done to placate the Pakistan ISI military intelligence.

[3] In 1997, responding to the pleas of the Afghan-American community and the recognized Afghanistan ambassador, I led an effort to stop the State Department from permitting the Afghanistan embassy in Washington from being taken under the control of a diplomat loyal to the Taliban. Instead of permitting a new ambassador who was assigned by the non-Taliban Afghan government that is still recognized at the United Nations, the State Department claimed 'we don't take sides,' and forced the embassy to be closed against the will of the Afghanistan United Nations office.

[4] During late 1997 and early 1998, while the Taliban imposed a blockade on more than two million people of the Hazara ethnic group in central Afghanistan, putting tens of thousands at risk of starving to death or perishing from a lack of medicine during the harsh winter months, the State Department undercut my efforts to send in two plane loads of medicines by the Americares and the Knightsbridge relief agencies. State

Department representatives made false statements that the humanitarian crisis was exaggerated and there was already sufficient medical supplies in the blockaded area. When the relief teams risked their lives to go into the area with the medicines—without the support of the State Department they found the hospitals and clinics did not have even aspirins or bandages, no generators for heat in sub-zero weather, a serious lack of blankets and scant amounts of food. The State Department, in effect, was assisting the Taliban's inhuman blockade intended to starve out communities that opposed their dictates.

[5] Perhaps the most glaring evidence of this administration's tacit support of the Taliban was the effort made during a Spring 1998 visit to Afghanistan by Mr. Inderfurth and U.N. Ambassador Bill Richardson. These administration representatives convinced the anti-Taliban Northern Alliance not to go on the offensive against a then-weakened and vulnerable Taliban. And instead convinced these anti-Taliban leaders to accept a cease-fire that was proposed by Pakistan. The cease fire lasted only as long as it took the Paks to resupply and reorganize the Taliban. In fact, within a few months of announcement of the US-backed 'Ulema' process, the Taliban, freshly supplied by the ISI and flush with drug money, went on a major offensive and destroyed the Northern Alliance. This was either incompetence on the part of the State Department and US intelligence agencies or indicative of the real policy of our government to ensure a Taliban victory.

[6] Can anyone believe that with the Taliban, identified by the United Nations and the DEA as one of the two largest producers of opium in the world, that they weren't being closely monitored by our intelligence services, who would have seen every move of the military build up that the Pakistanis and Taliban were undertaking. In addition, at the same time the US was planning its strike against the terrorist camps of Osama bin Laden in Afghanistan. How could our intelligence services not have known that Osama bin Laden's forces had moved north to lead the Taliban offensive, where horrendous brutality took place.

[7] In addition, there has been no major effort to end the flow of opium out of Afghanistan, which is the main source of the revenues that enables the Taliban to maintain control of the country, even though the US Government observes by satellite where the opium is grown."

[78] Rall, Ted, 'It's All About Oil,' *San Francisco Chronicle*, 2 November 2001.

[79] US House of Representatives, Statement by Representative Dana Rohrabacher, Hearing of the House International Relations Committee on 'Global Terrorism And South Asia,' Washington, DC, 12 July 2000.

[80] Ali, Nour, *US–UN Conspiracy Against the People of Afghanistan*, op. cit.

[81] Interview with Ahmed Rashid by Omar Samad, Azadi Afghan Radio, op. cit.

[82] Rashid, Ahmed, 'Special Report—Osama Bin Laden: How the US Helped Midwife a Terrorist,' Center for Public Integrity, Washington, DC, www.public-i.org/excerpts_01_091301.htm.

[83] Editor, 'UNOCAL & Afghanistan', *Oil & Gas International*, 29 October 2001, www.oilandgasinternational.com/departments/from_editor/10_29_01.html.[84] Starr, S. Frederick, 'Afghanistan Land Mine,' *Washington Post*, 19 December 2000.

[85] Ibid.

[86] *Toronto Sun*, 4 December 2000.

[87] Bedi, Rahul, 'India Joins Anti-Taliban Coalition,' *Jane's Intelligence Review*, 15 March 2001. The interests of India and Russia in joining the anti-Taliban policy under US leadership also mentioned in this report: "Oleg Chervov, deputy head of Russia's security council, recently described Taliban-controlled Afghanistan as a base of international terrorism attempting to expand into Central Asia. Radical Islamic groups are also trying to increase their influence across Pakistan, he said at a meeting of Indian and Russian security officials in Moscow. 'All this dictates a pressing need for close co-operation between Russia and India in opposing terrorism,' he said."

[88] 'Pipelineistan: The Rules of the Game', *Asia Times*, 25 January 2002. Available in *Alexander Oil & Gas Connections*, Vol. 7, No. 4, 21 February 2002, www.gasandoil.com/goc/features/fex20867.htm.

[89] Special Report, 'India in Anti-Taliban Military Plan,' *India Reacts*, 26 June 2001.

[90] Ahmad, Ishtiaq, 'How America Courted the Taliban,' op. cit.

[91] United Press International (UPI), 'Richardson Plans Afghan Mission', 8 April 1998.

[92] Iqbal, Anwar, 'US, Taliban Talk Frequently,' UPI, 15 August 1999.

[93] Iqbal, Anwar, 'Taliban, Foreign Allies, Foes Meet,' UPI, 4 March 2000.

[94] Godoy, Julio, 'US Taliban Policy Influenced by Oil,' op. cit.

[95] Ibid.

[96] Ibid.

[97] Leigh, David, 'Attack and Counter-attack,' *Guardian*, 26 September 2001.

[98] Steele, Jonathan, et. al., 'Threat of US Strikes Passed to Taliban Weeks Before NY Attack,' *Guardian*, 22 September 2001. The 'track two' stage of negotiations with the Taliban, reports Steele et. al., "was designed to offer a free and open-ended forum for governments to pass messages and sound out each other's thinking. Participants were experts with long diplomatic experience of the region who were no longer government officials but had close links with their governments."

[99] Arney, George, 'US "Planned Attack on Taleban",' BBC News, 18 September 2001, news.bbc.co.uk/hi/english/world/south_asia/newsid_1550000/1550366.stm.

[100] NBC News, 16 May 2002. Cited in Scott, Peter Dale, 'Bush Given Invasion Plan Two Days Before 9/11,' Online Resources on Al-Qaeda, ist socrates.berkeley.edu/~pdscott/qf911.html.

[101] Cited in Ruppert, Michael, 'A Time For Fear,' *From the Wilderness*, October 2001.

Chapter 2: Terrorism and Statecraft Part I

[1] Labeviere, Richard, *Dollars for Terror: The United States and Islam*, op. cit. See the book's Prologue at www.algora.com/Dollars_foreword.htm.

[2] Labeviere, Richard, *Dollars for Terror: The United States and Islam*, Algora Publishing, New York, 2000; AIM Report, 'Catastrophic Intelligence Failure,' op. cit.

[3] O'Neill, Brendan, 'How We Trained al-Qa'eda', *Spectator*, 13 September 2003.

[4] Aldrich, Richard J., 'America Used Islamists to Arm the Bosnian Muslims: The Srebrenica Report Reveals the Pentagon's Role in a Dirty War', *Guardian*, 22 April 2002, www.guardian.co.uk/yugo/article/0,2763,688327,00.html.

[5] Wiebes, Cees, *Intelligence and the War in Bosnia 1992–1995*, Lit Verlag, 2003, p. 159–162.

[6] Ibid., p. 167.

[7] Cited in Chossudovsky, Michel, 'Osamagate', Centre for Research on Globalisation, Montreal, 9 October 2001, www.globalresearch.ca/articles/CHO110A.html.

[8] Ibid., p. 207.

[9] Bodanksy, Yossef, *Some Call It Peace: Waiting for War in the Balkans*, International Media Corporation, London, 1996, Chapters 3 and 9. An online version is available at members.tripod.com/Balkania/resources/geostrategy/bodansky_peace.

[10] Chossudovsky, Michel, 'Osamagate,' Centre for Research on Globalisation, Montreal, 9 October 2001, globalresearch.ca/articles/CHO110A.html. Chossudovsky has taught as Visiting Professor at academic institutions in Western Europe, Latin America and Southeast Asia, has acted as economic adviser to governments of developing countries and has worked as a consultant for several international organizations, including the United Nations Development Program (UNDP), the African Development Bank, the United Nations African Institute for Economic Development and Planning (AIEDEP), the United Nations Population Fund (UNFPA), the International Labour Organization (ILO), the World Health Organization (WHO), the United Nations Economic Commission for Latin America and the Caribbean (ECLAC).

[11] International Media Corporation Defense and Strategy Policy, 'US Commits Forces, Weapons to Bosnia,' London, 31 October 1994; Cited in Chossudovksy, 'Osamagate,' op. cit.

[12] *Washington Post*, 22 Sept. 1996. Congressional Press Release, Republican Party Committee (RPC), US Congress, 'Clinton-Approved Iranian Arms Transfers Help Turn Bosnia into Militant Islamic Base,' 16 Jan. 1997, www.senate.gov/~rpc/releases/1997/iran.htm. Cited in Chossudovsky, 'Osamagate,' op. cit.

[13] Hoffman, David, *The Oklahoma City Bombing and the Politics of Terror*, Feral House, 1998, Chapter 11 'The Covert Cowboys', available online at www.constitution.org/ocbpt/ocbpt_11.htm.

[14] Weaver, Mary Anne, *Atlantic Monthly*, May 1996.

[15] Thomas, Evan, 'The Road to Sept. 11,' *Newsweek*, 1 October 2001, www.msnbc.com/news/632825.asp.

[16] Weaver, op. cit.

[17] Ibid.

[18] Associated Press, 'Alleged Terrorist Linked to CIA,' March 1995. Available online at wildcat.arizona.edu/papers/old-wildcats/spring95/March/March20,1995/06_1_m.html.

[19] Associated Press, 'Alleged Terrorist Linked to CIA,' op. cit.

[20] Grigg, William Norman, 'Behind the Terror Network,' *New American*, Vol. 17, No. 23, 5 November 2001, www.thenewamerican.com/tna/2001/11-05-2001/vo17no23_network.htm.

[21] 'Arab Veterans of Afghanistan War Lead New Islamic Holy War', *Compass*, 28 October 1994, www.fas.org/irp/news/1994/afghan_war_vetrans.html.

[22] Benjamin, Daniel and Simon, Steven, 'The New Face of Terrorism', *New York Times*, 4 January 2000.

[23] *Las Vegas Sun*, 1 August 1993. Cited in Hoffman, David, *The Oklahoma City Bombing*, op. cit.

[24] Cited in Friedman, Robert I., 'The CIA and the Sheik: The Agency Coddled Omar Abdel Rahman, Allowing Him to Operate in the US', *Village Voice*, 30 March 1993.

[25] Cited in Hoffman, op. cit.

[26] 'New York Trial in Rabbi's Death Planted an Explosive Seed', *Los Angeles Times*, 4 July 1993. Cited in Schoenman, Ralph, 'Who Bombed the US World Trade Center?—1993: Growing Evidence Points to Role of FBI Operative', *Prevailing Winds Magazine*, No. 3, 1993, www.wbaifree.org/takingaim/articles/wtc93.html.

[27] Jenkins, Brian, 'Terror Trial: Guilty on 25 Counts', CNN, 1 October 1995, edition.cnn.com/US/9510/terror_trial.

[28] Schoenman, op. cit.

[29] 'FBI Informant Recorded Agents', *Newsday*, 3 August 1993.

[30] Cited in Schoenman, op. cit.

[31] *Los Angeles Times*, 4 July 1993. Schoenman, op. cit.

[32] DeRienzo, Paul, Transcript of interview with William Kunstler about role of Emad Salem in the World Trade Center bombing trial, WBAI 3 August 1993, pdr.autono.net/kunstler_wtc.html.

[33] DiRienzo, Paul, et. al., 'Who Bombed the World Trade Center? FBI Bomb Builders Exposed', *The Shadow*, October 1994/January 1995, pdr.autono.net/WhoBombedWTC.html.

[34] Blumenthal, Ralph, 'Tapes Depict Proposal to Thwart Bomb Used in Trade Center Blast', *New York Times*, 28 October 1993, p. A1.

[35] Hoffman, op. cit.

[36] O'Neill, Brendan, op. cit.

[37] Craig, Larry E., *The Kosovo Liberation Army: Does Clinton Policy Support Group with Terror, Drug Ties?: From 'Terrorists' to 'Partners'*, United States Senate Republican Policy Committee, Washington, DC, 31 March 1999, www.fas.org/irp/world/para/docs/fr033199.htm.

[38] Bisset, James, 'War on Terrorism Skipped the KLA', *National Post*, 13 November 2001, available online at www.deltax.net/bissett/a-terrorism.htm.

[39] Seper, Jerry, 'KLA Rebels Train in Terrorist Camps', *Washington Times*, 4 May 1999.

[40] Grigg, William Norman, 'Behind the Terror Network,' *New American*, 5 November 2001, Vol. 17, No. 23, www.thenewamerican.com/tna/2001/11-05-2001/vol7no23.htm.

[41] *Sunday Times*, 12 March 2000.

[42] *The Herald*, 27 March 2000.

[43] Grigg, 'Behind the Terror Network,' op. cit.

[44] BBC News, 'Kostunica Warns of Fresh Fighting', 29 January 2001, news.bbc.co.uk/1/hi/world/europe/1142478.stm. Also see Beaumont, Peter, et. al., 'CIA's Bastard Army Ran Riot in Balkans, Backed Extremists', *Observer*, 11 March 2001, observer.guardian.co.uk/international/story/0,6903,449923,00.html.

[45] Bisset, James, op. cit.

[46] Taylor, Scott, 'Macedonia's Civil War: "Made in the USA"', AntiWar.com, Randolph Bourne Institute, 20 August 2001, www.antiwar.com/orig/taylor1.html.

[47] Szamuely, George, 'Happy Days, Here Again', *New York Press*, Vol. 15, No. 6, 6–12 February 2002, www.nypress.com/15/6/taki/bunker.cfm.

[48] Deliso, Christopher, 'European Intelligence: The US Betrayed Us in Macedonia', AntiWar.com, Randolph Bourne Institute, 22 June 2002, www.antiwar.com/orig/deliso46.html.

[49] Dettmer, Jamie, 'Al-Qaeda's Links in the Balkans', *Insight on the News*, 1 July 2002.

[50] Ibid.

[51] Taylor, Scott, 'Signs Point to a bin Laden-Balkan Link', *Halifax Herald*, 29 October 2001, www.balkanpeace.org/hed/archive/oct01/hed4292.shtml. .

[52] Cited in CPB Report, 'Bin Laden's Balkan Connection', Centre for Peace in the Balkans, Toronto, September 2001, www.balkanpeace.org/our/our09.shtml.

[53] *Neue Zürcher Zeitung*, 25 October 2001. Cited in Pascali, see note 91.

[54] CPB Research Analysis, 'Balkan–Albania–Kosovo–Heroin–Jihad', Center for Peace in the Balkans, Toronto, May 2000, www.balkanpeace.org/our/our03.shtml.

[55] Cited in Pascali, Umberto, 'Bin Laden Puppet Masters Smoked Out in the Balkans', *Macedonia TV*, 9 November 2001, www.makedonija.tv/bin_laden_puppetmasters_smoked_o.htm. Pascali is a veteran journalist based in Macedonia who writes for the respected daily *Dvnenik*.

[56] Cited in Pascali, 'US Protects Al-Qaeda Terrorists in Kosovo', Centre for Research on Globalisation, Montreal, 21 November 2001, globalresearch.ca/articles/PAS111A.html.

[57] Cited in Pascali, 'Bin Laden Puppet Masters', op. cit.

[58] FBI Most Wanted Terrorists, 'Ayman al-Zawahiri' (viewed 11th June 2004), www.fbi.gov/mostwant/terrorists/teralzawahiri.htm.

[59] Foden, Giles, 'The Hunt for "Public Enemy No 2": Egyptian May Now Be Running

Terror Operations from Afghanistan', *Guardian*, 24 September 2001, www.guardian.co.uk/international/story/0,3604,556872,00.html.

[60] Ibid.

[61] Sachs, Suan, 'Egyptian Raised Terror Funds in US in 1990s', *New York Times*, 23 October 2001, p. B4. Also see Williams, Lance, 'Top bin Laden Aide Toured California', *San Francisco Chronicle*, 11 October 2001.

[62] Hays, Tom and Theimer, Sharon, 'US Relying on Double Agent for Details of Al-Qaeda,' Associated Press, 30 December 2001.

[63] 'Ali Mohamed Served In the US Army—And bin Laden's Inner Circle,' *Wall Street Journal*, 26 November 2001.

[64] Neff, Joseph and Sullivan, John, *Raleigh News & Observer*, 24 October 2001.

[65] Hays, Tom and Theimer, Sharon, 'US Relying on Double Agent for Details of Al-Qaeda,' op. cit.

[66] Neff, Joseph and Sullivan, John, 'Al-Qaeda Terrorist Duped FBI, Army', *Raleigh News & Observer*, 21 October 2001.

[67] Berger, J. M., 'The Path Not Followed', *IntelWire: Special Reports on Terrorism*, 8 October 2003, www.intelwire.com/khalifa100803.

[68] 'Security Questions at Shooting Range', *New York Times*, 5 October 2003. Weiser, Benjamin, 'US Ex-Sergeant Charged as bin Laden Accomplice', *New York Times*, 30 October 1998.

[69] Emerson, Steve, 'Abdullah Assam: The Man Before Osama Bin Laden', International Association For Counterterrorism & Security Professionals (viewed 28 June 2004), www.iacsp.com/itobli3.html.

[70] Sullivan, John and Neff, Joseph, 'An Al-Qaeda Operative in Fort Bragg', *Raleigh News & Observer*, 12 November 2001, www.knoxstudio.com/shns/story.cfm?pk=SIEGE-SPECFORCES-11-13-01&cat=AN.

[71] Turnipseed, Tom, 'A Continuum of Terror: From Mujahideen to al-Qaeda', *Counterpunch*, 28 November 2001.

[72] Kelley, Kevin J., 'US Knew About Kenyan Embassy Bombers in '96', *East African*, 1 January 2001.

[73] Mohamed stated as follows: "In 1996, I learned from el-Hage that Abu Ubaidah had drowned. In 1998, I received a letter from Ihab Ali in early January 1998. The letter said that el-Hage had been interviewed by the F.B.I. in Kenya, and gave me a contact number for el-Hage. I called the number and then called someone who would pass the message to Fawwaz for bin Laden." (ICT Report, 'Bin Laden Associate Pleads Guilty in US Court', International Policy Institute for Counter Terrorism, Herzilya, 21 October 2001, www.ict.org.il/spotlight/det.cfm?id=508.)

[74] Hirschkorn, Phil, 'Embassy Bombings Jury Wraps Fourth Day of Deliberations', CNN, 15 May 2001, edition.cnn.com/2001/LAW/05/15/embassy.bombings.

[75] 'Bin Laden Had US Terror Cell for a Decade', *Sunday Times*, 11 November 2001.

76 Bodansky, Yossef, 'US Trade: Mubarak for S-For Safety?', *Defense and Foreign Affairs Strategic Policy*, January 1998. Available online as Bodansky, 'The Price of Washington's Bosnia Policy', Freeman Center for Strategic Studies, Houston, February 1998, www.freeman.org/m_online/feb98/bodansky.htm.

77 Egyptian reports cited in Pascali, 'Bin Laden Puppet Masters', op. cit.

78 Bodansky, 'US Trade', op. cit. [emphasis added]

79 Dyson, Mark and Lehrer, Jim, 'Terrorist Attack', PBS *Newshour* Transcript, 17 November 1997, www.pbs.org/newshour/bb/middle_east/july-dec97/egypt_11-17.html.

80 Bodansky, Yossef, *Bin Laden: The Man Who Declared War On America*, Prima Publishing, Roseville, CA, 1999, 2001, p. 213.

81 'Report: US warned of embassy bombing plot', *USA Today*, 1999, www.usatoday.com/news/world/bomb152.htm.

82 PBS Hunting Bin Laden, 'Warnings to the FBI: Could the Bombings Have Been Prevented?', April 1999 [updated September 2001], www.pbs.org/wgbh/pages/frontline/shows/binladen/bombings/warnings.html. Risen, James and Weiser, Benjamin, 'Before Bombings, Omens and Fears', *New York Times*, 9 January 1999, partners.nytimes.com/library/world/africa/010999africa-bomb.html.

83 Risen and Weiser, 'Before Bombings', op. cit.

84 Ibid.

85 Ibid.

86 Hirschkorn, Phil, 'Embassy bombings jury', op. cit. Hirschkorn, 'Defense Attorney Wants to Put America on Trial', CNN, 2 April 2001, edition.cnn.com/LAW/trials.and.cases/case.files/0012/embassy.bombing/trial.report/trial.report.04.02/index.html. Although presiding Judge Sand rightly rejected the argument as essentially morally irrelevant to the case—which was concerned with the role of the four conspirators—the argument itself is sound and well-documented.

87 Waller, Douglas, 'Was Hijack "Ringleader" in Bin Laden Orbit?', *Time*, 5 October 2001, www.time.com/time/nation/article/0,8599,178228,00.html.

Chapter 3: Terrorism and Statecraft Part II

1 Damrel, David, 'The Religious Roots of Conflict: Russia and Chechnya', *Religious Studies News*, Vol. 10, No. 3, September 1995. Masud, Enver, 'America's Disgraceful Silence Over Chechnya', The Wisdom Fund, Arlington, 28 September 1999, www.twf.org.

2 Margolis, Eric, 'US Aids Russia's Crimes in the Caucasus', *Toronto Sun*, 12 October 1999. For a short review of Russia's war-crimes in the first 1990 war on Chechnya see AI Report, *Brief Summary of Concerns About Human Rghts Violations in the Chechen Republic*, Amnesty International, London, April 1996.

3 Margolis, Eric, 'US Aids Russia's Crimes in the Caucasus', *Toronto Sun*, 12 October 1999.

4 *Economist*, 8 January 2000.

[5] Womack, Helen, 'Russian Agents "Blew Up Moscow Flats"', *Independent*, 6 January 2000.

[6] Dispatches, *Dying for the President*, Channel 4 [British television], 9 March 2000.

[7] Sweeney, John, 'Take Care Tony, That Man Has Blood on His Hands', *Observer*, 12 March 2000.

[8] Cited in Grigg, William Norman, 'Putin: Prophet or Provocateur?', *New American*, Vol. 18, No. 7, 8 April 2002, www.thenewamerican.com/tna/2002/04-08-2002/vo18no07_putin.htm.

[9] Cockburn, Patrick, 'Russia "Planned Chechen War Before Bombings"', *Independent*, 29 January 2000.

[10] Ibid.

[11] Ibid.

[12] Ibid.

[13] Nyquist, J. R., 'The Chechen War and Bin Laden's Nukes', Geopolitical Global Analysis, *Financial Sense*, 9 July 2002, www.financialsense.com/stormwatch/geo/pastanalysis/2002/0709.htm.

[14] Riebling, Mark and Eddy, R. P., 'Jihad@Work', *National Review*, 24 October 2002, www.nationalreview.com/comment/comment-riebling102402.asp.

[15] LaFreniere, Sharon, 'How Jihad Made Its Way To Chechnya', *Washington Post Foreign Service*, 26 April 2003, p. A01, www.washingtonpost.com/ac2/wp-dyn?pagename=article&node=&contentId=A39482-2003Apr25&notFound=true.

[16] Erikson, Mark, 'Bin Laden's Terror Wave 2', *Asia Times*, 29 October 2002, www.atimes.com/atimes/Central_Asia/DJ29Ag05.html.

[17] Montgomery, Dave, 'Bin Laden Helped Bankroll Dagestan War, Experts Say', *San Jose Mercury News*, 10 September 1999.

[18] Bodansky, Yossef, 'The Great Game for Oil', *Defense & Foreign Affairs Strategic Policy*, June/July 2000.

[19] 'US Confirms Meeting Between US, Chechen officials', *People's Daily* (Beijing), 25 January 2002, english1.peopledaily.com.cn/200201/25/eng20020125_89317.shtml.

[20] Press Release, 'On the Meeting of a US State Department Official with Ilyas Akhmadov', Ministry of Foreign Affairs of the Russian Federation, 24 January 2002, www.ln.mid.ru/BRP_4.NSF/0/acbefd4917cedad943256b4c004647e2?OpenDocument.

[21] Amirouche, Hamou, 'Algeria's Islamist Revolution: The People Versus Democracy?', *Middle East Policy*, Vol. V, No. 4, January 1998.

[22] Addi, Lahouari, 'Algeria's Tragic Contradictions', *Journal of Democracy*, 7.3, 1996, 94–107.

[23] Lombardi, Ben, 'Turkey: The Return of the Reluctant Generals', *Political Science Quarterly*, Vol. 112, No. 2, Summer 1997.

[24] Entelis, John P., *Democracy Denied: America's Authoritarian Approach Towards the*

Maghreb—Causes & Consequences, XVIIIth World Congress of the International Political Science Association, Quebec, 1–5 August 2000.

[25] Kjeilen, Tore, 'GIA', *Encyclopedia of the Orient*, 1996–2004, i-cias.com/e.o/gia.htm.

[26] Boudjemaa, M., 'Terrorism in Algeria: Ten Years of Day-to-Day Genocide' in Cilliers, Jakkie and Sturman, Kathryn (ed.), *Africa and Terrorism: Joining the Global Campaign*, Institute for Security Studies Monograph No. 74, Pretoria, July 2002, www.iss.co.za/PUBS/MONOGRAPHS/No74/Chap6.html.

[27] Robinson, Colin, 'Armed Islamic Group a.k.a. Groupement Islamique Arme', Center for Defense Information, Washington, DC, 5 February 2003, www.cdi.org/terrorism/gia_020503.cfm.

[28] ABC Asia Pacific, 'Cause & Effect: Terrorism in the Asia Pacific Region', 2004, abcasiapacific.com/cause/network/armed_islamic.htm.

[29] Gunaratna, Rohan and Hirschkorn, Phil, et. al., 'Blowback', *Jane's Intelligence Review*, Vol. 13, No. 8 1 August 2001.

[30] *Guardian*, 8 April 2004.

[31] 'Armed Islamic Group: Algeria, Islamists' in *Terrorism: Questions & Answers*, Council on Foreign Relations, Washington, DC, 2004, cfrterrorism.org/groups/gia.html.

[32] Cited in Hiel, Betsy, 'Algeria Valuable In Hunt For Terrorists,' *Pittsburgh Tribune-Review*, 18 November 2001.

[33] Sane, Pierre, Secretary General of Amnesty International, 'Algerians: Failed by their Government and by the International Community', Amnesty International, New York, 18 November 1997.

[34] Amirouche, Hamou, 'Algeria's Islamist Revolution: The People Versus Democracy?', *Middle East Policy*, Vol. V, No. 4, January 1998.

[35] *Paris Match*, 9 October 1997.

[36] *Independent*, 30 October 1997.

[37] *Sunday Times*, 16 July 2000.

[38] *Independent*, 30 October 1997.

[39] Sweeney, John and Dolye, Leonard, 'Algerian Regime Responsible for Massacres: Algerian Regime Was Behind Paris Bombs', *Manchester Guardian Weekly*, 16 November 1997.

[40] Chinade, M., 'Not So Secret Terrorist Junta', *Impact International*, Vol. 28, No. 2, February 1998.

[41] Television Swiss Romande (TSR), Switzerland, January 1998.

[42] Sweeney, John, 'Seven Monks Were Beheaded. Now the Whistleblower Has Paid With His Life', *Observer*, 14 June 1998.

[43] Interviewed by Yasser Za'atreh in *Palestine Times*, London, No. 72, June 1997.

[44] Simon, Daniel Ben, 'Arabs Slaughter Arabs in Algeria', *Ha'aretz*, 20 April 2001. Also

see Hadjarab, Mustapha, 'Former Officer Testifies To Army Atrocities', *Algeria Interface*, 9 February 2001. Souadia, for instance, admits accompanying commandos from the army's 'anti-terrorist' squad to Lakhdaria, an alleged rebel stronghold 50 miles from Algiers. The squad disguised themselves as bearded fundamentalists. "All the suspects of course ended up being killed. We arrested people, we tortured them, we killed them and then we burned their bodies." In that region alone, "I must have seen at least 100 people liquidated". (*Guardian*, 14 February 2001). See Souadia, Habib, *The Dirty War: The Testimony of a Former Officer of the Special Forces of the Algerian Army, 1992–2000*, La Decouverte, Paris, 2001.

[45] Cited in Italian Anti-Terrorist Judge Ferdinando Imposimato's Foreword to Souadia's book, *The Dirty War*, ibid.

[46] Review of Samraoui's book, *A Chronicle of the Years of Blood: How the Secret Services Manipulated Islamic Groups*, Denoel, 2003, in *Süddeutsche Zeitung*, 15 March 2004.

[47] Sweeney, John, 'We Accuse 80,000 Times', *Observer*, 16 November 1997.

[48] Bone, Alistair, 'The Running Man', *New Zealand Listener*, Vol. 189, No. 3301, 16–22 August 2003.

[49] Campbell, Gordon, 'The French Connection', *New Zealand Listener*, 14–20 February 2004.

[50] Sweeney, 'We Accuse 80,000 Times', op. cit.

[51] Norton-Taylor, Richard, 'Terrorist Case Collapses After Three Years', *Guardian*, 21 March 2000.

[52] Ibid.

[53] 'The Providential Fog of London', *Le Figaro*, 3 November 1995.

[54] *Le Parisien*, 4 November 1995.

[55] Ciment, James, 'The Battle of Algiers', *In These Times*, December 1997.

[56] Sweeney and Doyle, 'Algeria Regime Responsible for Massacres', op. cit.

[57] Sweeney, 'We Accuse 80,000 Times', op. cit.

[58] Fisk, Robert, 'France Supplies Covert Military Aid to Regime', *Irish Times*, 28 December 1994.

[59] Colvie, Marie, 'Britain Plans Algerian Arms Deal Despite Ethical Policy', *Sunday Times*, 16 July 2000.

[60] Reuters, 'Qatar Confirms British Arms to Go to Algeria', 19 July 2000, edition.cnn.com/2000/WORLD/meast/07/19/arms.qatar.reut.

[61] Strategic Export Controls, *Annual Report 1999*, Foreign and Commonwealth Offices, London, 2000; Strategic Export Controls, *Annual Report*, Stationary Office, London, 2001.

[62] HRW, *World Report 2000*, Human Rights Watch, New York, 2001, www.hrw.org/wr2k1/mideast/algeria3.html.

[63] Entelis, John, *Democracy Denied*, op. cit.

[64] Aldridge, Bob, *Understanding the 'War on Terrorism': The Oil & Gas Interests Part 2*—

(*Africa*), Pacific Life Research Center, Santa Clara, CA, 1 February 2003, p. 6–7, www.plrc.org/docs/030201.pdf. .

[65] 'Nothing to Lose But Our Illusions', *Sun Magazine*, June 2000.

[66] See 'Algeria', United States Energy Information Adminstration, February 1999, website at www.eia.doe.gov/emeu/cabs/algeria.html.

[67] Cooley, John K., *Unholy Wars: Afghanistan, America and International Terrorism*, Pluto Press, London, 1998, p. 205–6.

[68] HRW, *World Report 2000*, op. cit.

[69] Gershman, John, 'Moros in the Philippines', *Foreign Policy In Focus*, October 2001, www.selfdetermine.org/conflicts/philippines.html.

[70] Ibid.

[71] Ibid. Also see Turbiville, Graham H., 'Bearers of the Sword Radical Islam, Philippines Insurgency, and Regional Stability', *Military Review*, March–April 2002, fmso.leavenworth.army.mil/FMSOPUBS/ISSUES/sword.htm.

[72] Cooley, *Unholy Warriors*, op. cit., p. 227–233. Santuaro III, Edmundo, 'Abu Sayyaf: The CIA's Monster Gone Beserk', *Bulatlat*, No. 16, 1–7 June 2001, www.bulatlat.com/archive/016abu_us.htm.

[73] Berger, 'The Path Not Followed', *IntelWire*, op. cit.

[74] Clark, Emily, 'In the Spotlight: Abu Sayyaf', Center for Defense Information, Washington, DC, 5 March 2002, www.cdi.org/terrorism/sayyaf.cfm.

[75] York, Byron, 'The bin Ladens' Great Escape: How the US Helped Osama's Family Leave the Country after 9/11', *National Review*, 11 September 2002, www.nationalreview.com/york/york091102.asp.

[76] Berger, J. M., 'INS Deported al Qaeda-Linked Suspect Just Days After Oklahoma Bombing', *IntelWire: Special Reports on Terrorism*, 6 October 2003, www.intelwire.com/khalifa100603.html.

[77] Ibid.

[78] Privilege speech of Senator Aquilino Pimentel at the Philippine Senate, 'Treasonous Handling of the Abu Sayyaf', 31 July 2000, www.nenepimentel.org/speeches/20000802.shtml.

[79] Bengwayan, Michael A., 'US Forces in Philippines Facing CIA-Trained Abu Sayyaf Terrorists', *Bayani Magazine: Journal of Filipino Arts and Culture*, 10 March 2002, bayanimagazine.com/bayani.arch107.html.

[80] Conde, Carlos H., 'Dos Palmas hostages paid ransom, AFP officials took cut', *CyberDyaryo* 4 February 2002, www.cyberdyaryo.com/features/f2002_0204_02.htm.

[81] Special Feature: Inside the Abu Sayyaf, 'Edwin Angeles: The Spy Who Came in From the Cold', *Philippine Inquirer*, 2001, www.inq7.net/specials/inside_abusayyaf/2001/features/spy_turns_bandit.htm.

[82] Bersamin, Jun, 'American Blast Victim in Davao Tagged as Terrorist', ABS-CBN, 27

September 2002, available online at newsmine.org/archive/war-on-terror/alqaeda/cia-bomb-maker/american-blast-victim-phillipines-terrorist.txt.

[83] 'InPeace to Reyes, Corpus: Resign', *Minda News*, Mindanao News and Information Cooperative Center (MNICC), Davao, Vol. II, No. 82, 28 July 2003, www.mindanews.com/2003/07/28nws-inpeace.html.

[84] Regalado, Edith, 'CIA Whisks Away Brit-Am Blast Victim: Now in US', *Philippine Star*, 9 July 2002.

[85] Zumel-Sicat, Dorian, 'Treasure Hunter a Player in a More Absorbing Tale', *Manila Times*, 29 May 2002, www.manilatimes.net/national/2002/may/29/top_stories/20020529top5.html

[86] Zumel-Sicat, Dorian and Andrade, Jeannette, 'Treasure Hunter had White Supremacists for Associates', *Manila Times*, 30 May 2002, www.manilatimes.net/national/2002/may/30/top_stories/20020530top6.html

[87] Zumel-Sicat, Dorian, 'Spies, Terrorists Attracted to Treasure Hunters' Circles', *Manila Times*, 31 March 2002, www.manilatimes.net/national/2002/may/31/top_stories/20020531top6.html

[88] Capulong, Eduardo, 'US Intervention in the Philippines: Second Front in the "War on Terror,"' *International Socialist Review*, No. 22, March–April 2002.

[89] Ibid.

Chapter 4: The Anglo-American Axis: Protecting Osama

[1] *Jane's Intelligence Review*, 1 October 1995.

[2] *Washington Post*, 3 October 2001.

[3] Ibid.

[4] Gould, Jennifer, 'Thanks, But No Thanks: How the US Missed a Chance to Get Bin Laden,' *Village Voice*, 31 October-6 November 2001, www.villagevoice.com/issues/0144/gould.php.

[5] For extensive discussion of the US bombing of Al-Shifa in the context of US relations with Sudan, see Ahmed, Nafeez M., 'United States Terrorism in the Sudan: The Bombing of Al-Shifa and its Strategic Role in US–Sudan Relations,' Media Monitors Network, 22 Oct. 2001, www.mediamonitors.net/mosaddeq16.html. The matters raised in this paper were presented to the Policy Committee of the UK's National Union of Journalists in Oct. 2001.

[6] Rose, David, 'Resentful West Spurned Sudan's Key Terror Files,' *Observer*, 30 September 2001.

[7] 'Why Was Russia's Intelligence on Al-Qaeda Ignored?', *Jane's Intelligence Digest*, 5 October 2001.

[8] 'Avoiding the Real Wuestions,' *Jane's Intelligence Digest*, 28 May 2002, www.janes.com/security/international_security/news/jid/jid020528_1_n.shtml.

[9] Robinson, Gwen, 'CIA "Ignored Warning" on al Qaeda,' *Financial Times*, 12 January 2002; Baer, Robert, *See No Evil: The True Story of a Ground Soldier in the CIA's War on Terrorism*, Random House International, New York 2002.

[10] Baer, Robert, *See No Evil: The True Story of a Ground Soldier in the CIA's War on Terrorism*, op. cit., Preface.

[11] Ridgeway, James, 'The French Connection,' *Village Voice*, 2–8 January 2002, www.villagevoice.com/issues/0201/ridgeway.php.

[12] Gellman, Barton, 'A Strategy's Cautious Evolution', *Washington Post*, 20 January 2002, p. A01, www.washingtonpost.com/ac2/wp-dyn?pagename=article&node=&contentId=A8734-2002Jan19; CBS News, 'Infighting Delayed Osama Hunt', 25 June 2003, www.cbsnews.com/stories/2003/06/25/attack/main560293.shtml; Mayer, Jane, 'The Search for Osama', *New Yorker*, 4 August 2003, www.newyorker.com/fact/content/?030804fa_fact; 'Anti-Terror War's Missteps Detailed By Ex-NSC Staffers', *Washington Post*, 2 October 2002, p. A06, www.washingtonpost.com/ac2/wp-dyn?pagename=article&contentId=A30061-2002Oct1&notFound=true. Cited in Thompson, *Update [Complete 9/11 Timeline]*, op. cit. (section January 2001-4 September 2001)

[13] Labeviere, Richard, 'CIA Agent Allegedly Met Bin Laden in July,' *Le Figaro*, 31 October 2001.

[14] Sampson, Anthony, 'CIA Agent Alleged to Have Met Bin Laden in July,' *Guardian*, 1 November 2001.

[15] Sage, Adam, 'Ailing bin Laden "Treated for Kidney Disease",' *Times*, 1 Nov. 2001, www.thetimes.co.uk/article/0,,2001370005-2001380403,00.html.

[16] Bryant, Elizabeth, 'Radio Reports New CIA–Bin Laden Details,' United Press International, 1 November 2001.

[17] Ibid.

[18] Ibid. Agence France Presse, 31 October 2001.

[19] Chossudovsky, Michel, Introduction to *Le Figaro* article, Centre for Research on Globalisation, 2 November 2001, www.globalresearch.ca/articles/RIC111B.html.

[20] Johnston, David, *New York Times*, 19 August 2001.

[21] Marlowe, Lara, 'US Efforts to Make Peace Summed Up By Oil,' *Irish Times*, 19 November 2001. O'Neill's charges were also reported on CNN, 'American Morning with Paula Zahn,' 8 January 2001. Richard Butler of the Council on Foreign Relation and US ambassador-in-residence was unable to deny the veracity of the charges, instead promising a further investigation—which has not yet occurred.

[22] BBC *Newsnight*, 'Has Someone Been Sitting On The FBI?', BBC 2, 6 Nov. 2001, news.bbc.co.uk/hi/english/events/newsnight/newsid_1645000/1645527.stm.

[23] Palast, Gregory and Pallister, David, 'FBI Claims Bin Laden Inquiry Was Frustrated,' *Guardian*, 7 November 2001.

[24] 'Above the Law: Bush's Racial Coup d'Etat and Intelligence Shutdown,' *Green Press*, 14 February 2002, www.greenpress.org/html/GPress_2-14-02.html.

[25] Ibid.

[26] Omicinski, John, 'General: Capturing bin Laden Is Not Part of Mission,' *USA Today*, 23 November 2001.

[27] *Daily Mirror*, 16 November 2001.

[28] Letter to Honourable Charles O. Rossotti, Chairman of Internal Revenue Service, from Judicial Watch, 20 September 2001, www.judicialwatch.org/cases/78/hamascomplaint.htm.

[29] JW Press Release, 'Government Finally Begins to Investigate Alleged Terrorist Front Groups,' Judicial Watch, Washington, DC, 5 November 2001, www.judicialwatch.org/1071.shtml.

[30] Limbacher, Carl, 'Judicial Watch: Clinton IRD Turned Blind Eye to Terrorists,' *NewsMax*, 23 September 2001.

[31] JW Press Release, 'Government Finally Begins to Investigate Alleged Terrorist Front Groups,' op. cit.

[32] Jonathan Weiner in an interview with Linda Wertheimer, National Public Radio (NPR), 21 November 2001.

[33] Hersh, Seymour, M., 'King's Ransom: How Vulnerable Are Saudi Royals?', *New Yorker*, 22 October 2001.

[34] 'Saudi Arabia', Terrorism: Questions & Answers, Council on Foreign Relations, www.terrorismanswers.com/coalition/saudiarabia.html.

[35] For sources and further discussion see Flocco, Tom and Ruppert, Michael, 'The Profits of Death, Part III,' FTW Publications, 9 January 2002, www.copvcia.com/stories/dec_2001/death_profits_pt3.html.

[36] *Washington Post*, 29 September 2001; *Financial Times*, 29 November 2001. Cited in ibid. See the Flocco and Ruppert report for further damning revelations.

[37] 'Who Really Wants to Stop Bin Laden?' *Intelligence Online*, 16 March 2000, www.intelligenceonline.com/p_default.asp?rub=folders&name=dos_ioa_bin_laden.

[38] Horrock, Nicholas M., 'FBI Agent: I Was Stymied in Terror Probe,' *Washington Post*, 30 May 2002, www.washtimes.com/upi-breaking/30052002-054621-5800r.htm. This article is a re-print of a United Press International report.

[39] Irvine, Reed and Kincaid, Clive, 'Another FBI Whistleblower,' *Media Monitor*, Accuracy In Media, Washington D.C., 14 June 2002, www.aim.org/publications/media_monitor/2002/06/14.html.

[40] Walker, Thomas, 'Did bin Laden Have Help From US Friends?', *Toronto Star*, 27 November 2001.

[41] 'FBI Arrogance and Secrecy Dismay US,' *Times*, 3 November 2001.

[42] Rashid, Ahmed, 'Bin Laden "Has Network of Sleepers Across North America",'

Telegraph, 16 September 2001.

[43] Woodward, Bob and Pincus, Walter, 'Investigators Identify 4 to 5 Groups Linked to Bin Laden Operating in US. No Connection Found Between 'Cell' Members and 19 Hijackers, Officials Say,' *Washington Post*, 23 Sept. 2001.

[44] White, Michael and Wintour, Patrick, 'Blair Calls for World Fight Against Terror', *Guardian*, 12 September 2001, www.guardian.co.uk/wtccrash/story/0,1300,550524,00.html.

[45] Sweeney, John, 'Bin Laden Connected to London Dissident', BBC News, 10 March 2002.

[46] Fielding, Nick and Gadhery, Dipesh, 'Bin Laden Called UK 260 Times', *Sunday Times*, 24 March 2002.

[47] Kenyan Embassy Bombing, United States District Court, Southern District of New York, Indictment, *United States of America vs Usama Bin Laden*, S(9) 98 Cr. 1023 (LBS), www.terrorismcentral.com/Library/Incidents/USEmbassyKenyaBombing/Indictment/Count t1.html.

[48] Sweeney, op. cit.

[49] O'Neill, Sean, 'Britain a Perfect Haven for Islamic Radicals Looking for Recruits', *Telegraph*, 11 September 2002, www.telegraph.co.uk/news/main.jhtml?xml=/news/campaigns/war/recruit.xml.

[50] Greenslade, Nick, 'Who's Afraid of al-Masari?' *Tribune*, 27 February 2003, www.tribweb.co.uk/greenslade21022003.htm. [www.terrorismcentral.com/Library/Incidents/USEmbassyKenyaBombing/Indictment/Intro duction.html.]

[51] Kenyan Embassy Bombing, op. cit., www.terrorismcentral.com/Library/Incidents/USEmbassyKenyaBombing/Indictment/Introd uction.html.

[52] Laville, Sandra and Rozenberg, Gabriel, 'Al-Muhajiroun Recruiting Jihadis', Telegraph, 17 September 2001.

[53] Al-Muhajiroun Fatwa, 'Jihad Fatwa Against Israel' Case No. Israel/M/F50, 2 October 2000, available online at EmergencyNet News, Emergency Response and Research Institute, www.emergency.com/2000/fatwa2000.htm.

[54] Shahar, Yael and Karmon, Ely, 'London-Based Islamic Group Issues Fatwa against Israel', International Policy Institute for Counter Terrorism, Herzlia, 19 October 2000, www.ict.org.il/articles/articledet.cfm?articleid=131.

[55] Al-Muhajiroun Press Release, 'Advice and Warning to All Jews and Muslims in the UK', 17 October 2000. Also see Foster, Peter and Aldrick, Philip, 'Extremist Backs 'Kill Jews' Poster', *Telegraph*, 19 October 2000.

[56] Reuters, 'Al-Muhajiroun Issues Fatwa Against Musharraf', 18 September 2001.

[57] *Asian Times*, 21 December 1999. Cited in *British Muslim Monthly Survey*, December 1999, Vol. VII, No. 12, p. 9, artsweb.bham.ac.uk/bmms/1999/ 12December99.asp#Death%20threat%20against%20Yeltsin.

[58] 'Bin Laden Promises More Suicide Attacks', *Times*, 10 October 2001.

[59] *Sunday Telegraph*, 23 September 2001.

[60] *Times*, 22 September 2001.

[61] *Daily Mail*, 19 September 2001. Also see Whine, Michael, 'Al-Muhajiroun: The Portal for Britain's Suicide Terrorists', International Policy Institute for Counter Terrorism, Herzliya, 21 May 2003, www.ict.org.il/articles/articledet.cfm?articleid=484.

[62] Alleyne, Richard and Bunyan, Nigel, 'Briton's Boast of Recruiting for bin Laden May Lead to Charges', *Telegraph*, 19 December 2001, www.opinion.telegraph.co.uk/news/main.jhtml?xml=/news/2001/12/19/nbut19.xml.

[63] Demetriou, Danielle and Sawer, Patrick, 'Al-Muhajiroun Say 1000 Brit Muslims Have Joined Jihad', *This is London*, 29 October 2001.

[64] *Washington Post*, 7 January 2002. Womack, Sarah and Alleyne, Richard, 'Police Can't Stop Muslim Inciting Terror in Britain', *Telegraph*, 8 January 2002, www.telegraph.co.uk/news/main.jhtml?xml=/news/2002/01/08/nbutt08.xml.

[65] Bamber, David, 'Hunt for 1,200 Britons Who Trained with al-Qa'eda', *Telegraph*, 26 January 2003, www.telegraph.co.uk/news/main.jhtml?xml=/news/2003/01/26/nalq26.xml&sSheet=/news/2003/01/26/ixnewstop.html&secureRefresh=true&_requestid=52048.

[66] Banerji, Robin, 'Looking for Trouble', *Time* , 8 December 2002, www.time.com/time/europe/magazine/article/0,13005,901021216-397474,00.html.

[67] Doyle, Neil, 'Al Qaeda Uses Websites to Draw Recruits, Spread Propaganda', *Washington Times*, 11 September 2003.

[68] Gertz, Bill, 'Islamists to Honor 9/11 Hijackers', *Washington Times*, 30 August 2003, www.washtimes.com/national/20030829-113829-1065r.htm.

[69] Liberty Report, *Anti-Terrorism Legislation in the United Kingdom*, Liberty, London, 2001, www.liberty-human-rights.org.uk/resources/publications/pdf-documents/anti-terrornew.pdf.

[70] BBC News, 'Britain Sheltering al-Qaeda Leader', 8 July 2002, news.bbc.co.uk/1/hi/uk/2115371.stm. BBC News. 'Investigating Terror: People', 2001 (viewed 10 June 2004), news.bbc.co.uk/hi/english/static/in_depth/world/2001/war_on_terror/investigation_on_terror/people_4.stm. Cited in Watson, Paul Joseph, *Order Out of Chaos: Elite Sponsored Terrorism and the New World Order*, AEJ Productions, 2002.

[71] BBC Radio 4, 'West London Terror Suspect', 19 October 2001, www.bbc.co.uk/radio4/today/reports/politics/qatada.shtml.

[72] British Treasury, Bank of England, 'Terrorist Financing: List of Suspects' 12 October 2001, www.bankofengland.co.uk/sanctions/sanctionsconlistoct01a.pdf. Also see Watson, op. cit.

[73] Harris, Paul, et. al., 'Britain's Most Wanted: How was the terrorist hunted for plotting terrorist attacks across Europe allowed to disappear in the UK', *Observer*, 5 May 2002, observer.guardian.co.uk/focus/story/0,6903,710502,00.html.

[74] Leppard, David, 'Terror Links in Europe: MI5 Knew for Years of London Mosque's Role', *Sunday Times*, 25 November 2001.

[75] Ibid.

[76] Tapper, Jake, 'Muslim Spy Who Infiltrated bin Laden's Terror Network in London', *Times*, 16 January 2003, www.timesonline.co.uk/article/0,,5041-544935,00.html.

[77] Burke, Jason, 'How I Was Betrayed By the British', *Observer*, 18 February 2001, www.observer.co.uk/focus/story/0,6903,439639,00.html.

[78] Rotella, Sebastian and Sobart, Janet, 'British Flex Muscles in Raid', *Daily Iowan*, 21 January 2003, www.dailyiowan.com/news/2003/01/21/Nation/British.Flex.Muscles.In.Raid-347904.shtml.

[79] Barnett, Anthony, et. al., 'MI5 Wanted Me to Escape, Claims Cleric', *Observer*, 21 October 2001.

[80] Barnett, 'Bin Laden Mastermind "Still Hiding in Britain"', *Observer*, 5 May 2002, observer.guardian.co.uk/uk_news/story/0,6903,710330,00.html.

[81] Harris, Paul, 'Britain's Most Wanted', op. cit.

[82] Crumley, Bruce, 'Sheltering a Puppet Master?', *Time*, 7 July 2002, www.time.com/time/world/article/0,8599,300609,00.html.

[83] McGrory, Daniel and Ford, Richard, 'Al-Qaeda Cleric Exposed as an MI5 Double Agent', *Times*, 25 March 2004, www.timesonline.co.uk/article/0,,3-1050175,00.html.

[84] Open Judgement of Mr Justice Collins (Chairman), Special Immigration Appeals Commission, January 2004, p. 11–12, www.channel4.com/news/ftp_images2/2004/03/week_4/23_document.pdf.

[85] Gillan, Audrey, 'Detained Muslim cleric is spiritual leader to militants, hearing told', *The Guardian*, 20 November 2003.

[86] McKenna, Terence, 'The Recruiters', CBC News - The National, 16 March 2004, www.cbc.ca/national/news/recruiters/qatada.html.

[87] Ibid.

[88] Open Judgement, op. cit. The Judgement clarifies (p. 12) that Abu Qatada's early refusal to organize and/or legitimize terrorist attacks on British targets later developed into a very real willingness to allow and/or support the same.

[89] Ford, Richard and McGrory, Daniel, 'Blunket Fury as Privy Councillors Attach Terror Laws', *Times*, 19 December 2003, www.timesonline.co.uk/article/0,,2-936853,00.html.

[90] FBI Most Wanted Terrorists, 'Anas al-Liby' (viewed 11th June 2004), www.fbi.gov/mostwant/terrorists/teralliby.htm.

[91] Ross, Brian and Walter, Vic, 'Called Off the Trail? FBI Agents Probing Terror Link Say They Were Told "Let Sleeping Dogs Lie"', ABC News, 19 December 2002, abcnews.go.com/sections/primetime/DailyNews/FBI_whistleblowers021219.html.

[92] Ibid.

[93] Watson, op. cit.

[94] Shayler, David, 'MI6 Plot to Assassinate Colonel Gaddafi: Police Enquiries Confirms

Plot is Not "Fantasy'", Press Release, 11 November 2001, www.cryptome.org/shayler-gaddafi.htm.

[95] Shayler, David, 'Don't Shoot the Messenger', *Observer*, 27 August 2000, www.guardian.co.uk/Archive/Article/0,4273,4055752,00.html.

[96] Hollingsworth, Mark, 'Secrets, Lies and David Shayler: The Spy Agencies Are Pursuing the Press Because They Are Afraid', *Guardian*, 17 March 2000, www.guardian.co.uk/comment/story/0,3604,181807,00.html.

[97] McGowan, Patrick, 'Call for Secret Shayler Trial', *Evening Standard*, 7 October 2002, www.thisislondon.co.uk/news/articles/1488303.

[98] Bright, Martin, 'MI6 "Halted Bid to Arrest bin Laden'", *Observer*, 10 November 2002, observer.guardian.co.uk/print/0,3858,4543555-102279,00.html.

Chapter 5: Saudi Arabia: Bin Laden's Financial Base

[1] Mayer, Jane, 'The House of Bin Laden,' *New Yorker*, 12 November 2001, newyorker.com/fact/content/?011112fa_FACT3.

[2] Ibid.

[3] Ibid.

[4] York, Byron, 'The bin Ladens' Great Escape', op. cit.

[5] Ibid., Hosenball, Mark, 'Attacking the Money Machine', *Newsweek*, 7 November 2002, www.nationalreview.com/york/york091102.asp.

[6] Cited in *Baltimore Sun*, 24 April 2001.

[7] *San Antonio Express-News*, 14 September 1998.

[8] York, Byron, 'The bin Ladens' Great Escape', op. cit.

[9] Golden, Daniel, et. al., 'Bin Laden Family Could Profit from a Jump in US Defense Spending Due to Ties to US Banks,' *Wall Street Journal*, 27 September 2001.

[10] ABC News, 'Strained Family Ties,' 1 October 2001 [emphasis added].

[11] CBS News, 'Bin Laden Family Evacuated,' 30 September 2001, www.cbsnews.com/stories/2001/09/30/archive/main313048.shtml.

[12] Unger, Craig, 'The Great Escape', *New York Times*, 1 June 2004.

[13] York, Byron, 'The bin Ladens' Great Escape', op. cit.

[14] BBC *Newsnight*, 'Has Someone Been Sitting On The FBI?', BBC 2, 6 November 2001, news.bbc.co.uk/hi/english/events/newsnight/newsid_1645000/1645527.stm.

[15] Ibid.

[16] Palast, Gregory and Pallister, David, 'FBI Claims Bin Laden Inquiry Was Frustrated,' op. cit.

[17] 'Peeling Back the Layers of Saudi-funded Terror net,' *Pittsburgh Tribune-Review*, 23 June

2002, www.pittsburghlive.com/x/tribune-review/opinion/datelinedc/s_77535.html.

[18] Steele, Kathy, 'Phantom Flight from Florida', *Tampa Tribune*, 5 October 2001, archived at web.archive.org/web/20011108145853/www.tampatrib.com/MGA3F78EFSC.html.

[19] Unger, Craig, 'Unasked Questions', *Boston Globe*, 11 April 2004, www.boston.com/news/globe/ideas/articles/2004/04/11/unasked_questions.

[20] Isikoff, Michael and Hosenball, Mark, 'A Legal Counterattack', *Newsweek*, 16 April 2003, msnbc.msn.com/id/3067906.

[21] Ibid.

[22] Unger, Craig, 'Unasked Questions', op. cit.

[23] Mayer, Jane, 'The House of Bin Laden,' op. cit.

[24] Golden, Daniel, et. al., 'Bin Laden Family Could Profit from a Jump in US Defense Spending,' op. cit.

[25] Lazarus, David, 'Carlyle Profit from Afghan War,' *San Francisco Chronicle*, 2 December 2001

[26] JW Press Release, 'Judicial Watch to File FOIA Lawsuit Today Over Carlyle Group Documents,' op. cit.

[27] Golden, Daniel, et. al., 'Bin Laden Family Could Profit from a Jump in US Defense Spending,' op. cit.

[28] Ibid.

[29] Lazarus, David, 'Carlyle Profit from Afghan War,' op. cit.

[30] Gray, Geoffrey, 'Bush Sr. Could Profit From War,' *Village Voice*, 11 October 2001.

[31] Mayer, Jane, 'The House of Bin Laden,' op. cit.

[32] Ibid.

[33] *Wall Street Journal*, 19 September 2001. Credit to Chossudovsky for this source.

[34] Agence France Press and *Hindustan Times*, 7 November 2001.

[35] Martin S. Indyk is Senior Fellow of Foreign Policy Studies at the Brookings Institution in Washington, DC. His experience in government and international relations include the following: US Ambassador to Israel (1995–97, 2000–01); Assistant Secretary of State for Near East Affairs, US State Department (1997–2000); Special Assistant to the President and Senior Director for Near East and South Asian Affairs, National Security Council (1993–1995); Executive Director, Washington Institute for Near East Policy; adjunct professor, Johns Hopkins University.

[36] Indyk, Martin S., 'Back to the Bazaar,' *Foreign Affairs*, January/February 2002.

[37] 'Above the Law,' *Green Press*, op. cit.

[38] Hersh, Seymour, M., 'King's Ransom: How Vulnerable Are Saudi Royals?', *New Yorker*, 22 October 2001.

[39] Roslin, Alex, 'US Saudi Scandal,' *Now*, 22 November 2001, nowtoronto.com.

[40] Braun, Stephen and Pasternak, Judy, 'Long Before Sept. 11, Bin Laden Aircraft Flew Under the Radar,' *Los Angeles Times*, 18 November 2001.

[41] Labeviere, Richard, *Dollars for Terror: The United States and Islam*, Algora Publishing, New York, 2000.

[42] Associated Press, 'Saudi Prince Says Taliban Had Approved Bin Laden Handover,' 3 November 2001.

[43] Mayer, Jane, 'The House of Bin Laden,' op. cit. [emphasis added]

[44] Ali, Tariq, 'The Real Muslim Extremists,' *New Statesman*, 1 October 2001.

[45] Kaiser, Robert G., 'Enormous Wealth Spilled Into American Coffers,' *Washington Post*, 11 February 2002.

[46] Madsen, Wayne, 'Questionable Ties,' *In These Times*, Institute for Public Affairs, No. 25, www.inthesetimes.com/issue/25/25/feature3.shtml. Also see *Intelligence Newsletter*, 2 March 2000.

[47] Meyers, Jack, et. al., 'Saudi Clans Working With US Oil Firms May Be Tied to Bin Laden,' *Boston Herald*, 10 December 2001.

Chapter 6: Pakistan: Bin Laden's Power Base

[1] 'Creating the Taliban: "CIA Made a Historic Mistake",' *Rationalist International Bulletin*, No. 68, 19 March 2001, rationalistinternational.net.

[2] Risen, James and Miller, Judith, 'Pakistani Intelligence Had Links to Al-Qaeda, US Officials Say,' *New York Times*, 29 October 2001. Available online at tiger.berkeley.edu/sohrab/politics/isi_problems.html.

[3] US State Department, *Patterns of Global Terrorism*, Department of State, Washington, DC, 2000, www.state.gov/s/ct/rls/pgtrpt/2000. Credit to Chossudovsky for this source.

[4] Cienski, Jan, 'Murder Puts Focus on Ties Between Pakistan's Spy Agencies, Extremists,' *National Post*, 26 February 2002.

[5] Rashid, Ahmed, 'Special Report—Osama Bin Laden: How the US Helped Midwife a Terrorist,' op. cit.

[6] CBS Evening News, 'Bin Laden Whereabouts Before 9/11,' 28 January 2002.

[7] Raman, B., 'Musharraf, Bin Laden and the Lashkar,' SAPRA, 2 July 2001, www.subcontinent.com/sapra/terrorism/terrorism20010702a.html.

[8] 'Overt Assistance from Pakistan May Bring Dire Consequences,' *Jane's Intelligence Digest*, 20 September 2001, www.janes.com/security/international_security/news/jid/jid010920_1_n.shtml.

[9] Thompson, Paul, 'September 11's Smoking Gun: The Many Faces of Sheikh Saeed', Center for Cooperative Research, 25 February 2003, www.cooperativeresearch.org/timeline/main/essaysaeed.html.

[10] See Chossudovsky, Michel, 'Cover-up or Complicity of the Bush Administration? The

Role of Pakistan's Military Intelligence (ISI) in the September 11 Attacks', Centre for Research on Globalisation, Montreal, 2 November 2001, www.globalresearch.ca/articles/CHO111A.html.

[11] Editorial, 'Restore Democracy,' *Progressive Populist*, Vol. 7, No. 21, 1 December 2001, www.populist.com/01.21.html. Also see the following sources on Lt. Gen. Ahmad's visit cited in Chossudovsky, 'Cover-up or Complicity', op. cit.: *Daily Telegraph*, 14 September 2001; *Guardian*, 15 September 2001; Reuters, 13 September 2001; *New York Times*, 13 September 2001.

[12] McGeary, Johanna, 'The World's Toughest Job', *Time*, 22 October 2001, Vol. 158, No. 16.

[13] Mateen, Amir, 'ISI Chief's Parleys Continue in Washington,' *News*, 10 September 2001. Cited in Chossudovsky, 'Cover-up and Complicity', op. cit.

[14] *Weekly Standard*, Vol. 7, No. 7, October 2001.

[15] ABC News, 'Worldwide Probe Leading to Bin Laden,' 30 September 2001, abcnews.go.com/sections/us/DailyNews/WTC_Investigation010930.html.

[16] Joshi, Manoj, 'India Helped FBI Trace ISI–terrorist Links,' *Times of India*, 9 October 2001.

[17] Agence France Presse, 10 October 2001. Also see Gannon, Kathy, 'Police in Pakistan Charge Three in Kidnapping of Reporter,' Associated Press, 9 January 2002, archived at www.nctimes.net/news/2002/20020209/63933.html.

[18] Monitoring Desk, 'Gen Mahmud's Exit Due to Links with Umar Sheikh,' *Dawn*, 8 October 2001. Also see Madsen, Wayne, 'Afghanistan, the Taliban and the Bush Oil Team,' Democrats.Com, January 2002.

[20] Tarauto, James, 'Our Friends the Pakistanis,' *Wall Street Journal*, 10 October 2001.

[20] Swami, Praveen, 'A Sheikh and the money trail,' *Frontline*, Vol. 18, No. 21, 13–26 October 2001, www.flonnet.com/fl1821/18210150.htm. The *New York Times* also confirms that "One of the first signs of a large infusion of cash coming into the United States for use by the hijackers appears in bank records dating from 2000, when $100,000 was deposited in bank accounts controlled by some of the leading hijackers, including Mr. Atta and Marwan al-Shehhi, Mr. Lormel said. The F.B.I. has traced that money back to the United Arab Emirates and believes that it was sent to the hijackers by Mustafa Ahmed al-Hisawi, who is accused of helping to manage Osama bin Laden's finances." (Risen, James, 'Sept. 11 Hijackers Said to Fake Data on Bank Accounts,' *New York Times*, 10 June 2002)

[21] Candiotti, Susan et. al., 'Suspected Terrorist Leader Was Wired Funds Through Pakistan,' CNN, 1 October 2001, www.cnn.com/2001/US/10/01/inv.pakistan.funds/index.html.

[22] Sperry, Paul, 'Did Ally Pakistan Play Role in 9-11?', *WorldNetDaily*, 30 January 2002, www.worldnetdaily.com/news/article.asp?ARTICLE_ID=26249.

[23] MSNBC, 'Indictment: Zacarias Moussaoui,' 11 December 2001, www.msnbc.com/modules/wtc/moussaoui_indictment/default.asp?p=1.

[24] Eggen, Dan, 'Obscure Hijacker's Larger Role Revealed,' *Washington Post*, 13 December

2001, www.washingtonpost.com/ac2/wp-dyn?pagename=article&node=&contentId=A34751-2001Dec12&notFound=true.

[25] Eggen, Dan and Day, Kathleen, 'US Probe of Sept. 11 Financing Wraps Up,' *Washington Post*, 7 January 2002, www.washingtonpost.com/ac2/wp-dyn/A6076-2002Jan6.html.

[26] CNN, 'Suspected Hijack Bankroller Freed by India in 99', 6 October 2001, www.cnn.com/2001/US/10/05/inv.terror.investigation.

[27] Ibid.

[28] William, John, 'Attack on Terrorism—Inside Al-Qaeda,' *Financial Times*, 29 November 2001, specials.ft.com/attackonterrorism/FT3RNR3XMUC.html. [emphasis added]

[29] *New York Times*, 10 July 2002.

[30] Bamber, David, et. al., 'London House Linked to US Plot', *Telegraph*, 30 September 2001, news.telegraph.co.uk/news/main.jhtml?xml=/news/2001/09/30/nhunt30.xml.

[31] Mukherjee, Subroto, 'Omar Sheikh: Profile of a Kidnapper,' *South Asian Outlook*, March 2002, www.southasianoutlook.com/sao_back_issues/march_2002/omar_sheikh.htm.

[32] *New York Times*, 15 March 2002.

[33] *New York Times*, 19 March 2002.

[34] *New York Times*, 13 March 2002.

[35] Klaidman, Daniel, 'US Officials Are Eager to Try the Main Suspect in Daniel Pearl's Murder,' *Newsweek*, 13 March 2002, www.msnbc.com/news/723527.asp.

[36] Hirschkorn, Phil, 'Embassy Bombing Trial Revealed bin Laden Links,' CNN, 16 October 2001, www.cnn.com/2001/US/10/16/inv.embassy.bombings.connections/.

[37] 'Did Pearl Die Because Pakistan Deceived CIA?,' *Pittsburg Tribune-Review*, 3 March 2002, www.pittsburghlive.com/x/tribune-review/opinion/datelinedc/s_20141.html.

[38] Stock, Jon, 'Inside the Mind of a Seductive Killer', *Times*, 21 August 2002, archived at www.cooperativeresearch.org/timeline/2002/londontimes082102.html.

[39] 'Did Pearl Die Because Pakistan Deceived CIA?,' *Pittsburg Tribune-Review*, op. cit.

[40] Swami, Praveen, 'A Sheikh and the Money Trail,' *Frontline*, Vol. 18, No. 21, 13–26 October 2001, www.frontlinennet.com/fl1821/18210150.htm.

[41] *New York Times*, 15 March 2002.

[42] CNN, 28 February 2002.

[43] Hussain, Zahid and McGrory, Daniel, 'London Schoolboy Who Graduated to Terrorism', *The Times*, 16 July 2002, www.timesonline.co.uk/newspaper/0,,171-357086,00.html.

[44] Williams, David, 'Kidnapper-Guy Hotmail.com', *Daily Mail*, 16 July 2002, archived at www.cooperativeresearch.org/timeline/2002/dailymail071602.html.

[45] Press Trust of India, 'UK Move To Allow Entry To Ultra Alarms Abducted Britons', 3 January 2000, archived at www.cooperativeresearch.org/timeline/2000/pti010300.html.

[46] Anson, Robert Sam, 'The Journalist and the Terrorist', *Vanity Fair*, August 2002,

archived at www.cooperativeresearch.org/timeline/2002/vanityfair0802.html.

[47] BBC News, 'Profile: Omar Saeed Sheikh', 16 July 2002, news.bbc.co.uk/2/hi/uk/1804710.stm.

[48] BBC News, 'Militant Free to Return to UK', 3 January 2000, news.bbc.co.uk/1/hi/uk/588915.stm.

[49] 'Did Pearl Die Because Pakistan Deceived CIA?,' op. cit.

[50] Stuart News Company Press Journal, 12 September 2001. Cited in Chossudovsky, Michel, 'Political Deception: The Missing Link Behind 9-11,' Global Outlook, Summer 2002, No. 2, globalresearch.ca/articles/CHO206A.html.

[51] Interview with Michel Chossudovsky, 'Aftermath: Unanswered Questions from 9/11', Guerrilla News Network, www.guerrillanews.com/after_math.

[52] Thompson, Paul, 'September 11's Smoking Gun: The Many Faces of Sheikh Saeed', op. cit.

[53] Lumpkin, John J., 'Counterterrorism Official Points Finger at Kuwaiti as Mastermind of Sept. 11 Attacks,' Associated Press, 5 June 2002.

[54] Madsen, Wayne, 'Afghanistan, the Taliban and the Bush Oil Team', Centre for Research on Globalisation, Montreal, 23 January 2002, globalresearch.ca/articles/MAD201A.html.

[55] Lumpkin, John J., 'Atta Entered Germany as Student,' Associated Press, 8 February 2002.

[56] McGirk, Tim, 'The Taliban Guy the CIA Won't Question,' Time, 25 February 2002.

[57] Indo-Asian News Service, 'Pakistan Still Aiding Taliban: Northern Alliance,' 12 October 2001, www.rediff.com/us/2001/oct/12ny7.htm.

[58] 'Alliance Threatens to Massacre Taleban's Foreign Fighters,' Times, 16 November 2001, print edition (online version excludes the question put to Dawood).

[59] Hersh, Seymour, 'The Getaway,' New Yorker, 21 January 2002.

[60] Strmecki, Marin, Commentary, January 2002.

[61] Hersh, Seymour, 'The Getaway,' op. cit.

[62] Smucker, Philip, 'Blunder That Let Bin Laden Slip Away,' Telegraph, 23 February 2002, www.telegraph.co.uk/news/main.jhtml?xml=/news/2002/02/23/wbin223.xml&sSheet=/news/2002/02/23/ixnewstop.html.

[63] Bhatai, Shyam, 'How bin Laden's Huge Convoy Gave American Forces the Slip,' Times, 22 July 2002, www.timesonline.co.uk/article/0,,3-362078,00.html.

[64] LeBoutillier, John, 'CIA Snookered Again?,' Newsmax, 13 December 2001, www.newsmax.com/archives/articles/2001/12/13/83210.shtml.

[65] 'Pilots Had Leaders of al-Qaeda "in Their Gunsights,"' Times, 19 November 2002.

[66] Pisani, Francis, 'Best Story, Not the Biggest Bomb: How to Fight the Terror Networks,' Le Monde diplomatique, June 2002, MondeDiplo.com/2002/06/02networks.

Chapter 7: What They Knew, When

[1] Cited in Public Education Center, www.publicedcenter.org/faaterrorist.htm; *Washington Post*, 2 January 2001.

[2] FOX News, 'Airlines Say They Weren't Warned', 16 May 2002, www.foxnews.com/story/0,2933,52998,00.html.

[3] Staff Statement No. 11, *The Performance of the Intelligence Community*, National Commission on the Terrorist Attacks Upon the United States, 13–14 April 2004, www.9-11commission.gov/hearings/hearing10/staff_statement_11.pdf.

[4] Warrick, Jo and Stephens, Joe, 'Before Attack, US Expected Different Hit, Chemical, Germ Agents Focus of Preparation,' *Washington Post*, 2 October, 2001.

[5] Ibid.

[6] Wald, Matthew, 'Earlier Hijackings Offered Signals That Were Missed,' *New York Times*, 3 October 2001.

[7] Neumeister, Larry, 'Trade Center Bomber's Threat Foreshadowed September Terrorist Attacks,' Associated Press, 30 September 2001.

[8] Novak, Robert, *Chicago Sun-Times*, 27 September 2001.

[9] PEC Report, 'Terrorist Plans to Use Planes as Weapons Dates to 1995: WTC bomber Yousef confessed to US agents in 1995,' Public Education Center, Washington, DC, www.publicedcenter.org/faaterrorist.htm.

[10] Agence France Press, 'Western Intelligence Knew of Laden Plan Since 1995,' 7 December 2001. Printed in *Hindustan Times*.

[11] Garcia, Raphael M., 'Decoding Bojinka,' *Newsbreak Weekly*, 15 November 2001, Vol. 1, No. 43. Also see Cooley, John, *Unholy Wars: Afghanistan, American and International Terrorism*, Pluto Press, London, 1999, p. 247.

[12] Monk, Paul, 'A Stunning Intelligence Failure,' Australian Thinking Skills Institute, Melbourne, www.austhink.org/monk/index.htm.

[13] AFP, 'Similar Plot First Uncovered in Philippines, Says Police Chief,' *Sydney Morning Herald*, 13 September 2001.

[14] Timmerman, Kenneth R., 'What They Knew; When They Knew It,' *Insight On The News*, 27 May 2002. Also see Breitweiser, Kristen (Co-Chairperson, September 11th Advocates), Statement Concerning the Joint 9/11 Inquiry, Senate Select Committee on Intelligence, House Permanent Select Committee on Intelligence, 18 September 2002, www.fas.org/irp/congress/2002_hr/091802breitweiser.pdf.

[15] *Monterey Herald*, 18 July 2002.

[16] AIM Report No. 18, 'Catastrophic Intelligence Failure,' Accuracy In Media, Washington, DC, 24 September 2001, www.aim.org/publications/aim_report/2001/18.html.

[17] Timmerman, Kenneth R., 'What They Knew; When They Knew It,' op. cit.

[18] *San Francisco Chronicle*, 6 March 2002.

[19] *Washington Post*, 24 September 2001. The *Post* also discusses Project Bojinka and the plans to hurl civilian jets into key US buildings, including the WTC. Also see Ressa, Maria, 'US Warned in 1995 of Plot to Hijack Planes, Attack Buildings,' CNN, 18 September 2001.

[20] Fainaru, Steve and Grimaldi, James V., 'FBI Knew Terrorists Were Using Flight Schools,' *Washington Post*, 23 September 2001, www.washingtonpost.com/ac2/wp-dyn?pagename=article&node=&contentId=A10840-2001Sep22.

[21] Fineman, Mark and Pasternak, Judy, 'Suicide Flights and Crop Dusters Considered Threats at '96 Olympics,' *Los Angeles Times*, 17 November 2001.

[22] Gertz, Bill, 'For Years, Signs Suggested "That Something Was Up,"' *Washington Times*, 17 May 2002, www.washtimes.com/national/20020517-70217917.htm.

[23] Hill, Eleanor, Joint Inquiry Staff Statement Part I, House/Senate Joint Inquiry 18 September 2002. Available at Federation of American Scientists, www.fas.org/irp/congress/2002_hr/091802hill.html. "In June 1998, the Intelligence Conununity obtained information from several sources that Usama Bin Ladin was considering attacks in the US, including Washington, DC and New York. This information was provided to senior US Government officials in July 1998;

In August 1998, the Intelligence Community obtained information that a group of unidentified Arabs planned to fly an explosive-laden plane from a foreign country into the World Trade Center. The information was passed to the FBI and the FAA...;

In September 1998, the Intelligence Community prepared a memorandum detailing al-Qa'ida infrastructure in the United States, including the use of fronts for terrorist activities. This information was provided to senior US Government officials in September 1998;

In October 1998, the Intelligence Community obtained information that al-Qa'ida was trying to establish an operative cell within the United States. This information indicated there might be an effort underway to recruit US citizen Islamists and US-based expatriates from the Middle East and North Africa;

In the fall of 1998, the Intelligence Community received information concerning a Bin Ladin plot involving aircraft in the New York and Washington, DC areas;

In November 1998, the Intelligence Community obtained information that a Bin Ladin terrorist cell was attempting to recruit a group of five to seven young men from the United States to travel to the Middle East for training. This was in conjunction with planning to strike US domestic targets."

[24] Woodward, Bob and Eggen, Dan, 'Aug. Memo Focused on Attacks in US', *Washington Post*, 18 May 2002, www.washingtonpost.com/wp-dyn/articles/A35744-2002May17.html.

[25] Hudson, Rex A., Report Prepared for the National Intelligence Council, *The Sociology and Psychology of Terrorism*, Federal Research Division, Library of Congress, Washington, DC, September 1999, p. 8, www.loc.gov/rr/frd/pdf-files/Soc_Psych_of_Terrorism.pdf.

[26] National Intelligence Council website (viewed 9 July 2004), www.cia.gov/nic/NIC_home.html.

[27] National Intelligence Council website, NIC Mission (viewed 9 July 2004), www.cia.gov/nic/NIC_about.html.

[28] Shenon, Philip, 'Traces of Terrorism: The Warnings: FBI Knew for Years About Terror Pilot Training', *New York Times*, 18 May 2002.

[29] Limbacher, Carl, 'London Report: Bin Laden May Hit New York, Stock Exchange,' *NewsMax*, 5 October 1999.

[30] Hill, Joint Inquiry Staff Statement Part I, op. cit. "In the spring of 1999, the Intelligence Community obtained information about a planned Bin Ladin attack on a US Government facility in Washington, DC;

In September 1999, the Intelligence Conununity obtained information that Usama Bin Ladin and others were planning a terrorist act in the United States, possibly against specific landmarks in California and New York City...;

In late 1999, the Intelligence Community obtained information regarding the Bin Ladin network's possible plans to attack targets in Washington, DC and New York City during the New Year's Millennium celebrations;

On December 14, 1999, an individual named Ahmed Ressam was arrested as he attempted to enter the United States from Canada. An alert US Customs Service officer in Port Washington stopped Ressam and asked to search his vehicle. Chemicals and detonator materials were found in his car. Ressam's intended target was Los Angeles International Airport. Ressam, who was later determined to have links to Usama Bin Ladin's terrorist network, has not been formally sentenced yet."

[31] Cited in Grigg, William Norman, 'Could We Have Prevented the Attacks?', *New American*, Vol. 17, No. 23, 5 November 2001.

[32] Lines, Andy, 'Pentagon Chiefs Planned for Jet Attack,' *Mirror*, 24 May 2002, www.intellnet.org/news/2002/05/24/9488-1.html. Also see Ryan, Dennis, 'Contingency Planning Pentagon MASCAL Exercise Simulates Scenarios in Preparing for Emergencies', Military District of Washington News Service, 3 November 2000, www.mdw.army.mil/news/Contingency_Planning.html.

[33] Flocco, Tom, 'DOJ Asked FBI Translator To Change Pre 9-11 Intercepts', 911 Citizens Watch, New York, 24 March 2004, www.911citizenswatch.org/modules.php?op=modload&name=News&file=article&sid=146.

[34] Transcript of CBS *60 Minutes* interview with Sibel Edmonds, 'Lost in Translation', 27 October 2002, in Attachment 1 of US Department of Justice, *A Review of Allegations of a Continuing Double Standard of Discipline at the FBI*, Office of the Inspector General, Washington, DC, 6 November 2003, www.usdoj.gov/oig/special/0311/final.pdf.

[35] Ibid.

[36] Interview by Amy Goodman with Sibel Edmonds, 'Fmr. FBI Translator: White House Had Intel On Possible Airplane Attack Pre-9/11', *Democracy Now*, 31 March 2004, www.democracynow.org/article.pl?sid=04/03/31/1616221&mode=thread&tid=25.

[37] Grigg, William Norman, 'Could We Have Prevented the Attacks?', op. cit.

[38] Fainaru, Steve and Grimaldi, James V., 'FBI Knew Terrorists Were Using Flight Schools,' op. cit.

[39] Hill, Joint Inquiry Staff Statement Part I, op. cit. "In March 2001, an intelligence source claimed a group of Bin Ladin operatives were planning to conduct an unspecified

attack in the United States in April 2001. One of the operatives allegedly resided in the United States;

In April 2001, the Intelligence Community obtained information that unspecified terrorist operatives in California and New York State were planning a terrorist attack in those states for April;

Between May and July, the National Security Agency reported at least 33 communications indicating a possible, imminent terrorist attack... These reports were widely disseminated within the Intelligence Community;

In May 2001, the Intelligence Community obtained information that supporters of Usama Bin Ladin were reportedly planning to infiltrate the United States via Canada in order to carry out a terrorist operation using high explosives. This report mentioned an attack within the United States...

In July 2001, this information was shared with the FBI, the Immigration and Naturalization Service (INS), US Customs Service, and the State Department and was included in a closely held intelligence report for senior government officials in August 2001;

In May 2001, the Department of Defense acquired and shared with other elements of the Intelligence Community information indicating that seven individuals associated with Usama Bin Ladin departed various locations for Canada, the United Kingdom, and the United States;

In June 2001, the DCI's CTC had information that key operatives in Usama Bin Ladin's organization were disappearing while others were preparing for martyrdom;

In July 2001, the DCI's CTC was aware of an individual who had recently been in Afghanistan who had reported, 'Everyone is talking about an impending attack.' The Intelligence Community was also aware that Bin Ladin had stepped up his propaganda efforts in the preceding months."

[40] Drogin, Bob, 'US Tells of Covert Afghan Plan Before 9/11,' *Los Angeles Times*, 18 May 2002, www.latimes.com/news/nationworld/nation/la-051802strike.story.

[41] Breitweiser, Kristen, Statement Concerning the Joint 9/11 Inquiry, op. cit.

[42] Stafford, Ned, 'Newspaper: Echelon Gave Authorities Warning of Attacks,' *Newsbytes*, 13 September 2001, www.newsbytes.com/news/01/170072.html. ECHELON is a vast intelligence information collection system capable of monitoring all the electronic communications in the world. It is operated by the US, UK, Canada, Australia, and New Zealand. While no government agency has ever confirmed or denied its existence, an EU committee that investigated ECHELON for more than a year in early September 2001 confirmed that the system did exist. The EU committee reported that Echelon sucks up electronic transmissions "like a vacuum cleaner", using keyword search techniques to sift through enormous amounts of data. The system covers the whole world's electronic communications with 120 satellites. For more on ECHELON see Bamford, James, *Body of Secrets: Anatomy of the Ultra-Secret National Security Agency*, Doubleday, 2001.

[43] Hill, Joint Inquiry Staff Statement Part I, op. cit. [emphasis added]

[44] Wright, Lawrence, 'The Counter-Terrorist,' *New Yorker*, 14 January 2002. Under pressure from Congress, the White House has finally officially admitted that the US intelligence community had information that Al-Qaeda was planning an imminent attack

through hijacking. However, National Security Adviser Condoleezza Rice has gone on record denying that US intelligence had any other specific information, such as that the planes might be used as missiles (BBC *Newsnight*, 16 May 2002). This denial, however, is patently false, as demonstrated by the reports on the public record discussed here.

[45] *Washington Post*, 17 May 2002.

[46] Timmerman, Kenneth R., 'What They Knew; When They Knew It,' op. cit.

[47] Solomon, John, 'CIA Cited Risk Before Attack,' Associated Press, 3 October 2001.

[48] Pacenti, John, 'The Individuals That Mr. Glass Has Dealt With Are Essentially Terrorists', *Palm Beach Post*, 29 September 2001, www.cooperativeresearch.org/timeline/2001/palmbeachpost092901.html.

[49] Mintz, John, 'US Reopens Arms Case In Probe for Taliban Role', *Washington Post*, 2 August 2002, p. A01, www.washingtonpost.com/ac2/wp-dyn/A33797-2002Aug1?language=printer.

[50] Hansen, Chris, 'Charges to be Brought Against Arms Dealers Who Were Filmed in ATF Undercover Operation', MSNBC—Dateline NBC, 18 March 2003, www.cooperativeresearch.org/timeline/2003/msnbc031803b.html; Hansen and Curry, Ann, 'Trail of Terror: Never before broadcast tapes of how arms merchants who may have links to terrorism are buying arsenals of weapons, even components for nuclear bombs', Dateline NBC, 2 August 2002;

[51] Pacenti, John, 'Con Man Turned Patriot Tells All', Cox News Service, 2 August 2002, www.cooperativeresearch.org/timeline/2002/coxnews080202.html.

[52] Pacenti, 'Intelligence Panel Hears from Glass', *Palm Beach Post*, 17 October 2002, www.cooperativeresearch.org/timeline/2002/palmbeachpost101702.html.

[53] MSNBC, 'Stinger Missile Sting Operation', Dateline NBC, 18 March 2003, www.cooperativeresearch.org/timeline/2003/msnbc031803.html?0sl=-12.

[54] WPBF Channel 25, 'Informant: Terrorists Warned of WTC Collapse', 5 August 2002, www.cooperativeresearch.org/timeline/2002/wpbf080502.html.

[55] Pacenti, 'Con Man Turned Patriot Tells All', op. cit.

[56] Hansen and Curry, 'Trail of Terror', op. cit.

[57] Ibid.

[58] Mintz, 'US Reopens Arms Case', op. cit. [emphasis added]

[59] WPBF Channel 25, op. cit.

[60] Pacenti, 'Con Man Turned Patriot Tells All', op. cit.

[61] Pacenti, 'Intelligence Panel Hears from Glass', op. cit.

[62] WPTV Channel 5 (an NBC TV station in Florida), 'Tip Questions', 7 October 2002, www.cooperativeresearch.org/timeline/main/Glass-Graham.html. Full transcript at www.cooperativeresearch.org/timeline/2002/wptv100702.html.

[63] Ibid.

[64] Pacenti, 'Con Man Turned Patriot Tells All', op. cit.

[65] Burstein, Jon, 'Former Wall St. Bond Trader Cuts Plea Deal, Will Testify in Arms-trading Case', *South Florida Sun-Sentinel*, 23 August 2001, www.cooperativeresearch.org/timeline/2001/sunsentinel082301.html.

[66] Hansen and Curry, 'Trail of Terror', op. cit.

[67] Mintz, 'US Reopens Arms Case', op. cit.

[68] Burstein, '2 Pakistanis Indicted in Stinger Missile Deal in West Palm', *Palm Beach Post*, 20 March 2003.

[69] *National Post*, 20 May 2002.

[70] Schorr, Daniel, 'Washington's Secrecy Battles—From 9/11 to Enron,' *Christian Science Monitor*, 31 May 2002, www.csmonitor.com/2002/0531/p11s02-cods.html.

[71] *Commercial Appeal*, Memphis, 17 May 2002.

[72] *Washington Post*, 17 May 2002.

[73] *Washington Post*, 29 January 2002. Credit to Professor Michel Chossudovsky for these three sources on the Presidential Daily Brief prior to 9/11.

[74] Jehl, Douglas, 'A Warning, but Clear? White House Tries to Make the Point That New Details Add Up to Old News,' *New York Times*, 11 April 2004, p. A13.

[75] Presidential Daily Briefing, 'Bin Laden Determined to Strike on US Soil', Central Intelligence Agency, 6 August 2001, available online at www.gwu.edu/~nsarchiv/NSAEBB/NSAEBB116/pdb8-6-2001.pdf.

[76] Prothero, P. Mitchell, 'Administration Won't Release 9/11 Data,' United Press International, 18 September 2002, www.upi.com/view.cfm?StoryID=20020918-035035-1042r.

[77] Hill, Eleanor, *Joint Inquiry Staff Statement*, Part I, 18 September 2002. Available at Intelligence Resource Program, Federation of American Scientists, www.fas.org/irp/congress/2002_hr/091802hill.html.

[78] Ridgeway, James, 'Bush's 9-11 Secrets: The Government Received Warnings of Bin Laden's Plans to Attack New York and DC', *Village Voice*, 31 July 2003.

[79] Editorial, 'Evidence Mounts That September 11 Was Predictable,' *USA Today*, 15 September 2001.

[80] Wastell, David and Jacobson, Philip, 'Israeli Security Issued Warning to CIA of Large-scale Terror Attacks,' *Telegraph*, 16 September 2001. It has been claimed that the US intelligence community receives numerous warnings such as this which are red-herrings, thus explaining why the latest warning from Israeli intelligence was not taken seriously. This argument fails, however, in light of the fact that the US already knew for certain that Osama Bin Laden was planning to implement Project Bojinka very soon. Given this knowledge, the urgent warnings from other intelligence agencies, including Israel, would have obviously provided increasing confirmation of the plans, not disconfirmation. If not, then one wonders what other sort of criteria would be necessary for US intelligence to take a warning from Mossad seriously!

[81] MSNBC, 15 September 2001. Also see Steele, Johnathan, et. al., 'Threat of US Strikes Passed to Taliban Weeks Before NY Attacks,' *Guardian*, 22 September 2001, www.guardian.co.uk/international/story/0,3604,556254,00.html.

[82] Russian press reports translated by a former CIA official, cited in Ruppert, Michael C., 'This Was Not An Intelligence Failure,' *From The Wilderness* Publications, 24 September 2001. See *Izvestia*, 12 September 2002.

[83] Agence France Press, 'Russia Gave "Clear Warning,"' 16 September 2001.

[84] Rufford, Nicholas, 'MI6 Warned US of Al-Qaeda Attacks,' *Sunday Times*, 9 June 2002.

[85] Evans, Michael, 'Spy Chiefs Warned Ministers of al-Qaeda Attacks,' *Times*, 14 June 2002.

[86] *Le Figaro*, 31 October 2001.

[87] Gumbel, Andrew, 'Bush Did Not Heed Several Warnings of Attack,' *Independent*, 17 September 2001.

[88] *San Francisco Chronicle*, 14 September 2001.

[89] Cooley, John K., 'Other Unheeded Warnings Before 9/11,' *Christian Science Monitor*, 23 May 2002, www.csmonitor.com/2002/0523/p11s01-coop.html.

[90] Associated Press, 'Egypt Leader Says He Warned America,' 7 December 2001. Also see *Atlanta Journal and Constitution*, 8 Dec. 2001.

[91] Nicolson was formally the David Bruton Jr. Chair in Cancer Research and professor at the University of Texas M. D. Anderson Cancer Center in Houston, and professor of internal medicine and professor of pathology and laboratory medicine at the University of Texas Medical School at Houston. He was also adjunct professor of comparative medicine at Texas A & M University. Among the most cited scientists in the world, having published over 480 medical and scientific papers, edited 13 books, served on the Editorial Boards of 12 medical and scientific journals and currently serving as editor of two (*Clinical & Experimental Metastasis* and the *Journal of Cellular Biochemistry*), Professor Nicolson has active peer-reviewed research grants from the US Army, National Cancer Institute, National Institutes of Health, American Cancer Society and the National Foundation for Cancer Research. In 1998 he received the Stephen Paget Award from the Cancer Metastasis Research Society and the Albert Schweitzer Award in Lisbon, Portugal.

[92] Statement by Professor Garth L. Nicolson to the Institute for Policy Research & Development, 3 January 2002.

[93] Bonner, Raymond and Tagliabue, John, 'Eavesdropping, US Allies See New Terror Attack,' *New York Times*, 21 October 2001.

[94] Ruppe, David, 'Who Did It? US Searches for Terror Clues,' ABC News, 11 September 2001.

[95] NBC News, 4 October 2001. See *Toronto Globe & Mail*, 4 October 2001.

[96] Sale, Richard, 'NSA Listens to bin Laden', United Press International (UPI), 13 February 2001. This report provides empirical information disproving an earlier *WorldNetDaily* report alleging that the Clinton administration sold powerful encryption software to al-Qaeda that would allow the network to encrypt, and thus block US

surveillance of, the network's encrypted communications. This report shows that regardless of Osama bin Laden's attempts at encryption, the codes were broken by ECHELON and his communications monitored.

[97] Drogin, Bob, 'Hate Unites an Enemy Without an Army,' *Los Angeles Times*, 21 September 2001.

[98] *New York Times*, 14 October 2001.

[99] Shane, Scott, 'Bin Laden, Associates Elude Spy Agency's Eavesdropping,' *Baltimore Sun*, 16 September 2001.

[100] Crary, David and Schwartz, David, 'World Trade Center Collapses in Terrorist Attack,' Associated Press, 11 September 2001.

[101] ABC News, 'Missed Opportunities,' World News Tonight, 18–20 February 2001.

[102] Diamond, John, 'US Had Agents Inside al-Qaeda,' *USA Today*, 4 June 2002, www.usatoday.com/news/attack/2002/06/03/cia-attacks.htm.

[103] Ensor, David, et. al., 'Justice May Probe Leaked Pre 9-11 Intercepts,' CNN, 21 June 2002.

[104] Ibid.

[105] Sale, Richard, 'NSA Listens to bin Laden', op. cit.

[106] Milligan, Susan and Schlesinger, Robert, 'Panel Sets Wide Scope for Inquiry into 9/11', *Boston Globe*, 5 June 2002.

[107] 'The Proof They Did Not Reveal: Two key pieces of evidence were missing from the government's dossier on the US attacks, made public last week. Now full details of the case against Bin Laden can be disclosed', *Sunday Times*, 7 October 2001, www.sunday-times.co.uk/news/pages/sti/2001/10/07/stiusausa02012.html .

[108] CNN, 'Blair's Full Statement', 4 October 2001, edition.cnn.com/2001/WORLD/europe/10/04/gen.blair.statement.

[109] Waller, Douglas , 'Was Hijack "Ringleader" in Bin Laden Orbit?', *Time*, 5 October 2001, www.time.com/time/nation/article/0,8599,178228,00.html.

[110] Diamond, John, 'US Had Agents Inside al-Qaeda', *USA Today*, 4 June 2002. www.usatoday.com/news/sept11/2002/06/03/cia-attacks.htm.

[111] *Newsweek*, 1 October 2001.

[112] Holnut, Randolph T., 'Why is Bush Stonewalling 9/11 Probe?,' *Albion Monitor*, 17 May 2002, www.monitor.net/monitor/0205a/911carlyle.html. Also see CBS News, 26 July 2001.

[113] Sorenson, Harley, 'Heads-Up to Ashcroft Proves Threat Was Known Before 9/11,' *San Francisco Chronicle*, 3 June 2002, www.sfgate.com/cgi-bin/article.cgi?file=/gate/archive/2002/06/03/hsorensen.DTL.

[114] Turnipseed, Tom, 'The Fear Factor to Promote War and Trample the Truth,' Common Dreams News Center, 14 June 2002, commondreams.org and www.turnipseed.net.

[115] Pitt, William Rivers, 'The Terrorists Flew and Bush Knew,' *Truthout*, 16 May 2002,

www.truthout.org/docs_02/05.17A.WRP.Bush.NU.htm.

[116] *Idaho Observer*, October 2001, proliberty.com/observer/20011008.htm.

[117] Matier, Philip, 'Willie Brown Got Low-key Early Warning About Air Travel,' *San Francisco Chronicle*, 12 September 2001.

[118] Cockburn, Alexander and St. Clair, Jeffrey, *Counterpunch*, 14 Sept. 2001.

[119] Doran, James, 'Rushdie's AirBan,' *Times*, 27 September 2001.

[120] Ananova, 'Rushdie "Given US Air Ban Week Before Terrorist Attacks",' 27 September 2001.

[121] Thomas, Evan, *Newsweek*, 24 September 2001.

[122] Hirsh, Michael, 'We've Hit the Targets,' *Newsweek*, 13 Sept. 2001.

[123] Farah, Joseph, 'The Failure of Government,' op. cit.

[124] Ruppert, Michael C., 'Suppressed Details of Criminal Insider Trading Lead Directly into the CIA's Highest Ranks,' *From the Wilderness*, 9 October 2001, www.fromthewilderness.com/free/ww3/10_09_01_krongard.html.

[125] *San Francisco Chronicle*, 29 September 2001. Cited in Ruppert, 'Suppressed Details', op. cit.

[126] 'Black Tuesday: The World's Largest Insider Trading Scam?', Herzliya International Policy Institute for Counter-terrorism, 21 September 2001. Cited in Ruppert, 'Suppressed Details', op. cit.

[127] Ruppert, 'Suppressed Details', op. cit.

[128] Ruppert, Michael C., 'A Timeline Surrounding September 11th,' *From the Wilderness*, 2 November 2001, www.copvcia.com/stories/nov_2001/lucy.html. For further information on PROMIS, the software descended from it, as well as the use of this new software by the CIA to monitor stock trading, see FTW Publications, 26 October 2001, www.copvcia.com/members/magic_carpet.html; FTW Publications, Vol. IV, No.6, 18 September 2001, www.copvcia.com/members/sept1801.html; FTW Publications, Vol. 3, No 7, 30 September 2000, www.copvcia.com/stories/may_2001/052401_promis.html. Also see *Washington Times*, 15 June 2001; FOX News, 16 October 2001.

[129] Michael C. Ruppert, 'Guns and Butter: The Economy Watch,' Interview with Kellia Ramares and Bonnie Falkner, KPFA 94.1 FM, Berkeley, CA, 12 October 2001. Available online at 'The CIA's Wall Street Connections,' Centre for Research on Globalisation, Montreal, 3 November 2001, globalresearch.ca/articles/RUP111A.html.

[130] Flocco, Tom, 'Profits of Death—Insider Trading and 9-11,' FTW Publications, 6 December 2001 [emphasis added].

[131] UPI, 13 February 2001.

[132] Doran, James, 'Millions of Shares Sold Before Disaster,' op. cit.

[133] Hence, Kyle F., 'Making a Killing Part II—Billions in Pre-911 Insider Trading Profits Leaves a Hot Trail: How Bush Administration Naysayers May Have Let it go Cold,' Center for Research on Globalisation, Montreal, 21 April 2002, www.globalresearch.ca/articles/HEN204B.html. Reuters, 16 December 2002.

[134] Eichenwald, Kurt, et al, 'Doubt Intensifies That Advance Knowledge of Attacks Was Used for Profit,' *New York Times*, 28 September 2001.

[135] FOX News, 'EU Searches for Suspicious Trading,' 22 September 2001.

[136] Hooper, John, 'Terror "Made Fortune for Bin Laden",' *Observer*, 23 September 2001.

[137] Doran, James, 'Millions of shares sold before disaster,' *Times*, 18 September 2001.

[138] *USA Today*, October 2001.

[139] *Montreal Gazette*, 19 September 2001.

[140] CBS, *60 Minutes*, 19 September 2001.

[141] Flocco, Tom, 'Profits of Death—Insider Trading and 9-11,' op. cit.

[142] *Independent*, 10 October 2001, www.independent.co.uk/story.jsp?story=99402

[143] Ruppert, Michael C., 'Suppressed Details of Criminal Insider Trading Lead Directly into the CIA's Highest Ranks,' op. cit. The discussion in this paper on financial transactions leading up to September 11th is based on Ruppert's analysis. His comments on the CIA–Wall Street alliance are crucial, and have been reproduced here: "Clark Clifford—The National Security Act of 1947 was written by Clark Clifford, a Democratic Party powerhouse, former Secretary of Defense, and one-time advisor to President Harry Truman. In the 1980s, as Chairman of First American Bancshares, Clifford was instrumental in getting the corrupt CIA drug bank BCCI a license to operate on American shores. His profession: Wall Street lawyer and banker. John Foster and Allen Dulles—These two brothers 'designed' the CIA for Clifford. Both were active in intelligence operations during WWII. Allen Dulles was the US ambassador to Switzerland where he met frequently with Nazi leaders and looked after US investments in Germany. John Foster went on to become secretary of state under Dwight Eisenhower and Allen went on to serve as CIA director under Eisenhower and was later fired by JFK. Their professions: partners in the most powerful—to this day—Wall Street law firm of Sullivan, Cromwell. Bill Casey—Ronald Reagan's CIA director and OSS veteran who served as chief wrangler during the Iran–Contra years was, under President Richard Nixon, Chairman of the Securities and Exchange Commission. His profession: Wall Street lawyer and stockbroker. David Doherty—The current vice president of the New York Stock Exchange for enforcement is the retired general counsel of the Central Intelligence Agency. George Herbert Walker Bush—President from 1989 to January 1993, also served as CIA director for 13 months from 1976–7. He is now a paid consultant to the Carlyle Group, the 11th largest defense contractor in the nation, which also shares joint investments with the bin Laden family. A.B. 'Buzzy' Krongard—The current executive director of the Central Intelligence Agency is the former chairman of the investment bank A.B. Brown and former vice chairman of Banker's Trust. John Deutch—This retired CIA director from the Clinton Administration currently sits on the board at Citigroup, the nation's second largest bank, which has been repeatedly and overtly involved in the documented laundering of drug money. This includes Citigroup's 2001 purchase of a Mexican bank known to launder drug money, Banamex. Nora Slatkin—This retired CIA executive director also sits on Citibank's board. Maurice 'Hank' Greenberg—The CEO of AIG insurance, manager of the third largest capital investment pool in the world, was floated as a possible CIA director in 1995. FTW exposed Greenberg's and AIG's long connection to CIA drug trafficking and covert operations in a two-part series that was

interrupted just prior to the attacks of September 11. AIG's stock has bounced back remarkably well since the attacks. To read that story, please go to www.copvcia.com/stories/july_2001/part_2.html."

[144] Flocco, Tom, 'Profits of Death—Insider Trading and 9-11,' op. cit.

[145] Berenson, Alex, 'Stock Adviser Knew About 9/11 Attacks, US Suggests,' *New York Times*, 25 May 2002, www.nytimes.com/2002/05/25/business/25FRAU.html?pagewanted=print&position=bottom.

[146] *Wall Street Journal*, 2 October 2001.

[147] Pender, Kathleen, 'Terrorism's Long, Tangled Money Trail,' *San Francisco Chronicle*, 7 October 2001.

[148] Hamilton, Walter, *Los Angeles Times*, 18 October 2001.

[149] Hence, Kyle, 'Making a Killing Part II,' op. cit.

[150] For discussion see for example Grey, Barry, 'Suspicious Trading Points to Advance Knowledge by Big Investors of September 11 AZttacks,' World Socialist Web Site, 5 October 2001.

[151] Ibid.

[152] Hence, Kyle, 'Making a Killing Part II,' op. cit.

Chapter 8: Tracking the Terrorists

[1] Farah, Joseph, 'The Failure of Government,' *WorldNetDaily* Exclusive Commentary, 19 October 2001, www.wnd.com.

[2] Reuters, 13 September 2001.

[3] CBS, *60 Minutes II*, 8 May 2002.

[4] Cave, Damon, 'US Was Warned That Moussaoui Had Close Ties to al-Qaida, Analyst Says,' *Salon*, 23 May 2002, www.salon.com/news/feature/2002/05/23/warning/index_np.html.

[5] *Star-Tribune*, 29 December 2001.

[6] *New York Times*, 8 February 2002.

[7] Shenon, Philip, 'FBI Ignored Attack Warning: Flight Instructor Told Agency of Terror Suspect's Plan,' *San Francisco Chronicle*, 22 Dec. 2001.

[8] *New York Times*, 24 May 2002.

[9] Seper, Jerry, 'Justice Blocked FBI Warrant,' *Washington Times*, 3 October 2001.

[10] ABC News, 'Missed Opportunities,' *World News Tonight*, 18–20 February 2001.

[11] Gordon, Greg, 'FAA Security Took No Action Against Moussaoui,' *Corpus Christi Caller Times*, 13 January 2002.

[12] Isikoff, Michael and Klaidman, Daniel, 'Access Denied,' MSNBC, 1 October 2001.

[13] Walsh, Nick Paton, 'MI5 Blunders Over Bomber', *Observer*, 30 December 2001, observer.guardian.co.uk/international/story/0,6903,625797,00.html.

[14] *Washington Post*, 3 July 2002.

[15] ARD, 23 November 2001.

[16] *Washington Post*, 28 October 2001.

[17] Smith, Hedrick, 'Inside The Terror Network: Should We Have Spotted the Conspiracy?', PBS Frontline, www.pbs.org/wgbh/pages/frontline.

[18] Swain, Diana, Canadian Broadcasting Corporation, 14 September 2001.

[19] Garcia, Ken, 'Intelligence Agencies Fell Asleep at the Switch,' *San Francisco Chronicle*, 16 September 2001 [emphasis added].

[20] *Observer*, 30 September 2001.

[21] 'Terrorists Among Us,' *Atlanta Journal Constitution*, 16 September 2001.

[22] Hopsicker, Daniel, 'Mohamed Atta Kept Terrorist E-List,' *Online Journal*, 24 April 2002, www.onlinejournal.com/archive/04-30-02_Hopsicker.pdf.

[23] BBC News, 26 November 2001.

[24] Landay, Johnathan S., 'Agency Could Have Overheard Terror Dialogue,' *Miami Herald*, 7 June 2002, www.miami.com/mld/miami/news/nation/3417402.htm.

[25] Ibid.

[26] Buncombe, Andrew, 'Al-Qa'ida Still a Threat Despite Loss of Key Men,' *Independent*, 15 September 2002, news.independent.co.uk/world/asia_china/story.jsp?story=333411.

[27] Hill, Eleanor, Joint Inquiry Staff Statement, Part I, 18 September 2002. Available at Intelligence Resource Program, Federation of American Scientists, www.fas.org/irp/congress/2002_hr/091802hill.html.

[28] Sale, Richard and Iqbal, Anwar, 'UPI Exclusive: Pearl Tracked al-Qaida', United Press International, 30 September 2002, www.upi.com/view.cfm?StoryID=20020930-052952-9407r.

[29] Ibid.

[30] Blomquist, Brian, 'Meeting that Spawned 9/11', *New York Post*, 10 July 2003. Also see 'Operation Holy Tuesday Codename for 9/11 Attacks', *Irish Examiner*, 11 July 2003, archives.tcm.ie/irishexaminer/2003/07/11/story365226268.asp; Ananova, 'Al-Qaida Called Sept 11 Attacks Operation Holy Tuesday', 10 July 2003, www.ananova.com/news/story/sm_798520.html?menu.

[31] CNN, '2nd Material Witness in FBI Custody', 16 September 2001, edition.cnn.com/2001/US/09/15/investigation.terrorism.

[32] Blomquist, 'Meeting that Spawned 9/11', op. cit.

[33] CNN, 30 August 2002.

[34] *New York Times*, 22 September 2002.

[35] Reuters, 'CIA Knew 9-11 Hijackers Were in the US,' 2 June 2002. Also see *Newsweek*, 3 June 2002.

[36] Smyth, Patrick, 'CIA Was Aware of Hijackers, Magazine Claims,' *Irish Times*, 3 June 2002, www.ireland.com/newspaper/world/2002/0603/1328098541FR03SMYTH.html.

[37] Johnston, David and Becker, Elizabeth, 'CIA was Tracking Hijacker Months Earlier Than It Had Said', *New York Times*, 3 June 2002.

[38] Thompson, Paul, 'Alhazmi and Almihdhar: The 9/11 Hijackers Who Should Have Been Caught', Center for Cooperative Research, 30 September 2002, www.cooperativeresearch.org/timeline/main/essaykhalidandnawaf.html.

[39] Hill, Eleanor, 'The Intelligence Community's Knowledge of the September 11 Hijackers Prior to September 11, 2001,' House/Senate Intelligence Committee, Washington D.C., 20 September 2002, intelligence.senate.gov/0209hrg/020920/witness.htm.

[40] Ibid.

[41] Capital Briefs, 'Basic Failure,' *Human Events*, 24 September 2001, Vol. 57, No. 35, p. 2.

[42] Willman, David and Miller, Alan C., 'Authorities Failed to Alert Airline about Suspected Terrorists', *Los Angeles Times*, 20 September 2001.

[43] Isikoff, Michael, 'Exclusive: The 9-11 Report: Slamming the FBI', *Newsweek*, 28 July 2003, msnbc.com/news/941425.asp.

[44] Isikoff, Michael, 'Exclusive: The Informant Who Lived with the Hijackers', *Newsweek*, 16 September 2002.

[45] Thompson, Paul, 'Alhazmi and Almihdhar', op. cit.

[46] Crewdson, John, 'Hijacker Held, Freed Before Sept. 11 Attack,' *Chicago Tribune*, 13 December 2001, www.chicagotribune.com/search/chi-0112130293dec13.story. Also see *Baltimore Sun*, 14 December 2001.

[47] MacVicar, Sheila and Faraj, Caroline, 'September 11 Hijacker Questioned in January 2001,' CNN, 1 August 2002. edition.cnn.com/2002/US/08/01/cia.hijacker/index.html.

[48] Ibid.

[49] Ibid.

[50] CNN, 'Another Hijacker Was Stopped for Traffic Violation', 9 January 2002, edition.cnn.com/2002/US/01/09/inv.hijacker.traffic.stops/.

[51] MacVicar and Faraj, 'September 11 Hijacker Question', op. cit.

[52] McWethy, John, 'FBI Was Warned of Sept. 11 Hijacker', ABC News, 23 May 2002, abcnews.go.com/sections/wnt/DailyNews/FBI_informant020523.html.

[53] Report of the Joint Inquiry into the Terrorist Attacks of September 11, 2001, *Joint Inquiry into Intelligence Community Activities Before and After the Terrorist Attacks of September 11, 2001*, House Permanent Select Committee on Intelligence and Senate Select Committee on Intelligence, December 2002, p. 180–2, 191.

[54] AIM Report No. 18, 'Catastrophic Intelligence Failure,' op. cit.

[55] Mowbray, Joel, 'Visas That Should Have Been Denied', *National Review*, 9 October 2003, www.nationalreview.com/mowbray/mowbray100902.asp.

[56] BBC *Newsnight*, 'Has Someone Been Sitting on the FBI?', 6 November 2001.

[57] Interview with Michael Springmann, 'Dispatches,' CBC Radio One, 16 January 2002, radio.cbc.ca/programs/dispatches/audio/020116_springman.rm.

[58] Epstein, Edward Jay, 'The Jeddah Ciphers,' *Netherworld: September 11, 2001*, edwardjayepstein.com/nether_WWDK4.htm. Epstein writes for the *New Yorker*, *Wall Street Journal*, and *Atlantic Monthly*.

[59] Cited in CCR Outline, 'US Intelligence and the Terrorists: Pre-9-11,' Center for Cooperative Research (CCR), 5 August 2002, www.cooperativeresearch.org/US_intelligence_and_the_terrorists.htm. [emphasis added]

[60] Freedberg, Sydney P., 'Loopholes Leave US Borders Vulnerable,' *St. Petersburg Times*, 25 November 2001.

[61] Mowbray, Joel, 'Open Door for Saudi Terrorists,' *National Review*, 1 July 2002, www.nationalreview.com/mowbray/mowbray061402.asp.

[62] Wheeler, Larry, 'Pensacola NAS link faces more scrutiny,' *Pensacola News Journal*, 17 September 2001. www.pensacolanewsjournal.com/news/091701/Local/ST001.shtml

[63] 'Alleged Hijackers May Have Trained at US Bases,' *Newsweek*, 15 September 2001.

[64] *New York Times*, 16 September 2001.

[65] Gugliotta, Guy and Fallis, David S., '2nd Witness Arrested: 25 Held for Questioning', *Washington Post*, 16 September 2001, p. A29. Wheeler, Larry, et. al., 'Pensacola NAS Link Faces More Ccrutiny', *Pensacola News Journal*, 17 September 2001.

[66] *Washington Post*, 22 September 2001.

[67] Ibid.

[68] Hopsicker, Daniel, 'Did Terrorists Train at US Military Schools?', *Online Journal*, 30 October 2001, www.onlinejournal.com/archive/10-30-01_Hopsicker-printable.pdf.

[69] Ibid.

[70] Hopsicker, Daniel, 'Pentagon Lied: Terrorists Trained at US Bases,' *Mad Cow Morning News*, 14 October 2001, www.madcowprod.com/index6.html. [emphasis added]

[71] Fainaru, Steve and Grimaldi, James V., 'FBI Knew Terrorists Were Using Flight Schools,' op. cit.

[72] Hopsicker, Daniel, 'Death in Venice (Florida),' *Online Journal*, 28 September 2001, www.onlinejournal.com/archive/10-02-01_Hopsicker-printable.pdf.

[73] Hopsicker, Daniel, 'What Are They Hiding Down in Venice, Florida?', *Online Journal*, 9 October 2001, www.onlinejournal.com/archive/10-09-01_Hopsicker-printable.pdf.

[74] Ibid.

[75] Kuhnhenn, James and Koszczuk, Jackie, 'Airlines in Sept. 11 Attacks Got No Specific Warnings,' *Miami Herald*, 17 May 2002.

[76] Hopsicker, Daniel, 'Was the CIA Running a Terrorist Flight School?', *Online Journal*, 7 November 2001.

[77] Hopsicker, Daniel, 'Jackson Stephens Active in Venice, FL,' *Online Journal*, 25 November 2001.

[78] Hopsicker, Daniel, 'Rudi Dekkers and the Lone (nut) Cadre,' *Online Journal*, 24 October 2001, www.onlinejournal.com/archive/10-24-01_Hopsciker-printable.pdf.

[79] Hopsicker, Daniel, 'Venice, Florida, Flight School Linked to CIA: Firm has 'green light' from local DEA,' *Online Journal*, 2 March 2002, www.onlinejournal.com/archive/03-02-02_Hopsicker.pdf.

[80] Kirk, Don, 'Filipinos Recall Hijack Suspects Leading a High Life', *International Herald Tribune*, 5 October 2001, www.intellnet.org/news/2001/10/05/7357-1.html.

[81] Fagan, Kevin, 'Agents of Terror Leave Their Mark on Sin City: Las Vegas Workers Recall the Men They Can't Forget', *San Francisco Chronicle*, 4 October 2001, www.sfgate.com/cgi-bin/article.cgi?file=/chronicle/archive/2001/10/04/MN102970.DTL.

[82] Benjamin, Jody A., 'Suspect's Actions Don't Add Up', *South Florida Sun Sentinel*, 16 September 2001, www.sun-sentinel.com/news/local/southflorida/sfl-warriors916.story.

[83] McDermott, Terry, 'Early Scheme to Turn Jets into Weapons: Philippines: Police say Khalid Shaikh Mohammed Led a Cell Aiming to Blow Up Planes in '95', *Los Angeles Times*, 24 June 2002.

[84] Wiktorowicz, Quintan and Kaltner, John, 'Killing in the Name of Islam: Al Qaeda's Justification for September 11', *Middle East Policy*, Vol. X, No. 2, Summer 2003, www.mepc.org/public_asp/journal_vol10/0306_wiktorowiczkaltner.asp.

[85] Elliot, Michael, 'Hate Club: Al-Qaeda's Web of Terror', *Time*, 4 November 2001.

[86] Zeidan, David, 'Radical Islam in Egypt: A Comparison of Two Groups', *Middle East Review of International Affairs*, Vol. 3, No. 3, September 1999, meria.idc.ac.il/journal/1999/issue3/jv3n3a1.html.

[87] Rahman, B., 'Tricky Mush Does Another', *South Asia Analysis Group*, Paper No. 811, 7 October 2003.

[88] Hellen, Nicholas, 'Ultra Zealots: If You Think Bin Laden is Extreme—Some Muslims Want to Kill Him Because He's Soft', *Sunday Times*, 21 October 2001.

[89] Barnett, Anthony, et. al., 'London-based Terror Chief Plotted Mayhem in Europe', *Observer*, 30 September 2001.

[90] Kiefer, David, 'SF Attorney: Bush Allowed 9/11', *San Francisco Examiner*, 20 June 2002.

[91] Interview with US attorney Stanley Hilton, Alex Jones Show, Texas, 11 March 2003, transcript available at 9/11 Citizens Watch, www.unansweredquestions.org/timeline/2003/alexjonesshow031103.html.

Chapter 9: Intelligence Breakdown or Political Fiasco?

[1] For instance, in spite of the multiple dire warnings, the Federal Aviation Administration (FAA) failed to upgrade its security in accordance with repeated recommendations.

[2] Stratfor, 16 September 2001, www.stratfor.com.

[3] Stratfor, 'Sept 11: What Did Bush Know and When Did He Know It?', Strategic Forecasting LLC, 20 May 2002.

[4] Ibid.

[5] Deutch, John and Smith Jeffrey H., 'Smarter Intelligence,' *Foreign Policy*, January–February 2002.

[6] Betts, Richard K., 'Fixing Intelligence', *Foreign Affairs*, January/February 2002. Excerpt available at www.foreignaffairs.org/20020101faessay6556/richard-k-betts/fixing-intelligence.html.

[7] Karmon, Ely, *Intelligence and the Challenge of Counter-Terrorism in the 21st Century*, International Policy Institute for Counter-Terrorism, Herzilya, 5 November 1998, www.ict.org.il/articles/articledet.cfm?articleid=54.

[8] Hoffman, Bruce, 'Terrorism—a Policy Behind the Times,' *Los Angeles Times*, 12 November 2001.

[9] Johnson, Loch K., *Secret Agencies: US Intelligence in a Hostile World*, Yale University Press, 1996.

[10] Corn, David, 'The Loyal Opposition: The 9/11 X-Files', *Tom Paine*, 1 March 2002, www.tompaine.com/feature.cfm/ID/5206.

[11] US government source cited in Ruppert, Michael C., 'World War III: This Was Not An Intelligence Failure,' *From the Wilderness* Publications, 18 September 2001, www.fromthewilderness.com/free/ww3/09_18_01_ww3.html. Statement from Michael C. Ruppert, former LAPD narcotics detective and expert on CIA covert operations, to Institute for Policy Research & Development, Brighton 15 January 2001.

[12] Walsh, Edward and Vise, David A., 'Louis Freeh to Resign as Director of the FBI', *Washington Post*, 2 May 2001, p. A01.

[13] Vise, David A. and Adams, Lorraine, 'Bin Laden Weakened, Officials Say,' *Washington Post*, 11 March 2000.

[14] 'Congress Fattens Its Dossier on Sept. 11 Intelligence Errors,' *Los Angeles Times*, 6 June 2002.

[15] Dobbs, Michael, 'An Obscure Player in the US War on Terror,' *Washington Post*, 2 April 2000.

[16] Wright, Lawrence, 'The Counter-Terrorist,' *New Yorker*, 14 January 2002.

[17] Timmerman, Kenneth, 'What They Knew; When They Knew It,' *Insight On The News*, 27 May 2002, www.insightmag.com/main.cfm/include/detail/storyid/253605.html.

[18] Ibid.

[19] CFIBA report, 'Types of Intelligence,' *Intelligence Notebook*, Canadian Forces Intelligence Branch Association, (viewed 12 July 2004), www.intbranch.org/engl/intntbk/intro.html.

[20] Betts, Richard K., 'Intelligence Warning: Old Problems, New Agendas,' *Parameters* (US Army War College Quarterly), Spring 1998, p. 26–35.

[21] Staff Statement No. 9, *Law Enforcement, Counterterrorism, and Intelligence Collection in the United States Prior to 9/11*, National Commission on Terrorist Attacks Upon the United States, Washington, DC, April 2004, p. 7.

[22] Gordon, Greg, 'FAA Security Took No Action Against Moussaoui,' *Corpus Christi Caller Times*, 13 January 2002.

[23] Staff Statement No. 9, op. cit., p. 9.

[24] Ibid., p. 2.

[25] Ibid., p. 10.

[26] Ibid., p. 10.

[27] Ibid., p. 4.

[28] Ibid., p. 9.

[29] Ibid., p. 4.

[30] Ibid., p. 11.

[31] Staff Statement No. 11, *The Performance of the Intelligence Community*, National Commission on Terrorist Attacks Upon the United States, Washington, DC, April 2004 p. 3.

[32] Staff Statement No. 5, *Diplomacy*, National Commission on Terrorist Attacks Upon the United States, Washington, DC, March 2004, p. 6.

[33] Staff Statement No. 11, op. cit., p. 12.

[34] Statement for the Record, FBI Director Louis J. Freeh before the Senate Judiciary Committee, 3 September 1998, archived at www.fas.org/irp/congress/1998_hr/98090302_npo.html.

[35] Statement for the Record, FBI Director Louis J. Freeh before the Senate Committee on Appropriations, Subcommittee for the Departments of Commerce, Justice, and State, the Judiciary, and Related Agencies, 4 February 1999, archived at www.fas.org/irp/congress/1999_hr/990204-freehct2.htm.

[36] 'Avoiding the Real Wuestions,' *Jane's Intelligence Digest*, 28 May 2002.

[37] Burns, Margie, 'Why Did Bush Abolish Information Sharing and Route All National Security Information to Him, Via Condoleezza Rice?', *Online Journal*, 2 August 2003, www.onlinejournal.com/Special_Reports/080203Burns/080203burns.html. Also see the full NSPD of February 13th 2001 at the website of the Federation of American Scientists, www.fas.org/irp/offdocs/nspd/nspd-1.htm.

[38] McGovern, Ray, 'Signs of Attack Well-known', *Miami Herald*, 3 June 2002,

www.miami.com/mld/miami/3387673.htm.

[39] Rowley, Coleen, 'Memo to FBI Director Robert Mueller,' *Time*, 21 May 2002. Available at Centre for Research on Globalisation, globalresearch.ca/articles/ROW205A.html.

[40] ABC News, 'Missed Opportunities,' op. cit.

[41] ABC News, 'Canvass of Flight Schools Weighed Before 9/11?,' 3 May 2002, abcnews.go.com/sections/us/DailyNews/homefront020503.html.

[42] Timmerman, Kenneth R., 'What They Knew; When They Knew It,' *Insight On The News*, 27 May 2002.

[43] Cornwell, Rupert, 'Finger of Blame Points Directly at FBI for Ignoring Warnings that Might Have Averted 911,' *Independent*, 25 May 2002, news.independent.co.uk/world/americas/story.jsp?story=298692.

[44] *Los Angeles Times*, 25 May 2002, and summary of this piece by Martin, Patrick, 'New Evidence That US Government Suppressed September 11 Warnings,' World Socialist Web Site, 27 May 2002.

[45] Ibid.

[46] CNN, 20 May 2002.

[47] *Los Angeles Times*, 25 May 2002.

[48] Bruce, Ian, 'FBI "Super Flying Squad" to Combat Terror', *Herald*, 16 May 2002.

[49] Isikoff, Michael, 'FBI Agent's Notes Pointed to Possible World Trade Center Attack,' *Newsweek*, 20 May 2002. Available at www.apfa.org/public/articles/News-Events/UNHEEDED.HTML.

[50] Blomquist, Brian, 'FBI Man's Chilling 9/11 Prediction', *New York Post*, 9 May 2002, www.nypost.com/news/nationalnews/47581.htm.

[51] Lewis, Neil A., 'FBI Inaction Blurred Picture Before September 11,' *New York Times*, 27 May 2002.

[52] *Newsweek*, 3 June 2002.

[53] Eggen, Dan, 'Halting Some Hijackers Was "Possible,"' *Washington Post*, 27 May 2002.

[54] 'FBI Told to Explain Action,' *New York Times*, 26 May 2002.

[55] Vogler, Mark E., 'Methuen Native at Center of FBI Storm,' *Eagle-Tribune*, 30 May 2002.

[56] Eggen, Dan, 'Halting Some Hijackers Was "Possible,"' op. cit.

[57] Moore, Steve, 'The FBI's Radical Fundamentalist Unit in Washington D.C.,' Centre for Research on Globalisation, Montreal, 18 August 2002, globalresearch.ca/articles/MOO208B.html.

[58] Rowley, Coleen, 'Memo to FBI Director Robert Mueller,' op. cit.

[59] David P. Schippers served as chief counsel to the United States House of Representatives managers for the impeachment trial of President Bill Clinton in the US Senate from January 1 to February 28, 1999. He served as chief investigative counsel for

the United States House of Representatives' Committee on the Judiciary during 1998. From April to September he handled the investigative issues and investigations relating to the committee's oversight investigation of the US Dept. of Justice and all of its subagencies. From Sept. to Dec. 1998, he was charged with reviewing and reporting on the Referral of the Office of Independent Counsel concerning possible impeachment offenses committed by President Clinton. He was then responsible for conducting the impeachment inquiry authorised by the House of Representatives and reporting the results to the Committee on the Judiciary. An attorney in private practice since 1967, Schippers is the senior partner in the Chicago law firm Schippers & Bailey, which specializes in trust law, labor law, trials, and appeals in the state and federal courts of Illinois and throughout the country. From 1963 to 1967, Schippers served as a member and later the chief of the Organized Crime and Racketeering Section of the US Department of Justice at Chicago. He prepared and tried many major criminal cases in the federal courts and was also involved in a great number of major grand jury investigations. He previously served in the US Attorney's Office as an assistant United States attorney, trying major criminal cases on behalf of the government and preparing and arguing appeals on behalf of the government. Schippers earned both his undergraduate and J.D. degree from Loyola University in Chicago. He has served as a teacher of trial advocacy and advanced trial advocacy to senior law students at the Loyola University School of Law. He has also taught trial advocacy at the Williamette University School of Law in Salem, Oregon, and at the United States Air Force Air University in Montgomery, Alabama. Schippers served as one of five members of the Illinois State Police Merit Board from 1987 to 1993. He is the recipient of the Loyola University Law Alumni Medal of Excellence, the Loyola University Alumni Association citation for distinguished service to the legal profession, and the Award of Appreciation from the Federal Criminal Investigators Association.

[60] Jasper, William F., 'OKC Bombing: Precursor to 9-11?', New American, 28 January 2002, Vol. 18, No. 2.

[61] David P. Schippers, 'David Schippers Tells Metcalf Feds Ignored Warnings of WTC Attacks,' WorldNetDaily, 21 October 2001, wnd.com/news/article.asp?ARTICLE_ID=25008.

[62] David P. Schippers, 'Government Had Prior Knowledge,' Interview on Alex Jones Show, Talk Radio, Austin, Texas, 10 Oct. 2001, transcript available at www.infowars.com/transcript_schippers.html.

[63] EFI Report, 'What Does Nationally-renowned Attorney David Schippers Think of This Possibility?' Eagle Forum of Illinois, 30 September 2001, www.ileagles.net/schippers.htm.

[64] Telephone interview with Chief Investigative Counsel David P. Schippers, Institute for Policy Research & Development, Brighton, 26 February 2002.

[65] Telephone interview with Chief Investigative Counsel David P. Schippers, op. cit.

[66] Price, Joyce Howard, 'September 11 Attacks Called Avoidable,' Washington Times, June 9, 2002, www.washtimes.com/national/20020609-22093908.htm.

[67] Grigg, William Norman, 'Did We Know What Was Coming?', The New American, Vol. 18, No. 5, 11 March 2002, www.thenewamerican.com/tna/2002/03-11-2002/vol18no05_didweknow.htm.

[68] Interview with Tyrone Powers with Bob Slade on Open Line show, 98.7 Kiss FM, New York, 19 May 2002. Cited in Shipman, Dennis, 'The Spook Who Sat Behind The Door: A Modern Day Tale', IndyMedia, 20 May 2002, portland.indymedia.org/front.php3?article_id=11188&group=webcast. Emailed statement from Powers to the Institute for Policy Research & Deveopment, Brighton, 22 May 2002.

Chapter 10: Deconstructing the Commission's Chronology

[1] Israel, Jared and Bykov, Illarion, 'Guilty for 9-11: Bush, Rumsfeld, Myers Part 1,' The Emperor's New Clothes, 14 November 2001, Updated 17 November 2001, emperors-clothes.com/indict/indict-1.htm.

[2] Schiavo, Mary, 'FAA/Airline Accountability,' Transcript: 9/11 and the Public Safety, UnAnsweredQuestions Press Conference, National Press Club, Washington, DC, 10 June 2002, unansweredquestions.org/transcript.php#mary.

[3] Credit to Michael C. Ruppert for unearthing this fact from official FAA and DoD records. For details see Ruppert's forthcoming book *The Truth and Lies of 9/11: America's Descent into Fascism at the End of the Age of Oil*.

[4] Associated Press, 'Use of Military Jets Jumps Since 9/11', 13 August 2002.

[5] See FAA Order 7400.2E, 'Procedures for Handling Airspace Matters,' Effective Date: 7 December 2000 (Includes Change 1, effective 7 July 2001), Chapter 14-1-2. Full text posted at: www.faa.gov/ATpubs/AIR/air1401.html#14-1-2. Also see Dennis, Gregory and Torlak, Emina, 'Direct-To Requirements,' sdg.lcs.mit.edu/atc/D2Requirements.htm. Cited in Israel, Jared and Bykov, Illarion, 'Guilty for 9-11: Bush, Rumsfeld, Myers Part 1,' op. cit.

[6] MSNBC, 12 September 2001, www.msnbc.com/news/627524.asp. Cited in Israel and Bykov, 'Guilty for 9-11: Bush, Rumsfeld, Myers Part 1,' op cit.

[7] CNN, 26 October 1999.

[8] FAA 'Aeronautical Information Manual: Official Guide to Basic Flight Information and Air Traffic Control (ATC) Procedures,' (Includes Change 3 Effective: 12 July 2001) Chapter 5-6-4 'Interception Signals,' Full text posted at: www.faa.gov/ATpubs/AIM/Chap5/aim0506.html#5-6-4. Cited in Israel and Bykov, 'Guilty for 9-11: Bush, Rumsfeld, Myers Part 1,' op cit.

[9] FAA Order 7110.65M, 'Air Traffic Control,' (Includes Change 3 Effective: 12 July 2001), Chapter 10-2-5 'Emergency Situations,' Full text posted at: www.faa.gov/ATpubs/ATC/Chp10/atc1002.html#10-2-5. Cited in Israel and Bykov, 'Guilty for 9-11: Bush, Rumsfeld, Myers Part 1,' op cit.

[10] FAA Order 7110.65M, 'Air Traffic Control' (Includes Change 3 Effective: 12 July 2001), Chapter 10-1-1 'Emergency Determinations,' Full text posted at: www.faa.gov/ATpubs/ATC/Chp10/atc1001.html#10-1-1. Cited in Israel and Bykov, 'Guilty for 9-11: Bush, Rumsfeld, Myers Part 1,' op cit.

[11] FAA Order 7610.4J 'Special Military Operations' (Effective Date: 3 November 1998; Includes: Change 1, effective 3 July 2000; Change 2, effective 12 July 2001), Chapter 4, Section 5, 'Air Defense Liaison Officers.' Full text posted at: www.faa.gov/ATpubs/

MIL/Ch4/mil0405.html. Cited in Israel and Bykov, 'Guilty for 9-11: Bush, Rumsfeld, Myers Part 1,' op cit.

[12] Ibid., Chapter 7, Section 1-2, 'Escort of Hijacked Aircraft: Requests for Service.' Full text at: faa.gov/ATpubs/MIL/Ch7/mil0701.html. Cited in Israel and Bykov, 'Guilty for 9-11: Bush, Rumsfeld, Myers Part 1,' op cit.

[13] ABC News, 25 October 1999.

[14] FAA Order 7610.4J 'Special Military Operations', op. cit.

[15] Chairman of the Joint Chiefs of Staff Instruction 3610.01A, 1 June 2001, 'Aircraft Piracy (Hijacking) and Destruction of Derelict Airborne Objects,' 4.Policy (page 1) PDF file available at: www.dtic.mil/doctrine/jel/cjcsd/cjcsi/3610_01a.pdf.

[16] DoD Directive 3025.15, 'Military Assistance to Civil Authorities (MCSA)', 18 February 1997, 4.7.1, www.nici.org/publications/publications/ 32%20dod%203025.15.pdf. [emphasis added]

[17] Ibid.

[18] DoD Directive 3025.1, 'Military Support to Civil Authorities (MCSA)', 15 January 1993, www.nici.org/publications/publications/36%20%20dod%203025.1.pdf.

[19] Air Traffic Control Center, 'ATCC Controller's Read Binder,' Xavier Software, Aug. 1998, www.xavius.com/080198.htm. This software is a "fully realistic simulation of actual traffic flows, radar sectors, ATC procedures, and radar equipment currently used throughout the US. Designed by a real controller, ATCC is ideal for pilots [and] controller trainees." [emphasis added]

[20] CNN, 26 October 1999.

[21] Bretz, Elizabeth A., 'Hard Questions to Answer,' *Spectrum Magazine*, Institute of Electrical and Electronics Engineers, 13 July 2002, www.spectrum.ieee.org/WEBONLY/special/sept01/questions.html.

[22] Johnson, Glen, 'Facing Terror Attacks Aftermath: Otis Fighter Jets Scrambled Too Late to Halt the Attacks,' *Boston Globe*, 15 Sep. 2001.

[23] Walsh, Edward and Clairborne, William, 'Golfer Payne Stewart Dies in Plane Crash,' *Washington Post*, 26 October 1999, www.washingtonpost.com/wp-srv/national/daily/oct99/crash26.htm.

[24] NTSB Aircraft Accident Brief (DCA00MA005, South Dakota, October 25, 1999), National Transport Safety Board, 2000, www.ntsb.gov/Publictn/2000/AAB0001.htm.

[25] Walsh, Edward and Clairborne, William, 'Golfer Payne Stewart Dies in Plane Crash,' op. cit.

[26] AP Online/Nando Media, 'Payne Stewart fatal crash chronology,' 26 October 1999, archive.sportserver.com/generic/story/0,1673,500049709-500081423-500247865-0,00.html.

[27] Ibid.

[28] Sealey, Geraldine, 'Golfer Payne Stewart Dies,' ABC News, 25 October 1999,

abcnews.go.com/sections/us/DailyNews/plane102599.html.

[29] Interview with Jerry Quickley, KPFK Radio, The Morning Show 'Beneath the Surface,' August/September 2002, kpfk.org.

[30] Szamuely, George, 'Scrambled Messages,' New York Press, Vol. 14, No. 50, www.nypress.com/14/50/taki/bunker.cfm.

[31] Testimony of General Richard B. Myers, 'US Senator Carl Levin (DMI) Holds Hearing On Nomination of General Richard Myers to be Chairman of the Joint Chiefs of Staff,' Senate Armed Services Committee, Washington, DC, 13 September 2001.

[32] Johnson, Glen, 'Otis Fighter Jets Scrambled Too Late to Halt the Attacks,' Boston Globe, 15 September 2001.

[33] NBC News, 'Meet the Press,' 16 September 2001, stacks.msnbc.com/news/ 629714.asp?cp1=1 Stan Goff, a 26-year US veteran and expert in military science and doctrine, a retired Special Forces Master Sergeant who was tactics instructor at the US Army's Jungle Operations Training Center in Panama, taught Military Science at the US Military Academy at West Point, and was involved in operations in eight designated conflict areas from Vietnam to Haiti, has similarly concluded on analysis of the chronology of the events that no US Air Force jets at all were scrambled until after the Pentagon crash (Goff, Stan, 'The So-called Evidence is a Farce,' Narco News, 10 October 2001, www.narconews.com).

[34] Staff Statement No. 17, Improvising a Homeland Defense, National Commission on Terrorist Attacks on the United States, Washington, DC, June 2004, p. 4.

[35] Ibid., p. 5.

[36] Sheehy, Gail, '9/11 Tapes Reveal Ground Personnel Muffled Attacks', New York Observer, 15 June 2004.

[37] Ibid.

[38] Ibid.

[39] Ibid.

[40] News Release, 'NORAD's Response Times', North American Aerospace Defense Command, Peterson, AFB, 18 September 2001, web.archive.org/web/20020615115751/ www.norad.mil/presrelNORADTimelines.htm.

[41] Staff Statement No. 17, op. cit., p. 6.

[42] Clayton, Mark, 'Controllers' Tale of Flight 11', Christian Science Monitor, 13 September 2001, www.csmonitor.com/2001/0913/p1s2-usju.html.

[43] Mccartney, Scott and Carey, Susan, 'American, United Watched and Worked In Horror as Sept. 11 Hijackings Unfolded', Wall Street Journal, 15 October 2001.

[44] ABC News, '9/11: Interviews by Peter Jennings', 11 September 2002, archived at www.cooperativeresearch.org/timeline/2002/abcnews091102.html.

[45] ABC News, 'Terror Hits the Towers', 14 September 2001, abcnews.go.com/onair/ DailyNews/sept11_moments_1.html.

[46] Dwyer, Jim, 'Takeoffs Continued Until Second Jet Hit Trade Center', Transcripts Show', *New York Times*, 30 December 2002.

[47] Ragavan, Chitra and Mazzetti, Mark, 'Pieces of the Puzzle: A Top-secret Conference Call on September 11 Could Shed New Light on the Terrorist Attacks', *US News & World Report*, 8 September 2003.

[48] Seely, Hart, 'Amid Crisis Simulation, "We Were Suddenly No-Kidding Under Attack"', Newhouse News Service, 25 January 2002, www.newhousenews.com/archive/story1a012802.html.

[49] Clarke, Richard, *Against All Enemies: Inside America's War on Terror*, Free Press, New York, 2004, p. 2–4. See Paul Thompson, *Day of 9/11 Interim Update*, 17 June 2004, www.cooperativeresearch.org/061704-911timelineupdate.html.

[50] Staff Statement No. 17, op. cit., p. 6.

[51] Seely, Hart, 'Amid Crisis Simulation', op. cit.

[52] News Release, 'NORAD's Response Times', op. cit.

[53] Staff Statement No. 17, op. cit., p. 9.

[54] DelaHaya, Tech. Sgt. Rick, 'F-15 Eagle Celebrates Silver Anniversary', *Air Force News*, 30 January 1997, archived at www.ugamedia.com/f15/news/40.txt.

[55] Cited in Thompson, Paul, *Complete 9/11 Timeline* (United Airlines Flight 175), Center for Cooperative Research, 8:52 AM (viewed 27 June 2004), www.cooperativeresearch.org/timeline.jsp?timeline=complete_911_timeline&day_of_911=ua175.

[56] Staff Statement No. 17, op. cit., p. 10.

[57] Ibid., p. 11.

[58] Ibid., p. 11.

[59] Ibid., p. 13–14.

[60] Staff Statement No. 17, op. cit., p. 18–19.

[61] NORAD Timeline Presentation and Question and Answer Session, '9/11 Commission Testimony: Remarks of NORAD Personnel: Maj. Gen. Craig McKinley, Maj. Gen. Larry Arnold, Col. Alan Scott', National Commission on September 11 Terrorist Attacks, 23 May 2003, archived at www.cooperativeresearch.org/timeline/2003/noradtestimony052303.html and transcribed from www.c-span.org/VideoArchives.asp?Cat=Issue&Code=DESE.

[62] Thompson, Paul, *Complete 9/11 Timeline* (American Airlines Flight 77), Center for Cooperative Research, 8:46 AM (viewed 27 June 2004), www.cooperativeresearch.org/timeline.jsp?timeline=complete_911_timeline&day_of_911=aa77.

[63] Wald, Matthew I., 'Pentagon Tracked Jet but Found No Way to Stop It', *New York Times*, 15 September 2001, archived at emperor.vwh.net/9-11backups/nyt915.htm.

[64] Adcock, Sylvia, 'Air Attack on Pentagon Indicates Weakness', *Newsday*, 23 September 2001, www.newsday.com/ny-uspent232380681sep23.story.

[65] Staff and Wire reports, 'Timeline in Terrorist Attacks of Sept. 11, 2001', *Washington Post*, 12 September 2001, www.washingtonpost.com/wp-srv/nation/articles/timeline.html.

[66] Staff Statement No. 17, op. cit., p. 11.

[67] FAA clarification memo to 9/11 Independent Commission, 'FAA Communications with NORAD On September 11, 2001', 21 May 2003, archived at www.cooperativeresearch.org/timeline/2003/faa052203.html.

[68] Ibid.

[69] Thompson, Paul, 'The Failure to Defend the Skies on 9/11', Center for Cooperative Research (viewed 27 June 2004), www.cooperativeresearch.org/essay.jsp?article=essayairdefense.

[70] Staff Statement No. 17, op. cit., p. 13.

[71] Ibid., p. 13.

[72] Ibid., p. 13.

[73] Seely, 'Amid Crisis Simulation', op. cit., 9:24 AM.

[74] Staff Statement No. 17, op. cit., p. 14.

[75] ABC News, '9/11: Interviews by Peter Jennings', op. cit.; Thompson, *Complete 9/11 Timeline* (American Airlines Flight 77), op. cit., 9:27 AM.

[76] CNN, 'Government Failed to React to FAA Warning', 16 September 2001, www.cnn.com/2001/US/09/16/inv.flat.foot.

[77] Thompson, 'The Failure to Defend the Skies', op. cit.

[78] National Commission on September 11 Terrorist Attacks, '9/11 Commission Testimony: Remarks of Secretary of Transportation Norman Mineta', 23 May 2003, archived at www.cooperativeresearch.org/timeline/2003/commissiontestimony052303.html.

[79] Eggen, Dan and Branigin, William, 'Air Defenses Faltered on 9/11, Panel Finds: Report Documents Command and Communication Errors', *Washington Post*, 17 June 2004, www.washingtonpost.com/wp-dyn/articles/A48471-2004Jun17.html.

[80] Staff Statement No. 17, op. cit., p. 24.

[81] Donnelly, Sally, 'The Day the FAA Stopped the World', *Time*, 14 September 2001, www.time.com/time/nation/article/0,8599,174912,00.html. Cited in Thompson, 'The Failure to Defend the Skies', op. cit. [emphasis added]

[82] Scott, William B., 'Exercise Jump-Starts Response to Attacks', *Aviation Week and Space Technology*, 3 June 2002, www.aviationnow.com/content/publication/awst/20020603/avi_stor.htm.

[83] Thompson, 'The Failure to Defend the Skies', op. cit.

[84] Staff Statement No. 17, op. cit., p. 15, 17.

[85] Ibid., p. 16.

[86] Ibid., p. 17.

[87] CNN, 'Officials: Government failed to react to FAA warning', 17 September 2001, edition.cnn.com/2001/US/09/16/inv.hijack.warning.

[88] Staff Statement No. 17, op. cit., p. 18.

[89] Gibson, John, et. al., 'War on Terror', FOX News, 24 September 2001. Transcript archived at www.cooperativeresearch.org/timeline/2001/foxnews092401.html.

[90] Thompson, 'The Failure to Defend the Skies', op. cit.

[91] *Boston Globe*, 15 September 2001.

[92] Ibid. There are other disturbing reports that indicate that the government's failure with respect to Flight 93 was even more serious than this. Evidence of events on and around the flight garnered by *New York Times* correspondent Jere Longman in his book *Among the Heroes*—plus other credible accounts including cockpit voice recordings, recordings of passenger's phone calls with relatives, multiple eyewitness testimonials, and testimonials from military officials—strongly suggests that Flight 93 was in fact shot down by the US military, after passengers had taken control of the plane. It has been documented that the passengers had virtually succeeded in repelling the hijackers and taking control over the plane just before 10:00 AM. This takeover was known to military and law enforcement officials, because many phone calls from the passengers narrating events on the plane were relayed directly to the latter. Nevertheless, numerous credible eyewitness—including for instance a New Hampshire flight controller—saw Flight 93 being closely intercepted by a military plane. Multiple eyewitnesses on the ground independently confirmed that they had not only seen the fighter craft, but had distinctly heard the sound of a missile and witnessed the ensuing explosion as it impacted on the flight, before it had actually crash landed. Although this evidence in itself is by no means conclusive, it is more than sufficient to necessitate an urgent investigation—but the Commission has deliberately ignored this issue, just as it has ignored and glossed over the substance of the systematic violations of standard procedures on 9/11. If true, this account indicates that firstly, the US government had the capacity to intercept and shoot down the hijacked aircraft throughout the crisis, but selectively employed this power only against the last plane; secondly, that the government did not shoot down Flight 93 to save the lives of far larger numbers of civilians due to the plane's impact on highly populated buildings, because the plane had been taken over by the passengers; and thirdly, that the shooting down of the plane was in fact superfluous because it killed passengers who otherwise were likely to survive. Why, then, did the government wish to shoot down Flight 93 after it had been saved? Much of this evidence has been documented extensively by Thompson in his *Complete 9/11 Timeline* (United Airlines Flight 93) (viewed 28 June 2004), www.cooperativeresearch.org/timeline.jsp?timeline=complete_911_timeline&day_of_911 =ua93. David Ray Griffin offers some perturbing explanations of the evidence in his review of Thompson's material in *The New Pearl Harbor*, op. cit.

Chapter 11: The Paralysis of the National Security System on 9/11

[1] *USA Today*, 17 September 2001.

[2] *San Diego Union-Tribune*, 12 September 2001.

[3] DC Military, private website authorized by US military to provide information for members of the US armed forces, (viewed 19th November 2001), web.archive.org/web/20011129021913/www.dcmilitary.com/baseguides/airforce/andrews/partnerunits.html. The website was changed after 9/11 but has been archived here.

[4] DCANG Home Page, District of Columbia Air National Guard website, (viewed 8 April 2001), web.archive.org/web/20010205074600/www.dcandr.ang.af.mil/hq/index.htm. The website was changed after 9/11 but has been archived here. Strangely, this information was removed from the website in the aftermath of the September 11th terrorist attacks. See Israel, Jared, 'Powerful Evidence That Air Force Was Made To Stand Down on 9/11,' The Emperor's New Clothes, 1 July 2002, emperors-clothes.com/indict/update630.htm.

[5] Sunday Telegraph, 14 September 2001.

[6] Denver Post, 11 September 2001.

[7] NBC Nightly News (6:30 PM EST), 11 September 2001.

[8] NBC, Meet the Press (10:00 AM EST), 16 September 2001.

[9] Ibid.

[10] Also see Israel, Jared and Bykov, Illarion, 'Mr. Cheney's Cover Story: Guilty for 9/11: Bush, Rumsfeld, Myers Part 2,' The Emperors New Clothes, 20 November 2001, Updated 21 November 2001, emperors-clothes.com/indict/indict-2.htm.

[11] Testimony of US Vice President Dick Cheney, Meet the Press, NBC, 16 September 2001.

[12] 'Fighter Response After Attacks Questioned,' Washington Post, 14 September 2001.

[13] Szamuely, George, 'Nothing Urgent,' op. cit.

[14] Rhem, Kathleen T. (Sergeant 1st class), 'Myers and Sept. 11: "We Hadn't Thought About This",' American Forces Press Service, 23 October 2001, www.defenselink.mil/news/Oct2001/n10232001_200110236.html

[15] Szamuely, George, 'Nothing Urgent,' op. cit.

[16] Rhem, Kathleen T., 'Myers and Sept. 11: "We Hadn't Thought About This,"' op. cit.

[17] Testimony of General Richard B. Myers, 'US Senator Carl Levin (DMI) Holds Hearing On Nomination of General Richard Myers to be Chairman of the Joint Chiefs of Staff,' op. cit.

[18] Szamuely, George, 'Nothing Urgent,' op. cit.

[19] Special Report, 'Planes Crash into World Trade Center,' ABC News, 11 September 2001, 8:53 AM EST.

[20] Szamuely, George, 'Nothing Urgent,' op. cit.

[21] Gil-White, Francisco and Israel, Jared, 'Bush Betrayed Consciousness of Guilt on 9-11,' Emperor's Clothes, 11 September 2002, emperors-clothes.com/indict/conscious.htm.

[22] MSNBC, 'Sarasota, Fla.: Small school, big lessons,' www.msnbc.com/news/801474.asp.

[23] Ibid.

[24] White House Briefing, 'President Meets with Displaced Workers in Town Hall Meeting: Remarks by the President in Town Hall Meeting,' Office of the Press Secretary, Washington, DC, 4 December 2001, www.whitehouse.gov/news/releases/2001/12/20011204-17.html.

[25] Adcock, Sylvia, et. al., 'Air Attack on Pentagon Indicates Weaknesses,' *Newsday*, 23 September 2001, www.newsday.com/ny-uspent232380681sep23.story.

[26] Sheehy, Gail, 'Four 9/11 Moms Battle Bush', op. cit.

[27] United States Department of Defense News Transcript, 'Assistant Secretary Clarke Interview with WBZ Boston', 15 September 2001, www.defenselink.mil/transcripts/2001/t09162001_t0915wbz.html.

[28] Sprengelmeyer, M. E. and Alessi, Ryan, 'At the Pentagon, Fear and Anger', *Detroit News*, 11 September 2001, www.detnews.com/2001/nation/0109/11/nation-291261.htm.

[29] Chairman of the Joint Chiefs of Staff Instruction 3610.01A, 'Aircraft Piracy (Hijacking) and Destruction of Derelict Airborne Objects,' op. cit.

[30] Yen, Hope, 'As 9/11 Panel Ends, Victims' Families Share Anger, Hope', Associated Press, 18 June 2004, www.news-leader.com/today/0618-As911panel-114372.html.

[31] Scott, William B., 'Exercise Jump-Starts Response to Attacks', op. cit.

[32] Seely, Hart, 'Amid Crisis Simulation', op. cit.

[33] Bamford, James, 'Inside the Failed Air Force Scramble to Prevent the Sept. 11 Attacks', MSNBC News, 28 June 2004, msnbc.msn.com/id/5315883.

[34] First public hearing, Statement of Mindy Kleinberg to the National Commission on Terrorist Attacks Upon the United States, 31 March 2003, www.9-11commission.gov/hearings/hearing1/witness_kleinberg.htm.

[35] Simmie, Scott, 'Northern Guardian: The Scene at NORAD on Sept. 11', *Toronto Star*, 9 December 2001, p. B05. Also see NORAD News Release, 'NORAD Maintains Northern Vigilance', 9 September 2001, www.norad.mil/index.cfm?fuseaction=home.news_rel_09_09_01.

[36] News Release, 'NORAD's Response Times', op. cit.; Seely, Hart, 'Amid Crisis Simulation', op. cit.

[37] Ruppert, Michael C., 'TRIPOD II and FEMA: Lack of NORAD Response on 9/11 Explained', *From the Wilderness*, 5 June 2004, www.fromthewilderness.com/free/ww3/060704_tripod_fema.html.

[38] Scott, 'Northern Guardian: The Scene at NORAD on Sept. 11', op. cit.

[39] Komarow, Steven and Squitieri, Tom, 'NORAD Had Drills of Jets as Weapons', *USA Today*, 18 April 2004, www.usatoday.com/news/washington/2004-04-18-norad_x.htm.

[40] Ibid.

[41] Concept Proposal–Amalgam Virgo 01, *Scenario: Counter Terrorism–Combined (Joint) Training for Unconventional Threat*, The Strike, Land Attack and Air Defense Division,

National Defense Industrial Association, 1–2 June 2001, archived at www.ratical.org/ ratville/CAH/linkscopy/AmalgumVirgo.pdf.

[42] Scott, 'Northern Guardian', op. cit.

[43] Definition of the Joint Chiefs of Staff (JCS), JCS website, (viewed 30 June 2004), www.dtic.mil/jcs/core/jcs_defn.html.

[44] DCANG Home Page, District of Columbia Air National Guard website, 11 September 2001, web.archive.org/web/20010205074600/www.dcandr.ang.af.mil/hq/index.htm. The website was changed after 9/11 but has been archived here. Also see Thompson, 'Failure to Defend the Skies', op. cit.

[45] Scott, William B., 'F-16 Pilots Considered Ramming Flight 93', *Aviation Week and Space Technology*, 9 September 2002. www.aviationnow.com/avnow/news/ channel_awst.jsp?view=story&id=news/aw090971.xml. Archived at www.cooperativeresearch.org/timeline/2002/aviationweekspacetechnology090902.html.

[46] Ibid.

[47] Thompson, 'The Failure to Defend the Skies', op. cit.

[48] Statement from Kyle Hence, 9/11 Citizens Watch, 1 July 2004.

[49] Message via email from Kyle Hence, 9/11 Citizens Watch, 23 June 2004.

[50] National Reconnaissance Office website, www.nro.gov.

[51] Lumpkin, John J., 'Agency Planned Exercise on Sept. 11 Built Around a Plane Crashing into a Building', Associated Press, 21 August 2002, www.sfgate.com/cgi-bin/ article.cgi?f=/news/archive/2002/08/21/national1518EDT0686.DTL.

[52] National Law Enforcement and Security Institute announcement, 'Homeland Security: America's Leadership Challenge', www.nlsi.net/hs-alc-info.htm.

[53] United States Joint Forces Command website, (viewed 30 June 2004) www.jfcom.mil/ about/about1.htm.

[54] USFJCOM Project Alpha website, (viewed 30 June 2004) www.jfcom.mil/about/ fact_alpha.htm.

[55] See for example USFJCOM Project Alpha, Millenium Challenge website, (viewed 30 June 2004) www.jfcom.mil/about/experiments/mc02.htm.

[56] USFJCOM Air Combat Command website, (viewed 30 June 2004) www.jfcom.mil/ about/com_acc.htm.

[57] Lumpkin, 'Agency Planned Exercise on Sept. 11', op. cit.

[58] *Washington Post*, 16 September 2001. Credit to Barbara Honneger for this source, cited in her article 'The US Government, Not the Hijackers, "Chose" the Date of the 9-11 Attacks'.

[59] Testimony of the Honorable Rudolph W. Giuliani before the National Commission on Terrorist Attacks Upon the United States, 19 May 2004. Can be heard online at WNYC radio, www.wnyc.org/news/articles/28147.

[60] OEM Press Release, 'New York City Office of Emergency Management Holds Trial Point-of Dispensing Drill', Office of Emergency Management, New York, 22 May 2002, www.nyc.gov/html/oem/html/other/sub_news_pages/tripod05_22_02.html.

[61] US Embassy Islamabad Press Release, 'Cheney to Oversee Domestic Counterterrorism Efforts', 9 May 2001, usembassy.state.gov/islamabad/wwwh01050902.html. CBS News, 'New Terror Task Force', 8 May 2001, www.cbsnews.com/stories/2001/05/08/national/main290081.shtml.

[62] The Pentagon: Headquarters of the United States Department of Defense website, www.defenselink.mil/pubs/pentagon.

[63] CSP Decision Brief, 'Know Thy Enemy', Center for Security Policy, Washington, DC, 9, December 2002, No. 02-D 62, www.centerforsecuritypolicy.org/index.jsp?section=papers&code=02-D_62; 'Justice: Ptech no security risk', *Washington Technology*, 16 December 2002, Vol. 17, No. 18, www.washingtontechnology.com/news/17_18/datastream/19630-1.html.

[64] Guidera, Jerry and Simpson, Glenn R., 'US Probes Terror Ties to Boston Software Firm', *Wall Street Journal*, 6 December 2002, available online at www.centerforsecuritypolicy.org/index.jsp?section=static&page=ptech.

[65] Ibid.

[66] Ibid. Ranalli, Ralph, 'FBI Reportedly Didn't Act on Ptech Tips', *Boston Globe*, 7 December 2002.

[67] Hopsicker, Daniel, 'FBI Shut Down Investigation into Saudi Terror Cell in Boston', Mad Cow Morning News, 5 February 2003, www.madcowprod.com/ mc4522004.html. NPR Weekend All Things Considered, 'FBI's Continuing Investigation of Boston-area Software Company Ptech and Its Possible Ties to Terrorism', National Public Radio, 8 December 2002, transcript available online at www.globalsecurity.org/org/news/2002/021208-secure01.htm.

[68] CNN, 'Customs Searches Software Firm Near Boston: Fears That Funds May Have Gone to al Qaeda', 6 December 2002, archives.cnn.com/2002/US/Northeast/12/06/ptech.raid.

[69] Ranalli, 'FBI Reportedly Didn't Act on Ptech Tips', op. cit.

[70] NPR, 'FBI's Continuing Investigation', op. cit.

[71] Hopsicker, 'FBI Shut Down Investigation into Saudi Terror Cell in Boston', op. cit.

[72] CNN, 'Customs Searches Software Firm Near Boston', op. cit.

Chapter 12: A Two-Pronged Military Strategy

[1] *Frontier Post*, 10 October 2001.

[2] Scott, Peter Dale, 'Many Signs Warlordism Returning to Afghanistan,' Online Resource on al-Qaeda and Osama Bin Laden, 5 January 2002, socrates.berkeley.edu/~pdscott/qfla.html. Also see Scott's *Drugs, Oil and War: The United States in Afghanistan, Colombia and Indochina*, Rowman & Littlefield, Lanham, MD, 2003.

[3] Viviano, Frank, *San Francisco Chronicle*, 26 September 2001.

[4] White House Statement, 28 November 2001.

[5] 'As the War Shifts Alliances, Oil Deals Follow,' *New York Times*, 15 December 2001.

[6] *Le Monde*, 5 December 2001, *Al-Watan*, 15 December 2001. *Le Monde* reported that Karzai "has a wide knowledge of the western world. After studying law in Kabul and India, he completed his training in the United States where he was for a time a consultant for the American oil company Unocal, when it was studying the construction of a pipeline in Afghanistan." Al-Watan reported that "Karzai found no contradiction between his ties with the Americans and his support for the Taliban movement as of 1994, when the Americans had—secretly and through the Pakistanis—supported the Taliban's assumption of power... At the time, Karzai worked as a consultant for the huge US oil group Unocal, which had supported the Taliban movement and sought to construct a pipeline to transport oil and gas from the Islamic republics of Central Asia to Pakistan via Afghanistan." Also see *Pravda*, 9 January 2002.

[7] For discussion see Martin, Patrick, 'Oil Company Adviser Named US Representative to Afghanistan,' World Socialist Web Site, www.wsws.org.

[8] Cited in Fisher, Daniel, 'Afghanistan: Oil Execs Revive Pipeline from Hell', Forbes.com, 4 February 2002.

[9] Madsen, Wayne, 'Afghanistan, the Taliban and the Bush Oil Team', Centre for Research on Globalisation, Montreal, 23 January 2002, globalresearch.ca/articles/MAD201A.html.

[10] Agence France Press and Reuters, 'Musharraf, Karzai Agree Major Oil Pipeline in Cooperation Pact,' *Irish Times*, 9 February 2002.

[11] Agence France Presse, 'World Bank Holds Talks Over Massive Central Asian Pipeline', *Alexander's Gas & Oil Connections*, 15 May 2002, www.gasandoil.com/goc/news/nts22408.htm.

[12] 'Pakistan Steps Up Efforts to Reactivate Turkmen Gas Pipeline Project', *Dawn*, 9 May 2002. Available at *Alexander's Oil & Gas Connections*, Vol. 7, No. 11, 29 May 2002, www.gasandoil.com/goc/news/nts22268.htm. Credit to Michael C. Ruppert and Dave Allen Pfieffer writing for *From the Wilderness* for these, and some other, sources.

[13] BBC News, 13 May 2002.

[14] 'Pipelineistan: The Rules of the Game', *Asia Times*, 25 January 2002, www.gasandoil.com/goc/features/fex20867.htm.

[15] 'Pakistan, Turkmenistan and Afghanistan to Sign Accord', *Dawn*, 17 May 2002, www.gasandoil.com/goc/news/nts22404.htm.

[16] Reuters, 'Central Asia's Great Game Turned on its Head,' 25 Sept. 2001.

[17] Arkin, William, *Los Angeles Times*, 6 January 2001.

[18] Peuch, Jean-Christophe, 'Central Asia: US Military Build-up Shifts Sphere of Influence,' Radio Free Europe/Liberty, 11 January 2002.

[19] Ibid.

[20] Arkin, William M., 'The Secret War: Frustrated by Intelligence Failures, the Defense Department is Dramatically Expanding Its "Black World" of Covert Operations', Los Angeles Times, 27 October 2002, www.latimes.com/news/nationworld/nation/la-op-arkin27oct27.story.

[21] Hess, Pamela, 'Panel Wants $7 Billion Elite Counter-Terror Unit', United Press International, 26 September 2002, www.upi.com/view.cfm?StoryID=20020925-041703-4695r.

[22] Berkowitz, Bill, 'Hellzapoppin' at the Pentagon: Rumsfeld's Defense Science Board Proposes "Prodding" Terrorists to Terrorism', Working For Change, 13 November 2002, www.workingforchange.com/article.cfm?ItemID=14076.

[23] Floyd, Chris, 'Into the Dark: The Terrorist Plan to Provoke Terrorist Attacks', Counterpunch, 1 November 2002, www.counterpunch.org/floyd1101.html.

[24] BBC News, 'Al-Qaeda "Claims Madrid Bombings,"' 14 March 2004, news.bbc.co.uk/2/hi/europe/3509426.stm.

[25] National Public Radio, 'Key Suspect in Madrid Bombings Had Al Qaeda Ties: Spain Says Cell of 20 Moroccans Planned, Executed Attacks', 17 March 2004, www.npr.org/display_pages/features/feature_1760742.html.

[26] DEBKAFile Exclusive Report, 'Bin Laden Orchestrated Madrid Attacks in Person', 20 March 2004, www.debka.com/article.php?aid=809.

[27] Smith, Lee, 'Jihad Without End: The Madrid Bombings Weren't About Iraq', Slate, 18 March 2004, slate.msn.com/id/2097370.

[28] DEBKAFile, 'Bin Laden Orchestrated Madrid Attacks', op. cit.

[29] DEBKAFile Special Analysis, 'Who's Next After Madrid?', 13 March 2004, www.debka.com/article.php?aid=804.

[30] CBS News, 'Turkey: Blasts Bear Al-Qaeda Marks', 1 December 2003, www.cbsnews.com/stories/2003/12/02/terror/main586392.shtml.

[31] Owen, Edward, 'Bomb Squad Links in Spanish Blasts', Times, 19 June 2004, avantgo.thetimes.co.uk/services/avantgo/article/0,,1150429,00.html.

[32] BBC News, 'Spain Probes Bomb Suspect Reports', 29 April 2004, news.bbc.co.uk/1/hi/world/europe/3670627.stm.

[33] BBC News, 'Frenchman Held Over Morocco Blast', 3 June 2003, news.bbc.co.uk/1/hi/world/africa/2960192.stm. BBC News, 'Death sentences for Morocco bombings', 19 August 2003, news.bbc.co.uk/1/hi/world/africa/3162285.stm.

[34] News 24 (South Africa), 'Suspect Linked to French Trial', 8 September 2003, www.news24.com/News24/Africa/Features/0,,2-11-37_1413226,00.html.

[35] BBC News, 'Suspect claims intelligence link', 8 September 2003, news.bbc.co.uk/1/hi/world/africa/3091624.stm.

[36] DebkaFile Special Report, 'Bin Laden Videotape Was Hit-and-Run Assault on US Election', 31 October 2004, debka.com/article.php?aid=928.

Chapter 13: The Grand Design

[1] Krakowski, Elie, 'The Afghan Vortex,' *IASPS Research Papers in Strategy*, Institute for Advanced Strategic and Political Studies, Jerusalem, No. 9, April 2000.

[2] Chin, Larry, *Online Journal*, 7 Feb. 2002, www.onlinejournal.com.

[3] Cited in 'How Oil Interests Play Out in the US Bombing of Afghanistan,' *Drillbits and Trailings: Electronic Monthly on the Mining & Oil Industries*, 31 Oct. 2001, Vol. 6, No. 8, www.moles.org/ProjectUnderground/drillbits/6_08/1.html.

[4] Editor, 'UNOCAL & Afghanistan', op. cit.

[5] Croissant, Michael P. and Aras, Bulent (ed.), *Oil and Geopolitics in the Caspian Sea Region*, Praeger, London, 1999.

[6] Baryiski, Robert V., 'The Caspian Oil Regime: Military Dimensions,' *Caspian Crossroads Magazine*, Volume 1, Issue No. 2, Spring 1995.

[7] Blank, Stephen J., 'The United States: Washington's New Frontier in the Trans-Caspian,' in Croissant, Michael P. and Aras, Bulent (ed.), *Oil and Geopolitics in the Caspian Sea Region*, op. cit.

[8] Cited in Cohn, Marjorie, 'The Deadly Pipeline War: US Afghan Policy Driven By Oil Interests,' Jurist: The Legal Education Network, University of Pittsburgh, 7 December 2001, jurist.law.pitt.edu.

[9] Cited in Monbiot, George, 'A Discreet Deal in the Pipeline,' *Guardian*, 15 February 2001.

[10] Silk Road Strategy Act of 1999, 106th Congress, posted at EurasiaNet, www.eurasianet.org/resource/regional/silkroad.html.

[11] Pentagon draft document cited in *New York Times*, 8 March 1992; *International Herald Tribune*, 9 March 1992; *Washington Post*, 22 March 1992; *Times*, 25 May 1992. For further discussion of US global strategies see Ahmed, Nafeez M., 'America in Terror—Causes and Context: The Foundational Principles of Western Foreign Policy and the Structure of World Order,' Media Monitors Network, 12 September 2001, mediamonitors.net/mosaddeq12. html.

[12] Blank, Stephen J., 'The United States: Washington's New Frontier in the Trans-Caspian,' op. cit., p.250.

[13] For further discussion see Chossudovsky, Michel, 'America at War in Macedonia,' Transnational Foundation for Future Peace and Research (TFF), TFF Meeting Point, June 2001. Chossudovsky is professor of economics at the University of Ottawa.

[14] Blank, Stephen J., 'The United States: Washington's New Frontier in the Trans-Caspian,' op. cit., p. 256.

[15] Cited in ibid., p. 252.

[16] Ibid., p. 250.

[17] Cited in ibid., p. 252.

[18] Ibid., p. 266–267.

[19] Rose, Stephen Peter, *Harvard Magazine*, May–June 2002, p. 30–31.

[20] Brzezinski, Zbigniew, *The Grand Chessboard: American Primacy and its Geostrategic Imperatives*, Basic Books, 1997. Brzezinski holds a 1953 PhD from Harvard University. His other achievements include: counselor, Center for Strategic and International Studies; professor of american foreign policy, Johns Hopkins University; national security advisor to President Jimmy Carter (1977–81); trustee and founder of the Trilateral Commission International; advisor of several major US/global corporations; member of National Security Council and Defense Department Commission on Integrated Long-Term Strategy; under Ronald Reagan, member of the President's Foreign Intelligence Advisory Board; past member, Board of Directors, The Council on Foreign Relations; 1988, co-chairman of the Bush National Security Advisory Task Force. Michael C. Ruppert must be credited for his very useful selection of quotes from Brzezinski's study, in 'A War in the Planning for 4 Years,' *From the Wilderness* Publications, 7 November 2001.

[21] Brzezinski, Zbigniew, *The Grand Chessboard: American Primacy and its Geostrategic Imperatives*, op. cit., p. xiii.

[22] Ibid, p. 124–125.

[23] Ibid., p. 130.

[24] Ibid., p. 132–133.

[25] Ibid., p. 139.

[26] Ibid., p. 141.

[27] Ibid., p. 145.

[28] Ibid., p. 148.

[29] Ibid., p. 149.

[30] Ibid., p. 194–195.

[31] Ibid., p. xiii.

[32] Ibid., p. xiv.

[33] Ibid., p. 30.

[34] Ibid., p. 31.

[35] Ibid., p. 40.

[36] Ibid., p. 55.

[37] Ibid., p. 121.

[38] Ibid., p. 197–198.

[39] Ibid., p. 209.

[40] Ibid., p. 211.

[41] Ibid., p. 24–25.

[42] Leach, Gerald, 'The Coming Decline of Oil,' *Tiempo*, December 2001, No. 42.

Available online at 'The Global Economy,' Centre for Political Analysis, Institute for Policy Research & Development, Brighton, globalresearch.org/view_article.php?aid=457120250.

[43] Campbell, Colin J., 'Peak Oil: An Outlook on Crude Oil Depletion,' *Mbendi Energy News*, February 2002, www.mbendi.co.za/indy/oilg/p0070.htm.

[44] Dfieffer, Dave Allen, 'Is the Empire About Oil?' *From the Wilderness*, 8 August 2002, www.fromthewilderness.com/free/ww3/080802_oil_empire.html.

[45] Duncan, Richard C., 'The Peak of World Oil Production and the Road to the Olduvai Gorge,' presented at Summit 2000, Geological Society of America, Nevada, 13 November 2000, dieoff.com/page224.htm.

[46] Campbell, Colin J., 'Peak Oil: An Outlook on Crude Oil Depletion,' op. cit.

[47] Mackay, Neil, 'Bush Planned Iraq "Regime Change" Before Becoming President,' *Sunday Herald*, 15 September 2002, www.sundayherald.com/27735.

[48] Bookman, Jay, 'The President's Real Goal in Iraq,' *Atlanta-Journal Constitution*, 29 September 2002, www.accessatlanta.com/ajc/opinion/0902/29bookman.html.

[49] For full document, see PNAC Report, *Rebuilding America's Defenses: Strategies, Forces and Resources for a New Century*, Project for the New American Century, Washington D.C., September 2000, www.newamericancentury.org/RebuildingAmericasDefenses.pdf.

[50] Mackay, Neil, 'Bush Planned Iraq "Regime Change" Before Becoming President,' op. cit.

[51] These documents are as follows: *Defense Planning Guidance for the 1994–1999 Fiscal Years* (Draft), Office of the Secretary of Defense, 1992; *Defense Planning Guidance for the 1994–1999 Fiscal Years* (Revised Draft), Office of the Secretary of Defense, 1992; *Defense Strategy for the 1990s*, Office of the Secretary of Defense, 1993; *Defense Planning Guidance for the 2004–2009 Fiscal Years*, Office of the Secretary of Defense, 2002.

[52] Armstrong, David, 'Dick Cheney's Song of America: Drafting a Plan for Global Dominance,' *Harpers Magazine*, October 2002, Vol. 305, No. 1892.

[53] PNAC Report, op. cit., p.62–63.

[54] ABC News Nightline, 'The Plan', 5 March 2003, abcnews.go.com/sections/nightline/DailyNews/pnac_030310.html.

[55] See, for example, 'The Wrong Way to Fix the Vote,' *Washington Post*, 10 June 2001; Borger, Julian and Palast, Gregory, 'Inquiry into New Claims of Poll Abuses in Florida,' *Guardian*, 17 February 2001; BBC *Newsnight*, 'Theft of the Presidency,' 15 Feb. 2001; 'Florida's "Disappeared Voters": Disenfranchised by the GOP,' *Nation*, 5 February 2001; 'A Blacklist Burning for Bush,' *Observer*, 10 December 2000; 'Florida's Flawed "Voter Cleansing" Program: Salon.com's Politics Story of the Year,' *Salon*, 4 December 2000, www.salon.com. These reports discuss how the actual vote count means that Gore should have been President. Bush was able to win power through the deliberate disenfranchisement of black voters in Florida.

[56] Letter from House of Representatives Committee of the Judiciary (signed by Rep. John Conyers, Jr., Rep. Melvin Watt, Rep. Jerrold Nadler, Rep. Tammy Baldwin on behalf of 12 members of the Committee) to J. Kenneth Blackwell, Ohio Secretary of State,

Washington, DC, 2 December 2004, available online at www.house.gov/
judiciary_democrats/ohblackwellltr12204.pdf.

[57] UC Berkeley Press Release, 'UC Berkeley Research Team Sounds "Smoke Alarm" for
Florida E-Vote Count: Research Team Calls for Investigation', University of California,
Berkeley, 18 November 2004, available online at globalresearch.ca/articles/
BER411A.html. Also see Hout, Michael, et. al., The Effect of Electronic Voting
Machines on Change in Support for Bush in the 2004 Florida Elections, University of
California, Berkeley, November 2004, ucdata.berkeley.edu/new_web/VOTE2004/
index.html.

[58] Palast, Greg, 'Kerry Won…', TomPaine.com (A Project of the Institute for America's
Future), 4 November 2004, www.tompaine.com/articles/kerry_won_.php.

[59] Benson, Jocelyn and Weaver, Vesla, Democracy Spoiled: National, State, and County
Disparities in Disfranchisement Through Uncounted Ballots, The Civil Rights Project,
Harvard University, Cambridge, MA, July 2002, www.civilrightsproject.harvard.edu/
research/electoral_reform/residual_ballot.php.

[60] Palast, 'Kerry Won', op. cit.

Chapter 14: The Failure of the 9/11 National Commission

[1] Chossudovsky, Michel, 'New Chairman of 9/11 Commission had Business Ties to
Osama's Brother in Law', Centre for Research on Globalisation, Montreal, 27 December
2002, www.globalresearch.ca/articles/CHO212A.html.

[2] Azerbaijan International, 'Delta Hess Alliance in Azerbaijan,' 2002,
www.azer.com/aiweb/categories/services/services_company/deltahess.html. Cited in ibid.

[3] Energy Compass, 15 November 2002. Cited in Chossudovsky, 'New Chaiman of 9/11
Commission', op. cit.

[4] Testimony of former CIA Director James Woolsey, Senate Judiciary Committee, Federal
News Service, 3 September 1998. Cited in Chossudovsky, 'New Chairman', op. cit.

[5] Wells, Jonathan, et. al., 'Saudi Elite Linked to bin Laden Financial Empire', Boston
Herald, 14 October 2001, www.bostonherald.com/news/americas_new_war/
aussaud10142001.htm.

[6] Chossudovsky, 'New Chaiman', op. cit.

[7] Flocco, Tom, 'Chairman Kean's Link to Bin Laden's Brother-in-Law', Scoop, 2 April
2004, www.scoop.co.nz/mason/archive/scoop/stories/ 42/f2/200404021119.00e63b79.html.

[8] Homeland Security Project (viewed 1 July 2004), www.homelandsec.org/ABOUTUS/
index.htm.

[9] Associated Press, 'A Summary of Financial Disclosure Reports, Covering 2002', Mercury
Times, 28 March 2003, www.dfw.com/mld/bayarea/news/
5500832.htm?template=contentModules/printstory.jsp&1c.

[10] Chossudovsky, 'Who's Who on the 9-11 "Independent" Commission', Centre for
Research on Globalisation, Montreal, 17 July 2003, www.globalresearch.ca/articles/
CHO307B.html.

[11] Ibid. President's Foreign Intelligence Advisory Board website, www.whitehouse.gov/pfiab and Zelikow's bio at www.9-11commission.gov/about/bio_zelikow.htm.

[12] Kojm's bio, www.9-11commission.gov/about/bio_kojm.htm.

[13] Chossudovsky, 'Who's Who', op. cit. See Marcus' bio at www.9-11commission.gov/about/bio_marcus.htm, and CBS News, 'Sept. 11 Families Sue Saudis, Sudan', 16 August 2002, www.cbsnews.com/stories/2002/08/15/attack/main518849.shtml.

[14] Hopsicker, Daniel, Barry and the Boys: The CIA, the Mob, and America's Secret History, Madcow Press, 2001, p. 325–330.

[15] Hopsicker, Daniel, 'Six Degrees of Richard Ben-Veniste', Mad Cow Morning News, No. 35, 20 December 2004, www.madcowprod.com/issue35.html.

[16] CBS News, 'Conflicts of Interest on Sept. 11 Panel?', 5 March 2003, www.cbsnews.com/stories/2003/03/05/eveningnews/main542868.shtml.

[17] Associated Press, 'A Summary of Financial Disclosure Reports', op. cit.

[18] Fielding bio at www.9-11commission.gov/about/bio_fielding.htm.

[19] CBS News, 'Conflicts of Interest on Sept. 11 Panel?', op. cit. ABC News, 'Suit Limits, Panel's Airline Connections', 14 February 2003, abcnews.go.com/wire/Politics/ap20030214_1409.html.

[20] Associated Press, 'A Summary of Financial Disclosure Reports', op. cit.

[21] Gorelick bio, www.9-11commission.gov/about/bio_gorelick.htm.

[22] Associated Press, 'A Summary of Financial Disclosure Reports', op. cit.

[23] Political Friendster, 'Connection Between Boeing and Slade Gorton', Stanford University (viewed 2 July 2004), politicalfriendster.stanford.edu/showConnection.php?id1=62&id2=219.

[24] CBS News, 'Conflicts of Interest', op. cit.

[25] New York Times, 26 October 2003. Cited in Scamming America: The Official 9/11 Cover-Up Guide, NY 9/11 Truth, New York, May 2004, septembereleventh.org/documents/9-11_coverup_booklet.pdf.

[26] Salon, November 2003. Cited in Scamming America, op. cit.

[27] Eggen, Dan, 'Kerrey Replacing Member of 9/11 Panel', Washington Post, 10 December 2003, p. A14, www.voicesofsept11.org/911ic/archive/2003/121003.php.

[28] Right Web, 'Profile: Committee for the Liberation of Iraq', Interhemispheric Resource Center, New Mexico, 18 December 2003, rightweb.irc-online.org/org/cli.php.

[29] Vistica, Gregory L., One Awful Night in Thangh Pong', New York Times Magazine, 25 April 2001, www.nytimes.com/2001/04/25/magazine/25KERREY.html?ex=1088913600&en=cf64b9d78b26814f&ei=5070; Raimondo, Justin, 'Is Bob Kerrey a War Criminal? Yes', AntiWar.com, 27 April 2001, www.antiwar.com/justin/j042701.html.

[30] Lehman bio, www.9-11commission.gov/about/bio_lehman.htm.

[31] Ball Corporation, 'John F. Lehman Biography' (viewed 2 July 2004), www.ball.com/bios/lehman.html. BATC News Release, 'Ball Aerospace Celebrates 45th Anniversary', Ball Aerospace & Technologies Corp., (a wholly owned subsidiary of Ball), Boulder, CO., 17 July 2001, www.ball.com/aerospace/media/nr07_17_01.html.

[32] Roemer bio, www.9-11commission.gov/about/bio_roemer.htm.

[33] Chossudovsky, 'Who's Who', op. cit.

[34] CBS News, 'Conflicts of Interest', op. cit.

[35] Thompson bio, www.9-11commission.gov/about/bio_thompson.htm. Winston & Strawn, 'Firm Overview' (viewed 2 July 2002), www.winston.com/WSHome.nsf/pFrameFO?OpenPage.

[36] CBS News, 'Conflicts of Interest', op. cit.

[37] Associated Press, 'A Summary of Financial Disclosure Reports', op. cit.

[38] CBS News, 'Conflicts of Interest', op. cit.

[39] Shenon, Philip, 'Deal on 9/11 Briefings Lets White House Edit Papers', New York Times, 13 November 2003, archived at www.commondreams.org/headlines03/1114-05.htm.

Chapter 15: Summary of Findings

[1] Joshi, Manoj, 'India Helped FBI Trace ISI–terrorist Links,' op. cit.

[2] Moss, Stephen, 'There Isn't a Target in Afghanistan Worth a $1m Missile,' Guardian, 10 October 2001.

[3] Goff, Stan, 'The So-Called Evidence is a Farce,' op. cit.

[4] Interview with Milton Bearden by Dan Rather, Special Report, CBS Evening News, 12 September 2001.

[5] Hersh, Seymour, 'What Went Wrong', New Yorker, 1 October 2001, www.newyorker.com/fact/content/?011008fa_FACT.

[6] Baer, Robert, See No Evil, op. cit. Also see book extracts in Guardian, 12 January 2002, books.guardian.co.uk/extracts/story/0,6761,631434,00.html.

[7] Gannon, Kathy, Associated Press, 11 September 2001.

[8] Bollyn, Chris, 'Euro Intel Experts Dismiss 'War on Terrorism' as Deception,' American Free Press, 4 December 2001.

[9] Tagesspiegel, 13 January 2001, www2.tagesspiegel.de/archiv/2002/01/12/ak-sn-in-558560.html.

[10] Transcript of presentation by Dr. Mahmoud Khalaf at Center for Asian Studies, University of Cairo, 5 December 2001.

[11] PBS NewsHour, 'Improving Intelligence', 11 December 2002, www.pbs.org/newshour/

bb/congress/july-dec02/intelligence_12-11.html.

[12] Monbiot, George, 'The Need for Dissent,' *Guardian*, 18 Sept. 2001.

[13] See Ahmed, Nafeez Mosaddeq, *Behind the War on Terror: Western Secret Strategy and the Struggle for Iraq*, Clairview Books, London, 2002.

[14] Ibid.

[15] *Guardian*, 29th January 2002.

[16] Joint Inquiry into Intelligence Community Activities Before and After the Terrorist Attacks of September 11, 2001, 'Report of the Joint Inquiry into the Terrorist Attacks of September 11, 2001', House Permanent Select Committee on Intelligence and Senate Select Committee on Intelligence, 107th Congress, 2D Session, December 2002, www.gpoaccess.gov/serialset/creports/911.html.

[17] JW Press Release, 'Judicial Watch Seeks Names of Those Responsible for Intelligence Failures', Judicial Watch, Washington, DC, 24 September 2002, available at foi.missouri.edu/whistleblowing/jwseeksnames.html.

[18] 'Avoiding the Real Questions', *Jane's Intelligence Digest*, 28 May 2002.

[19] CBS News, 'New Terror Task Force', 8 May 2001, www.cbsnews.com/stories/2001/05/08/national/printable290081.shtml.

Chapter 16: Terrorism as Historical Geostrategy

[1] McMurtry, John, 'Reply to ZNet Commentary of May 22, 2002: What Did Bush Know?,' ZNet, 8 June 2002, www.zmag.org/content/TerrorWar/mcmurty.cfm.

[2] Rippy, Ed, 'How the U.S. has Gotten into Wars,' IndyMedia, July 2002, www.indymedia.org/display.php3?article_id=182889&group=webcast.

[3] Miller, John C., *Sam Adams: Pioneer in Propaganda*, Stanford University Press, 1936, p. 178–9f. Cited in Rippy, op. cit.

[4] Ibid., p. 186–191.

[5] Stockwell, John, 'The CIA and the Gulf War,' Speech at Louden Nelson Community Center, Santa Cruz, CA, 20 February 1991, serendipity.magnet.ch/cia/stock2.html. Cited in Sanders, Richard, 'How to Start a War', *Global Outlook*, Summer 2002, No. 2.

[6] The Learning Center, 'The White House and Western Expansion,' White House Historical Association, www.whitehousehistory.org/02_learning/subs_4/frame_b_405a.html.

[7] Powers, Betsy, 'The U.S.–Mexican War of 1846–48,' War, Reconstruction and Recovery in Brazoria County, Brazoria County Historical Museum, Texas, www.bchm.org/wrr/war/p4cw.html.

[8] Rippy, op. cit. Also see Offner, John, 'Why Did the United States Fight Spain in 1898?,' *OAH Magazine of History*, Organization of American Historians, Vol. 12, No. 3, Spring 1998, www.oah.org/pubs/magazine/1898/offner.pdf.

[9] Combs, Jerald A., *The History of American Foreign Policy*, Alfred A. Knopf, New York, 1986, p. 144f. Cited in Rippy, op. cit.

[10] Ibid., p. 153. See Foner, Philip S., *The Spanish–Cuban–American War and the Birth of American Imperialism, 1895–1902*, Monthly Review Press, New York, 1972 (2 Volumes).

[11] McSherry, Patrick, 'The Loss of the Battleship Maine and the World Trade Center Towers: An Historical Comparison,' The Spanish American War Centennial Website, www.spanamwar.com/MaineWTC.htm.

[12] Miller, Tom, 'Remember the Maine,' *Smithsonian*, February 1998, www.smithsonianmag.si.edu/smithsonian/issues98/feb98/maine.html.

[13] Rippy, op. cit.

[14] Cited in Perloff, James, 'Pearl Harbor,' *New American*, 8 December 1986, Vol. 2, No. 30.

[15] Cited in Raico, Ralph, 'Rethinking Churchill,' in Denson, John V., *The Costs of War: America's Pyrrhic Victories*, Ludwig von Mises Institute, 1997. Relevant excerpts available at www.lewrockwell.com/orig/raico-churchill2.html.

[16] Ibid.

[17] Rippy, op. cit.

[18] History Channel, 'Betrayal at Pearl Harbor,' 7 December 2001.

[19] Stinnett, Robert B., *Day of Deceit: The Truth About FDR and Pearl Harbor*, Simon & Schuster, New York, 2000.

[20] Ibid., p. 7. Cited in Rippy, op. cit.

[21] Ibid., p. 4

[22] Ibid., p. 11

[23] Stinnett, Robert B., 'Pentagon Still Scapegoats Pearl Harbor Fall Guys,' *Providence Journal*, The Independent Institute, Oakland, CA, 7 December 2001.

[24] Ibid., p. 8.

[25] Ibid., p. 9.

[26] Borgquist, Daryl S., 'Advance Warning? The Red Cross Connection,' *Navy History*, The Naval Institute, May/June 1999.

[27] Bamford, James, *Body of Secrets: Anatomy of the Ultra-Secret National Security Agency*, Doubleday, New York, 2001. See ABC News, 'Friendly Fire,' 1 May 2001; Shane, Scott and Bowman, Tom, 'New Book on NSA Sheds Light on Secrets,' *Baltimore Sun*, 24 April 2001; Spannaus, Edward, 'When U.S. Joint Chiefs Planned Terror Attacks on America,' *Executive Intelligence Review*, 12 October 2001.

[28] See Madsen, Wayne, 'Anthrax and the Agency: Thinking the Unthinkable', *Counterpunch*, 8 April 2002, www.counterpunch.org/madsenanthrax.html.

[29] Cohen, Jeff and Solomon, Norman, '30-Year Anniversary: Tonkin Gulf Life Launched Vietnam War,' *Media Beat*, Fairness and Accuracy in Reporting (FAIR), New York,

27 July 1994, www.fair.org/media-beat/940727.html.

[30] Bradley, Mark P., 'Gulf of Tonkin,' The Vietnam War, University of Wisconsin, www.uwm.edu/People/mbradley/gulfoftonkin.html.

[31] Cohen and Solomon, op. cit.

[32] Combs, op. cit., p. 401.

[33] Cited in Ford, Captain Ronnie E., 'New Light on Gulf of Tonkin,' The History Network, 28 July 1997, available at www.hartford-hwp.com/archives/54/106.html.

[34] Ibid. For further discussion and sources see Rippy, op. cit.

[35] This point is discussed lucidly and concisely by US military expert Stan Goff, a former US Special Forces master sergeant and Lecturer in military science and doctrine at the West Point Military Academy: "Start with Bush. Start with the de facto president right now. He was the CEO of Harken Energy. That is his own little company, you know. As it turns out, he wasn't very good at it. You know, his dad, was an oil man. So you've got two generations in oil right there. Okay. And his dad was also you know the former president, the former vice president, the director of Central Intelligence. George Herbert Walker Bush is on the board of Carlyle Group. Carlyle Group is right now a $12 billion dollar equity company, but it's heavily invested in all kinds of things, including oil and it's also I think 11th or 12th whatever, biggest defense contractors in the country right now. It's getting very incestuous. And in fact, Carlyle put Bush junior on the board of one of its subsidiaries, which is Cater Air. A little shuttle service, a little puddle jumper service. Sort of as a sop to dad. The new ambassador to Saudi Arabia, Robert Jordan, is a Dallas lawyer and an old Bush booster. Jordan works for a Baker Botts. That's a firm with offices in Riyadh. And Baker Botts represents Carlyle Group over there. And the Baker in Baker Botts is James Baker, who was secretary of state for George Herbert Walker Bush, but he is also the guy that engineered the whole Florida coup d'etat, in the 2000 election. He was the midwife of that little venture. Some of the other folks in Carlyle, Fidel Ramos, former chief of the Philippines. Park Tae Joon of South Korea. John Major. Everybody remember John Shalikashvili, former chairman of the Joint Chiefs? And you can go back with the Bush family. Prescott Bush, Rockefellers, Duponts, Standard Oil, Morgans, Fords, all these other folks were anti-Semites and anti-Communists way back. They also actually financed the rise to power of Adolf Hitler. They financed it. I mean, that's a historical fact. It's irrefutable. And Prescott Bush did business with the Nazis all the way up to 1942 until he was censured by the United States under the Trading with the Enemy Act. And after the War, he turned right around and ran for Congress in Connecticut and won. This is an interesting family. Anyway, Dick Cheney, CEO of Halliburton Oil. Got $34 million before he took office in stock options from Halliburton. As the CEO, Cheney, and I'm looking at my notes, oversaw $23.8 billion dollars in oil industry contracts to Iraq alone. Now this is interesting, because Cheney found the loopholes in the embargo on Iraq. Now the attack on Iraq was done when Cheney was the secretary of defense. He stepped down as secretary of defense and turned right around and became the CEO of Halliburton, took advantage of the loopholes and went back there and made $23.8 billion dollars in Iraq by rebuilding the infrastructure that we bombed out of existence. Halliburton is also involved with the Russian mob. They've got sort of two things going on. One is oil and the other is drug trafficking. Halliburton is a story all by itself. Secretary of State, Colin Powell. This man has no diplomatic credentials. He was the former chairman of Joint Chiefs of Staff and all of sudden he is in charge of the entire

diplomatic corps of the United States. That's interesting just by itself. He has cash holdings or stock holdings in a number of defense contractors. Tony Prinicipi, secretary of foreign affairs. Lockheed Martin, defense contractor. The biggest defense contractor in the world. Andrew Card, chief of staff, General Motors. Secretary of the Navy, Gordon England. General Dynamics. Secretary of the Airforce, James Roche, Northrup Grummond. Secretary of the Army, General Thomas White retired. Enron Energy. These folks are [chuckles] all defense contractors or oil people. The whole bunch of them are. Donald Rumsfeld is secretary of defense. What people don't realize is he is also the former CEO of Searle Pharmaceuticals. They get big defense contracts. But he is also with General Signal Corporation, a defense contractor. And interestingly enough, he is also heavily invested in biotech, which is probably gonna make a killing here pretty soon with whatever Anthrax vaccines.... I've got a picture of Cheney and Rumsfeld in May 2000 at the Russian-American business leaders forum together. Arms around each other, and smiling. Dick Armitage. Deputy Secretary of Defense, he's a guy like me, he's a former special ops guy, SEAL. He had to leave the Reagan Administration because he was up to his neck in Iran–contra drug problems. And now he's working directly with the Russian Mafia. And he is also a board member of Carlyle. Remember that? Chief of Carlyle is Mr. Carlucci, who is also with the Middle East Policy Council, you see how this stuff intersects? Commerce Secretary is Donald Evans who owns Colorado Oil Company. You have to take a very close look at this cabinet, which I think was constructed in a very systematic way to figure out what their foreign policy priorities are." (Interview with Stan Goff by Mike McCormick, 24 October 2001, www.interlog.com/~cjazz/goff.htm)